Handbook Integrated Care

Volker Amelung · Viktoria Stein
Nicholas Goodwin · Ran Balicer
Ellen Nolte · Esther Suter
Editors

Handbook Integrated Care

 Springer

Editors
Volker Amelung
Institute for Epidemiology, Social
    Medicine and Health System Research
Medical School Hannover
Hannover, Germany

Viktoria Stein
International Foundation for Integrated Care
Oxford, United Kingdom

Nicholas Goodwin
International Foundation for Integrated
    Care
Oxford, United Kingdom

Ran Balicer
Health Policy Research and Planning
Clalit Health Services
Tel-Aviv, Israel

Ellen Nolte
European Observatory on Health Systems
    and Policies
London School of Economics and Political
    Science, London School of Hygiene &
    Tropical Medicine
London, UK

Esther Suter
Workforce Research & Evaluation
Alberta Health Services Calgary
Calgary, Alberta
Canada

ISBN 978-3-319-56101-1   ISBN 978-3-319-56103-5   (eBook)
DOI 10.1007/978-3-319-56103-5

Library of Congress Control Number: 2017942954

Printed on acid-free paper

This Springer imprint is published by Springer Nature
The registered company is Springer International Publishing AG
The registered company address is: Gewerbestrasse 11, 6330 Cham, Switzerland

Preface

Over the years, integrated care has evolved into a dominant topic in healthcare management and health systems design. A wide range of approaches and models have been developed and implemented, extending from more narrow, indication-based disease management programs to complex population-oriented whole system models. The common and central goal in all these programs is the quest to optimize the interface between different sectors and professional groups from the patient's perspective. At the core is the provision of the right care, at the right time by the appropriate service provider in a timely manner, irrespective of organizational boundaries or financial flows. From an individual service user perspective, it will be of less importance who is mandated to provide the services (and who pays for them), as long as they are easily accessible, are of high quality, and meet their expectations. Yet, health systems remain organized according to the traditional, episodic model of care which is ill-equipped to meet the needs created by any demographic, epidemiological, medical, and technological changes. Differences in cultures, conflicting remuneration and incentive systems, budget constraints, varying regulations, and different geographical locations within and across organizations continue to create barriers to seamless provision of care.

Integrated care approaches are widely seen as a means to overcome these challenges, which are complex in nature, but questions remain about how integrated care is to be achieved and sustained. The international literature has documented successful pilots and initiatives which provide valuable lessons on the design and implementation of complex, system-wide changes toward better integration and coordination of services. While there remains question about the transferability of entire models of integrated care, there is growing evidence on essential elements, tools, and interventions that have been shown to facilitate successful implementation of integrated care approaches.

This handbook seeks to bring together, for the first time, the evidence on the key concepts, management elements, and tools that have been implemented internationally to enhance integrated care, illustrated by a multitude of good practice examples from around the world. The target audience of this handbook are both healthcare politicians seeking for inspiration for legislations and also practioners, learning from best practice.

The first part of this handbook describes the conceptual basis of integrated care. The varying characteristics of integrated care in different health systems make this outline vital. Just as an example, in state-run health systems such as in Great Britain and Canada, integrated care is a concept toward health system design that is also discussed at a meta-level. In contrast, in predominantly market-oriented health systems, such as in the United States and Switzerland, integrated care is understood as a competitive strategy for individual market players at a micro level. Despite these seemingly opposing approaches, integrated care in any country consistently focuses on redesigning the processes of service provision from the patient perspectives.

The second part sheds light on the different management aspects of integrated care that vary significantly across different systems. Nonetheless, many aspects of integrated care management are generic. For instance, health systems with strong hierarchical governing institutions lend themselves for network-oriented integrated care. This approach requires understanding of a particular set of leadership and governance structures. Another vital management aspect is performance measurement. Effective integration mechanisms of complex care systems are often difficult to quantify and demand innovative methods of evaluation. Despite the plethora of pilot projects around the world, there is a knowledge deficit on what works in what context to guide the design and evaluation of integrated care projects.

In the third part, the potential of integrated care in select patient groups is analyzed to elevate the practical applicability of this handbook. Design and implementation concepts for fields such as geriatrics, pediatrics, and young adults medicine or care for rare diseases are illustrated. In line with the goal of this handbook, these illustrations strike a balance between the theoretical discourse, conceptual design, and practical examples.

While integrated care as a concept is applicable to any system, the models, tools, and instruments must be contextualized and different system environments require different approaches for implementation. The fourth part of the book illustrates examples from eight distinct health systems. The ideas are not to reinvent but rather to learn from the experiences of other countries, transfer the knowledge, and adapt it to local context. Successful integrated care programs are often a mosaic of ideas and concepts from a variety of settings that are intelligently woven together.

This extensive handbook would not have been realized without the help of many colleagues and staff members. A special thanks goes to Dominika Urbanski, who dedicated many hours and emails to integrating the different pieces of this book into one coherent volume. Thank you also to Mudathira Kadu for proofreading the manuscript in record time. We are also grateful to Dr. Martina Bihn of Springer Verlag for her patience and continual support in the realization of this project. Ultimately, this book could not have been done without the contributions of the many authors and their willingness to share their expertise and experience with the reader.

Hannover, Germany   Volker Amelung
Oxford, United Kingdom   Viktoria Stein
Oxford, United Kingdom   Nicholas Goodwin
Tel-Aviv, Israel   Ran Balicer
London, United Kingdom   Ellen Nolte
Calgary, Canada   Esther Suter

Contents

Part I   Foundations of Integrated Care

1   **What Is Integrated Care?**   3
Nicholas Goodwin, Viktoria Stein, and Volker Amelung

2   **Evidence Supporting Integrated Care**   25
Ellen Nolte

3   **Patients Preferences**   39
A. Mühlbacher and Susanne Bethge

Part II   Tools and Instruments

4   **Case-Managers and Integrated Care**   55
Guus Schrijvers and Dominique Somme

5   **Disease Management**   73
Ellen Nolte

6   **Discharge and Transition Management in Integrated Care**   97
Dominika Urbanski, Anika Reichert, and Volker Amelung

7   **Mobile Sensors and Wearable Technology**   113
Christopher A. Yao and Kendall Ho

8   **Data Integration in Health Care**   121
Maya Leventer-Roberts and Ran Balicer

Part III   Management of Integrated Care

9   **Strategic Management and Integrated Care in a Competitive**
Environment   133
Volker Amelung, Sebastian Himmler, and Viktoria Stein

10   **Governance and Accountability**   149
Sara Mallinson and Esther Suter

11   Financing and Reimbursement 165
     Ellen Nolte

12   Planning 189
     Susanne Ozegowski

13   Integrated Care and the Health Workforce 209
     Loraine Busetto, Stefano Calciolari, Laura Guadalupe González Ortiz,
     Katrien Luijkx, and Bert Vrijhoef

14   Leadership in Integrated Care 221
     Volker Amelung, Daniela Chase, and Anika Reichert

15   Culture and Values 237
     Robin Miller, Marisa de Andrade, Rommy Marjolein Don,
     Volker Amelung, Viktoria Stein, Nicholas Goodwin, Ran Balicer,
     Ellen Nolte, and Esther Suter

16   Change Management 253
     Nick Goodwin

17   How to Make a Service Sustainable? An Active Learning
     Simulation Approach to Business Model Development
     for Integrated Care 277
     Ingo Meyer, Reinhard Hammerschmidt, Lutz Kubitschke,
     and Sonja Müller

Part IV   Evaluation and Health Services Research

18   Evaluating Complex Interventions 297
     Apostolos Tsiachristas and Maureen P.M.H. Rutten-van Mölken

19   Economic Evaluation of Integrated Care 315
     Apostolos Tsiachristas and Maureen P.M.H. Rutten-van Mölken

20   Claims Data for Evaluation 333
     Enno Swart

Part V   Client Groups

21   Children 353
     Ingrid Wolfe

22   Integrated Care for Frail Older People Suffering from Dementia
     and Multi-morbidity 369
     Henk Nies, Mirella Minkman, and Corine van Maar

23   Physical and Mental Health 383
     Chris Naylor

24   Integrated Palliative and End-of-Life Care 399
     Emilio Herrera Molina, Arturo Álvarez Rosete, Silvia Librada Flores,
     and Tania Pastrana Uruena

25 Rare Diseases 413
    Raquel Castro, Juliette Senecat, Myriam de Chalendar, Ildikó Vajda,
    Silvia van Breukelen, Maria Montefusco, Stephanie Jøker Nielsen,
    and Dorica Dan

26 Pathways in Transplantation Medicine: Challenges in Overcoming
    Interfaces Between Cross-Sectoral Care Structures 429
    Lena Harries, Harald Schrem, Christian Krauth, and Volker Amelung

27 Integrated Care Concerning Mass Casualty Incidents/Disasters:
    Lessons Learned from Implementation in Israel 439
    Bruria Adini and Kobi Peleg

28 Integrated Care for People with Intellectual Disability 449
    Marco O. Bertelli, Luana Salerno, Elisa Rondini,
    and Luis Salvador-Carulla

29 Integrated Care for Older Patients: Geriatrics 469
    Sofia Duque, Elisa Giaccardi, and Tischa J.M. van der Cammen

Part VI Case Studies

30 Canada: Application of a Coordinated-Type Integration Model
    for Vulnerable Older People in Québec: The PRISMA Project . . . 499
    Réjean Hébert

31 Germany: Evolution and Scaling Up of the Population-Based
    Integrated Health Care System "Healthy Kinzigtal" 511
    Oliver Groene and Helmut Hildebrandt

32 Scotland 525
    Elaine Mead

33 USA: Innovative Payment and Care Delivery Models—Accountable
    Care Organizations 541
    Andreas Schmid

34 Switzerland 551
    Isabelle Peytremann-Bridevaux, Peter Berchtold,
    and Isabelle Hagon-Traub

35 Netherlands: The Potentials of Integrating Care via Payment
    Reforms 561
    Jeroen N. Struijs, Hanneke W. Drewes, Richard Heijink,
    and Caroline A. Baan

36 New Zealand: Canterbury Tales 573
     Brian Dolan, Carolyn Gullery, Greg Hamilton, and David Meates

**37 Israel: Structural and Functional Integration at the Israeli
     Healthcare System** 587
     Ran Balicer, Efrat Shadmi, Orly Manor, and Maya Leventer-Roberts

Part I

Foundations of Integrated Care

What Is Integrated Care?

1

Nicholas Goodwin, Viktoria Stein, and Volker Amelung

1.1 Introduction

Integrated care is a concept that is now widely used and accepted in different health and care systems across the world. Yet the concept is not new since concerns about fragmentations in the way care is designed and delivered has a long historical lineage. The origins of the term date back to the ancient Greeks who recognised the need to treat people's mental health alongside their physical symptoms. In more recent times, integrated care as a terminology became commonplace in the 1970s in the fields of child and adolescent health as well as long-term care for the elderly.

By the late 1970s, one of the strongest drives towards more integrated and coordinated care provision emerged from the birth of the primary health care (PHC) movement following the World Health Organisation's Alma-Ata Declaration on Primary Health Care in 1978 (WHO 1978). Strengthening primary health care has subsequently been the cornerstone for action in health sector reforms worldwide with good evidence to demonstrate its impact in terms of health system strengthening and promoting universal health coverage (WHO 2008).

A key element to the PHC movement has been to improve what Barbara Starfield termed the 'four C's' of primary care: accessible contact; service coordination; comprehensiveness, and continuity of care (Starfield 2002). So, in the most fundamental of ways, a key role of the PHC movement has been to promote the delivery of more integrated care to people living in local communities. This PHC movement has been sustained to the present day. Many present-day initiatives,

N. Goodwin (✉) • V. Stein
International Foundation for Integrated Care, Wolfson College, Oxford OX6 2UD, UK
e-mail: nickgoodwin@integratedcarefoundation.org

V. Amelung
Institute for Epidemiology, Social Medicine and Health System Research, Medical School Hannover, Hannover, Germany

© Springer International Publishing AG 2017
V. Amelung et al. (eds.), *Handbook Integrated Care*,
DOI 10.1007/978-3-319-56103-5_1

such as multi-speciality community providers in England and the patient-centred medical home model that originated in the USA, underpin their rationale through such evidence.

In parallel to the PHC movement, though not often aligned to it, has been the response of care systems globally to the growth of age-related chronic illnesses and comorbidities. Of specific importance has been the development of the Chronic Care Model (CCM) and its variants (Wagner et al. 1999). The CCM has become accepted in many countries as the comprehensive framework for the organization of healthcare to integrate care and improve outcomes for people with chronic conditions. The model focuses on six key and inter-related components including: support for self-management; decision-support to professionals; care co-ordination and case management; clinical information systems; and community resources to promote healthy living; and health system leadership (Wagner et al. 1999).

The development of the CCM came in recognition that most health systems were failing to meet the needs of people with chronic illnesses since they remained largely built on acute, episodic models of care rather than care that focuses on more longitudinal, preventive, community-based and integrated approaches. The CCM has thus been a catalyst to help reorient systems of care to become more integrated in the management of chronic illness that has strengthened PHC and promoted self-management and patient empowerment.

More recent variations of the CCM model have focused on including the broader determinants of health with coordinated interventions that cut across the primary, secondary and tertiary levels of care and that extend beyond the boundaries of the health care system to cover issues such as public health (i.e. population health promotion, prevention, screening and early detection), rehabilitation and palliative care (Barr et al. 2003; WHO 2002). Indeed, approaches to develop population-based 'managed care' organisations have emerged not only as a policy imperative in many countries (e.g. such as through the development of Integrated Service Organisations in the Basque Country) but also as a business strategy [e.g. such as Kaiser Permanente in the USA and Gesundes Kinzigtal in Germany—see the Case Studies (Part 6)].

PHC, CCM and approaches to 'managed care' have been significant steps towards integrated care. Yet, many existing programmes continue to use a vertical and disease-oriented approach to care when the evidence suggests that better outcomes occur through adopting an integrated approach between health care and other sectors that is more preventative and community-based. Disease-based approaches tend to foster duplication and the inefficient use of resources and produce gaps in the care of patients with multi-morbidity. The structural solutions in the way care has been organised to promote chronic care requires reappraisal if the ultimate objective is to promote more people-centred integrated care. Table 1.1 attempts to provide an understanding of how the characteristics of integrated care should be distinguished from that of conventional care and approaches to disease management.

Most recently, there has been a surge in interest in how integrated care needs to be 'people-centred' and embrace patients and service users as partners in care and

Table 1.1 Aspects of care that distinguish conventional health care from integrated care (adapted from WHO 2008, p.43)

Conventional ambulatory medical care in clinics or outpatient departments	Disease management programmes	Integrated care
Focus on illness and cure	Focus on priority diseases	Focus on holistic care to improve people's health and wellbeing
Relationship limited to the moment of consultation	Relationship limited to programme implementation	Continuous care to individuals, families and communities across the life course
Episodic curative care	Programme-defined disease control interventions	Co-ordinated and people-centred care integrated around needs and aspirations
Responsibility limited to effective and safe advice to the patient at the moment of consultation	Pro-active management of a patient's risk factors to meet targets	Shared responsibility and accountability for population health, tackling the determinants of ill-health through systems-thinking and inter-sectoral partnerships
Users are consumers of the care they purchase	Population groups are targets of specific disease-control interventions	People and communities are empowered to become co-producers of care at the individual, organizational and policy levels

to ensure services are well co-ordinated around their needs (e.g. see Blomfield and Cayton 2009; Ferrer 2015; The Health Foundation 2011, 2012). More broadly still, the notion of integrated care has gone beyond the borders of the health and social care systems to think more strategically about how to embrace the social determinants of ill-health through bringing together the wider range of community assets to promote public health, prevent ill-health, and secure wellbeing to populations.

This complex and emergent story of the focus and rationale for integrated care perhaps explains why there remains a lack of a common definition for integrated care which is universally accepted. Integrated care is, and remains, a polymorphous concept that has been applied from several disciplinary and professional perspectives and which is associated with diverse objectives. This diversity therefore represents a challenge to policy-makers, managers, professionals and researchers alike in developing 'common ground' in their understanding to the meaning and logic of integrated care.

This opening chapter, therefore, seeks to respond to the commonly asked question *'what is integrated care?'* To do so, the chapter briefly examines the rationale that lies behind integrated care before seeking to make sense of the various attempts that have been made to define it. The chapter then seeks to outline the core aspects of integrated care and reviews how a range of models and frameworks have been (and are being) created to understand the building blocks and dynamics of integrated care systems. The chapter concludes with some forward thinking on integrated care as an evolving science.

1.2   The Rationale for Integrated Care

Notwithstanding the long history to the origins of the term, integrated care as an ongoing policy concern has come as a response to the significant shift in global demographics that has seen age-related and long-term chronic conditions replace communicable disease as the most significant challenge facing all health and care systems. This shift means that the economic burden of chronic illness now represents as much as 80% of expenditure on health (Nolte and McKee 2008). This growth is significantly associated with ageing populations. For example, it has been estimated that by 2034 more than 5% of all people in Western Europe will be aged over 85 with more than one-fifth of these living with five or more co-morbidities (concurrent physical and mental health needs) (European Commission and Economic Policy Committee 2009).

Coupled with ageing populations is a dramatic increase in the use of long-term care by older people. For example, a comparative analysis on long-term care services in Europe projected dramatic increases in the use and costs of long-term care (more than 300% in the case of Germany) between 2000 and 2050 (Comas-Herrera and Wittenberg 2003). Therefore, community-based and home-based alternatives to institutionalisation in residential homes through the deployment of multi-disciplinary professional teams has become a commonplace response (e.g. Leichsenring et al. 2013).

These projections in the future demands on health and long-term care systems is observed to be so acute that even the World Health Organisation has passed a resolution across its 194 member states to adopt a *Framework on Integrated People-Centred Health Services* (WHO 2016). In their interim report it was argued that unless a people-centred and integrated health services approach is adopted, health care will become increasingly fragmented, inefficient and unsustainable (WHO 2015, p.7). In other words, integrated care represents a fundamental paradigm shift in the way health and care services must be funded, managed and delivered.

The case for making such a change towards integrated care is a compelling one. Since the future of our health and care systems is increasingly shaped by ageing populations, urbanization, and the globalization of unhealthy lifestyles it is clear that current approaches to care that focus on curative, specialist-led and hospital-based services need to be revised. People living with non-communicable diseases (NCDs), mental health problems, and long-term and multiple comorbidities need to make strenuous efforts to access the care they need and too often find themselves disempowered, disengaged and unable to manage their health needs. By missing the opportunity to promote health and prevent complications care has become more complex and more expensive.

The hypothesis underpinning integrated care, therefore, is that it represents an approach to promote quality improvement amongst people and populations where care is currently fragmented and poorly coordinated. Indeed, it has increasingly been recognised that integrated care should be seen as a means to promoting the 'Triple Aim' goals in care system reform (Berwick et al. 2008): greater cost efficiency; improved care experiences; and improved health outcomes. It is for this reason, in times of scarce resources and growing demands, that so much hope and weight has been placed on the integrated care movement as a mechanism for system transformation. Integrated care represents an approach to strengthen and/or introduce a set of fundamental design features for health systems that can generate significant benefits to the health and health care of citizens, whether rich or poor.

As this Handbook will reveal, the positive impact of integrated care can be seen to accrue at the level of the individual patient as well as to communities and care systems. Yet, in many areas such as health economics, such impact remains contested and there are also significant issues in understanding how best to deploy integrated care initiatives in practice. Nonetheless, given the projections on the future demand for health and care services, we are past the 'tipping point' where action needs to be taken to transform care systems. The move to more people-centred and integrated care is a core strategy in that task.

1.3   Defining Integrated Care

Integrated care is a concept that is widely used but recent literature reviews have uncovered more than 175 overlapping definitions and concepts linked with the term (Armitage et al. 2009). This large number of definitional possibilities demonstrate that they tend to be either generic or disaggregated in nature to reflect the complexity and multidimensionality of the concept. Over many years, a plethora of terms have been used including: 'managed care', 'coordinated care', 'collaborative care', disease management', 'case management', 'transmural care', 'continuity of care', 'seamless care', 'service-user-centred care' and many others.

This 'confusion of languages' stems from the different meaning and objectives that various stakeholders within care systems attribute to the term. This might relate to differing professional points of view (e.g. clinical vs. managerial; professional vs. patient) or from the disciplinary perspective of the observer (e.g. public administration, public health, social science, or psychology) (Nolte and McKee 2008). Work by Shaw et al. (2011) provides a graphic representation of some of these different viewpoints (see Fig. 1.1). It should be recognised from this that the different interpretations and meaning of integrated care are *all* potentially legitimate. This suggests that integrated care as a concept cannot be narrowly defined in its meaning, but must be seen as an umbrella term—perhaps linked to set of broader ideas and principles—that captures this wide ranging set of viewpoints.

In considering the variability in the way integrated care has been defined, let us consider the four definitions presented in Box 1.1. The first of these definitions, from the World Health Organisation, imbues integrated care with the qualities of care co-ordination as a continuous support process over time. It is focused on the

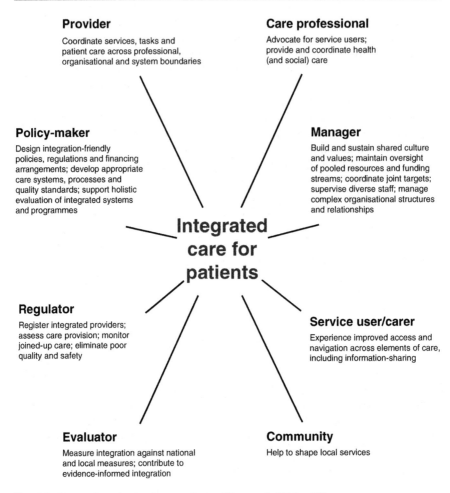

Provider

Coordinate services, tasks and patient care across professional, organisational and system boundaries

Care professional

Advocate for service users; provide and coordinate health (and social) care

Policy-maker

Design integration-friendly policies, regulations and financing arrangements; develop appropriate care systems, processes and quality standards; support holistic evaluation of integrated systems and programmes

Manager

Build and sustain shared culture and values; maintain oversight of pooled resources and funding streams; coordinate joint targets; supervise diverse staff; manage complex organisational structures and relationships

Integrated care for patients

Regulator

Register integrated providers; assess care provision; monitor joined-up care; eliminate poor quality and safety

Service user/carer

Experience improved access and navigation across elements of care, including information-sharing

Evaluator

Measure integration against national and local measures; contribute to evidence-informed integration

Community

Help to shape local services

Fig. 1.1 Perspectives shaping integrated care (Shaw et al. 2011, p.13)

delivery of public health or clinical interventions and is largely bounded within the confines of health care (WHO 2015). The second definition, used for example to underpin integrated care strategies in the Basque country, is again different since it primarily discusses the importance of the structural re-organisation required to enable care organisations to work together collaboratively (Contandriapolous et al. 2003). The third definition, and one used to define integrated care for articles in the International Journal of Integrated Care (IJIC, no date). The definition is lengthier but seeks to describe the complexity and inter-sectoral nature of integrated care. It also has the added advantage of distinguishing between integration (the process by which professionals and organisations come together) and integrated care (which is the outcome as experienced by service users). This is an important distinction since it implies integrated care should only be judged successful if it contributes to better care experiences and outcomes for people (Goodwin and Smith 2012).

Box 1.1 Four commonly used definitions of integrated care

1. A health system-based definition

"The management and delivery of health services such that people receive a continuum of health promotion, disease prevention, diagnosis, treatment, disease-management, rehabilitation and palliative care services, through the different levels and sites of care within the health system, and according to their needs throughout the life course" (WHO 2015)

2. A health and care managers' definition

"The process that involves creating and maintaining, over time, a common structure between independent stakeholders (and organisations) for the purpose of coordinating their interdependence in order to enable them to work together on a collective project" (Contandriapoulos et al. 2003)

3. A social science-based definition

"Integration is a coherent set of methods and models on the funding, administrative, organizational, service delivery and clinical levels designed to create connectivity, alignment and collaboration within and between the cure and care sectors. The goal of these methods and models is to enhance quality of care and quality of life, consumer satisfaction and system efficiency for people by cutting across multiple services, providers and settings. Where the result of such multi-pronged efforts to promote integration lead to benefits for people the outcome can be called 'integrated care'" (adapted from Kodner and Spreeuwenberg 2002)

4. A definition based on the perspective of the patient (person-centred coordinated care)

"I can plan my care with people who work together to understand me and my carer(s), allow me control, and bring together services to achieve the outcomes important to me." (National Voices, no date)

However, the criticisms behind these three well-used definitions is that they treat integrated care as a set of systemic or organisational processes as opposed to the essential quality of 'caring' for people. Hence, the fourth definition, seeks to define integrated care from the person's perspective such that the terms might have meaning to the end user (National Voices, 2011). This definition was developed by National Voices in the UK to create for NHS England a defining narrative for the national strategy to promote integrated care and support. By consulting with people across its 130 health and social care charities, National Voices asked what matters most to patients and service users and produced a series of 'I statements' on how

Alzheimer Web of Care

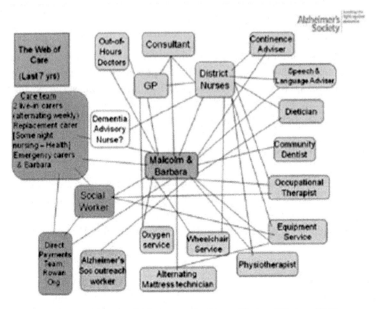

Fig. 1.2 Tackling complexity: the Alzheimer web of care (National Voices 2011)

care and services should be integrated around their needs with a core focus on care planning, care transitions, communication, information, and shared decision-making towards specific goals and outcomes.

What is implicit to all of the four definitions presented in Box 1.1 is the notion that integrated care should be centred on the needs of services users, their families and the communities to which they belong (Shaw et al. 2011). Indeed, there is evidence to suggest that the more successful integrated care programmes require the common language of *people-centeredness* to create a unifying narrative across stakeholders with potentially very different professional, organisational and political objectives (Ham and Walsh 2013).

As Goodwin and Alonso (2014) point out, there is good reasoning behind developing such a 'people-led' definition to integrated care. For example, in reflecting on the real-life context of a patient with advanced dementia and his principal carer (his spouse), it has been demonstrated how a highly diverse, complex and largely unconnected 'web of care' can result from fragmented health and care systems (National Voices 2011) (Fig. 1.2). These fragmentations are manifest in a range of key problems including:

- *a lack of ownership* from the range of care providers to support 'holistic' care needs;
- *a lack of involvement of the patient/carer in* supporting them to make effective choices about their care and treatment options or enabling them to live better with their conditions;

- *poor communication between professionals and providers*, exacerbated by the inability to share and transfer data, silo-based working, and embedded cultural behaviours;
- *simultaneous duplication of care* (e.g. repeated tests) *and gaps in care* (e.g. as appointments are missed or medications mismanaged);
- *a poor and disabling experience for the service users*;
- *reduced ability for people to live and manage their needs* effectively; and ultimately
- *poor system outcomes*, for example in terms of the inability to prevent unnecessary hospitalisations (Goodwin and Alonso 2014)

A key aspect of integrated care, then, is the ability to effectively co-ordinate care around people's needs. What is important to understand is that effective care co-ordination can be achieved without the need for formal integration of structures or organisations. Within single providers, integrated care can often be weak unless internal communication or silo-based working have been addressed. As Curry and Ham (2010) demonstrate in their review of the literature, it is the co-ordination of care at a clinical and service-level that matters the most.

Whilst a user-centred definition appears to be the most logical and useful approach to take to define integrated care, it is not for this Handbook to provide the overarching definition of integrated care that should be adopted by all. If the evidence for adoption tells us one thing it is that there is a requirement for all local stakeholders to come together agree on their own definition and meaning for integrated care as a means to guide their collective actions. However, in many ways, our overall understanding of the definition of integrated care should be made very simple. Integration (from the Latin *integer*, meaning whole or entire) generally means combining parts so that they work together or form a whole. Care, which can have many meanings, does in this context refer to providing attentive assistance or treatment to people in need. Hence *integrated care* results when the former (integration) is required to optimise the latter (care) and so is particularly important where fragmentations in care delivery have led to a negative impact on care experiences and outcomes.

The advantage to such a simple definition is that it might help overcome the tendency to focus on structural or organisationally-based solutions, or those that focus purely on integration as a means to create cost efficiencies (which as we will see later in this Handbook might often lead to negative results). Rather, by providing the definition of integrated care with a purpose, so integrated care is given a compelling logic as to its objectives and, therefore, leads to a recognition for how success through integrated care might be judged (Lewis et al. 2010).

In conclusion, integrated care is an approach for any individuals where gaps in care, or poor care co-ordination, leads to an adverse impact on care experiences and care outcomes. Integrated care may be best suited to frail older people, to those living with long-term chronic and mental health illnesses, and to those with medically complex needs or requiring urgent care. However, integrated care should *not* be solely regarded as a response to managing medical problems, the principles extend to the wider definition of promoting health and wellbeing.

1.4   The Core Dimensions of Integrated Care

One of the key problems to understanding integrated care is its complexity. To support this, there have been a number of different taxonomies developed in order to manage our understanding. Typically, these have examined (after Nolte and McKee 2008; Goodwin and Alonso 2014):

- the *process* of integration (i.e. the mechanisms—both technical and behavioural—required to integrate the work of people and organisations);
- the *degree* or *intensity* of integration (i.e. whether the process involves the 'full integration' of health and social care organisations into a new organisational model or whether the approach supports the creation of non-binding linkages or ties that support better co-ordination between them);
- the *breadth* of integration (i.e. whether it is fully oriented to: a whole population group; a specific client group—say older people or children; or a specific illness, such as diabetes);
- the *types* of integration (i.e. organisational, professional, cultural, technological);
- the *time-span* for integration (i.e. whether it is a 'life-course' approach to people over time, or whether focused on specific episodes of care); and
- the *level* at which integration occurs (i.e. macro-, meso- and micro- and even nano- at the point of care with the individual)

Moreover, integrated care appears to have taken a number of key forms, including (after Goodwin and Smith 2012; IJIC, no date):

- *Horizontal integration.* Integrated care between health services, social services and other care providers that is usually based on the development of multi-disciplinary teams and/or care networks that support a specific client group (e.g. for older people with complex needs)
- *Vertical integration.* Integrated care across primary, community, hospital and tertiary care services manifest in protocol-driven (best practice) care pathways for people with specific diseases (such as COPD and diabetes) and/or care transitions between hospitals to intermediate and community-based care providers
- *Sectoral integration.* Integrated care within one sector, for example combining horizontal and vertical programmes of integrated care within mental health services through multi-professional teams and networks of primary, community and secondary care providers;
- *People-centred integration:* Integrated care between providers and patients and other service users to engage and empower people through health education,

shared decision-making, supported self-management, and community engagement; and

- *Whole-system integration:* Integrated care that embraces public health to support both a population-based and person-centred approach to care. This is integrated care at its most ambitious since it focuses on the multiple needs of whole populations, not just to care groups or diseases.

One of the most important issues when adopting integrated care as a service design principle is the extent to which funders and/or care delivery organisations should opt to formally create new structural entities or otherwise seek to coordinate their activities in a less formal network. As discussed above, what really appears to matter is not the organisational solution but the service-level and clinical-level integration that occurs with and around service users. Yet there is evidence to suggest that the more severe the need of the patient, the more appropriate it might be to develop 'fully integrated' organisations to manage their complex needs (see Fig. 1.3).

Hence, there appears to be a continuum of forms of integrated care from a 'linkage' approach (sometimes referred to as 'virtual' integration) that might seek to ensures effective information sharing and focus on effective referral practices; to a 'coordination' model that might develop more formal connections such as care pathway agreements to enable effective care transitions between service providers; to a 'fully integrated' service where new organisational forms, perhaps using pooled budgets, become dedicated to the management of care to defined patient groups or populations (Ahgren and Axelson 2005).

Moreover, the intensity of the organisational solution to integrated care has been argued to reflect the severity of the needs of the patient or service user. As Table 1.2 demonstrates, full integration is argued to work best when aimed at people with severe, complex and long-term needs. Hence, for a person with lower levels of need, an appropriate response to care integration might focus more on a 'linkage' model. This might encourage systems that seek to identify people in local communities with emergent needs (e.g. are at risk of becoming frail and/or having one or more chronic conditions) and support the appropriate follow-up and information sharing. Conversely, for people with high needs, integrated care might require the development of intensive multi-disciplinary care teams, common management structures enabled through pooled funding, and shared information systems (Leutz 1999).

The ability to match resources to the needs of population groups, for example as means to promote care management to high risk individuals, has become one of the most well-established approaches to integrated care strategies. Pioneered by Kaiser Permanente in the USA, stratifying populations to their risk profiles (see Fig. 1.4) can enable targeted, community-based and pro-active approaches to care that seeks to prevent unnecessary institutionalisation (Singh and Ham 2006).

However, there is a countervailing argument that suggests that fully integrated systems for people with highly complex needs might not necessarily be an

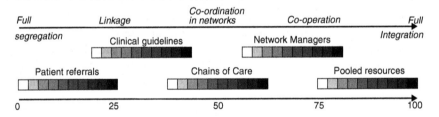

Full integration

Formally pooling resources,
allowing a new organisation to be
created alongside development of
comprehensive services attuned to the needs
of specific patient groups.

Coordination

Operating through existing organisational units so as to
coordinate different health services, share clinical information
and manage transition of patients between different units
(for example chains of care, care networks).

Linkage

Taking place between existing organisational units with
a view to referring patients to the right unit at the right time,
and facilitating communication between professionals involved in order
to promote continuity of care. Responsibilities are clearly aligned to
different groups with no cost shifting.

Full	*Linkage*	Co-ordination in networks	Co-operation	*Full*
segregation	Clinical guidelines		Network Managers	*Integration*
Patient referrals		Chains of Care		Pooled resources
0	25	50	75	100

Fig. 1.3 The intensity of integration (Leutz 1999 cited in Shaw et al. 2011, p.15 and adapted from Ahgren and Axellson 2005)

appropriate solution and does not necessarily lead to the better management of their needs (6 P et al. 2006). This is because it can be very difficult to predict the variable demands of the high-risk patient on a day-to-day basis and, as a result, the creation of care management organisations might not have the human and financial resources available to respond effectively (Ross et al. 2012). Recent research on care co-ordination to people with complex needs suggests that a 'core team' is required to support day-to-day needs but a responsive provider network is also needed to support people when unmanageable complexities in care arise (Goodwin et al. 2013, 2014).

Table 1.2 Matching client needs with approaches to integrated care (Leutz 1999)

Client needs	Linkage	Co-ordination	Full integration
Severity	Mild to moderate	Moderate to severe	Moderate to severe
Stability	Stable	Stable	Unstable
Duration	Short to long-term	Short to long-term	Long-term to terminal
Urgency	Routine/non-urgent	Mostly routine	Frequently urgent
Scope of need	Narrow to moderate	Moderate to broad	Broad
Self-direction	Self-directed	Moderate self-directed	Weak self-directed

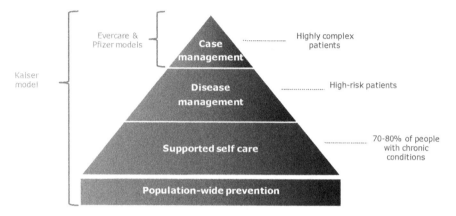

Fig. 1.4 The 'Kaiser Triangle': deploying different strategies for integrated care according to the risk profiles of populations (adapted from Singh and Ham 2006)

1.5   The Building Blocks of Integrated Care

Many frameworks have been developed to understand the key elements, or building blocks, that comprise a successful integrated care programme. The most influential framework, as described above, has been the CCM that set out the design of integrated chronic care initiatives to improve quality and outcomes. The CCM was developed from a Cochrane systematic review of factors in recognition of the failures of health systems in meeting the needs of people with chronic illnesses since they remain largely built on acute, episodic models of care rather than care that focuses on more longitudinal, preventative, community-based and integrated approaches. The CCM aimed to provide a comprehensive framework for the organization of healthcare in order to improve outcomes for people with chronic conditions (see Box 1.2).

Box 1.2 The six interrelated components of the Chronic Care Model

1. self-management support,
   a. patient education
   b. patient activation/psychosocial support
   c. self-management assessment
   d. self-management resources and tools
   e. collaborative decision-making with patients
   f. guidelines/education
2. decision support,
   a. decision-support tools and guidelines
   b. provider education
   c. expert consultation support
3. delivery system redesign,
   a. care management roles
   b. team practice
   c. care coo-ordination and care coordinators
   d. pro-active follow-up
   e. planned visits
4. clinical information systems,
   a. patient registries
   b. information use for care management
   c. feedback on performance data
5. community resources
   a. for patients
   b. for community
6. health system (support)
   a. leadership
   b. provider engagement
   c. system to spread innovation and improvements

Further revised since to include: cultural competency; patient safety; care
coordination; community policies; and case management.
Source: Wagner et al. (1999)

Several variations of the CCM, including the *Expanded Chronic Care Model* and
the *Innovative Care for Chronic Conditions* have focused on the importance of the
broad determinants of health (Barr et al. 2003; WHO 2002). They stress the
importance of coordinated interventions that cut across the primary, secondary
and tertiary levels of care and beyond the boundaries of the health care system to
cover issues such as public health (i.e. population health promotion, prevention,
screening and early detection), management of diagnosed cases, rehabilitation and
palliative care).

For example, the *Expanded Chronic Care Model* identified a number of additional domains to the original CCM including: community resources and policies (such as healthy public policy, a focus on influencing the socio-determinants of ill-health through the living environment, and strengthening community action); self-management support; decision-support to professionals through evidence-based guidelines; a focus on quality of life and holistic needs rather than just clinical outcomes; and the importance of data systems that integrate information across sectors (Barr et al. 2003).

The *Innovative Care for Chronic Conditions,* developed by the WHO as part of a 'road map' for countries and their health systems to deal with the rising burden of chronic illness, placed a specific premium on prevention through 'productive partnerships' between patients and families, community partners and health care teams to create informed, prepared and motivated communities. Eight strategies for action were presented to support the model become reality (WHO 2002; see Fig. 1.5).

Other framework developments have included the *patient centred medical home (PCMH)* that represents an evidence-based model of enhanced primary care developed in the USA that can provide care which is accessible, continuous, comprehensive and co-ordinated and delivered in the context of family and community (National Committee for Quality Assurance 2016). PCMH evolved as a response in how to manage *all* patients in a particular community, rather than those with

Fig. 1.5 Innovative care for chronic conditions framework (adapted from WHO 2002)

chronic illness as in CCM, and was particularly targeted at children and adolescents and other people requiring more holistic care and treatment. PCMH was piloted as an approach within Medicare and Medicaid insurance programmes, including the creation of new payments and incentives for group practices that meet the core criteria associated with being designated as a PCMH. The key domains of the approach include: having a personal physician (continuity of care); physician-directed medical practice; whole person orientation; care that is co-ordinated and/or integrated around a person's individual needs; quality and safety targets; and enhanced access (to primary care).

The frameworks and models for care systems described above have primarily evolved from the USA and been confined in their thinking to *within* health systems and not sought to identify the wider range of actions that decision-makers would need to adopt to enable integrated care to be adopted. One knowledge synthesis conducted in Canada, however, that sought to address this was able to develop 'ten principles of successful integrated systems' (Suter et al. 2007) from which some care systems in Canada derived a simple scorecard to reflect on their capabilities (see Box 1.3). The research is currently being updated and validated through a series of Delphi exercises and a revised version was due later in 2016 (Suter et al. 2015).

Box 1.3 Ten Principles for Successfully Integrated Systems (Suter et al. 2007)

1. *Care across the continuum.* Recognizing the importance of providing seamless health care despite the multiple points of access
2. *Patient focus.* Encouraging active participation by the patients, families, or informal caregivers while focusing on population-based needs assessment
3. *Geographic coverage and rostering.* Rostering to maximize accessibility and minimize duplications
4. *Standardized care delivery through inter professional teams.* Using provider developed and evidence-based clinical care guidelines and protocols
5. *Performance measurement.* Evaluating the process of integration and measuring system, provider, and patient outcomes
6. *Appropriate information technology and communication.* Collecting data through electronic patient records systems to effectively track utilization and outcomes
7. *Organizational culture and leadership.* Sharing a vision of an integrated health care delivery system through strong leadership and cohesion
8. *Physician engagement.* Integrating physicians, particularly primary care physicians, by a variety of methods such as compensation mechanisms, financial incentives, and non-financial ways of improving quality of life
9. *Strong governance structure.* Implementing a strong governance structure that includes community and physician representatives
10. *Sound financial management.* Encouraging fiscal responsibility

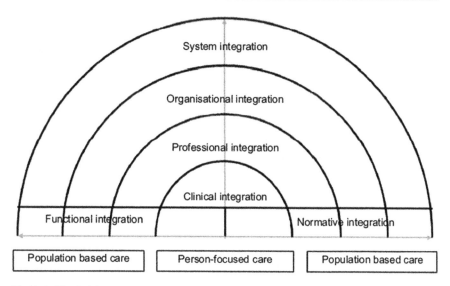

Fig. 1.6   The Rainbow Model of integrated care (after Valentijn et al. 2013)

Of the range of interpretations and conceptual frameworks through which to understand and study the complexities of integrated care it is the comparatively recent work by Valentijn et al. that provides one of the more elegant approaches (Valentijn 2016; Valentijn et al. 2013 and see Fig. 1.6). By placing people-focused and population-based co-ordinated care as the guiding principle or objective of integration, their research describes the range of different integration processes at the macro-level (system integration), meso-level (organisational and professional integration) and micro-level (clinical, service and personal integration). Functional integration (e.g., communication and the use of ICT) sits alongside normative integration (e.g., shared cultural values) to ensure effective connectivity between the functioning of the integrated care system between the various levels. Hence, information and communication is regarded as a key transversal issues with a role as a 'connector' of processes that has the dual quality of both being the 'glue' through which people and organisations come together to provide more integrated services, but also the 'grease' in making these relationships dynamic through creating effective channels of communication and data sharing.

Valentijn et al.'s *Rainbow Model* of integrated care (Fig. 1.6) is a very useful way to conceptualise the inter-relationships among the different dimensions of integrated care though it does drive a 'process-driven' rather than 'user-centred' understanding. In a final taxonomy of integrated care elements positively associated with each of the different levels (see Box 1.4) the research did not focus on core issues related to person-centred care nor on the wider issues that other frameworks had identified regarding the ability to tackle the socio-determinants of ill-health or integrate public health approaches into integrated care strategies. This is not to criticise the *Rainbow Model* but demonstrates the problems in developing a generic template or tool through which to judge the key success factors across what is a complex service innovation. This leads to the recognition that the concept of integrated care should be seen as so much more than the sum of complex organisational and systemic processes but be regarded as a fundamental design principle in the future of care systems (Goodwin 2013a).

Box 1.4 The Rainbow Model of Integrated Care: Final Taxonomy Summary (from Valentijn 2016)

Clinical integration: case management, continuity of care, multi-disciplinary care plans, supportive relationship with client *Professional integration*: inter-professional education, inter-disciplinary teams *Organisational integration*: shared governance and accountability; shared strategy; trust	*System integration*: aligned regulatory frameworks to support care coordination and team work *Functional integration*: shared information systems; collective learning and joint research; regular feedback on performance measures *Normative integration*: shared vision; reciprocity of behaviour; mutual gain; visionary leadership; distributed leadership; shared norms and values

---

Most recently, the World Health Organisation has published a series of papers examining the transformational processes necessary to achieve people-centred and integrated health services delivery. WHO Europe, for example, has published its European Framework for Action on Integrated Health Services Delivery (WHO Regional Office for Europe 2016). The Framework provides an 'implementation package' designed for people and institutions in political and technical roles responsible for integrated care policy and practice.

In parallel to this, and based on its own examination of the evidence internationally, the WHO at the global level has since published its *Framework on Integrated People-Centred Services* (WHO 2016). Having been ratified by WHO's General Assembly in May 2016, it implies that all WHO member states (including across the EU) have signed up to the formal commitment to implement integrated care. In terms of implementation, the Framework sets out five interwoven strategies that need to be implemented for health service delivery to become more integrated and people-centred: empowering and engaging people and communities; strengthening governance and accountability; reorienting the model of care; coordinating services within and across sectors; and creating an enabling environment.

1.6   Conclusions

Without the full alignment of political, regulatory, organisational and professional support for the goals of integrated care, a significant degree of local leadership and commitment is needed at a clinical and service level to make change happen. This does not appear to be a sustainable proposition for the long-term future of integrated care, nor will it allow the widespread uptake of these approaches. Perhaps all countries need to re-evaluate and recalibrate their health and social care systems such that local service innovations can be supported to integrate services that can better meet the growing needs of [older] people with complex and multiple conditions (Goodwin et al. 2014, p.22)

Integrated care is difficult to define and understand since it represents a complex service innovation in the way health and care services should be redesigned around people's needs. Consequently, integrated care has come to mean different things to different people and the resulting conceptual 'soup' has often acted as a barrier when it comes to developing commonly understood strategies to support implementation and change. However, as this chapter has attempted to outline, there are three distinct dimensions to what integrated care means in practice:

- First, integrated care is a necessary response to overcome fragmentations in care delivery where this adversely impacts on the ability to co-ordinate care effectively around people's needs and so leads to sub-optimal results in terms of people's care experiences and outcomes.
- Second, integrated care represents an approach to improve the quality and cost-effectiveness of care by ensuring that services are well coordinated around people's needs. Integrated care is by definition, therefore, both 'people-centred' and 'population-oriented'.
- Third, it is this people-centred focus that becomes the organising principle for integrated care as a service innovation, whether this be related to individual patients, the carer/family, or the wider community to which they belong.

However, our understanding of integrated care, its complexities, its components, and the ways to implement it remain an emerging scientific discipline. There is a significant and emerging body of knowledge that helps us understand and appreciate the building blocks that need to be put in place for the effective development of integrated care in policy and practice. Yet, as the next chapters in this Handbook make clear, what appears to be more difficult is our understanding of the impact of integrated care programmes and the relationship between the component parts of an integrated care solution that contributes to improving outcomes.

It has been observed that the implementation science to integrated care remains weak (Goodwin 2013b). In part this is a reflection on how many integrated care programmes are immature, often ill-defined, and lacking in focus. Much still needs to be done through research to broaden our conceptual and empirical understanding, but in a way that pro-actively supports adoption to meet the 'Triple Aim' goals that have been adopted as the core hypothesis behind the integrated care movement.

References

6 P, Goodwin, N., Peck, E., & Freeman, T. (2006). *Managing networks of 21st century organizations*. Basingstoke: Palgrave-McMillan.

Ahgren, B., & Axelsson, R. (2005). Evaluating integrated health care: A model for measurement. *International Journal of Integrated Care, 5*(3), e01.

Armitage, G., Suter, E., Oelke, N., & Adair, C. (2009). Health systems integration: State of the evidence. *International Journal of Integrated Care, 9*(2), 1–11.

Barr, S., Robinson, S., Marin-Link, B., & Salivaras, S. (2003). The expanded chronic care model: An integration of concepts and strategies from population health promotion and the Chronic Care Model. *Hospital Quarterly, 7*(1), 73–82.

Berwick, D. M., Nolan, T. W., & Whittington, J. (2008). The triple aim: Care, health, and cost. *Health Affairs (Millwood), 27*(3), 759–769.

Blomfield, M., & Cayton, H. (2009). *Community engagement: A report for the Health Foundation*. London: The Health Foundation.

Comas-Herrera, A., & Wittenberg, R. (Eds.) (2003). *European study of long-term care expenditure*. Report to the European Commission, Employment and Social Affairs DG. Personal Social Services Research Unit, London School of Economics, London. PSSRU Discussion Paper 1840.

Contandriapoulos, A., Denis, J. L., Touati, N., & Rodriguez, C. (2003). *The integration of health care: Dimensions and implementation*. Retrieved from http://nelhin.on.ca/assets/0/16/2100/3734/3736/6cab135d-87c1-45bd-88cd-2c1d5404ec9b.pdf

Curry, N., & Ham, C. (2010). *Clinical and service integration: The route to improved outcomes*. London: The King's Fund.

European Commission and Economic Policy Committee. (2009). *2009 Ageing Report: Economic and budgetary projections for the EU-27 Member States (2008–2060)*. Luxembourg: Office for Official Publications of the European Communities.

Ferrer, L. (2015). *Engaging patients, carers and communities in the provision of coordinated/integrated health services: Strategies and tools*. Copenhagen: WHO Regional Office for Europe.

Goodwin, N. (2013a). Understanding integrated care: A complex process, a fundamental principle. *International Journal for Integrated Care,* Jan–Mar, URN:NBN:NL:UI:10-1-114416.

Goodwin, N. (2013b). How do you build programmes of integrated care? The need to broaden our conceptual and empirical understanding. *International Journal for Integrated Care*, Jul–Sep, e040.

Goodwin, N., & Alonso, A. (2014). Understanding integrated care: The role of information and communication technology. In S. Muller, I. Meyer, & L. Kubitschke (Eds.), *Beyond Silos: The way and how of eCare*. Hershey, PA: IGI Global.

Goodwin, N., & Smith, J. (2012). *The evidence base for integrated care*. London: The King's Fund.

Goodwin, N., Sonola, L., Thiel, V., & Kodner, D. (2013). *Co-ordinated care for people with complex chronic conditions. Key lessons and markers for success*. London: The King's Fund.

Goodwin, N., Dixon, A., Anderson, G., & Wodchis, W. (2014). *Providing integrated care for older people with complex needs. Lessons from seven international case studies*. London: The King's Fund.

Ham, C., & Walsh, N. (2013). *Making integrated care happen at scale and pace: Lessons from experience*. London: The King's Fund.

International Journal of Integrated Care (IJIC). (no date). *IJIC guidelines for research and theory papers*. Retrieved from https://s3-eu-west-1.amazonaws.com/ubiquity-partner-network/up/journal/ijic/IJIC-research-and-theory-guidelines.pdf

Kodner, D., & Spreeuwenberg, C. (2002). Integrated care: Meaning, logic, applications and implications – a discussion paper. *International Journal of Integrated Care, 2*(14), e12.

Leichsenring, K., Billings, J., & Nies, H. (Eds.). (2013). *Long-term care in Europe. Improving policy and practice*. Palgrave Macmillan: Basingstoke.

Leutz, W. (1999). Five laws for integrating medical and social services: Lessons from the United States and the United Kingdom. *The Milbank Quarterly, 77*(1), 77–110.

Lewis, R., Rosen, R., Goodwin, N., & Dixon, J. (2010). *Where next for integrated care organisations in the English NHS?* London: The Nuffield Trust.

National Committee for Quality Assurance. (2016, September). *Latest evidence: Benefits of NCQA patient-centred medical home recognition.* Washington: NCQA.

National Voices. (no date). *A narrative for person-centred coordinated ('integrated') care.* National Voices. Retrieved from www.nationalvoices.org.uk/sites/www.nationalvoices.org. uk/files/narrative-coordinated-care.pdf

National Voices. (2011). *Webs of Care. What does care look like from the individual's perspective?* London: National Voices. Available at: http://www.nationalvoices.org.uk/sites/default/ files/public/publications/webs_of_care.pdf

Nolte, E., & McKee, M. (2008). Integration and chronic care: A review. In E. Nolte & M. McKee (Eds.), *Caring for people with chronic conditions: A health system perspective* (pp. 64–91). Maidenhead: Open University Press.

Ross, S., Curry, N., & Goodwin, N. (2012). *Case management. What it is and how it can best be implemented.* London: The King's Fund.

Shaw, S., Rosen, R., & Rumbold, B. (2011). *What is integrated care?* London: The Nuffield Trust.

Singh, D., & Ham, C. (2006). *Improving Care for people with long-term conditions. A review of UK and international frameworks.* Health Services Management Centre, University of Birmingham, Birmingham.

Starfield, B. (2002). Policy relevant determinants of health: An international perspective. *Health Policy, 60*, 201–218.

Suter, E., Oelke, N., Adair, C., Waddell, C., Armitage, G., & Huebner, L. (2007 October). Health Systems Integration. Definitions, processes & impact: A research synthesis. Ottawa, ON: Canadian Institutes of Health Research (CIHR).

Suter, E., Oelke, N., Lima, M., Vliet-Brown, C., Hepp, S., & Stiphout, M. (2015). Indicators and measurement tools for health system integration: Results from a knowledge synthesis. *International Journal of Integrated Care, 4*, 99.

The Health Foundation. (2011). *Evidence: Helping people help themselves.* London: The Health Foundation.

The Health Foundation. (2012). *Leading the way to shared decision making.* London: The Health Foundation.

Valentijn, P. (2016). *Rainbow of chaos. A study into the theory and practice of integrated primary care.* Dissertation, Tilburg University, The Netherlands.

Valentijn, P. P., Schepman, S. M., Opheij, W., & Bruijnzeels, M. A. (2013). Understanding integrated care: A comprehensive conceptual framework based on the integrative functions of primary care. *International Journal of Integrated Care, 13*, e010.

Wagner, E., et al. (1999). Improving chronic illness care: Translating evidence into action. *Health Affairs, 20*(6).

World Health Organization. (1978). *Declaration of Alma-Ata, International Conference on Primary Health Care 1978.* Geneva: World Health Organization.

World Health Organization. (2002). *Innovative care for chronic conditions. Building blocks for action.* Geneva: World Health Organization.

World Health Organization. (2008). Primary health care: Now more than ever. World Health Report. Geneva: World Health Organization.

World Health Organisation. (2015). *WHO global strategy on people-centred and integrated health services: Interim report.* Geneva: World Health Organization.

World Health Organisation. (2016, April 15). *Framework on integrated, people-centred health services.* Report by the Secretariat, 69th World Health Assembly, World Health Organisation, Geneva.

WHO Regional Office for Europe. (2016). *Towards people-centred health systems: An innovative approach for better health systems.* Copenhagen: WHO Regional Office for Europe.

Evidence Supporting Integrated Care

2

Ellen Nolte

2.1   Introduction

An ageing population coupled with a rising burden of chronic diseases, growing consumer expectations and technological advances challenge health care delivery in many countries. Against a backdrop of increasing financial constraints, this creates a pressing need for efficient use of resources. There is increasing concern about health systems' continued focus on acute, episodic illness with their dependence on hospital-based care delivery. Apart from being very costly, there are questions about the suitability and efficiency of such services in light of the changing disease burden (Rechel et al. 2009), and the rising proportion of people with multiple health problems (Barnett et al. 2012). Chronic conditions create a spectrum of long-term and fluctuating needs. In combination with increasing frailty at old age, these conditions require the development of delivery systems that bring together a range of professionals and skills from both the cure and care sectors, as well as active service user engagement (Holman and Lorig 2000; Nolte and McKee 2008a).

Yet, service delivery has developed in ways that have tended to fragment care both within and between sectors. For example, structural and financial barriers dividing providers at the primary and secondary care and at the health and social care interface, distinct organisational and professional cultures, and differences in terms of governance and accountability all contribute to care fragmentation (Glasby et al. 2006). As a consequence, people typically receive care from many different providers, often in different settings or institutions; they are frequently called upon

E. Nolte (✉)
European Observatory on Health Systems and Policies, London School of Economics and Political Science, London School of Hygiene & Tropical Medicine, London, UK
e-mail: E.Nolte@lse.ac.uk

© Springer International Publishing AG 2017
V. Amelung et al. (eds.), *Handbook Integrated Care*,
DOI 10.1007/978-3-319-56103-5_2

to monitor, coordinate, or carry out their own care plan, often with limited guidance on how to do so (House of Commons Health Committee 2014; Nolte et al. 2008). Failure to better coordinate services along the care continuum may result in suboptimal outcomes, such as potentially preventable hospitalisations, medication errors, and other adverse events (Vogeli et al. 2007).

It is against this background that, globally, systems have set out to explore new approaches to health care delivery that can bridge the boundaries between professions, providers, and institutions and so provide appropriate support to people with long-standing health and care needs (Nolte et al. 2008; WHO Regional Office for Europe 2016; World Health Organization 2015). At the policy level, countries have sought to create regulatory and policy frameworks to promote approaches that better integrate care and improve coordination between sectors and levels of care. This often occurs alongside efforts to shift specialist services from hospital into the community as a means to increase the accessibility of services and the responsiveness of the system, and, potentially, reduce costs (Ettelt et al. 2006; Nolte et al. 2014; Winpenny et al. 2016). In Europe, this development has been supported by the 2011 European Council Conclusion recommending countries introduce innovative approaches and models of health care to move towards more integrated care systems, enhance equitable access to high quality care, and reduce inequalities (Council of the European Union 2011).

The move to more integrated care systems is often associated with high expectations and a goal of increasing the effectiveness, efficiency, and sustainability of service delivery more broadly (European Commission 2011). This chapter provides an overview of available evidence supporting integrated care. Building on our earlier work, we begin by briefly describing conceptualisations of integrated care against which to assess the evidence, followed by an overview of the literature that examines the impacts of integrated care. We then discuss some of the key challenges of interpreting the existing evidence base and the extent to which it permits drawing robust conclusions on the effects of integrated care approaches on various outcomes. We close with a set of overarching observations.

2.2   Conceptualising Integrated Care

Depending on the context, strategies to integrate care are sometimes driven by a need to contain cost, sometimes by the need to improve care, and often by both. Central to the development of integrated care is an expectation that it might support achievement of the 'Triple Aim' approach of a simultaneous focus on improving health outcomes, enhancing patient care experience, and reducing the per capita costs of care for populations (Berwick et al. 2008). Available evidence points to a positive impact of integrated care programmes on the quality of patient care and on selected outcomes (Martinez-Gonzalez et al. 2014; Ouwens et al. 2005). However, the effectiveness and consequences of different forms of care integration, including their economic impacts, remain uncertain (Nolte and Pitchforth 2014). This is in

part because of the lack of a common understanding of what is being referred to as
'integrated care', as well as inconsistencies in describing component approaches
and interventions (Martinez-Gonzalez et al. 2014; Nolte and Pitchforth 2014;
Ouwens et al. 2005). This section provides a summary of ways to think about
integrated care; a detailed review of relevant conceptualisations is presented in
Chap. 1.

Integrated care is a concept that has been widely used in many ways by different
scholars and in different health systems (Nolte and McKee 2008b). Traditionally, it
has been discussed in the health and social care fields, with reference to linking the
cure and care sectors (Kodner and Spreeuwenberg 2002). Some authors also
suggest linking in broader human services systems such as education and housing
in order to improve outcomes (Leutz 1999). The application of the concept of
integrated care to health and social care is not clear cut, however, and different
conceptualisations have been put forward emphasising, for example, the health care
perspective ("a concept bringing together inputs, delivery, management and organization of services related to diagnosis, treatment, care, rehabilitation and health
promotion" (p. 7) (Groene and Garcia-Barbero 2001), or interpreting integration in
terms of financing and delivery functions in the context of managed care (Ovretveit
1998; Shortell et al. 1994).

The common denominator of integrated care concepts and approaches is their
primary aim of improving outcomes for, traditionally, frail older people and other
population groups with diverse and complex needs who require assistance with
activities of daily living (Nolte and McKee 2008b). It is important, however, to
recognise that integration is a much broader concept that applies to many other
areas such as urgent care, maternity and child health care, and public health, among
others. A common element is the notion that integrated care should be centred on
the needs of service users, their families, and the communities to which they belong
(Shaw et al. 2011). Lewis et al. (2010) highlighted that a user-centred vision for
care delivery is more likely to overcome the tendency to opt for structural or
organisation-based solutions, and it also provides a compelling logic regarding
the objectives for integrated care and how success might be evaluated.

Systematic understanding of the evidence of the impacts of integrated care has
long been hampered by the absence of a "sound paradigm through which to
examine the process" (p. 311) (Goodwin et al. 2004), and it has only been more
recently that more formal analytical frameworks have been proposed (Minkman
et al. 2013; Valentijn et al. 2013; van der Klauw et al. 2014). For example, in an
attempt to develop a typology of integration in health and social care that enables
systematic assessment of the structures and processes involved, their prerequisites,
and their effects on service organisation, delivery, and outcomes, analysts have
identified different dimensions of integration. The most commonly used
dimensions differentiate the *type*, the *breadth*, the *degree*, and the *process* of
integration (Nolte and McKee 2008b). Valentijn et al. (2013) brought these different ways of conceptualising integration together in the form of the Rainbow Model
of Integrated Care, which sees integrated care as a person-focused and population-
based care approach across the care continuum. In the model, integration occurs at

the micro (clinical integration), meso (professional and organisational integration), and macro (system integration) levels, along with functional and normative integration linking the different levels (see Chap. 1) (Valentijn et al. 2013). It is important to recognise that the process of integration typically requires simultaneous action at the different levels and across different functions, which develop in distinct phases (Minkman 2011). Thus, care integration is not likely to follow a single path and variations will be inevitable.

2.3 The Evidence Supporting Integrated Care

There is now a series of reviews, and reviews of reviews, of the published and grey literature on integrated care models or strategies for people with (specific) chronic conditions (Busetto et al. 2016; Kruis et al. 2013; Martinez-Gonzalez et al. 2014; Ouwens et al. 2005), those with mental health co-morbidity (Lemmens et al. 2016; Rodgers et al. 2016), or for broader population groups (Nolte and Pitchforth 2014). Reviews typically consider a range of approaches that can be subsumed under the heading of integrated care, such as collaborative care, case management, care coordination, or disease management. Indeed, in a review of systematic reviews by Ouwens et al. (2005), which sought to assess the effectiveness, definitions, and components of integrated care programmes for chronically ill patients, the majority of the studies assessed disease management programmes (see Chap. 5) (Ouwens et al. 2005). Similarly, in a more recent meta-review of integrated care programmes for adults with chronic conditions, two-thirds of included studies were reviews of disease management interventions (Martinez-Gonzalez et al. 2014).

Both reviews found evidence of beneficial effects for some outcomes, such as functional health status, clinical outcomes, patient satisfaction, and quality of life. Frequently there was evidence of a positive trend only, rather than of statistically significant improvements (Martinez-Gonzalez et al. 2014; Ouwens et al. 2005). Evidence of impacts on mortality tended to be mixed. There was also evidence of reduced health care utilisation but again observed trends were often not statistically significant. Evidence of beneficial impacts of integrated care programmes on costs tended to be weak. Based on these observations, review authors concluded that integrated care programmes can lead to improvements in the quality of care and in selected health and resource use outcomes. At the same time, authors also reported a lack of precision among reviewed studies in describing programmes, with variation in definitions and components of care analysed, which made it difficult to arrive at overarching conclusions about the 'best approach'. Indeed, as Ouwens et al. (2005) noted, such heterogeneity might lead to inappropriate conclusions about programme effectiveness and the application of findings.

This raises the question about the usefulness of seeking to assess the effectiveness of integrated care as such and, more specifically, whether the concept lends itself to evaluation in a way that would allow for the generation of definitive evidence given its complex and polymorphous nature. Indeed, if integrated care is seen as a means to improve outcomes by overcoming issues of fragmentation through linkage or coordination of services of different providers along the continuum of care, related initiatives will have to be targeted to the needs of a given population, which in turn will be highly context-dependent. Therefore, while it may not be possible to generate clear-cut evidence as to the effectiveness of integrated care as a whole, there is potential for transferable lessons to be learned across different studies to identify core elements that will support better outcomes.

Such an approach was taken in the World Health Organization's global strategy on people-centred and integrated health services. Published in 2015, work presented in support of the strategy focused on the evidence of effects of interventions and approaches within each of five key strategic directions (World Health Organization 2015). These strategic directions were: empowering and engaging people, strengthening governance and accountability, reorienting the model of care, coordinating services, and creating an enabling environment. For example, under the heading of 'empowering and engaging people' the most common and effective interventions were identified to be in the areas of health education, shared decision-making, supporting self-management, and personalised care planning (Ferrer 2015).

Similarly, there is good evidence that coordination, described as a strategy, or rather a range of strategies that can help to achieve integrated care (Leutz 1999; Van Houdt et al. 2013), can positively impact selected outcomes. For example, a systematic review by Powell-Davies et al. (2006) examined the effects of different strategies of coordination within primary care and other sectors (Table 2.1). The review assessed outcomes in terms of the percentage of studies that reported significant positive results. It showed that, generally, strategies that helped build relationships between service providers, through co-location, case management, or the use of multidisciplinary teams tended to be the most successful in achieving positive health outcomes and service user satisfaction. Also, strategies that involved providing systems and structures to support coordination tended to be more effective in terms of health outcomes than those providing support for service providers.

The review by Powell-Davies et al. (2006) highlighted the need to recognise the context within which approaches are being implemented, whether individually or as part of a broader strategy, as well as the populations that are being targeted, in order to assess their impact and likelihood of success. This will be of particular importance where individual strategies can themselves be considered complex interventions.

This context specificity can be illustrated by the example of case management. Powell-Davies et al. (2006) noted that this may be a promising coordination strategy for some populations and settings, particularly in mental health and aged care (Powell Davies et al. 2006). A 2015 Cochrane review of the effectiveness of case management approaches to home support for people with dementia found, based on 13 randomised controlled trials, that it was beneficial for some outcomes at certain time points. There was evidence of a significantly reduced likelihood of being institutionalised among those with dementia in the short- and medium term, reduced carer burden, and reduced overall health care costs (Reilly et al. 2015). Conversely, a systematic review and meta-analysis of the effectiveness of case

Table 2.1 Summary of the evidence on the effectiveness of interventions to improve coordination in health care

Strategy	Proportion (%) of studies with positive outcome for health	Proportion (%) of studies with positive outcome for service user satisfaction	Proportion (%) of studies with positive outcome for cost saving
Coordination of clinical activities			
Structured arrangements for coordinating service provision between providers, including joint consultations, shared assessments and priority access to another clinical service (n = 37 studies)	19/31 (61.3%)	4/12 (33.3%)	3/15 (20%)
Communication between service providers			
Interventions designed to improve communication between service providers, such as case conferences (n = 56 studies)	26/47 (55.3%)	12/22 (54.5%)	3/21 (14.3%)
Support for service providers			
Interventions include support or supervision for clinicians, training (joint or relating to collaboration), and reminder systems (n = 33 studies)	16/28 (57.1%)	8/14 (57.1%)	1/12 (8.3%)
Support to service users			
Interventions include joint education, reminders and assistance in accessing care (n = 19 studies)	6/17 (35.3%)	3/6 (50.0%)	1/7 (14.3%)
Systems to support coordination			
Interventions include shared care plans, decision support, pro formas, service user held or shared records; shared information or communication systems; register of service users (n = 47 studies)	23/38 (60.5%)	7/19 (36.8%)	2/13 (15.4%)
Relationships between service providers			
Structured relationships between service providers including co-location, case management, multidisciplinary teams or assigning service users to a	19/29 (65.5%)	8/12 (66.7%)	2/12 (16.7%)

(continued)

Table 2.1 (continued)

Strategy	Proportion (%) of studies with positive outcome for health	Proportion (%) of studies with positive outcome for service user satisfaction	Proportion (%) of studies with positive outcome for cost saving
particular primary care provider (n = 33 studies)			
All studies (n = 80)	36/65 (55.4%)	14/31 (45.2%)	5/28 (17.9%)

Source: Adapted from Powell-Davies et al. (2006)

management of patients in primary care that are 'at-risk' of hospitalisation failed to demonstrate significant differences in service utilisation, mortality, or total cost among those receiving the intervention compared to usual care (Stokes et al. 2015). There was, however, some evidence of a (small) benefit for self-reported health and patient satisfaction.

It is beyond the scope of this chapter to assess the evidence base for case management, or indeed other strategies, tools, and instruments supporting integration, which are reviewed in greater detail elsewhere in this book. However, the example of case management provides a useful illustration of how a given approach or strategy seeking to enhance coordination and support integration may not always provide the most suitable strategy to enhance outcomes. Practitioners need to carefully consider the appropriateness for the target population. The review of case management of 'at-risk' patients also demonstrated that its effectiveness may be increased when delivered by a multidisciplinary team, when a social worker was involved, and when delivered in a setting rated as low in initial 'strength' of primary care (Stokes et al. 2015). These observations concur with the aforementioned review by Powell-Davies et al. (2006), which showed that coordinated care strategies that used multiple strategies tended to be more successful in enhancing health outcomes than those using a single strategy only. Specifically, those that helped structure relationships between providers and between providers and patients through, for example, co-location or multidisciplinary teams, were more likely to be successful.

2.4 The Economic Impacts of Integrated Care

As noted in earlier sections of this chapter, the move to more integrated care systems is often driven by the need to contain costs and associated with expectations of improved efficiency of service delivery. Yet, reviews that have also assessed the impacts on cost that can be attributed to integrated care programmes tend to report weak effects only (Martinez-Gonzalez et al. 2014; Ouwens et al. 2005). The following summarises the findings of our 2014 review of reviews, which sought to systematically assess the economic impacts of approaches and strategies supporting integrated care (Nolte and Pitchforth 2014). That review considered 19 systematic reviews and meta-analyses of diverse strategies that targeted a diverse group of people or populations. Reviewed studies focused on adults with specific chronic conditions including pain (Brink-Huis et al. 2008), depression (Gilbody et al. 2006a; van Steenbergen-Weijenburg et al. 2010), stroke (Langhorne et al. 2005), asthma (Maciejewski et al. 2009), heart failure (Phillips et al. 2004), COPD (Steuten et al. 2009) or those with multimorbidity (Smith et al. 2012). Others considered strategies for older people in the community considered to be frail (Oeseburg et al. 2009), who had long-term medical or social care needs (Tappenden et al. 2012), or who were to be discharged from hospital (Chiu and Newcomer 2007). Three reviews focused on adults with dementia or memory loss (Pimouguet et al. 2010), those with severe mental health problems (Smith and Newton 2007), or those who received mental health care services (Steffen et al. 2009), while the remainder addressed populations defined by patterns of health service utilisation (Althaus et al. 2011; Shepperd et al. 2008; Simoens et al. 2011).

Strategies frequently targeted the interface between hospitals and primary care or community services, most often in the context of discharge planning or care transition (Althaus et al. 2011; Chiu and Newcomer 2007; Langhorne et al. 2005; Phillips et al. 2004; Simoens et al. 2011; Steffen et al. 2009). Several studies examined initiatives that sought to coordinate primary care and community services, often, although not always, involving medical specialists (Brink-Huis et al. 2008; Gilbody et al. 2006a; Smith et al. 2012; van Steenbergen-Weijenburg et al. 2010) or extending further into social care services (Pimouguet et al. 2010; Smith and Newton 2007; Tappenden et al. 2012; van Steenbergen-Weijenburg et al. 2010). The latter type of interventions tended to target older people with multiple care needs, those with dementia or with mental health problems. About half of primary studies considered by reviews were set in the USA, followed by the United Kingdom, Australia, Canada, New Zealand, the Netherlands, Spain, Italy, and Sweden.

The most common economic outcome measures were utilisation and cost, but reporting of measures was inconsistent and the quality of the evidence was often low. The majority of economic outcomes focused on hospital utilisation such as (re) admission rates, length of stay or admission days, and emergency department visits. For example, among reviews that considered care coordinating activities at the hospital-primary care or community services interface the majority reported evidence of reduced hospital utilisation (Chiu and Newcomer 2007; Langhorne et al. 2005; Phillips et al. 2004; Simoens et al. 2011; Steffen et al. 2009).

Most studies reported cost in terms of health care cost savings, most frequently in relation to hospital costs. Avoided costs or cost savings were typically derived from reduced hospital and emergency room utilisation. There was some evidence of cost reduction in a number of reviews although findings were frequently based on a small number of original studies, or studies that only used a before-after design without control, or both (Althaus et al. 2011; Brink-Huis et al. 2008; Chiu and

Newcomer 2007; Phillips et al. 2004; Shepperd et al. 2008; Simoens et al. 2011; Steffen et al. 2009). Philips et al. (2004) highlighted the impact of health system setting on costs, demonstrating that pooled cost differences of comprehensive discharge planning for those with heart failure ranged from −$359 compared to usual care in non-USA based trials to −$536 in USA trials. Tappenden et al. (2012) further noted, in a review of structured home-based, nurse-led health promotion, the importance of differentiating between initial and longer-term costs (Tappenden et al. 2012). They reported that a community-based nursing programme for patients with Parkinson's disease had initially increased costs but over 2 years costs were lower.

Reviews also assessed the cost-effectiveness of selected integrated care approaches but again the evidence base was weak, frequently relying on single trials of a given intervention. For example, one review of approaches targeting frequent hospital emergency department users found only one trial that reported the intervention to be cost effective (Althaus et al. 2011). One other review of structured home-based, nurse-led health promotion for older people at risk of hospital or care home admission concluded, based on three economic studies, that there was a high likelihood of cost savings associated with the intervention (Tappenden et al. 2012). However, one of the three primary studies suggested that there was little or no evidence for gains in quality-adjusted life years over usual care. Overall the evidence was difficult to interpret.

2.5   How to Interpret the Evidence Supporting Integrated Care

There is a wide and diverse evidence base, which appears to support a range of strategies and methods towards achieving more integrated care. However, it remains difficult to arrive at overarching conclusions about what works best in what composition and in what context. This is in part because the available evidence captures a wide range of, at times, very varied strategies and care approaches, which are not necessarily equivalent or comparable in relation to the type of service model, or the health and social care system context within which they are embedded. This challenge is greater where more complex combinations of interventions and service delivery changes are being implemented.

We have argued elsewhere that the interpretation of evaluation findings such as those presented here needs to be placed in the broader context of programme implementation specifically and issues around evaluation more widely (Nolte et al. 2012). For example, where an evaluation finds improvements in health outcomes but not in economic impacts, this might be because the length of evaluation was not sufficient to demonstrate economic gain. Likewise, an evaluation might find that a given care approach improved outcomes for a subgroup of participants only; this might indicate that the intervention was suboptimal or not sufficiently targeted at those who would benefit most. Also, intervention effects will differ by target population and, importantly, by setting, in particular where initiatives involve a complex interplay of different actors as is the case with integrated care approaches.

Against this background, it will be particularly important to understand the quality of the available evidence in order to make sense of the variation in findings. Concerning economic evaluations for example, several authors highlighted their low quality as a major impediment to arrive at a robust evidence base suitable to inform decision making. Studies frequently rely on before-after studies without appropriate control, reducing the ability to attribute observed cost reductions to the actual intervention (Althaus et al. 2011). Other challenges include small sample sizes (Chiu and Newcomer 2007), the type of costs and cost categories considered (de Bruin et al. 2011), and whether these are limited to the health care sector or also consider the wider societal impact of (successful) integrated care strategies (Gilbody et al. 2006b), alongside lack of reporting on reliability of estimates. All of this highlights the need for higher quality studies.

At the same time, to support this process, there may be a need to revisit the way in which evidence in the field of integrated care is being generated to advance our understanding of 'what works'. At the core remains the clear definition of what constitutes effectiveness (or 'success') and, perhaps more critically, the hypothesised mechanism(s) of expected effect(s), which requires good theoretical understanding of how the intervention causes change and of the links within the causal chain (Craig et al. 2008). Much of the available evidence on outcomes rests on explicitly quantitative methods. However, as Cretin et al. (2004) have suggested in the context of chronic care, the complexity and variability of related interventions and programmes calls for the use of mixed-method research. While there is an increasing body of work in this field, there remains relatively little research on methodological, analytical, or conceptual aspects of the use of qualitative approaches in the evaluation of complex care programmes. Recently, there has been a move towards emphasising 'realistic evaluation' (Pawson and Tilley 1997), which uses pluralistic quasi-experimental methods for evaluating complex interventions that are highly influenced by contextual factors. Realistic evaluation involves understanding what works for whom under what circumstances, and places equal emphasis on external validity, generalisability and cumulative learning.

2.6 Conclusions

This chapter has provided an overview of available evidence supporting integrated care. It highlights that evidence of the impacts of integrated care as a whole is difficult to derive, given the complex and polymorphous nature of a concept that has been approached from different disciplinary and professional perspectives. Instead, it may be more instructive for decision-makers and practitioners to draw on evidence of impact of core elements and strategies that can help to achieve integrated care. One such element is care coordination which in itself can be seen to comprise a series of strategies, including case management, co-location and the use of multidisciplinary teams, along with support strategies such as shared care plans and decision support, which have been shown to enhance processes and the quality of care as well as health outcomes although the evidence of impact on cost remains weak.

A fundamental question that remains is whether integrated care is to be considered as an intervention that, by implication, ought to be cost-effective and support financial sustainability, or whether it is to be interpreted, and evaluated, as a complex strategy to innovate and implement long-lasting change in the way services in the health and social care sectors are being delivered and that involve multiple changes at multiple levels. Evidence reviewed here and in other sections of this book strongly supports the latter. This means that initiatives and strategies underway will require continuous evaluation over extended periods of time that will enable assessment of their impacts on both economic and health outcomes. Such an approach will require sustained investment in research and in the development and implementation of integrated care initiatives to ensure that evaluation will inform service development in particular (Goodwin et al. 2012).

References

Althaus, F., Paroz, S., Hugli, O., et al. (2011). Effectiveness of interventions targeting frequent users of emergency departments: A systematic review. *Annals of Emergency Medicine, 58* (41–52), e42.

Barnett, K., Mercer, S., Norbury, M., et al. (2012). Epidemiology of multimorbidity and implications for health care, research, and medical education: A cross-sectional study. *Lancet, 380*, 37–43.

Berwick, D., Nolan, T., & Whittington, J. (2008). The triple aim: Care, health, and cost. *Health Affairs, 27*, 759–769.

Brink-Huis, A., van Achterberg, T., & Schoonhoven, L. (2008). Pain management: A review of organisation models with integrated processes for the management of pain in adult cancer patients. *Journal of Clinical Nursing, 17*, 1986–2000.

Busetto, L., Luijkx, K., Elissen, A., et al. (2016). Intervention types and outcomes of integrated care for diabetes mellitus type 2: A systematic review. *Journal of Evaluation in Clinical Practice, 22*, 299–310.

Chiu, W. K., & Newcomer, R. (2007). A systematic review of nurse-assisted case management to improve hospital discharge transition outcomes for the elderly. *Professional Case Management, 12*, 330–336. quiz 337-338.

Council of the European Union. (2011). *Council conclusions: Towards modern, responsive and sustainable health systems*. Accessed February 15, 2016, from https://www.consilium.europa. eu/uedocs/cms_data/docs/pressdata/en/lsa/122395.pdf

Craig, P., Dieppe, P., Macintyre, S., et al. (2008). *Developing and evaluating complex interventions: New guidance*. London: Medical Research Council.

Cretin, S., Shortell, S., & Keeler, E. (2004). An evaluation of collaborative interventions to improve chronic illness care: Framework and study design. *Evaluation Review, 28*, 28–51.

de Bruin, S., Heijink, R., Lemmens, L., et al. (2011). Impact of disease management programs on healthcare expenditures for patients with diabetes, depression, heart failure or chronic obstructive pulmonary disease: A systematic review of the literature. *Health Policy, 101*, 105–121.

Ettelt, S., Nolte, E., Mays, N., et al. (2006). *Health care outside hospital. Accessing generalist and specialist care in eight countries*. Copenhagen: World Health Organization on behalf of the European Observatory on Health Systems and Policies.

European Commission. (2011). *Strategic implementation plan for the European Innovation Partnership on Active and Healthy Ageing*. Steering group working document. Final text adopted by the steering group on 7/11/11. Accessed February 15, 2016, from http://ec.europa.eu/research/innovation-union/pdf/active-healthy-ageing/steering-group/implementation_plan.pdf#view=fit&pagemode=none

Ferrer, L. (2015). *Engaging patients, carers and communities for the provision of coordinated/integrated health services: Strategies and tools*. Copenhagen: WHO Regional Office for Europe.

Gilbody, S., Bower, P., Fletcher, J., et al. (2006a). Collaborative care for depression: A cumulative meta-analysis and review of longer-term outcomes. *Archives of Internal Medicine, 166*, 2314–2321.

Gilbody, S., Bower, P., & Whitty, P. (2006b). Costs and consequences of enhanced primary care for depression: Systematic review of randomised economic evaluations. *The British Journal of Psychiatry, 189*, 297–308.

Glasby, J., Dickinson, H., & Peck, E. (2006). Guest editorial: Partnership working in health and social care. *Health & Social Care in the Community, 14*, 373–374.

Goodwin, N., 6, P., Peck, E., et al. (2004). *Managing across diverse networks of care: Lessons from other sectors*. London: National Co-ordinating Centre for NHS Service Delivery and Organisation R&D.

Goodwin, N., Smith, J., Davies, A., et al. (2012). *Integrated care for patients and populations: Improving outcomes by working together*. London: The King's Fund.

Groene, O., & Garcia-Barbero, M. (2001). Integrated care. A position paper of the WHO European office for integrated health care services. *International Journal of Integrated Care, 1*, 1–16.

Holman, H., & Lorig, K. (2000). Patients as partners in managing chronic disease. Partnership is a prerequisite for effective and efficient health care. *BMJ, 320*, 526–527.

House of Commons Health Committee. (2014). *Managing the care of people with long-term conditions* (Vol. I). Second Report of Session 2014–15. London: The Stationery Office.

Kodner, D., & Spreeuwenberg, C. (2002). Integrated care: Meaning, logic, applications, and implications – a discussion paper. *International Journal of Integrated Care, 2*, 1–6.

Kruis, A. L., Smidt, N., Assendelft, W. J., et al. (2013). Integrated disease management interventions for patients with chronic obstructive pulmonary disease. *Cochrane Database of Systematic Reviews, 10*, CD009437.

Langhorne, P., Taylor, G., Murray, G., et al. (2005). Early supported discharge services for stroke patients: A meta-analysis of individual patients' data. *Lancet, 365*, 501–506.

Lemmens, L., Molema, C., Versnel, N., et al. (2016). Integrated care programs for patients with psychological comorbidity: A systematic review and meta-analysis. *Journal of Psychosomatic Research, 79*, 580–594.

Leutz, W. (1999). Five laws for integrating medical and social services: Lessons from the United States and the United Kingdom. *The Milbank Quarterly, 77*, 77–110.

Lewis, R., Rosen, R., Goodwin, N., et al. (2010). *Where next for integrated care organisations in the English NHS?* London: The Nuffield Trust.

Maciejewski, M. L., Chen, S. Y., & Au, D. H. (2009). Adult asthma disease management: An analysis of studies, approaches, outcomes, and methods. *Respiratory Care, 54*, 878–886.

Martinez-Gonzalez, N. A., Berchtold, P., Ullman, K., et al. (2014). Integrated care programmes for adults with chronic conditions: A meta-review. *International Journal for Quality in Health Care, 26*, 561–570.

Minkman, M. (2011). A development model for integrated care. *International Journal of Integrated Care, 11*, e099.

Minkman, M., Vermeulen, R., Ahaus, K., et al. (2013). A survey study to validate a four phases development model for integrated care in the Netherlands. *BMC Health Services Research, 13*, 214.

Nolte, E., & McKee, M. (2008a). *Caring for people with chronic conditions: A health system perspective*. Maidenhead: Open University Press.

Nolte, E., & McKee, M. (2008b). Integration and chronic care: A review. In E. Nolte & M. McKee (Eds.), *Caring for people with chronic conditions. A health system perspective* (pp. 64–91). Maidenhead: Open University Press.

Nolte, E., & Pitchforth, E. (2014). *Integrated care: A rapid review of the evidence on economic impacts*. Copenhagen: WHO Regional Office for Europe and European Observatory on Health Systems and Policies.

Nolte, E., Conklin, A., Adams, J., et al. (2012). *Evaluating chronic disease management. Recommendations for funders and users*. Santa Monica: RAND Corporation.

Nolte, E., Knai, C., & McKee, M. (2008). *Managing chronic conditions: Experience in eight countries*. Copenhagen: World Health Organization on behalf of the European Observatory on Health Systems and Policies.

Nolte, E., Knai, C., & Saltman, R. (2014). *Assessing chronic disease management in European health systems. Concepts and approaches*. Copenhagen: World Health Organization (acting as the host organization for, and secretariat of, the European Observatory on Health Systems and Policies).

Oeseburg, B., Wynia, K., Middel, B., et al. (2009). Effects of case management for frail older people or those with chronic illness: A systematic review. *Nursing Research, 58*, 201–210.

Ouwens, M., Wollersheim, H., Hermens, R., et al. (2005). Integrated care programmes for chronically ill patients: A review of systematic reviews. *International Journal for Quality in Health Care, 17*, 141–146.

Ovretveit, J. (1998). *Integrated care: Models and issues*. A Nordic School of Public Health Briefing Paper. Goteborg: Nordic School of Public Health.

Pawson, R., & Tilley, N. (1997). *Realistic evaluation*. London: Sage.

Phillips, C. O., Wright, S. M., Kern, D. E., et al. (2004). Comprehensive discharge planning with postdischarge support for older patients with congestive heart failure: A meta-analysis. *JAMA, 291*, 1358–1367.

Pimouguet, C., Lavaud, T., Dartigues, J. F., et al. (2010). Dementia case management effectiveness on health care costs and resource utilization: A systematic review of randomized controlled trials. *The Journal of Nutrition, Health & Aging, 14*, 669–676.

Powell Davies, G., Harris, M., Perkins, D., et al. (2006). *Coordination of care within primary health care and with other sectors: A systematic review*. Sydney: University of New South Wales.

Rechel, B., Wright, S., Edwards, N., et al. (2009). *Investing in hospitals of the future*. Copenhagen: World Health Organization, on behalf of the European Observatory on Health Systems and Policies.

Reilly, S., Miranda-Castillo, C., Malouf, R., et al. (2015). Case management approaches to home support for people with dementia. *Cochrane Database of Systematic Reviews, 1*, CD008345.

Rodgers, M., Dalton, J., Harden, M., et al. (2016). Integrated care to address the physical health needs of people with severe mental illness: A rapid review. *Health Services and Delivery Research, 4*, 1–129.

Shaw, S., Rosen, R., & Rumbold, B. (2011). *What is integrated care? An overview of integrated care in the NHS*. London: The Nuffield Trust.

Shepperd, S., Doll, H., Angus, R., et al. (2008). Admission avoidance hospital at home. *Cochrane Database of Systematic Reviews, 8*, CD007491.

Shortell, S., Gillies, R., & Anderson, D. (1994). The new world of managed care: Creating organized delivery systems. *Health Affairs, 13*, 46–64.

Simoens, S., Spinewine, A., Foulon, V., et al. (2011). Review of the cost-effectiveness of interventions to improve seamless care focusing on medication. *International Journal of Clinical Pharmacy, 33*, 909–917.

Smith, L., & Newton, R. (2007). Systematic review of case management. *The Australian and New Zealand Journal of Psychiatry, 41*, 2–9.

Smith, S., Soubhi, H., Fortin, M., et al. (2012). Interventions for improving outcomes in patients with multimorbidity in primary care and community settings. *Cochrane Database of Systematic Reviews, 4*, CD006560.

Steffen, S., Kosters, M., Becker, T., et al. (2009). Discharge planning in mental health care: A systematic review of the recent literature (Structured abstract). *Acta Psychiatrica Scandinavica, 120*, 1–9.

Steuten, L., Lemmens, K., Nieboer, A., et al. (2009). Identifying potentially cost effective chronic care programs for people with COPD. *International Journal of Chronic Obstructive Pulmonary Disease, 4*, 87–100.

Stokes, J., Panagioti, M., Alam, R., et al. (2015). Effectiveness of case management for 'at risk' patients in primary care: A systematic review and meta-analysis. *PLoS ONE, 10*, e0132340.

Tappenden, P., Campbell, F., Rawdin, A., et al. (2012). The clinical effectiveness and cost-effectiveness of home-based, nurse-led health promotion for older people: A systematic review. *Health Technology Assessment, 16*, 1–72.

Valentijn, P., Schepman, S., Opheij, W., et al. (2013). Understanding integrated care: A comprehensive conceptual framework based on the integrative functions of primary care. *International Journal of Integrated Care, 13*, e010.

van der Klauw, D., Molema, H., Grooten, L., et al. (2014). Identification of mechanisms enabling integrated care for patients with chronic diseases: A literature review. *International Journal of Integrated Care, 14*, e024.

Van Houdt, S., Heyrman, J., Vanhaecht, K., et al. (2013). An in-depth analysis of theoretical frameworks for the study of care coordination. *International Journal of Integrated Care, 13*, e024.

van Steenbergen-Weijenburg, K. M., van der Feltz-Cornelis, C. M., Horn, E. K., et al. (2010). Cost-effectiveness of collaborative care for the treatment of major depressive disorder in primary care. A systematic review. *BMC Health Services Research, 10*, 19.

Vogeli, C., Shields, A., Lee, T., et al. (2007). Multiple chronic conditions: Prevalence, health consequences, and implications for quality, care management, and costs. *Journal of General Internal Medicine, 22*, 391–395.

WHO Regional Office for Europe. (2016). *Lessons from transforming health services delivery: Compendium of initiatives in the WHO European Region*. Copenhagen: World Health Organization.

Winpenny, E., Miani, C., Pitchforth, E., et al. (2016). Outpatient services and primary care: Scoping review, case studies and international comparisons. *Health Services and Delivery Research, 4*, 1–322.

World Health Organization. (2015). *People-centred and integrated health services: An overview of the evidence*. Interim Report. Geneva: World Health Organization.

Patients Preferences

3

A. Mühlbacher and Susanne Bethge

3.1 Patients' Priorities for Integrated Health Care Delivery Systems

Integrated care (IC) suits patient needs better than fragmented health services. It is needed to organize care around the patient (Davis et al. 2005) and is seen as a critical factor in a high-performance healthcare system (McAllister et al. 2007). Care coordination is a process that addresses the health needs and wants of patients, including a range of medical and social support services (Rosenbach and Young 2000; Tarzian and Silverman 2002). Still there are problems in defining care coordination (Wise et al. 2007) which may be caused by the lack of knowledge about patient priorities. Hence patients must play a major role in designing the infrastructure and policies that will support the care coordination and integrated care approaches (Laine and Davidoff 1996).

If current trends continue, health care spending will leave governments bankrupt within decades (Henke et al. 2002). The problem is not lack of knowledge, nor is it the peoples' unwillingness to spend money. Rather, the difficulties lie in the understanding of peoples' priorities and preferences. Porter and Teisberg state "health care is on a collision course with patient needs and economic reality." (Porter and Teisberg 2006). This is one of the biggest problems policymakers are facing in the coming years and it raises questions of how services should be provided. The Institute of Medicine report "Crossing the Quality Chasm" (2001)

A. Mühlbacher (✉)
Health Economics and Health Care Management, Hochschule Neubrandenburg, Neubrandenburg, Germany

Center for Health Policy and Inequalities Research, Duke University, Durham, NC, USA
e-mail: muehlbacher@me.com; muehlbacher@hs-nb.de

S. Bethge
Innovation Committee at the Federal Joint Committee (Healthcare), Berlin, Germany
e-mail: susannebethge@googlemail.com

© Springer International Publishing AG 2017
V. Amelung et al. (eds.), *Handbook Integrated Care*,
DOI 10.1007/978-3-319-56103-5_3

emphasizes that health decisions should be customized based on patients' needs and values. Most, if not all, newly developed programs so far are conceptualized in a 'top–down' manner by the government and healthcare administration with little involvement of the general public (Wismar and Busse 2002). "Healthcare systems are challenged to effectively meet the wants and needs of patients by tailoring interventions based on each person's (. . .) preferences as well as personal and social context" (Sevin et al. 2009). In health policy terms, this refers to services "closely congruent with, and responsive to patients' wants, needs and preferences." (Laine and Davidoff 1996). The most powerful structural innovation will be based on a paradigm shift—patient-centred care. Patient-centred care takes numerous forms and should be based on patient evidence as provided by preference data.

Patient Preferences The term 'patient preferences' still lacks a consistent definition; despite this, there appears to be convergence in the view that patient preferences are statements made by individuals regarding their needs, values and expectations and the relative importance of treatment properties. Therefore, these preferences refer to the individual evaluation of dimensions of health outcomes, treatment characteristics or health system attributes. Based on the existing literature, integrated care can be differentiated into attributes, such as:

(1) **Organisation of care:** The organisation of care can be seen as a function that helps to ensure that patients' preferences for health services and information are met (National Quality Forum 2006). It is widely acknowledged that care coordination across all health care settings and related disciplines will improve the quality of health care and therefore satisfy the preferences of the patients involved (Adams and Corrigan 2003). Physicians in larger medical groups, particularly those who are part of integrated care programs, perform more favorably on all patient experience measures than those in smaller, less-integrated practice settings (Rodriguez et al. 2009). Some findings have shown that individuals within an integrated care system had shorter average hospital stays and lower costs than comparison groups (Criscione et al. 1995; Liptak et al. 1998). When addressing different social, developmental, educational and financial needs, the design of services has to take heterogeneity of patients and families into account. One of the biggest challenges in care coordination and integrated care is identification of the necessary set of attributes that are needed to obtain optimal results. Clinicians need to understand and tailor care to the wider whole-person context—including whatever non-medical factors may affect the success of medical care (Peek 2009).

(2) **Interpersonal care:** In integrated care, physician-patient communication is the fundamental platform for health service delivery. An important component is the creation of individualized care plans "that establish a partnership among practitioners, patients and their families (when appropriate), to ensure that decisions respect patients' needs and preferences" (Institute of Medicine 2001). Patients placed the highest value on seeing a physician who knew them well, followed by seeing a physician who was interested in their ideas,

one who asked about social and emotional issues and one who involved them in decisions (Cheraghi-Sohi et al. 2008). Preference studies using discrete choice experiments have shown that communication is highly valued (Vick and Scott 1998; Scott and Vick 1999; Morgan et al. 2000; Chapple et al. 2002; Scott et al. 2003; Gerard and Lattimer 2005; Rao et al. 2006; Al Mulley et al. 2012). Although patients with chronic diseases valued shared decision-making, it was of lower relevance than whether the physician seemed to listen (Longo et al. 2006). Longo et al. question the high priority patients place on communication issues and suggest critical examination (Longo et al. 2006).

(3) **Technical care:** Technical care—the quality of clinical care—is another key dimension (Campbell et al. 2000). A Discrete choice experiment reported that technical care was the most important factor in determining patient choice of a physician (accounting for 27% of the variance), compared with waiting time (15%), billing problems (20%), time to get a referral (18%), and who made health care decisions (20%) (Markham et al. 1999). Cheraghi-Sohi et al. (2008) argue that attributes used to test the priorities placed on patient-centred care in published studies have not accurately reflected the complexity of the patient-centred care concept. Little is known about patients' assessment of technical care and how these assessments correlate with other objective measures (Rao et al. 2006). A study conducted in the United States asked patients to choose between physician report cards with different scores for interpersonal and technical care. Findings showed that more patients preferred the physician with high technical care scores (Fung et al. 2005). The three described meta-dimensions of IC can further be explained by seven sub-domains. In qualitative and quantitative research these seven preference dimensions with three attributes each could be evaluated and identified as patient relevant in respect of IC (Juhnke and Mühlbacher 2013):

1. Access → described by waiting time for an appointment, travel time care provider, out of pocket costs
2. Service & facilities → described by guidance within the facility, medical devices & furnishings, friendliness & helpfulness of staff
3. Data & information → described by patient's health record, information about performance, accurate health information
4. Professional care → described by treatment guidelines, experience of care provider, patient education
5. Coordination & continuity → described by multidisciplinary care, care transition, clinical information exchange
6. Individualized healthcare → described by proactive care, case management, attention to personal situation
7. Personal care → described by trust & respect, attentiveness of care providers, shared decision making

The Question What do patients want from integrated care? Much work remains to be done for care coordination to become a standard feature of health care.

Integrated care aims to achieve higher-quality care, lower costs and greater patient satisfaction. Individual preferences on integrated care must be considered for a range of attributes, such as technical and interpersonal care. Designing services that are sensitive to patients' preferences in the context of limited resources may require policy and decision-makers to choose between attributes (Wensing et al. 1998; Campbell et al. 2000; Coulter 2005). Two of the core contributions needed to achieve this goal are: assessment of the value of integrated care for different patient populations and development of measures for integrated care quality (Antonelli et al. 2009). The published literature does not clearly specify the relative importance patients place on these attributes. In order to promote integrated care, policymakers need to understand patients' priorities and preferences.

In order to make integrated care more congruent with patients' needs, patients' preferences for different attributes need to be analyzed (Laine and Davidoff 1996). Moreover, meeting expectations on a range of attributes may be difficult within the constraints of limited budgets; this has led to interest in methods for assessing priorities (Ryan et al. 2001a). "One promising method is the Discrete choice experiment, used in psychology, marketing and economics." (Ryan et al. 2001a). McFadden (1973) introduced feasible techniques for estimating a complete characteristics-based model of demand.

3.2   Stated Preference Studies: Method and Study Design

Discrete Choice Experiment The value of goods and services depends on the nature and level of the underlying attributes (Lancaster 1966, Lancaster 1971). Health care interventions, services or policies can be described by their attributes (Hauber 2009). A key feature of these methods is the specification of utilities associated with the alternatives in terms of choice characteristics and individual preferences (Ben-Akiva and Lerman 1985). Stated preference studies focus on investigating the trade-offs between crucial attributes (Ryan and Hughes 1997; Ryan and Farrar 2000; Ryan and Gerard 2003). Discrete choice experiments are the most important form of stated preference studies and determine whether consumers are willing to trade-off some of the attributes against others (Ryan et al. 2001b). DCEs have recently gained importance in the study of innovative health technologies and non-market goods (Lancsar et al. 2007; Lancsar and Louviere 2008; Ryan et al. 2008) or where market choices are severely constrained by regulatory and institutional factors (Ryan and Farrar 2000). The US Food and Drug Administration (FDA) has already considered preference data within a regulatory decision for medical devices (U.S. Food and Drug Administration (FDA) 2014) and the German Institute for Quality and Efficiency in Health Care (IQWiG) has conducted two pilot studies to preference methods (Danner et al. 2011, Mühlbacher et al. 2016).

The Discrete Choice technique is already used to elicit preferences in primary care (Vick and Scott 1998; Scott and Vick 1999; Morgan et al. 2000) and gaining more and more importance (de Bekker Grob et al. 2010; Clark et al. 2014). The application of DCEs has been extended to take account of provider preferences (Ubach et al. 2003), or insured preferences for health system attributes (Telser 2008). Moreover, the technique has been used to evaluate patient-centred outcomes in the provision of care (Mühlbacher et al. 2008, 2009, 2014; Mühlbacher and Bethge 2014, 2015; Ostermann et al. 2015). For policy analysis, it might be interesting to calculate how choice probabilities vary with changes in attributes or attribute levels, or to calculate secondary estimates of money equivalence (Willingness to pay (WTP) or Willingness to accept (WTA)) (Kleinman et al. 2002), risk equivalence (maximum acceptable risk (MAR)) (Johnson et al. 2007) or time equivalence for various changes in attributes or attribute levels (Johnson et al. 2009). Findings on the reliability and validity of DCEs in health care settings are encouraging (Bryan et al. 2000; Bryan and Parry 2002). A DCE can be described in terms of detailed checklists (Bridges et al. 2011; Johnson et al. 2012, 2015; Mühlbacher et al. 2013).

To analyze patient and insuree preferences in IC, two very similar studies have been conducted in US (Mühlbacher et al. 2015a) and Germany (Mühlbacher et al. 2015b) and should help to illustrate preference measurement in IC. An identical stated preferences method was used to assess patient preferences in different health care systems and cultural backgrounds. For that reason as an identical survey was applied in US and in Germany. Furthermore a study was realized that explored the impact of the contextual factor of the communicator of IC programs and the resulting effects within choice behaviour (Bethge et al. 2015).

3.3 Preference for Integrated Health Care Delivery Systems

Qualitative Methods Both studies in the US and in Germany included an identical conceptual framework linking organisational structure to potential preferences. The framework was developed by systematic literature reviews as well as quantitative surveys and factor analysis about the very differentiated needs and expectations in respect of integrated care (Juhnke and Mühlbacher 2013). The final framework included the specification of different organisational levels of health care delivery and corresponding preference dimensions as described in the first part of this chapter and as can be seen in Fig. 3.1.

Quantitative data were obtained by means of two identical discrete choice experiments (DCE) integrated in online surveys. Within the experiment, participants were presented two alternative scenarios of hypothetical health care delivery systems and asked to choose between them. Each scenario included six attributes with three specific levels.

Based on the assumption that patients' choices are influenced by latent concepts such as sociodemographic characteristics, experience, knowledge, and attitudes, it was also important to elicit respondent-specific experiences, attitudes, and sociodemographic information. These characteristics may influence preferences in a systematic way, and heterogeneity within subgroups can be analyzed. Therefore, this additional data were included in the survey.

Level	Preference Dimension	Attributes		
Individual Level	Interpersonal Care	Shared Decision-Making	Attentiveness of Care Providers	Trust and Respect
	Individualised Healthcare	Attention to Personal Situation	Case Management	Proactive Care
Process Level	Coordination & Continuity	Multidisciplinary Care	Care Transition	Clinical information Exchange
	Professional Care	Experience of Care Provider	Treatment Guidelines	Patient Education
Organizational Level	Data & Information	Patient's health Record	Information about Performance	Accurate health Information
	Service & Facilities	Friendliness and Helpfulness of Staff	Medical Devices and Furnishings	Guidance within the Facility
	Access	Waiting Time for an Appointment	Travel Time to Care Provider	Out of Pocket Costs

Fig. 3.1 Framework: patient-centred health care delivery (Mühlbacher et al. 2015a)

Sample Characteristics Within the two studies n = 3900 participants (only patients assigned in health care system) in the US as well as n = 1322 participants (insuree sample) in Germany could be included within the final preference estimations. Table 3.1 presents some sociodemographic characteristics of both study samples.

US Preference Results The feature "Out of pocket costs" was a very important attribute within the DCE in the US study. In DCE 1 regarding patient involvement, "trust and respect" (0.65600) was slightly higher than cost. "Attention to personal situation" (0.42178) was as well of great importance. In DCE 2 addressing preferences at the point of care, "shared decision making" (0.71058) and "access to patient health record" (0.46432) were highly valuable to patients. In DCE 3 focusing on personnel in healthcare delivery systems, "multidisciplinary care" (0.74096) was ranked highest. Lastly, in DCE 4 analyzing features of the organisation of healthcare delivery systems, "treatment guidelines" (0.44834), "clinical information exchange" (0.38334) and "case management" (0.37689) were of almost equal value to patients. Differences in individual living conditions influenced respondents' preferences.

German Preference Results The additional costs (Out of Pocket costs) were again of highest relevance in patients' choice. Next to the "costs" attribute, in DCE 1 (patient involvement) "patient education" (coef.: 0.2196) was of great

Table 3.1 Respondent characteristics of US and German participants

Characteristic	US Patient sample (N = 3900) No. (%)	German Insuree sample (N = 1322) No. (%)
Sex		
Men	1347 (34.5)	652 (49.3)
Women	2553 (65.5)	670 (50.7)
Marital status		
Married	2431 (62.3)	605 (45.8)
Single	568 (14.6)	278 (21.0)
Divorced or separated	432 (11.1)	143 (10.8)
In a committed relationship, but not married	311 (8.0)	277 (21.0)
Widowed	158 (4.1)	19 (1.4)
Self-rated health		
Excellent	408 (10.5)	34 (2.6)
Very good	1249 (32.0)	252 (19.1)
Good	1270 (32.6)	708 (53.6)
Fair	741 (19.0)	295 (22.3)
Poor	216 (5.5)	33 (2.5)
Not sure	16 (<0.1)	–

importance, in DCE 2 (point of care) it was "waiting for an appointment" (coef.: 0.335). In DCE 3 (personnel) "experience of care provider" (coef.: 0.289) had strong influence on decisions. In the fourth DCE (organisation) "medical devices and furnishings" (coef.: 0.464) were highly relevant. *(Detailed results of the German study can be found at* (Mühlbacher et al. 2015a*) and details for the US study are available at* (Mühlbacher et al. 2015b*))*.

Comparison of Results The inclusion of an identical cost attribute across all content blocks provides the means to compute a common metric across all 21 attributes. Figure 3.2 represents the comparison of the relative importance of the attributes for the US and the German study (not discussing the issue of scale heterogeneity). The estimates are sorted in relation to the US results beginning with the most important. It can be seen that the US participants were most influenced by shared decision making, multidisciplinary care and trust and respect within their decision for an integrated care program. These are attributes that relate to individual or process aspects of integrated care. On the contrary, the German participants valued medical devices and furnishings, waiting time for an appointment as well as the experience of care provider highest. This means the German population is more focused on organisational aspects of health care delivery and puts a high value on the state of medical equipment.

The differentiation of the first five ranks in comparison between both study groups can be seen in the following chart (Fig. 3.3).

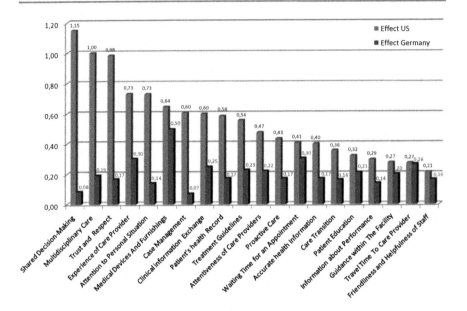

Fig. 3.2 Overall assessment of all attributes in relation to cost attribute

Level	Preference Dimension	Attributes		
Individual Level	Interpersonal Care	Shared Decision-Making (1)	Attentiveness of Care Providers	Trust and Respect (3)
	Individualized Healthcare	Attention to Personal Situation (5)	Case Management	Proactive Care
Process Level	Coordination & Continuity	Multidisciplinary Care (2)	Care Transition	Clinical information Exchange (5)
	Professional Care	Experience of Care Provider (4) (3)	Treatment Guidelines	Patient Education
Organizational Level	Data & Information	Patient's Health Record	Information about Performance	Accurate health Information
	Service & Facilities	Friendliness and Helpfulness of Staff	Medical Devices and Furnishings (1)	Guidance within the Facility
	Access	Waiting Time for an Appointment (2)	Travel Time to Care Provider (4)	Out of Pocket Costs

○ = Overall ranking US   ● = Overall ranking Germany

Fig. 3.3 Rankorder comparison US and Germany, place 1–5

Conclusion The presented results display the complexity of preferences and their dependency on cultural and health care system differences. As stated by the WHO *"There is no perfect combination or a "one size fits all" solution"* for patient-centred and integrated health services. Nevertheless the person with its needs and expectations is/and needs to be in the centre of integrated care (World Health Organization (WHO) 2015).

The novelty of the presented results is the combination of qualitative and quantitative methods for building a conceptual map of patient-centred outcomes that can be used to plan comprehensive assessment of patients' preferences in integrated care. The framework concludes important attributes and endpoints and allows sorting them in categories and subcategories. Further research is needed to distinguish the possible interpretations of the presented attitudes or preference dimensions and to take notice of heterogeneity within patient population. In addition, the development of a conceptual framework can be used as foundation of further stated preference measures.

It is necessary to evaluate what patient preferences are to help researchers, payers, regulators, physicians, and patients to understand the relative importance of each treatment attribute and the willingness of patients to trade among treatment attributes. Designing integrated care around patients' preferences has the potential to improve the effectiveness of health care by improving adoption of, and adherence to clinical treatments or public health programs. An important area for future research is the question: what are the implications of patient-centred care? Understanding how patients and other stakeholders perceive and value different aspects of integrated care is vital to the optimal design and evaluation of programs.

3.4 Discussion and Outlook

Patient-centred outcomes will provide objective information about the impact on patient involvement, the experiences of patients, and their needs and wants. The publication of patient preference data will help insurers, policymakers and others to promote patient-centred integrated care as the new standard of primary care. The data can be communicated through medical and economic journals, congresses and media.

Because of the lack of information on patient needs in the decision-makers' assessment of health services, the individuals' preferences often play a subordinate role at present. The patients' perspectives and desires in health care decisions are often not sufficiently considered. However, shared decision-making with the involvement of patients in treatment decisions have been encouraged in recent years.

Though not examined in this chapter that has focused on patient preferences, it should be noted that a key aspect in the development of interpersonal care is the ability to engage and empower patients as partners in their own care. There is good evidence to demonstrate the value of empowerment strategies with patients suggesting that approaches such as health literacy, shared decision-making and self-management support should be better embedded in integrated care programmes than currently seems to be the case (Ferrer 2015). The recent publication of a Global Strategy on Integrated People-Centred Health Services by the World Health Organisation presents evidence that enabling individuals to make informed choices and supporting them to understand their responsibilities as well as their rights can significantly enhance health outcomes. The WHO go further to argue that an equal and reciprocal relationship' between health professionals and patients is required to support more sustainable care systems (World Health Organization (WHO) 2015).

The findings of such studies supply important information on the benefits of integrated care from the patients' point of view. If patient needs are taken into account adequately, it is safe to assume that this will increase their satisfaction with integrated care programs. Heterogeneity within preferences due to racial and ethnic disparities, age or illness can be documented and considered in the design of health care services. Integrated care schemes will not work unless it is accepted that different patient groups need different care programs and that sensitivity to cultural factors and the local context of application are important to engage patients and support their needs and preferences effectively.

The presented studies reviewed in this chapter also support efforts for increased consideration of patient benefit as an essential quality criterion in the assessment of integrated care. Especially where it is difficult to clearly differentiate between services in terms of medical and financial aspects, comprehensive information on patient benefits (and to that of communities as well) can be very useful in prioritizing approaches to care and treatment. Studies of this type can thus help to stimulate fresh discussion and lead to the formulation of increasingly person-centred care concepts in the long term.

Acknowledgements Within the US study, the SSRI at DUKE University and DUKE Health View supported the recruitment of patient for the patient preference study. The study was financially supported by the Commonwealth Fund and the Harkness Fellowship in Healthcare Policy and Practice, New York, USA granted to Axel Mühlbacher. Susanne Bethge received a stipend from the International Academy of Life Science, Hannover, Germany. The German study was financially supported by Berlin Chemie AG.

References

Adams, K., & Corrigan, J. (2003). *Priority areas for national action: Transforming health care quality*. Institute of Medicine of the National Academies, The National Academies Press.

Antonelli, R., McAllister, J., & Popp, J. (2009). *Making care coordination a critical component of the pediatric health system: A multidisciplinary framework*. New York: The Commonwealth Fund.

Ben-Akiva, M. E., & Lerman, S. R. (1985). *Discrete choice analysis: Theory and application to travel demand*. Cambridge, MA: MIT Press.

Bethge, S., Mühlbacher, A., & Amelung, V. (2015, November 7–11). *The importance of the communicator for an integrated care program – A comparative preference analysis with Discrete Choice Experiments*. International Society for Pharmacoeconomics and Outcomes Research (ISPOR) 18th Annual European Congress, Milan, Italy.

Bridges, J., Hauber, A., Marshall, D., Lloyd, A., Prosser, L., Regier, D., Johnson, F., & Mauskopf, J. A. (2011). Conjoint analysis applications in health—a checklist: A Report of the ISPOR Good Research Practices for Conjoint Analysis Task Force. *Value in Health, 14*(4), 403–413.

Bryan, S., & Parry, D. (2002). Structural reliability of conjoint measurement in health care: An empirical investigation. *Applied Economics, 34*(5), 561–568.

Bryan, S., Gold, L., Sheldon, R., & Buxton, M. (2000). Preference measurement using conjoint methods: An empirical investigation of reliability. *Health Economics, 9*(5), 385–395.

Campbell, S. M., Roland, M. O., & Buetow, S. A. (2000). Defining quality of care. *Social Science and Medicine, 51*(11), 1611–1625.

Chapple, A., Campbell, S., Rogers, A., & Roland, M. (2002). Users' understanding of medical knowledge in general practice. *Social Science and Medicine, 54*(8), 1215–1224.

Cheraghi-Sohi, S., Hole, A. R., Mead, N., McDonald, R., Whalley, D., Bower, P., & Roland, M. (2008). What patients want from primary care consultations: A discrete choice experiment to identify patients' priorities. *Annals of Family Medicine, 6*(2), 107–115.

Clark, M. D., Determann, D., Petrou, S., Moro, D., & de Bekker-Grob, E. W. (2014). Discrete choice experiments in health economics: A review of the literature. *PharmacoEconomics, 32*(9), 883–902.

Coulter, A. (2005). What do patients and the public want from primary care? *BMJ, 331*(7526), 1199–1201.

Criscione, T., Walsh, K. K., & Kastner, T. A. (1995). An evaluation of care coordination in controlling inpatient hospital utilization of people with developmental disabilities. *Mental Retardation, 33*(6), 364–373.

Danner, M., Hummel, J. M., Volz, F., Van Manen, J. G., Wiegard, B., Dintsios, C. M., Bastian, H., Gerber, A., & IJzerman, M. J. (2011). Integrating patients' views into health technology assessment: Analytic hierarchy process (AHP) as a method to elicit patient preferences. *International Journal of Technology Assessment in Health Care, 27*(04), 369–375.

Davis, K., Schoenbaum, S. C., & Audet, A. M. (2005). A 2020 vision of patient-centered primary care. *Journal of General Internal Medicine, 20*(10), 953–957.

de Bekker Grob, E. W., Ryan, M., & Gerard, K. (2010). Discrete choice experiments in health economics: A review of the literature. *Health Economics, 21*(2), 145–172.

Ferrer, L. (2015). *Engaging patients, carers and communities for the provision of coordinated/integrated health services.* Working paper, WHO Regional Office for Europe: Copenhagen.

Fung, C. H., Elliott, M. N., Hays, R. D., Kahn, K. L., Kanouse, D. E., McGlynn, E. A., Spranca, M. D., & Shekelle, P. G. (2005). Patients' preferences for technical versus interpersonal quality when selecting a primary care physician. *Health Services Research, 40*(4), 957–977.

Gerard, K., & Lattimer, V. (2005). Preferences of patients for emergency services available during usual GP surgery hours: A discrete choice experiment. *Family Practice, 22*(1), 28–36.

Hauber, A. B. (2009). Healthy-years equivalent: Wounded but not yet dead. *Expert Review of Pharmacoeconomics & Outcomes Research, 9*(3), 265–270.

Henke, K.-D., Mackenthun, B., & Schreyögg, J. (2002). *Gesundheitsmarkt Berlin: Perspektiven für Wachstum und Beschäftigung.* Baden-Baden: Nomos-Verl.-Ges.

Institute of Medicine. (2001). *Crossing the quality chasm: A new health system for the 21st century.* Washington, DC: National Academy Press.

Johnson, F. R., Hauber, A. B., & Özdemir, S. (2009). Using conjoint analysis to estimate healthy-year equivalents for acute conditions: An application to vasomotor symptoms. *Value in Health, 12*(1), 146–152.

Johnson, F. R., Lancsar, E., Marshall, D., Kilambi, V., Mühlbacher, A., Regier, D. A., Bresnahan, B. W., Kanninen, B., & Bridges, J. F. P. (2012). *Constructing experimental designs for discrete-choice experiments.* Report of the ISPOR Conjoint Analysis Experimental Design Task Force.

Johnson, F. R., Ozdemir, S., Mansfield, C., Hass, S., Miller, D. W., Siegel, C. A., & Sands, B. E. (2007). Crohn's disease patients' risk-benefit preferences: Serious adverse event risks versus treatment efficacy. *Gastroenterology, 133*(3), 769–779.

Johnson, R. F., et al. (2015). Sample size and utility-difference precision in discrete-choice experiments: A meta-simulation approach. *Journal of Choice Modelling, 16*, 50–57.

Juhnke, C., & Mühlbacher, A. (2013). Patient-centredness in integrated healthcare delivery systems-needs, expectations and priorities for organised healthcare systems. *International Journal of Integrated Care, 13*, 1–14.

Kleinman, L., McIntosh, E., Ryan, M., Schmier, J., Crawley, J., Locke III, G. R., & De Lissovoy, G. (2002). Willingness to pay for complete symptom relief of gastroesophageal reflux disease. *Archives of Internal Medicine, 162*(12), 1361–1366.

Laine, C., & Davidoff, F. (1996). Patient-centered medicine. A professional evolution. *JAMA, 275* (2), 152–156.

Lancaster, K. J. (1966). *A new approach to consumer theory.* Indianapolis, IN: Bobbs-Merrill.

Lancaster, K. (1971). *Consumer demand: A new approach.* New York: Columbia University Press.

Lancsar, E., & Louviere, J. (2008). Conducting discrete choice experiments to inform healthcare decision making: A user's guide. *PharmacoEconomics, 26*(8), 661–678.

Lancsar, E., Louviere, J., & Flynn, T. (2007). Several methods to investigate relative attribute impact in stated preference experiments. *Social Science & Medicine, 64*(8), 1738–1753.

Liptak, G. S., Burns, C. M., Davidson, P. W., & McAnarney, E. R. (1998). Effects of providing comprehensive ambulatory services to children with chronic conditions. *Archives of Pediatrics & Adolescent Medicine, 152*(10), 1003–1008.

Longo, M. F., Cohen, D. R., Hood, K., Edwards, A., Robling, M., Elwyn, G., & Russell, I. T. (2006). Involving patients in primary care consultations: Assessing preferences using discrete choice experiments. *The British Journal of General Practice, 56*(522), 35–42.

Markham, F. W., Diamond, J. J., & Hermansen, C. L. (1999). The use of conjoint analysis to study patient satisfaction. *Evaluation & The Health Professions, 22*(3), 371–378.

McAllister, J. W., Presler, E., & Cooley, W. C. (2007). Practice-based care coordination: A medical home essential. *Pediatrics, 120*(3), e723–e733.

McFadden, D. (1973). *Conditional logit analysis of qualitative choice behavior.* Berkeley, CA: University of California.

Morgan, A., Shackley, P., Pickin, M., & Brazier, J. (2000). Quantifying patient preferences for out-of-hours primary care. *Journal of Health Services Research & Policy, 5*(4), 214–218.

Mühlbacher, A. C., & Bethge, S. (2014). Patients' preferences: A discrete-choice experiment for treatment of non-small-cell lung cancer. *The European Journal of Health Economics, 6,* 657–670.

Mühlbacher, A., & Bethge, S. (2015). Reduce mortality risk above all else: A discrete-choice experiment in acute coronary syndrome patients. *PharmacoEconomics, 33*(1), 71–81.

Mühlbacher, A., Bethge, S., & Eble, S. (2015a). Präferenzen für Versorgungsnetzwerke: Eigenschaften von integrierten Versorgungsprogrammen und deren Einfluss auf den Patientennutzen. *Das Gesundheitswesen, 77*(5), 340–350.

Mühlbacher, A. C., Bethge, S., Reed, S. D., & Schulman, K. A. (2015b). Patient preferences for features of health care delivery systems: A discrete-choice experiment. *Health Services Research, 51,* 704–727.

Mühlbacher, A., Bethge, S., & Tockhorn, A. (2013). Präferenzmessung im Gesundheitswesen: Grundlagen von Discrete-Choice-Experimenten. *Gesundheitsökonomie & Qualitätsmanagement, 18*(4), 159–172.

Mühlbacher, A., Bridges, J. F. P., Bethge, S., Dintsios, C. M., Schwalm, A., Gerber-Grote, A., & Nübling, M. (2016). *Preferences for antiviral therapy of chronic hepatitis C: A discrete choice experiment.* European Journal of Health Economics.

Mühlbacher, A. C., Junker, U., Juhnke, C., Stemmler, E., Kohlmann, T., Leverkus, F., & Nubling, M. (2014). Chronic pain patients' treatment preferences: a discrete-choice experiment. *Eur J Health Econ, 16,* 613–628.

Mühlbacher, A., Lincke, H., & Nübling, M. (2008). Evaluating patients' preferences for multiple myeloma therapy, a discrete choice experiment. *GMS Psycho-Social-Medicine, 5,* PMC2736517.

Mühlbacher, A., Nübling, M., Rudolph, I., & Linke, H. J. (2009). *Analysis of patient preferences in the drug treatment of Attention-Deficit Hyperactivity Disorder (ADHD): A discrete choice experiment.* BMC Health Services Research.

Mulley, A., Trimble, C., & Elwyn, G. (2012). *Patients' preferences matter – Stop the silent misdiagnosis.* London: The King's Fund.

National Quality Forum. (2006, August). *National Quality Forum*.

Ostermann, J., Njau, B., Mtuy, T., Brown, D. S., Muhlbacher, A., & Thielman, N. (2015). One size does not fit all: HIV testing preferences differ among high-risk groups in Northern Tanzania. *AIDS Care, 27*, 595–603.

Peek, C. J. (2009). Integrating care for persons, not only diseases. *Journal of Clinical Psychology in Medical Settings, 16*(1), 13–20.

Porter, M. E., & Teisberg, E. O. (2006). *Redefining health care: Creating value-based competition on results*. Boston, MA: Harvard Business School Press.

Rao, M., Clarke, A., Sanderson, C., & Hammersley, R. (2006). Patients' own assessments of quality of primary care compared with objective records based measures of technical quality of care: Cross sectional study. *BMJ, 333*(7557), 19.

Rodriguez, H., von Glahn, T., Rogers, W., & Gelb Safran, D. (2009). Organizational and market influences on physician performance on patient experience measures. *Health Services Research, 44*, 880–901.

Rosenbach, M., & Young, C. (2000). Care coordination and medicaid managed care: Emerging issues for states and managed care organizations. *Spectrum, 73*(4), 1–5.

Ryan, M., & Farrar, S. (2000). Using conjoint analysis to elicit preferences for health care. *BMJ, 320*(7248), 1530–1533.

Ryan, M., & Gerard, K. (2003). Using discrete choice experiments to value health care programmes: Current practice and future research reflections. *Applied Health Economics and Health Policy, 2*(1), 55–64.

Ryan, M., & Hughes, J. (1997). Using conjoint analysis to assess women's preferences for miscarriage management. *Health Economics, 6*(3), 261–273.

Ryan, M., Gerard, K., & Amaya-Amaya, M. (2008). *Using discrete choice experiments to value health and health care*. Dordrecht: Springer.

Ryan, M., Bate, A., Eastmond, C. J., & Ludbrook, A. (2001a). Use of discrete choice experiments to elicit preferences. *Quality in Health Care, 10*(Suppl 1), i55–i60.

Ryan, M., Scott, D. A., Reeves, C., Bate, A., van Teijlingen, E. R., Russell, E. M., Napper, M., & Robb, C. M. (2001b). Eliciting public preferences for healthcare: A systematic review of techniques. *Health Technology Assessment, 5*(5), 1–186.

Scott, A., & Vick, S. (1999). Patients, doctors and contracts: an application of principal-agent theory to the doctor-patient relationship. *Scottish Journal of Political Economy, 46*(2), 111–134.

Scott, A., Watson, M. S., & Ross, S. (2003). Eliciting preferences of the community for out of hours care provided by general practitioners: A stated preference discrete choice experiment. *Social Science and Medicine, 56*(4), 803–814.

Sevin, C., Moore, G., Shepherd, J., Jacobs, T., & Hupke, C. (2009). Transforming care teams to provide the best possible patient-centered, collaborative care. *The Journal of Ambulatory Care Management, 32*(1), 24–31.

Tarzian, A. J., & Silverman, H. J. (2002). Care coordination and utilization review: Clinical case managers' perceptions of dual role obligations. *The Journal of Clinical Ethics, 13*(3), 216–229.

Telser, H., Becker, K., & Zweifel, P. (2008). Validity and reliability of willingness-to-pay estimates: Evidence from two overlapping discrete-choice-experiments. *The Patient, Patient-Centered Outcome Research, 1*, 283–293.

U.S. Food and Drug Administration (FDA). (2014). *The patient preference initiative: Incorporating patient preference information into the medical device regulatory processes*. Public Workshop, September 18–19, 2013. FDA White Oak Campus, Silver Spring, MD.

Ubach, C., Scott, A., French, F., Awramenko, M., & Needham, G. (2003). What do hospital consultants value about their jobs? A discrete choice experiment. *BMJ, 326*(7404), 1432.

Vick, S., & Scott, A. (1998). Agency in health care. Examining patients' preferences for attributes of the doctor-patient relationship. *Journal of Health Economics, 17*(5), 587–605.

Wensing, M., Jung, H. P., Mainz, J., Olesen, F., & Grol, R. (1998). A systematic review of the literature on patient priorities for general practice care. Part 1: Description of the research domain. *Social Science and Medicine, 47*(10), 1573–1588.

Wise, P., Huffman, L., & Brat, G. (2007). *A critical analysis of care coordination strategies for children with special health care needs.* Technical Review No. 14. Rockville, MD: Agency for Healthcare Research and Quality. AHRQ Publication No. 07-0054.

Wismar, M., & Busse, R. (2002). Outcome-related health targets-political strategies for better health outcomes – A conceptual and comparative study (part 2). *Health Policy, 59*(3), 223–242.

World Health Organization (WHO). (2015). *WHO global strategy on people-centred and integrated health services.* Interim report. WHO reference number: WHO/HIS/SDS/2015.6.

Part II

Tools and Instruments

Case-Managers and Integrated Care

4

Guus Schrijvers and Dominique Somme

This chapter on case management starts with a case story about Julia, a person with dementia, and her case manager, John (Sect. 4.1). It shows six innovations which are necessary to introduce case managers. Julia and John live in the year 2025, in a rich western country with a health system that supports integrated care by means of adequate financing and digitalization of care. Section 4.2 introduces a definition of the concept of case management and discusses important terms in it. Then (Sect. 4.3), two specific competences of case managers are discussed: (1) the assessments of care and social needs and (2) empowering interviewing of clients. The chapter continues (Sect. 4.4) with the comparison of the "ideal world" in the case story in 2025 with the real world in 2015 by focusing on case management practices in The Netherlands and France. The chapter ends (Sect. 4.5) by offering theories to support the implementation of the case manager. The chapter emphasises that case managers are not only for clients with dementia but are relevant as an approach to support other people with health, educational and financial problems; clients with developmental disorders; patients with severe mental illness; patients with cancer and metastases; and persons with more than one chronic condition. In this chapter, the words clients, patients and persons are used as synonyms occurring in different care contexts.

G. Schrijvers (✉)
Public Health at the University Medical Center Utrecht, Utrecht, The Netherlands
e-mail: mail@guusschrijvers.nl

D. Somme
Geriatrics Department, University of Rennes 1, CRAPE, UMR 6051, Rennes, France
e-mail: Dominique.SOMME@chu-rennes.fr

© Springer International Publishing AG 2017
V. Amelung et al. (eds.), *Handbook Integrated Care*,
DOI 10.1007/978-3-319-56103-5_4

4.1   The Story of Julia and John in 2025

In the story below an added asterix means: this kind of services generally does not exist in 2016, neither in The Netherlands nor in France. However, they exist in small innovative, experimental projects. They are necessary for an implementation of case managers in the year 2025. They are summarized (Box 4.2) and discussed in Sect. 4.4.

It is 2025. Julia is 84 years old. She lives with her husband Peter, also 84, in a small old apartment in a lower middle class neighbourhood in a city. They own this apartment, which is mortgage-free. In previous years she was a school teacher. Peter was a machine operator. Several years earlier, he had a foot amputated after an accident and now he is in constant pain. The couple has a modest pension. They have one son, living with his family 20 km away.

Julia suffers from dementia, periodical heart rhythm disorder and chronic itch. If an itch attack occurs, she does not stop scratching. She is not able to do her skin care by herself. She takes five different medications, three times each day. Julia cannot be alone and must always be supervised. Peter is somewhat healthy, except for the pain, but frail. He is unable to supervise his wife 24 h a day. Much of their health care is provided by non-profit care providers and financed by their social insurance companies and the municipality where they live. However, the insurance and municipal payment for the services is not enough. Julia and Peter pay hundreds of euros per month out of pocket.

John, a case manager, came into the picture a year ago after Julia fell in her home; she tripped over a small table in the living room and hurt herself. Julia's general practitioner Carla was called and did a home visit. She introduced Julia and Peter to John*. He is a nurse specialist with an academic background specializing in care for persons with dementia*. He works for the group practice in which Carla is one of the five GP's*. After being introduced, John did a couple of things. He introduced himself as the first contact person and care coordinator for Julia. He left his business card under a magnetic button on the fridge door. Then he did a care assessment of both Julia and Peter. Peter, Julia and John made a live/care plan for the next 6 months*.

Later, John organized a "non-professional potential caregivers conference," to which he and Peter invited members of the family, neighbours, friends and old colleagues*. They were asked to be a buddy for Julia and Peter and to offer respite care (to relieve Peter), transportation services, technical help and social support for Julia and Peter. Because this conference did not yield enough buddies, John mobilized voluntary organisations to send volunteers a couple of mornings and afternoons during the week. He also asked the local pharmacist to review Julia's medication* and to introduce some technical devices to improve Julia's medication therapy adherence. John also involved the fall prevention service from the department of geriatrics at the local hospital*. They sent a nurse, advised the couple to take some vitamins and inspected the apartment. She further advised them to remove small tables and to install a stair lift and extra railings in the bathrooms, toilet and hallway. Peter and Julia complied, although they had to pay the cost out *of their own pocket. This meant that they had to take out a small mortgage on their apartment. John also found that Julia was undernourished because of dental complaints. She was reluctant to go for a consult but he convinced Julia to visit a local dentist, although that meant additional expenses.*

John also showed Peter and Julia how to use an Internet connected tablet PC to have contact with him, Carla, their son and other buddies*. A simple screen with big buttons, a 2-h course and a helpdesk were enough to introduce the telecare. Peter and Julia bought a new Internet connected tablet PC and a better and faster modem. This was an option because in the last 10 years the bandwidth was much enlarged in the city where they live. Peter was less stressed with caregiving and John convinced him to ask Carla for a referral to a pain specialist.

John was consulted during Julia's next heavy itch attack. He organized a short stay in an assisted living facility in the neighbourhood*. There he visited Julia daily, sometimes accompanied by Carla, the GP. Care assistants helped Julia with bathing, skin care and clothing. John encouraged Peter to visit his wife daily. The short stay was partly paid from a personal budget from the insurance company*; Peter, being the mentor of Julia, could decide how to spend the funds.

As Julia's dementia progressed, John arranged for Julia to sleep at the assisted living facility to give Peter a good night's rest. During the days, she was at her own apartment. After a year and a half, Julia died sitting in her chair with Peter nearby. After her death John visited Peter several times to provide comfort and to help him start a new life as a single person*.

4.2   The Definition of Case Manager

This section introduces a definition of case manager as used in The Netherlands and in France. The concepts used in the definition are explained in the order of their place in the definition. At the end of the section, broader definitions receive attention as well as the arguments why these are rejected. Box 4.1 shows the definition of a case manager.

Box 4.1 The definition of a case manager
A case manager is a professional who:

1. *has regular contact with persons in complex situations*,*
2. *evaluates all of their care and social needs*,*
3. *cooperate with physicians and other professionals**
4. *makes a life/careplan* for the health and social domain,*
5. *organizes the formal and informal care* of the client*
6. *works within a program,**

(continued)

Box 4.1 (continued)
7. *use all communication means including digital information and communication technology**
8. *works only for persons who are not able to organize their life/careplan and are without a sufficient network of relatives to assist with this.**

The words with an asterix are explained in Sect.4.2.

This definition is based on definitions used in France[1] and in The Netherlands (Mahler et al. 2013). It is also in accordance with the definition of the Case Management Society of America (CMSA).[2] The definition is broad, as illustrated by the story of Julia and John. Case managers are involved in the health and social domain, in formal and informal care and in financial and non-financial affairs. Such a broad array of responsibilities for a case manager is rare at the present time.

4.2.1 Complex Situations

The first words with an asterix in the definition in Box 4.1 are *complex situations*. As a concept, complexity can be related to instability, unpredictably and intensity.[3] Persons in complex situations will probably experience some disruptions in the evolution of their situation (instability), some of which are not anticipated even by professionals (unpredictability) and the disruptions are frequently severe (intensity). Clinicians and case managers, even when they can't say very clearly why a situation is complex, are often skilled in detecting complexity. Usually, a complex situation requires collaboration between clients, clinicians, case managers and informal carers to be properly handled. A difference has to be underlined between persons in complex situations and frail persons, for example, frail elderly, frail families and frail persons with severe mental illness. Frail persons have a high risk to become persons in a complex situation. However, they do not belong to that group. Case managers could work for frail persons without complex situations. This has the advantage that the relation between them and the client already exists. They are able to help with preventive measures such as mobilizing other relatives to

---

[1]Décret n° 2011-1210, 29 sept 2011 implementing the houses for Autonomy and integrated care for people suffering from Alheimer's disease and related disorder. Journal Officiel de la République Française JORF n°0227 p 16463, text 30 and Arrêté 16 nov 2012 fixing the activities and skills repository for case-managers in houses for Autonomy and integrated care for people suffering from Alzheimer's disease and related disorder. Journal Officiel de la République Française JORF n°0271, p 18343, text 22.

[2]http://www.cmsa.org, consulted on September 29, 2015.

[3]A National Interprofessional Competency Framework Canadian Interprofessional Health Collaborative, Fev 2010. See: http://www.cihc.ca/files/CIHC_IPCompetencies_Feb1210.pdf

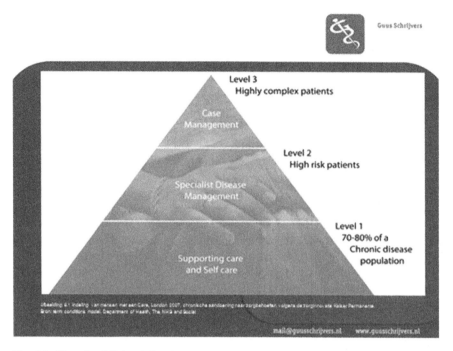

Fig. 4.1 Three-level Kaiser Triangle

extend the time during which the partner of the patient can provide care. They could inform clients about opportunities and the possible (dis)advantages of options and coach the clients in their choices. Nevertheless, extending the target population to "frail" people obviously and dramatically increases the societal need for case managers. This increases their caseloads with a risk of decreasing the quality of the intervention for people in complex situations. Kaiser Permanente, a healthcare organisation in California, introduced the three-level Kaiser Triangle (see Fig. 4.1). Most patients with a chronic condition deal with their diseases with support of primary care as usual. This is the first level. At the second level they are in need of a disease management program. Only in the case of complexity (level 3) are they in need of a case-manager.

4.2.2 All the Needs

The second set of words in Box 4.1 with an asterix is *evaluates all of their care and social needs*. Case managers have to be careful about all possible expressions of needs, preference and priorities. In fact, even when people say that they can't express an opinion, this is rarely the case for all the dimensions of the situation. Understanding one aspect frequently helps a lot in understanding the other. The point is that case management is related to person-centred care. The coaching abilities of the case managers are thus crucial (Corvol et al. 2015; Balard et al. 2013). This in important whether the classification of the client is a family with many problems, a person with dementia, a person with psychiatric disorders or a person with cancer.

4.2.3   Physicians' Cooperation

In the definition of Box 4.1, the third set of words with an asterix is: the case manager cooperates with physicians and other professionals. In our case story, the case manager cooperates with a general practitioner and is part of the primary healthcare team of which the GP is also a member. This is only one of the options. Case managers also work in a setting with geriatricians, treating Alzheimer patients at home and in nursing homes. If case managers work for cancer patients, they could cooperate with oncologists working in a hospital. In all these settings the physician is responsible for diagnosis, therapy, prognosis and the prescription of medication. However, case managers are responsible for the continuity of care and other services and for the making of the life/careplan. They can also coach clients or patients to raise questions to physicians and other professionals, to express their preferences and to ask to improve the quality of their care (Parrish et al. 2009; Coleman et al. 2004; Parry et al. 2008).

4.2.4   The Life/Care Plan

This life/careplan, the fourth concept in the definition in Box 4.1 with an asterix, describes five elements: (1) the health and social needs of the person in the complex situation; (2) the support of the informal carers to satisfy these needs; (3) the supply of care and services by professionals; (4) the allocation of tasks and responsibilities to informal carers and professionals and; (5) the time scheduling of informal and formal carers. The plan also has formal aspects showing who is the case manager; who is the first contact person (the client or a relative) within the informal carers; and who is the first responsible physician. It has also a validity period depending on the stability of the situation: 6 weeks? 6 months? A year?

A life/careplan contains a crisis section. This describes what the client and their informal carer have to do in case of a calamity, for example, illness of informal carer, failure of nursing or medical equipment or sudden worsening of the complex situation. In the story of Julia and Peter, the crisis paragraph describes what to do when Peter himself becomes ill, when the stair lift does not function and who to consult in case of a severe itch attack. Sometimes, the case manager or even the whole professional team is convinced that something is required to prevent a crisis. However, the client refuses it. It is important that the relationship is not severed by this refusal. On the contrary, the risk assessments of crises on one side and patient's rights on the other side have to be very carefully weighted. That is an important role of case managers.

Does a case manager make a life/careplan for an individual person or for a household? In The Netherlands, families exist with multiple problems at the same time with all members as clients or patients. For example, the father is unemployed, the mother has breast cancer and the kids do not function in the school and neighbourhood. For this kind of family the professional mantra is: *One family, one plan and one case manager.* In The Netherlands, the concept of a life-careplan is under scientific discussion and not crystallised in a new paradigm.[4] A debate exist in scientific, professional and financial circles about the content and other aspects of such plans, since in 2015 it is mandatory to develop one under the new Act of Long Term Care.[5,6]

Finally, the plan can entitle an individual to use public or insurance paid resources to assist the client. This position of advocacy for the client and gate-keeping of some scarce resources can put case managers in ethical dilemmas for which they must be trained (Corvol et al. 2013). A professional or policy maker other than the case manager could do this job. However, it seems less bureaucratic that one and the same case manager decides about payments based on life/careplan within financial guidelines. If case managers have the power to allocate resources, their decisions are faster made than in a context with a back office deciding about that.

4.2.5 Informal Care and the Case Manager

Informal care (the fifth set of words with an asterix mentioned in the definition of Box 4.1) is divided into care by relatives (or family care) and by volunteers. The latter are united in an organisation, for example, a church or a charity. Often they provide supportive services such as friendly visiting, transport, garden maintenance or small jobs like repairing a wall plug. Care such as washing patients or helping to go to the toilet is mostly done by relatives or eventually by professionals; that is too intimate for volunteers. Within the group of family carers a central person (the partner, a son or daughter) often offers most of the informal care. Often this person is healthy but frail. It is not simple for a case manager to define who the primary informal carer is, because sometimes appearances are misleading; for example a partner who lives with the person could be less involved in the informal care than a daughter living elsewhere. The assessment of the informal care network is one of the most important skills that a case manager has to possess.

---

[4]Inventarisatie individuele zorgplannen. http://www.vilans.nl/Pub/Home/Ons-aanbod/Producten/Inventarisatie-Individuele-zorgplannen.html

[5]http://www.rijksoverheid.nl/documenten-en-publicaties/kamerstukken/2014/03/10/wetsvoorstel-wet-langdurige-zorg.html

[6]http://www.rijksoverheid.nl/documenten-en-publicaties/kamerstukken/2014/03/10/memorie-van-toelichting-wet-langdurige-zorg.html

4.2.6   Within a Program

The case manager works within a program is the sixth phrase with an asterix in the definition of Box 4.1. Such a program could be the Chronic Care Model of Wagner (Wagner et al. 1996; Coleman et al. 2009) an integrated care program in Dutch style or German style. Such a program defines multidisciplinary professional pathways, decision trees, referral guidelines and treatment options. The program is also the link between case management and integrated care. The relation between case management and integrated care is not simple. *Per se*, the addition in a health and social services of a new service (the case managers) is at risk of increasing the fragmentation of the system (with new interfaces with this professional and the organisation hiring them etc. . . . In fact, case managers can participate in the integrated care movement only if their action is "translated" by a dedicated professional in organisational transformation leading to a more integrated health and social services system (Somme et al. 2014a).

4.2.7   Target Population

The last phrase in the definition with an asterix is *about persons who are not able to organize their care/life plan and are without a sufficient network of relatives.* A representative survey in The Netherlands of persons between 57 and 77 years of age showed four types of profiles of potential clients and patients (Doekhie et al. 2014). The first group (46%) lives pro-actively and wants to make decisions about their own life and care delivery. The second group (28%) could plan their own life but like to be cared for. This type of person doesn't like self-service in a restaurant and wants to be served. The third group (10%) asks professionals to make decisions and accepts advice as an order. The fourth and last group (16%) is unable to express their needs and to think on a longer term. Persons in this group often live alone, have a lack of money, and have a low education and quality of life. In social services and in the public health domain, persons in the last two groups are eligible for case managers. For the second group there seems to be a market for commercial case managers who organize for them care and services if complex situations arise.

4.2.8   Rejected Broader Definitions

Although the definition in Box 4.1 is broad, emotional support could also be included but is not mentioned. This is included in the task of case-managers: it strengthens their relation with the clients. However, they may offer tissues for the tears and listening ears for the complaints, but they don't take over the feelings of the clients. They don't give them hugs. In The Netherlands this professional attitude is called detached commitment.

The definition could also be extended to include continuous supervision, if a patient or client can't be alone. However, this is not a special task for case managers.

Generally, they have a caseload of 30–40 clients of the same target group: persons with dementia, cancer patients at home with metastases or multiproblem families. They help during a longer period and not only during transfers from one facility to another. Sometimes case managers work for a group of patients living in an assisted living house for persons of the same target group. But even in that case, they have to keep confidential the personal relationship they have with each individual. All clients have to be assessed in a one-to-one exchange (and not as a part of a whole group) about their own needs.

The third extension could be that a case manager is also involved with treatment, for instance giving injections to cancer patients. In The Netherlands case managers for cancer patients do this. However, in youth health and in care for persons with dementia, it is unusual. That is why inclusion of therapeutic interventions is not necessary to be a case manager.

4.2.9   Competencies and Skills of Case Managers

The qualifications of case managers are given in their definition. They have competencies (knowledge and skills) about health and social needs, the functioning of informal networks, the local supply of professionals and the mechanisms of cooperating with them. They know a lot about the regulations and financial limitations. Two competencies, communication skills and integrity, are discussed in more detail here.

Case managers must be able to apply different communication styles. Evidence seems to be in favor of an empowering style offering different options for life and care in a neutral way. However, sometimes case managers have to persuade clients/patients that their demands for help are unrealistic or too expensive for the municipality or social insurance agency. Case managers have professional autonomy: they are not waiters serving whatever the client demands. They have empathy for the clients or patients but also have to keep a professional distance.

The second competency, integrity, is in danger if case managers are on the payroll of suppliers of care and services. Then they could be pushed or seduced to create work for the supplying organisation. If they are on the payroll of a municipality or a social insurance, integrity is in danger because of cost control goals of these organisations. It should be recommended to adopt an independent position. How to realize this, is not easy to answer and is under discussion in The Netherlands. Above that, a professional organisation for case managers is necessary to resolve ethical questions and with its own disciplinary rules.

Case managers have responsibility for the continuity of care for the clients. Here, a tension may exist with clinicians. If patients are hospitalized and their case managers judge that there is an issue at home, they have almost no authority to contradict hospital clinicians even if they have more information on the home arrangements. Another source of tension occurs in conflicts between clinicians about the best therapy for a patient. Such a conflict causes delays in the start of treatment and makes clients unsure. Then case managers do not typically have the power to insist that the two come to consensus. In the Dutch oncological world a dog metaphor exists: a case manager should be a kind labrador for the patients and a pitbull for arguing doctors. It is not easy for nurses to combine both characteristics.

4.3 Specific Tools for Case Managers

This section discusses the contribution of scientists to make case managers more professional with their own scientific tools: (1) to evaluate health and social needs and (2) to empower patients and clients. Not discussed are here other necessary skills of case managers such as negotiation skills, coordination and management skills, inter-professional and inter-disciplinary working and patient and family support. Neither is discussed the role of the case manager as care-giver, and so the need for advanced nursing skills. All these skills are necessary for all professionals working in an integrated setting. They are discussed elsewhere in this book.

4.3.1 Evaluating Health and Social Needs

Case managers have to assess all the social and healthcare needs of their clients, and also living arrangement needs and psychological needs. They have to assess these needs with a formal assessment process. Otherwise arbitrariness and personal preferences of the case manager could play a role.

There is no international assessment tool approved by the authorities for the assessment task. In Canada, some parts of France and parts of Australia case managers use the FAMS or derivations of it (Somme et al. 2014b; Nugue et al. 2012). FAMS means Functional Autonomy Measurement System. It was developed by the Prisma Program originating from the province of Quebec (Stewart et al. 2013). It allows the classification of personal situations in 14 groups with very similar care or social needs. Germany uses a three level assessment model to evaluate health and social needs. Its focus is on nursing needs. A debate is going on to broaden the assessment and to include also communicative and cognitive limitations (Büscher 2011). In 2003 The Netherlands introduced an assessment system based on the International Classification of Functioning, Disabilities and Health (World Health Organization 2001). This system facilitated assessment of health, limitations and disorders without mentioning what kind of professional care should be offered. Based on this system The Netherlands uses now six kinds of care needs: (1) personal care on the body like washing; (2) technical nursing care (e.g. wound cleaning); (3) supporting and supervising (if the client cannot be alone); (4) Psychological treatment; (5) special conditions for housing (for instance bars in the bath room) and (6) short stay in a nursing home (e.g., after a hospital admission).

In Scandinavian countries no assessment instruments exist. It is up to the professional to make an assessment. In the UK and the USA local instruments are that are not necessarily based on scientific research. In the rehabilitation sector in France,

Canada and The Netherlands the Resident Assessment Instrument (RAI) (Morris et al. 1990) and the Barthel Index (Mahoney and Barthel 1965) are popular: case managers here measure the mobility of persons and clients and the need for support if it is limited.

Until now, a universal assessment instrument covering all health and social needs is not available. In The Netherlands, there is hesitation to make better (and longer) questionnaires to assess the client and patient needs. The latest strategy is that a case manager goes immediately to the experienced problems of the client without analysing the interaction between different needs. This is popular in youth health and is known as solution focused therapy (Molnar et al. 1987; Visser 2012). However, clients' situations have to be assessed on all their dimensions and not only the "obviously problematic" ones. This is because it permits preventive action on dimensions that are unstable but not overly problematic and because it allows examination of all the causes of the situation and thus finding the best solution (Somme 2014). Another new development is the structured dialogue between case manager and client or patient. Here, case managers assess health needs, for example limited mobility within the house. If there is a problem, they assess immediately what solutions the client or the partners have. They offer a professional solution only if there is absolutely no informal one.

In 2012, the Skidelskys, a father and son who are an economist and a philosopher, respectively, wrote a bestseller with the title *How much is enough?* (Skidelsky and Skidelsky 2012). Their book is interesting for case managers working in the field of supporting clients' quality of life within financial limitations. They studied the theories of Keynes, Aristoteles, Rawls, Sen and Nussbaum. Based on their publications they formulated seven basic needs of human beings: (1) Health; (2) A safe and trusted environment; (3) Respect from others; (4) Personal autonomy; (5) Harmony with nature; (6) Friendships and other affective relations and (7) Free time for pleasant activities. They put these seven needs on the same level. This is in contradiction with Maslow's pyramid showing a hierarchy in which physical needs are more basic than, for example, free time for pleasant activities (Maslow 1943).

In most countries, case managers work with assessment systems in which health needs and physical needs are more important than the Skidelskys' social needs (numbers 3–7). To our knowledge, only in Sweden do professional personal assistants exist. They are assigned to a client by case managers. Together with the client they decide whether they spend their time fulfilling the client's physical needs or they drink friendly coffee as to build affective relations.[7] In the Bible the competition between physical and social needs is also discussed. In the parable of the two sisters, Maria and Martha provide housing and care to the Lord, who appears as a traveller. Martha starts immediately with washing the feet of the Lord and preparing a meal. For her physical needs were most important. Maria started with a conversation with the Lord about his trip. For her, social needs like

---

[7]http://www.independentliving.org/docs5/jag.html visited on September 27, 2015.

attention and love come first. The Lord appreciated Maria more than Martha. We, as authors of this chapter, do not follow the Bible or the Beatles with their song *All you need is love*. We prefer the Swedish model where clients and professionals share decisions about priorities between physical and social needs.

4.3.2   Empowering Interviewing of Patients, Clients and Relatives

Stimulating self-management by client, patient or relatives is called patient empowerment or patient activation. There are four types of self-management (Heijmans et al. 2012): (1) Medical self-care, e.g. the intake of drugs; (2) Dealing with professionals e.g. making appointments with a professional; (3) Coping with the effects of the disease or limitation, e.g. coping with pain and (4) Adapting the lifestyle, e.g. doing physical exercises. Empirical Dutch research teaches that persons with chronic conditions have the most problems with self-management of the third and fourth type. English studies show that it is not enough to educate them on these domains by giving information and instructions in a leaflet or on a website (Kennedy et al. 2013; De Jong et al. 2014; Bardsley et al. 2013). Three other aspects are also necessary.

First, it is important to measure current self-management before introducing new forms. The PAM (Patient Activation Measure) is an example of a measurement tool for this (Hibbard et al. 2004).The designers of this instrument distinguish four phases of self-management: (1) Belief that the patient's role is important; (2) Self-confidence and know-how to apply self-management; (3) The self-management action and (4) Self-management in stressful periods.

Second, an educational theory is necessary to check that information is understood, and applied. Educational theories are the triangle (from knowing to doing) of Miller (1990) and the learning style theory of Kolb (1984).

The third necessary aspect is the use of the motivational interviewing designed by Miller et al. (2012). He distinguishes four phases in his interview technique: (1) Creating a relationship of trust between professional and client/patient; (2) Focusing on behavioural change goals in the client or patient; (3) Enforcing these goals and (4) Making a plan with practical steps to implement the goals.

Patient empowering interviewing is a crucial role for case managers. Their skills are distinguishing different types of self-care, applying the PAM instrument, using an educational theory and motivational interviewing. Although case managers are focused on clients and patients, they also have to activate the relatives. Behaviours to be activated are: (1) Perseverance of supporting of their loved patients or clients; (2) Assertiveness (How to say no to a patient without feeling guilty); (3) Physical support (how to lift your partner from bed into a chair?). Courses for relatives seem to be cost effective (Livingston et al. 2013; Knapp et al. 2013; Long et al. 2014).

4.4   The Real World and the Ideal World of the Case Story

Section 4.1 contains the story Julia and Peter. Six types of services are mentioned with an asterix. They do not exist nationwide, neither in France nor in The Netherlands. However, they exist in small experiments and innovations, mostly not officially published in scientific journals. These six types of services are summarized in Box 4.2.

Box 4.2 Services of case managers with do not exist in 2016

1. *Advanced nursing specialist working as case manager in primary health care for target groups as persons with dementia, multimorbidity, cancer or families with many problems*
2. *Making a care-lifeplan for a period of e.g. a year*
3. *a pharmacist reviewing the medication of patients with many shifts a day*
4. *an outreaching fall prevention service within primary health care*
5. *an IT expert helping patients and their relatives using their Tablet PC to communicate with their formal and informal care providers*
6. *Providing comfort and relaunch tips for informal carers with a deceased partner*

The six show the differences between the ideal world of the authors and the reality in their countries. The reality exists in The Netherlands because of a lack of consensus about the aims of the Dutch health care policy. The most important stakeholders, government, professional organisations, health care providers, labour unions and patient organisations, disagree about the triple aim of improving health, enhancing quality of care and controlling costs as formulated by Berwick and colleagues in 2008 (Berwick et al. 2008) and Bisognano in 2012 (Bisognano et al. 2012). First, there is a difference in the timeframe of the policy aims. Broadly speaking, scientific advisory institutes and professional organisations think in term of 8–12 years or more. The government and its agencies think in periods of 4 years until the next election. Commercial firms and innovations subsidizing charities have a time horizon of 2 years. Second, the aims of the stakeholders are different. For the government, all policy was focused on health care cost control and decentralisation of power to municipalities. Case managers and continuity of care were low on the policy agenda. Contrary to this, research and professional institutes for health services embrace these two policy aims. Third, if there are case managers and integrated care programs within which they have to work, they are not supported by an adequate health information technology (IT) system and financing system.

In France, there has been a shift towards more case managers, especially in care for persons with dementia. However, case managers are not recognized as a profession. Instead, it is mandatory to have a professional qualification before being hired as a case manager. There is no case management professional organisation (order or syndicate). There is no specialized journal. Nevertheless, the "professional field" is defined in a regulation. Case managers have to fulfill four conditions:

- they have to be hired by a local leader in charge of a local integrated care project
- they have to be a professional from a limited list of professions which are authorized to make "in-home" assessments of a person's entire situation. These professions are: social services workers (with a certain level of responsibility corresponding to a licence level at least), medical auxiliary (a group of professionals in which there are nurses, occupational therapists, physiotherapists, and so on), or clinical psychologist (with a Master degree)
- they have to have professional experience with in-home care arrangement for people with loss of autonomy and in complex situations
- they have to take a 100 h university training program with a minimum of 20 days of practical course with a licensed case manager during the first 3 years of the contract.

Case management for clients with dementia was implemented in France as one part of a vast program for improving the integration of social and healthcare systems. It was not the only means of improving integration but just one part.

4.5 Implementation Strategies to Disseminate the Function of Case Managers

This chapter started with an ideal case story in the year 2025. It has been mentioned above that best practices exist in The Netherlands, France and also in other countries. Or said in a slogan: the future is already invented in best practices. The problem is how to disseminate the best practices. Evidence does not support (de Stampa et al. 2010) a top down, big bang introduction of case managers in a state or a nation. That creates only chaos and makes case managers unpopular in the population and within professional groups. Our rejection is based on bad experiences in the period from 2009 to 2014 with the introduction of case managers within family centres for Dutch families with multiple problems. On the other hand, it is probably inefficient to "wait" for integrated care, because professionals and organizations have no direct interest in working in an integrated (often more complex) way. Thus what is needed from the top down is not to define "how" to do what is to be done but why and when to do that and to help the change happen rather than making it or letting it happen. The fact is that without political will, integrated care never appears "naturally", but without sufficient margins at an operational level, integration will always be rejected (Greenhalgh et al. 2004).

Instead of the top-down approach the model by Rogers (2003) to gradually disseminate case managers in a country is interesting. Figure 4.2 shows the Roger Model. In it, innovation 1 is disseminated faster than Innovations 2 and 3. The three innovations have comparable introduction phases. In the first phase, only early adopters use the innovation. The innovation is relatively slow

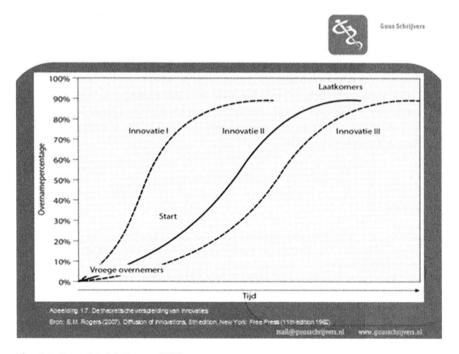

Fig. 4.2 Roger Model (Rogers 2003)

implemented. Then the curve goes up fast: the early and late majority takes over the innovation. In the last phase only laggards remain, explaining why the implementation speed is again low.

Rogers shows five conditions that decrease the implementation speed. One of these is the complexity of the innovation. A monodisciplinary guideline is implementable faster than the new role of case manager. The latter changes the roles of many professionals, redefines the relations with physicians and changes access to health and social services.

For the introduction of complex innovations another scientist, Christensen, has a theory (Christensen et al. 2009). He is the author of the bestseller *The Innovator's Prescription*. Christensen emphasizes the simultaneous innovation of care, the payment system and the health information system. Let us explain this theory with the innovation of the broad case manager as an example. If professionals have designed this care innovation, it only has a chance for implementation if simultaneously a fee and payment system for the new function is introduced. Otherwise there is no business case for this innovation. Alongside that, the IT system has to be changed or else the case manager (often a nurse) cannot communicate with physicians, nurses and social workers in the social domain.

Are the models of Rogers and Christensen enough to design an implementation strategy for the introduction of case managers in a country? We think that these are necessary but not enough. On a micro level, the case manager integrates health and social services. On the macro level there should be a sense of urgency to stimulate this by means of adaptation of current regulation. In The United Kingdom the legislation for the health services and social services were already integrated. In The Netherlands this is the case for long term care. In France, this integration on a national level is being prepared for clients with dementia.

If the implementation of the function of case manager is simultaneously supported on micro and macro levels from professional, financial and digital sides, in 2025 the case story of Julia and John would become a reality.

Utrecht, Rennes 07052016

References

Balard, F., et al. (2013). Exploring representations and experiences of case-management users: Towards difficulties and solutions to leading qualitative interviews with older people with complex living conditions. *Quality in Primary Care, 21*, 229–235.

Bardsley, M., et al. (2013). Impact of telehealth on general practice contacts: Findings from the whole systems demonstrator cluster randomised trial. *BMC Health Services Research, 13*, 395.

Berwick, D. M., et al. (2008). The triple aim: Care, health, and cost. *Health Affairs (Millwood), 27*(3), 759–769.

Bisognano, M., et al. (2012). *Pursuing the triple aim. Seven innovators show the way to better care, better health and lower costs.* San Francisco: Jossey-Bass.

Büscher, A. (2011, May 31). *Determining eligibility for long-term care—lessons from Germany* (Vol. 11). URN:NBN:NL:UI:10-1-101447, ijic2011-19.

Christensen, C. M., et al. (2009). *The innovator's prescription: A disruptive solution for health care.* New York: McGraw Hill.

Coleman, E. A., et al. (2004). Reparing patients and caregivers to participate in care delivered across settings: The care transitions intervention. *Journal of the American Geriatrics Society, 52*(11), 1817–1825.

Coleman, K., et al. (2009). Evidence on the chronic care model in the new millennium. *Health Affairs (Millwood), 28*(1), 75–85.

Corvol, A., et al. (2013). Ethical issues in the introduction of case management for elderly people. *Nursing Ethics, 20*(1), 83–89.

Corvol, A., et al. (2016). What ethics for case managers? Literature review and discussion. *Nursing Ethics, 23*(7), 729–742.

De Jong, C. C., et al. (2014). The effects on health behavior and health outcomes of internet-based asynchronous communication between health providers and patients with a chronic condition: A systematic review. *Journal of Medical Internet Research, 16*(1), e19. doi:10.2196/jmir.3000.

de Stampa, M., et al. (2010). Diagnostic study, design and implementation of an integrated model of care in France: A bottom-up process with continuous leadership. *International Journal of Integrated Care, 10*, e034.

Doekhie, K. D., et al. (2014). *Ouderen van de toekomst. Verschillen in de wensen en mogelijkheden voor wonen, welzijn en zorg, een overzichtsstudie.* Utrecht: Nivel.

Greenhalgh, T., et al. (2004). Diffusion of innovations in service organizations: Systematic review and recommendations. *The Milbank Quarterly, 82*(4), 581–629.

Heijmans, M., et al. (2012). *Ontwikkelingen in de zorg voor chronisch zieken, Rapportage 2010.* Utrecht: NIVEL.

Hibbard, J. H., et al. (2004). Development of the patient activation measure (PAM). Conceptualizing and measuring activation in patients and consumers. *Health Services Research, 39*(4 Pt 1), 1005–1026.

Kennedy, A., et al. (2013). Implementation of self management support for long term conditions in routine primary care settings: Cluster randomised controlled trial. *BMJ, 346*, f2882.

Knapp, M., et al. (2013). Cost effectiveness of a manual based coping strategy programme in promoting the mental health of family carers of people with dementia (the START (STrAtegies for RelaTives) study): A pragmatic randomised controlled trial. *BMJ, 347*, f6342.

Kolb, D. A. (1984). *Experiential learning: Experience as the source of learning and development.* Englewood Cliffs, NJ: Prentice-Hall.

Livingston, G., et al. (2013). Clinical effectiveness of a manual based coping strategy programme (START, STrAtegies for RelaTives) in promoting the mental health of careers of family members with dementia: Pragmatic randomised controlled trial. *BMJ, 347*, f6276.

Long, K., et al. (2014). Estimating the potential cost savings from the New York University Caregiver Intervention in Minnesota. *Health Affairs (Millwood), 33*(4), 596–604.

Mahler, M., et al. (2013). *Case management, Op weg naar passende zorg en ondersteuning dichtbij.* Utrecht: Vilans.

Mahoney, F. I., & Barthel, D. W. (1965). Functional evaluation: The Barthel Index. *Maryland State Medical Journal, 14*, 61–65.

Maslow, A. H. (1943). A theory of human motivation. *Psychological Review, 50*(4), 370–396.

Miller, G. E. (1990). The assessment of clinical skills/competence/performance. *Academic Medicine, 65*, 563–567.

Miller, W. R., et al. (2012). *Motivational interviewing.* New York: Guilford Press.

Molnar, A., et al. (1987). Solution-focused therapy: Toward the identification of therapeutic tasks. *Journal of Marital and Family, 13*(4), 349–358.

Morris, J. N., et al. (1990). Designing the national resident assessment instrument for nursing homes. *The Gerontologist, 30*(3), 293–307. doi:10.1093/geront/30.3.293.

Nugue, M., et al. (2012). Use of standardized multidimensional evaluation tools and the emergence of the case manager's professional identity in France. *Care Management Journals, 13*(4), 184–193.

Parrish, M. M., et al. (2009). Implementation of the care transitions intervention: Sustainability and lessons learned. *Professional Case Management, 14*(6), 282–293.

Parry, C., et al. (2008). Assessing the quality of transitional care: Further applications of the care transitions measure. *Medical Care, 46*(3), 317–322.

Rogers, E. M. (2003). *Diffusion of innovations* (5th ed.). New York: Free Press. (1st edition 1962).

Skidelsky, R., & Skidelsky, E. (2012). *How much is enough, Money and the Good life.* New York: Other Press.Paperback

Somme, D. (2014). Integrated care in France: Dream or reality? *Intenational Journal of Integrated Care, 14*, e053.

Somme, D., et al. (2014a). The French society of geriatrics and gerontology position paper on the concept of integration. *International Journal of Integrated Care, 14*, e052.

Somme, D., et al. (2014b). Adapting the Quebecois method for assessing implementation to the French National Alzheimer Plan 2008–2012: Lessons for gerontological services integration. *International Journal of Integrated Care, 14*, e016.

Stewart, M. J., et al. (2013). Successfully integrating aged care services: A review of the evidence and tools emerging from a long-term care program. *International Journal of Integrated Care, 13*, e003.

Visser, C. F. (2012). *The solution-focused mindset: An empirical test of solution-focused assumptions.*

Wagner, E. H., et al. (1996). Organizing care for patients with chronic illness. *The Milbank Quarterly, 74*(4), 511–544.

World Health Organization. (2001). *International classification of functioning, disability and health (ICF).* Geneva: WHO.

Disease Management

5

Ellen Nolte

5.1 Introduction

Structured disease management has been suggested as a potential means to improve the quality and reduce the cost of healthcare, and to enhance health outcomes for people with chronic conditions. Health professionals, policymakers and institutions in many countries in Europe and elsewhere have begun introducing some form of disease management programme and similar approaches in order to address the rising burden of chronic disease. However, attempts to do so have varied and the nature and scope of programmes and care models differ (Nolte et al. 2008, 2014). Some, such as Germany and the Netherlands, and more recently, Denmark, France and Italy, have introduced large-scale, population-based structured disease management programmes while others are experimenting with smaller-scale care approaches, although this is now changing (Nolte and Knai 2015).

As approaches to chronic disease management vary, so does the evidence about their effectiveness, about the value of different approaches, and about what works in what contexts and for what populations (Nolte and McKee 2008b). It has been noted that this is in part because of the variety of terms and concepts that are used to describe efforts to improve chronic illness care and its components. Coleman et al. (2009) have further highlighted the relative lack of scientific rigour in evaluating these approaches and the reporting of the results of such interventions, which tend to be complex in nature and scope, with several interrelated components often acting at different levels of service delivery (Craig et al. 2008).

E. Nolte (✉)
European Observatory on Health Systems and Policies, London School of Economics and Political Science, London School of Hygiene & Tropical Medicine, London, UK
e-mail: E.Nolte@lse.ac.uk

© Springer International Publishing AG 2017
V. Amelung et al. (eds.), *Handbook Integrated Care*,
DOI 10.1007/978-3-319-56103-5_5

In this chapter we explore the nature of disease management as a tool or strategy for integrated care. We examine the evidence base for disease management and identify requirements for advancing the debate, building on and updating our earlier work around chronic disease management and integrated care (Nolte 2017; Nolte and McKee 2008b; Nolte and Pitchforth 2014). We close with some overarching observations.

5.2   What Is Disease Management?

One of the key challenges to describing disease management as a strategy is that definitions of this concept vary widely (Krumholz et al. 2006; Schrijvers 2009). Disease management, by definition, traditionally targets patient groups with a specific condition, such as diabetes, and focuses on addressing the clinical needs of those affected (Nolte and McKee 2008b). However, more recent definitions are explicitly adopting a population-based approach that may also consider the needs that arise from multiple chronic conditions (Care Continuum Alliance 2010).

Disease management was first mentioned as a concept in the United States in the 1980s. It was initially used mainly by pharmaceutical companies offering educational programmes to employers and managed care organisations to promote medication adherence and behaviour change among people with chronic conditions such as diabetes, asthma and coronary artery disease (Bodenheimer 1999; The Boston Consulting Group 2006). From the mid-1990s, disease management strategies were adopted more widely across the private and public sectors in the USA (Krumholz et al. 2006), and, more recently, in several European countries (Nolte and Knai 2015; Rijken et al. 2012), Australia (Glasgow et al. 2008; Hamar et al. 2015), Israel (Goldfracht et al. 2011), and Singapore (Tan et al. 2014), among others. This occurred in parallel with an emerging body of evidence, which pointed to the potential for disease management to improve care quality and lead to cost savings.

However, approaches vary widely in focus, nature and scope of interventions, and populations covered. For example, in the USA, descriptions range from "discrete programs directed at reducing costs and improving outcomes for patients with particular conditions" (Rothman and Wagner 2003, p.257) to "a population-based systematic approach that identifies persons at risk, intervenes, measures the outcomes, and provides continuous quality improvement" (Epstein and Sherwood 1996, p.832). Ellrodt et al. (1997, p.1687) defined disease management as "an approach to patient care that coordinates medical resources for patients across the entire delivery system". More recently, the Population Health Alliance (previously Care Continuum Alliance and, before that, Disease Management Association of America) defined disease management as "a system of coordinated health care interventions and communications for populations with conditions in which patient self-care efforts are significant" (Care Continuum Alliance 2010, p.55). The definition provided by the Population Health Alliance further stipulates for full-service disease management programmes to include six components: population identification processes; evidence-based practice guidelines; collaborative practice models to include physician and support-service providers; patient self-management education; process and outcomes measurement, evaluation, and management; and routine reporting or feedback loop. Approaches that use fewer than these six components are to be considered disease management support services only.

Although authors have increasingly adopted the definition proposed by the Population Health Alliance, variation in what is referred to as disease management has remained (Coelho et al. 2014; Coleman et al. 2009; Lemmens et al. 2009; Martinez-Gonzalez et al. 2014; Peytremann-Bridevaux et al. 2015; Pimouguet et al. 2011). Norris et al. (2003) observed that programmes tend to vary "in breadth, in focus or purpose ...[they] may also vary with the writer's perspective (economic, research, clinical) and the delivery system to which the term is being applied (e.g. primary care, specialty-based services contracted to another delivery system, pharmacy services)" (p.478–9). This appears to have changed little since Norris and colleagues published their observations in 2003, as we shall see below. While variation may be necessary to focus a given programme to the needs of a given population, it poses challenges for comparison and the assessment of effect in particular. Furthermore, in many settings, the focus continues to be on single diseases, albeit with some adjustment to consider comorbidity (Fullerton et al. 2011), and there remain concerns overall about the suitability of current approaches to disease management to address the complex needs of those with multiple disease processes (Aspin et al. 2010; Nolte et al. 2012b; Rijken et al. 2012).

5.3   What Are the Impacts of Disease Management?

As noted in the introduction to this chapter, structured disease management has been proposed as a means to improve the quality and reduce the cost of health care, and ultimately improve health outcomes for the chronically ill. However, the evidence on the ability of such approaches to achieve this varies by type of approach and target group. What is known is mainly based on small studies of high-risk patients, often undertaken in academic settings (Mattke et al. 2007). Evidence of the impact of large-scale, population-wide programmes is slowly becoming available, such as from Australia (Hamar et al. 2015), Denmark (Smidth et al. 2013), Germany (Fuchs et al. 2014; Jacob et al. 2015; Mehring et al. 2014), and the Netherlands (de Bakker et al. 2013; Elissen et al. 2012; Tsiachristas et al. 2015).

There is now a wide range of systematic reviews, reviews of reviews and meta-analyses of the evidence on (chronic disease-) specific interventions and disease management programmes. However, reflecting the variation in the interpretation and use of the term 'disease management', it remains challenging to arrive at an overarching conclusion. This is particularly the case where terms such as disease management are being used interchangeably with 'collaborative care', 'case management', or, indeed, 'integrated care', reflecting the challenges that have been discussed in the context of assessing the evidence base for the impacts of integrated care, as reported in Chap. 4. For example, Ouwens et al. (2005) presented a review of systematic reviews of approaches seeking to improve the care for people with chronic conditions. While broadly referring to 'integrated care' programmes, of the 13 systematic reviews considered, 8 were reviews of disease management interventions, each employing a distinct definition of disease management. The remainder reviewed some form of care or case management (two reviews), multi-disciplinary teams/structures (two), and more generally management of patients with chronic health problems (one). Similarly, Martinez-Gonzalez et al. (2014) provided a meta-review of integrated care programmes for adults with chronic conditions, of which the majority reported on disease management interventions.

As we noted elsewhere in this book (see Chap. 2), this issue is not only of academic relevance but has important implications for practice. Empirical evidence of approaches that can be subsumed under the above terms is often difficult to compare because of a lack of clarity in defining and describing the approach being studied. This challenge was also highlighted by Ouwens et al. (2005). They concluded, on the basis of their review of reviews, although there was considerable heterogeneity in interventions, patient populations, and processes and outcomes of care, programmes under review appeared to have led to improvements in the quality of care. Yet, they noted that the variation in definitions and components of care, and failure to recognise these variations, could lead to inappropriate conclusions about programme effectiveness and the application of findings in practice.

Building on the work by Ouwens et al. (2005), this section updates and amends an earlier rapid review of the evidence base for chronic disease management (Nolte 2017; Nolte and Pitchforth 2014). Our earlier work assessed the evidence identified in 15 systematic reviews and meta-analyses that were published between 2004 and 2012. We complemented these with an additional eight systematic reviews, which we identified from a separate search of PubMed (NCBI 2016) carried out to inform Chapter 2. The review presented here is not intended to be exhaustive. Instead, we sought to provide an overview of the nature of evidence that has been published since the work by Ouwens et al. (2005) and to examine the extent to which recent evidence has provided more certainty around the impacts of disease management on service and health outcomes, and the implications of these findings in the context of integrated care. Table 5.1 provides a summary overview of the main observations of the 23 systematic reviews considered here.

Conditions most frequently considered in reviews were heart failure (Drewes et al. 2012; Gonseth et al. 2004; Roccaforte et al. 2005, 2006; Takeda et al. 2012; Whellan et al. 2005; Yu et al. 2006), diabetes (Egginton et al. 2012; Elissen et al. 2013b; Knight et al. 2005; Pimouguet et al. 2011), asthma or chronic obstructive pulmonary disease (COPD) (Adams et al. 2007; Boland et al. 2013; Kruis et al. 2013; Lemmens et al. 2011; Niesink et al. 2007; Peytremann-Bridevaux et al. 2008, 2015), depression (Archer et al. 2012; Ekers et al. 2013; Neumeyer-Gromen et al. 2004; Thota et al. 2012), or a combination of these (de Bruin et al. 2011; Ofman et al. 2004; Tsai et al. 2005). Definitions of disease management varied among

Table 5.1 Evidence of effect of disease management programmes as reported in 23 systematic reviews

	Number studies reviewed	Condition/s targeted	Definition disease management	Functional status, clinical outcomes	Hospitalisation	Quality of life	Patient satisfaction	Mortality	Process	Cost
Chronic heart failure										
Gonseth et al. (2004)	54 studies: 27 RCT, 27 non-RCT	Heart failure (ages 65+)	An intervention designed to manage heart failure and reduce hospital readmissions using a systematic approach to care and potentially employing multiple treatment modalities (adapted from Weingarten et al. (2002), who used the definition by Ellrodt et al. (1997))		⇩					(⇩)
Roccaforte et al. (2005)	33 RCT	Heart failure	None specified; description of DMP characteristics of included studies: multidisciplinary approach, use of specialist nurse or case manager, (patient) education, planned home/outpatient clinic visits, regular phone contacts		⇩	?		⇩	+ (Roccaforte et al. 2006)	
Whellan et al. (2005)	19 RCT	Heart failure	None specified; focus on postdischarge interventions		⇩			(⇩)		(⇩)
Göhler et al. (2006)	36 RCT	Heart failure	None specified; considered		⇩			⇩		

(continued)

Table 5.1 (continued)

	Number studies reviewed	Condition/s targeted	Definition disease management	Functional status, clinical outcomes	Hospitalisation	Quality of life	Patient satisfaction	Mortality	Process	Cost
			interventions ranging from patient education on self-monitoring and knowledge of disease to electronic home monitoring; all had to have scheduled interventions after discharge							
Yu et al. (2006)	21 RCT	Heart failure (ages 60+)	A programme that uses multiple interventions in a systematic manner to manage heart failure across different health care delivery systems (adapted from Ellrodt et al. (1997) and Weingarten et al. (2002))		⇩	(+)		(⇩)		(⇩)
Drewes et al. (2012)	46 studies: 32 RCT, 4 CT, 9 before/after, 1 chart review[b]	Heart failure (adults)	Interventions that contained two or more elements of the Chronic Care Model (health care system, community resources and policies, self-management support, delivery system design, decision support, clinical information system) (Wagner 1998)		⇩	+		⇨		

Takeda et al. (2012)	25 RCT (of which 2 represented disease management)	Heart failure (adults)	Broad conceptualisation of 'clinical services interventions', including case management, clinic models and multidisciplinary interventions, and disease management, which was defined as 'a system of coordinated health care interventions and communications for populations with long-term conditions in which patient self-care is significant' (adapted from Royal College of Physicians 2004)		⇓ᵃ	(+)ᵃ		(⇓)ᵃ
Diabetes								
Knight et al. (2005)	24: 19 RCT; 5 non-RCT	Diabetes (adult patients)	Programmes that used a systematic approach to care and included more than one intervention component. A systematic approach to care was defined as one that includes of any of the following components: guidelines, protocols, algorithms, care plans, or systematic patient or provider education programmes	+/(+)	(⇓)	(+)	(+)	(+)

(continued)

Table 5.1 (continued)

	Number studies reviewed	Condition/s targeted	Definition disease management	Functional status, clinical outcomes	Hospitalisation	Quality of life	Patient satisfaction	Mortality	Process	Cost
Pimouguet et al. (2011)	41 RCT	Diabetes type 1 or type 2	Ongoing and proactive follow-up of patients that includes at least two of five components: patient education; coaching; treatment adjustment; monitoring; care coordination	+				=		
Egginton et al. (2012)	52 studies: 45 RCT, 7 non-RCT	Diabetes type 2	Not defined; uses the term 'care management', distinguishes delivery mode (office (interaction or chart review in outpatient setting), web (interaction using computer/internet) and telephone (interaction using telephone/pager)) and leader type (physician, other (e.g. multidisciplinary team, nurse))	+		(+)			(+)	?
Elissen et al. (2013b)	61 studies: 41 RCT, 6 CT, 4 before/after, 10 observational studies[b]	Diabetes mellitus (adult patients)	Interventions that included at least two components of the Chronic Care Model (Wagner 1998)	+					+	

Asthma and/or chronic obstructive pulmonary disease (COPD)

Lemmens et al. (2009)	36 studies: 28 RCT, 8 controlled before/after	Asthma or COPD (adults aged 16+)	Multiple interventions in the context of disease management targeting the patient (e.g. patient education, self-management support), professional practice (e.g. professional education, audit, feedback) or organisational structure (e.g. role redesign, follow-up)	=	⇩	+	(+)	(+)
Peytremann-Bridevaux et al. (2015)	20 RCT	Asthma (adults aged 16+)	Interventions that met five criteria: at least one organisational component targeting patients (elements that interfere with the care process or that aim to improve continuity of care); at least one organisational component targeting health care professionals (e.g., physicians, nurses, etc.), the health care system, or both; presence of a patient education or self-management support component, or both; active involvement of two or more health	+/(+)	?	+		

(continued)

Table 5.1 (continued)

	Number studies reviewed	Condition/s targeted	Definition disease management	Functional status, clinical outcomes	Hospitalisation	Quality of life	Patient satisfaction	Mortality	Process	Cost
			care professionals; and minimum duration of 3 months							
Adams et al. (2007)	32 studies: 20 RCT; 5 CT; 7 before/after	COPD	Interventions that contained at least one element of the Chronic Care Model (self-management support, delivery system design, decision support, clinical information system) (Wagner 1998)	+/(+)	⇩	?		=		(⇩)
Niesink et al. (2007)	10 RCT	COPD	Programmes that contained at least one of the following components: (1) multidisciplinary care team, (2) clinical pathway, (3) clinical follow-up, (4) case management, or (5) self-management or patient education	(+)		(+)				
Peytremann-Bridevaux et al. (2008)	13 studies: 9 RCT; 1 CT; 3 before/after	COPD	Interventions included two or more different components (e.g. physical exercise, self-management, structured follow-up), active involvement of two or more health	+/(+)	⇩	(+)		=		

Reference	Studies	Condition	Intervention description						
			care professionals in patient care; consideration of patient education; at least one component of the intervention lasted a minimum of 12 months						⇨
Boland et al. (2013)	11 studies: 7 RCT, 2 before/after, 2 case-control	COPD	Interventions that contained two or more elements of the Chronic Care Model (Wagner et al. 2001): organisational support, community resources and policies, self-management support, delivery system design, decision support, clinical information system; programme had minimum duration of 12 months		⇨	+		⇨	⇨
Kruis et al. (2013)	26 RCT	COPD	Integrated disease management intervention which includes at least two of the following components: education/self-management; exercise; psychosocial; smoking cessation; medication; nutrition; follow-up and/or communication;	+/(+)	⇨	+/(+)	n/r	=	n/r

(continued)

Table 5.1 (continued)

	Number studies reviewed	Condition/s targeted	Definition disease management	Functional status, clinical outcomes	Hospitalisation	Quality of life	Patient satisfaction	Mortality	Process	Cost
			multidisciplinary team; financial intervention; and which includes active involvement of at least two different categories of health care providers; minimum duration of 3 months							
Depression										
Neumeyer-Gromen et al. (2004)	10 RCT	Depression (adults aged 18+)	'Complete DMP' comprising use of evidence-based guidelines, patient self-management education, provider education, collaborative care, reminder systems, monitoring *(detailed definition not provided, inferred from the text)*	+		+	+		+	?
Archer et al. (2012)	79 RCT	Depression or anxiety (any age)	Collaborative care intervention that included (i) multi-professional approach to patient care, (ii) structured management plan, (iii) scheduled patient follow-up, and (iv) enhanced	+ (adults)		+ (adults)	+ (adults)		+ (adults)	

			interprofessional communication				
Thota et al. (2012)	32 studies: 28 RCT, 5 quasi-experimental	Major depression, minor depression, dysthymia	Collaborative care intervention that included at least a case manager, primary care provider, and mental health specialist with collaboration among these roles	+	+	+	+
Ekers et al. (2013)	14 RCT	Depression plus one or more physical health problems (adults aged 16+)	Nurse-delivered collaborative care with at least two of the following components: proactive follow-up of participants, assessment of patient adherence to psychological and pharmacological treatments, monitoring of patient progress using validated measure, provision of psychological support, regular communication and supervision with mental health specialists and/or primary care physician	+			

(continued)

Table 5.1 (continued)

	Number studies reviewed	Condition/s targeted	Definition disease management	Functional status, clinical outcomes	Hospitalisation	Quality of life	Patient satisfaction	Mortality	Process	Cost
Combined										
Ofman et al. (2004)[c]	102 experimental or quasi-experimental	Asthma (9 studies), back pain (6), COPD (6), chronic pain (2), heart failure (9), coronary artery disease (6), depression (20), diabetes (22), hyperlipidaemia (6), hypertension (7), rheumatoid arthritis (9)	An intervention designed to manage or prevent a chronic disease using a systematic approach to care and potentially employing multiple treatment modalities (adapted from Ellrodt et al. 1997)	+/(+)	(⇓)	(+)	+	(⇓)	+/(+)	(⇓)
Tsai et al. (2005)	112 randomised and nonrandomised trials	Asthma (27 studies), chronic heart failure (21), depression (33), diabetes (31)	Interventions that included at least one of the six elements deemed to be essential for providing high-quality care to patients with chronic illnesses: delivery system design, self-management support, decision support, clinical information systems, community resources, and health care organisation (adapted from Wagner et al. 1999)	+		+/(+)			+/(+)	

| de Bruin et al. (2011) | 31 studies: 18 RCT, 3 quasi-experimental, 3 cross-sectional, 2 descriptive, 2 before/after, 2 prospective observational, 1 longitudinal analysis of paid claims | Diabetes (14 studies), depression (4), heart failure (8), COPD (5) | Interventions that contained two or more elements of the Chronic Care Model (health care system, community resources and policies, self-management support, delivery system design, decision support, clinical information system) (Wagner 1998) | | | | (⇩) |

Note: Symbols in bold indicate a significant finding: ⇩ significant reduction in more than half of studies reviewed or as demonstrated in meta-analysis; (⇩) some evidence of reduction; + significant improvement in more than half of studies reviewed or as demonstrated in meta-analysis; (+) some evidence of improvement; +/(+) significant improvement in some outcomes; = no significant change in outcome concerned; ? evidence inconclusive

[a]Considered two RCTs of disease management only

[b]Study also reviewed 15 systematic reviews which were not included in the meta-analysis

[c]Assessed percentage of statistically significant comparisons per outcome (number of statistically significant comparisons for selected outcomes favouring treatment/total number of comparisons)

studies, although all adopted a fairly comprehensive conceptualisation. Earlier studies tended to draw on the definition by Ellrodt et al. (1997), which we described earlier in this chapter as "an approach to patient care that coordinates medical resources for patients across the entire delivery system"(p.1687), while more recent reviews built on the Chronic Care Model (CCM) proposed by Wagner (1998), which considers six elements as essential for improving chronic illness care. Several reviews analysed primary studies that included a minimum of two discrete interventions considered beneficial for chronic illness care, such as patient self-management, provider feedback, structured follow-up, or role re-design (Boland et al. 2013; de Bruin et al. 2011; Drewes et al. 2012; Knight et al. 2005; Kruis et al. 2013; Lemmens et al. 2009; Peytremann-Bridevaux et al. 2008, 2015) or a variation of this conceptualisation (Egginton et al. 2012; Göhler et al. 2006; Gonseth et al. 2004; Neumeyer-Gromen et al. 2004; Roccaforte et al. 2005; Tsai et al. 2005). Three reviews focusing on depression explicitly used the concept of 'collaborative care', considered to include a multiprofessional approach to patient care and care or case management (Archer et al. 2012; Ekers et al. 2013; Thota et al. 2012). Typically, at least half of primary studies covered by reviews were set in the USA, followed by Australia, the United Kingdom, Canada, Sweden and the Netherlands. Two reviews focused on studies set in the USA only (Egginton et al. 2012; Neumeyer-Gromen et al. 2004).

Studies reported on a diverse set of outcomes, reflecting the condition being targeted. In brief, available reviews provided fairly consistent evidence of a positive impact of disease management interventions targeting those with depression. For example, an early meta-analysis of 102 experimental or quasi-experimental studies targeting 11 conditions by Ofman et al. (2004) found that disease management interventions for those with depression had the highest proportion of studies demonstrating substantial improvements in patient care (48% statistically significant), which was supported by evidence of significant improvements of disease management programmes for depression severity (Neumeyer-Gromen et al. 2004). More recent reviews focused on the impacts of disease management conceptualised as 'collaborative care', and these demonstrated significant improvements in depression symptoms, patient adherence to treatment, response to treatment and satisfaction with care, among other outcomes (Archer et al. 2012; Ekers et al. 2013; Neumeyer-Gromen et al. 2004; Thota et al. 2012).

A similar consistency was found for disease management interventions targeting heart failure. These showed for example statistically significant reductions in the frequency of disease-specific and all-cause hospitalisations of at least 15% up to 30% and more (Drewes et al. 2012; Gonseth et al. 2004; Roccaforte et al. 2005; Whellan et al. 2005; Yu et al. 2006), with a significant reduction in all-cause mortality demonstrated in three of the seven reviews considered (Drewes et al. 2012; Göhler et al. 2006; Roccaforte et al. 2005). A 2012 meta-review of meta-analyses of heart failure disease management programmes noted that out of a total 13 reviews that reported on all-cause mortality, 6 had identified statistically significant improvements, with effect sizes varying from 3% to 25%, mostly clustering around 15–20% (Savard et al. 2011). Drewes et al. (2012) highlighted the substantial heterogeneity among findings of primary studies included in their review, which they were unable to explain by the quality of studies, the length of follow-up, or the number of components considered beneficial in chronic care. Two reviews reported evidence that programmes which had incorporated a multidisciplinary team approach had a stronger impact on outcome measures (Göhler et al. 2006; Roccaforte et al. 2005).

Evidence for the impact of disease management on diabetes also tended to show beneficial effects overall, with significantly improved glycaemic control among diabetes disease management populations compared to usual care, along with improvements in the quality of care as measured through, for example, adherence to treatment guidelines (Elissen et al. 2013b; Knight et al. 2005; Pimouguet et al. 2011). The overall clinical significance of observed improvements in glycaemic control remains uncertain, although there was evidence that disease management may be more effective for patients with poor control (Pimouguet et al. 2011). Elissen et al. (2013b) noted that the most promising results were attained in studies with limited follow-up (<1 year) and by programmes that included more than two chronic care components. The review by Knight et al. (2005) further showed that observed effects were larger for studies conducted in the USA, although the number of trials outside the USA considered in their review was small. Overall there was considerable variation across studies included in individual reviews in terms of intervention delivery methods, duration and populations covered, leading Egginton et al. (2012) to conclude that findings from their review would not allow for recommendations for a particular type of intervention to be more effective than another one.

Such variation was also observed in studies that examined the evidence base for disease management targeted at people with asthma or COPD. Among these, there was consistent evidence of significantly reduced hospitalisations among those receiving disease management for COPD (Adams et al. 2007; Boland et al. 2013; Lemmens et al. 2009; Peytremann-Bridevaux et al. 2008), and, possibly, asthma (Lemmens et al. 2009). There was evidence that patients who received three or more chronic care interventions in disease management programmes for COPD had lower rates of hospitalisations (Boland et al. 2013). Impacts on health outcomes were mixed across reviews, with evidence of significant improvements in some outcomes, such as exercise capacity in COPD patients (Peytremann-Bridevaux et al. 2008), and measures of quality of life among patients with asthma (Lemmens et al. 2009; Pimouguet et al. 2011) or with COPD (Boland et al. 2013; Niesink et al. 2007; Peytremann-Bridevaux et al. 2008). Evidence of impact on mortality was more difficult to interpret. For example, Peytremann-Bridevaux et al. (2008) estimated, on the basis of ten studies, a trend for reduced mortality, while Boland et al. (2013), based on the findings of six primary studies, found a small but significant reduction in all-cause mortality (0.70, 95% CI 0.51–0.97). However, similar to reviews of disease management targeting diabetes or heart failure, findings of primary studies included in reviews of COPD interventions were heterogeneous, varying by study-, intervention-, and disease-characteristics, and it remains unclear which specific components of interventions have the greatest benefit.

Few studies explicitly considered costs, and where they did, the evidence tended to be inconsistent (Egginton et al. 2012; Neumeyer-Gromen et al. 2004; Ofman et al. 2004). De Bruin et al. (2011) reviewed the impact of disease management programmes on health care expenditures for patients with diabetes, depression, heart failure or COPD. Of 31 studies reviewed, 21 reported incremental health care costs per patient per year, and of these, 13 demonstrated evidence of cost savings but observed effects were typically not statistically significant or not tested for statistical significance. Conversely, Boland et al. (2013), in a review of the economic impact of disease management programmes targeting COPD specifically, found these to lead to hospitalisation savings of 1060 € (95% CI: 80–2040 €) per patient per year and savings in total health care utilisation of 898 € (95% CI: 231–1566 €). The review further demonstrated indicative evidence that COPD disease management led to greater savings in studies of patients with severe COPD or those with a history of exacerbations. However, heterogeneity of studies included in either review remains a considerable challenge, with variation in the intervention (content and type) and study design. De Bruin et al. (2011) highlighted variation in the economic evaluative approach chosen, the type of direct health care costs and cost categories considered, alongside lack of reporting on reliability of estimates as a particular challenge to deriving comparative estimates. This highlights the need for higher quality studies.

5.4   Interpreting the Existing Evidence Base

The interpretation of evaluation findings such as those presented here will have to be placed in the context of programme implementation specifically and issues around evaluation more broadly (Nolte et al. 2012a). For example, where an evaluation finds improvements in process indicators (suggesting improved quality of care) but not in outcomes, this might be because the length of evaluation was not sufficient to demonstrate health improvements. Likewise, an evaluation might find that a given intervention improved outcomes for a subgroup of participants only; this might indicate that the intervention was suboptimal or not sufficiently targeted at those who would benefit most. Also, intervention effect will differ by disease type.

This is reflected in the overarching findings of our review. We found fairly consistent evidence that disease management can have beneficial impacts on outcomes for those with depression, both in terms of disease severity and treatment response. Similarly, for those with heart failure, existing evidence points to beneficial effects of disease management on measures of utilisation (reduced hospital use) and outcomes (reduced mortality). Evidence of the impact of disease management on diabetes outcomes remains less certain, however. While some interventions are frequently found to have statistically significant impacts on glycaemic control, which typically forms the primary outcome, the clinical importance of observed reductions remains questionable. Likewise, for COPD, the impact of disease management on outcomes tends to be less consistent, with the possible exception of exercise capacity and quality of life. However, available evidence does consistently demonstrate reduced hospitalisation, which has been shown to lead to actual savings in one review (Boland et al. 2013).

The majority of studies reviewed here echo the concerns reported by Ouwens et al. (2005), confirmed by a recent review of the same topic (Martinez-Gonzalez et al. 2014). Thus, it remains challenging to interpret the evidence from existing primary studies, which tend to be characterised by heterogeneity in the definition and description of the intervention and components of care under study. In this respect, the conclusions by Ouwens et al. (2005) still seem to hold, namely that variation in definitions and components of care, and failure to recognise these variations, might lead to inappropriate conclusions about programme effectiveness and the application of findings. While this further underlines the continued need for the use of consistent definitions and of better description of the content of interventions to enable comparison, evidence presented here does allow for some observations suitable to inform the further development of approaches to more effectively address chronic conditions.

Thus, available evidence points to the value of multifaceted approaches to enhance outcomes of those with chronic disease. For example, reviews that examined the impact of different care components highlighted an association between the format or 'modality' of the intervention and reported outcomes (Elissen et al. 2013b; Göhler et al. 2006; Roccaforte et al. 2005). Evidence from collaborative care models for the management of depressive disorders suggested that interventions were more effective when based in the community or that involved nurses as case managers (Thota et al. 2012). Further, Ekers et al. (2013) found that nurse-delivered treatment based on a collaborative care approach was effective in the treatment of depression in patients who also had at least one physical health problem, such as arthritis, cancer, coronary heart disease or stroke. Similarly, for persons with heart failure, the impact on outcomes was found to be stronger for those interventions that incorporated a multidisciplinary team approach (Göhler et al. 2006; Roccaforte et al. 2005), while disease management interventions that had a multimodal format according to the Chronic Care Model resulted in lower hospitalisation rates among patients with COPD compared with control groups (Adams et al. 2007; Boland et al. 2013), which in turn was linked to cost savings (Boland et al. 2013).

Other evidence points to the need to develop approaches that more specifically target those who are most likely to benefit. For example, Pimouguet et al. (2011) showed how diabetes disease management may be more effective for patients with poor glycaemic control. Similar findings were reported for a large population-based diabetes care intervention in the Netherlands (Elissen et al. 2012), although requiring further confirmation (Elissen et al. 2013a).

It is notable that in selected studies reviewed here the reported evidence tended to be stronger for primary studies undertaken in the USA compared to elsewhere. This was the case for disease management for diabetes (Knight et al. 2005) and collaborative care programmes for depression (Ekers et al. 2013). Given that much of the available evidence tends to originate from the USA, these findings highlight a need for caution when considering transferring models across countries with different health systems, and for developing a more robust evidence base to demonstrate that relevant models are effective outside the US context (Nolte and McKee 2008b; Ekers et al. 2013).

5.5   Conclusions

This chapter has reviewed the recent evidence base on the effectiveness of disease management strategies and programmes. We show that, overall, disease management holds promise to improve processes and outcomes of care but evidence that is available tends to be limited to a small set of conditions only. Arguably, by restricting the review reported here on published systematic reviews we will have missed more recent evidence from primary studies that have investigated the impact of disease management on a broader range of conditions.

We show that there is emerging evidence that provides important insights into how disease management approaches that employ a multifaceted strategy and target those most likely to benefit are more likely to enhance outcomes of those with chronic disease. However, one fundamental issue remains, which is related to the need to develop a system-wide model of care for patients with chronic disease. Disease-specific approaches such as disease management programmes are ill-suited to meet the needs of the typical patient in primary care who frequently has multiple health problems with complex needs (Nolte and McKee 2008b). The rapid rise of those with multiple care needs is of particular concern to all health systems. The nature of multiple chronic conditions creates a challenging spectrum of health care needs in itself, with further complexity added to in cases of increasing frailty at old age in particular, involving physical, developmental, or cognitive disabilities. This complexity of health and care needs requires the development of delivery systems that bring together a range of professionals and skills from both the cure (healthcare) and care (long-term and social care) sectors (Nolte and McKee 2008a).

More generalist approaches such as integrated care models that are being implemented in a range of European countries are potentially better equipped to respond to more complex patient needs, while disease management can form an important instrument within integrated care strategies. There remains a need for more systematic evaluation of new models of care as a means to inform the development of efficient and effective interventions to address the growing burden of chronic conditions in Europe and elsewhere.

References

Adams, S., Smith, P., Allan, P., et al. (2007). Systematic review of the chronic care model in chronic obstructive pulmonary disease prevention and management. *Archives of Internal Medicine, 167*, 551–561.

Archer, J., Bower, P., Gilbody, S., et al. (2012). Collaborative care for depression and anxiety problems. *Cochrane Database of Systematic Reviews, 10*, CD006525.

Aspin, C., Jowsey, T., Nolte, E., et al. (2010). Health policy responses to rising rates of multi-morbid chronic illness in Australia and New Zealand. *Australian and New Zealand Journal of Public Health, 34*, 386–393.

Bodenheimer, T. (1999). Disease management–promises and pitfalls. *The New England Journal of Medicine, 340*, 1202–1205.

Boland, M. R., Tsiachristas, A., Kruis, A. L., et al. (2013). The health economic impact of disease management programs for COPD: A systematic literature review and meta-analysis. *BMC Pulmonary Medicine, 13*, 40.

Care Continuum Alliance. (2010). *Outcomes guidelines report* (Vol. 5). Washington, DC: Care Continuum Alliance.

Coelho, A., Leone, C., Ribeiro, V., et al. (2014). Integrated disease management: A critical review of foreign and Portuguese experience. *Acta Médica Portuguesa, 27*, 116–125.

Coleman, K., Mattke, S., Perrault, P., et al. (2009). Untangling practice redesign from disease management: How do we best care for the chronically ill? *Annual Review of Public Health, 30*, 385–408.

Craig, P., Dieppe, P., Macintyre, S., et al. (2008). *Developing and evaluating complex interventions: New guidance*. London: Medical Research Council.

de Bakker, D., Struijs, J., Baan, C., et al. (2013). Early results from adoption of bundled payment for diabetes care in the Netherlands show improvement in care coordination. *Health Affairs, 31*, 426–433.

de Bruin, S., Heijink, R., Lemmens, L., et al. (2011). Impact of disease management programs on healthcare expenditures for patients with diabetes, depression, heart failure or chronic obstructive pulmonary disease: A systematic review of the literature. *Health Policy, 101*, 105–121.

Drewes, H., Steuten, L., Lemmens, L., et al. (2012). The effectiveness of chronic care management for heart failure: Meta-regression analyses to explain the heterogeneity in outcomes. *Health Services Research, 47*, 1926–1959.

Egginton, J., Ridgeway, J., Shah, N., et al. (2012). Care management for type 2 diabetes in the United States: A systematic review and meta-analyis. *BMC Health Services Research, 12*, 72.

Ekers, D., Murphy, R., Archer, J., et al. (2013). Nurse-delivered collaborative care for depression and long-term physical conditions: A systematic review and meta-analysis. *Journal of Affective Disorders, 149*, 14–22.

Elissen, A., Duimel-Peeters, I., Spreeuwenberg, C., et al. (2012). Toward tailored disease management for type 2 diabetes. *The American Journal of Managed Care, 18*, 619–630.

Elissen, A., Adams, J., Spreeuwenberg, M., et al. (2013a). Advancing current approaches to disease management evaluation: Capitalizing on heterogeneity to understand what works and for whom. *BMC Medical Research Methodology, 13*, 40.

Elissen, A. M., Steuten, L. M., Lemmens, L. C., et al. (2013b). Meta-analysis of the effectiveness of chronic care management for diabetes: Investigating heterogeneity in outcomes. *Journal of Evaluation in Clinical Practice, 19*, 753–762.

Ellrodt, G., Cook, D., Lee, J., et al. (1997). Evidence-based disease management. *JAMA, 278*, 1687–1692.

Epstein, R., & Sherwood, L. (1996). From outcomes research to disease management: A guide for the perplexed. *Annals of Internal Medicine, 124*, 832–837.

Fuchs, S., Henschke, C., Blumel, M., et al. (2014). Disease management programs for type 2 diabetes in Germany: A systematic literature review evaluating effectiveness. *Deutsches Ärzteblatt International, 111*, 453–463.

Fullerton, B., Nolte, E., & Erler, A. (2011). Qualität der Versorgung chronisch Kranker in Deutschland. *Zeitschrift für Evidenz, Fortbildung und Qualität im Gesundheitswesen, 105*, 554–562.

Glasgow, N., Zwar, B., Harris, M., et al. (2008). Australia. In E. Nolte, C. Knai, & M. McKee (Eds.), *Managing chronic conditions. Experience in eight countries.* Copenhagen: World Health Organization on behalf of the European Observatory on Health Systems and Policies.

Göhler, A., Januzzi, J., Worrell, S., et al. (2006). A systematic meta-analysis of the efficacy and heterogeneity of disease management programs in congestive heart failure. *Journal of Cardiac Failure, 12*, 554–567.

Goldfracht, M., Levin, D., Peled, O., et al. (2011). Twelve-year follow-up of a population-based primary care diabetes program in Israel. *International Journal for Quality in Health Care, 23*, 674–681.

Gonseth, J., Guallar-Castillon, P., Banegas, J. R., et al. (2004). The effectiveness of disease management programmes in reducing hospital re-admission in older patients with heart failure: A systematic review and meta-analysis of published reports. *European Heart Journal, 25*, 1570–1595.

Hamar, G., Rula, E., Coberley, C., et al. (2015). Long-term impact of a chronic disease management program on hospital utilization and cost in an Australian population with heart disease or diabetes. *BMC Health Services Research, 15*, 174.

Jacob, L., Hadji, P., Albert, U., et al. (2015). Impact of disease management programs on women with breast cancer in Germany. *Breast Cancer Research and Treatment, 153*, 391–395.

Knight, K., Badamgarav, E., Henning, J., et al. (2005). A systematic review of diabetes disease management programmes. *The American Journal of Managed Care, 11*, 241–250.

Kruis, A. L., Smidt, N., Assendelft, W. J., et al. (2013). Integrated disease management interventions for patients with chronic obstructive pulmonary disease. *Cochrane Database of Systematic Reviews, 10*, CD009437.

Krumholz, H., Currie, P., Riegel, B., et al. (2006). A taxonomy for disease management: A scientific statement from the American Heart Association Disease Management Taxonomy writing group. *Circulation, 114*, 1432–1445.

Lemmens, K., Nieboer, A., & Huijsman, R. (2009). A systematic review of integrated use of disease-management interventions in asthma and COPD. *Respiratory Medicine, 103*, 670–691.

Lemmens, K., Lemmens, L., Boom, J., et al. (2011). Chronic care management for patients with COPD: A critical review of available evidence. *Journal of Evaluation in Clinical Practice, 19*, 734–752.

Martinez-Gonzalez, N. A., Berchtold, P., Ullman, K., et al. (2014). Integrated care programmes for adults with chronic conditions: A meta-review. *International Journal for Quality in Health Care, 26*, 561–570.

Mattke, S., Seid, M., & Ma, S. (2007). Evidence for the effect of disease management: Is $1 billion a year a good investment? *The American Journal of Managed Care, 13*, 670–676.

Mehring, M., Donnachie, E., Fexer, J., et al. (2014). Disease management programs for patients with COPD in Germany: A longitudinal evaluation of routinely collected patient records. *Respiratory Care, 59*, 1123–1132.

NCBI. (2016). *Pubmed.* Retrieved from http://www.ncbi.nlm.nih.gov/pubmed

Neumeyer-Gromen, A., Lampert, T., Stark, K., et al. (2004). Disease management programs for depression: A systematic review and meta-analysis of randomized controlled trials. *Medical Care, 42*, 1211–1221.

Niesink, A., Trappenburg, J., de Weert-van Oene, G., et al. (2007). Systematic review of the effects of chronic disease management on quality-of-life in people with chronic obstructive pulmonary disease. *Respiratory Medicine, 101*, 2233–2239.

Nolte, E. (2017). Disease management. In R. Busse, N. Klazinga, J.-A. Røttingen, et al. (Eds.), *Quality strategies in European health systems: A systematic assessment of their nature, use and effectiveness.* Maidenhead: Open University Press.

Nolte, E., & Knai, C. (2015). *Assessing chronic disease management in European health systems. Country reports.* Copenhagen: World Health Organization (acting as the host organization for, and secretariat of, the European Observatory on Health Systems and Policies).

Nolte, E., & McKee, M. (2008a). *Caring for people with chronic conditions: A health system perspective.* Maidenhead: Open University Press.

Nolte, E., & McKee, M. (2008b). Integration and chronic care: A review. In E. Nolte & M. McKee (Eds.), *Caring for people with chronic conditions. A health system perspective* (pp. 64–91). Maidenhead: Open University Press.

Nolte, E., & Pitchforth, E. (2014). What we know: A brief review of the evidence of approaches to chronic care. In E. Nolte, C. Knai, & R. Saltman (Eds.), *Assessing chronic disease management in European health systems. Concepts and approaches* (pp. 9–22). Copenhagen: World Health Organization (acting as the host organization for, and secretariat of, the European Observatory on Health Systems and Policies).

Nolte, E., McKee, M., & Knai, C. (2008). Managing chronic conditions: An introduction to the experience in eight countries. In E. Nolte, C. Knai, & M. McKee (Eds.), *Managing chronic conditions: Experience in eight countries* (pp. 1–14). World Health Organization on behalf of the European Observatory on Health Systems and Policies: Copenhagen.

Nolte, E., Conklin, A., Adams, J., et al. (2012a). *Evaluating chronic disease management. Recommendations for funders and users.* Santa Monica: RAND Corporation.

Nolte E, Knai C, Hofmarcher MC, A, et al. (2012b) Overcoming fragmentation in healthcare: Chronic care in Austria, Germany and the Netherlands. *Health Economics, Policy, and Law* 7: 125-146.

Nolte, E., Knai, C., & Saltman, R. (2014). *Assessing chronic disease management in European health systems. Country reports.* Copenhagen: World Health Organization (acting as the host organization for, and secretariat of, the European Observatory on Health Systems and Policies).

Norris, S., Glasgow, R., Engelgau, M., et al. (2003). Chronic disease management. A definition and systematic approach to component interventions. *Disease Management and Health Outcomes, 11,* 477–488.

Ofman, J., Badamgarav, E., Henning, J., et al. (2004). Does disease management improve clinical and economic outcomes in patients with chronic diseases? A systematic review. *The American Journal of Medicine, 117,* 182–192.

Ouwens, M., Wollersheim, H., Hermens, R., et al. (2005). Integrated care programmes for chronically ill patients: A review of systematic reviews. *International Journal for Quality in Health Care, 17,* 141–146.

Peytremann-Bridevaux, I., Staeger, P., Bridevaux, P., Ghali, W., et al. (2008). Effectiveness of chronic obstructive pulmonary disease-management programs: Systematic review and meta-analysis. *The American Journal of Medicine, 121,* 433–443.

Peytremann-Bridevaux, I., Arditi, C., Gex, G., et al. (2015). Chronic disease management programmes for adults with asthma. *Cochrane Database of Systematic Reviews, 5,* CD007988.

Pimouguet, C., Le Goff, M., Thiébaut, R., et al. (2011). Effectiveness of disease-management programs for improving diabetes care: A meta-analysis. *CMAJ, 183,* E115–E127.

Rijken, M., Bekkema, N., Boeckxstaens, P., et al. (2012). Chronic Disease Management Programmes: An adequate response to patients' needs? *Health Expectations, 17,* 608–621.

Roccaforte, R., Demers, C., Baldassarre, F., et al. (2005). Effectiveness of comprehensive disease management programmes in improving clinical outcomes in heart failure patients. A meta-analysis. *European Journal of Heart Failure, 7,* 1133–1144.

Roccaforte, R., Demers, C., Baldassarre, F., et al. (2006). Corrigendum to "Effectiveness of comprehensive disease management programmes in improving clinical outcomes in heart failure patients. A meta-analysis" [Eur J Hear Fail 7 (2005) 1133–1144]. *European Heart Journal, 8,* 223–224.

Rothman, A., & Wagner, E. (2003). Chronic illness management: What is the role of primary care? *Annals of Internal Medicine, 138,* 256–261.

Royal College of Physicians. (2004). *Clinicians, services and commissioning in chronic disease management in the NHS. The need for coordinated management programmes.* London: Royal College of Physicians of London, Royal College of General Practitioners, NHS Alliance.

Savard, L., Thompson, D., & Clark, A. (2011). A meta-review of evidence on heart failure disease management programs: The challenges of describing and synthesizing evidence on complex interventions. *Trials, 12,* 194.

Schrijvers, G. (2009). Disease management: A proposal for a new definition. *International Journal of Integrated Care, 9,* e06.

Smidth, M., Christensen, M., Fenger-Grøn, M., et al. (2013). The effect of an active implementation of a disease management programme for chronic obstructive pulmonary disease on healthcare utilization–a cluster-randomised controlled trial. *BMC Health Services Research, 13,* 385.

Takeda, A., Taylor, S. J., Taylor, R. S., et al. (2012). Clinical service organisation for heart failure. *Cochrane Database of Systematic Reviews, 9,* CD002752.

Tan, W., Ding, Y., Xia, W., et al. (2014). Effects of a population-based diabetes management program in Singapore. *The American Journal of Managed Care, 20,* e388–e398.

The Boston Consulting Group. (2006). *Realizing the promise of disease management.* Boston: The Boston Consulting Group.

Thota, A., Sipe, T., Byard, G., et al. (2012). Collaborative care to improve the management of depressive disorders: A community guide systematic review and meta-analysis. *American Journal of Preventive Medicine, 42,* 525–538.

Tsai, A., Morton, S., Mangione, C., et al. (2005). A meta-analysis of interventions to improve care for chronic illness. *The American Journal of Managed Care, 11,* 478–488.

Tsiachristas, A., Burgers, L., & Rutten-van, M. M. (2015). Cost-effectiveness of disease management programs for cardiovascular risk and COPD in The Netherlands. *Value in Health, 18,* 977–986.

Wagner, E. (1998). Chronic disease management: What will it take to improve care for chronic illness. *Effective Clinical Practice, 1,* 2–4.

Wagner, E., Davis, C., Schaefer, J., et al. (1999). A survey of leading chronic disease management programs: Are they consistent with the literature? *Managed Care Quarterly, 7,* 56–66.

Wagner, E., Glasgow, R., Davis, C., et al. (2001). Quality improvement in chronic illness care: A collaborative approach. *Joint Commission Journal on Quality Improvement, 27,* 63–80.

Weingarten, S., Henning, J., Badamgarav, E., et al. (2002). Interventions used in disease management programmes for patients with chronic illness – which ones work? Meta-analysis of published reports. *BMJ, 325,* 925–932.

Whellan, D. J., Hasselblad, V., Peterson, E., et al. (2005). Metaanalysis and review of heart failure disease management randomized controlled clinical trials. *American Heart Journal, 149,* 722–729.

Yu, D. S., Thompson, D. R., & Lee, D. T. (2006). Disease management programmes for older people with heart failure: Crucial characteristics which improve post-discharge outcomes. *European Heart Journal, 27,* 596–612.

Discharge and Transition Management in Integrated Care

6

Dominika Urbanski, Anika Reichert, and Volker Amelung

6.1 Introduction

A key part of integrated care is to ensure a continuous pathway for a patient when being transferred from one healthcare sector to another. Discharge planning and management tries to achieve exactly that. The discharge process demonstrates excellently the need for integrated care. In almost no other part within the care process one can see a clearer clash of different (a) settings and capacities, (b) personal resources and professional cultures, (c) reimbursement and payment schemes, (d) care and medication procedures, (f) usage of (information) technologies, (e) professional cultures and (f) interests. The importance of each of these aspects depends significantly on the degree of pressure each entity within the healthcare system and their sub-systems has to face. For example, the higher the pressure in the hospital sector, the more likely hospitals will optimize their part in the value chain according to their specific interests. This is not necessarily in the best interest of the entire healthcare system—or even the patient.

The following chapter describes what discharge management entails, why it is needed in health care systems and in what different ways it can be organized. In conclusion, discharge management is an essential part of providing integrated care in all health systems, but there is still a long way to go to guarantee adequate transitions for patients in most (if not all) health systems.

D. Urbanski (✉)
inav GmbH - Institute for Applied Health Services Research, Berlin, Germany
e-mail: urbanski@inav-berlin.de

A. Reichert
Centre for Health Economics, University of York, York, UK

V. Amelung
inav GmbH - Institute for Applied Health Services Research, Berlin, Germany

Institute for Epidemology, Social Medicine and Health System Research, Medical School Hannover, Hannover, Germany

© Springer International Publishing AG 2017
V. Amelung et al. (eds.), *Handbook Integrated Care*,
DOI 10.1007/978-3-319-56103-5_6

6.2   What Is Discharge Management?

Despite its importance there is no universal definition of the concept of discharge management. Instead, various descriptions can be found in the literature. Taking a very broad perspective, discharge and/or transition management encompasses any transfer of patients between sectors of care delivery, between care givers or providers, or from one setting to another (Chenoweth et al. 2015). It not only describes the planning and guaranteeing of continuity of care (Wong et al. 2011), it also entails "the transfer of professional responsibility and accountability for some or all aspects of care for a patient, [. . .], to another person or professional group, on a temporary or permanent basis" (Toccafondi et al. 2012, p.i58), including the transfer of budgetary responsibility (Wong et al. 2011).

In the following we focus on a more narrow scope and use the term discharge management to describe the process of patients leaving the temporary inpatient care setting and entering the outpatient care setting, which can be either the patient's home or long-term care institution. The inpatient setting does not only refer to an acute hospital, it also includes inpatient rehabilitation settings (Müller and Deimel 2013).

6.3   Why Discharge Management?

Discharge management appears to be almost an inevitable component of (health) care delivery in modern healthcare systems. The desire to enhance patient empowerment and their satisfaction in order to improve medical outcomes, save costs and meet the demographic challenges supports the need for organizing and optimizing the discharge process. The relevance of well-organized and planned discharge processes arises from the fact that patients who are discharged from hospitals experience higher mortality and morbidity risks which are not only related to medical factors, but may also be linked to social and health service backgrounds (Escobar et al. 2015; Yiu et al. 2013). Patients are especially vulnerable in the period during or directly after discharge (Philibert and Barach 2012). Therefore, the need for discharge planning results from several different factors interacting with each other. The following trends within healthcare systems contribute to the growing importance of managing the interface between out- and inpatient care adequately.

6.3.1 Demographic Challenges

The starting point is -as in many other respects -the demographic challenge as one of the main drivers for the need of discharge management. First of all, there is a simple numeric effect: with an increased average life expectancy the risk of being hospitalised once or more often in life also rises. Hospitalised patients often suffer from worse health and are on average older than those treated in outpatient settings

(Abad-Corpa et al. 2013; Mohr 2009). For example, older people make up only 13% of the U.S. population and 14% of the Canadian population but they are responsible for 45% (USA) respectively 50% (Canada) of the hospital costs (Fox et al. 2013). In older age, not only chronic illnesses are more common, also multi-morbidity becomes more likely. This means that in many societies the share of people who are dependent on repeated inpatient medical care which needs to be coordinated with long-term and social care is increasing.

Besides the simple effect of higher age, changes lifestyles and family situations play a role when it comes to discharge management. In many western societies an increasing number of people -especially the elderly -lives alone without the support of families or communities readily available. This is why the patient's living situation and social network needs to be considered at the point of discharge and when planning follow-up care. For example, the type and amount of care needed by an old patient with a hip fracture who lives with family members in a house with a ground floor will differ from the care needed by a patient with the same age and condition who lives alone in an apartment on the fifth floor with no elevator (Wehmeier and Schäfer 2013). Transition planning is particularly necessary as the treatment process and its outcome within the inpatient sector are mutually interconnected with the medical, but also the social and nursing situation of a patient. Not only do patient factors impact whether and how a patient needs to be treated in hospital. A patient's mobility, quality of life, need for care and nursing, and ability for social inclusion may all be changed as a consequence of hospitalization (Deimel 2013). Patients may (at least temporarily) lose their independence-especially if they are older (Bender 2013).

6.3.2   Rising Costs and Financial Pressure

Financial pressure has increased dramatically in almost every health system due to constantly rising costs. This however increases the tendency of single providers or sectors to act in their own interests which may not necessarily be in the best interest of the entire healthcare system - and most likely even less in the interest of the patient. One result of the ongoing budget constraints in the inpatient sector is the trend of shifting procedures from the inpatient setting into the outpatient setting. However, in the long run this may lead to higher total costs. In the US, almost 20% of elderly patients are readmitted to a hospital within one month after discharge (Shu et al. 2011). This does not only lead to rising costs, it also leads to increased suffering by the patients. Studies have shown that discharge management can reduce readmission and mortality rates (Shu et al. 2011). The financial incentives for effective discharge planning are considerable and relate to reduced readmissions, keeping patients in their homes and out of residential care (Chenoweth et al. 2015) or freeing up acute beds (Atwal et al. 2002). It is assumed that approximately 30% of discharges in the United States are delayed due to non-medical reasons, including inadequate assessment of the patient and lacking knowledge of a patient's social environment, problems in the organization of follow-up care, delays in the ordering of transportation means for the patient (to their homes etc.) and poor communication between hospitals and outpatient service providers (Shepperd et al. 2013). More and more reimbursement systems focus on some kind of guarantees which have to be met by the hospitals. For example in the German DRG system, insurance companies will not reimburse the hospitals for patients with certain defined indications if they had been readmitted within a defined period of time after discharge.

6.3.3 Declining Length of Stay

The average length of hospital stay has declined in many countries over the past years (see Fig. 6.1, also Eurostat 2015). In the EU member states it dropped from 9.6 to 7.8 days between 2000 and 2012 (OECD 2014). Even though these numbers do not say much about the quality of care as such, they do imply that the process of entering and leaving the hospital setting needs to be optimized to guarantee the same quality of care in a shorter period of inpatient time. It also means that patients leave the hospital more vulnerable than they used to. They often still require intensive and specific care -which should preferably be closely coordinated with the care received in the inpatient setting. However, it may be challenging for the outpatient setting to maintain the intensity of care provided in the inpatient unit (Deimel 2013). In Germany for example, hospitals have access to more expensive medications. The continuous treatment with the same products can therefore cause financial problems for ambulatory care providers due to their more restrictive budgets. A decline in the length of stay further implies an increase in interfaces as patients have more care needs and thus more providers need to be involved and coordinated. Given this context, it is particularly important that the transition between hospitals, general practitioners (GPs), social care and other providers works well.

6.3.4 Financing and Reimbursement Systems

As mentioned before, there is a variety of financing systems and responsibilities involved in the process of discharge management and they usually co-exist without cooperation between systems. Discharge management is especially needed in systems that are still organized in silo-structures. The silo-analogy refers to the coexistence of structures which are not interacting with each other. For example, in Germany both the in- and the outpatient sector have strictly separate budgets and the health and social care sector are even financed by a different insurance system.

The DRG (Diagnosis-Related Groups) systems, and other comparable systems which are used for reimbursement in the hospital sector in many countries, provide a fixed payment per patient based on the average costs of patients with a comparable condition. The less the patient costs - i.e. the shorter the stay of the patient - the more the hospital can profit. Increasing competition between hospitals adds to the

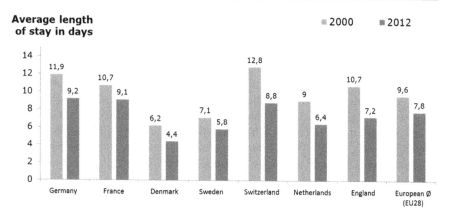

Fig. 6.1 Average length of stay in hospitals for all causes, 2002 and 2012 (or nearest year). Source: OECD Health Statistics, 2014, own diagram

pressure hospital providers face nowadays. These factors lead to a strong focus on economic efficiency and cost reductions. In the example of Germany, the introduction of the DRG system has brought about some important changes, highlighting the importance of discharge management. Previously, the financing system allowed the hospital to take into consideration the individual situation of a patient and even postpone the discharge if there was nobody to care for the patient in the outpatient setting. This became less common (and financially unbearable) under the DRG system (Mohr 2009). The revolving-door effect mentioned in this context refers to a situation where patients are discharged "too early" and re-enter the inpatient setting within a few days after discharge. Reasons for this include a lack of or inappropriate provision of care in the outpatient setting. Numbers from the United States underline this vividly: approximately one fifth of Medicare beneficiaries who are discharged from the hospital re-enter the inpatient setting within 30 days of discharge. Half of them had no contact to a GP during the outpatient time (Hennessey and Suter 2011).

Organising care in a coherent and coordinated way is particularly difficult in the context of economic pressure that most or many health systems face today. This, together with the divided financing and reimbursement systems, does not foster but work against integration and cooperation. Services that focus on organizing and managing the transition of patients are oftentimes not or not sufficiently remunerated as each sector calculates their costs separately. This means that shifting cost from the inpatient to the outpatient sector by discharging as early as possible appears rational from the perspective of the inpatient sector but may in the long run lead to higher costs for the health system - and to a poorer medical outcome for the patient. However, this does not mean that discharging patients early is never an optimal choice. Looking at COPD patients for example, finding alternative ways to treat patients outside of hospitals is an important factor for minimizing cost. The key is well-designed discharge planning to make early discharge a fruitful way for all actors, including the patients (Escarrabill 2009).

6.3.5 The Need to Manage Complexity

Discharging a patient from the hospital into the outpatient sector or the long-term care sector is a process involving many different actors and systems. According to Deimel et al. (2013), there are six main areas that the discharge process potentially has to cover: medicine, rehabilitation, nursing care, medical aids, social care and relatives (see Table 6.1). Usually, more than one of these areas or actors has to be involved in the discharge process. It is important to note again that the process does not only involve professional actors, but also the social environment of a person. Discharge management is thus a multidisciplinary process focusing on many aspects of a patient's life.

Given a high degree of specialization of hospitals, the complexity and the number of actors that have to be coordinated increases. Instead of one regional hospital there are often many specialized clinics treating patients. In many countries, the general practitioner (GP) takes a large share of the responsibility in guaranteeing the follow-up treatment but is often not sufficiently informed about the treatment the patient received in the hospital (Hesselink et al. 2014; Harbord 2009). The fact that various independently operating actors - such as social care institutions, specialists and therapists, nursing providers, or pharmacists - may be responsible for the same patient further adds to the challenge of providing continuous care. To guarantee seamless care, sectors must communicate and exchange information (Mohr 2009). This does not only require the exchange of medical or social information but also the clarification of responsibilities between actors. The latter is often unclear, especially when multi-morbid patients leave the hospital setting, needing services of different specialized providers (Hennessey and Suter 2011). Gaps in the delivery of care may particularly result from patients being discharged on weekends, when the GP or a follow-up care specialist are not available, or adequate medication, medical aids or else cannot be provided in time. Furthermore, many communication systems are not compatible between sectors or providers. These factors may lead to patients receiving wrong or inappropriate treatment and increase the risk of adverse effects such as a longer length of stay or a higher proportion of readmissions. This in turn, may cause patient dissatisfaction and increased health care expenditure (Drachsler et al. 2012). To guarantee seamless delivery of care, professional discharge and transition management is key (Harbord 2009) and implementing it successfully requires a clearly defined regulatory and legal framework.

6.4 How to Put Discharge Management into Practice

  „Effective discharge planning requires capacity planning, performance review, hospital discharge policies, and healthcare providers/stakeholders agreements. There is clear evidence and wide agreement among healthcare providers/stakeholders that a standardized and policy-driven protocol [is] important to an effective discharge planning."
  (Wong et al. 2011, p. 9)

Table 6.1 Sectors and actors involved in follow-up care, Source: Adapted from Deimel et al. (2013)

Follow-up care sectors	
Medicine	*Nursing care*
Physician and specialist care	Ambulatory care services
Diagnostics	Care consultation services
Therapy in another hospital	Partial in-patient and in-patient care services
Wound management	
Nutrition therapy	
Drug management	
Rehabilitation	*Aids*
In- and out-patient rehabilitation	Movement
Physiotherapy	Home support
Ergotherapy	Medical devices
Speech therapy	
Social	*Relatives*
Housing and financing matters	Out-patient assistance/support
Psychosocial services	In-patient care services
Severe disability	Short-term nursing

To date, many different attempts and models to organize the discharge and transition process exist. They vary not only across but also within health systems. However, this diversity has not yet led to a clear "best-practice" model. Instead, discharge management processes in general leave a lot of room for improvement to guarantee optimal care for the patients, but also their relatives, the caring institutions and other partners (Deimel 2013).

Overall, research draws a rather negative picture of the situation of discharge management, pinpointing to a lack of effectiveness in daily practice, a lack of clear strategies and challenges in evaluating interventions (Hesselink et al. 2014). Among others, the difficulty of changing behaviours of providers is being widely emphazised and discussed. Inefficiencies caused by poor information exchange, poor coordination of care and poor communication between the various providers as well as between providers and patients lead to - oftentimes preventable - readmissions (Hesselink et al. 2014). The HANDOVER project which was initiated in 2008 and funded by the European Union's Seventh Framework Programme aimed at investigating and defining how to best improve the discharge process. In this project, researches from Italy, the Netherlands, Poland, UK, Spain and Sweden as well as from the United States and Australia worked together (Philibert and Barach 2012). The research group identified among other things barriers to transitions, which include "time constraints and low prioritisation of discharge communication, pressure on available hospital beds, and variability in patient and family member involvement in discharge planning" (Philibert and Barach 2012, p.i1).

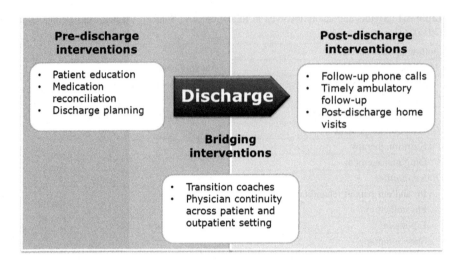

Fig. 6.2 Discharge interventions according to Tang et al. (2014)

The diversity in discharge practice is reflected in the various categorizations of discharge management that can be found in the literature. For example, interventions or models can be categorized based on the time of care they focus on. Tang et al. (2014) suggest a categorization into pre-discharge, post-discharge and bridging-interventions (see Fig. 6.2).

For each of these three phases of discharge management, various different models of integrating health care and organizing discharge management can be further identified and applied. Burns and Pauly (2002, p.136ff) for example suggest four models of integrated health care within hospitals, which can be also applied to models of organizing discharge management:

1. Customized integration and disease management, describing the tailored integration around diseases or individuals (case management and disease management), oftentimes covered by public health insurance programs
2. Co-location of care, describing joint-venture collaborations including the relocation of personnel to foster interaction and integration.
3. IT-integrated health care, describing the integration through technologies such as electronic health records, automated drug dispensing, remote patient monitoring etc.
4. Patient-integrated health care, empowering the individuals as gatekeepers of their own health.

If the outpatient and social care sector would be added, the list would likely grow longer. Nevertheless, these four models show clearly how many different ways exist to put discharge management into practice. No matter which phase of the discharge process and which model is chosen, it is important to take a professional approach.

6.4.1 Professionalization of Discharge Planning

Discharge management, if primarily understood as the process of leaving the inpatient setting, is to a large extent seen as the responsibility of the hospitals. Even though the process is multi-professional and multi-dimensional, it is (or should be) initiated in the hospital - some argue as soon as the patient enters the hospital (Deimel 2013; Müller and Deimel 2013). Planning and managing the discharge process of patients is, as should be evident by now, a very complex task. Therefore, it is quite surprising that a recent survey of hospital managers in the United Kingdom found that case managers responsible for discharges seldomly had certifications or long time experiences in discharge planning (Chenoweth et al. 2015).

Effective discharge management needs the cooperation of various actors within a complex setting: The hospitals with their doctors, social services, nursing services, the specialists and practitioners in the outpatient setting, pharmacies, and rehabilitation or care institutions (Pilgrim and Kittlick 2013). In this context, the call for a professional and qualified discharge manager who is responsible for navigating the patient through this complex system is not surprising (Deimel et al. 2013; Harbord 2009; Hennessey and Suter 2011; Wong et al. 2011). Communication among the various actors needs to be organized and professionalized since they are not used to interact in their regular day-to-day work (Mohr 2009). Defining a responsible person in charge of this process has proven to be helpful to achieve successful communication (Wong et al. 2011). In Germany, the responsibility for discharge management was for the longest time with the social services, but over time has been shifted to the nursing services of the hospital. The responsible departments guarantee that the patients receive all services they are entitled to, manage the initiation of nursing care, help with financial as well as housing questions, and initiate psychosocial interventions if needed. However, the degree to which these agencies are responsible and capable varies from hospital to hospital. In the Anglo-American health care systems, it is common to find a "discharge planner" who is responsible for the adequate discharge of the patients. In these systems, discharge management also includes the empowerment and active involvement of the patients (Müller and Deimel 2013). Still, the work initiated in the hospital is often not adequately continued once the patient leaves the inpatient setting (Pilgrim and Kittlick 2013).

Frequently, GPs take the lead and responsibility for coordinating the patient's care. However, it was found that they are often very challenged by these tasks, especially due to a lack of communication and information. They further do not feel sufficiently rewarded for this work (Philibert and Barach 2012). Short-notice releases of patients from the hospital that do not allow enough time to initiate follow-up care add to the challenge (Müller 2013). Not only the outpatient doctors see the inter-sectoral cooperation as being problematic at times; the inpatient doctors also voice concerns. They complain, for example, about the resistance of GPs to continue or at least take into account the care provided in the inpatient setting (Dienst 2013). The outpatient doctors, in contrast, point out delays in receiving discharge documents from the hospital or receiving incomplete documentations. Information technology may help improving this process in the future.

6.4.2 Integrating Various Components

Evidence seems to suggest that only discharge programs including various interventions are successful in improving care and reducing hospital readmissions. "In a recent systematic review, no single intervention was found to be associated with a reduced risk for 30-day readmissions" (Tang et al. 2014, p.1513).

Even though many tools currently in use have been evaluated, there is a lack of clear evidence of their effectiveness. Limited evidence exists for the effectiveness of discharge planning reminders, financial incentives and penalties. The effects of including discharge management in the medical curriculum and of feedback forms and other ways to trigger provider reflections are also not clear (Hesselink et al. 2014). A systematic review of literature assessing post-discharge telephone calls and their impacts found no clear evidence of their effects on readmission, emergency department use, patient satisfaction and well-being as well as follow-ups (Bahr et al. 2014).

However, evidence regarding models that integrate various components into the discharge process seem to be more conclusive. In the United States, for example, an integrated post-discharge transitional care program entailing a disease-specific care plan, follow-up phone calls, hotline counselling and referrals to hospital-run clinics significantly decreased readmissions within 30 days after discharge (Shu et al. 2011).

The finding that integrated approaches are more fruitful is not surprising when keeping in mind that inefficiencies are rooted in various factors. These can be divided into those related to attitudes and behaviours, to processes (such as missing guidelines), to technical problems (such as lacking electronic information exchanges) or patients (Hesselink et al. 2014). Addressing just one factor is unlikely to have a strong impact given the complex context. Effective tools need to go hand in hand with training, reimbursement, policies and enabling organizational structures. Further they must include the patient's preferences (Drachsler et al. 2012; Hesselink et al. 2014).

6.4.3 Patient Involvement

Patients who experience discharge management are more satisfied with the care they received in and outside the hospital than those who did not receive this service

(Abad-Corpa et al. 2013; Shepperd et al. 2013). This introduces another important actor of the discharge process, who is often not sufficiently included as an active participant in the care process: the patient. The mostly passive role of the patient to date is slowly changing in many aspects of the health care system, but particularly in successful discharge management. The patient is an important, if not the most important, actor in the process of care after treatment. This is also reflected in the shift of responsibilities: Patients are becoming increasingly responsible for their own health and wellbeing. One crucial component needed for patients to assume a more active role is information and education which they increasingly demand and wish for (Mohr 2009). Research shows that the patient's involvement is positively influenced when she or he is provided with information regarding the discharge - written or verbal - and when she or he isgiven guidance, for example via counselling, follow-up calls, or home visits (Hesselink et al. 2014). If not informed and integrated appropriately, patients may not be able to meet the expectations of being responsible actors in this process (Philibert and Barach 2012). Discharge management should not only aim at improving coordination of care, but also at including the patients into decision-making processes (Abad-Corpa et al. 2013).

Bender (2013) summarizes the findings of various studies highlighting the main problems patients and their relatives experience during the discharge process. These problems can be encountered pre-discharge, inside the hospital setting during the discharge process and post-discharge, in the outpatient setting (see Fig. 6.3).

Besides the patients themselves, their relatives are important actors to be involved in discharge management. Relatives often bear a large share of the responsibility of providing and guaranteeing immediate follow-up care after patients are discharged (Pilgrim and Kittlick 2013). Informing them in a timely manner about the various challenges, changes and needs will lead to better care for the patients.

6.4.4 Information Exchange and Technology

Another common challenge related to planning discharge processes is connecting the various actors. Technology can help improve this process by, for example, enabling care providers to communicate via a common electronic patient record (Pilgrim and Kittlick 2013). In many countries, such records are already being widely used. Other countries, such as Germany, are far behind—especially due to restrictive data protection policies (Amelung et al. 2016).

For successful discharge planning, it is crucial that relevant information is exchanged between care providers and that it is available for the follow-up care givers as soon as possible. This also includes the need for complete, accurate and understandable documents as well as the adequate transmission of information which can be via the patient or electronic means (Hesselink et al. 2014). The review by Hesselink et al. (2014) finds that using standardised procedures such as discharge letter templates, planning guidelines, or medication reconciliation checklists has proven to be an effective tool.

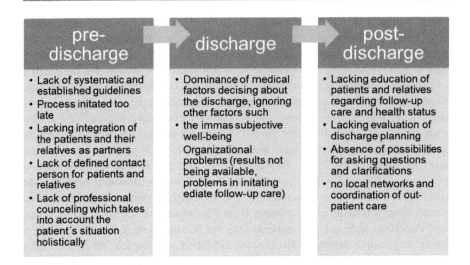

Fig. 6.3 Problems experienced with discharge management by patients and relatives. Source: Adapted from Bender (2013)

6.4.5 Early Initiation and Predictive Models for Discharge Management

Besides coordinated communication, the importance of an early initiation of the discharge process is emphasized, so that the various actors involved can be contacted and coordinated as needed (Harbord 2009). This should also include early screening of high-risk patients upon admission (Wong et al. 2011; Müller and Deimel 2013). Early initiation of discharge processes has been shown to lead to a significant reduction in re-admission rates one and twelve months after discharge from the hospital compared to standard care (Fox et al. 2013). Early initiation of discharge management was defined as initiation during the acute phase of the medical condition. If patients were readmitted, early discharge management reduced the average hospital stay by 2½ days. Mortality, however, did not vary between the treatment and the control group. Not just early discharge management, but any discharge management has been shown to have a positive effect on the length of hospital stay, especially for elderly patients, and re-admission rates (Shepperd et al. 2013; Rennke et al. 2013).

Models that predict the likelihood of readmission and the occurrence of health problems are a useful tool to support early initiation of the discharge process. Such models can be used to guide discharge planning before the patient gets discharged. Administrative data are fed into the system. However, Escobar et al. (2015) found such models to rarely incorporate clinical and patient-reported data. In the United States, organisations such as Kaiser Permanente are increasingly using information from electronic medical records (EMR) for predictive models to generate scores indicating the severity of illness and longitudinal comorbidity (Escobar et al. 2015). Using the information and infrastructure available, Escobar et al. (2015) developed a predictive model that calculates a 7- and 30-day risk estimate to inform inpatient care givers as well as case managers outside the hospital setting to help preparing service delivery.

6.5   Conclusion

Discharge management is an essential—if not the essential—part of providing integrated care in all health systems. However, there is still a long journey towards guaranteeing adequate transitions for patients in most (if not all) health systems. Discharge management is one of the traditional managed care approaches which potentially leads to both—higher quality and reduced costs. The major challenge for its success is the existence of conflicting interests within the different sectors of the health care provision which come together in this process. If hospitals are not integrated in a larger system with a single financial responsibility for a defined population they will continue to optimize their individual value chain. Therefore, an adequate reimbursement system such as bundled payments is essential to enable a functioning discharge management system. Secondly, the different professional cultures in the various sectors need to be addressed adequately to be of value to the patient and not a barrier to optimal treatment. It must be in the interest of all parties to internalize the discharge management interfaces within a network of providers.

One factor is important to keep in mind: organizing and sustaining successful discharge management requires resources and comes at a cost (Shepperd et al. 2013). However, in the long run discharge management has high potential for increasing the efficiency of health systems. It has been shown that professionalising discharge management can lead to reduced costs for health care provision (Shepperd et al. 2013). Nevertheless, coherent and reliable evidence is still missing.

References

Abad-Corpa, E., Royo-Morales, T., Iniesta-Sánchez, J., Carrillo-Alcaraz, A., Rodríguez-Mondejar, J. J., Saez-Soto, A. R., & Vivo-Molina, M. C. (2013). Evaluation of the effectiveness of hospital discharge planning and follow-up in the primary care of patients with chronic obstructive pulmonary disease. *Journal of Clinical Nursing, 22*, 669–680.

Amelung, V., Bertram, N., Binder S., Chase, D. P. & Urbanski, D. (2016). Die elektronische Patientenakte. Fundament einer effektiven und effizienten Gesundheitsversorgung. Stiftung Münch (Hrsg.), medhochzwei.

Atwal, A., & Caldwell, K. (2002). Do multidisciplinary integrated care pathways improve interprofessional collaboration? *Scandinavian Journal of Caring Sciences, 16*, 360–367.

Bahr, S. J., Solverson, S., Schlidt, A., Hack, D., Smith, J. L., & Ryan, P. (2014). Integrated literature review of postdischarge telephone calls. *Western Journal of Nursing Research, 36*, 84–104. doi:10.1177/0193945913491016.

Bender, T. (2013). Kritische Analyse aus Sicht des Patienten/Angehörigen. In D. Deimel & M. L. Müller (Eds.), *Entlassmanagement. Vernetztes Handeln durch Patientenkoordination* (pp. 12–14). Stuttgart: Thieme.

Burns, L. R., & Pauly, M. V. (2002). Integrated delivery networks: A detour on the road to integrated health care? *Health Affairs, 21*, 128–143. doi:10.1377/hlthaff.21.4.128.

Chenoweth, L., Kable, A., & Pond, D. (2015). Research in hospital discharge procedures addresses gaps in care continuity in the community, but leaves gaping holes for people with dementia: A review of the literature. *Australasian Journal on Ageing, 34*, 9–14.

Deimel, D. (2013). Einleitung allgemeiner Teil. In D. Deimel & M. L. Müller (Eds.), *Entlassmanagement. Vernetztes Handeln durch Patientenkoordination* (pp. 2–5). Stuttgart: Thieme.

Deimel, D., Kuß, A., & Ossege, M. (2013). Positionspapier: Entlassmanagement im Krankenhaus. Retrieved from http://www.bmcev.de/fileadmin/Daten/Positionspapiere/BMC-Positionspapier-Entlassmanagement_Langfassung.pdf

Dienst, S. (2013). Kiritsche Analyse aus Sicht eines Krankenhauses. In D. Deimel & M. L. Müller (Eds.), *Entlassmanagement. Vernetztes Handeln durch Patientenkoordination* (pp. 21–25). Stuttgart: Thieme.

Drachsler, H., Kicken, W., van der Klink, M., Stoyanov, S., Boshuizen, H. P. A., & Paul, B. P. (2012). The Handover Toolbox. A knowledge exchange and training platform for improving patient care. *BMJ Quality and Safety, 21*, i114–i120. doi:10.1136/bmjqs-2012-001176.

Escarrabill, J. (2009). Discharge planning and home care for end-stage COPD patients. *The European Respiratory Journal, 34*, 507–512. doi:10.1183/09031936.00146308.

Escobar, G. J., Ragins, A., Scheirer, P., Liu, V., Robles, J., & Kipnis, P. (2015). Nonelective rehospitalizations and postdischarge mortality. Predictive models suitable for use in real time. *Medical Care, 53*, 916–923.

Eurostat. (2015). *Hospital discharges and length of stay statistics*. Retrieved from http://ec.europa.eu/eurostat/statistics-explained/index.php/Hospital_discharges_and_length_of_stay_statistics

Fox, M. T., Persaud, M., Maimets, I., Brooks, D., O'Brian, K., & Tregunno, D. (2013). Effectiveness of early discharge planning in acutely ill or injured hospitalized older adults: A systematic review and meta-analysis. *BMC Geriatrics, 13*, 1–9.

Harbord, A. (2009). Ernährung in der ambulanten häuslichen Versorgung. In C. von Reibnitz (Ed.), *Homecare* (pp. 47–58). Bern: Verlag Hans Huber.

Hennessey, B., & Suter, P. (2011). The community-based transitions model: One agency's experience. *Home Healthcare Nurse, 29*, 218–230.

Hesselink, G., Zegers, M., Vernooij-Dassen, M., Barach, P., Kalkman, C., Maria Flink, M., Öhlén, G., Olsson, M., Bergenbrant, S., Orrego, C., Suñol, R., Toccafondi, G., Venneri, F., Dudzik-Urbaniak, E., Kutryba, B., Schoonhoven, L., & Wollersheim, H. (2014). Improving patient discharge and reducing hospital readmissions by using intervention mapping. *Health Services Research, 14*, 389.

Mohr, A. (2009). Integrierte Versorgung – eine Perspektive für Homecare. In C. von Reibnitz (Ed.), *Homecare* (pp. 176–177). Bern: Verlag Hans Huber.

Müller, T. (2013). Kritische Analyse aus Sicht eines ambulanten ärztlichen Dienstleisters. In D. Deimel & M. L. Müller (Eds.), *Entlassmanagement. Vernetztes Handeln durch Patientenkoordination* (pp. 28–31). Stuttgart: Thieme.

Müller, M. L., & Deimel, D. (2013). Begriffsbestimmung und heute bereits umgesetzte Modelle. In D. Deimel & M. L. Müller (Eds.), *Entlassmanagement. Vernetztes Handeln durch Patientenkoordination* (pp. 6–11). Stuttgart: Thieme.

OECD. (2014). Average length of stay in hospitals. In *Health at a Glance: Europe 2014*. Paris: OECD. Retrieved from http://www.oecd-ilibrary.org/docserver/download/8114211ec031.pdf?expires=1456492455&id=id&accname=guest&checksum=DC093FF3F544DB13E2B62F26D608D522.

Philibert, I., & Barach, P. (2012). The European HANDOVER Project: A multi-nation program to improve transitions at the primary care-inpatient interface. *BMJ Quality and Safety, 21*, i1–i6. doi:10.1136/bmjqs-2012-001598.

Pilgrim, T., & Kittlick, C. (2013). Kritische Analyse aus Sicht des Versorgungsmanagements. In D. Deimel & M. L. Müller (Eds.), *Entlassmanagement. Vernetztes Handenln durch Patientenkoordination* (pp. 15–18). Stuttgart: Thieme.

Rennke, S., Nguyen, O. K., Shoeb, M. H., Magan, Y., Wachter, R. M., & Ranji, S. R. (2013). Hospital-initiated transitional care interventions as a patient strategy. *Annals of Internal Medicine, 158,* 433–441.

Shepperd, S., Lannin, N. A., Clemson, L. M., McCluskey, A., Cameron, I. D., & Barras, S. L. (2013). Discharge planning from hospital to home (Review). *Cochrane Database of Systematic Reviews, 1,* CD000313.

Shu, C. C., Hsu, N. C., Lin, Y. F., Wang, J. Y., Lin, J. W., & Wen-Je Ko, W. J. (2011). Integrated postdischarge transitional care in a hospitalist system to improve discharge outcome: An experimental study. *BMC Medicine, 9,* 96.

Tang, N., Fujimoto, J., & Karliner, L. (2014). Evaluation of a primary care-based post-discharge phone call program: Keeping the primary care practice at the center of post-hospitalization care transition. *Journal of General Internal Medicine, 29*(11), 1513–1518. doi:10.1007/s11606-014-2942-6.

Toccafondi, G., Albolino, S., Tartaglia, R., Guidi, S., Molisso, A., Venneri, F., Peris, A., Pieralli, F., Magnelli, E., Librenti, M., Morelli, M., & Barach, P. (2012). The collaborative communication model for patient handover at the interface between high-acuity and low-acuity care. *BMJ Quality and Safety, 21,* i58–i66. doi:10.1136/bmjqs-2012-001178.

Wehmeier, D., & Schäfer, A. (2013). Kritische Analyse aus Sicht einer Rehaklinik. In D. Deimel & M. L. Müller (Eds.), *Entlassmanagement. Vernetztes Handenln durch Patientenkoordination* (pp. 25–27). Stuttgart: Thieme.

Wong, E. L. Y., Yam, C. H. K., Cheung, A. W. L., Leung, M. C. M., Chan, F. W. K., Wong, F. Y. Y., & Yeoh, E. K. (2011). Barriers to effective discharge planning: A qualitative study investigating the perspectives of frontline healthcare professionals. *BMC Health Services Research, 11,* 242.

Yiu, R., Fung, V., Szeto, K., Hung, V., Siu, R., Lam, J., Lai, D., Maw, C., Cheung, A., Shea, R., & Choy, A. (2013). Building electronic forms for elderly program: Integrated care model for high risk elders in Hong Kong. *Medinfo.* doi:10.3233/978-1-61499-289-9-1016.

Mobile Sensors and Wearable Technology

7

Christopher A. Yao and Kendall Ho

The recent surge of innovative approaches to improve health has garnered a lot of public interest and become a major frontrunner in the consumer technology market. With this gaining momentum, wearable devices to measure individuals' physiology such as heart rate and activity levels have become highly popular, increasingly pervasive, and are creating a cultural shift to help people to collect, quantify, and observe their own data relating to their behaviours in day-to-day life. This "quantified self" can increase self-awareness regarding their behaviour and impact positively on their overall health and well-being (Swan 2009). With the potential to change health behaviour through these platforms, the general public has the ability to be more engaged and participatory in their own health.

7.1 Commercial Mobile Sensors and Wearable Technologies

The allure of these commercially available devices is the ability to provide an array of program features such as reward systems, opportunities for social interaction, and measured behavioural outcomes, which can increase motivation to engage in healthier behaviours. With these novel features, along with perceptions of affordability, practicality, and ease of use, overall attitudes and adoption of these devices have improved considerably (Gao et al. 2010; Kim and Shin 2015). One of the most compelling features is the use of various self-regulation strategies to help individuals improve exercise motivation and behaviour. Individuals can understand and recognize the necessary steps to change their own behaviour through the use of these devices, which can create a foundation for integrated approaches to health and patient care.

C.A. Yao • K. Ho (✉)
University of British Columbia Faculty of Medicine, Vancouver, BC, Canada
e-mail: kendall.ho@ubc.ca

© Springer International Publishing AG 2017
V. Amelung et al. (eds.), *Handbook Integrated Care*,
DOI 10.1007/978-3-319-56103-5_7

Currently, consumers keen on adopting a healthy and fitness-based lifestyle can purchase wearable technology from a plethora of manufacturers from Fitbit, Jawbone, Garmin, Apple, Samsung, Motorola, and even Swarovski. These devices are able to consolidate the various functions found in accelerometers, pedometers, GPS, and heart rate monitors into one device. They can then provide useful measurements and feedback on variables such as step counts, physical activity intensity, total daily energy expenditure, sedentary activity and sleep quality. Recent literature has suggested that some of these commercially available devices are fairly reliable and capable of providing accurate measures of step counts (Evenson et al. 2015). Furthermore, there is additional evidence to support that some of these products are able to yield physical activity estimates comparable to research-grade accelerometers (Lee et al. 2014; Ferguson et al. 2015). However, the validity regarding variables like energy expenditure and sleep has yet to be thoroughly investigated (Evenson et al. 2015).

At the crux of the commercial devices are the program features, either embedded on the device itself or with accompanied software, that incorporate multiple self-regulation strategies to help individuals adopt and maintain their behaviour. Similar to previous content analyses performed on smartphone apps (West et al. 2012; Abroms et al. 2011; Cowan et al. 2013; Azar et al. 2013; Breland et al. 2013), a recent investigation was conducted to examine the various behaviour change techniques implemented in 13 commercially available sensors (Lyons et al. 2014). In all the appraised devices, features like self-monitoring and feedback on behaviour, adding activity monitors to the environment, setting goals, and outlining potential discrepancies between measured performance and goal were identified. Conversely, strategies like problem solving, action planning, prompting or cues to action were less prevalent. According to intention-based behaviour theories, these less frequently incorporated strategies may be critical components to translate intention into behaviour and habit formation (Rhodes and Yao 2015). Despite these gaps, preliminary evidence has suggested that these devices can facilitate short-term changes to physical activity behaviour (Lewis et al. 2015).

7.2   Mobile Sensors and Wearable Technologies in Health Care

Mobile and wearable sensor technologies have also begun to expand into the health care landscape. Unlike commercial mobile sensors, which have been relatively established and centred on increasing physical activity levels, mobile sensors in the clinical domain have been in development and primarily focus on continuous monitoring and precise diagnostics to inform treatment and care of various health conditions and diseases (Chen et al. 2011; Appelboom et al. 2014; Chan et al. 2012; Alemdar and Ersoy 2010). These devices have been integrated into materials like adhesive bandages and clothing, and can track and monitor cardiac function (i.e., electrocardiography), heart rate, blood pressure, respiration, oxygen saturation (i.e., pulse oximetry), galvanic skin response, glucose levels, kinematics, body and ambient temperature, and global positioning. With aggregated measures of these variables, insight into medical status (e.g., vital signs, level of diabetes self-care), chronic disease risk, and physiological anomalies can be observed and captured to inform clinicians and patients about appropriate treatment. An example of how mobile sensors can be applied in preventative health care is the detection of heart conditions. For instance, atrial fibrillation can be fairly transient and asymptomatic, and is not often diagnosed until a serious health incident like a stroke or syncope occurs. Devices such as AliveCor have been used to monitor the electrical activity of the heart via a bipolar electrode in clinical and non-clinical populations, and allow patients to share ultrasound and electrocardiogram data with their healthcare provider (Haberman et al. 2015; Ferdman et al. 2015; Baquero et al. 2015).

Clinical sensors can also extend beyond the patient and be integrated into a broader wireless network, linking the patient to his or her immediate surroundings and to the health care provider. An early illustrations of this was the alert portable telemedical monitor (AMON) project which proposed a wearable monitoring system to remotely track and relay health information and data between the patient and clinician (Anliker et al. 2004). Aimed at individuals at risk of cardiac and respiratory disease, this prototype featured multifactor tracking of vital signs (blood pressure, oxygen saturation, pulse, ECG) and physical activity, online analysis and emergency detection, and a communication interface (e.g., SMS) in a wrist-worn device. Despite having issues regarding measurement accuracy, the device showed a clear indication that it was a feasible approach to improve outpatient care while encouraging patients to self-monitor and live independently. Overall, devices such as the AliveCor and AMON are diagnostic tools that have an immense potential to prevent and detect serious health conditions and diseases, and as these devices continue to develop, so will the proliferation of these technologies.

7.3 Using Mobile Sensors and Wearable Technologies to Change Health Behaviour

One area that requires further exploration is the coupling of precise clinical measurement and monitoring with behavioural change theory to improve health-related behaviours and health outcomes. A recent qualitative investigation exploring the role of sensor technology to sustain behaviour change found that simply tracking health data alone may not be sufficient enough to sustain patient motivation to achieve health goals (Miyamoto et al. 2016). Applying behaviour change theory to the development of these devices may address the dynamic nature of patient motivation.

The importance of theoretical models lie in their ability to produce a nomenclature of psychosocial determinants, understand the mechanisms for why a behaviour might occur, and subsequently, target key constructs to elicit changes to behaviour (Davis et al. 2014). For instance, theoretical frameworks such as the social cognitive theory indicate goal setting and reflection on own performance are both necessary in order to stimulate and anchor behavioural modification (Bandura 1986). A recent systematic review examining the potential of smartphone technology to measure and influence physical activity behaviour found that the most commonly applied theoretical framework was the social cognitive theory (Bort-Roig et al. 2014). Moreover, the review further highlighted five behaviour change strategies commonly found on these devices that were associated with changes in physical activity behaviour: physical activity profiling, goal setting, real-time feedback, social support networking, and online expert consultation.

Based on these specific recommendations, a recent feasibility study investigated the use of wireless blood pressure monitors and weight scales along with glucose monitoring and the effects of these devices on diabetes self-management and health outcomes (Ho et al. 2015). Measurements from these devices were uploaded to a secure online profile in real-time and made accessible to the patients and their caregivers. In addition to these monitoring systems, social support was provided in the forms of a secure online discussion board for participants and researchers to connect with each other; patients also received biweekly text messages from a health professional with evidence-based information to improve diabetes self-management. After 3 months, patients saw improvements to physiological outcomes like weight, systolic blood pressure, and blood glucose (hemoglobin A1C values decreased into the recommended target ranges for diabetes management i.e., <7) (Ho et al. 2015). As well, patients reported lower level of distress regarding their health condition and felt more empowered in managing their diabetes (Ho et al. 2015). Overall, these findings demonstrated the prospective use of mobile technologies to elicit behaviour change and improve the health of clinical populations.

7.4   Current Limitations and Potential Impact on Health

Undoubtedly, the research and development around mobile sensors and wearable technology still require further development, and the long-term impact of these devices remains unknown. One of the major barriers to understanding the long-term impact to health behaviour and health outcomes has been adherence to the wearable sensor itself. Previous research has shown that adherence to commercial devices tends to decline after 6 months (Kim and Shin 2015). Potential reasons for this may be related to equipment itself (e.g., usability, comfort, and battery life) and a diminishing novelty effect (Alemdar and Ersoy 2010), lack of professional support to help the user to understand the context and meaning of the data collected (Miyamoto et al. 2016), and inability of these devices to target important psychosocial constructs associated with intention-behaviour discordance and habit formation (Rhodes and Yao 2015). Wearable sensor technology in the clinical domain may experience a similar fate with regards to adherence outcomes.

Despite the current limitations, mobile sensors and wearable devices can positively impact patient delivery and care. In terms of patient care, these sensors will be able to continuously collect personal data in various environmental contexts as part of an all-encompassing health network. In turn, the amassed data can be used in multifactor analyses to identify the user's specific needs and prevent further decline in health (Banaee et al. 2013). As well, clinicians will be able to remotely monitor their patient's current condition in real-time and appraise overall data trends, be notified of any immediate changes to health status (e.g., irregularities, decompensation), and better administer appropriate actions and treatment (e.g., modify medication dosage, curtail adverse events). While in healthy populations, the data collected would allow for the prediction and detection of anomalies in behaviours to encourage and support healthy lifestyle behaviours.

This technology can also ease the care process and establish a sense of patient safety. The devices can allow health professionals to remotely monitor and concurrently manage their patients and the data collected can expedite continuous care (e.g., from emergency medical care to community care and patient's home), while allowing patients to feel supported and safe by being closely monitored by their provider. Moreover, the ability for health care professionals to remotely monitor patients will be able to extend services into previously underserved areas.

With these overall effects, health care professionals will be able to considerably increase their ability to provide adequate and timely care through active provider-patient engagement; thus, improving overall health outcomes and patient experiences. In addition to this, the preventative effects of mobile and wearable technologies will be able to reduce health care costs, like unnecessary emergency care admissions and reducing the length of patient hospital stays, while bettering health care efficiency though continuous care.

7.5 Integrating Mobile Sensors and Wearable Technologies in the Clinical Setting

As these wearable sensor technologies inevitably evolve and become integrated into a larger network that moves beyond the patient and the patient home, these devices will become increasingly relevant to clinical practice. From a health care perspective, it will be important to utilize these tools as complementary tools in treatment and prevention of health conditions and disease. Both clinicians and patients can stay informed about the current developments and look for ways to personalize the technology to compliment the individual's goals towards better health. For patients who are in the initial phases of changing their health behaviour and consider the adoption of a commercial device, health care professionals can guide patients toward the most appropriate, empirically supported wearable applications in terms of content, validity, and reliability.

Along with these benefits, certain risks related to the use of this technology may arise. Issues such as self-diagnosis and self-management without the integrated care or support of health professionals, over reliance on technologies that may be underdeveloped, data misinterpretation and a strong belief in own data to override professional advice, can contribute to a fragmented care pathway. To resolve these issues and encourage collaborative efforts to promote health behaviour change, clinicians should provide patient education, highlight the limitations of this technology, and tailor the use of the device to the patient's goal of improving their health.

In order to advance the area of mobile and wearable sensors, further scientific evidence is needed. Despite the current state of this technology, the promise and potential benefits of mobile sensors and wearable technologies certainly outweigh the conceivable drawbacks. Both the commercial and medical sectors will continue to find innovative ways to improve wearable sensors technology, which will lead to improved acceptance among clinicians and patients. Inevitably, as these sensors gain popularity and expand into our environment, patients will become more participatory in their own health—shifting to a more preventative and collaborative patient-centred paradigm (Swan 2009). Due to the novelty of this approach, it will be important to build strong and trusting partnerships between health professionals and patients to encourage the adoption and integration of mobile sensors and wireless technology into health care.

References

Abroms, L. C., Padmanabhan, N., Thaweethai, L., & Phillips, T. (2011). iPhone apps for smoking cessation: A content analysis. *American Journal of Preventive Medicine, 40*(3), 279–285.

Alemdar, H., & Ersoy, C. (2010). Wireless sensor networks for healthcare: A survey. *Computer Networks, 54*(15), 2688–2710.

Anliker, U., Ward, J., Lukowicz, P., Tröster, G., Dolveck, F., Baer, M., et al. (2004). AMON: A wearable multiparameter medical monitoring and alert system. *IEEE Transactions on Information Technology in Biomedicine, 8*(4), 415–427.

Appelboom, G., Camacho, E., Abraham, M. E., Bruce, S. S., Dumont, E. L., Zacharia, B. E., et al. (2014). Smart wearable body sensors for patient self-assessment and monitoring. *Archives of Public Health, 72*(1), 28.

Azar, K. M. J., Lesser, L. I., Laing, B. Y., Stephens, J., Aurora, M. S., Burke, L. E., et al. (2013). Mobile applications for weight management. *American Journal of Preventive Medicine, 45*(5), 583–589.

Banaee, H., Ahmed, M. U., & Loutfi, A. (2013). Data mining for wearable sensors in health monitoring systems: A review of recent trends and challenges. *Sensors, 13*(12), 17472–17500.

Bandura, A. (1986). *Social foundations of thought and action: A social cognitive theory* (617 p). Englewood Cliffs, NJ: Prentice-Hall.

Baquero, G. A., Banchs, J. E., Ahmed, S., Naccarelli, G. V., & Luck, J. C. (2015). Surface 12 lead electrocardiogram recordings using smart phone technology. *Journal of Electrocardiology, 48* (1), 1–7.

Bort-Roig, J., Gilson, N. D., Puig-Ribera, A., Contreras, R. S., & Trost, S. G. (2014). Measuring and influencing physical activity with smartphone technology: A systematic review. *Sports Medicine, 44*(5), 671–686.

Breland, J. Y., Yeh, V. M., & Yu, J. (2013). Adherence to evidence-based guidelines among diabetes self-management apps. *Translational Behavioral Medicine, 3*(3), 277–286.

Chan, M., Estève, D., Fourniols, J.-Y., Escriba, C., & Campo, E. (2012). Smart wearable systems: Current status and future challenges. *Artificial Intelligence in Medicine, 56*(3), 137–156.

Chen, M., Gonzalez, S., Vasilakos, A., Cao, H., & Leung, V. C. M. (2011). Body area networks: A survey. *Mobile Networks and Applications, 16*(2), 171–193.

Cowan, L. T., Van Wagenen, S. A., Brown, B. A., Hedin, R. J., Seino-Stephan, Y., Hall, P. C., et al. (2013). Apps of steel: Are exercise apps providing consumers with realistic expectations?

A content analysis of exercise apps for presence of behavior change theory. *Health Education Behavior, 40*(2), 133–139.

Davis, R., Campbell, R., Hildon, Z., Hobbs, L., & Michie, S. (2014). Theories of behaviour and behaviour change across the social and behavioural sciences: A scoping review. *Health Psychology Review*, 1–36.

Evenson, K. R., Goto, M. M., & Furberg, R. D. (2015). Systematic review of the validity and reliability of consumer-wearable activity trackers. *International Journal of Behavioral Nutrition and Physical Activity, 12*(159).

Ferdman, D. J., Liberman, L., & Silver, E. S. (2015). A smartphone application to diagnose the mechanism of pediatric supraventricular tachycardia. *Pediatric Cardiology, 36*(7), 1452–1457.

Ferguson, T., Rowlands, A. V., Olds, T., & Maher, C. (2015). The validity of consumer-level, activity monitors in healthy adults worn in free-living conditions: A cross-sectional study. *International Journal of Behavioral Nutrition and Physical Activity, 12*(1), 42.

Gao, Y., Li, H., & Luo, Y. (2010). An empirical study of wearable technology acceptance in healthcare. *Industrial Management & Data Systems, 115*(9), 1704–1723.

Haberman, Z. C., Jahn, R. T., Bose, R., Tun, H., Shinbane, J. S., Doshi, R. N., et al. (2015). Wireless smartphone ECG enables large-scale screening in diverse populations. *Journal of Cardiovascular Electrophysiology, 26*(5), 520–526.

Ho, K., Newton, L., Booth, A., & Novak, L. H.. (2015). *Mobile digital access to a web-enhanced network (mDAWN): Assessing the feasibility of mobile health tools for self-management of type 2 diabetes.* American Medical Informatics Association 2015 Annual Symposium, San Francisco, CA.

Kim, K. J., & Shin, D. H. (2015). An acceptance model for smart watches: Implications for the adoption of future wearable technology. *International Rescuer, 25*(4), 527–541.

Lee, J.-M., Kim, Y., & Welk, G. J. (2014). Validity of consumer-based physical activity monitors. *Medicine and Science in Sports and Exercise, 46*(9), 1840–1848.

Lewis, Z. H., Lyons, E. J., Jarvis, J. M., & Baillargeon, J. (2015). Using an electronic activity monitor system as an intervention modality: A systematic review. *BMC Public Health, 15*, 585.

Lyons, E. J., Lewis, Z. H., Mayrsohn, B. G., & Rowland, J. L. (2014). Behavior change techniques implemented in electronic lifestyle activity monitors: A systematic content analysis. *Journal of Medical Internet Research, 16*(8), e192.

Miyamoto, S. W., Henderson, S., Young, H. M., & Pande, A. (2016). Tracking health data is not enough: A qualitative exploration of the role of healthcare partnerships and mHealth technology to promote physical activity and to sustain behavior change. *JMIR mHealth and uHealth, 4*(1), 1–12.

Rhodes, R. E., & Yao, C. A. (2015). Models accounting for intention-behavior discordance in the physical activity domain: A user's guide, content overview, and review of current evidence. *International Journal of Behavioral Nutrition and Physical Activity, 12*, 1–14.

Swan, M. (2009). Emerging patient-driven health care models: An examination of health social networks, consumer personalized medicine and quantified self-tracking. *International Journal of Environmental Research and Public Health, 6*(2), 492–525.

West, J. H., Hall, P. C., Hanson, C. L., Barnes, M. D., Giraud-Carrier, C., & Barrett, J. (2012). There's an app for that: Content analysis of paid health and fitness apps. *Journal of Medical Internet Research, 14*(3), e72.

Data Integration in Health Care

8

Maya Leventer-Roberts and Ran Balicer

Health data integration is considered a key component and, in some cases, a pre-requisite in nearly every systematic attempt to achieve integrated care. In the context of health care, data integration is a complex process of combining multiple types of data from different sources into a single infrastructure, allowing multiple levels of users to access, edit, and contribute to an electronic record of health services (EHRs). The types of data integration that are performed depend on the quality, quantity, and capability of the service performing the integration as well as the needs of the current and future users of the new framework (Johnson et al. 2008). In the following chapter we describe six basic types of data integration, the pathways by which data integration facilitates integrated care, the main players of health care data integration, and key challenges to integrating data.

8.1 Types of Data Integration

8.1.1 Horizontal Integration

Horizontal data integration occurs when the data segments being combined originate from similar kinds of sources. Two examples are combining data from multiple nursing shifts in an inpatient setting (Flaks-Manov et al. 2015) or from various community health care providers within a single clinic (Balicer et al. 2014).

M. Leventer-Roberts
Clalit Research Institute, Clalit Health Services, Tel-Aviv, Israel

Icahn School of Medicine at Mount Sinai, New York, USA

R. Balicer (✉)
Clalit Research Institute, Clalit Health Services, Tel-Aviv, Israel

Faculty of Health Sciences, Ben-Gurion University of the Negev, Beersheba, Israel
e-mail: rbalicer@gmail.com

© Springer International Publishing AG 2017
V. Amelung et al. (eds.), *Handbook Integrated Care*,
DOI 10.1007/978-3-319-56103-5_8

121

Horizontally integrated data is inherently non-hierarchical and there is no inherent weight or priority given to the different sources of data. The main obstacle to horizontal integration is combining the data in a way that all the data is consistently represented: one source may measure and record weight in kilograms (kgs) while another, in pounds (lbs) and one may not weigh at all, resulting in missing values. We delve deeper into data consistency later in the chapter when we discuss data quality.

8.1.2 Vertical Integration

Vertical data integration occurs when data from different types of sources are combined into one database. For example, vertical data integration would combine the information documented by a nurse who performs weekly home visits with the information recorded by a physician who performs a quarterly physician review of a diabetic treatment regimen. This type of integration requires a thoughtful organization of how to nest and correlate the findings from each assessment, which contains a hierarchical provider structure. Sources are likely to serve both independent and yet interrelated goals; A nurse may monitor patient medication compliance in a weekly visit which may drive a physician to change treatment goals at the subsequent review. Alternatively, ranking or prioritizing a single diagnosis when a patient has been seen by multiple general practitioners and referred to varying sub-specialists creates challenges when data managers have to apply subjective interpretations to previously objective documentation.

8.1.3 Historical Integration

The merging of patient health records from multiple systems and of different formats (including paper charts) often requires additional processing or review in order to reconcile basic or summary information to serve as a reference for future use. This manual compilation of data can be tedious, costly and full of error, all of which are reasons EHRs were not adopted quickly (Evans 2016).

8.1.4 Longitudinal Integration

The data captured on a patient is a dynamic process over time; As certain conditions resolve and others may develop. Therefore, health care data integration requires flexibility to allow for new entries and new types of entries. Furthermore, as our understanding and management of treatment advances over time, we are increasingly in need of the new methods of capturing and storing data that can still be merged consistently with less precise information.

8.1.5   Cross-Indexing Integration

The ability to relate an individual's medical records with their family member's current medical care or medical history presents a unique opportunity to expand the detail present and accessible across multiple generations as well as multiple exposures (living within the household of smokers identifies ones as exposed to second-hand smoke or to other health risks increased by a shared living environment, such as type 2 diabetes). Such a level of data integration requires a cross-indexing mechanism to ensure that multiple records can be updated simultaneously.

8.1.6   Alternative Sources

Patient reported outcomes, social media, biomonitoring data from various sensors, genome sequencing, and even open chart models are increasingly becoming relevant sources of data for holistic processing of patient health records (Frey et al. 2015). Data integration that includes these types of data can offer new dimensions of insight.

8.2   The Importance of Data Integration

Data integration is a key facilitator of integrated people-centred care. Un-integrated data strongly hinders any attempt to integrate the provision of care and to empower patients. Decision-making processes that occur in isolation of known, documented, and managed data are inherently problematic, from both the managerial and legal standpoint. While not all types of data will necessarily contribute to a given clinical decision, such as initiation of a therapy or transfer to an assisted living facility, an integrated system provides critical support for decisions that weigh the short- and long-term implications of a change in care to patient experience.

Recent studies have shown that it is beneficial for patient records be readily accessible not only to the care provider but also to patients themselves (Esch et al. 2016; Sustains 2014). Some organizations have taken this principle to the most extreme and adopted an open-chart system that allows for co-creation and management of EHRs by providers, care-givers, and patients. One recent study on such a system (Esch et al. 2016) found a direct relationship between "open notes" health records and improved medication adherence, self-care, and a high level of patient empowerment. This example of data integration demonstrates the importance of a thorough understanding of the quality and quantity of data that needs to be managed in a fully integrated record.

8.3   Impact of Data Integration

In addition to serving the needs of the patients and providers, data integration has a potential measurable impact on two key components of a high quality health care delivery system: reducing waste and improving decision-making capacity.

8.3.1   Types of Waste That Can Be Reduced with Data Integration

8.3.1.1 Repeat Testing

One of the most commonly cited examples of the beneficial impacts of data integration is the ability to reduce repeat testing (Menachemi and Collum 2011). Patients who undergo testing at one institution, if upgraded to another more acute facility, do not necessarily have to undergo repeat testing for the purposes of internal or external validation.

8.3.1.2 Manual Integration of Data

In the absence of data integration, each provider that sees a patient may find themselves entering data into an unstructured format the reports symptoms, laboratory findings, mediation list, medical history, and additional key components of a medical history. This type of complete history and physical exam, which may be instructive as an exercise for the individual physician, is repetitive and prone to error when applied multiple times at multiple facilities.

8.3.1.3 Informal Reports

The sharing of information between providers may occur informally, particularly if there is no avenue for routine data integration. Specifically, there may be telephone or conversational discussions regarding patient care and management that are not readily documented for verification and for future reference which is important if there are follow up questions to the decisions made during the transfer of care. While it is highly likely that these types of integration will continue and even potentially increase in frequency, it is, nonetheless, important to provide a platform for their inclusion in health records so they are not lost or repeated unnecessarily.

8.3.2   Improving Decision-Making Capacity

8.3.2.1 Individual Level

Patient-centred care requires not only the ability of the provider to consider the consequences of their decision-making on the daily management on the part of the patient but also the ability of the patient to determine and direct the priorities in his or her own management. Data integration creates a streamlined library from which a patient can review and respond to multiple aspects of their medical history and treatment pathways in order to play a proactive role in a conversation regarding his or her health.

8.3.2.2 Provider Level

Logic follows that providers who can actively and easily access complete medical records are more likely to prevent issues resulting from drug-interactions or allergic reactions. Furthermore, using integrated medical records, they may be able to base their clinical decision-making processes on the most up-to-date information, which is important if a patient is unable to provide detailed history.

8.3.2.3 Policy Level

Both provider and payer organizations benefit from the collective input of multiple parties when reviewing their management of individual patients and of larger populations (at the clinic or district level). At the clinic level, data integration allows for real-time monitoring and evaluation of interventions and the quality of service delivery. At the district level, data integration supports the ability to compare the needs and outcome of various clinics, resulting in the ability to focus on granular information, such as practice variation, needs-based planning, and quality improvement measures. Furthermore, the ability for an umbrella organization to proactively distribute resources (vaccines, nursing educators, and social workers) can be supported by the demonstrated and predicted needs within and between communities.

8.3.2.4 International Level

Standards of care, as supported by randomized control trials and large observational studies and driven by a panel of experts and policy makers, have much to gain from all types and all levels of data integration (Bloomrosen and Detmer 2010). When organizations are able to integrate the health care utilization and practice patterns on a large scale, they are able to predict future needs, identify trends, and isolate previously untapped potentials for interventions such as practice variation and hot spots of disease or highly effective delivery of care. Ultimately, comparisons of local findings are best able to have global significance when they can be directly compared to similar system among various health-care and resources utilization outcomes.

8.4   Key Challenges in Integrating Data

The main challenges that concern advocates of data integration include access to, quality of, and ongoing monitoring of integrated data (Lampsas et al. 2002).

8.4.1   Access and Privacy

Designing a system to provide meaningful access to data can range from simple access, which is open to everyone to complicated, in which different levels of access are required for each part of an EHR, determined by the privacy needs of the patient and the differing levels of responsibility multiple different decision-makers.

The majority of systems find themselves with a combination of access levels, where the majority of integrated data is available to the patient and providers, with some key sensitive material flagged as requiring additional clearance (infectious disease data, for example). Some may argue that providers must be able to access all types of data, such as a patient's psychiatric history when assessing medication adherence, and others argue that certain types of health records are at risk for a breach of privacy and at worst embarrassing and at best irrelevant, such as revealing the occurrence of a treated sexually transmitted disease on an asthma treatment plan several decades later. However, the decision-making power rarely rests with one person and often requires a case-by-case review. Patient-driven input is increasingly suggested as an important contribution in order to maximize the utility of a patient medical record (Sacchi et al. 2015).

8.4.2 Security

Data security is a challenge for all large datasets and is important for maintenance of both privacy and accuracy of the data stored. Data security issues may arise when there are outside forces seeking to access the data warehouse, but more frequently can arise when there is an unintentional breach in data security by a provider who is not sufficiently attentive to the needs of security. While the primary responsibility for the maintenance of a data security system rests on the central organization, any person with access to the data has the ability to compromise the data security, therefore their use and modification of the data should be monitored accordingly.

8.4.3 Quality

The overall quality of integrated data is likely to be no greater than that of the lowest quality component. Integrated data is inherently dependent on its components, and a marked difference in quality in one component can have a substantial impact on the interpretation of other components.

8.4.3.1 Quality Assessment

Quality assessment may refer to both routine and random chart reviews in order to understand the extent to which data is inconsistent, contradictory, or nonsensical (Scheurwegs et al. 2015). Consistent data deliver the same message regardless of the format. Two examples of varying data formats are structured (coded) and unstructured (uncoded) data. Seemingly contradictory data can present due to various health care providers documenting different assessments. Adopting a blanket hierarchical nature of data quality would prevent the documentation of nuances that may later serve the patients treatment. For example, a patient may report in a brief interaction to physician that he is overall experiencing "no pain," but to a nurse may reveal "reduced pain" or a "change in pain." These reports are not necessarily contradictory but, nonetheless, create a challenge to maintaining within an integrated system. Finally, the integration of data increases the risk for the presence nonsensical raw data due to the typographical errors in coding or transferring of data from one system to another. Each of these factors requires a different approach to minimize their impact on the overall quality of the data.

8.4.3.2 Quality Control

Quality control outlines the distinct steps undergone by a managing body to review and revise integrated data based on a quality assessment. Quality control may be a tedious process and may uncover minor and significant errors at similar rates that are difficult to distinguish. However, a perception of a high level of quality control is critical to achieve successful data integration because the extent at which patients and providers will use the data for their decision-making is inherently dependent on their perception of the quality of available data.

8.4.4   Tracking Use of Integrated Data

Monitoring the use of integrated data is the first step to evaluating its impact and limitations.

8.4.4.1 Providers

While the majority of users are likely to be the health care providers, the extent to which they create versus utilize data in an integrated system is an important marker in the ongoing monitoring process. Logic follows that the more accessibility a provider has to their system, the more likely he or she will use the clinical decision-making process. For example, providers who lack the ability to review, modify, and incorporate patient-reported data are probably less likely to invest in reviewing or applying it to their decision making process. Furthermore, once fully situated, the use of an integrated system could reduce a provider's time spent recording and reviewing clinical data.

8.4.4.2 Patients

Use of medical records by a patient might be an excellent barometer as to whether the relevant types of information are being stored and catalogued in a useful manner. Patient-centred care, which focuses on employing patients as driving factor in determining the integration of services, should substantially inform the characteristics of data that are being created through the use in the ongoing delivery of care. When patients are found to be actively accessing and responding to their providers' notes and messages, it is more likely that providers are capturing relevant information to the goals of their patients (Evans 2016).

8.4.4.3 Policy Makers

Policy makers are likely to be less concerned about the detailed interactions between social work and home nursing care, and more likely to be concerned about the overall coordination of care between various levels of providers and the various levels of acuity. Transfers to long term facilities or discharges from lengthy inpatient stays are transition points of high concern to policy makers that have a high likelihood of benefiting from data integration. The extent to which the adoption of a comprehensive chart review and medication reconciliation is indeed a reality in practice upon transfer between facilities, and whether it has a successful and meaningful impact, must be assessed through strategic planned review between the institutions (MacLeod 2015).

8.4.4.4 Insurers

While patient privacy must be maintained and ownership is ultimately shared in various combinations between the creators of the data (i.e., patient, provider, insurer), policies which unduly limit data dissemination between parties involved in care provision and quality assessments can diminish the impact of integrated data on the delivery of care. When an insurer's priority is to know that the correct treatment is being delivered to the right patient, integrated data can provide a strong source for support in the decision-making processes for fee-for-service, bundled payments, and pay-for-performance, alike. The combination of documentation of services along with the documentation of provider reports and justification for those services can ultimately benefit not only the patient but also the overall efficiency of the health care system.

8.5   Summary

Health care data integration is a complex task, but is considered a cornerstone of every systematic attempt to achieve integrated patient care. It requires detailed planning and ongoing assessment to ensure accurate and effective coordination of information. Ultimately, data integration has the potential to provide multiple stakeholders with critical, timely, and detailed information for short- and long-term decision-making, documentation, and it supports attempts to achieve structural and functional health care coordination and integration.

References

Balicer, R. D., Shadmi, E., & Israeli, A. (2014). Interventions for reducing readmissions – are we barking up the right tree? *Israel Journal of Health Policy Research, 2,* 2.

Bloomrosen, M., & Detmer, D. E. (2010). Informatics, evidence-based care, and research; implications for national policy: A report of an American Medical Informatics Association health policy conference. *Journal of the American Medical Informatics Association, 17*(2), 115–123. doi:10.1136/jamia.2009.001370.

Esch, T., Mejilla, R., Anselmo, M., Podtschaske, B., Delbanco, T., & Walker, J. (2016). Engaging patients through open notes: An evaluation using mixed methods. *BMJ Open, 6*(1), e010034. doi:10.1136/bmjopen-2015-010034.

Evans, R. S. (2016). Electronic health records: Then, now, and in the future. *IMIA Yearbook of Medical Informatics, Suppl 1,* S48–S61.

Flaks-Manov, N., Shadmi, E., Hoshen, M., & Balicer, R. D. (2015). Health information exchange systems and length of stay in readmissions to a different hospital. *Journal of Hospital Medicine*. doi:10.1002/jhm.2535.

Frey, L. J., Sward, K. A., Newth, C. J., Khemani, R. G., Cryer, M. E., Thelen, J. L., Enriquez, R., Shaoyu, S., Pollack, M. M., Harrison, R. E., Meert, K. L., Berg, R. A., Wessel, D. L., Shanley, T. P., Dalton, H., Carcillo, J., Jenkins, T. L., & Dean, J. M. (2015). Virtualization of open-source secure web services to support data exchange in a pediatric critical care research network. *Journal of the American Medical Informatics Association, 22*(6), 1271–1276. doi:10.1093/jamia/ocv009. Epub 2015 Mar 21.

Johnson, P. J., Blewett, L. A., Ruggles, S., Davern, M. E., & King, M. L. (2008). Four decades of population health data: The integrated health interview series as an epidemiologic resource. *Epidemiology, 19*(6), 872–875.

Lampsas, P., Vidalis, I., Papanikolaou, C., & Vagelatos, A. (2002). Implementation and integration of regional health care data networks in the Hellenic National Health Service. *Journal of Medical Internet Research, 4*(3), E20.

MacLeod, H. (2015). Local health integration networks: Build on their purpose. *Health Management Forum, 28*(6), 242–246. doi:10.1177/0840470415600127. Epub 2015 Sep 28. Review.

Menachemi, N., & Collum, T. H. (2011). Benefits and drawbacks of electronic health record systems. *Risk Management and Healthcare Policy, 4*, 47–55. doi:10.2147/RMHP.S12985.

Sacchi, L., Lanzola, G., Viani, N., & Quaglini, S. (2015). Personalization and patient involvement in decision support systems: Current trends. *IMIA Yearbook of Medical Informatics, 10*, 106–118.

Scheurwegs, E., Luyckx, K., Luyten, L., Daelemans, W., & Van den Bulcke, T. (2015). Data integration of structured and unstructured sources for assigning clinical codes to patient stays. *Journal of the American Medical Informatics Association, 23*, e11–e19.

Sustains. (2014, May 14). *Patient access to their health records becomes a reality in Europe.* Press Releases. European Commission. Retrieved October 30, 2016, from http://www.sustains project.eu/pressreleases?lang=sv

Part III

Management of Integrated Care

Strategic Management and Integrated Care in a Competitive Environment

9

Volker Amelung, Sebastian Himmler, and Viktoria Stein

9.1 Integrated Care as a Strategic Option: Preliminary Remarks

Few integrated care-related issues depend on health system design as much as the question of integrated care as a strategic option. The question is whether integrated care is a suitable competitive positioning strategy in a competition-oriented health care system. For example, a hospital can consider whether it should expand into upstream and/or downstream service sectors in order to improve its strategic position. In addition to improving patient care, other potential targets of focus may include the growth of market share, the creation of barriers to entry for competitors, capacity utilization, the use of synergy potentials, product line expansion, risk diversification and entry into more profitable market segments. Integrated care in this context is regarded as an instrument for achieving pre-defined objectives. Although these goals may be fundamentally very different, the hospital's perspective remains that of a sole trader striving to optimize its position in a competitive environment. The integrated care strategy can in this context be regarded as an approach promising a rapid return on investment, albeit with certain risks.

V. Amelung (✉)
Institute for Epidemology, Social Medicine and Health System Research, Medical School Hannover, Hannover, Germany

inav - Institute for Applied Health Services Research, Berlin, Germany
e-mail: amelung@inav-berlin.de

S. Himmler
inav - Institute for Applied Health Services Research, Berlin, Germany

University of Bayreuth, Bayreuth, Germany

V. Stein
International Foundation for Integrated Care, Oxford, UK

© Springer International Publishing AG 2017
V. Amelung et al. (eds.), *Handbook Integrated Care*,
DOI 10.1007/978-3-319-56103-5_9

133

In a national health care system, integrated care is viewed as an overall strategy for the respective health care system. The focus is not on the various players' strategies, but on the extent to which integrated care is a strategy that benefits the entire system. The ultimate goal is to provide a population the best possible health care while taking both cost and quality considerations into account. However, even within national health care systems such as in the UK, there is a significant degree of competition that exists amongst contractees seeking to work together to provide health and social care services (for example, between independent GP practices, semi-autonomous hospital trusts, social enterprises and the third sector). Hence, even with the most regulated health and care systems, competitive behaviours within system remain. This is a challenge for planners and purchasers of care seeking more integrated solutions since there is a need to broker mutual gain across partners in care with competing interests.

Differentiation is very important because it explains behavioural patterns and can generate a need for regulation. In a competitive environment an organisation's goal will be to be better than the others. Accordingly, the objective cannot be that all players must necessarily be involved. Moreover, where competition exists there are often incentives to obscure information on one's own success factors or withhold them with others (patent protection, for example, is an essential aspect of competition). There is a need for regulatory action because the compatibility of these strategies with the core values of many health care systems is limited.

Important tools needed to implement the competitive strategies described in detail on the following pages are not available or are only partially available to stakeholders in the health care system. Pricing, for example, is an instrument that is unavailable, or only partially available, in nearly all health care systems. Therefore, if a hospital's health care system has a diagnosis related groups-based payment system, it cannot implement any type of pricing strategy—i.e., raise or lower its prices. Pricing in this case is more or less under state control (administrated) and therefore cannot be used as a strategic tool. In product design, there is a similar situation, leaving most health care systems very little room for manoeuvre. State regulations (forbidding hospitals in Germany to fully diversify into outpatient care, for example) and demand and volume planning—the predominant strategies in most health care systems—are the underlying causes. Consequently, many health care players basically have a monopoly that is legitimized by the state. There is almost no other sector where the level of regulation is as extensive as in health care. This by no means exhaustive list of restrictions on our strategic positioning options clearly shows that the health care system is in this respect fundamentally different from other markets, and that strategic options must be considered in the regulatory framework of each country.

Also worth considering is that health care is characterized by a high degree of complexity and change. Unlike many other sectors, its value chains are not clearly definable but are often iterative processes. In many indications, treatment is not a clearly structured process (outpatient → inpatient → rehabilitation), but a series of long-term pathways characterized by the individual patient's comorbidities and courses of treatment. This considerably limits the possibilities for standardization despite the existence of guidelines. What is more, because medical knowledge changes very rapidly (e.g., via the potentials of personalized medicine), the system's structures must be designed to be flexible.

In the following sections, we will mainly focus on the first variant, which is competition-oriented, and will explain what is generally meant by the term "competitive strategy", how they are developed, and which strategic options are available. Rather than concentrating on the strategy development process in general, we will focus specifically on how to utilize integrated care as a strategic management option (e.g., instead of or in addition to concentrating on a focus) and on what factors must be considered when doing so.

9.2   Strategic Management: Definition and Differentiation

In the general management discussion, strategic management is a topic characterized by scores of definitions. Some of these definitions are only minimally different from others, and new definitions are constantly being added. Nevertheless, some cornerstones for understanding strategic management exist that are generally accepted, at least in the scientific discourse (cf. Hungenberg, p. 4f). Decisions are considered strategic if they affect the basic direction of company development and are thus intended to have sustained effect. The aim is to ensure a firm's long-term success and to secure its position in relevant markets. In this case, market positioning and the necessary resource endowments are considered to be at least partially influenceable. The decisive factor is that the focus is on a higher-level perspective, and it is crucial to consider the overall perspective and that of the individual entities.

In the following section, we will start by defining key terms and will then describe various instruments used for aforementioned purpose.

9.2.1   Strategy

The term "strategy" is a greatly over-used term today. It is derived from the Greek word "strategos", which means the art of war. Von Clausewitz (1976, p. 84) defined strategy as "the use of engagements for the object of war". The important thing is that in this concept of strategy the means of achieving the goal rather than the goal itself is an element of the definition. Transferred to the context of integrated care, the goal could be to provide comprehensive care to a given population with a given budget. Integrated care concepts are then implemented in order to achieve this goal.

Mintzberg (1979) defined strategy as "a pattern in a stream of decisions. His well-known "Five Ps for Strategy" (Mintzberg 1992) framework differentiates five definitions of strategy—strategy as plan, pattern, position, perspective and ploy. First, he describes strategy as a plan—a course of action to achieve a desired state or condition. This is based on a number of individual decisions that can be intentional or simply emerge (strategy as pattern). Strategy as position comprises recognizing attractive positions and striving to get there. Due to the higher-layer, he also describes strategy as a perspective. Strategy as a ploy refers to the fact that tactics are used in the game of outwitting competitors.

9.2.2   Principles of Management

The term "management" can be defined as the organization of processes and structures. General distinctions can be made between different management functions, institutions, and levels. Management functions and responsibilities, depending on the respective definition, may include planning and organization, leadership and supervision, as well as personnel placement (see the respective chapters). The institution of management refers to the hierarchy level of an organization. The functions associated with management vary considerably by country and cultural region. Normative, strategic, and operational management levels can be distinguished. Normative management defines the self-image of a company or organization and thus sets the foundations for its legitimation. It finds expression in corporate governance and corporate culture. The importance of strategic management, which is effectively positioned between normative and operational management, was already discussed. Operative management is the level involved with converting strategic concepts into concrete measures.

9.3   The Strategic Planning Process

In strategic planning, organizations decide which markets they want compete in and with which products and at what prices, and how they wish to position themselves in the competition. Strategic planning thus addresses:

- An organisation's range of services and the values of the players involved,
- An organisation's relationship to other market players or stakeholders and

    Assessment of developments in the markets and one's own organization.

    Traditionally, this workflow starts by performing a strategic analysis and then formulating and implementing a strategy derived from it. The two basic types of strategic analyses are internal analysis and external analysis. This will be explained later in terms of a Strengths-Weaknesses-Opportunities-Threats (SWOT) analysis. Based on the knowledge gained from the analysis, the company identifies the available strategic options and chooses one, which it then implements and, by necessity, monitors continuously. Since this course of action involves constantly recurring tasks, it can be characterized as an iterative process. It does not need to be a formalized process, but can also occur implicitly by people taking an appropriate course of action.

    Methodologically speaking, the basic strategic process is fundamentally the same in health care as in other industries. However, a number of players in the health care sector place less emphasis on strategic planning and generally tend to focus on filling health care contracts. Nevertheless, the question of how a health care company wishes to position itself becomes more and more important as the level of competitiveness in which it must operate increases. In contrast to other branches of business, health care companies generally have less room to manoeuvre (for example, due to health care contracts), and it takes much longer to implement changes.

9.4 Instruments for Strategic Planning

A range of instruments are used for strategic planning in practice. Two essential concepts will be discussed in detail below: the classic SWOT analysis, which differentiates strengths and weaknesses and opportunities and threats, and Porter's analysis of competitive environments, which is much more strategically oriented and analyses five competitive forces.

9.4.1 SWOT Analysis

In order to decide on a strategy, one must first collect and analyse all relevant information. This has become increasingly difficult in the age of "information overload." The Strengths-Weaknesses-Opportunities-Threats (SWOT) matrix, developed at Harvard Business School in the 1960s, is a simple analytical framework for operationalising the indispensable strategic position assessments (Kotler et al. 2010, p. 30). The collected information is divided into four quadrants: the strengths (S) and weaknesses (W) of internal factors, and the opportunities (O) and threats (T) of external factors. The strategy to be formulated is, therefore, the result of opportunities and threats arising from the changing economic and political environment in which a company operates as well as the strengths and weaknesses of the company (Kohlöffel 2000, p. 155). The most difficult step of SWOT analysis is to identify the strengths and weaknesses of a company's internal factors and link them to the opportunities and threats of its external factors in a meaningful manner. For example, a company looks for ways to utilize its strengths so as to avoid potential risks (David 2011, p. 210). The elements of a SWOT matrix and examples of the four dimensions are shown in Fig. 9.1. The different types of strategies resulting from combining the dimensions are explained below.

The four basic types of strategies delineated by SWOT analysis are SO, ST, WO and WT. SO strategies use a business's internal strengths to take advantage of external opportunities. This represents the ideal case. WO, WT and ST strategies are aimed at getting the company in a position to be able to use SO strategies (David 2011, p. 210). In health care, for instance, a hospital could exploit its above-average knowledge about the treatment of a given disease in the outpatient setting. Rigid sectoral boundaries have prevented this until now, but integrated care provides opportunities to overcome this.

WO strategies involve utilizing changes in the business environment (e.g., new legislation) as an opportunity to convert internal improvement potentials into strengths to ultimately be able to use an SO strategy. In many cases, great external opportunities exist, but internal weaknesses prevent a company from exploiting them. One possible WO strategy is to acquire human capital in order to obtain the

External factors / Internal factors	Opportunities • New business segments • Reforms	Threats • New competitors • Market saturation
Strengths • Know-how • Market position	SO strategies	ST strategies
Weaknesses • Growing costs • Poor brand recognition	WO strategies	WT strategies

Fig. 9.1 SWOT analysis [original illustration based on Kohlöffel (2000), p. 155)]

necessary skills in the area of opportunity. Even if, for instance, a service provider has weaknesses in communication and IT, it can use a government-supported e-Health initiative as an opportunity to invest in its IT capabilities. It can do this either by hiring external IT service providers or by educating and training its existing personnel. Another WO strategy is to form technology partnerships with competitors. Such partnerships can be established within the framework of an integrated care concept (Kohlöffel 2000, p. 156; David 2011, p. 210).

In ST strategies, a company uses existing strengths to ward off impending external threats. The goal is to avoid or at least mitigate risks (Kohlöffel 2000, p. 156). If, for instance, the corporate success of a financially well-situated hospital is threatened by an intensely competitive environment, the hospital could use its strength (money) to acquire a competitor. In addition to mitigating the competitive situation, this would allow the hospital to benefit from the economies of scale. Integrated care also provides opportunities for approaches in this regard. Intense competition for patients can be lessened by embedding the hospital in a network. This also serves to secure patient streams.

WT strategies are defensive tactics that aim to overcome internal weaknesses and avoid external risks. Here, the greatest changes must be made and innovative solutions found to ensure the viability of a company or division. If too many weaknesses and risks collide, options such as the divestment of business units, mergers or workforce reductions must be considered as well (David 2011, p. 211). To illustrate a possible WT scenario, take for example a networked health care provider with a small, low-profit gym who is looking for a way out of that highly competitive segment. Divestment of this business unit is a possible WT strategy.

Many important points must be considered when performing a SWOT analysis. Strengths and weaknesses should be portrayed in purely descriptive terms without interpretation. If, for example, a given characteristic cannot be clearly defined as a weakness/risk or strength/opportunity, it should be included in both categories in order to avoid interpretation. The information-gathering process should purposefully focus on collecting data for the external analysis, which takes much more time and effort. Conversely, it is relatively easy to obtain information on a company's internal strengths and weaknesses, for example, via controlling and benchmarking.

It is also important to mention that a SWOT analysis should attempt to be as abstract and descriptive as possible. Since it does not make recommendations or set priorities, a SWOT analysis can only serve as a starting point for determining a company's strategic direction (Kotler et al. 2010, pp. 30–33). Still, it is a very useful tool for visualizing a company's current situation. Nevertheless, SWOT analyses are just one out of numerous strategic management tools.

9.4.2   Analysis of Value Chains and Competitive Environments

Porter's value chain (Porter 1999) is another potential analysis model used to analyse a business's relative competitive position. This analytical tool systematically tries to explain the causes of competitive advantages based on all of a company's activities (Bea and Haas 2009, p. 120). A value chain is a set of activities that a business must perform in order to produce and sell a product or service. In addition to a company's own value chain, the upstream and downstream value chains of its suppliers and customers play an important role (Porter 1999, pp. 67–68).

The value chain itself can be defined as the sum total of the value-added yields of the individual value activities and the profit margin. The profit margin is defined as the difference between the added value and cost of all activities (Porter 1999, p. 68). There are two basic types of activities in the value chain: primary activities and support activities (Fig. 9.2). *Primary activities* can be divided into five categories and are responsible for the primary production and sale of a product. *Support activities* serve to support the primary activities.

As shown in the illustration, the value chain activities are geared towards the traditional operational functions of logistics, production and sales. The novel aspect of Porter's concept is that all parts of the value chain are regarded as sources of costs and differentiation advantages and, thus, of competitive advantages. However, Porter's model does not directly show how to achieve strategic advantages within a given value activity (Bea and Haas 2009, p. 121). Porter explicitly states that the value chains of suppliers and distribution channels (Fig. 9.3) or, more generally, of players operating downstream or upstream also contribute to the margin. They are part of the total costs to the customers and, thus, are factors affecting a company's strategic competitive advantages (Porter 1999, p. 68).

In health care, the integration of upstream and downstream players could also improve a hospital's competitive position by helping it to better control its profit margins. An integrated value chain system in health care is illustrated below based on the concepts in Fig. 9.4.

In order to formulate a competitive strategy, a company must be in a relationship with its environment (Porter 2013, p. 37). Because the external factors in Porter's value chains only exist in the form of upstream and downstream value systems, Porter developed another instrument that specifically addresses the competitive environment: the Five Forces model. The intensity of competition within an industry is the central factor that shapes the industry structure and business

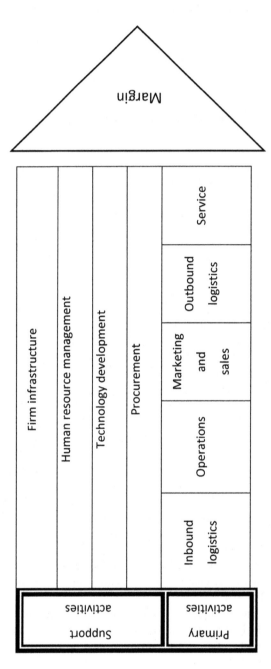

Fig. 9.2 Porter's value chain (Porter 1999, p. 66)

environment in which a company operates. Porter identified five competitive forces that determine the intensity of competition. Porter's Five Forces model (Fig. 9.5) defines the five forces driving industry competition as rivalry among existing firms, the bargaining power of suppliers, the bargaining power of buyers, the threat of substitute products or services, and potential entrants or competitors (Swayne et al. 2008, pp. 94–95; Porter 2013, p. 37). The higher the collective strength of these competitive forces, the lower the profit potential in the respective industry (Kotler et al. 2010, p. 47).

Fig. 9.3 Porter's value chain (Porter 1999, p. 64)

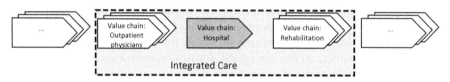

Fig. 9.4 Integrated value chain (VC) system in health care (original illustration)

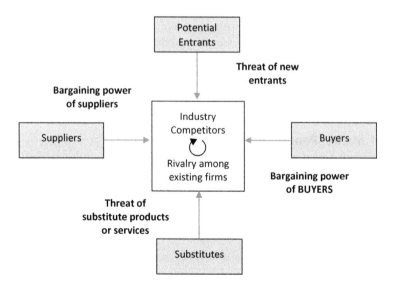

Fig. 9.5 Porter's Five Forces model for analysis of the competitive environment (Porter 2013, p. 38)

Due to high barriers to entry, the threat of new competitors is much lower in health care than in other industries. Hospital planning considerations, licensing requirements for outpatient clinics, and a large number of regulations prevent free market access. This is complicated by the fact that there are relatively rigid restrictions on the range of products that can be offered in health care, and alternative products cannot be introduced to the health care market as easily as in other industries (Swayne et al. 2008, pp. 95–98). An integrated care concept can allow for exceptions in some circumstances, Standard care models with sharp sector boundaries can be replaced, at least in part, by implementing a networked integrated care system. Moreover, integrated care can provide companies in the healthcare industry a competitive advantage because integrated care systems give them the potential to internalize suppliers and buyers and thus decrease their bargaining power.

9.5   Options for Strategic Positioning

A range of different strategic concepts are used in practice. Two basic concepts will be discussed in detail below: Ansoff's Product/Market Matrix from the 1960s focuses on the fundamental question of which products should be supplied in which markets. Porter, on the other hand, focuses on uniqueness as perceived by the customer and the scope of a company's strategy.

9.5.1   Ansoff's Product/Market Matrix

Ansoff's product/market matrix (Ansoff 1966; Fig. 9.6) is a tool for analysing corporate growth potential that divides the corporate environment into four possible product/market combinations characterized by the dimensions "existing" and "new" to delineate four different growth strategies that can be used by firms or hospitals: market penetration, product development, market development, and diversification (Ansoff 1966, pp. 131–132).

9.5.1.1 Market Penetration
Market penetration is a growth strategy intended to increase a firm's market share in a current market segment. The firm can usually accomplish this by increasing its market share by using various marketing instruments or by expanding its market

PRODUCT / MARKET	Present	New
Present	Market penetration	Product development
New	Market development	Diversification

Fig. 9.6 Ansoff's product/market matrix (Ansoff 1966, p. 132)

volume (Waldecker 1995, p. 136). The main goal is to increase the market share of products (increased number of cases) and the fastest way to do so is through mergers and acquisitions.

Whereas companies outside the health care sector are usually relatively free to determine what goes into their marketing mix, companies in the healthcare sector are often very limited in their choice of marketing instruments. Communications policy is the only marketing tool available because the fixed standard care catalogue and fixed fee per case rules do not allow for independent product and pricing policies; moreover, distribution policy is hardly relevant in patient-related services. Opportunities for action via communication policy are also extremely limited due to statutory provisions (e.g., the Law on Advertising in the Health Care System) designed to protect the patient (Schlüchtermann 2013, pp. 176–177). Integrated care provides an additional option because patient flows are easier to steer through a networked regional system. This creates opportunities for service providers to increase their market share.

Increasing the market volume can also lead to increased market penetration and thus growth. From a business perspective, the aim is to increase the volume of utilization and to arouse latent needs in the population, i.e., to acquire customers who did not use a given service before (Waldecker 1995, p. 136). If a service provider chooses to generate growth this way, it must first determine whether there is objective evidence of such a need in the population. This task is much more difficult for an independent service provider than for a member of a supply network because members can selectively refer patients to the services offered by other members of the network.

9.5.1.2 Product Development

Product development is a growth strategy that aims at introducing new or more or less extensively modified products into existing markets (Ansoff 1966, pp. 132–136). Despite major restrictions in health care, providers of care still have different opportunities for product development. They can, for example, supplement existing health care services by adding certain characteristics and thus marginally alter the services such that they offer (seemingly) greater benefit to the patient. Another product development option is to use an innovative technology or treatment method that is markedly superior to the existing technology or method in order to generate additional revenues in an existing market (Waldecker 1995, pp. 132–137). Potentials for growth through product development can also be exploited by offering related services in areas where needs have not yet been satisfied, but the existing care contract of the respective service provider must be taken into account. For example: A hospital could set up a cardiac catheter laboratory to meet the additional needs of its existing cardiac patients and thus generate more revenue. A second possibility is to develop and provide specific prevention services for an existing customer segment. If, for instance, a care provider treats a lot of overweight patients, they could offer their patients additional services such as sports or cooking classes. Integrated care gives product developers in health care the opportunity to place truly new products on the market through the integration of other service providers. Integrated care can generate potentials for growth in this industry where product development opportunities are greatly limited.

9.5.1.3 Market Development

The third potential area of growth is market development. According to Ansoff's Product/Market Matrix, market development consists of introducing virtually unchanged services into a new market segment (Waldecker 1995, p. 137). The new market segment could be either a customer group that the company has not addressed fully or a segment where the company is not yet regionally present. Mergers or takeovers are effective external growth strategies in the latter case. However, they have the disadvantage of being either very expensive or associated with the partial abandonment of corporate sovereignty. An integrated care contract can help to avoid these disadvantages. For example, the creation of a network can enable a hospital to address customer groups in yet untapped regions as thus reap the benefits of broader regional distribution through network partners.

9.5.1.4 Diversification

Diversification is the last of the four growth strategies in Ansoff's Product/Market Matrix (Ansoff 1966, pp. 131–139). The aim of diversification is to achieve corporate growth by increasing the number of branches of industry in which a business is involved (Alberts and Segall 2003, p. 31). Diversification can be accomplished by creating new products and services or related products and services that expand the existing portfolio and offering them on untapped markets to generate additional revenue. Diversification strategies can be classified as horizontal, vertical and lateral. In **horizontal diversification**, a hospital adds new services that are technically or commercially related to current hospital services and offers them in a new market segment. **Vertical diversification** in the hospital environment is a growth strategy along the healthcare value chain that integrates upstream and downstream services into the range of services provided by the hospital. This can, for example, enable a hospital to enter the outpatient, rehabilitation or nursing market. Integrated care provides many opportunities for vertical diversification. In an integrated care system, all players along the healthcare value chain have the possibility to tap upstream and downstream markets. **Lateral diversification** gives care providers almost unlimited possibilities for growth because it allows the provider to market new products or services that are technically or commercially unrelated to the original hospital services (Arnold 2008, pp. 553–554).

9.5.2 Porter's Competitive Strategies

Whereas Porter's Five Forces model tries to explain business success based on the attractiveness of an industry, Porter's generic competitive strategies deal with strategic considerations. Porter developed this concept to more deeply analyse strategies that will result in sustainable competitive advantages over direct

COMPETITIVE ADVANTAGE

		Low cost	Uniqueness perceived by the customer
	Broad	**1. Cost leadership**	**2. Differentiation**
TARGET SCOPE	Narrow	**3A. Focus strategy** (low cost)	**3B. Focus strategy** (differentiation)

Fig. 9.7 Porter's generic strategies to sustain a competitive advantage (Porter 1999, p. 38)

competitors within an industry. According to Porter, the number of strategic opportunities to gain long-term competitive advantage over a competitor, or competitors, is very limited. Although other strategies may be successful for companies operating in less competitive markets, it is generally very useful to follow Porter's recommendations in most industries (Müller 2007, p. 7). As a rule, a company must be fully committed to a given strategy to ensure that it is executed effectively. The basic types of strategic options, which will be described in detail below, arise from two levels: *competitive advantage* and *target scope* (Fig. 9.7). The two basic types of competitive advantage according to Porter are low cost and differentiation. These advantages arise when a company's strengths allow it to deal with the five competitive forces better than its competitors. Market scope, or the width of the competitive field, is the second level of this strategy matrix. Porter states that companies operate either in the overall market (industry-wide) or focus on a narrow niche market (particular segment only). This yields the four ideal types of generic strategies illustrated below (Porter 1999, pp. 37–38).

Hybrid strategies, Porter maintains, are possible but are only successful in exceptional cases, for example, when there is low-level competition.

9.5.2.1 Cost Leadership

Cost leadership is a competitive strategy in which a firm strives to gain a cost advantage over its competitors in a number of industry segments via a number of measures (Porter 1999, p. 74). Many of these measures are based on exploiting economies of scale and scope. Relevant instruments for this include increasing the number of products, establishing an efficient corporate size, selectively exploiting experience in cost reduction, and minimizing costs in all business units (Müller 2007, pp. 12–14). The ultimate goal of this strategy is to become the industry's absolute lowest cost producer. This protects a company from the competitive forces in the industry because the cost advantages resulting from the economies of scale create barriers to entry for competitors. Secondly, the cost leader's earnings remain higher than those of its competitors, even in highly competitive markets. Cost leadership also strengthens a company's negotiating position against its customers and suppliers (Porter 2013, pp. 74–75). Integrated care also gives health care players opportunities for cost leadership. Cost reductions can be achieved through better integration of upstream and downstream service providers.

9.5.2.2 Differentiation

Differentiation is a competitive strategy in which a company strives to modify a product based on existing or latent consumer needs to the extent that the product will be perceived as unique within the industry and can be sold at a higher price because of its uniqueness (Porter 1999, pp. 40–41). Unlike cost leadership, differentiation focuses on the supply side rather than the resource side. Offering additional services, creating noticeable quality differences, and establishing a "brand experience" are examples of differentiation strategies (Müller 2007, p. 15). The uniqueness of its product protects a company from competitive forces and can increase profitability.

9.5.2.3 Low Cost and Differentiation Focus Strategies

The two focus strategies, which are also called *niche strategies*, follow the competitive advantages of cost leadership and differentiation. The difference, however, is that the company then only addresses a certain segment of the market. Focus strategies are based on the assumption that a very narrow strategic focus leads to advantages over competitors within a given niche. Cost leadership and uniqueness can be achieved more efficiently in a small market segment than in the entire market (Porter 2013, pp. 77–79).

9.5.2.4 "Stuck in the Middle"

Another scenario by Porter is called "stuck in the middle". This occurs when a company does not succeed in focussing on only one of the discussed strategies, but is virtually stuck between the two. The company then has no competitive advantages and will have under-average performance over the long term because other companies striving to achieve cost leadership, differentiation or focus will achieve a better competitive position in each segment. The way out of this situation is for the company to make a conscious decision for one of these strategies (Porter 1999, p. 44).

9.6 Integrated Care as a Quality Improvement Strategy

It should be emphasized that integrated care is a means to an end, not an end in itself. It serves merely as a strategy aimed at providing better services for patients and populations. The aim of integrated care is to improve quality, not to reduce costs. As illustrated throughout this book, an integrated care strategy may be implemented on different levels, but in order to be sustainable and effective, it must permeate all tiers of the healthcare value chain—from the system level to the individual level. When health care managers accept these basic principles, they can learn a lot from classic management literature and practical experience in other sectors (6 P et al. 2006).

The management side of health care has long been neglected because many care providers consider it to be a necessary part of business, but not of health care. However, due to the manifold and often stated challenges of the twenty-first century and the slow speed of development new forms of care delivery, such as integrated care, the need for more strategic thinking, planning, management and implementation approaches has become evident. As described in this chapter, strategic management requires not only a clear vision and common goals shared by all stakeholders involved, but also a thorough understanding of one's partners, providers and "clients," i.e. patients. This is essential for implementing changes in the process of transitioning to integrated care as well as for realising sustainable integrated care solutions. The following chapters will go more into detail on these and other key elements of integrated care design, implementation and management.

References

6 P, Goodwin, N., Peck, E., & Freeman, T. (2006). *Managing networks of 21st century organizations*. Basingstoke: Palgrave-McMillan.

Alberts, W. W., & Segall, J. E. (2003). *The corporate merger*. Chicago: Beard Books.

Ansoff, H. I. (1966). *Management-Strategie*. München: Verlag Moderne Industrie.

Arnold, A. (2008). Marketing. In B. Schmidt-Rettig & S. Eichhorn (Eds.), *Krankenhaus-Managementlehre: Theorie und Praxis eines integrierten Konzepts, Kohlhammer Krankenhaus* (1. Aufl., pp. 521–583). Stuttgart: Kohlhammer.

Bea, F. X., & Haas, J. (2009). *Strategisches Management, Grundwissen der Ökonomik Betriebswirtschaftslehre* (5., neu bearb. Aufl., Vol. 1458). Stuttgart: Lucius & Lucius.

David, F. R. (2011). *Strategic management: Concepts* (13th ed., Global ed.). Boston: Pearson.

Kohlöffel, K. (2000). *Strategisches Management: Alle Chancen nutzen - neue Geschäfte erschliessen; mit großer Praxis-Fallstudie*. München: Hanser.

Kotler, P., Berger, R., & Bickhoff, N. (2010). *The quintessence of strategic management: What you really need to know to survive in business*. Heidelberg: Springer.

Mintzberg, H. (1979). *The structuring of organizations*. Englewood Cliffs, NJ: Prentice Hall.

Mintzberg, H. (1992) Five Ps for strategy. In H Mintzberg and JB Quinn (Eds.), The strategy process, pp 12-19, 1992, Prentice-Hall, Englewood Cliffs, NJ.

Müller, B. (2007). *Porters Konzept generischer Wettbewerbsstrategien: Präzisierung und empirische Überprüfung, Gabler Edition Wissenschaft* (1. Aufl.). Wiesbaden: Dt. Univ.-Verl.

Porter, M. E. (1999). *Wettbewerbsvorteile: Spitzenleistungen erreichen und behaupten* (5., durchges. und erw. Aufl.) Frankfurt/Main: Campus-Verlag.

Porter, M. E. (2013). *Wettbewerbsstrategie: Methoden zur Analyse von Branchen und Konkurrenten* (12, erweiterte und aktualisierte Auflage). Frankfurt am Main: Campus.

Schlüchtermann, J. (2013). *Betriebswirtschaft und Management im Krankenhaus: Grundlagen und Praxis* (1., Auflage). Berlin: MWV Medizinisch Wissenschaftliche Verlagsgesellschaft.

Swayne, L. E., Duncan, W. J., & Ginter, P. M. (2008). *Strategic management of health care organizations* (6th ed.). Hoboken, NJ: Wiley.

Von Clausewitz, C. (1976). *On war* (M. Howard & P. Paret, Trans.). Princeton: Princeton University Press.

Waldecker, P. (1995). *Strategische Alternativen in der Unternehmensentwicklung*. Wiesbaden: Deutscher Universitätsverlag.

Governance and Accountability

10

Sara Mallinson and Esther Suter

Governance may not be a top priority when debating health care transformation for the twenty-first century but it is a critical instrument to strengthen public and institutional performance (Van Kersbergen and Van Waarden 2004; Chhotray & Stoker 2009). Governance matters, and never more so than in times of crisis. "For example, since 2008, in the UK approximately one in three NHS foundation trusts have been subject to formal regulatory action on at least one occasion, with poor governance a contributing factor in almost all the cases." (Monitor et al. 2014, p. 4). The first two sections of this chapter cover theoretical aspects, including how governance and accountability are conceptualized and specific considerations of governance and accountability in integrated health systems. The latter two sections focus on the practical aspects of implementing governance and accountability into integrated health systems and the tools needed to support its implementation. We have tried to present a balanced view by drawing on a wide range of published literature, thus, while many of the innovative examples we discuss originate in the UK, we believe, they can easily be applied in to types of health system.

10.1 What Is Governance and Accountability?

In the following, governance is understood as the policy tools and processes needed to steer a system towards population health goals (Barbazza and Tello 2014; Task Team 2013). Governance is a multi-faceted concept that became an established part of the health system lexicon in the early 2000s. With the publication of the World

S. Mallinson
Alberta Health Services Calgary, Workforce Research & Evaluation, Calgary, Canada
e-mail: Sara.Mallinson@albertahealthservices.ca

E. Suter (✉)
Faculty of Social Work, University of Calgary, Calgary, Canada
e-mail: Suter@ucalgary.ca

© Springer International Publishing AG 2017   149
V. Amelung et al. (eds.), *Handbook Integrated Care*,
DOI 10.1007/978-3-319-56103-5_10

Health Organization (WHO) landmark report "Health Systems: Improving Performance" (WHO 2000), governance was adopted and adapted to health system contexts. Stewardship, leadership, strategic direction and regulation became important concepts to actualize health system priorities. The later 2000s saw the publication of a burgeoning literature on how to achieve large scale change, including WHO's 2007 'building blocks' framework for health system strengthening (WHO 2007). This reflected governments' ongoing struggle to manage health needs along with increasing health services expenditure.

The literature contains a number of different conceptualizations of health governance. They share some common features but none are universally accepted (Barbazza and Tello 2014; Mikkelsen-Lopez et al. 2011; Brinkerhoff and Bossert 2008):

- Governance must encompass all aspects of managing health services delivery to support health system goals, including financing, human resources, information and medicine and technology.
- A systems perspective is required to understand the interdependencies between these domains and devise appropriate governance mechanisms.
- Governance mechanisms and processes must support achievement of overall health systems goals; this requires a number of conditions:
  - Clear accountability of key actors to beneficiaries,
  - Responsible leadership and a clear vision,
  - An equitable policy process that allows influencing of policymaking by all players equally,
  - Transparency,
  - Sufficient state capacity to manage health care policy and service delivery effectively, and
  - Public engagement and participation.

There is agreement that 'good' governance leads to health improvement (Brinkerhoff and Bossert 2008; Mikkelsen-Lopez et al. 2011), but the lack of clarity in the nomenclature and in models and measures of governance has failed to produce clear evidence on the impact of governance models (Barbazza and Tello 2014; van Olmen et al. 2012). Developing appropriate governance processes that respond to the complexities of health care systems is important but so is understanding the situations in which governance is working and is delivering the outcomes desired by all stakeholders.

Most descriptions of governance highlight accountability as an important governance tool. Well-defined accountability structures, along with high-quality systems to monitor processes and outcomes towards agreed upon goals, are intertwined with successful governance (George 2003; Brinkerhoff 2004; Hammer et al. 2011; Lewis and Pettersson 2009; Barbazza and Tello 2014; Suter and Mallinson 2015; Baez-Camargo 2011).

Accountability discussions tend to focus on the relationships between different stakeholder groups on three levels (Fig. 10.1). Firstly, there is accountability at the level of the state, which may include various ministries (health, finance, social care,

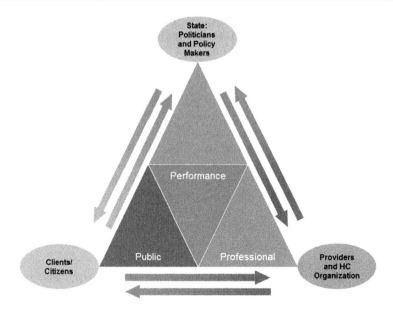

Fig. 10.1 Accountability relationships in integrated healthcare systems. Adapted from Brinkerhoff and Bossert (2008)

education). Secondly, there is accountability at the level of healthcare organizations, regulatory bodies, and service providers. Thirdly, there is accountability to clients/citizens (individuals and families, communities, and populations). Accountability mechanisms with the State have traditionally been vertical and unidirectional (Kickbusch and Behrendt 2013) with a focus on financial accountability and health system performance (Brinkerhoff 2003, 2004; Deber 2014). Service providers and healthcare organizations are accountable to state funders for the ethical use of resources and to clients for service delivery. Mechanisms focus on organizational performance and oversight and service delivery according to legal, ethical and professional standards (Brinkerhoff 2003, 2004; Deber 2014; Fooks and Maslove 2004). Failure to meet the goals and objectives needs to trigger real and enforceable actions. Lastly, accountability to clients/citizens has a number of potential functions: helping the public to hold the state and local healthcare organizations to account on electoral promises and services; supporting public engagement through increased transparency which, in turn, is a mechanism for checking that health systems represent the public's interest, values, needs and expectations (Brinkerhoff 2003). The interweaving of transparent public accountability mechanisms with improved public engagement can lead to better informed, accountable and legitimate decision-making (Abelson and Gauvin 2004; Kickbusch and Behrendt 2013).

10.2 Appropriate, Agile, and Effective: New Directions for Governance and Accountability in Integrated Health Systems

In the second decade of the twenty-first century, the thinking around governance underwent a shift. Governments, organizations, communities and individuals began grappling with the changing global context in which influences on health and well-being transcend traditional boundaries in an increasingly globalized 'knowledge society' (Wilke 2007; Kickbusch and Gleicher 2014). This has required a re-focusing on whole-system health, one which cuts across political, economic, and social landscapes, and demands an evolution in governance models (WHO 2013). This has in turn led to a distinction being drawn between health governance (i.e., structures, processes and mechanisms that govern health care) and governance for health. Governance for health is a much broader idea, tying in wider changes in globalization, knowledge, participation, and co-production of health (Kickbusch and Gleicher 2012).

In parallel with calls to refocus on the broader idea of governance for health there has been an evolution in health service integration. Integrated care systems, networks or models, often regarded as Complex Adaptive Systems, are moving beyond horizontal integration between organizations at same level or delivering similar services. There are efforts to integrate more broadly across community-based services, including other sectors, and partnerships between communities, primary and acute care [i.e., vertical integration, Evans et al. (2013)]. The challenge is that many innovative cross-sectoral service arrangements require more flexibility and different accountability mechanisms to initiate and sustain change. They create new and ambiguous governance and accountability relationships (Brinkerhoff 2004; Deber 2014; Fooks and Maslove 2004; Kickbusch and Behrendt 2013; Maybin et al. 2011). In this context, the focus is increasingly on relationships and alliances, management of boundaries, shared information, best practice guidelines, and establishing a common culture.

In addition, organizations have to respond to an increasingly informed public that demands better leadership in publically funded organizations and greater accountability for allocation and use of resources (WHO 2008). Some authors maintain that creating a strong public voice through appropriate governance and accountability is critical for the success of integrated health systems (Abelson and Gauvin 2004; CIHR 2012; Fooks and Maslove 2004). There is also a key role for people in monitoring system quality and performance, including reporting on people's experiences in the health system. These broader trends—global interdependence, a new understanding of the complexity of health, the changing roles of citizens in co-production of health and health care—are the impetus for new and smarter governance approaches (Kickbusch and Behrendt 2013). Governance and accountability processes have to keep pace with the diverse contexts within which they operate, and be responsive to people in diverse roles and relationships. A recent high-level review of governance in UK health services (Grant Thornton 2015) suggested that partnerships needed agile governance rather than the command and control styles of more traditional, siloed models of health service delivery. The review also noted the need for a mature risk management strategy and for genuine empowerment for governance boards so their 'risk appetite' (Bullivant and Corbett-Nolan 2012) allows innovative arrangements to flourish. The problem for health system leaders is that these dimensions of new governance depend on a degree of culture change.

The idea of 'soft governance' to support collaborative care across multiple stakeholders is not new, but, as Fierlbeck (2014) argues, it has become particularly relevant as governments grapple with complex health problems across overlapping jurisdictions. She concludes that new 'experimental' governance models need to respond to limitations of hierarchical, vertical governance arrangements that do not allow a constellation of interests to negotiate alternative health care models. Kickbusch and Gleicher (2014) highlight global examples of whole-of government (WOG) and whole of society (WOS) approaches to manage complex policy processes that govern health and might be fitting for integrated health systems. WOG indicates a commitment to health at all levels of government with joint working across sectors as a core premise. WOS goes beyond institutions and influences/ mobilizes communities and other relevant policy sector, media and the private sector to co-create health. WOS approaches emphasize coordination through normative values and trust building amongst actors, which ultimately strengthens resiliency of communities. Their focus is on new forms of communication and collaboration in complex network settings, using social movements and negotiation to align diverse priorities, values and approaches.

Overall, this new vision points to the diffusion of governance from a state/health services centred model to a collaborative model where a range of actors including state, private industry, the public, media and international organizations across levels co-produce governance by Kickbusch and Gleicher (2012).

10.3 Implementing Innovation: Next Steps for Governance and Accountability in Integrated Health Systems

Although many health systems in developed nations are experimenting with integrated health care systems, recent policy initiatives and implementation projects in the UK provide a timely and interesting example of the drive to move integration forward. Successive UK governments have explored ways to tackle health system pressures through integrated health systems. Substantive policy changes in the Health and Social Care Act (Department of Health 2012) and increasing focus on the challenges of improving health care quality compel a new look at how services are organized, regulated, monitored, and directed. In the following, we describe these new developments in more detail with special consideration of their impact on governance.

In *NHS Five Year Forward,* the National Health Service sets out a vision for an updated agenda View (NHS England et al. 2014) that reflects the significant changes in science and technology and the increasing complexity of health and social care delivery. Central to the vision is a renewed focus on prevention, public health and primary care through new partnerships that cut across traditional boundaries. A combined health and social care budget and capitated arrangements are some of the innovations outlined on the financial side. There are also a series of new care models in primary, emergency and specialist care, many of them focusing on multidisciplinary teams and networks. The challenge, as encapsulated in this plan, is the need for meaningful local flexibility in service delivery models, funding mechanisms and regulatory requirement to accommodate diverse contexts. These are vital to build new relationships with patients and the community that enhance patient empowerment and engagement in care decisions.

The new care models envisioned in the NHS Five Year Forward View will have implications on all domains of governance and accountability. Shared budgets and capitated arrangements will challenge how funds are distributed and managed between social and health care partners; local flexibility in service delivery models puts more onus on service providers and organizations to maintain quality standards; the focus on patient and communities demands more effective mechanisms for engagement and public reporting. Two commissioned reports have explored the governance challenges inherent in the new vision in more detail.

The Dalton Review (Dalton 2014) explored the organizational forms needed to support the vision of the renewed NHS. The review strongly promotes the creation of different organisational models that are adaptable to local contexts. Organisational models comprise the structures of governance, accountability and management to achieve specific aims and objectives in delivering services. The report outlines a number of different models of service integration with different types of partnership and degrees of integration. They caution that embracing different models would require a shift in mind-set of boards towards achieving what is best for patients and communities through joint ownership. Such collaborative arrangements require careful consideration of governance structures and processes that will likely have to deviate from the status quo.

Building on the Dalton Review, the NHS Governance Review (Grant-Thornton 2015) offers a comprehensive discussion of NHS governance challenges emerging from the Five Year Forward View vision. In a similar vein to Dalton (2014), the authors stress the need for "…NHS leaders to engender cultural change, support innovation and build a modern workforce—all will need to be underpinned by robust corporate and quality governance arrangements." (p. 5). The report authors argue that cultural changes depend on transparent and robust performance monitoring across all major care pathways, especially where they are linked to payment mechanisms. However, their survey indicated ongoing uncertainty about accountability and delegation of authority between Care Commissioning Groups and NHS Trusts (p. 2). Collaboration and partnership governance with all health and wellbeing partners (including social enterprises, third sector, HealthWatch, and private sector) is essential but the relationships and systems are still evolving.

10.3.1 Vanguard Integration Sites

The Five Year Forward View is using three waves of Vanguard sites to operationalise different integrated care models (NHS England 2014). All share the fundamental aims of improving patient experience and continuity of care while also dealing with the financial and resource pressures facing the NHS. This translates into four core values for the re-design: clinical engagement; patient engagement; local ownership; national support.

The Northumbria Healthcare NHS Foundation Trust, for example, is one of eight Vanguard sites to spearhead the implementation of an integrated primary care-acute care model (https://www.northumbria.nhs.uk/about-us/vanguard). The trust already had a strong integration record and effective governance and accountability mechanisms in place to advance the integration agenda. An established Integration Committee had created a detailed integration plan (Freake 2013) and a dashboard to track progress against integration objectives, including patient experience.

As a Vanguard site, the focus is on the development of the primary care-acute care systems integration with partners at Northumberland Care Commissioning Group and Northumberland County Council (https://www.northumbria.nhs.uk/sites/default/files/images/Vanguard_270815_LR.PDF). Specifically, Northumberland Vanguard will create a new Specialist Emergency Care Hospital that will act as an extension of primary care to create 'hubs' of primary care provision across the county. This new model will allow patients to access their primary care physician 7 days a week. Cutting across organisational boundaries, the model will enhance access to community nursing services and coordinated discharge through shared information technology. The ultimate goal is to provide care closer to home.

Although the launch of the first group of Vanguards in spring 2015 was reportedly met with lots of goodwill, they have a difficult balancing act to perform. They must embrace local context with innovative, experimental forms of service delivery while also setting the pace for system-wide transformation. Vanguards use a 'learn as we go' approach that emphasizes the importance of ongoing monitoring of outcomes for patients, staff and the wider population. Sharing of processes, metrics, and learnings from high performing integrated systems is also being encouraged, and all Vanguards who are implementing variations of a component will be asked to participate in 'action research' (NHS England 2015, p. 9).

This approach to health care reform may seem much riskier because it builds on demand-led rather than supply-led local service planning and extends well beyond traditional organizational boundaries. Collaborative leadership, commissioning and delivery of care will depend on agile governance supported boards that are open to risk. Clearly, this kind of innovation depends on leadership that advances system-wide cultural change, but there are concerns about whether organizations can overcome the inertia that has characterized previous cycles of reform. Vanguards will have access to appropriate national, clinical, and program expertise to collaborate in the change process. As such they will be able to share clinical pathways, outcome based commissioning, and improvement methodologies. Evidence-based, replicable models and frameworks built for scale are the driving force for the implementation process. Joint leaders and supporting groups are responsible for developing processes to monitor impact for all stakeholders at national and local levels to support shared learning. Identifying appropriate tools to measuring patient-centred care is a particular area of interest. Initially, a suite of core metrics for each of the Vanguard models along with a standard dashboard showing its trajectory compared to its baseline and to other Vanguards is being proposed (England, N. H. S. 2015, p.11–13).

10.4   Tools for Governance and Accountability

The Dalton Report (2014) and the NHS Governance Review (Grant-Thornton 2015) have both highlighted the formidable governance and accountability challenges facing integrated care networks. In the sections below, we highlight some of the growing number of frameworks and tools available to help governments, health care organizations, and citizens grapple with governance and accountability in innovative integrated care models.

10.4.1 Frameworks

Well-led framework for governance review
Monitor, the national regulator for health services in England, developed the Well-led framework for governance reviews (Monitor et al. 2014). The framework aims to support the NHS Foundation trusts, in line with the Code of Governance, to complete an external review every 3 years. This tool allows boards to have robust oversight of quality, operations, and finance in the face of uncertain future income and new care models. It also supports Trusts in regular reviews of governance to ensure they remain fit for purpose.
The four domains for governance reviews are:

1. Strategy and planning—how well is the board setting direction for the organisation?
2. Capability and culture—is the board taking steps to ensure it has the appropriate experience and ability, now and into the future, and can it positively shape the organisation's culture to deliver care in a safe and sustainable way?
3. Process and structures—do reporting lines and accountabilities support the effective oversight of the organization?
4. Measurement—does the board receive appropriate, robust and timely information and does this support the leadership of the trust?

The framework is a 'core' reference document to shape the depth and focus of assurance processes. It also contains helpful guidance on how to conduct a governance review.

Good Governance Handbook
The Health Quality Improvement Partnership (HQIP) and the Good Governance Institute have released a new edition of the Good Governance Handbook (Corbett-Nolan et al. 2015). HQIP is an independent organisation led by the Academy of Medical Royal Colleges, The Royal College of Nursing and National Voices in the UK (http://www.hqip.org.uk/). Established in 2008, HQPI promotes quality in healthcare by enhancing the impact of clinical audit. To that effect, HQIP commissions a series of clinical outcomes review programmes that complement the work of other agencies such as the Care Quality Council.
Structured around ten themes, the Good Governance Handbook includes self-assessment questions for good governance at the levels of the board, division and department.

Pathway to accountability II
The Global Accountability Framework originated from the One World Trust (Blagescu et al. 2005) and incorporated self-check lists in the areas of transparency, participation, evaluation, and complaint and response mechanisms. The Pathway to Accountability II (Hammer et al. 2011) is a revised version aimed to support capacity building and system development. The revised version still focuses on the four domains of transparency, participation, evaluation and complaints but acknowledges the interdependencies and hence the need for a crosscutting, inter-sectoral approach. It introduces a graded scoring system and a series of quality management indicators within each of these domains. It is being widely used in WHO initiatives to support global accountability assessments across health systems.

Results-based accountability framework
This framework was developed by the Fiscal Policy Studies Institute and Mark Friedman (Friedman 2015). It involves "turn the curve" thinking—reverse-engineering solutions to problems by identifying desired outcomes and working back towards appropriate mechanisms and processes to achieve those ends, along with the data required to track performance. It focuses on three key questions: How much did we do? How well did we do it? Is anyone better off? It has been widely applied in social and community programs, and is being adapted to health system applications. For an example, see work in New Zealand (New Zealand Ministry of Health 2015) or Washington (Washington County Mental Health Services 2015).

10.4.2 Tools

The frameworks described above help to assess the status quo of governance and accountability in integrated care networks and highlight gaps. Other tools target more specifically accountability domains of performance, financial and public accountability. For example, the ***Health Data Navigator*** (Hofmarcher and Smith 2013) is an interactive platform for researchers, policy makers, and healthcare professionals to access health data from Austria, Estonia, Finland, France, Germany, Israel, Luxembourg and the UK. It contains information and links to support performance measurement of the health system including a list of international frameworks that can be adapted to national settings and methods for performance measurement. There is also a toolkit to promote generic standards for performance assessment and relevant data sources for comparative evaluations under the OECD health care quality indicators domains of quality, efficiency and access (Kelley and Hurst 2006).

Dashboards of health information have emerged to support public reporting on performance. One used by the Department of Health in Vermont, US allows the public to easily track the health status of Vermont residents through more than 100 goals in 21 focus areas (http://www.healthvermont.gov/hv2020/). This real-time dashboard presents measures, indicators and trends and helps to keep the Vermont government accountable in their health strategy. Similarly, the Canadian Institute for Health Information (CIHC) has developed an interactive website that allows the public to review performance data and health systems spending (http://www.cihi.ca/CIHI-ext-portal/internet/EN/Home/home/cihi000001).

Citizen/community score cards and surveys are a mechanism to promote civil engagement and demand-side accountability, and empower individuals to express their views to government bodies. The surveys allow citizens to contribute to oversight and regulation and therefore aim to improve the quality and integrity of public services (Singh and Shah 2007). Different types of citizen report cards and community score cards can be found at the World Bank's participation and civic engagement webpage: http://www.worldbank.org/socialaccountability_source book/Resources/pub4.html

Identifying new governance and accountability mechanisms for financial management of resources and for engaging patients and the public will need to be a priority for the Vanguards and other innovation sites. People Powered Health was an innovative programme in the UK between 2011 and 2013 that focused on co-production of health for people and by people (Horne et al. 2013). They advocated bottom-up redesign of monitoring and outcome assessment as a mechanism to drive change. NESTA and the Innovation Unit bring together examples of collaborative action from across the UK in a *Coproduction Catalogue* to illustrate what co-production looks like on the ground (Nesta 2013).

The catalogue outlines a number of different projects and models of co-production. It also lists a range of tools to assess impacts and outcomes from different perspectives when service innovations are rolled-out. For example, the NHS Five Year Forward View calls for new ways to distribute and manage funds and an example of this are the personal health budgets introduced for specific populations receiving health and social care services. A national evaluation of the pilot projects in over 60 primary care trusts showed favourable results with positive user feedback. Current work focuses on using a *personal outcomes evaluation tool* for annual, routine evaluation of user experience (Hatton and Waters 2015). It focuses on meaningful goals and capacity for people and communities. This includes a broad set of patient reported outcomes with focus on confidence and control over own health, behaviour change and lifestyle, measure of quality social networks and social support. Wider measures could look at satisfaction with equal and effective relationships, level of patient engagement using tools like the Patient Activation Measure, and levels of participation.

These are just a few examples of the guidance and tools that are available to support service integration and build collaboration. For a more complete description of innovative governance and accountability tools see Suter and Mallinson (2015).

10.5 Conclusions

We are at the advent of new relationships in integrated services. Large health systems are unpacking the challenges of whole system approaches to health and the best ways to meet future challenges is through new organizational forms. There is a push for radical, bottom-up change with patients, clinicians and communities as co-creators in all aspects of health service design, delivery and governance. As the roles of patients, communities and other stakeholders as partners for health evolve, we need tools and processes that create clear and transparent accountability relationships.

The challenges for governing these new models are significant and given their novelty there is little evidence about what works in a given context. Commentators have noted that the monitoring of accountability is the least developed element of health system leadership and governance (Smith et al. 2012). Some have pushed for "integrated governance", which focuses on partnerships between and within organizations (Delaney 2015; Jackson et al. 2008; Nicholson et al. 2014). Managing the interactions of governance structures associated with the different partnerships may be one of the biggest challenges (Delaney 2015). Jupp (2015) posits that we may be able to draw on experiences of other sectors that have undergone significant restructuring (such as education or the prison services in the UK).

Despite the uncertainty of what these new governance structures will look like or how they will operate, there is general agreement that governance will be an essential element of successful integrated care system reform (Brinkerhoff and Bossert 2008; Mikkelsen-Lopez et al. 2011). Some argue for a new or enhanced role of independent inspectorates to deliver on public accountability promises (Kickbusch and Behrendt 2013; Michels and Meijer 2008; World Bank 2013). Such agencies may also have a role in collecting and disseminating information on good practice and performance. One example is the Canada Health Council, implemented on the recommendation of an expert committee report on the state of the Canadian health care system. The agency had a vital role in monitoring progress on electoral promises and during its life span released a series of critical public reports (http://healthcouncilcanada.ca/reports.php). It also hosted a health innovation portal profiling best practice approaches across the continuum of care. Stacked with political appointees and representatives, however, it faced an up-hill battle to earn the trust and credibility it needed to make a difference and to satisfy citizens' demands for greater accountability (Flood and Archibald 2005). It disbanded in 2014.

Investing in good, smart systems to increase transparency across a wide variety of indicators of quality is likely to be central to improving accountability in a system with more autonomous providers (Jupp 2015). In addition, mechanisms for co-creation and patient empowerment will continue to play an important role. Power imbalances have been on the agenda for many years but unravelling traditional relationships to respond to new partnerships and shared-responsibility remains challenging. Strategic policy frameworks combined with effective coalition building and governance remain important tools to strengthen the coordination and integration of health services delivery (Goodwin 2002; Kickbusch and Behrendt 2013; Kickbusch and Gleicher 2012; Maslin-Prothero and Bennion 2010; Suter et al. 2009; Williams and Sullivan 2009; WHO 2013). In contrast to earlier governance approaches that focused on structures and organizational boundaries, newer approaches will need to pay increasing attention to the dispersion of power within integrated systems and accountability relationships across the four domains.

In summary, the multiple models of integrated care that are evolving globally raise the possibility of a period of experimentation and learning (Jupp 2015). Governance that is agile and can respond quickly to emerging changes is required to manage the complex interdependent partnerships in integrated care systems.

References

Abelson, J., & Gauvin, F. (2004). *Engaging citizens: One route to health care accountability.* Health Care Accountability Papers No. 2. Canadian Policy Research Networks Inc. (CPRN), Ottawa, ON.

Baez-Carmago, C. (2011). *Accountability for better healthcare provision: A framework and guidelines to define understand and assess accountability in health systems.* Working Paper Series no. 10. Basel Institute on Governance, Basel, Switzerland.

Barbazza, E., & Tello, J. E. (2014). A review of health governance: Definitions, dimensions and tools to govern. *Health Policy, 116*(1), 1–11.

Blagescu, M., de Las Casa, L., & Lloyd, R. (2005). *Pathways to accountability: The GAP framework.* London: One World Trust. Retrieved from www.oneworldtrust.org.

Brinkerhoff, D. (2003). *Accountability and health systems: Overview, framework and strategies, partners for health reformplus.* Bethesda, MD: Abt Associates.

Brinkerhoff, D. (2004). Accountability and health systems: Toward conceptual clarity and policy reference. *Health Policy and Planning, 19*(6), 371–379.

Brinkerhoff, D. W., & Bossert, T. J. (2008). *Health governance: Concepts, experience, and programming options.* Washington, DC: U.S. Agency for International Development, Health Systems 20/20.

Bullivant, J., & Corbett-Nolan, A. (2012). *Risk appetite for NHS organisations. A matrix to support better risk sensitivity in decision taking.* GGI Ltd. Retrieved from http://www.good-governance.org.uk/risk-appetite-for-nhs-organisations-a-matrix-to-support-better-risk-sensitivity-in-decision-taking/

Canadian Institutes for Health Research (CIHR). (2012). *CIHR's Citizen engagement handbook.* Ottawa, ON: CIHR.

Chhotray, V., & Stoker, G. (2009). *Governance theory and practice: A cross-disciplinary approach*. Hampshire: Palgrave-Macmillan.

Corbett-Nolan, A., Bullivant, J., Godfrey, K., Merret, H., Sutton, D., & Baltruks, D. (2015). *Good governance handbook*. London: Good Governance Institute and Healthcare Quality Improvement Partnership. Retrieved from http://www.good-governance.org.uk/wp-content/uploads/2015/01/GGH-Main-.pdf.

Dalton, D. (2014). *Examining new options and opportunities for providers of NHS care: The Dalton Review*. Salford: Salford Royal NHS Foundation Trust. Retrieved from https://www.gov.uk/government/uploads/system/uploads/attachment_data/file/384126/Dalton_Review.pdf.

Deber, R. B. (2014). Thinking about accountability. *Healthcare Policy/Politiques de Santé, 10* (Special Issue), 12–24.

Delaney, L. (2015). The challenges of an integrated governance process in healthcare. *Clinical Governance: An International Journal, 20*(2), 74–81.

Department of Health. (2012). *Health and Social Care Act 2012*. London: HMSO. Retrieved from http://www.legislation.gov.uk/ukpga/2012/7/pdfs/ukpga_20120007_en.pdf.

Evans, J. M., Baker, G. R., Berta, W. B., & Barnsley, J. (2013). The evolution of integrated healthcare strategies. *Advances in Health Care Management, 15*, 125–161.

Fierlbeck, K. (2014). The changing contours of experimental governance in European health care. *Social Science & Medicine, 108*, 89–96.

Flood, C., & Archibald, T. (2005). *Hamstrung and hogtied: Cascading constraints on citizen governors in medicare*. Health Care Accountability Papers No. 6. Canadian Policy Research Networks Inc. (CPRN), Ottawa, ON.

Fooks, C., & Maslove, L. (2004). *Rhetoric, fallacy or dream? Examining the accountability of Canadian health care to citizens*. Health Care Accountability Papers No. 1. Canadian Policy Research Networks Inc. (CPRN), Ottawa, ON.

Freake, D. (2013). *Report to the Board of Directors – Trust integrated care plan*. Alnwick: Northumbria Healthcare NHS Foundation Trust. Retrieved from https://www.northumbria.nhs.uk/sites/all/themes/northumbria_nhs/pdfs/enc-8a-integrated-care-plan.original.pdf.

Friedman, M. (2015). *Trying hard is not good enough 10th anniversary edition: Measurable improvements for customers and communities*. Santa Fe: PARSE Publishing.

George, A. (2003). *Accountability in health services: Transforming relationships and contexts*. Harvard Center for Population and Development Studies Working Paper Series, vol. 13, no. 1, Boston, MA.

Goodwin, N. (2002). Creating an integrated public sector? Labour's plans for the modernisation of the English health care system. *International Journal Integrated Care, 2*, e05.

Grant-Thornton UK. (2015). *NHS governance review 2015*. Uncharted waters, Grant Thornton, United Kingdom. Retrieved from http://www.grantthornton.co.uk/en/insights/nhs-governance-review-2015-uncharted-waters/

Hammer, M., Lloyd, R., Cumming, L., & Obrecht, A. (2011). *Pathways to accountability II: The 2011 revised global accountability framework*. London: One World Trust. Retrieved from www.oneworldtrust.org.

Hatton, C., & Waters, J. (2015). *Personal health budget holders and family carers*. The POET surveys 2015, In-Control and Lancaster University, UK. Retrieved from http://www.in-control.org.uk/what-we-do/poet-%C2%A9-personal-outcomes-evaluation-tool.aspx

Hofmarcher, M., & Smith, C. (Eds.). (2013). *Health data navigator. Your toolkit for comparative performance analysis. A EuroREACH product*. Vienna: Centre for Social Welfare Policy & Research. Retrieved from http://www.healthdatanavigator.eu/HDN_Toolkit_Final.pdf.

Horne, M., Kahn, H., & Corrigan, P. (2013). *People powered health: Health for people, by people and with people*. London: Nesta. Retrieved from https://www.nesta.org.uk/sites/default/files/health_for_people_by_people_and_with_people.pdf.

Jackson, C. L., Nicholson, C., Doust, J., Cheung, L., & O'Donnell, J. (2008). Seriously working together: Integrated governance models to achieve sustainable partnerships between health care organizations. *Medical Journal of Australia, 188*(8), S57–S60.

Jupp, B. (2015). *Reconsidering accountability in an age of integrated care-viewpoint*. London: Nuffield Trust. Retrieved from http://www.nuffieldtrust.org.uk/publications/reconsidering-accountability-integrated-care.

Kelley, E., & Hurst, J. (2006). *OECD working paper 23 -Health care quality indicators project conceptual framework*. Paris: OECD.

Kickbusch, I., & Behrendt, T. (2013). *Implementing a health 2020 vision: Governance for health in the 21st century. Making it happen*. WHO Regional Office for Europe: Copenhagen.

Kickbusch, I., & Gleicher, D. (2012). *Governance for health in the 21st century*. Copenhagen: WHO Regional Office for Europe.

Kickbusch, I., & Gleicher, D. (Eds.). (2014). *Smart governance for health and well-being: The evidence*. Copenhagen: WHO Regional Office for Europe.

Lewis, M., & Pettersson, G. (2009). *Governance in health care delivery: Raising Performance*. Policy Research Working Paper no. 5074. The World Bank, Washington, DC. Retrieved from http://www-wds.worldbank.org/servlet/WDSContentServer/WDSP/IB/2009/10/13/000158349_20091013151915/Rendered/PDF/WPS5074.pdf

Maslin-Prothero, S. E., & Bennion, A. E. (2010). Integrated team working: A literature review. *International Journal of Integrated Care, 10*, e043.

Maybin, J., Addicott, R., & Dixon, A. (2011). *Accountability in the NHS: Implications of the government's reform programme*. London: The King's Fund. Retrieved from http://www.kingsfund.org.uk/sites/files/kf/Accountability-in-the-NHS-June-Kings-Fund-2011.pdf.

Michels, A., & Meijer, A. (2008). Safeguarding public accountability in horizontal government. *Public Management Review, 10*(2), 165–173.

Mikkelsen-Lopez, I., Wyss, K., & de Savigny, D. (2011). An approach to addressing governance from a health system framework perspective. *BMC International Health and Human Rights, 11* (13), 1–11.

Monitor, Care Quality Commission, & NHS Trust Development Authority. (2014). *Well-led framework for governance reviews*. Government of UK. Retrieved from https://www.gov.uk/government/publications/well-led-nhs-foundation-trusts-a-framework-for-structuring-governance-reviews#history

Nesta. (2013). *People powered health co-production catalogue*. London: Nesta. Retrieved from http://www.nesta.org.uk/sites/default/files/co-production_catalogue.pdf.

New Zealand Ministry of Health. (2015). *Results based accountability – A quick guide*. Wellington: Ministry of Health. Retrieved from http://www.health.govt.nz/about-ministry/what-we-do/streamlined-contracting/results-based-accountability.

England, N. H. S. (2014). *Five year forward view into action: Planning for 2015–16*. London: NHS England. Retrieved from www.england.nhs.uk/wp-content/uploads/2014/12/forward-view-plning.pdf.

England, N. H. S. (2015). *The forward view into action – new care models: Update and initial support*. London: NHS England. Retrieved from https://www.england.nhs.uk/wp-content/uploads/2015/07/ncm-support-package.pdf.

NHS England, Care Quality Commission, Health Education England, Monitor, Public Health England, & Trust Development Authority. (2014). *NHS five year forward view*. London: NHS England. Retrieved from https://www.england.nhs.uk/ourwork/futurenhs/.

Nicholson, C., Jackson, C. L., & Marley, J. E. (2014). Best-practice integrated health care governance — applying evidence to Australia's health reform agenda. *The Medical Journal of Australia, 201*(Suppl. 3), S64–S66.

Singh, J., & Shah, P. (2007). *Community score card process—a short note on the general methodology for implementation*. Washington, DC: The World Bank. Retrieved from http://siteresources.worldbank.org/INTPCENG/1143333-1116505690049/20509286/comscorecardsnote.pdf.

Smith, P., Anell, A., Busse, R., Crivello, L., Healy, J., Lindahl, A. K., Westert, G., & Kene, T. (2012). Leadership and governance in seven developed health systems. *Health Policy, 106* (1), 37–49. doi:10.1016/j.healthpol.2011.12.009.

Suter, E., & Mallinson, S. (2015). *Accountability for coordinated/integrated health services delivery*. Working Paper. WHO Regional Office for Europe, Copenhagen. Retrieved from http://www.euro.who.int/__data/assets/pdf_file/0003/286149/Accountability_for_coordinated_integrated_health_services_delivery.pdf

Suter, E., Oelke, N. D., Adair, C. E., & Armitage, G. D. (2009). Ten key principles for successful health systems integration. *Healthcare Quarterly, 13*, 6–23.

Task Team. (2013). *Health in the post-2015 agenda*. Report of the Global Thematic Consultation on Health.

Van Kersbergen, K., & Van Waarden, F. (2004). "Governance" as a bridge between disciplines: Cross-disciplinary inspiration regarding shifts in governance and problems of governability, accountability and legitimacy. *European Journal of Political Research, 43*(2), 143–171.

Van Olmen, J., Marchal, B., Van Damme, W., Kegels, G., & Hill, P. S. (2012). Health systems frameworks in their political context: Framing divergent agendas. *BMC Public Health, 12* (774), 1–13. Retrieved from http://www.biomedcentral.com/1471-2458/12/774.

Washington County Mental Health Services. (2015). *Outcomes report 2014*. Montpellier, VT: WCMHS. Retrieved from https://www.wcmhs.org/assets/files/docs/WCMHS%20FY14%20Outcomes%20Report%20Compressed.pdf.

Willke, H. (2007). *Smart governance – governing the global knowledge society*. Chicago: University of Chicago Press.

Williams, P., & Sullivan, H. (2009). Faces of integration. *International Journal of Care, 9*, e100. Retrieved from http://www.ijic.org/index.php/ijic/article/view/509/1016.

World Bank. (2013). *Local governance and innovation: The role of 'horizontal associations'*. The World Bank Group. Retrieved from http://web.worldbank.org/WBSITE/EXTERNAL/COUNTRIES/EASTASIAPACIFICEXT/0,,contentMDK:22499278~pagePK:146736~piPK:146830~theSitePK:226301,00.html

World Health Organization. (2000). *The world health report 2000 – Health systems: Improving performance*. Geneva: WHO.

World Health Organization. (2007). *Everybody's business: Strengthening health systems to improve health outcomes*. Geneva: WHO.

World Health Organization. (2008). *Toolkit on monitoring health systems strengthening: Health systems governance*. Geneva: WHO.

World Health Organization. (2013). *Health 2020: A European policy framework and strategy for the 21st century*. Copenhagen: WHO Regional Office for Europe.

Financing and Reimbursement

11

Ellen Nolte

11.1   Introduction

Problems of care coordination and integration typically arise at the interfaces between primary and secondary care, health and social care, curative and public health services, and among specialities and professional groups (Nolte and McKee 2008b). Financial factors such as differences in financing mechanisms and sources and in the allocation and flows of funding, including payment mechanisms, are frequently cited as a major barrier for the implementation of more integrated approaches to service delivery (Calnan et al. 2006; Cameron et al. 2014; Dickinson and Glasby 2010; Hardy et al. 1999).

Leutz (1999) argued that successful integration requires sustained investment in staff and support systems, funding for start-up costs, and flexibility to respond to needs that emerge during implementation. Several countries have, directly or indirectly, set aside dedicated resources to support the development and implementation of innovative care models seeking to achieve better service integration, such as through targeted payments or the use of start-up grants (Nolte and Knai 2015; Nolte et al. 2014; Nolte and McKee 2008b). Countries are also increasingly experimenting with new forms of paying providers in order to incentivise coordination and integration. Examples include the introduction of 'bundled payment' schemes for a defined package of chronic care such as in the Netherlands (de Bakker et al. 2012; Tsiachristas et al. 2013). This can be seen to form part of a move to what has been referred to as 'value-based payment' more broadly, including mechanisms such as shared savings and global budgets (Hayen et al. 2015; Miller 2009). Such

E. Nolte (✉)
European Observatory on Health Systems and Policies, London School of Economics and Political Science, London School of Hygiene & Tropical Medicine, London, UK
e-mail: E.Nolte@lse.ac.uk

© Springer International Publishing AG 2017   165
V. Amelung et al. (eds.), *Handbook Integrated Care*,
DOI 10.1007/978-3-319-56103-5_11

schemes recognise that payment systems that encourage multiple providers with different incentives are unlikely to provide well-coordinated care (Roland and Nolte 2014). Several countries have additionally introduced pay-for-performance (P4P) schemes in primary care, incentivising chronic and coordinated care in particular, although the evidence of their benefits remain mixed (Cashin et al. 2014a; Eijkenaar et al. 2013; Scott et al. 2011). Furthermore, a number of countries have experimented with different financing mechanisms. Examples include the shifting of responsibility for funding of particular components of service delivery between funding agencies, such as local and regional authorities (Frølich et al. 2015) or health and long-term care insurers (Maarse and Jeurissen 2016), or introducing pooled budgets to integrate health and social care (Hultberg et al. 2005; Mason et al. 2015).

This chapter provides an overview of the ways countries have sought to change financing and payment mechanisms at different levels in order to enable better coordination among providers in the delivery of health services and between health and social care and thus support integration. The chapter begins with a brief overview of the principles underlying the financing of and payment for services and the advantages and challenges inherent in different approaches. It then reviews examples from several countries that have experimented with innovative ways to enhance coordination and integration of service delivery. It then reflects on the evidence of impact of different approaches. It concludes with a set of overarching observations.

11.2   Principles of Financing of and Payment for Services

This section briefly discusses the principles of financing of health and social care as well as the payment mechanisms for service delivery. It is beyond the scope of this chapter to provide a comprehensive account of financing and payment forms, which have been described in detail elsewhere (Allen et al. 2011; Robertson et al. 2014; Thomson et al. 2009). Instead, it focuses on those aspects that are immediately relevant to the integration of care. Much of the discussion presented here relates to high-income countries, although it is important to recognise that the challenges arising from financing and payment systems are universal (World Health Organization 2010).

11.2.1 Financing of Health and Social Care

Health (and social care) financing encompasses a range of functions: the collection of funds for care, the pooling of funds (and therefore risks) a both cross time and populations, and the purchasing of services (Kutzin 2001). It also includes policies that relate to determining the coverage of the population (breadth), the range of benefits that are being provided (scope), and the proportion of benefit cost covered, that is, user charges (depth) (Busse et al. 2007). Countries differ in the way they carry out these functions and implement related policies. This has implications for important policy goals such as financial protection, equity of access, efficiency of service organisation and delivery (Thomson et al. 2009). Choices largely reflect individual countries' institutional, political, social and historical contexts.

Among high-income OECD countries, health care is largely financed from public sources, although the extent varies. In 2013, public funding accounted for just under 60% of total health expenditure in Israel up to 85% in Norway and 88% in the Netherlands (OECD 2015). In contrast, in the USA, just over half of health expenditure (52%) was from private sources. High-income countries use national or local taxation and/or statutory insurance to fund public health care, and the majority of countries provide (almost) universal coverage. Residence in the given country is the most common basis for entitlement to health care. In the USA, health care coverage is only gradually expanding following the 2010 Patient Protection and Affordable Care Act (ACA) (French et al. 2016).

Most high-income countries also provide public support for social or long-term care, although the nature and scope of what is funded varies (Scheil-Adlung 2015). Social care is typically financed from (local) taxes; a small number of countries, including the Netherlands, Germany, Japan and France, have introduced mandatory long-term care insurance, and Sweden has established a right to tax-funded social care (Robertson et al. 2014). The term 'social care' does not equally apply to all systems, however. For example, in England, adult social care has been defined as "the care and support provided by local social services authorities pursuant to their responsibilities towards adults who need extra support" (The Law Commission 2011, p.2), essentially capturing those services that are not provided by other organisations under different legislation. Other systems conceptualise social care differently and for example in Australia, Finland and the Netherlands 'social care' also includes parts of child and youth care (Schweppenstedde et al. 2014). Long-term care may (implicitly) be captured under social care although it is frequently referred to as a separate entity or sector. In Germany, the term 'social care' as an overarching concept does not exist while long-term care forms an established sector (Busse and Blümel 2014). For ease of comparison, in the following we will use the notion of social care as a generic term and synonymously with long-term care while recognising country-specific differences in the nature and scope of this sector.

The main difference between health and social care systems is the nature of entitlement for publicly funded services. In health care, entitlement is typically based on residency status as noted above, or in case of insurance systems, contribution or enrolment status. In contrast, in social care, entitlement is typically determined on the basis of need (means-tested) with the exception of countries that have introduced insurance or a right to social care (Robertson et al. 2014). This difference in service entitlement can create challenges for collaboration between the health and social care sectors, in particular as these systems are frequently administered separately. There are exceptions such as in Germany, where long-term care insurance is administered by the health insurance funds. Similarly, only a small number of countries provide more integrated health and social care financing at the system level, for example the publicly financed Medicaid system in some states in the USA (Crawford and Houston 2015). Scotland has been moving towards integrated partnerships between health and social care following its 2014 public service reform. Starting in 2016, 31 local partnerships have been set up in which NHS and local government care services are responsible for the planning, resourcing and delivery of all integrated health and social care services (see Chap. 32) (Health and Social Care Integration Communications Group 2015). Likewise, Finland has, in 2015, embarked on a major social welfare and health care reform, foreseeing the "complete horizontal and vertical integration of services" (p.30) (Prime Minister's Office 2015) through the creation of 18 autonomous regions. The regions are expected to take on responsibility for the organisation of social welfare and health services, among other public services, and central government supervision is expected to be strengthened. Several countries are experimenting with more integrated financing schemes at regional or local levels, examples of which we discuss below.

11.2.2 Payment Mechanisms in Health Care

There are a range of methods to pay different types of health care providers. The methods can be categorised in different ways, for example, whether they are prospective or retrospective, or the extent to which payments bring together ('bundle') components of health care services (Charlesworth et al. 2012; Thomson et al. 2009). This is further illustrated in Table 11.1, which also outlines some advantages and disadvantages of the four main forms of provider payment. These are: block budget, capitation, case-based payment and fee-for-service.

The principal forms of provider payment vary in their ability to support overarching system goals such as preventing health problems, delivering services to effectively address health problems, or responding to the legitimate expectations of the population and containing health care costs (Charlesworth et al. 2012; World Health Organization 2000). For example, payment systems based on capitation offer, in principle, the incentive for providers to invest in prevention. However, this is often not translated into practice, due, at least in part, to the often short-term nature of contracts, which are not sufficiently long for potential savings to be realised by providers (Marshall et al. 2014). Likewise, fee-for-service payments do not encourage preventive activities, unless these are specifically paid for. Furthermore, different payment systems vary in their ability to support patient choice, with block budgets and capitation providing only limited options in contrast to case-based and fee-for-service payments, which allow for money to follow the patient.

Against this background, systems tend to use several types of payment simultaneously or indeed combine different methods in the form of blended payment in order to influence provider behaviour (Marshall et al. 2014). For example, in Europe, primary or ambulatory care providers are typically paid through a combination of capitation and fee-for-service payments while the most common way of paying hospitals is prospectively using case-mix adjusted diagnosis-related groups (DRGs), often complemented with grants or budgets for specific services (Table 11.2) (Nolte et al. 2014; Thomson et al. 2009).

Table 11.1 Types of provider payments in healthcare

	Type of payment	Description	Advantages	Disadvantages
Bundled	Block budget/ salary	Periodic global lump sum; independent of number of patients	– Low transaction costs – Predictable expenditure/ income if budget has fixed cap – Provides flexibility for (cost-neutral or -reducing) provider innovation	– Lack of transparency and accountability – Disincentivises increases in activity – Disincentivises cost-increasing innovations; innovation may be constrained with limited access to capital – May lead to service rationing or lower quality where demand is high – Does not reward good performance
	Capitation	Periodic lump sum per enrolled patient for a range of services	– Low transaction costs – Supports cost containment and financial control – Incentivises attracting more patients and possibly improved care quality in selected dimensions of care	– Disincentivises provision of additional or costlier services – Providers might avoid patients with high levels of needs where payments are not fully risk-adjusted – May incentivise shifting of services to other providers where payments cover only part of the care pathway (e.g. primary care)
	Per period	Periodic lump sum per patient diagnosed with a particular condition		
	Per patient pathway	Lump sum for all services required for a defined pathway of care		

(continued)

Table 11.1 (continued)

	Type of payment	Description	Advantages	Disadvantages
	Per case/ diagnosis/ procedure	Payment per case based on grouping of patients with similar diagnoses/ procedures or resource needs	– Incentivises reducing costs per episode, which is only advantageous if it improves productivity and does not reduce quality – Incentivises increasing activity, which is only advantageous if this activity is cost-effective and appropriate	– Transaction costs are higher because of the need for billing and sophisticated costing systems – Incentive to increase activity may encourage unwanted activity (supplier-induced demand) – Challenges financial control where there are no limits on the volume of services provided – Where prices are fixed quality may fall as a result of attempts to increase profit by reducing costs
	Per day	Payment per day of stay in a hospital or other facility		
Unbundled	Fee-for-service	Payment for each item of service and patient contact	– Disincentivises withholding care and may support quality and comprehensive care – Providers are paid for all services they choose to deliver and may thus promote equity – Supports rapid uptake of innovations that expand or change use or services and technologies that are already reimbursed	– Challenges financial control and likely increases spending through increases in activity (supplier-induced demand) – Does not incentivise improving efficiency or joint working – Does not incentivise investing in prevention efficiency or joint working – Can delay uptake of innovations of services or technologies that are not yet reimbursed and require negotiation for reimbursement

Source: Adapted from Charlesworth et al. (2012) and Marshall et al. (2014)

Table 11.2 Selected features of healthcare provider payment in 12 countries in Europe

	Provision of primary/ generalist and specialist care outside hospital	General practitioner (GP) gatekeeping	Payment of physicians in primary/ ambulatory care	Payment of hospitals (year introduced)
Austria	Office-based primary and specialist care physicians; outpatient clinics	No	Blended system of fee-for-service with capitated element for basic services; determined by payment schemes based on public services or private law and supplemented by bonuses defined by the state	Performance-oriented hospital financing system (LKF) (1997)
Denmark	GPs in private practice	Yes; access to specialist care upon referral only except for ophthalmologists and dentists	A combination of capitation per patient and fee-for-service, in addition to special fees for out-of-hours services, telephone consultations and home visits	Combination of global budget and activity-based funding using DRGs
England	GPs in community-based practices or health centres	Yes	Weighted capitation based on General Medical Services contract, negotiated nationally between NHS Employers and the General Practitioners Committee of the British Medical Association; plus elements of fee-for-service and performance-related payment	Activity-based 'Payment by results' (PbR) using health resource groups for acute services (2003)

(continued)

Table 11.2 (continued)

	Provision of primary/ generalist and specialist care outside hospital	General practitioner (GP) gatekeeping	Payment of physicians in primary/ ambulatory care	Payment of hospitals (year introduced)
Estonia	GPs in independent family practice	Yes; direct access to selected specialties and follow-up consultation for chronic disease	Combination of basic allowance, capitation fee, fee-for-service, with additional compensation for those practicing in remote areas; based on negotiations between the statutory health insurance (SHI) and the Society of Family Physicians for a period of 5 years	Diagnosis-related groups (DRG) (2004), complemented by per-diem and fee-for-service payments
France	Office-based primary and specialist care physicians	Yes, of a soft type ('preferred doctor scheme'); with strong financial incentives for service users	Fee-for-service; nationally set coverage of fees based on agreements between professional organisations and the social security administration; extra-billing (concerns 50% of patients); P4P element since 2009 based on individual contracts between physicians and SHI	Diagnosis-related groups (DRGs) (phased in from 2004), supplemented by additional payments for specific areas/ services
Germany	Office-based primary and specialist care physicians	Voluntary ('GP contracts')	Combination of capitation and fee-for service based on centrally negotiated 'uniform value scale' by the Federal Association of SHI physicians and the National Association of SHI Funds	German diagnosis-related groups (G-DRG) (phased in from 2003)

(continued)

Table 11.2 (continued)

	Provision of primary/ generalist and specialist care outside hospital	General practitioner (GP) gatekeeping	Payment of physicians in primary/ ambulatory care	Payment of hospitals (year introduced)
Hungary	Office-based family physician; specialist care in policlinics and dispensaries	Yes, in principle, but wide range of specialist services are accessible without referral	Weighted capitation plus adjustments based on provider characteristics	Diagnosis-related groups (DRGs) (1993); outpatient specialist services on a fee-for-service basis
Italy	Office-based GPs, typically in solo practice; office-based specialists	Yes; direct access to certain specialists, e.g. gynaecologists	Capitation fee plus a share based on participation in public health interventions (vaccination and screening), based on national contract and regional agreements	Diagnosis-related groups (DRGs) (1995), complemented by capitation and/or grants for selected services
Latvia	Typically GPs in independent practice; health centres	Yes; direct access to certain specialists	Age-weighted capitation plus fees for defined activities, bonus payments and fixed allowances	Case-based payment, per diem plus fee-for-service points
Lithuania	Family physicians in independent practice; specialist outpatient care in health centres	Yes	Age-weighted capitation plus payment for people living in rural areas and incentive payments for certain listed services	Global budgets plus case-based payment
The Netherlands	General practitioners in group practices	Yes; access to specialist care upon referral only	Combination of capitation and fee-for-service; maximum remuneration fees for GPs negotiated between National Association of GPs, Health Insurers Netherlands and Ministry of Health, Welfare and Sport	Diagnosis and treatment combinations (DBCs) (2005)

(continued)

Table 11.2 (continued)

	Provision of primary/ generalist and specialist care outside hospital	General practitioner (GP) gatekeeping	Payment of physicians in primary/ ambulatory care	Payment of hospitals (year introduced)
Switzerland	Office-based primary and specialist care physicians	No, except for those enrolled in managed care plans (12% of residents)	Independent healthcare professionals are generally paid on a fee-for-services basis; some managed-care plans operate capitation models	Per-diem plus diagnosis-related groups (SwissDRG) (from 2009)

Source: Adapted from Nolte et al. (2014)

As indicated in Table 11.2, a number of countries have introduced additional payments for providers in primary or ambulatory care. The intent is to incentivise delivery of certain activities and services to enhance accessibility and improve the quality of care, in particular for those with chronic health problems. We will discuss examples of these in the following section.

11.3 Incentivising Coordination and Integration of Service Delivery: Examples from Different Countries

This section provides an overview of select countries' experiences of innovative approaches to enhance coordination and integration of service delivery, focusing on three strategies: committing additional funding, introducing innovative payment schemes and changing financing mechanisms. Where appropriate, it will also reflect on the evidence of impact of different approaches. In the space available, it is not possible to provide a comprehensive inventory of the entirety of initiatives and mechanisms that are being used across countries; instead, the chapter offers insights into a small number of examples for illustrative purposes, building on our previous work (Nolte and Knai 2015; Nolte and McKee 2008a; Nolte et al. 2008). Country case studies in Part 6 provide details on further examples.

11.3.1 Commitment of Additional Funding

A number of countries have set aside resources to support the development and implementation of innovative care models to achieve better service integration (Nolte and Knai 2015; Nolte and McKee 2008b). The precise mechanisms have varied, reflecting the diverse lines of accountability and responsibility for financing care and allocating resources. Targeted payments have been used where tiers of government have direct control over delivery, while more decentralised systems have tended to use start-up grants to support the development of new approaches, although this distinction is not clear cut.

Examples include provider health networks in France, which were tasked with strengthening the coordination, integration and continuity of health care for those with complex needs (Chevreul et al. 2015; Durand-Zaleski and Obrecht 2008). Emerging from the late 1990s, they include disease-specific networks, such as for diabetes, and networks targeting particular population groups, for example older people. Provider networks were supported by the state and the statutory health insurance to finance both infrastructure and operating costs as well as new services, with for example a total of €650 million invested between 2000 and 2005 (Durand-Zaleski and Obrecht 2008).

Several countries have used project or start-up grants to support the development of new approaches to care. For example, the federal government in Canada has supported provincial reform initiatives through the CA$800 million Primary Healthcare Transition Fund (~€560 million in 2006),[1] which operated over a period of 6 years (2000–2006) (Health Canada 2007; Jiwani and Dubois 2008). Financial support involved direct funding of primary care reform activities in the provinces, many of which were concerned with strengthening collaborative and multidisciplinary working among primary care providers and enhancing the IT infrastructure to support integration. The fund also supported a range of national initiatives, such as the National Strategy on Collaborative Care. In Australia, the central government has been allocating funds within the National Primary Care Collaboratives programme to improve service delivery, access and integration of care for patients with complex and chronic conditions since 2004 (The Department of Health 2014). The first three phases, running until 2012, were supported by an estimated AU$45 million (~€30 million) (Russell 2013). In Denmark, the government allocated a pool of DKK 585 million (~€80 million) over the period 2010–2012 for the development and implementation of regional disease management programmes as well as patient education and self-management, to be shared by regions and municipalities responsible for the organisation and financing of health and social care services (see also below) (Frølich et al. 2015). In Austria, the 2005 health reform established a financial pool at the level of the states (reform pool) to promote the coordination of and cooperation between ambulatory and hospital care. Administered by the statutory health insurance funds, the aim was to shift care from the inpatient to the ambulatory care sector, with 1–2% of health expenditure to be set aside for the reform pool to cover the associated costs (Hofmarcher and Quentin 2013). In Germany, reform efforts seeking to strengthen integrated care involved, among other things, enabling statutory health insurance

---

[1]Source: OANDA. Average exchange rates. https://www.oanda.com/currency/average. Accessed 29 June 2016.

funds to designate a total of 1% of their revenues to develop integrated care contracts with providers from 2004 (see Chap. 31) (Erler et al. 2015).

The impacts of these initiatives, where they have been evaluated, have been varied. For example, in France, the financing mechanism to support provider health networks was changed from 2008 to incentivise quality improvement strategies more widely and network funding became less secure (Chevreul et al. 2015). A 2014 assessment noted that attempts to enhance care coordination in primary care in France had led to numerous activities but that these had remained patchy, with networks perceived to be too specialised and there was a perceived risk of duplication of service delivery (Blanchard et al. 2014). As a result, and in an effort to further improve primary care services and the coordination of care, the 2016 health reform set out a series of measures, including the promotion of coordination support platforms (*plateformes territoriales d'appui, PTAs*) (Legifrance.gouv.fr 2016), a role that could potentially be taken on by provider networks (UNR.Sante 2016). In Germany, the number of integrated care contracts that had been executed since the introduction of start-up funding in 2004 had remained small, covering, in 2008, around 6% of the population with statutory health insurance (Grothaus 2010). Fewer than half of the contracts had incorporated elements of intersectoral care, and, following the discontinuation of start-up funding, an estimated 20% of contracts were terminated during 2008 and 2009 (Sachverständigenrat zur Begutachtung der Entwicklung im Gesundheitswesen 2009). There is little robust evidence of the overall impacts of integrated care contracts in Germany, with only a small number of exceptions (see Chap. 31). In an effort to further strengthen intersectoral collaboration, the 2015 health care reform committed a total of €300 million per annum over the period 2016–2019 to further support the implementation of innovative forms of care delivery, with funding to be allocated centrally (Gemeinsamer Bundesausschuss 2016).

11.3.2 Innovative Payment Schemes

Several countries have used financial incentives to strengthen care coordination through pay-for-improvement or pay-for-performance schemes (Nolte and Knai 2015). These are usually targeted at providers, most often physicians, although payers or purchasers of care have also benefitted from resources earmarked for care coordination (Nolte et al. 2012). Examples of incentive schemes targeting *payers* are disease management programmes (DMPs) in Germany, which were introduced in 2002 in an effort to promote evidence-based, coordinated treatment and care across primary and secondary care (Erler et al. 2015). Their introduction was enabled by an additional payment to the statutory health insurance (SHI) funds ('DMP risk-adjuster') for each enrolled SHI member joining a DMP. This provided considerable financial incentives for the SHI funds to offer such programmes and it facilitated their rapid nationwide implementation.

Financial incentives targeted at *providers*, most frequently physicians, can involve additional reimbursement for documentation, patient enrolment or regular assessment. Such payments are typically, although not exclusively, used in the context of disease management programmes such as those implemented in Austria (Sönnichsen et al. 2015), Germany (Erler et al. 2015), selected diabetes care programmes in Italy (Ricciardi et al. 2015) and France (Sophia diabetes and asthma care programmes, diabetes provider networks) (Chevreul et al. 2015; L'Assurance Maladie 2016). Incentive payments may also specifically target quality improvement activities aimed at enhanced coordination. Examples include Estonia, which introduced in 2006 a bonus payment system for GPs to encourage the prevention and management of diabetes type 2 and cardiovascular diseases (Lai and Knai 2015). In Switzerland, physicians participating in the Delta health network in the canton of Geneva, a health maintenance organisation formed in the early 1990s, receive a lump sum each time they participate in a quality circle (Peytremann-Bridevaux et al. 2015). This is in addition to their regular reimbursement, which consists of a combination of fee-for-service payments and capitation fee per insured person.

Several countries have additionally introduced specific pay-for-performance (P4P) schemes in order to incentivise chronic and coordinated care in particular. Such schemes make payment conditional on the achievement of specified targets linked to the provision of evidence-based care and the implementation of (integrated) care pathways. The most prominent examples in Europe include the Quality and Outcomes Framework (QOF) in the UK (Box 11.1) (Doran and Roland 2010; Nolte et al. 2015) and the Remuneration Based on Public Health Objectives (*rémunération sur objectifs de santé publique, ROSP*) scheme in France (Chevreul et al. 2015), along with smaller schemes implemented in some regions in Italy (Ricciardi et al. 2015).

Box 11.1 The Quality and Outcomes Framework in the United Kingdom
The Quality and Outcomes Framework (QOF) was implemented with the 2004 national GP contract (Nolte et al. 2015). It introduced a new voluntary payment scheme that initially linked up to 25% of GP practice income to performance as part of a wider government programme of initiatives to increase the quality of care delivered by NHS (Doran and Roland 2010).

The QOF involves the award of 'achievement points' for practices demonstrating that they have met several stages in the management of a given, usually chronic, condition, for a proportion of the relevant population. There have been several updates to the QOF since the original 2004 contract, successively including or redefining a wider range of indicators. For example, in 2009/2010, there were over 130 quality indicators in four domains: clinical, organisational, patient experience and additional services (Nolte et al. 2015) while the 2014/2015 QOF measured achievement in three domains (clinical, public health and public health/additional services) against 81 indicators (Health and Social Care Information Centre 2016). The

(continued)

Box 11.1 (continued)

payment scheme is voluntary for GP practices and patients join it by virtue of being registered with a given practice participating in the scheme (Nolte et al. 2015). When introduced in 2004, the scheme applied to across the United Kingdom and most practices had joined. From April 2013, the QOF was different between England and the devolved administrations. In 2014/2015, the scheme covered just under 8000 GP practices with over 56 million registered patients in England (Health and Social Care Information Centre 2016). Notably, while the QOF initially accounted for about 25% of GP practice income, this proportion has fallen over time to 15% in 2015. The future of QOF is being discussed, with Scotland set to abolish the scheme in 2017 (Health and Social Care Information Centre 2016).

France introduced in 2009 the *contrat d'amélioration des pratiques individuelles* (CAPI), a pay-for-performance scheme complementing the prevailing fee-for-service reimbursement in primary care (Chevreul et al. 2015). It comprised voluntary individual contracts between GPs and the statutory health insurance, whereby the GP agreed to meet specific goals including the management of chronic diseases and preventive health care. The scheme (renamed ROSP in 2011) was subsequently incorporated into the physicians' collective bargaining agreement with an expanded list of objectives and extended to additional medical specialties. Participation in the ROSP scheme is voluntary for a 3-year period and participating GPs receive payments in addition to their regular fee-for-service income, based on the number of patients treated and 29 quality indicators. In 2012, more than 75,000 physicians participated in the programme, receiving an average annual performance-based payment of €3746 (Chevreul et al. 2015). Pay-for-performance schemes seeking to strengthen coordination across primary care services have also been implemented in Australia (the Practice Incentives Program), New Zealand (the Primary Health Organisation (PHO) Performance programme) and in various states in the USA (for example, the California Integrated Healthcare Association physician incentive programmes) (Cashin et al. 2014b).

However, decision-makers are increasingly recognising the limitations of the traditional ways of paying providers in health care, which tend to fragment service delivery because of a misalignment of incentives across providers. Countries are therefore experimenting with innovative payment schemes by introducing, for example, episode-based payment involving a fixed amount for a package of services delivered to a patient for a complete episode of care (Charlesworth et al. 2012). These include the aforementioned 'bundled payment' schemes for a defined package of services for people with selected chronic conditions that were introduced in the Netherlands from 2007 onwards (see Chap. 35) (de Bakker et al. 2012; Tsiachristas et al. 2013), and related schemes in various states in the USA (Conrad et al. 2015). Other innovative payment schemes include shared savings programmes and comprehensive care payments, often referred to as global payments models. Under shared savings programmes, the payer or payers share the risk of rising expenditure with the care providers (Hayen et al. 2015). This means that providers that succeed in lowering their growth in health care costs while continuing to meet quality standards will be financially rewarded; savings can be reinvested in the programme. Shared savings programmes in health care are a comparatively recent development; examples include the Medicare Shared Savings Program in the USA (see Chap. 33) (Centers for Medicare and Medicaid Services 2015; Conrad et al. 2015) and the Healthy Kinzigtal integrated care programme in Germany (see Chap. 31) (Hildebrandt et al. 2013), with similar pilots in the Netherlands ongoing (Drewes et al. 2014). Examples of global payment models, which involve fixed payments for the care of a patient during a specified time period, include the Massachusetts Alternative Quality Contract in the USA (Box 11.2) (Song et al. 2014).

> **Box 11.2 The Alternative Quality Contract in Massachusetts, USA**
> The Alternative Quality Contract (AQC) is a two-sided contract implemented in 2009 by the non-profit health insurer Blue Cross Blue Shield of Massachusetts (BCBSMA) (Song et al. 2014). The AQC is a risk-adjusted global budget payment model in which provider organisations agree to accept responsibility for managing care within a specified annual budget and they share the risk if spending exceeds the budget (or share savings if spending is below budget) (Chernew et al. 2011). The model sought to improve quality and outcomes while moderating health care spending growth. The contract includes about 85% of the physicians in the BCBSMA network. Participating organisations receive bonus payments based on 64 process (e.g., preventive screening, medication management), outcome (e.g., high blood pressure control) and patient experience indicators (e.g., access to care, quality of communication), in ambulatory and hospital care. Shared savings (or deficits) are linked to the quality of care delivered, with higher levels of quality implying a larger share of savings and smaller share of deficits to providers. The AQC is among the largest private payment reform initiatives in the USA and seen to provide a model for state and national policy makers (Blue Cross Blue Shield of Massachusetts 2016).

The evidence of how well these financial incentives and innovative payment schemes are working is inconclusive. In Germany, the financing mechanism to incentivise roll-out of disease management programmes across SHI funds was changed from 2009, with the abolishment of the DMP-risk adjuster and the introduction of a morbidity-adjusted risk compensation scheme (Busse and Blümel 2014). This scheme seeks to compensate for differences in health care needs of populations enrolled with different SHI funds. The change resulted in lower payments for SHI members joining a DMP as SHI funds now only receive a fixed amount for each enrolled patient to cover programme operating costs. Whether SHI funds continue to benefit from offering DMPs thus depends on whether a given DMP can reduce costs. The impact of this change in financing on DMP enrolment is difficult to assess. Since their introduction in 2002, the number of patients signing up to DMPs increased steadily but the rate of increase slowed from 2009 (Erler et al. 2015). DMPs have remained the predominant approach to chronic illness care in Germany while the evidence of their impact on health outcomes remains subject to debate.

The evidence of impact of pay-for-performance schemes on health outcomes also remains mixed (Eijkenaar et al. 2013). Reviews of the Quality and Outcomes Framework in the UK found that while there was evidence of modest improvements in the quality of care for chronic diseases covered by the QOF, its impacts on costs, professional behaviour and patient experience had remained uncertain (Gillam et al. 2012). Other work noted that the QOF has had limited impact on improving health outcomes, and although there were small mortality reductions for a composite outcome of targeted disorders, the QOF was not associated with significant changes in mortality (Ryan et al. 2016). It has been noted that the impact of pay-for-performance schemes is dependent on the underlying payment mechanisms into which such schemes are introduced. Reviews have pointed to the potential of pay-for-performance to improve the quality of care while also highlighting the risk of unintended consequences related to incentive payments that need to be taken into account when designing such schemes (Markovitz and Ryan 2016; Roland and Dudley 2015).

There is some evidence that innovative payments schemes such as bundled payments and shared savings programmes may be associated with lower spending growth and possibly actual savings. However, effects vary across payment and care models, as do impacts on outcomes as demonstrated by the varied experiences of accountable care organisations in the USA (see Chap. 33) (McWilliams et al. 2015; Nyweide et al. 2015). Assessments of the Alternative Quality Contract in Massachusetts (Box 11.2) point to lower spending growth and generally greater quality improvements among those enrolled with participating organisations compared to comparable populations elsewhere in the USA (Song et al. 2014).

11.3.3 Changes to Financing Mechanisms

Some countries have also experimented with changing the mechanisms by which health and/or social care are being financed in order to encourage better coordination across sectors. One example is Denmark, which, in the context of the 2007 structural reform of the administrative system, reallocated responsibilities in the health care sector to 5 newly established regions and 98 municipalities (Olejaz et al. 2012). Specifically, the reform made municipalities responsible for the co-financing (20%) of regional health care activities to encourage municipalities to increase preventative services to reduce hospitalisations (Frølich et al. 2015).

Others have moved to experimenting with different ways of financing to help integrate health and social care services (Hultberg et al. 2005; Mason et al. 2015).

Mason et al. (2015), in a review of the evidence of impact of such approaches in Australia, Canada, England, Scotland, Sweden and the United States, distinguished different types of financial integration. These types of financial integration can be seen to lie on a continuum, which includes, at one end, 'simple' transfer payments, in which purchasers of public social or long-term care services (e.g., municipalities) make financial contributions to health bodies to support specific additional services (and vice versa). At the other end are pooled funds, in which each partner (health and social care) makes contributions to a common fund to pay for agreed projects or services, and structurally integrated budgets, in which responsibilities for health and social care are combined within a single body under single management. However, distinctions are not clear-cut and schemes tend to use more than one financial integration mechanism. Importantly, the range and scope of services covered under integrated financing schemes vary widely.

The PRISMA (Program of Research to Integrate Services for the Maintenance of Autonomy) model in Quebec, Canada is an example of an integrated financing scheme in which one partner leads the purchasing of services based on jointly agreed aims (see Chap. 30) (Mason et al. 2015). In this model, all public, private and voluntary health and social service organisations are involved in delivering services for older people in a given area. Each organisation retains its own structure but agrees to participate under an umbrella system and to adapt its operations and resources to the agreed requirements and processes. Budgets are negotiated between partner organisations, and a joint governing board, with representatives from all the health and social care organisations and community agencies, decides on the allocation of the resources to the integrated system.

A similar model has been adopted by NHS Highland in Scotland, in which responsibility for adult social care services were transferred to NHS Highland while the local authority (Highland Council) remains accountable for social care (see Chap. 32). The transaction is delivered through a 5-year plan, which is reviewed annually and monitored with regard to the delivery of agreed outcomes. The process also involved the creation of a single budget ('pooled funds') through the transfer of budget lines across the two bodies.

One example of a system involving structural integration is the Integrated Health and Social Care Board in Northern Ireland, which is responsible for the commissioning of services, resource and performance management. Five Health and Social Care Trusts responsible for the provision of integrated health and social care services across Northern Ireland (Ham et al. 2013).

As with innovative payment mechanisms described above, the evidence of impact of novel financing mechanisms, where this has been evaluated, remains patchy. There is little robust data on the effects of municipal co-financing in Denmark. One study sought to assess its impact on hospital services but it failed to demonstrate a clear link between local efforts to reduce hospitalisations and the number of hospital admissions among older people during the first 3 years following the reform (Vrangbæk and Sørensen 2013). At the same time, municipalities were found to have increased investments into public health efforts overall. A review of the evidence of impact of integrating financing for health and social care also failed to establish empirically robust positive effects of such schemes on health outcomes, secondary care use or costs (Mason et al. 2015). There was some anecdotal evidence of unintended consequences such as premature hospital discharge and increased risk of readmission. Identified barriers included difficulties of implementing financial integration, limited control of budget holders over access to services, difficulties in linking different information systems, and, among schemes in the UK, differences in priorities and governance among those involved. At the same time, most schemes succeeded in improving access to care, with substantial levels of unmet need identified in some, which then led to an increase in total costs. The authors concluded that the link between integrating funding, better health outcomes and lower costs is likely to be weak. However, there was reason to believe that even with additional costs integration can offer value for money if it delivers improvements in quality of life.

11.4   Conclusions

Differences in financing mechanisms and sources and in the allocation and flows of financial resources can pose a critical challenge for efforts to better coordinate and integrate across functions, professions and sectors. This chapter has provided an overview of ways in which countries have sought to overcome these challenges. While numerous innovative approaches have been implemented, the evidence base for what works best in each context is still under-developed.

Importantly, as Leutz (1999) has pointed out when reviewing attempts in the United States and United Kingdom to integrate health and social services there is often a failure to understand that "integration costs before it pays" (p.89). Indeed, Mason et al. (2015) found, in their review of different ways of financing to help integrate health and social care services in different countries, that some innovative models were associated with an increase in cost, mainly because they uncovered unmet needs. Frequently, there is an expectation that integration initiatives will self-fund from savings arising when a new service is substituted for an existing one. Yet, available evidence suggests that the creation of new coordinating mechanisms will not compensate for lack of resources (Freeman et al. 2007). There may be a temptation to inject one-off extra funding to pay for new services, but this will not necessarily ensure long-term sustainability. Success often depends on new approaches being incorporated into routine care, and while sustained financing will be a necessary requirement it may not be sufficient, especially where the innovation challenges established ways of working (May 2006).

Finding the right payment mix to support integrated care can be challenging, and countries are increasingly using some form of blended payment through combining different approaches, often involving some form of pay-for-performance element. The right mix will be important however, with evidence on performance-related pay in particular highlighting the need to carefully consider the existing payment structure into which new incentives are introduced and to design the structure of reward schemes to maximise the likelihood of intended outcomes and minimise the likelihood of unintended consequences (Roland and Dudley 2015).

Overall, there is a need to ensure that payment systems encourage rather than discourage coordination. Particular attention needs to be paid to changes in health services which appear likely to further fragment care, such as payment based on activity, which is now being used for paying hospitals in the majority of European countries, or the introduction of competition among service providers (Dickinson et al. 2013).

References

Allen, K., Bednárik, R., Campbell, L., et al. (2011). *Governance and finance of long-term care across Europe*. Birmingham, Vienna: HSMC and European Centre for Social Welfare Policy and Research.

Blanchard, P., Eslous, L., & Yeni, I. (2014). *Evaluation de la coordination d'appui aux soins*. Retrieved June 28, 2016, from http://www.igas.gouv.fr/IMG/pdf/2014-010R_Evaluation_coordination_appui_soins.pdf

Blue Cross Blue Shield of Massachusetts. (2016). *Alternative quality contract*. Retrieved June 28, 2016, from https://www.bluecrossma.com/visitor/about-us/affordability-quality/aqc.html

Busse, R., & Blümel, M. (2014). Germany: Health system review. *Health Systems in Transition, 16*, 1–296.

Busse, R., Schreyoegg, J., & Gericke, C. (2007). *Analyzing changes in health financing arrangements in high-income countries. A comprehensive framework approach*. Washington, DC: The World Bank.

Calnan, M., Hutten, J., & Tiljak, H. (2006). The challenge of coordination: The role of primary care professionals in promoting care across the interface. In R. Saltman, A. Rico, & W. Boerma (Eds.), *Primary care in the driver's seat? Organizational reform in European primary care* (pp. 85–104). Maidenhead: Open University Press.

Cameron, A., Lart, R., Bostock, L., et al. (2014). Factors that promote and hinder joint and integrated working between health and social care services: A review of research literature. *Health & Social Care in the Community, 22*, 225–233.

Cashin, C., Chi, Y.-L., Smith, P., et al. (2014a). Health provider P4P and strategic purchasing. In C. Cashin, Y.-L. Chi, P. Smith, et al. (Eds.), *Paying for performance in health care. Implications for health system performance and accountability* (pp. 3–21). Maidenhead: Open University Press.

Cashin, C., Chi, Y.-L., Smith, P., et al. (2014b). *Paying for performance in health care. Implications for health system performance and accountability*. Maidenhead: Open University Press.

Centers for Medicare & Medicaid Services. (2015). *Shared savings program*. Retrieved June 28, 2016, from https://www.cms.gov/Medicare/Medicare-Fee-For-Service-Payment/sharedsavingsprogram/index.html

Charlesworth, A., Davies, A., & Dixon, J. (2012). *Reforming payment for health care in Europe to achieve better value*. London: The Nuffield Trust.

Chernew, M., Mechanic, R., Landon, B., et al. (2011). Private-payer innovation in Massachusetts: The 'alternative quality contract'. *Health Affairs (Millwood), 30*, 51–61.

Chevreul, K., Brunn, M., Durand-Zaleski, I., et al. (2015). France. In E. Nolte & C. Knai (Eds.), *Assessing chronic disease management in European health systems. Country reports* (pp. 43–54). Copenhagen: World Health Organization (acting as the host organization for, and secretariat of, the European Observatory on Health Systems and Policies).

Conrad, D. A., Vaughn, M., Grembowski, D., et al. (2015). Implementing value-based payment reform: A conceptual framework and case examples. *Medical Care Research and Review, 73* (4), 437–457.

Crawford, M., & Houston, R. (2015). *State payment and financing models to promote health and social service integration.* Retrieved May 31, 2016, from http://www.chcs.org/media/Medic aid_-Soc-Service-Financing_022515_2_Final.pdf

de Bakker, D., Struijs, J., Baan, C., et al. (2012). Early results from adoption of bundled payment for diabetes care in the Netherlands show improvement in care coordination. *Health Affairs (Millwood), 31,* 426–433.

Dickinson, H., & Glasby, J. (2010). 'Why partnership working doesn't work': Pitfalls, problems and possibilities in English health and social care. *Public Management Review, 12,* 811–828.

Dickinson, H., Shaw, S., Glasby, J., et al. (2013). The limits of market-based reforms. *BMC Health Services Research, 13,* 11.

Doran, T., & Roland, M. (2010). Lessons from major initiatives to improve primary care in the United Kingdom. *Health Affairs, 29,* 1023–1029.

Drewes, H., Heijink, R., Struijs, J., et al. (2014). *Landelijke monitor populatiemanagement. Deel 1: Beschrijving proeftuinen [Monitor rural population management. Part 1: Description labs].* Bilthoven: National Institute for Public Health and the Environment (RIVM).

Durand-Zaleski, I., & Obrecht, O. (2008). France. In E. Nolte, C. Knai, & M. McKee (Eds.), *Managing chronic conditions – experience in eight countries* (pp. 55–73). Copenhagen: World Health Organization on behalf of the European Observatory on Health Systems and Policies.

Eijkenaar, F., Emmert, M., Scheppach, M., et al. (2013). Effects of pay for performance in health care: A systematic review of systematic reviews. *Health Policy, 110,* 115–130.

Erler, A., Fullerton, B., & Nolte, E. (2015). Germany. In E. Nolte & C. Knai (Eds.), *Assessing chronic disease management in European health systems. Country reports* (pp. 55–68). Copenhagen: World Health Organization (acting as the host organization for, and secretariat of, the European Observatory on Health Systems and Policies).

Freeman, G., Woloshynowych, M., & Baker, R. (2007). *Continuity of care 2006: What have we learned since 2000 and what are policy imperatives now?* London: National Co-ordinating Centre for NHS Service Delivery and Organisation R&D.

French, M., Homer, J., Gumus, G., et al. (2016). Key provisions of the patient protection and affordable care act (ACA): A systematic review and presentation of early research findings. *Health Services Research, 51*(5), 1735–1771.

Frølich, A., Jacobsen, R., & Knai, C. (2015). Denmark. In E. Nolte & C. Knai (Eds.), *Assessing chronic disease management in European health systems. Country reports* (pp. 17–26). Copenhagen: World Health Organization (acting as the host organization for, and secretariat of, the European Observatory on Health Systems and Policies).

Gemeinsamer Bundesausschuss. (2016). *Der Innovationsfonds und der Innovationsausschuss beim Gemeinsamen Bundesausschuss.* Retrieved June 28, 2016, from https:// innovationsfonds.g-ba.de/

Gillam, S., Siriwardena, A., & Steel, N. (2012). Pay-for-performance in the United Kingdom: Impact of the quality and outcomes framework: A systematic review. *Annals of Family Medicine, 10,* 461–468.

Grothaus, F-J. (2010). *Entwicklung der integrierten Versorgung in der Bundesrepublik Deutschland 2004–2008. Gemeinsamen Registrierungsstelle zur Unterstützung der Umsetzung des § 140 d SGB V.* Retrieved June 28, 2016, from http://www.bqs-register140d.de/

Ham, C., Heenan, D., Longley, M., et al. (2013). *Integrated care in Northern Ireland, Scotland and Wales. Lessons for England.* London: The King's Fund.

Hardy, B., Mur-Veemanu, I., Steenbergen, M., et al. (1999). Inter-agency services in England and The Netherlands. A comparative study of integrated care development and delivery. *Health Policy, 48,* 87–105.

Hayen, A., van den Berg, M., Meijboom, B., et al. (2015). Incorporating shared savings programs into primary care: From theory to practice. *BMC Health Services Research, 15,* 580.

Health and Social Care Information Centre. (2016). *QOF 2014/15 results.* Retrieved June 28, 2016, from http://qof.hscic.gov.uk/

Health and Social Care Integration Communications Group. (2015). *Communications toolkit – A guide to support the local implementation of health and social care integration.* Edinburgh: The Scottish Government.

Health Canada. (2007). *Primary health transition fund: Summary of initiatives* (Final edition). Retrieved June 26, 2016, from http://www.hc-sc.gc.ca/hcs-sss/pubs/prim/2007-initiatives/index-eng.php#a00

Hildebrandt, H., Schulte, T., & Stunder, B. (2013). Triple aim in Kinzigtal, Germany. Improving population health, integrating health care and reducing costs of care – lessons for the UK? *Journal of Integrated Care, 20,* 205–222.

Hofmarcher, M., & Quentin, W. (2013). Austria: Health system review. *Health Systems in Transition, 15,* 1–292.

Hultberg, E., Glendinning, C., Allebeck, P., et al. (2005). Using pooled budgets to integrate health and welfare services: A comparison of experiments in England and Sweden. *Health & Social Care in the Community, 13,* 531–541.

Jiwani, I., & Dubois, C. (2008). Canada. In E. Nolte, C. Knai, & M. McKee (Eds.), *Managing chronic conditions – experience in eight countries* (pp. 161–181). Copenhagen: World Health Organization on behalf of the European Observatory on Health Systems and Policies.

Kutzin, J. (2001). A descriptive framework for country-level analysis of health care financing arrangements. *Health Policy, 56,* 171–203.

L'Assurance Maladie. (2016). *Le service Sophia.* Retrieved June 28, 2016, from https://www.ameli-sophia.fr/service-sophia/presentation-du-service-sophia.html

Lai, T., & Knai, C. (2015). Estonia. In E. Nolte & C. Knai (Eds.), *Assessing chronic disease management in European health systems. Country reports* (pp. 37–42). Copenhagen: World Health Organization (acting as the host organization for, and secretariat of, the European Observatory on Health Systems and Policies).

Legifrance.gouv.fr. (2016). *LOI n° 2016-41 du 26 janvier 2016 de modernisation de notre système de santé (1) - Article 74.* Retrieved June 28, 2016, from https://www.legifrance.gouv.fr/eli/loi/2016/1/26/AFSX1418355L/jo/article_74

Leutz, W. (1999). Five laws for integrating medical and social services: Lessons from the United States and the United Kingdom. *Milbank Quarterly, 77,* 77–110.

Maarse, J., & Jeurissen, P. (2016). The policy and politics of the 2015 long-term care reform in the Netherlands. *Health Policy, 120,* 241–245.

Markovitz, A., & Ryan, A. (2016). Pay-for-performance: Disappointing results or masked heterogeneity? *Medical Care Research and Review.* doi:10.1177/1077558715619282. [Epub ahead of print].

Marshall, L., Charlesworth, A., & Hurst, J. (2014). *The NHS payment system: Evolving policy and emerging evidence.* London: The Nuffield Trust.

Mason, A., Goddard, M., Weatherly, H., et al. (2015). Integrating funds for health and social care: An evidence review. *Journal of Health Services Research & Policy, 20,* 177–188.

May, C. (2006). A rational model for assessing and evaluating complex interventions in health care. *BMC Health Services Research, 6,* 86.

McWilliams, J., Chernew, M., Landon, B., et al. (2015). Performance differences in year 1 of pioneer accountable care organizations. *The New England Journal of Medicine, 372,* 1927–1936.

Miller, H. (2009). From volume to value: Better ways to pay for health care. *Health Affairs (Millwood), 28,* 1418–1428.

Nolte, E., & Knai, C. (2015). *Assessing chronic disease management in European health systems. Country reports.* Copenhagen: World Health Organization (acting as the host organization for, and secretariat of, the European Observatory on Health Systems and Policies).

Nolte, E., & McKee, M. (2008a). *Caring for people with chronic conditions. A health system perspective*. Copenhagen: World Health Organization on behalf of the European Observatory on Health Systems and Policies.

Nolte, E., & McKee, M. (2008b). Making it happen. In E. Nolte & M. McKee (Eds.), *Caring for people with chronic conditions: A health system perspective* (pp. 222–244). Maidenhead: Open University Press.

Nolte, E., McKee, M., & Knai, C. (2008). Managing chronic conditions: An introduction to the experience in eight countries. In E. Nolte, C. Knai, & M. McKee (Eds.), *Managing chronic conditions: Experience in eight countries* (pp. 1–14). Copenhagen: World Health Organization on behalf of the European Observatory on Health Systems and Policies.

Nolte, E., Knai, C., Hofmarcher, M., Conklin, A., et al. (2012). Overcoming fragmentation in healthcare: Chronic care in Austria, Germany and the Netherlands. *Health Economics, Policy, and Law, 7*, 125–146.

Nolte, E., Knai, C., & Saltman, R. (2014). *Assessing chronic disease management in European health systems. Concepts and approaches*. Copenhagen: World Health Organization (acting as the host organization for, and secretariat of, the European Observatory on Health Systems and Policies).

Nolte, E., Brereton, L., Knai, C., et al. (2015). England. In E. Nolte & C. Knai (Eds.), *Assessing chronic disease management in European health systems. Country reports* (pp. 27–36). Copenhagen: World Health Organization (acting as the host organization for, and secretariat of, the European Observatory on Health Systems and Policies).

Nyweide, D., Lee, W., Cuerdon, T., et al. (2015). Association of pioneer accountable care organizations vs traditional medicare fee for service with spending, utilization, and patient experience. *JAMA, 313*, 2152–2161.

OECD. (2015). *OECD Health statistics*. Retrieved May 31, 2016, from http://stats.oecd.org/Index. aspx?DataSetCode=SHA

Olejaz, M., Juul Nielsen, A., Rudkjøbing, A., et al. (2012). Denmark: Health system review. *Health Systems in Transition, 14*, 1–192.

Peytremann-Bridevaux, I., Burnand, B., Cassis, I., et al. (2015). Switzerland. In E. Nolte & C. Knai (Eds.), *Assessing chronic disease management in European health systems. Country reports* (pp. 111–120). Copenhagen: World Health Organization (acting as the host organization for, and secretariat of, the European Observatory on Health Systems and Policies).

Prime Minister's Office. (2015). *Finland, a land of solutions. Strategic programme of Prime Minister Juha Sipilä's Government, 29 May 2015*. Helsinki: Government Publications.

Ricciardi, W., de Belvis, A., Specchia, M., et al. (2015). Italy. In E. Nolte & C. Knai (Eds.), *Assessing chronic disease management in European health systems. Country reports* (pp. 79–90). Copenhagen: World Health Organization (acting as the host organization for, and secretariat of, the European Observatory on Health Systems and Policies).

Robertson, R., Gregory, S., & Jabbal, J. (2014). *The social care and health systems of nine countries*. London: The King's Fund.

Roland, M., & Dudley, R. (2015). How financial and reputational incentives can be used to improve medical care. *Health Services Research, 50*, 2090–2115.

Roland, M., & Nolte, E. (2014). The future shape of primary care. *The British Journal of General Practice, 64*, 63–64.

Russell, L. (2013). *Primary care and general practice in Australia 1990–2012: A chronology of federal government strategies, policies, programs and funding*. Canberra: The Australian National University, Australian Primary Health Care Research Institute.

Ryan, A., Krinsky, S., Kontopantelis, E., et al. (2016). Long-term evidence for the effect of pay-for-performance in primary care on mortality in the UK: A population study. *Lancet, 388*, 268–274.

Sachverständigenrat zur Begutachtung der Entwicklung im Gesundheitswesen. (2009). *Koordination und Integration - Gesundheitsversorgung in einer Gesellschaft des längeren Lebens*. Bonn: Sachverständigenrat zur Begutachtung der Entwicklung im Gesundheitswesen.

Scheil-Adlung, X. (2015). *Long-term care protection for older persons: A review of coverage deficits in 46 countries.* Geneva: International Labour Organization.

Schweppenstedde, D., Hinrichs, S., Ogbu, U., et al. (2014). *Regulating quality and safety of health and social care: International experiences.* Santa Monica: RAND Corporation.

Scott, A., Sivey, P., Ait Ouakrim, D., et al. (2011). The effect of financial incentives on the quality of health care provided by primary care physicians. *Cochrane Database of Systematic Reviews, 9*, CD008451.

Song, Z., Rose, S., Safran, D., et al. (2014). Changes in health care spending and quality 4 years into global payment. *The New England Journal of Medicine, 371*, 1704–1714.

Sönnichsen, A., Flamm, M., & Nolte, E. (2015). Austria. In E. Nolte & C. Knai (Eds.), *Assessing chronic disease management in European health systems. Country reports* (pp. 7–16). Copenhagen: World Health Organization (acting as the host organization for, and secretariat of, the European Observatory on Health Systems and Policies).

The Department of Health. (2014). *Australian primary care collaboratives programme (APCCP).* Retrieved June 29, 2016, from http://www.health.gov.au/internet/main/publishing.nsf/Content/health-pcd-programs-apccp-index.htm

The Law Commission. (2011). *Adult social care.* London: The Law Commission.

Thomson, S., Foubister, T., & Mossialos, E. (2009). *Financing health care in the European Union. Challenges and policy responses.* Copenhagen: World Health Organization, on behalf of the European Observatory on Health Systems and Policies.

Tsiachristas, A., Dikkers, C., Boland, M. R., et al. (2013). Exploring payment schemes used to promote integrated chronic care in Europe. *Health Policy, 113*, 296–304.

UNR.Sante. (2016, Juin). *L'UNR.Santé en action. La Lettre de l'UNR.Santé.* Retrieved June 28, 2016, from http://media.wix.com/ugd/bf2047_331c431140874e59b9f9a9dab23a1591.pdf

Vrangbæk, K., & Sørensen, L. (2013). Does municipal co-financing reduce hospitalisation rates in Denmark? *Scandinavian Journal of Public Health, 41*, 616–622.

World Health Organization. (2000). *The World Health Report: Health systems: Improving performance.* Geneva: World Health Organization.

World Health Organization. (2010). *The World Health Report: Health systems financing: The path to universal coverage.* Geneva: World Health Organization.

Planning

12

Susanne Ozegowski

"Plans are worthless, but planning is everything"
(Dwight D. Eisenhower, 1957)

12.1 Introduction

12.1.1 The Need for Planning

Resource planning plays a central role in health care. There are many supplies which we consider essential to our daily lives, such as food, clothing, fuel etc. Nonetheless, there is no public planning of supermarkets, warehouses, or gas stations. Health care, however, is different: Firstly, there is a broad consensus in many societies that prices and volume in health services markets should not be determined (solely) by supply and demand as health is a fundamental human right (Dussault et al. 2010; WHO 2013). Equitable access to health care is deemed to be one of the central building blocks of that right (WHO 2013). Thus, in the context of this rights-based framework planning is required in order to allocate resources to health care by normative and ethical standards, and not simply market mechanisms.

Another reason for planning in health care is the need for excess capacity in order to be prepared for emergency situations. Since the time to treatment can be a decisive factor in emergencies, excess capacity for health care provision is necessary, especially in locations where it would not be efficient by market standards. That applies, for instance, to workforce planning: On the one hand, policymakers do not want to risk a shortage of health professionals which would put a timely provision of health care at risk. On the other hand, payer organizations and the (healthy) population seek to avoid a costly oversupply. Therefore, the challenge lies

S. Ozegowski (✉)
German Managed Care Association, BMC e.V., Berlin, Germany
e-mail: ozegowski@bmcev.de

© Springer International Publishing AG 2017
V. Amelung et al. (eds.), *Handbook Integrated Care*,
DOI 10.1007/978-3-319-56103-5_12

in estimating exactly the "right" number of health professionals required in the future. This is especially difficult for the physician workforce as medical education takes up to 15 years, meaning that forecasts have to be made for a considerable time span in order to bridge the time lag between recognizing a gap between supply and demand and being able to close that gap (Dussault et al. 2010).

12.1.2 Planning Taxonomy

The allocation of health care resources and the planning process can be looked at from a variety of angles:

- By stakeholder: Who is planning?
- By time frame: What time span does the planning process cover?
- By geography: Which catchment area is covered?
- By criteria: By what criteria and methodology are resources allocated?
- By subject: Which resources are considered?

In terms of **stakeholders**, the responsibility for planning can lie with national, regional, and/or local governments. It can be devolved to public authorities (like the National Health Service (NHS) in the UK) or multi-stakeholder bodies (such as the Joint Federal Commission in Germany assembling insurers and providers) (Ono et al. 2013). It can also be up to insurers, provider organizations, or integrated care providers.

The **time frame** for planning varies widely based on the specific subject of planning. As elaborated above, modifying the intake of medical students is rather a long-term measure in order to influence the future number of available physicians. Changing the number of nurses in an intensive care unit, on the other hand, has an immediate effect on the quality of care.

Planning can take place on all **geographical levels**: Large pharmaceutical and medical technology companies, for instance, are serving the global market. Therefore, when the avian influenza virus H5N1 started to spread in the early 2000s, the World Health Organization (WHO) issued a recommendation to all governments to stockpile the antiviral drug Tamiflu® for at least 25% of its population. As many countries followed that recommendation, the license holder Roche ran into considerable shortages of the drug on a global level (Greene and Moline 2006). Many other planning activities take place on a national, regional or local level. Medical student intake, for instance, is determined at a national level in many Western countries (Bloor and Maynard 2003). Training posts for nurses, on the other hand, are either planned on a national, a regional level or not at all, as an overview by the Organisation for Economic Co-operation and Development (OECD) showed (Simoens et al. 2005). The planning process for a certain type of resource does not necessarily have to rest exclusively with one institution for a certain catchment area. Instead, there may be competing or coexisting organizations which are planning health care resources for the same catchment area. In the Netherlands, for instance, competing insurance companies sign contracts with different hospitals based on their own criteria—yet, all of the companies have to ensure adequate access to hospital care for their insured (Krabbe-Alkemade et al. 2017).

Planning criteria also differ immensely. Allocations of health care resources are planned to ensure accessibility in terms of quantity, quality, and an adequate distance. At the same time (cost) efficiency and profitability of health care institutions also plays an important role as resources are limited. The goals of service provision can easily contrast with financial objectives, requiring decisions between competing criteria. In addition, there are typically complex webs of regulatory requirements that need to be observed. In Germany, for instance, hospitals are subject to minimum-volume standards for certain complex surgeries, e.g., hospitals are required to demonstrate 20 liver transplantations and 50 knee arthroplasties per year in order to be allowed to perform the respective intervention (de Cruppé et al. 2015). On January 2016, a new law was enacted, which excludes those hospital services not meeting the standards from reimbursement (Art 136b para. 4 German Social Code V). In addition to the two sometimes competing criteria addressed above, insurers and providers are usually motivated to maintain positive reputations—both in terms of patient satisfaction and as employers. These considerations can also influence decisions on resource allocation.

Finally, the question of what is being planned is, of course, crucial for any of the variables mentioned before: There are various resources that are **subject** to planning: Infrastructure, such as hospitals, emergency care units, medical devices and further equipment need to be sufficiently available. Denmark, for instance, has recently sought to strengthen the efficiency and quality of its inpatient care by cutting the number of hospitals by at least half and re-building many older hospitals according to state-of-the-art equipment and technology (Møller Pedersen 2009). Schools and faculties for medical studies and other health care professions are also an important resource. In addition, budget planning plays an important role: Investments in infrastructure, technology, and human resources require sufficient levels of financial resources. However, in the largely publicly-owned or public policy-driven health care sector, funding may not necessarily be available when needed and be subject to political cycles (e.g., elections) and the general economic environment (as both taxes and contributions to the statutory health insurance suffer during an economic downturn).

Many of the examples cited above relate to workforce planning as it is one of the most central resources in health care—due to the fact that health care is highly labour-intensive (Baumol and De Ferranti 2012). The health care workforce includes a large variety of professions: medical doctors, dentists, nurses, midwives, physiotherapists, and many others—with each profession containing many different sub-specializations. These complexities make workforce planning a great challenge. At the same time, workforce planning is also difficult since human capital cannot be easily shifted from one location to another and their output is challenging to quantify. Therefore, this chapter will largely focus on workforce planning.

Workforce planning would be impossible without a sound estimate of patient numbers and interventions both for the present and the future. Understanding (future) demand is essential to avoid both excess capacities and shortages. Therefore, this aspect will also be looked at in more detail throughout this chapter.

12.2 Workforce Planning Methodologies

Workforce planning always pertains to two essential components: supply on the one hand, and demand/need on the other (Roberfroid et al. 2008). We require an estimate for both components in order to identify possible gaps between the two and define appropriate actions.

As straightforward as this model is—the crux of planning lies in the details. The selection of variables for the forecasting model, the size of the catchment area as well as the choice between forecasting either expected actual utilization of health care services or expected need for services are not only technically complex, but they also rely on fundamental normative assumptions regarding equity, access, and health system responsiveness.

This purpose of this section is to give a broad overview of the different methodologies and their pros and cons, especially as it relates to health workforce planning in an integrated care setting.

Researchers differentiate between four different methodologies of workforce planning (Roberfroid et al. 2008): Many workforce plans start by forecasting physician and/or non-physician workforce **supply**. Then there are **demand-based** and **needs-based models** projecting the population's future health care requirements. A fourth approach to forecasting lies in **benchmarking** which relates to both, the supply and the demand side.

12.2.1 Planning of Supply

Supply analyses usually rely on a stock inflow-outflow model. Based on the current number of health workers (differentiated by specialty) the following drivers of future supply are quantified (Ono et al. 2013; Roberfroid et al. 2008):

- *Education*: The number of graduates from medical studies, training posts for medical specializations, and figures for the various non-physician training programs (nurses, midwives, physician assistants, physiotherapists, etc.) need to be taken into account. In addition, their location should also be a matter of concern: Studies show that maintaining medical schools and training posts in or close to rural, remote or underserved areas increases the chance of a more equitable geographic distribution of staff (Laven and Wilkinson 2003; Wilson et al. 2009).
- *Migration:* Immigration rates of health professionals from other countries and emigration of health professionals trained domestically need to be considered. Mobility within a country becomes relevant when workforce planning is to be applied to a certain region only.

- *Retirement and retention/attrition*: The number of health professionals retiring from work as well as those leaving the medical field to work in other industries are decisive variables.
- *Productivity*: The change in workload carried by health professionals is an important variable. Recently, this aspect has moved to the centre of attention, as the generation of so called "Millenials" is less willing to work long hours and puts greater emphasis on maintaining a work-life balance. Therefore, even with a stable headcount, overall productivity may decrease, so it becomes highly important to measure health professionals not in terms of headcount, but rather as full time equivalents (FTEs) (Ono et al. 2013). Ideally, FTEs should not be measured by the budgeted but rather by actual working hours. That is particularly relevant for physicians and other health professions who do not work on a salaried basis. As data on working hours is often unavailable, many forecasts estimate FTEs by benchmarking individual service provision against a peer group average (JAHWPF 2015; Roberfroid et al. 2008). Alternatively, productivity gains may be achieved through new treatment methods, higher quality of care (e.g., avoiding readmission), the use of technology (e.g., clinical decision support systems), and larger practice size with more efficient processes (Cunningham 2013). In a systematic review, Weiner et al. (2013) estimated that health information technology (IT)-supported workflow changes may lower the number of required physicians by 4–8% (assuming that 70% of physicians make full use of health IT available, such as electronic health records, and clinical decision support).
- *Delegation of tasks*: Delegation of tasks from higher to lower qualified personnel as well as an increasing differentiation of health professions may significantly reduce the need for highly qualified professionals: Altschuler et al. (2012) modelled three different scenarios varying by the degree of delegation. Based on their models, they identified a potential for increasing panel sizes per physician (and team) by 40–100%. Weiner et al. (2013) estimated that health IT-induced delegation from specialists (SPs) to general practitioners (GPs) or from GPs to nurses may decrease the need for physicians by a total of 12–26% (again at 70% penetration).

The reliability of supply models is, of course, highly dependent on the reliability of these driver variables. While some of these input variables are fairly predictable or controllable, such as retirement rates or number of graduates, other variables are less reliable: Macroeconomic trends impacting the labour market, generational trends (such as "Millenials"), and the potential of health IT are difficult to accurately forecast. An important determinant for the reliability is the longevity of the forecast: In order to account for the uncertainties inherent in long-term forecasts, many workforce plans calculate multiple scenarios (Crettenden et al. 2014).

Another aspect to consider is the geographic area for which the supply model is estimated: Within the geographic area qualifications and degrees should be largely recognized and there should be a reasonable degree of mobility of health care professionals. Otherwise, the overall supply may appear sufficient but large geographic variations could arise.

12.2.2 Demand-Based Planning

The **demand-based** or utilization-based **approach** aims at projecting future demand for health care in the population. It is based on current and/or historical utilization data, e.g., from claims data, and tries to project that information into the future. Basic models only take into account demographics, however, there are also highly complex forecasting models in order to account for various dynamics:

- *Demographics*: The change in size, age and sex structure of the population is the most common variable in demand projections. However, the impacts of these shifts are not always understood. For instance, it is up for debate whether the ageing of the population will lead to a compression or expansion of morbidity as there is evidence for both hypotheses (Crimmins and Beltran-Sanchez 2011; Fries et al. 2011). Therefore, the Swiss Health Care Observatory has, for instance, modeled separate scenarios for both hypotheses in its projections of health workforce requirements until 2030 (Seematter-Bagnoud et al. 2008).
- *Socioeconomics*: People with a lower socioeconomic status suffer from higher morbidity and mortality rates that in turn lead to higher utilization of health care resources. There is mixed evidence on the level of health care utilization when controlling for morbidity: Shadmi et al. (2011) find no difference in utilization by socioeconomic status among the Israeli population when controlling for morbidity. Thode et al. (2005), on the other hand, conclude that persons with the same morbidity level but low socioeconomic status consult more GPs compared to people with a high socioeconomic status while the effect are reversed for SPs.
- *Technology*: Health IT is accredited an enormous potential to fundamentally change the delivery of care. Not only could it affect the supply side (in terms of communication efficiency between health care providers), but it could also change communication and utilization patterns between health care providers and patients. Weiner et al. (2013) concluded that health IT may decrease physician demand as it enables more self-care and it allows for asynchronous care. This might reduce physician demand by 4–11% (at 70% penetration rate of health IT) (Weiner et al. 2013).
- *Health System Changes*: Health system variables have an important influence on utilization. For instance, limitations on direct access to certain providers or changes in the patients' benefits package have a good chance of influencing (supplier-induced) demand. One example is gatekeeping: Gatekeeping is generally thought to have the potential to optimize patient pathways, thereby leading to fewer unnecessary visits to SPs. In a systematic review, Garrido et al. (2011)

found a decrease in specialized care utilization and mixed evidence on the effect of gatekeeping on overall ambulatory care. Thus, if regulators chose to introduce (or incentivize) gatekeeping, this may have an impact on the demand for health services. Another example for the effect of a change in the benefits package is the reimbursement of chemotherapy drugs in the US: As of 2004, the Medicare Prescription Drug, Improvement, and Modernization Act cut payment rates for chemotherapy drugs administered to Medicare patients after Congress realized there had been a significant overpayment for certain drugs. Prices for some drugs were reduced by as much as 90%. In consequence, Jacobson et al. (2010) showed that prescription patterns of physicians changed while overall access to chemotherapy was not hampered.

- *Insurance Status*: Data from the United States show that utilization rates of health care vary significantly by insurance status (Bureau of Health Professions 2008): Namely, patients with "traditional" insurance contracts remunerating physicians on a fee-for-service basis displayed significantly higher levels of service use as opposed to patients enrolled in Health Maintenance Organizations (HMOs). That gap was even more apparent when comparing these figures to those that are uninsured: For instance, service use levels for surgery and internal medicine was between to three- to fivefold higher for people in traditional contracts compared to uninsured persons (Bureau of Health Professions 2008). Therefore, the reduction in number of uninsured persons resulting from the Affordable Care Act is expected to impact physician demand (Petterson et al. 2012). In addition, the US is one of the most dynamic health care markets when it comes to provider models. Medicare as well as private insurers have experimented with new models of care, e.g., through HMOs, Accountable Care Organizations (ACOs), Patient-Centered Medical Homes (PCMH), and Preferred Provider Organizations. These models are aimed at managing the patient and his or her pathway through the health care system and realigning provider incentives accordingly. Therefore, they have a significant impact on the required number of health professionals (Weiner 2004; Weiner et al. 1986). As the share of the population registered in these different provider models has seen relevant fluctuations, demand forecasts also need to take these changes into account.

The fundamental critique of demand-based models lies in the fact that current levels of health care utilization are strongly influenced by current supply levels and structure: A shortage of locally accessible physicians may lead to lower utilization in ambulatory care and, possibly, in a higher number of hospitalizations (Ozegowski and Sundmacher 2014; Sundmacher and Kopetsch 2014). An oversupply of physicians may, as explained above, induce higher utilization than "objectively" needed. Remuneration systems are also known to have a considerable effect on utilization of care: Fee-for-service models increase utilization, while health systems with capitation or salary-based remuneration usually have lower utilization rates (Gosden et al. 2000). Quarterly lump-sum fees might induce physicians to set the next appointment for their patients for the next quarter even when a lower (or higher) frequency would be appropriate.

Therefore, demand-based models have a tendency to reproduce current levels of over- or under-supply rather than estimating an optimal allocation of resources.

12.2.3 Needs-Based Planning

Needs-based planning is an attempt to overcome the problems rooted in demands-based models and, therefore, takes a fundamentally different approach.

The United States' Graduate Medical Education National Advisory Committee (GMENAC), which undertook one of the most comprehensive efforts in setting up a needs-based model, defined 'need' as "that quantity of medical services which expert medical opinion believes ought to be consumed over a relevant time period in order for its members to remain or become as healthy as possible given by existing medical knowledge" (GMENAC 1980, 5). This definition implies that there is a "right" level and type of health care services for each patient and that these decisions are not made by the patient him- or herself but rather by an "objective" medical expert.

In order to arrive at a needs-based estimation of health care services, it is necessary to approximate the morbidity of the population, the type and complexity of care (per provider) required for each morbidity, and to project future changes in both morbidity and (evidence-based) health care service provision.

Case Example 1
The GMENAC was chartered from 1976 to 1980 by the US Department of Health and Human Services to develop such an approach. The committee was comprised of 22 health care experts and it was supported by more than 300 consultants (McNutt 1981). Its goal was to estimate physician requirements for 23 different specialty groups as of 1990. In order to do so it set up Delphi panels for each physician specialty group consisting of 8–10 experts with different professional backgrounds. Each of these Delphi panels applied the following methodology (GMENAC 1980):

- It identified the incidence and prevalence of the major diseases based on epidemiological data;
- it determined the relevance of each disease for the specific specialty based on utilization data and expert judgment;
- it projected the changes in morbidity for each disease considered until the year 1990 based on changes in population size and (age- and sex-specific) structure;
- it adjusted for known measurement problems;

(continued)

- it took into account the "knowledge of the realities of provider and consumer behavior" (GMENAC 1980, 11), i.e., supplier- or patient-induced over-supply as well as undersupply from unmet needs, e.g., due to the limited ability to pay;
- it added a lump sum for the diseases which were not considered specifically.

These steps left each panel with an estimation of the burden of disease relevant for the health system. In the next step it converted these figures into resource requirements:

- It estimated the number and time of required units of care;
- it adjusted these findings by assumptions on increased potential for delegation of services to non-physician practice staff;
- it estimated physician productivity.

Thereby, each panel arrived at an estimation of the number of physicians required for each specialty. In order to account for the uncertainties in the model, the panels phrased their outcome in terms of a range of required physicians. The size of these ranges oscillated between $\pm 1\%$ (hematology/oncology) and $\pm 25\%$ (psychiatry) (own calculations based on GMENAC 1980, 22). Overall, the committee came to the conclusion that there would be a 15% surplus in physicians by 1990 and a 30% surplus by 2000.

The GMENAC was chartered from 1976 to 1980 by the US Department of Health and Human Services to forecast future physician supply requirements based on a needs-based planning approach. In a complex process that took more than three years to be completed it developed an analytical framework based on projecting changes in morbidity and applied it to all major physician specialties (see Case Example 1 for further details). The GMENAC findings led to an outcry at the time of publication and have been questioned by stakeholders (Reinhardt 1981). Harris (1986) brought forward many examples where the GMENAC projections were significantly off the reality (e.g., with regards to HIV, caesarean sections, etc.). Especially since the 2000s, many feared a shortage of physicians rather than a 30% surplus, mainly due to an expected surge in demand and lower productivity per physician (Cooper 1995; Weiner 2002). Nonetheless, the GMENAC work has remained the largest effort in implementing an (adjusted) needs-based model to date. The physician-patient ratios the GMENAC predicted are still used by providers today despite the heavy criticism and the fact that they were only updated once in 1990 (Camden Group 2011).[1]

---

[1]To the merit of the GMENAC, it should also be said that the US health care system is probably one of the most difficult for which to forecast physician supply requirements. First of all, it is a very large country with many different subcultures affecting health demand and patient

12.2.4 Benchmarks

A fourth approach to workforce planning is benchmarking. Benchmarks are formulated in terms of physician-population ratios, nurse-population ratios or other ratios of health professionals set in relation to the population. The degree of refinement of benchmarks can vary immensely: On the broadest level there may be a health workforce-to-population ratio. On a very refined level, it is possible to derive benchmarks for each specialty health professional group in relation to age- and sex-specific population cohorts.

There are various sources for benchmarks: The GMENAC ratios are still used, as mentioned above. Other benchmarks have been retrieved from HMOs or hospital referral regions (Goodman et al. 1996). A clear advantage of benchmarks is that they are simple to use and easy to apply. Also they may avert some of the problems rooted in demand-based models: Namely, demand-based models usually rest on the assumption that current utilization and supply levels reflect optimal care, without proving that assumption. Benchmarks, on the other hand, are drawn from integrated care systems which are deemed best practice (e.g., HMOs), from national average ratios or they rely on scientific evidence (e.g., GMENAC ratios). These benchmark staff ratios are then applied to the specific setting of the workforce planner, possibly after being modified to reflect the specificities of the setting. While this approach is easy to implement, it also has its disadvantages: Benchmarks show an immense variation based on their source. Therefore, the choice of the "right" benchmark is highly critical. Weiner (2004) compared three different HMOs (Kaiser Permanente, Group Health Cooperative, HealthPartners) against the national US average health workforce density. Despite adjustments for differences in demographics and services provided, HMO ratios ranged between 62% and 86% (primary care physicians), 63% and 71% (specialist physicians), and 63% and 93% (nonphysician health professionals) compared to the US average. In an older survey of 54 HMOs, Dial et al. (1995) also reported wide variations in physician-population ratios between HMOs and identified the HMO size to be one of the critical determinants for staffing ratios: HMOs with more than 80,000 enrollees were much more homogeneous in their physician-to-population ratios than were smaller ones. In a more recent comparison between nine patient-centred medical homes[2] (PCMH), Patel et al. (2013) found a variation in panel sizes from 625 to 2500. Even within

---

preferences. Secondly, the provider structure is highly fragmented leaving providers with very different abilities in managing patient demand.

[2]PCMH is a model of care from the United States which puts primary care in the centre and rests on the notion of transforming health care structures to ensure patient-centred, accessible, and coordinated health care (Agency for Healthcare Research and Quality, n.d.).

one HMO (Kaiser Permanente), differences in panel sizes between sites were reported due to different models of care (Neuwirth et al. 2007).

Therefore, the use of benchmarks is certainly helpful as it reduces complexity of planning. However, the applicability of a benchmark ratio should be critically reviewed when used in a different setting.

12.2.5 Limitations of Current Planning Approaches in Integrated Care Settings

Despite the extensive research and practical experience, workforce planning remains a difficult task. The fundamental challenge to workforce planning is that it is subject to a large degree of uncertainty. Planning models have dealt with that uncertainty by applying one of two available strategies: They have either used very simple models, e.g., benchmarks or rules of thumb, which were then adjusted in the daily operations or timeline models extrapolating future trends based on past levels of physician demand and supply (Dial et al. 1995). A second strategy is to build complex models assessing all possible influencing variables and requiring the planner to make assumptions for those variables that are uncertain. An example of that is the needs-based approach.

A study estimating the future need for otolaryngologists in the US has illustrated these challenges: Applying the demand-based model by the US Bureau of Health Professionals, the needs-based model according to the GMENAC methodology, and benchmarks from different HMOs, Anderson et al. (1997) resulted in a large variability of results both within and between models. Each model could predict both, a considerable shortage or a considerable oversupply of otolaryngologists, based on the precise assumptions and despite the fact that the forecasting period of six years was rather short. Similarly, in a retrospective analysis of different forecasts, Roberfroid et al. (2009) found considerable margins of error between forecast and reality. This underlines that workforce planning will never become an exact science but should be seen as a dynamic process requiring regular re-evaluation in light of actualities.

A second challenge in these modelling approaches arises with respect to integrated care: These models are rooted in systems with a single physician at the nexus of care. Hence these planning models attempt to estimate the "right" number of each physician specialty and non-physician provider separately. This ignores the fact that many patients suffer from multiple chronic conditions requiring team-based approaches to care. Dial et al. (1995) showed that the model of care played a large role for staffing levels of HMOs: HMOs with fewer primary care physicians had a much higher ratio of advanced practice nurses in comparison, and vice versa. Thus, applying the primary care physician ratio of one HMO to another setting may be very misleading if the models of care are different.

Thirdly, recent changes in models of care also involve a shift in the physician-patient relationship which in turn clashes with some of the planning models outlined above (Institute of Medicine 2001). The needs-based planning model in particular is rooted in a paternalistic notion of the physician-patient relationship: It is the physician who determines by "objective" criteria the "projected biologic requirements" (GMENAC 1980, 6) of patients. Taking into account patients' preferences and subjectively perceived needs, which is standard in a physician-patient relationship with shared decision making, is in clear contradiction to that planning model.

12.3 New Approaches to Workforce Planning in Integrated Care

In order to address these limitations, new approaches have evolved over the past several years. With regard to integrated care, the techniques applied by managed care-based provider models, such as HMOs and PCMHs, are of interest.

12.3.1 Team-Based Workforce Planning

As outlined above, modelling the demand for single professional groups has serious limitations in an integrated care setting. As integrated care relies on the notion of sharing the patient across different professional groups—both physicians and non-physicians—according to the specific qualification of each professional role, the team-based model of care also needs to be reflected in workforce planning. The Veterans Health Administration in the US has adopted such a team-based planning model. Each team consists of 1 FTE primary care practitioner (PCP) and a support staff of 2.17 FTE (such as registered nurses, pharmacists, medical assistants, etc.) and is expected to handle a panel size of 1200 patients of an average case-mix. However, teams with larger support staff are encouraged: For every additional (reduced) 10% of FTE support staff, panel sizes are expected to increase (decrease) by 2.5%. If the PCP is not a medical doctor, but a nurse practitioner or physician assistant, expected panel sizes are decreased by 25% (Department of Veterans Affairs 2009). These benchmarks have been collected over time from the Veterans Health Administration.

Are these benchmarks applicable to other providers? A comparison of several studies of integrated healthcare delivery systems showed that the fraction of primary care visits handled by nurse practitioners varied between 9 and 70% (Green et al. 2013). Such large ranges are also found for advanced practice nurses (Grover and Niecko-Najjum 2013). These variations clearly illustrate that it can be very misleading to pick out benchmarks for just one professional group from an integrated healthcare delivery system. Instead, the benchmarks can only be reliably copied when the entire model of care is comparable.

Another challenge for learning from international best practices in team-based workforce planning lies in the differences in regulatory requirements. In the US, for instance, each state has different regulatory requirements for non-physician professionals, which makes workforce planning and transferability of proven models of care rather difficult (Grover and Niecko-Najjum 2013). In Germany, both regulatory and political aspects play a large role when it comes to non-physician health care professionals: There is strong opposition to a greater differentiation of health workforce qualifications. Especially the Physicians' Chamber and the Federal Association of SHI Physicians fear that physicians may lose their exclusive right to the vast set of tasks that they perform today, and that they might in conjunction have to render a share of their budget to other professional groups. Therefore, the recent setup of academic programs for physician assistants has been met by an outcry by the Federal Association of SHI Physicians (Beerheide 2014). In that context, workforce planning becomes a real challenge: On the one hand, the Associations of SHI Physicians have the obligation (as public institutions) to ensure adequate access to outpatient care, which is a challenge for primary care in many rural areas. On the other hand, the associations represent the political interests of outpatient care physicians and, therefore, combat any changes that (seemingly) dilute current privileges of physicians.

12.3.2 Pro-active Management of Health Care Utilization

The application of managed care instruments, such as gatekeeping, case management/panel management, disease management, and financial incentives, plays a large role in patient pathways and influences actual utilization patterns. Kaiser Permanente has, for instance, developed the concept of total panel ownership which advocates a proactive role for primary care teams in identifying unmet patient needs (Livaudais et al. 2006; Neuwirth et al. 2007). GroupHealth, an integrated care provider based in Seattle (US), piloted a project in 2006 in which it significantly reduced panel sizes for primary care physicians, extending the time physicians spent with each patient by 50%, and introducing further care modules, such as Chronic Care Management, to its model of care. These reforms resulted in a significant decrease in emergency care visits, an increase in patient satisfaction, and a decrease in total costs compared to other GroupHealth sites (Reid et al. 2010).

Another important factor is the degree of integration, e.g., whether long-term care providers and social services are also part of the system. Montefiore Medical Center, which serves 500,000 residents in the Bronx, one of the poorest urban communities in the United States, has tightly integrated health and social care services (Chase 2010). It considers this as one of its key success factors as it shifts demand from physicians to nurses and social workers, which conserves physician resources and is expected to be more sustainable in the long-term.

Finally, during the 1990s and early 2000s, many HMOs struggled with significant wait times for their patients, which both hurt their reputation as a provider among patients and as an employer among health professionals (Murray and Berwick 2003). In response, the model of "advanced access" (or "open access") was developed. It was based on queuing theory which shows that transferring work to the future leads to inefficiencies. Thus, advanced access rejects appointment-based practice management and triage systems and, instead, relies on the idea of "doing today's work today" (Murray and Berwick 2003). Any patient who calls for an appointment is offered an appointment on the same day with his or her preferred provider. Implementing advanced access has significant consequences for panel sizes and, thus, workforce planning (Murray et al. 2007). However, empirical results of advanced access are mixed: While some provider-specific studies reported significant improvements in workforce productivity (Lewandowski et al. 2006), a systematic review reported mixed results on patient satisfaction and patient outcomes (Rose et al. 2011). Thus, it remains to be seen to what degree advanced access models will be implemented in the future.

12.3.3 Tackling Geographic Variations Through Technology

The use of technology and its (future) impact on health services has been commented on several times. One of its potentials lies in alleviating problems related to the geographic location of health care providers. A recent Cochrane systematic review illustrated that interactive telemedicine can substitute for face-to-face care while health outcomes remain comparable to usual care or improved (Flodgren et al. 2015). Structured telephone support, telemonitoring and text messaging have also shown to improve outcomes compared to usual care (Free et al. 2013; Inglis et al. 2010).

Kaiser Permanente Hawaii introduced two new elements in its delivery system: (1) an electronic health record to facilitate communication and coordination between health professionals, and (2) telephone access and secure messaging services between patients and their PCP. An initial study revealed that the number of total office visits decreased by 26% within three years; at the same time, scheduled phone calls and secure messaging rose considerably (Chen et al. 2009). Overall, ambulatory care contacts rose by 8% within the 3-year study period. Unfortunately, as the study did not include a control group, it remains unknown whether previously unmet needs were addressed by the new delivery model. Also, possible effects on process or outcomes quality were not assessed. However, this study and the systematic reviews cited above illustrate that the importance of geographic vicinity for service delivery may be reduced through the use of technology. This also impacts workforce planning: If patients need to visit their health care provider less frequently, longer travel times may be acceptable, which in turn allows for larger catchment areas in the planning process. In fact, if certain services no longer require face-to-face visits, geographic vicinity would no longer be a constraint for these services/providers.

12.4   Conclusion

Planning, especially workforce planning, has been high on the agenda of health policy makers, practitioners, and researchers for the past 40 years. Various methods have been developed and become more and more refined. Recent changes to models of care have again called into question much of the established methodologies. That applies in particular to integrated care where clearly specified tasks for single practitioners are replaced by a team-based, pro-active approach to care delivery.

Where does that leave us in terms of planning? I propose four key lessons:

1) Setting objectives and standards of care
Before making a plan, it is central to formulate the objectives and minimum service level standards of the specific delivery system—either in terms of structural and process indicators (such as minimum service level standards, geographic catchment areas, or maximum wait times), and/or in terms of health outcomes. This step is essential for assessing the performance of a plan—especially, if we accept the hypothesis that demand for health care services is infinite and will thus never be fully met.

2) Aligning planning approaches with the specific model of care
As we have seen, there is not one perfect methodology for workforce planning. A number of methodologies exist all of which have their pros and cons. The chosen planning approach and in particular the use of benchmarks should be tightly linked to the specified objectives, the specific model of care, and its particular setting.

3) Monitor and adapt constantly
Workforce planning is not a one-time exercise, but should be seen as a dynamic process which serves to (1) set a baseline for the required (human) resources at the start, and (2) on a meta level establish an agreement on the objectives of the delivery system and consistently verify and re-negotiate that agreement. Once adopted, the assumptions made in the workforce plan should be monitored against reality and adapted accordingly.

4) Integrated care calls for integrated planning
Integrated care moves away from the narrow focus on physicians as the central providers of health care, makes extensive use of technology, and aims for patient-centred, proactive models of care. Such a fundamental change in the understanding of health care also implies a fundamental change in workforce planning: It requires team-based, integrated planning approaches, it involves taking into account all the available communication channels, and it implies a shift of resources towards care coordination as well as fast and easy access to primary care in order to avert unnecessary utilization of highly-specialized (and often costly) care providers.

References

Agency for Healthcare Research and Quality. (n.d.). *Defining the PCMH*. Retrieved February 28, 2016, from https://pcmh.ahrq.gov/page/defining-pcmh

Altschuler, J., Margolius, D., Bodenheimer, T., & Grumbach, K. (2012). Estimating a reasonable patient panel size for primary care physicians with team-based task delegation. *Annals of Family Medicine, 10*(5), 396–400.

Anderson, G. F., Han, K. C., Miller, R. H., & Johns, M. E. (1997). A comparison of three methods for estimating the requirements for medical specialists: The case of otolaryngologists. *Health Services Research, 32*(2), 139–153.

Baumol, W. J., & De Ferranti, D. M. (2012). *The cost disease: Why computers get cheaper and health care doesn't*. London: Yale University Press.

Beerheide, R. (2014). *Scharfe Kritik an neuen Studiengängen*. Ärzte Ztg. Retrieved October 18, 2015, from http://www.aerztezeitung.de/politik_gesellschaft/berufspolitik/article/861854/substitution-scharfe-kritik-neuen-studiengaengen.html

Bloor, K., & Maynard, A. (2003). *Planning human resources in health care: Towards an economic approach. An international comparative review*. Ottawa: Canadian Health Services Research Foundation. Retrieved October 18, 2015, from http://www.chsrf.ca/Migrated/PDF/ResearchReports/CommissionedResearch/bloor_report.pdf

Bureau of Health Professions. (2008). *The physician workforce: Projections and research into current issues affecting supply and demand* (p. 111). Retrieved October 20, 2015, from http://bhpr.hrsa.gov/healthworkforce/supplydemand/medicine/physiciansupplyissues.pdf

Camden Group (2011). *Final physician needs assessment*. Report as of July 2010. Bellingham, Washington. Retrieved October 20, 2015, from http://www.whatcomalliance.org/wp-content/uploads/2011/02/Camden1-28-11.pdf

Chase, D. (2010). Montefiore medical center: Integrated care delivery for vulnerable populations. Case study. *The Commonwealth Fund, 53*(1448). Retrieved October 20, 2015, from http://www.commonwealthfund.org/~/media/files/publications/case-study/2010/oct/1448_chase_montefiore_med_ctr_case_study_v2.pdf

Chen, C., Garrido, T., Chock, D., Okawa, G., & Liang, L. (2009). The Kaiser Permanente electronic health record: Transforming and streamlining modalities of care. *Health Affairs, 28*(2), 323–333.

Cooper, R. A. (1995). Perspectives on the physician workforce to the year 2020. *Journal of the American Medical Association, 274*(19), 1534–1543.

Crettenden, I. F., McCarty, M. V., Fenech, B. J., Heywood, T., Taitz, M. C., & Tudman, S. (2014). How evidence-based workforce planning in Australia is informing policy development in the retention and distribution of the health workforce. *Human Resources for Health, 12*, 7.

Crimmins, E. M., & Beltran-Sanchez, H. (2011). Mortality and morbidity trends: Is there compression of morbidity? *The Journals of Gerontology. Series B, Psychological Sciences and Social Sciences, 66B*(1), 75–86.

Cunningham, R. (2013). Health workforce needs: Projections complicated by practice and technology changes. *Issue Brief George Washington University. National Health Policy Forum., 851*, 1–15.

de Cruppé, W., Malik, M., & Geraedts, M. (2015). Minimum volume standards in German hospitals: Do they get along with procedure centralization? A retrospective longitudinal data analysis. *BMC Health Services Research, 15*.

Department of Veterans Affairs (2009). *VHA handbook 1101.02: Primary care management module (PCMM)*. Washington, DC. Retrieved October 18, 2015, from http://www.va.gov/vhapublications/ViewPublication.asp?pub_ID=2017

Dial, T. H., Palsbo, S. E., Bergsten, C., Gabel, J. R., & Weiner, J. (1995). Clinical staffing in staff- and group-model HMOs. *Health Affairs, 14*(2), 168–180.

Dussault, G., Buchan, J., Walter, S., & Padaiga, Z. (2010). *Assessing future health workforce needs*. Retrieved October 20, 2015, from http://www.euro.who.int/__data/assets/pdf_file/0019/124417/e94295.pdf

Flodgren, G., Rachas, A., Farmer, A. J., Inzitari, M., & Shepperd, S. (2015). Interactive telemedicine: Effects on professional practice and health care outcomes. In The Cochrane Collaboration (Ed.), *Cochrane database of systematic review*. Chichester: Wiley.

Free, C., Phillips, G., Galli, L., Watson, L., Felix, L., Edwards, P., et al. (2013). The effectiveness of mobile-health technology-based health behaviour change or disease management interventions for health care consumers: A systematic review. *PLoS Medicine, 10*(1), e1001362.

Fries, J. F., Bruce, B., & Chakravarty, E. (2011). Compression of morbidity 1980–2011: A focused review of paradigms and progress. *Journal of Aging Research, 2011*, 1–10.

Garrido, M. V., Zentner, A., & Busse, R. (2011). The effects of gatekeeping: A systematic review of the literature. *Scandinavian Journal of Primary Health Care, 29*(1), 28–38.

GMENAC (1980). *Report of the graduate medical education national advisory committee to the secretary, department of health and human services: Vol. II. Modeling, research, and data technical panel* (p. 348). Hyattsville, MD: The US American Graduate Medical Education National Advisory Committee. Report No. HRA-81-652. Retrieved October 20, 2015, from http://eric.ed.gov/?id=ED203766

Goodman, D. C., Fisher, E. S., Bubolz, T. A., Mohr, J. E., Poage, J. F., & Wennberg, J. E. (1996). Benchmarking the US physician workforce: An alternative to needs-based or demand-based planning. *Journal of the American Medical Association, 276*(22), 1811–1817.

Gosden, T., Forland, F., Kristiansen, I., Sutton, M., Leese, B., Giuffrida, A., et al. (2000). Capitation, salary, fee-for-service and mixed systems of payment: Effects on the behaviour of primary care physicians. *Cochrane Database of Systematic Review, 3*, CD002215.

Green, L. V., Savin, S., & Lu, Y. (2013). Primary care physician shortages could be eliminated through use of teams, nonphysicians and electronic communication. *Health Affairs, 32*(1), 11–19.

Greene, J., & Moline, K. (2006). *The bird flu pandemic: Can it happen? Will it happen? How to protect yourself and your family if it does* (1st ed.). New York: Thomas Dunne Books.

Grover, A., & Niecko-Najjum, L. M. (2013). Primary care teams: Are we there yet? Implications for workforce planning. *Academic Medicine, 88*(12), 1827–1829.

Harris, J. E. (1986). How many doctors are enough? *Health Affairs, 5*(4), 73–83.

Inglis, S. C., Clark, R. A., McAlister, F. A., Ball, J., Lewinter, C., Cullington, D., et al. (2010). Structured telephone support or telemonitoring programmes for patients with chronic heart failure. *Cochrane Database of Systematic Review, 8*, CD007228.

Institute of Medicine (2001). *Crossing the quality chasm: A new health system for the 21st century*. Washington, DC: National Academy Press.

Jacobson, M., Earle, C. C., Price, M., & Newhouse, J. P. (2010). How medicare's payment cuts for cancer chemotherapy drugs changed patterns of treatment. *Health Affairs, 29*(7), 1391–1399.

JAHWPF (2015). *Handbook on health workforce planning – methodologies across EU countries*. Release 1. Retrieved October 20, 2015, from http://euhwforce.weebly.com/uploads/2/3/0/5/23054358/d052_-_handbook_on_planning_methodologies_-_release_1.pdf

Krabbe-Alkemade, Y. J. F. M., Groot, T. L. C. M., & Lindeboom, M. (2017). Competition in the Dutch hospital sector: An analysis of health care volume and cost. *European Journal of Health Economics, 18*(2), 139–153.

Laven, G., & Wilkinson, D. (2003). Rural doctors and rural backgrounds: How strong is the evidence? A systematic review. *The Australian Journal of Rural Health, 11*(6), 277–284.

Lewandowski, S., O'Connor, P. J., Solberg, L. I., Lais, T., Hroscikoski, M., & Sperl-Hillen, J. M. (2006). Increasing primary care physician productivity: A case study. *The American Journal of Managed Care, 12*(10), 573–576.

Livaudais, G., Unitan, R., & Post, J. (2006). Total panel ownership and the panel support tool--"It's all about the relationship". *The Permanente Journal, 10*(2), 72–79.

McNutt, D. R. (1981). GMENAC: Its manpower forecasting framework. *American Journal of Public Health, 71*(10), 1116–1124.

Møller Pedersen, K. (2009). *Restructuring & modernizing the hospital sector.* Health Policy Monitor. Retrieved October 20, 2015, from http://www.hpm.org/survey/dk/a13/5

Murray, M., & Berwick, D. M. (2003). Advanced access: reducing waiting and delays in primary care. *Journal of the American Medical Association, 289*(8), 1035–1040.

Murray, M., Davies, M., & Boushon, B. (2007). Panel size: How many patients can one doctor manage? *Family Practice Management, 14*(4), 44–51.

Neuwirth, E. B., Schmittdiel, J. A., Tallman, K., & Bellows, J. (2007). Understanding panel management: A comparative study of an emerging approach to population care. *The Permanente Journal, 11*(3), 12–20.

Ono, T., Schoenstein, M., & Lafortune, G. (2013, June). *Health workforce planning in OECD countries: A review of 26 projection models from 18 countries* (Report No. 62). Retrieved October 20, 2015, from http://www.oecd-ilibrary.org/social-issues-migration-health/health-workforce-planning-in-oecd-countries_5k44t787zcwb-en

Ozegowski, S., & Sundmacher, L. (2014). Understanding the gap between need and utilization in outpatient care—The effect of supply-side determinants on regional inequities. *Health Policy, 114*(1), 54–63.

Patel, M. S., Arron, M. J., Sinsky, T. A., Green, E. H., Baker, D. W., Bowen, J. L., et al. (2013). Estimating the staffing infrastructure for a patient-centered medical home. *The American Journal of Managed Care, 19*(6), 509–516.

Petterson, S. M., Liaw, W. R., Phillips, R. L., Rabin, D. L., Meyers, D. S., & Bazemore, A. W. (2012). Projecting US primary care physician workforce needs: 2010–2025. *Annals of Family Medicine, 10*(6), 503–509.

Reid, R. J., Coleman, K., Johnson, E. A., Fishman, P. A., Hsu, C., Soman, M. P., et al. (2010). The group health medical home at year two: Cost savings, higher patient satisfaction, and less burnout for providers. *Health Affairs, 29*(5), 835–843.

Reinhardt, U. E. (1981). The GMENAC forecast: An alternative view. *American Journal of Public Health, 71*(10), 1149–1157.

Roberfroid, D., Leonard, C., & Stordeur, S. (2009). Physician supply forecast: Better than peering in a crystal ball? *Human Resources for Health, 7*, 10.

Roberfroid, D., Stordeur, S., Camberlin, C., Van de Voorde, C., Vrijens, F., & Léonard, C. (2008). *Physician workforce supply in Belgium: Current situation and challenges.* Health Services Research (HSR). Brussels: Belgian Health Care Knowledge Centre (KCE). Retrieved October 20, 2015, from https://kce.fgov.be/sites/default/files/page_documents/d20081027309.pdf

Rose, K. D., Ross, J. S., & Horwitz, L. I. (2011). Advanced access scheduling outcomes: A systematic review. *Archives of Internal Medicine, 171*(13), 1150–1159.

Seematter-Bagnoud, L., Junod, J., Ruedin, H. J., Roth, M., Foletti, C., & Santos-Eggimann, B. (2008). *Offre et recours aux soins médicaux ambulatoires en Suisse - Projections à l'horizon 2030.* Neuchâtel: Schweizerisches Gesundheitsobservatorium (Obsan). Retrieved October 20, 2015, from http://www.obsan.admin.ch/sites/default/files/publications/2015/arbeitsdokument-33.pdf

Shadmi, E., Balicer, R. D., Kinder, K., Abrams, C., & Weiner, J. P. (2011). Assessing socioeconomic health care utilization inequity in Israel: Impact of alternative approaches to morbidity adjustment. *BMC Public Health, 11*(1), 609.

Simoens, S., Villeneuve, M., & Hurst, J. (2005). *Tackling nurse shortages in OECD countries* (OECD Health Working Papers Report No. 19). Retrieved October 20, 2015, from http://www.oecd-ilibrary.org/social-issues-migration-health/tackling-nurse-shortages-in-oecd-countries_172102620474

Sundmacher, L., & Kopetsch, T. (2014). The impact of office-based care on hospitalizations for ambulatory care sensitive conditions. *European Journal of Health Economics, 16*(4), 365–375.

Thode, N., Bergmann, D. E., Kamtsiuris, P., & Kurth, B.-M. (2005). Einflussfaktoren auf die ambulante Inanspruchnahme in Deutschland. *Bundesgesundheitsblatt Gesundheitsforsch Gesundheitsschutz, 48*(3), 296–306.

Weiner, J. P. (2002). A shortage of physicians or a surplus of assumptions? *Health Affairs, 21*(1), 160–162.

Weiner, J. P. (2004). Prepaid group practice staffing and U.S. physician supply: Lessons for workforce policy. *Health Affairs.* Suppl Web Exclusives:W4-43-59.

Weiner, J. P., Steinwachs, D. M., & Williamson, J. W. (1986). Nurse practitioner and physician assistant practices in three HMOs: Implications for future US health manpower needs. *American Journal of Public Health, 76*(5), 507–511.

Weiner, J. P., Yeh, S., & Blumenthal, D. (2013). The impact of health information technology and e-health on the future demand for physician services. *Health Affairs, 32*(11), 1998–2004.

WHO. (2013). *The right to health.* Retrieved October 20, 2015, from http://www.who.int/mediacentre/factsheets/fs323/en/

Wilson, N. W., Couper, I. D., De Vries, E., Reid, S., Fish, T., & Marais, B. J. (2009). A critical review of interventions to redress the inequitable distribution of healthcare professionals to rural and remote areas. *Rural and Remote Health, 9*(2), 1060.

Integrated Care and the Health Workforce 13

Loraine Busetto, Stefano Calciolari, Laura Guadalupe González Ortiz, Katrien Luijkx, and Bert Vrijhoef

13.1 Background

The past decades have been characterised by the growing prevalence of chronic diseases, the rising number of older and often multi-morbid patients, and changes in the definitions of health and illness (Imison and Bohmer 2013; Centre for Workforce Intelligence 2011; Calciolari and Ilinca 2011a). These developments have led to an increased demand for complex, long-term care (Vrijhoef 2014). However, most health systems are currently ill-equipped to respond to this demand (Chap. 12). Specifically, chronically ill patients too often have to consult multiple providers who lack coordination among themselves and across settings, resulting in care that is ineffective and inefficient (Coleman et al. 2009). In addition, World Health Organization (WHO) statistics estimate that workforce shortage amounts to 2.4 million physicians, nurses and midwives within Europe (World Health Organization 2016).

L. Busetto (✉) • K. Luijkx
Tranzo Scientific Center for Care and Welfare, Tilburg University, Tilburg, The Netherlands
e-mail: L.Busetto@uvt.nl; loraine.busetto@med.uni-heidelberg.de; k.g.luijkx@tilburguniversity.edu

S. Calciolari • L.G. González Ortiz
Institute of Economics (IdEP), Università della Svizzera Italiana, Lugano, Switzerland
e-mail: stefano.calciolari@usi.ch; laura.guadalupe.gonzales.ortiz@usi.ch

B. Vrijhoef
Tranzo Scientific Center for Care and Welfare, Tilburg University, Tilburg, The Netherlands

Panaxea B.V., Amsterdam, The Netherlands

Department of Patient and Care, Maastricht University Medical Center, Maastricht, The Netherlands

Department of Family Medicine and Chronic Care, Vrije Universiteit Brussel, Brussels, Belgium
e-mail: vrijhoef_hubertus@nuhs.edu.sg; b.vrijhoef@mumc.nl

© Springer International Publishing AG 2017   209
V. Amelung et al. (eds.), *Handbook Integrated Care*,
DOI 10.1007/978-3-319-56103-5_13

There is an obvious mismatch between the most prevalent health problems, i.e. (multiple) chronic diseases, and the preparation of the workforce to deal with them, since training in most countries still relies on models that emphasise diagnosis and treatment of acute diseases (Pruitt and Epping-Jordan 2005). This is likely to result in an imbalance between the increasing demand for complex long-term care and the low supply of health professionals equipped to work in these areas. Although this global crisis in the health care workforce has been noticed for more than a decade (Pruitt and Epping-Jordan 2005; World Health Organization 2004), new care models and initiatives to integrate care services have paid only minor attention to how to deal with this. Since these misalignments are likely to influence the quality of care negatively, changes are needed to cope with the necessity of matching knowledge and competences of the workforce with current and future needs (Imison and Bohmer 2013). According to Pruitt and Epping-Jordan, patients with on-going health problems are in need of

> ...treatment that is continuous across settings and across types of providers; care for chronic conditions needs to be coordinated over time. Healthcare workers need to collaborate with each other and with patients to develop treatment plans, goals, and implementation strategies that centre on the needs, values, and preferences of patients and their families. Self-management skills and behaviours to prevent complications need to be supported by a workforce that understands the fundamental differences between episodic illness that is identified and cured and chronic conditions that require management across years (Pruitt and Epping-Jordan 2005).

Many health systems have endorsed integrated care strategies as a means to approach the above challenges. These are expected to lead to better outcomes, increased efficiency and improved access for service users (Center for Workforce Intelligence 2013). Generally, integrated care strategies include changes to patient-provider relationships, care process designs, communication infrastructures and staffing provisions. Given health professionals' involvement in all aspects of integrated care, it is assumed that workforce and staffing interventions will affect the implementation of integrated care strategies profoundly (Imison and Bohmer 2013; Deloitte Center for Health Solutions 2012). Consider, for example, the additional demands that are put on the skill set of health professionals when they are expected to provide person-centred care to well-informed patients wanting to take part in decision-making processes. Or consider the differences in culture between those working in health care as opposed to community care, who are expected to cooperate closely and efficiently around complex patients. Another example is the adoption of information technology in health care whose implementation necessarily requires workers to adjust their skill sets and may sometimes even replace certain activities or tasks currently employed by humans.

The WHO argues that there is a need for new competencies to complement existing ones for caring for people with chronic conditions:

> First, the workforce needs to organize care around the patient, i.e. adopt a patient-centred approach. This focus has been described as one in which the provider tries to enter the

patient's world, to see the illness through the eyes of the patient. Second, providers need communication skills that enable them to collaborate with others. They need not only to partner with patients, but to work closely with other providers and join with communities to improve outcomes for patients with chronic conditions. Third, the workforce needs skills to ensure that the safety and quality of patient care are continuously improved. Fourth, the workforce needs skills that assist them in monitoring patients across time, using and sharing information through available technology. Finally, the workforce needs to consider patient care and the provider's role in that care from the broadest perspective, including population-based care, multiple levels of the health care system, and the care continuum (World Health Organization 2005).

Human resources in health care (hereafter also called *health workforce* or, simply, *workforce*) are "the different types of clinical and non-clinical staff responsible for public and individual health interventions" (Kabene et al. 2006). As explained by Glouberman and Mintzberg (2001a, b), the health workforce delivers health care in different professional "worlds" in terms of setting (e.g. acute or chronic care) or service focus (e.g. cure or care). A high degree of specialisation within these worlds can serve the interests of the patients, but only as long as the different worlds are appropriately integrated, thus keeping complexity under control at the point of service (Glouberman and Mintzberg 2001a).

As argued above, it has become clear that patients with complex health and social problems require a mix of providers that can collectively address their needs, as one provider cannot possibly have all the necessary skills. This involves two essential steps. The first step is to design the appropriate staff and skill mix of the group of health professionals providing care to a specific patient population; the second step is to organise and manage the interaction of this group of health professionals in practice.

13.2   Staff Mix and Skill Management

According to Dubois and Singh, health workforce management may entail strategies with regard to *staff mix* and *skill management* (Dubois and Singh 2009; Griffiths 2012). While the former concept is concerned with the different staff members that hold certain skills, the latter concept is concerned with the different skills that are held by the staff members. Or as Dubois and Singh explain, staff mix refers to "achieving a specific mix of different types of personnel", whereas skill management refers to "adapting workers' attributes (...) and roles to changing environmental conditions and demands" (Dubois and Singh 2009).

Specifically, *staff mix* concerns the mix of posts, grades or occupations in a system or organisation. It includes the following aspects:

a. *number of workers* in defined occupational groups, holding a certain volume of work assigned to staff members, e.g., number of full-time equivalent workers, such as nurses per patient;

b. *mix of qualifications* refers to the proportion of highly qualified staff members in the respective health workforce or occupational group, e.g. registered or specialised nurses, physicians with specialty certifications;

c. *balance between junior and senior staff members*, i.e. the proportion of experienced staff in the health workforce;

d. *mix of disciplines* refers to gathering together personnel from different professions and/or professionals with different specialties. In this respect, interventions are intended to foster comprehensive care through professional cooperation (Dubois and Singh 2009).

While staff mix aims at reaching a certain mix of personnel, *skill management* relates more specifically to how the use of staff members' skills can be optimised by adapting their roles, knowledge, skills, and know-how. In doing so, skill management may entail two different areas of intervention, namely (a) *skill development* and (b) *skill flexibility*. Skill development does not entail adding functions from other professions. In particular, it concerns:

a. *role enhancement/enrichment:* enable groups of workers to acquire new competencies and skills by designing new roles for them, with expanded tasks and wider and/or higher range of responsibilities;

b. *role enlargement:* extending activities and taking on roles at parallel or lower levels (Dubois and Singh 2009).

Skill flexibility relies on multi-skilled workers who can switch from one professional role to another. It concerns:

a. *role substitution*, which refers to extending the practice scope by encouraging the personnel to work across and beyond traditional professional divides;

b. *role delegation*, which consists of transferring tasks from one grade to another by breaking down traditional job demarcations (Dubois and Singh 2009).

Organisations may not be able to control all aspects of the above staff mix and skill management strategies. For example, the maximum number of workers is probably limited by an organisation's budget, and the mix of qualifications may be limited by a workforce shortage in a certain health profession. Also, staff mix and skill management strategies are not independent choices, but often the feasibility of one strategy tends to influence the implementation of another, or the other way around. For example, if the total number of workers in a certain organisation is low, the number of skills that are needed may exceed the number of workers that are available. In rural regions, those skill-sets typically held by specialist doctors might not be available, but some of their skills might still be needed to provide appropriate care to the patient population. In those cases, instead of increasing the number of workers, it can be beneficial to invest in role enhancement or enlargement by means of provider education so that specialised nurses can perform certain tasks traditionally held by specialised doctors. This would ensure that a relatively wide range of tasks and responsibilities can be performed by a relatively small number of people (Dierick-van Daele et al. 2008).

It should be noted that it may not always be clear which of the above staff mix and skill management strategies one is concerned with in practice, as often the knowledge of a number of details is necessary to identify subtle distinctions between different strategies. Consider for example the inclusion of a case manager in an integrated diabetes care team. Does this change the number of workers, the mix of qualifications, the balance between junior and senior staff members, the mix of disciplines, or some or all of the above? Does it concern role enhancement, enlargement, substitution or delegation? To answer these questions, we would need to know whether the case manager role was introduced as a new, additional one (and thereby increasing the number of workers), or whether tasks were delegated from a higher grade to the case manager (and thereby constituting role delegation), and so on. In other words, extensive information on the intervention itself, as well as the situation prior to the implementation of the intervention, is needed to identify which type of strategy one is concerned with. It is therefore not surprising that the performance of certain tasks by nurses, which are traditionally held by general practitioners (GPs), has been used as an example for both role substitution and role delegation (Dubois and Singh 2009; Kislov et al. n.d.). Nevertheless, the above classification system provides a useful and comprehensive overview of the types staff mix and skill management strategies that are available and can be implemented in practice.

13.3 Multidisciplinary Team Work

Once the most appropriate staff mix and skill management strategies are identified and the group of providers with a certain skill set is assembled, organisations still need to organise the way in which this group of providers cooperates and delivers care in practice. Generally, this is referred to by the umbrella term "multidisciplinary team work", which is an especially popular and frequently implemented intervention within integrated care strategies (Drewes et al. 2012; Meeuwissen et al. 2012; Elissen et al. 2012; Ouwens et al. 2005). Multidisciplinarity is also referred to as interdisciplinarity, multiprofessionalism or interprofessionalism (Nancarrow et al. 2013; American Association of Colleges of Nursing 2015). These concepts are generally not used interchangeably, but it is difficult to provide clear distinctions, because different authors attribute different meanings to the concepts. Here, we will only use the term multidisciplinarity, by which we mean a group of health professionals from different disciplines or with different medical specialties.

Often team work is defined as or assumed to be multidisciplinary in nature, without this being explicitly addressed as such (Langins and Borgermans 2015; World Health Organization 2013, 2014; Nolte and McKee 2008; Firth-Cozens 2001). In contrast, a recent study on workforce interventions in integrated care strategies (Busetto et al. unpublished) has looked at the following three distinct aspects of multidisciplinary team work:

a. *multidisciplinary staff* refers to a group of health professionals from different disciplines or with different medical specialties;
b. *multidisciplinary protocols or pathways* refer to protocols or pathways that involve tasks for health professionals from different disciplines or with different medical specialties;
c. *team meetings* refer to a group of health professionals that works around a patient or group of patients and that meets on a regular basis to discuss the patients' treatment. These meetings may be real or virtual.

These three aspects are often implemented together in practice, but do not need to be necessarily. The differences between these concepts can best be demonstrated by using two practice examples. The first example relates to the delivery of integrated care for people with type 2 diabetes in the Netherlands. Here, care is facilitated by care groups, i.e. legal entities that establish contracts with health insurers and health professionals in order to coordinate the so-called 'care chain' of chronic care from diagnosis to after care (De Wildt et al. 2009). Bundled payments are made by the health insurers to the care groups for the whole package of diabetes care per patient per year. However, the care groups are not care providers, but management organisations who pay health professionals to deliver the care included in the diabetes package. The content and price of these packages are negotiated in a stepped approach between the health insurers, care groups and health professionals. The main locus of diabetes care is the GP's practice. For services that cannot be performed at the GP practice, the patient is referred to other health professionals or to a hospital, but always goes back to the GP's practice that holds responsibility for the patient's continuous care.

A recent study has shown that the above described example of integrated care is characterised by two of the three aspects of multidisciplinary team work (Busetto et al. 2015). In the Netherlands, integrated care for people with type 2 diabetes is delivered by multidisciplinary staff. This includes practice nurses (PNs), GPs, diabetes nurse specialists (DNSs), internists, dieticians, podiatrists, pedicurists, optometrists, and sometimes physical therapists and pharmacists. These health professionals may, and often are, based at different locations. The PN and GP are located at the GP's practice, the DNS is located at the GP's practice and hospital, the internist and the optometrist at the hospital, and dieticians, pedicurists and podiatrists often have their own practices but may also be located in the GP's practice or at the hospital. The division of tasks between these health professionals is specified in multidisciplinary protocols. These are based on national care standards of good practice diabetes care and on the negotiations between the care group, health insurers and health professionals. However, team meetings do not take place. Instead, the communication between the health professionals involved is facilitated and formalised via the clinical information system, a common patient database that is used by the care group and all health professionals involved in the delivery of integrated diabetes care. The health professionals can access and enter patient data and the practice nurses can use the system to refer patients to other health professionals.

The second example describes integrated care as implemented by a geriatric hospital in Germany. The hospital was founded in 1999 and intentionally planned and developed as a multidisciplinary and integrated geriatric care centre. The hospital offers comprehensive services for patients with complex, multiple age-related conditions who are in temporary need of acute care. Patients generally stay at the hospital for up to 21 days, depending on their health status and potential for rehabilitation. They are then discharged to their home setting or transferred to a nursing home for long-term care. The hospital consists of five wards. On each ward multidisciplinary staff delivers care, which includes doctors, nurses, neuropsychologists, physical therapists, occupational therapists, speech therapists and social workers. Together, they perform a comprehensive geriatric assessment of each patient that is admitted to the hospital. Moreover, all patients are treated by the doctor, physical therapists and occupational therapists. They are also all cared for by the nurses and social workers. Whether patients receive further treatment by the speech therapists and neuropsychologists depends on their specific condition and wishes. A short team meeting takes place every morning with an extended one happening once a week. All health professionals are present during these meetings. During the morning meetings, the nurses report on occurrences during the late and night shift and the doctor introduces the new admissions of the day. The purpose of these team meetings is to keep everyone abreast of the latest developments of the patients on the ward and to give the health professionals the chance to ask questions and set priorities for the day's treatments. During the weekly team meetings, every patient is discussed in detail and all health professionals comment in turn from their own professional perspective. Together, the team maps the patients' development over time and agrees on a discharge plan, either to the patients' home setting or in the form of a transfer to a nursing home.

The division of tasks between the multidisciplinary staff is not described in multidisciplinary protocols or pathways. There are job descriptions for each individual professional, and there are rules about which assessment each health professional has to perform as part of the comprehensive geriatric assessment. But there are no protocols that specify a division of tasks in relation to the tasks of the other health professionals. Instead, the division of tasks has developed over time and is addressed and discussed by the health professionals when there is overlap or disagreement. For example, overlap often occurs between the physical therapists and occupational therapists, the occupational therapists and neuropsychologists, and the neuropsychologists and doctors. This may cause frustration among the health professionals and activities or assessments may be repeated unnecessarily. Ideally, however, ambiguities may be resolved by agreeing on tasks through personal interaction between the different health professionals. This can lead to a higher quality of care because it includes more perspectives on the same problem (Busetto et al. 2017).

13.4 Workforce à la carte

From these examples, it can be concluded there are different and distinct aspects of multidisciplinary team work which should be taken into account. One could even argue that these three aspects—multidisciplinary staff, multidisciplinary protocols or pathways and team meetings—are necessary conditions for multidisciplinary team work. Creating a group of health professionals from different professional backgrounds is not sufficient in itself, and neither are multidisciplinary protocols or team meetings. Hence, it may not come as a surprise that one of the reasons why the bundled payment scheme was introduced in the Netherlands was the fact that the multidisciplinary protocols (or care standards back then) alone were not enough to facilitate collaboration between individual professionals (Elissen 2013; Struijs et al. 2012). The bundled payments were created as a financial incentive framework to integrate a multidisciplinary staff consisting of all health professionals involved in the delivery of integrated diabetes care. Moreover, today there are worries about whether the PN has taken over too many tasks from the GP, for which he or she might not be sufficiently qualified (Busetto et al. 2015). One of the causes of this problem can be seen in the fact that the PN provides the care to the diabetes patients relatively independently, instead of consulting with the GP (and other health professionals) during team meetings. In the German case, these team meetings do exist, but the multidisciplinary staff complains about an unclear division of tasks, which can be traced back to the absence of multidisciplinary protocols or pathways. Of course, saying that these aspects are necessary conditions does not mean that they are sufficient, even if all of them are implemented. Other less tangible aspects such as motivation, team culture, common goals, or a tradition of cooperation also play a crucial role (Busetto et al. 2015; Lemieux-Charles and McGuire 2006; Xyrichis and Lowton 2008).

We can also take another step back and look at the connection between the staff mix and skill management strategies discussed earlier and how they relate to the organisation of multidisciplinary team work in practice. For example, if there is a certain mix of qualifications in which a certain staff member holds a certain qualification and corresponding skill set, it may be relatively easy to draft multidisciplinary protocols that specify the tasks and responsibilities of the specific staff members. For example, the division of tasks between internists and specialised nurses can be written down in detail and the respective staff members can follow the procedures defined in the protocols. If an internist is replaced by a different person, the multidisciplinary protocol would not have to be changed, because the new person can be expected to hold a similar skill set as the previous one. The same holds true for a group with a certain mix of disciplines for which the protocols define the division of tasks between, for example, physical therapists and occupational therapists and for which these positions can be held by different persons from the respective discipline. The above is more difficult when skill development and flexibility strategies are applied, as these change the skills and tasks of a staff member beyond their traditional function, role or qualification. This makes it more challenging to formalise task divisions in protocols because the skills, and therefore tasks, of a certain person are likely to evolve and change over time. However, in improving the care for people with chronic conditions we will have to rethink and revise written protocols once in a while and improve them where necessary, which should also be incentivised by new skill management strategies.

It is possible that certain staff mix and skill management strategies are more or less effective when matched with a certain way of organising multidisciplinary team work in practice. For example, balancing junior and senior staff within a group of health professionals is often based on the assumption that senior staff members can teach certain on-the-job skills to the junior members, who in turn have new ideas and ways of doing things that senior staff members can learn from. However, for this effect to take place, it seems necessary that a certain degree of interaction between the two groups takes place, which is unlikely to be achieved where there is a highly sequential organisation of care and in the absence of team meetings as we saw in the Dutch example. On the other hand, once there are a certain number of workers, team meetings become less easy to organise and discussions will likely diminish in efficiency. In those cases, a digital and/or more formalised interaction between team members may be a more worthwhile option. A similar interaction occurs between patients and members of the care team and has to be reflected in skill management strategies as well.

To put the above in an even bigger picture i.e. health care system reform, the WHO perspective on preparing a health workforce for the twenty-first century needs to be taken into account. According to the WHO, a transformation of the workforce is only one component of the more general health care system reform that is needed to improve care for patients with chronic conditions. However, transformation in health care organisations is impossible without a corresponding transformation in the workforce that provides the care (World Health Organization 2005).

13.5 Conclusions

As is the case for integrated care in general, workforce interventions need to be well planned, implemented, and evaluated. The Center for Workforce Intelligence offers three recommendations to support a more systematic consideration of the implications of integrated care for the health workforce (Center for Workforce Intelligence 2013). First, one must realise that there is no universal approach to integration. Instead, different (local) routes to integration exist, and each requires particular workforce interventions and management responses. One such route, as mentioned above, is the multidisciplinary team which requires focussing on specific aspects including the creation of a climate for team building or establishing shared values, legal considerations around the use of information and working protocols, as well as the planning of new roles and responsibilities. Second, one must take appropriate measures to make sure that the right health professionals with the appropriate expertise are in place to deliver tailored integrated care. These may include multidisciplinary training programs or a socialisation of health professionals to consider themselves part of a multidisciplinary team in the service of an autonomous patient in need of care. Finally, one must identify those factors that are critical for the success of workforce changes in integrated care interventions. The impact of integrated care on health outcomes is defined by the interaction of all its components within the health care setting as well as with those in the community (Elissen et al. 2012). It goes without saying that many, if not all, of these components have consequences for the health care workforce, and vice versa.

The key message for practitioners and policymakers is to take into account the complexity and heterogeneity inherent to integrated care strategies (Calciolari and Ilinca 2011b). When workforce interventions are implemented as part of these strategies, they are not implemented in isolation but in combination with other changes. These may concern changes as diverse as bundled payment systems, shared patient databases or self-management support initiatives. The common denominator remains that for these changes to be implemented and executed effectively, they need to be well-aligned with workforce and staffing changes. A bundled payment system incentivising a care chain will incentivise actions by different health professionals that are linked to each other in a chain of successive treatments, but it will not necessarily support multidisciplinary team work when no regular team meetings are in place. Similarly, implementing shared patient databases and self-management support initiatives requires a workforce with the appropriate skill-set to execute, or at least support, these interventions.

As part of new care models, workforce changes are needed to cope with the risk of a dwindling supply and the necessity of matching knowledge and competences of the workforce with the future needs. In contrast to the growing amount of literature that supports the current drive towards integrated care, little is published about its associated workforce and staffing interventions. Given that the success of integrated care strategies depends to a large extent on the health workforce executing them, it is time for all of us involved to broaden our horizons and start discussing how to address workforce interventions as part of integrated care strategies. For example, attention should increasingly shift to patient perspective on staffing issues and what is needed according to the patients themselves. Moreover, practitioners and policy-makers should be aware of the emergence of new stakeholders on the scene who are assuming more important roles in long-term care, including both for-profit and not-for-profit private enterprises (Center for Workforce Intelligence 2013). In particular, practitioners and politicians will need to shift their attention from single-focus solutions to more complex approaches.

The journey to improved health outcomes by means of integrated care is a relatively recent one, but it has demonstrated that workforce changes form an area of attention that is essential for the understanding and success of integrated strategies as a whole. Even if integrated care should be surpassed by a superior approach in the future, workforce changes as part of complex improvement strategies will necessarily remain on the radar of every health care system working towards improved population health.

References

American Association of Colleges of Nursing. (2015). *Interdisciplinary Education and Practice*. Retrieved October 13, 2015, from http://www.aacn.nche.edu/publications/position/interdisciplinary-education-and-practice

Busetto, L., Luijkx, K. G., Huizing, A., & Vrijhoef, B. (2015). Implementation of integrated care for diabetes mellitus type 2 by two Dutch care groups: A case study. *BMC Family Practice, 16*, 105.

Busetto, L., Kiselev, J., Luijkx, K. G., Steinhagen-Thiessen, E., & Vrijhoef, H. J. M. (2017). Implementation of integrated geriatric care at a German hospital: A case study to understand when and why beneficial outcomes can be achieved. *BMC Health Services Research, 17*, 180. doi:10.1186/s12913-017-2105-7. https://bmchealthservres.biomedcentral.com/articles/10.1186/s12913-017-2105-7 (unpublished 2017).

Calciolari, S., & Ilinca, S. (2011a). Organizing integrated care for frail elderly patients in Switzerland, Italy, United States, and Canada. In A. Bergmann (Ed.), *Yearbook of Swiss administrative sciences*. Zurich: SGVW.

Calciolari, S., & Ilinca, S. (2011b). Comparing (and learning from) integrated care initiatives: An analytical framework. *Journal of Integrated Care, 19*(6), 4–13.

Center for Workforce Intelligence. (2011). Accessed March 31, 2017, from http://www.cardiffandvaleuhb.wales.nhs.uk/sitesplus/documents/1143/updated_integrated-carefor-older-people%5B1%5D.pdf

Center for Workforce Intelligence. (2013). Accessed March 31, 2017, from http://www.cfwi.org.uk/publications/think-integration-think-workforce-three-steps-to-workforceintegration-1

Coleman, K., Mattke, S., Perraulth, P. J., & Wagner, E. H. (2009). Untangling practice redesign from disease management: How do we care for the chronically ill? *Annual Review of Public Health, 30*, 385–408.

De Wildt, J. E., Baroch, N., & Maas, L. (2009). *Handboek van Zorggroep naar ketenzorg*. Sanofi Aventis: Gouda.

Deloitte Center for Health Solutions. (2012). *The new health care workforce: Looking around the corner to future talent management*. Retrieved from http://www.deloitte.com/assets/Dcom-UnitedStates/Local%20Assets/Documents/Health%20Reform%20Issues%20Briefs/us_chs_NewHealthCareWorkforce_032012.pdf

Dierick-van Daele, A. T., Spreeuwenberg, C., Derckx, E. W., Metsemakers, J. F., & Vrijhoef, B. J. (2008). Critical appraisal of the literature on economic evaluations of substitution of skills between professionals: A systematic literature review. *Journal of Evaluation in Clinical Practice, 14*(4), 481–492.

Drewes, H. W., Steuten, L. M., Lemmens, L. C., Baan, C. A., Boshuizen, H. C., Elissen, A. M., et al. (2012). The effectiveness of chronic care management for heart failure: Meta-regression analyses to explain the heterogeneity in outcomes. *Health Services Research, 47*(5), 1926–1959.

Dubois, C., & Singh, D. (2009). From staff-mix to skill-mix and beyond: Towards a systemic approach to health workforce management. *Human Resources for Health, 7*, 87.

Elissen, A. M. J. (2013). *Going beyond the 'grand mean': Advancing disease management science and evidence*. Dissertation, Universitaire Pers Maastricht, Maastricht.

Elissen, A. M. J., Steuten, L. M. G., Lemmens, L. C., Drewes, H. W., Lemmens, K. M. M., Meeuwissen, J. A. C., et al. (2012). Meta-analysis of the effectiveness of chronic care management for diabetes: Investigating heterogeneity in outcomes. *Journal of Evaluation in Clinical Practice, 19*(5), 753–762.

Firth-Cozens, J. (2001). Multidisciplinary teamwork: The good, bad, and everything in between. *Quality in Health Care, 10*, 65–69.

Glouberman, S., & Mintzberg, H. (2001a). Managing the care of health and the cure of disease – Part I: Differentiation. *Health Care Management Review, 26*(1), 56–69.

Glouberman, S., & Mintzberg, H. (2001b). Managing the care of health and the cure of disease – Part II: Integration. *Health Care Management Review, 26*(1), 70–84.

Griffiths, P. (2012). Inaugural lecture: Doing away with doctors? Workforce research and the future of nursing. *Working Papers in the Health Sciences, 1*(1), 1–11.

Imison, C., & Bohmer, R. (2013). *NHS and social care workforce: Meeting our needs now and in the future?* London: The King's Fund.

Kabene, S. M., Orchard, C., Howard, J. M., Soriano, M. A., & Leduc, R. (2006). The importance of human resources management in health care: A global context. *Human Resources for Health, 4*, 20.

Kislov, R., Nelson, A., Normanville, C. D., Kelly, M. P., & Payne, K. (n.d.). *Word redesign and health promotion in healthcare organisations: A review of the literature.* National Health Service.

Langins, M., & Borgermans, L. (2015). *Strengthening a competent health workforce for the provision of coordinated/integrated health services.* Working document.

Lemieux-Charles, L., & McGuire, W. L. (2006). What do we know about health care team effectiveness? A review of the literature. *Medical Care Research and Review, 63*(3), 263–300.

Meeuwissen, J. A. C., Lemmens, L. C., Drewes, H. W., Lemmens, K. M. M., Steuten, L. M. G., Elissen, A. M. J., et al. (2012). Meta-analysis and meta-regression analyses explaining heterogeneity in outcomes of chronic care management for depression: Implications for person-centered mental healthcare. *The International Journal of Person Centered Medicine, 2*(4), 716–758.

Nancarrow, S. A., Booth, A., Ariss, S., Smith, T., Enderby, P., & Roots, A. (2013). Ten principles of good interdisciplinary team work. *Human Resources for Health, 11*(19).

Nolte, E., & McKee, M. (2008). *Caring for people with chronic conditions: A health system perspective.* European Observatory on Health Systems and Policies: Maidenhead.

Ouwens, M., Wollersheim, H., Hermens, R., Hulscher, M., & Grol, R. (2005). Integrated care programmes for chronically ill patients: A review of systematic reviews. *International Journal for Quality in Health Care, 17*(2), 141–146.

Pruitt, S. D., & Epping-Jordan, J. E. (2005). Preparing the 21st century global healthcare workforce. *BMJ, 330*, 637–639.

Struijs, J., de Jong-van Til, J., Lemmens, L., Drewes, H. W., de Bruin, S., & Baan, C. (2012). *Drie jaar integrale bekostiging van diabeteszorg: Effecten op zorgproces en kwaliteit van zorg.* Bilthoven: Ministerie van Volksgezondheid, Welzijn en Sport. 260224003.

Vrijhoef. (2014). Presentation at the mini symposium: Improving chronic care – Rheumatology, an example. March 13, 2014.

World Health Organization. (2004). *The health workforce: Current challenges.* Geneva: WHO.

World Health Organization. (2005). *Preparing a health care workforce for the 21st century: The challenge of chronic conditions.* Geneva: WHO.

World Health Organization. (2013). *Transforming and scaling up health professionals' education and training: World Health Organization Guidelines.* Geneva: World Health Organization.

World Health Organization. (2014). In E. Nolte, C. Knai, & R. B. Saltman (Eds.), Observatory studies series (Vol. 37). Accessed March 31, 2017, from http://www.euro.who.int/__data/assets/pdf_file/0009/270729/Assessing-chronic-diseasemanagement-in-European-health-systems.pdf

World Health Organization. (2016). *Data and statistics: Dynamic health labour markets in the European Region.* Retrieved April 26, 2016, from http://www.euro.who.int/en/health-topics/Health-systems/health-workforce/data-and-statistics

Xyrichis, A., & Lowton, K. (2008). What fosters or prevents interprofessional teamworking in primary and community care? A literature review. *International Journal of Nursing Studies, 45*(1), 140–153.

Leadership in Integrated Care

14

Volker Amelung, Daniela Chase, and Anika Reichert

14.1 The Neglected Topics in Designing Integrated Care

Leadership is certainly one of the neglected topics in integrated care. This is surprising, as the leadership challenge is greater in networks for integrated care than in typical organizations (Sydow et al. 2011). This is due to, on the one hand, network structures that require leadership of and in networks, and on the other hand, a higher level of complexity in the health care sector (see Figure 14.2).

Structures in health care seem to be very complex due to numerous reasons:

- Services are usually provided by more than one person which brings in complexity as communication about various services and coordination of these need to take place.
- Care providers act within a specific setting and its respective management.

The figure clearly demonstrates the need for a more complex leadership approach than in traditional hierarchical organizations.

V. Amelung (✉)
Medical School Hannover, Institute for Epidemiology, Social Medicine and Health System Research, Hannover, Germany

inav – Institute for Applied Health Service Research, Berlin, Germany
e-mail: amelung@inav-berlin.de

D. Chase
inav – Institute for Applied Health Service Research, Berlin, Germany

A. Reichert
Centre for Health Economics, University of York, York, UK

© Springer International Publishing AG 2017
V. Amelung et al. (eds.), *Handbook Integrated Care*,
DOI 10.1007/978-3-319-56103-5_14

14.2   No Coincidence: What Management Literature Tells Us About Leadership

In common management literature there is a discussion about whether management or leadership approaches are appropriate to successfully lead modern companies (Mintzberg 2013). Whether an organization is *"overmanaged and underled"* or *"overled and undermanaged"* is difficult to assess from the outside. Clearly management and leadership need to be synthesized and well-balanced in an organization since they depend on each other (Mintzberg 2013; The King's Fund 2011). Thus, it is the leader's task to communicate the organisation's goal and align management and administration to take aim at these goals (The King's Fund 2011).

14.2.1 Manager Versus Leader

> *"Management is doing things right; leadership is doing the right things"*
> (Peter F. Drucker)

In this chapter, the focus is to provide an overview of leadership and management. For this reason we give a rather broad definition of leadership and management although there is a plethora of definitions for both.

> *"Leadership is a process whereby an individual influences a group of individuals to achieve a common goal"* (Northouse 2013).

Management necessarily takes place in every organisation and functions as the interface for people, information, and action (Mintzberg 2013). Interestingly enough, the word "to manage" originates from the Latin expression *"manus agere"* which basically means to lead from the hand and reportedly was used in the context of leading or taming horses (Mintzberg 2010).

In Kotter's (2001) paper on the differences between managers and leaders, the main characteristics and tasks of each are outlined (see Table 14.1).

Table 14.1 Differences between leadership and management

Leadership	Management
Preparing a system for change	*Coping with complexity*
Example: The leader knows the conditions of a market which oftentimes lead to change (e.g. new competitors) and prepares the system for change.	*Example:* The manager oversees structures and tasks in a system in order to prevent chaos, specifically in large organizations.
• Setting the direction • Aligning people • Motivating and inspiring	• Planning and budgeting • Organizing and staffing • Controlling and problem solving

Source: Kotter (2001)

Table 14.2 Types and styles of leadership

Theories	Principles	
Leadership theories	*Individual leadership styles*	
• Den Hartog and Koopman (2011) • Blessin and Wick (2014)	Individual examples of "role models"	Examples based on empirical research
	• J. Welch • Powell (2013)	• Kouzes and Posner (2009) • Schoemaker et al. (2013) • Battilana et al. (2010)

14.2.2 Types and Styles of Leadership

The general discussion on leadership takes place on the continuum between more and less abstract theories and practical principles. Literature on leadership contains many approaches and entails quite a history. Many sources have roots in the field of psychology and human resources research. Thus, this overview makes no claim to completeness. Newer literature focuses on key qualifications of leaders, which we will outline towards the end of this chapter. In the following paragraph only a restricted selection can be introduced (overview, see Table 14.2).

In the first part of this overview we will elaborate on four historical leadership eras.

14.2.2.1 Theories

Throughout the vast literature on leadership theories, Den Hartog and Koopman (2011) demarcate four leadership eras throughout the twentieth century. Elaborating on each of the theories' leadership styles would go beyond the scope of this overview. According to Den Hartog and Koopman (2011), leadership developed from "*who leaders are*" (trait) to "*what leaders do*" (behaviour). Over the course of the century other important topics emerged: "*how leaders act in certain situations*" (contingency) and finally "*how leaders engage followers for common goals*" (new leadership) (Table 14.3).

14.2.2.2 Learning from the Big Bosses' Experience

Religious role models like Mahatma Gandhi, entrepreneurs like Jack Welch or Steve Jobs, politicians like Ronald Reagan or military leaders like Colin Powell: they all were great leaders. Over time they gained invaluable experience leading people and are entitled to pass on their lessons learned on this topic. Two big leaders of modern times, Jack Welch from competitive industry and Colin Powell from the U.S. Army where hierarchies are part of the system, were selected to highlight their leadership credo in this summary. We chose two out of many examples to illustrate the line of argumentation in these approaches.

Table 14.3 Overview of four leadership eras throughout the course of the twentieth century

Leadership theory	Explanation/leadership style
Trait approach (search for "the great man") → *Up to late 1940s*	*Focus on innate characteristics of the leader and his influence on the success/change achieved*
Style approach → *Late 1940s–late 1960s*	*The leader's behaviour is pivotal to success/change achieved. Leadership behaviour can be learned.* → *e.g. authoritarian, democratic, laissez-faire*
Contingency approaches → Late 1960s–early 1980s	The leader's behaviour needs to be congruent with aspects of the situation; the effectiveness of leadership is contingent on the situation. Thus, there is not only a single leadership style appropriate for the situation but many. The leader must be capable of distinguishing between and carefully applying these.
New Leadership → Since early 1980s	E.g.: Transformational, charismatic, inspirational, visionary leadership. New leaders attain extraordinary levels of followers' motivation and engagement to accomplish the organization's goals.

Source: Adapted from Blessin and Wick (2014), Den Hartog and Koopman (2011)

Table 14.4 Jack Welch's "Four E's" of his best players as prerequisites for leadership

Energy	*Energize*
Fascinated by ideas and eager to open new doors even though this might involve risks.	Sharing this enthusiasm with others in order to have a common vision.
Edge	*Execution*
Being a strong competitor and not hesitating to make tough calls (e.g. firing someone) for the good of the company.	Always eager to perform and deliver results. Leaders can turn vision into results.

Source: Bartlett and Wozny (1999), Krames (2005)

Jack Welch: Former CEO of General Electric

Over the course of 20 years (1981–2001) Jack Welch was CEO of General Electric. In order to sustain success he needed to reorganize one of the world's largest companies several times to achieve his goal of being among the best companies. This entails understanding and forming the skill- and mind-set of 290,000 employees by overcommunicating new strategic and organizational goals (Bartlett and Wozny 1999; Krames 2005).

Jack Welch himself spent a vast majority of his time on people's issues, by training and developing them. He aimed to create so-called *A Players with four E's* (see Table 14.4).

The vision of excellence in every competitive market is only one of many possible ways to lead people. Different branches afford different ways of leadership. Next, Colin Powell's leadership style will be shortly illustrated.

Table 14.5 Colin Powell's principles to excel in leadership

Topic	Examples of principles
Being a provocateur	*Always being diplomatic and polite will not bring forward ideas of change.* Change needs to be a top priority in the organization and has to be communicated clearly.
Promoting discourse	*Promote an open dialogue* with all levels of staff by establishing an open-door policy. Everyone can participate in communication and information flow, diverse opinions are more than welcome. *Leaders must avoid the ego trap* by accepting new facts and change. Do not be too focused on your own path if it is not aligned with the organization's vision. *When instituting change* keep authority and their GO in mind, yet in some cases it is fundamental to go forward with alternatives.
Overwhelming strength	*Define your own strategic interests* by stating your mission clearly but only if you are capable of implementing it. Implement change only in certain parts of an organization while being open for alternatives in other parts.
People over plans	*Choose people on your team* who are loyal, integer, and energetic and let them perform by decentralizing your organization's structure. Leadership can take place on all levels and does not need to rely on job position or seniority. The organization should be balanced out and a fun working environment for others. This means that individuals need to be balanced as well by spending time on home and family life.
Detail diligent	Leaders are aware of details in their own organization, i.e., know all the information flowing to prevent mistakes. Details open doors for extraordinary opportunities.

Source: Harari (2002), Powell (2013)

Colin Powell: Former U.S. Secretary of State

Serving for the U.S. Army as four-star general as well as in the George W. Bush administration from 2001 to 2005 as Secretary of State, Colin Powell was confronted with the topic of leadership for a long time and published his *Leadership Secrets* in 2002. A summary of his leadership principles is provided in Table 14.5.

Even these two leadership approaches are from very different settings, they add significant value for the discussion about leadership in health care. Both focus on principles and values.

14.2.3 Leadership Learnings from Empirical Data

Separate from situational theories of leadership, there are different standpoints regarding whether one needs to be a born leader or one can learn to be a leader.

14.2.3.1 Fundamental Practices by Kouzes and Posner (2009)

In their book, Kouzes and Posner (2009) discuss pivotal prerequisites to be a leader based on their empirical research since 1983. By interviewing leaders and their followers, the authors could identify five fundamental principles for leadership which are summarized in Table 14.6.

Table 14.6 Summary of fundamental leadership practices (A–E) and derived leadership commitments (1–10)

Fundamental practice	Short explanation
A. Set an example	Leaders are always willing to go first and set an example as they have a detailed operational plan.
1. Strengthen others, give away power, assign critical tasks and offer support. 2. Make your behaviour consistent with shared values. Achieve small wins that promote consistent progress and build commitment. 3. Achieve small wins that promote consistent progress and build commitment.	
B. Inspire a shared vision	At the beginning of every successful business is a vision of the ideal future state of the organization.
4. Experiment, take risks and learn from your mistakes. 5. Envision a future that is more uplifting and ennobling.	
C. Challenge the process	Leaders are pioneers who are open to new grounds and the unknown.
6. Seek challenging opportunities to grow, change, innovate and improve.	
D. Enable others to act	Enforcing your team for action, building trust and solid relationships and competencies are key for collaboration and a sense for responsibility.
7. Appeal to others people's values, dreams and hopes to share your common vision. 8. Foster collaboration by promoting cooperative goals and building trust.	
E. Encouraging the heart	Build a culture where values and success are appreciated and celebrated.
9. Recognize individual contributions that lead to the success of each project. 10. Celebrate team achievement, not just individual ones.	

Source: Adapted from Kouzes and Posner (2009)

14.3 Leadership in Networks

Leadership in networks differentiates itself fundamentally from that in traditional hierarchies. There are five crucial aspects of leading networks:

1. Network structures resemble new hierarchies that have to be embedded in well-established structures;
2. Networks render it possible that individuals can lead other individuals, likewise organizations can lead other organizations (Sydow et al. 2011);
3. Fundamentally, network structures are parallel structures with little power and are predominantly free of hierarchy. Specifically rules and resources create power.
4. Negotiations are more important than 'Command and Control' and are therefore a matter of more complex and invisible structures (Sydow et al. 2011);
5. The leadership complexity is considerably greater than in traditional structures, as stakeholders represent various sectors and professional cultures.

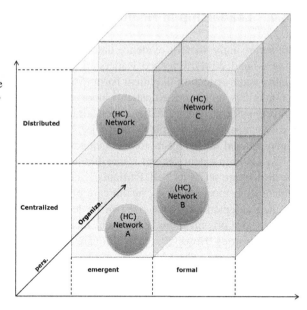

Fig. 14.1 Example of (Health Care)-Networks localized within dimensions of organizational structure (HC=Health care). Size and location of network within the dimensions does not relate to quality of organization and leadership. Source: Adapted from Sydow et al. (2011)

Sydow et al. (2011) have developed a regulatory framework in order to describe the type of leadership applied in the respective network. In its basic form it can be transferred to any system, e.g., health care systems. Its fundamental purpose is the classification of leadership style rather than evaluating it.

In Figure 14.1 four different networks, e.g. leadership in health care networks such as integrated care systems, are illustrated, embedded within three axes:

- Organization of the network: emergent—formal
- Nature of leadership: centralized—distributed
- Leadership attribution: individual person—organization

All three dimensions pertain to both leading a network and leading within a network.

The first dimension refers to the structure and style of organization. It reaches from emergent/ad hoc/informal organizations to formally organized structures. Within the network structures one can detect both forms in parallel, meaning in different areas of the network various forms of structures might apply.

The second dimension differentiates according to the degree of centralization concerning leadership. Here, within the network structures, one can distinguish between very centralized and decentralized/distributed structures.

The third dimension considers the question of whether leadership refers to persons or organizations.

14.4   Leadership in Health Care: Learning from Best Practice

Not surprisingly, there is evidence that leadership matters in health care, too (The King's Fund 2011). Engaged leadership can achieve an increase in health care quality and a reduction of patient harm (Swensen et al. 2013). Regulators, payers, communities, and informed patients increase the pressure for leaders of health care delivery systems to achieve better performance. Efforts that have been tried so far focused most times on micro- or project-level. Achieving improvements on an organizational level appears to be much harder (Reinertsen et al. 2008).

To a certain extent general leadership theories and principles can be applied in the health care sector as well. Particularly nowadays, with increasingly competitive structures in most countries, health care organizations have evolved to be more - business-oriented units that need to be led appropriately. Therefore, leaders of health care organizations often are facing challenges similar to leaders in other industries. However, the health care sector also has some unique characteristics which need to be addressed.

14.4.1   What Is Different in Health Care: The Logic of Health Care Delivery

Health care organisations can be described as complex adaptive systems which can are difficult to manage and organize in detail (Reinertsen et al. 2008). Delivery processes can be compared to value chains with structurally fragmented activities (Amelung 2013). Each medical intervention is delivered in small disconnected applications, yet they interfere with each other (Glouberman and Mintzberg 2001).

Furthermore, health care interventions always take place for persons and communities. Den Hertog et al. (2005) illustrate how different sectors in health care (walls; sectors and interdisciplinarity) and system levels (ceilings; policy-makers, managers, and professionals) create a hard to manage and innovation-hampering system (see Fig. 14.2). These walls and ceilings are embedded in a patient-centred and community-based environment in which leadership needs to design and implement change.

Berwick et al. (2008) introduced the idea of the Triple Aim. This idea requires the simultaneous pursuit of three aims in order to improve a health care system:

- Improvement of the individual experience of care
- Improvement of population health
- Reduction of costs of care

These goals need to be treated interdependently as changes made to achieve one of the goals can affect the other two, often negatively. That means the aim lies in balancing the triple aim (Berwick et al. 2008). To achieve triple aim results, high-impact leadership is needed (Swensen et al. 2013).

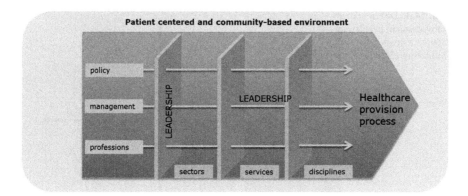

Fig. 14.2 Walls and ceilings within health care systems. Source: Adapted from Den Hertog et al. (2005)

Triple aim results represent a shift from volume to value (Swensen et al. 2013). All too often quality in health care organizations is seen as an expense or regulatory requirement but leaders need to develop a fundamental understanding of quality as a business strategy and part of their core work. As quality improvement is rarely part of the medical school curriculum, leadership must be familiar with the science and potential of such methods (Swensen et al. 2009).

New invasive interventions often carry significant risks and costs. Leadership in health care needs to understand when interventions are beneficial and evidence-based. This stresses the importance of data in this sector. Health care is dominated by data, e.g., from clinical trials or health care services delivery data which build the basis for guidelines. Guidelines are the summary of best evidence and foster the triple aim. They can be an effective tool to develop a core standard work based on best practice where deviations from the rule are expected only for patient-centred reasons, not because the physician *"likes to practice this way"*. Standardization is important to create a culture of safety in health care delivery (Swensen et al. 2009). But standardization in medicine always causes an inherent tension between excellence and physician autonomy which leads us to the next section—the role of professional cultures in health care.

14.4.2 Professional Cultures in Health Care

Delivering high-quality health care requires the creation of a collective mind characterised by optimal teamwork, communication skills, and an attitude of transparency and psychological safety, that is a professional culture. For the establishment of this professional culture, physicians have played a major role as leading persons. In many countries health care systems only have scarce resources for big challenges, e.g., increase of chronic diseases or age of the population. For this reason there is a demand for more, respectively different, leadership and

Fig. 14.3 Differentiated
subsystems in health care.
Source: Glouberman and
Mintzberg (2001)

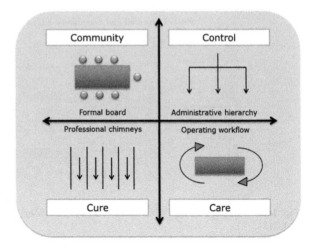

management in the health care sector than what traditionally was provided by physicians. For effective leadership and management, difficult and controversial decisions are required to make which may infringe on the autonomy of health care providers. Doctors strongly believe that physician autonomy is crucial to quality in health care. The challenge in health care is that even with increasing leadership and management efforts physicians do not feel a loss of control or want to reject new forms of leadership and management (Schmitz and Berchtold 2009).

Glouberman and Mintzberg (2001) characterize health care organizations by four main subsystems: Cure, Care, Control and Community (see Fig. 14.3). All are highly differentiated. Physicians, representing subsystem Cure, as well as the nursing staff, subsystem Care, work in the operative core business of patient care. But they are divided by completely different roles. Physicians work *in* the hospital but not *for* it. They intervene with the patients in short visits and control treatment decisions before they depart, leaving most of the care to the nursing staff. They distinguish themselves by their medical discipline. In some countries such as Germany, the nursing staff can hardly specialize within their profession. They are tightly committed to the institution and provide care on a rather continuous basis seeking to coordinate complex workflows.

Control—representing the organization's management—is responsible for the system at large and controls the resources. As administrators they exercise formal authority trying to control a patchwork of more or less autonomous staff groups. Community represents the societal level, i.e. elected politicians, advocacy, and various advisory groups seeking to exercise influence. They supervise the organization's management and build the formal connection to the outside world.

Professional cultures are pronounced and powerful. Leadership needs to address those subsystems and their professional identities in order to be successful (Schmitz and Berchtold 2009). Therefore, clinicians—particularly, but not only doctors—need to be engaged in management and leadership. But health care providers—

similar to the situation in other industries and sectors—must recognise that the type of leadership is changing. The old model of 'heroic' leadership by individuals will be replaced by models of shared leadership both within organisations and across organisations (The King's Fund 2011).

The 'post-heroic' model of leadership described by Turnbull (2011) involves multiple actors with leadership roles working together collaboratively across organisational or professional boundaries. Thus, leadership represents practices and organisational interventions, rather than just personal behavioural style or competencies. But as mentioned, this does not apply only to health care, but also for other sectors.

14.4.3 Leading a Health Care Organization: Personal Skills and Institutional Habits

Often leaders are struggling with how to focus their efforts. There is abundant literature on what personal skills or behaviour leaders should bring with them in order to be successful. All approaches are helpful in different ways. Just to take one example, Swensen et al. (2013) defined five critical behaviours that are inherent in most of these theories (Table 14.7). The list is intended to be open-ended. Adopting these behaviours can be a starting point to move the organization from volume to value—driving to better performance.

Another area of the literature does not focus on the leader as a person but on the organization and its success factors. Though there seems to be no dominant delivery model so far, there may be certain activities, behaviours, and ways of thinking that high performance organizations do share. Bohmer (2011) for example identified four so called "*habits*" that high-value health care organizations typically do have in common (see Table 14.8).

The expression of these habits may be unique for each organization depending on the individual regulatory and reimbursement environment. However, successful approaches to care management are based on the same habits.

Table 14.7 The behaviour of leaders in health care organizations

Person-centredness	Frequent interaction with patients and families in daily routines (e.g., participation in rounds, discussing results in terms of patients)
Front-line engagement	Establish an understanding of the work at the front lines of care—being visible and building trust (e.g., asking questions, sharing concerns, engaging in problem solving)
Relentless focus	Creating focus and urgency on high-priority efforts by framing the vision and strategy
Transparency	Forcing transparency in e.g. results, progress, aims, and defects as a catalyst to create understanding for change and thus functions
Boundarilessness	Establish a culture open for change and innovation (e.g., deliver health services across the continuum and person-centred)

Source: Swensen et al. 2013

Table 14.8 Four habits of high-value health care organizations

Specification and planning
• **criteria-based decision making** for both patient flow related as well as clinical decisions; manifested e.g. in treatment algorithms, discharge planner, pre-procedure checklists, standardized patient assessments
• **advanced planning** to specify choices, transitions, subgroups, and patient pathways
→ shift from expensive resources to problems these are designed to solve
Infrastructure design
• **designing microsystems** to match defined subpopulations and pathways including staff, IT, physical space, business processes, policies and procedures
→ shift from single platform, general-services-organization designs to patient group specific approaches maximizing use of scarce resources
Measurement and oversight
• **internal process control** and **performance management** by collecting more measurements than those required for external reporting
→ shift to measurement as an integral part of accountability and performance management
Self-study
• **examination of positive and negative deviance** in care and outcomes

Source: Bohmer (2011)

14.5 Lessons to Be Learned for Leadership in Integrated Care

As already noted, leadership structures in networks differ from those in typical hierarchies. Network structures *"provide a unique context for leadership that is characterized by ambiguity, diversity, dynamism, and complexity; the genuine failure of hierarchical fiat; and the importance of networks or relationships"* (Sydow et al. 2011, p. 341). In integrated care concepts seven aspects could be identified as particularly deviating from structures in other sectors and could be considered as potential pitfalls (see Fig. 14.4).

14.5.1 System-Related Pitfalls (Dark Blue)

First of all, governance structures and service delivery processes are important. Integrated care needs to adjust governance structures in order to steer patients through the system. Governance structures are health care policy on a macro level, the process of health care provision on the meso level, and the individual patient on the micro level. As mentioned above the complexity for leadership in health care emerges because of the importance of patients (and communities) as well as the highly complex legislative structure. Health policy usually entails fragments of other fields of expertise, such as the judicial or social authorities.

The service delivery (process) takes place in three (simplified) sectors, primarily outpatient care, inpatient care, and rehabilitation. Yet, care delivery is much more complex in practice as it takes place in a whole system of stakeholders. Next to the

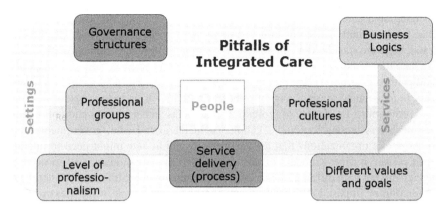

Fig. 14.4 The pitfalls of integrated care hamper successful implementation. Source: Own illustration

typical sectors, other areas such as nursing services, pharmacists, medical engineering, service providers and various others are involved.

14.5.2 People-Related Pitfalls (Yellow)

The second area comprises the dimensions of professional groups and cultures. Integrated care needs to encompass various occupational groups that distinguish themselves through strong professional cultures that have grown over years (e.g. nurses and physicians). The medical profession has distinctive inner differentiations (medical specialists vs. general practitioners, outpatient vs. inpatient physicians). Leadership in integrated care needs to work towards acceptance of these professions and cultures. Yet, it becomes clear that leadership should not become "*one more burden that comes with the job*" for professionals but that people need to be trained in leadership and they need to be paid for leading. A well-balanced approach is needed: the King's Fund Commission on Leadership and Management in the NHS elaborates on how much systems invest in professional management. Whereas the primary care trusts in England spent approximately 1–2% of their budgets on management, there are American organizations which invest around 12.5% of their budget for professional management and leadership (The King's Fund 2011). We postulate that a well-balanced investment is indispensable to sustain professional leadership in health care.

14.5.3 Organization-Related Pitfalls (Light Blue)

The third area is more complex and comprises the dimensions of different target systems and business mindsets as well as the degree of professionalization.

Integrated care often engages Public-Private-Partnership approaches, meaning that fundamentally different target systems need to be harmonized. On the one hand, there are stakeholders interested in common welfare (e.g. municipalities), and on the other hand, there are Non-Profit-Organizations, such as religious hospitals, and private institutions like pharmaceutical companies. For leadership it is necessary to understand these divergent mindsets in order for them to cooperate.

Furthermore, the degree of professionalization as well as the structure of organization differs among various stakeholders. In integrated care, governmental and other public organizations that act according to public law might need to interact with private business models of all sizes. These organizations are all in need of leadership but with different demands to it. Leadership in health care does not mean regulation or imposed change. It means that there are people who—next to their medical profession—understand the necessity of a strategic line of approach towards higher quality. They understand that better care, i.e. integrated care, will not *"just happen"* but needs conceptual input from different perspectives. Most certainly, appropriate resources (e.g., generated through participation fees of the individual stakeholders or governmental subsidies) are required for the implementation of integrated care concepts.

14.6   Conclusion

Leadership in integrated care does not differ fundamentally from leadership challenges in other network structures and needs to be addressed adequately. Beside the general underestimation of the importance of leadership in health care, several aspects have to be considered specifically. The following general recommendations highlight the importance of the topic for integrated care:

1. **Integrated care concepts are strategic assets**
   Integrated care concepts have to be recognized as strategic assets by the relevant institutions. Independent of their actual importance for the business model, integrated care concepts need strategic tailwind. This tailwind can be fostered by leadership.
2. **Leadership in integrated care is necessary**
   Leadership structures should be implemented separately from already well-established structures; meaning, the implementation should not be carried out solely by physicians or other service providers along the way but has to be organized separately and professionally, ideally within a management company.
3. **Leadership in integrated care requires investment**
   The expenditures for leadership need to be budgeted. Leadership is an integral field of activity and has to be remunerated separately. Expenditures on proper leadership and management skills as part of the budget assignment document an appreciation for it.

4. **Leadership in integrated care must build a culture of shared values**

Expert knowledge and professional authority are indispensable for the leadership of integrated care concepts. Leadership should be embedded in existing structures—nearly invisible—and occur indirectly through pointing out direction and growing a culture of shared values. Otherwise, resistance will build up.

5. **Leadership in integrated care needs time**

Leadership needs to motivate all parties involved in integrated care. The longer structures have been in place, the longer it needs to force them open.

6. **Leadership in integrated care needs to be focused**

Leadership needs to focus on the components and occupational groups that are most difficult to integrate. Generally, this is the medical profession. But leadership should also initiate local activities (e.g. regional conferences, workshops, quality circles, groups of regulars) in order to strengthen and document the solidarity within and between the groups and the involvement of the broader community.

7. **Leadership in integrated care needs to be data-based**

Medical care is strongly influenced by data. Therefore, in order to lead successfully, a comprehensive data-warehouse is crucial. Health care professionals will be mainly convinced by strong evidence of the suggested pathway. But data needs to be transparently accessible for all partners and should not be a source of power.

Leadership is still a highly underdeveloped and underestimated topic in health care management. But beside several important differences in health care, the main challenges are very similar to those in general management. Therefore the main focus should be on adapting general management approaches in the health care setting.

References

Amelung, V. E. (2013). *Healthcare management – Managed care organisations and instruments*. Berlin: Springer.

Amelung, V. E., Hildebrandt, H., & Wolf, S. (2012). Integrated care in Germany – A stony but necessary road! *International Journal of Integrated Care, 12*, e16.

Bartlett, C. A., & Wozny, M. (1999). GE's two-decade transformation: Jack Welch's leadership. Harvard Business School Case 9-399-150.

Battilana, J., Gilmartin, M., Sengul, M., Pace, A., & Alexander, J. A. (2010). Leadership competencies for implementing planned organizational change. *The Leadership Quarterly, 21*, 422–438. doi:10.1016/j.leaqua.2010.03.007.

Berwick, D. M., Nolan, T. W., & Whittington, J. (2008). The triple aim: Care, health, and cost. *Health Affairs, 27*(3), 759–769. doi:10.1377/hlthaff.27.3.759.

Blessin, B., & Wick, A. (2014). *Führen und führen lassen* (7th ed.). UVK Verlagsgesellschaft mbH: Konstanz.

Bohmer, R. M. J. (2011). The four habits of high-value health care organizations. *The New England Journal of Medicine, 365*(22), 2045–2047.

Den Hartog, D. N., & Koopman, P. L. (2011). Leadership in organizations. In N. Anderson, D. S. Ones, H. K. Sinangil, & C. Viswesvaran (Eds.), *Handbook of industrial, work & organizational psychology* (Vol. 2). London: SAGE.

Den Hertog, F., Groen, M., & Weehuizen, R. (2005). *Mapping health care innovation: Tracing walls and ceilings MERIT Research Memorandum series.* Maastricht: Maastricht Economic Research Institute on Innovation and Technology (MERIT); International Institute of Infonomics.

Glouberman, S., & Mintzberg, H. (2001). Managing the care of health and the cure of disease – Part I: Differentiation. *Health Care Management Review, 26*(1), 56–69.

Harari, O. (2002). *The leadership secrets of Colin Powell.* New York: McGraw-Hill.

Kodner, D. L., & Spreeuwenberg, C. (2002). Integrated care: Meaning, logic, applications, and implications – A discussion paper. *International Journal of Integrated Care, 2*, e12.

Kotter, J. P. (2001, December). What leaders really do. *Harvard Business Review.*

Kouzes, J. M., & Posner, B. Z. (2009). *The leadership challenge.* Weinheim: Wiley-VCH Verlag GmbH & Co. KGaA.

Krames, J. A. (2005). *Jack Welch and the 4E's of leadership. How to put GE's leadership formula to work in your organization.* New York: McGraw-Hill.

Mintzberg, H. (2010). *Managen.* Gabal Verlag GmbH: Offenbach.

Mintzberg, H. (2013). *Simply managing What managers do – and can do better.* San Fransisco: Berett-Koehler.

Northouse, P. G. (2013). *Leadership: Theory and practice* (6th ed.). Thousand Oaks: SAGE.

Powell, C. (2013). *Leadership – Regeln, die mich durchs leben führten.* Hoffmann und Campe: Hamburg.

Reinertsen, J. L., Bisognano, M., & Pugh, M. D. (2008). *Seven leadership leverage points for organization-level improvement in health care* (2nd ed.). Cambridge: Institute for Healthcare Improvement.

Schmitz, C., & Berchtold, P. (2009). Managing professionals – Führung im Krankenhaus. In V. E. Amelung, J. Sydow, & A. Windeler (Eds.), *Vernetzung im Gesundheitswesen Wettbewerb und Kooperation.* Stuttgart: W. Kohlhammer Druckerei GmbH + Co. KG.

Schoemaker, P. J. H., Krupp, S., & Howland, S. (2013, January–February). Managing yourself strategic leadership: The essential skills. *Harvard Business Review.*

Swensen, S. J., Dilling, J. A., Miliner, D. S., Zimmerman, R. S., Maples, W. J., & Lindsay, M. E. (2009). Quality: The Mayo Clinic approach. *American Journal of Medical Quality, 24*(428). doi:10.1177/1062860609339521.

Swensen, S. J., Pugh, M., McMullan, C., & Kabcnell, A. (2013). *High-impact leadership: Improve care, improve the health of populations and reduce costs.* Cambridge: Institute for Healthcare Improvement.

Sydow, J., Lerch, F., Huxham, C., & Hibbert, P. (2011). A silent cry for leadership: Organizing for leading (in) clusters. *The Leadership Quarterly, 22*, 328–343.

The King's Fund. (2011). *The future of leadership and management in the NHS No more heroes.* London: The King's Fund.

Turnbull, J. K. (2011). *Leadership in context: Lessons from new leadership theory and current leadership development practice.* Retrieved from www.kingsfund.org.uk/leadershipcommission

Culture and Values

15

Robin Miller, Marisa de Andrade, Rommy Marjolein Don, Volker
Amelung, Viktoria Stein, Nicholas Goodwin, Ran Balicer, Ellen
Nolte, and Esther Suter

15.1 Introduction

There is increasing recognition of the importance of culture and values in the
running and improvement of health, care and wider community services. Culture,
or 'the way we do things round here', has been connected to the quality and safety
of such services both positively and negatively. An enabling and learning culture is
seen to promote opportunities for identifying, reflecting and acting on any concerns,

R. Miller (✉)
Health Services Management Centre, University of Birmingham, Birmingham, UK
e-mail: R.S.Miller@bham.ac.uk

M. de Andrade
School of Health in Social Science, University of Edinburgh, Edinburgh, UK
e-mail: marisa.deandrade@ed.ac.uk

R.M. Don
NHS Forth Valley, Larbert, UK

V. Amelung
Institute for Epidemiology, Social Medicine and Health System Research, Medical School
Hannover, Hannover, Germany

V. Stein • N. Goodwin
International Foundation for Integrated Care, Oxford, United Kingdom

R. Balicer
Health Policy Research and Planning, Clalit Health Services, Tel-Aviv, Israel

E. Nolte
European Observatory on Health Systems and Policies, London School of Economics and Political
Science, London School of Hygiene & Tropical Medicine, London, UK

E. Suter
Workforce Research & Evaluation, Alberta Health Services Calgary, Calgary, Alberta, Canada

© Springer International Publishing AG 2017   237
V. Amelung et al. (eds.), *Handbook Integrated Care*,
DOI 10.1007/978-3-319-56103-5_15

whilst a controlling and blaming culture is seen to stifle such concerns being raised and so responded to appropriately. In turn values, both those expressed by an organization within its mission and strategy and those which practically underpin the everyday decisions made by teams are a key component of institutional culture. Personal values based on professional standards and individual beliefs further influence the choices and priorities of practitioners. Any organization seeking to achieve effective change must take account of these multi-layered and multi-dimensional factors. Integrated care initiatives, which commonly bring together professionals, practitioners and services from established silos add yet more complexity. The clashes in values and culture which can emerge through their new arrangements can be a powerful obstacle as the parties involved are exposed to alternative ways of seeing and interpreting the world.

These dynamics are commonly reflected in research regarding integration within health and care services (see Box 15.1). This reflects study outside these sectors, where organisational culture and an alignment of personal and professional values have been recognised as key enablers of positive change management for many decades (e.g. Cummings and Worley 2014). 'Values alignment. . . could well be the bedrock, the foundation, upon which all truly successful organisational change depends' (Branson 2008, p392).

In this chapter, we will begin with a consideration of what is meant by 'culture' and 'values' and how they have been connected in relation to the field of integration. We will then focus on two key approaches to developing them positively—teamwork and inter-professional learning. We conclude with a reflection on what this means for those leading and working in integrated settings, and provide resources for further learning and reading.

Box 15.1 Examples of culture and values within evidence reviews and evaluations

Minkman (2012): The process of integration in itself is described as multi-faceted in nature, requiring the integration of structures, processes, cultures and social relationships (p348).

Petch (2014): Much of the achievement of integrated care and support is dependent on successful culture change. Both professions and organisations are likely to have developed particular cultures which help to shape their identity and foster allegiance (p8).

Cameron et al. (2012): By its very nature, joint working brings together professionals with different philosophies and values as well as divergent professional cultures. Not surprisingly, these differences can act as barriers to effective joint working (p13)

RAND Europe and Ernst & Young LLP (2012): The realisation of a given pilot's intended changes relied on its ability to modify existing systems and practices and to make new ones possible. This ability was especially dependent on organisational culture.... pilots often found integration activities were hampered by a lack of openness that several staff perceived to inhibit discussion, and which was part of a wider 'blame culture (p82).

15.2   What Is Meant by Culture?

Despite organisational culture being a regular feature of health, social care and integrated care policy and practice guidance, there remains considerable debate about what is meant by this concept. The definition by Schneider and Barbera (2014) encapsulates many of the elements that are regularly associated with contemporary interpretations—'the values and beliefs that characterize organizations, as transmitted by socialization processes that newcomers have, the decisions made by management, and the stories and myths people tell and retell about their organizations' (p10). This reflects the view that staff members are inducted into the culture of the organisation through socialisation with others. Also that culture is developed, conveyed and reinforced by influences as variable as the concrete actions taken by key players and the informal anecdotes and personal reflections of individuals and teams. Bissell (2012, p82) provides a simpler account—'deeply held beliefs about success'—which underlines the sense that culture is something that can be resistant to change through the strength of attachment, and that it can relate to what ends are aspired to (i.e. why we do what we do) as well as the processes through which these can be achieved (i.e. the way we do things around here).

One of the most commonly deployed models of organisational culture in current use is that of Schein (2010)—'a pattern of shared basic assumptions learned by a group as it solved its problems of external adaptation and internal integration' (p18). This again picks up on culture's deeply rooted nature. It provides the additional dimension of culture as being the process through which organisations respond to the challenges they face through collaboration between the individuals and functions within them. Schein proposes that culture can be seen to be operating in three domains—values (ideologies or charters), artefacts (physical manifestations such as dress code, company reports and environment) and assumptions (thought processes, feelings and behaviour). However Meyerson and Martin (1987) contest the notion that organisations have a single culture, suggesting that it is more common for them to have differentiation (separate sub-cultures within departments that can be in a state of harmony, conflict or ambivalence and which combine to compose the organisation) or fragmentation (in which there are no whole organisation or fixed sub-cultures, but rather varying and fluid relationships between individuals and groups).

Sullivan and Williams (2012) highlight the importance of physical artefacts (or 'objects') to understanding the cultural dynamics within an integrated care initiative. They recall a comment made by one staff member in such an initiative on the symbolism of shared or separate refreshment arrangements between the different teams—with different kettles being seen to reflect a failure to achieve a common and shared identity. Gale et al. (2014) have developed a helpful framework which combines theoretical insights with the practice experience of those responsible for health and care redesign. This is suggests that the three domains identified by Schein can be considered as working on three levels—that of 'patients' (i.e. those accessing a service and their families and carers), 'people' (i.e. those working, managing and leading services), and 'place' (the physical

Table 15.1 Observable artefacts commonly encountered in integrated care initiatives across health and care (based on Miller et al. 2016)

Domain	Example of common artefacts within integrated care initiatives
Patients	*Terminology*: Along with patients, service users, customers or clients are terms commonly used to denote those who are receiving support. Each of these terms highlights different interpretations of their relationship with the service provider. *Documentation*: Are assessments and care plans in a format that encourages service recipients to access and engage with this information? *Care co-ordination*: Do processes expect decisions to be made with full participation of those receiving services and are adjustments made for those with alternative communication styles?
People engaged in delivering service	*Staff dress*: Uniforms commonly worn by health staff which differentiate between them and non-health staff, and between different health disciplines *Terms & Conditions*: Staff may be entitled to different holidays or opportunities for learning and development *Payment*: Salary differentials lead to distinct variations in holidays, cars and housing
Place in which services are delivered	*Locations:* Are people required to come to a discrete building or are they supported in their own homes? *Standard of building*: Is the building in a good state of repair and/or specifically designed for the needs of the service in question? *Facilities for staff*: Are there different expectations on office and desk arrangements, and facilities for refreshments between teams and professionals?

environment and locality in which a service is based). Table 15.1 suggests common artefacts of integration through which organisational culture can be observed.

A good example of the impact of culture within an integrated care organisation is that of 'Care Trusts'. The option of developing a Care Trust as an integrated health and social care organization in England was announced following long-standing concerns about the ability of the statutory bodies responsible for health and social care to work together. It was envisaged by central government that Care Trusts would become the norm for the planning and delivery of community services for older people, and they were also developed to deliver services for people with mental health problems and/or learning disabilities. Care Trusts were therefore primarily an example of structural integration, but (dependent on the individual trust) also sought to develop 'linkage', 'coordination' and 'networks' with other local health and social care organizations (see Miller et al. (2011) for overview of care trust policy and practices).

The initial policy intentions did not explicitly mention 'culture' as this was before the term's rise to prominence. However, it is clear that developing a particular approach to the 'way we do things around here' and the subsequent impact on patients, service users and their families was at the forefront of policy makers' aspirations:

'They will enable staff to shape a new organisation around patient and user needs and provide a system that supports them in doing their jobs and rewards them for working together. For users, carers and patients, this will mean greater potential for tailored and integrated care, greater accessibility, and one stop shops for services that used to entail repeated conversations and a procession of different faces at times of illness, stress and vulnerability.' (DH 2002)

Evaluations of some Care Trusts (e.g. Torbay) did suggest that positive impacts had been achieved, although the extent to which these could be attributed to the development of an integrated organisation rather than other factors was not established (Thistlethwaite 2011). Senior managers in other Care Trusts suggested that using such a structural approach to achieving integration could cause as many problems as it solved and were less convinced that it provided an effective and efficient means to deliver the expected outcomes (Miller et al. 2011). In relation to cultural aspects in particular, it would appear that the ways of working, beliefs regarding the potential of partnerships and the likely response of key actors were central to their success even before the organisations were launched. In areas in which there was an existing inter-agency culture of joint working, care trusts appear to have had a positive impact as the next step in a shared journey. However, in areas where such a culture was not present and care trusts were being imposed as a means to force collaboration, there was considerable tension and mistrust which delayed or in some cases derailed success.

Once established, there were numerous reports of the importance of culture within these integrated care organisations acting as an enabler or as a barrier (Dickinson et al. 2007). Barriers included the 'clash' in cultures between health and social care staff, failure to address intransigent cultures within teams and professions which might otherwise facilitate innovation, and the culture within partner agencies viewing the new organisations as something separate. There were also examples of the opposite experience, such as development of a shared culture, new ways of working, and successful partnerships being achieved. Key factors that contributed to more positive engagement with culture were: a transformational leadership style with consistency in vision over time; the development of shared artefacts through branding, mission statements and promotional materials emphasizing a shared identity; incentive structures which rewarded collaborative practice and were supported by relevant development; and a focus both on improving relationships between different professionals and practitioners as well as with local patients, service users and communities (Miller et al. 2011). A common reflection of senior leaders within care trusts was that they should have had a greater focus on cultural issues and if such an undertaking is repeated they should be put at the forefront of the process.

15.3   What Is Meant by Values?

There is also a range of interpretations for the concept of 'values'. Woodbridge and Fulford (2004) suggest that amongst health care professionals 'values are often synonymous with ethics' (p14). They highlight though that the term is also commonly applied to 'wishes, desires, needs' (i.e. quality of life) and 'self-fulfill-ment'. In social care, the difference between values, ethics and practice principles has been defined as follows (BASW 2012):

Values: What people commonly believe is worthy or valuable in social care practice.

Ethical principles: General statements about the attitudes, rights and duties that should underpin social care. For example, to promote inclusion in society, to co-produce solutions, to protect those who are vulnerable, etc.

Practice principles: General statements about how service users and their families can be supported to achieve the desired outcomes. For example, 'putting the person at the centre of any decisions', 'communicating clearly the options available', and 'treating people with respect'.

In this framing, 'values' can be summarised as 'what we see as important', with 'principles' providing guidance about how these values can be 'translated into practice'. Values are not always well defined, which means that people may not fully understand what they or others mean by them. This results in individuals, organisations and policy makers having different views about what the key values are, how they interpret these, and how they would implement the values in practice. For example, independence could be interpreted as someone not being dependent on public sector funding, living outside of an institutional setting and/or being able to make decisions over their own life without interference or control by someone else. Empowerment may mean being able to choose how to deploy the public service resources to which someone is entitled, being involved in the planning or management of services, or being enabled to be more assertive over one's overall rights. Whilst some values and principles will be similar over the decades, others and/or their definitions will be added, omitted or amended as professional and societal values and insights change. Finally, there may be a clash between the values that underpin the different duties and responsibilities that professionals and practitioners are expected to undertake. For example, there may be a clash between responsibilities to 'control' peoples' behaviour in order to keep them safe versus the responsibility to promote autonomy and independence.

Different professions have their own 'ethical codes' which set out a 'framework of values' that individuals within this profession are expected to follow (Woodbridge and Fulford 2004). Whilst there are many areas of similarity (e.g. respect for individuals, do no harm), there is also the potential for differing emphasis which can lead to some tension within inter-professional settings (Cameron 2011, Mangan et al 2015). For example, Cameron et al. (2012) highlight that 'the emphasis placed on professional specific knowledge and socialisation shapes the values and identities of the different professions, ultimately causing separation' (p55). People accessing services will also bring their own values leading to the potential for very different interpretations of the same set of social and health conditions. 'Values-based practice (VBP)' has been suggested as means to enable effective collaboration and decision making in situations in which alternative (and hence potentially conflicting) values are in play (Woodbridge and Fulford 2004). Perry et al. (2013) describe VBP as seeking to put people accessing services at the head of any decisions. It requires professionals and practitioners to be respectful of each other and patients' values rather than trying to impose their own beliefs, and this may necessitate a new set of skills relating to negotiation and facilitation. Heginbotham (2012) suggests that VBP can also move from the realm of direct work with patients and services to the planning and purchasing of services. The core principles of VBP that are commonly promoted include communication, person-centredness and partnership (Woodbridge and Fulford 2004), and as such they connect with common principles behind collaborative practice and the competencies that this requires (see Box 15.2 and 15.3).

Box 15.2 Collaborative practice

'Interprofessional collaboration is the process of developing and maintaining effective interprofessional working relationships with learners, practitioners, patients/clients/families and communities to enable optimal health outcomes. Elements of collaboration include respect, trust, shared decision making, and partnerships.' (CIHC 2010, p8)

Box 15.3 Value based competences within collaborative practice (IPEC 2011)

Place the interests of patients and populations at the centre of interprofessional health care delivery.

Respect the dignity and privacy of patients while maintaining confidentiality in the delivery of team-based care.

Embrace the cultural diversity and individual differences that characterize patients, populations, and the health care team.

Respect the unique cultures, values, roles/responsibilities, and expertise of other health professions.

Work in cooperation with those who receive care, those who provide care, and others who contribute to or support the delivery of prevention and health services.

Develop a trusting relationship with patients, families, and other team members

Demonstrate high standards of ethical conduct and quality of care in one's contributions to team-based care.

Manage ethical dilemmas specific to inter-professional patient/population centred care situations.

Act with honesty and integrity in relationships with patients, families, and other team members.

Maintain competence in one's own profession appropriate to scope of practice.

15.4 How Do We Positively Develop Values and Cultures?

> **Box 15.4 Alternative approaches to culture change**
> 'Culture cannot easily be mandated—it develops over time as a successful adaptation to conditions, bringing desired results and defining desired norms and values. It is tempting for senior managers just to announce new behaviours or new values, but if they do not clearly specify what is desired and how it connects to meaningful consequences... they will not give people a chance to learn that the new behaviours work better than current practices. This process is much more likely to succeed if key individuals are involved in helping to design new ways of doing things that solve real problems and thereby engage their internal motivation. Once enough people realise that things work better, the values that lay behind the mandated new behaviours become more accepted, and new assumptions arise to support how these behaviours are "the way we do things around here"' (Carroll and Quijada 2004, pii17)

It will be apparent then that culture and values are deeply embedded within individuals, organisations, and ways of working, and that seeking to alter these is unlikely to be simple or quick. Furthermore, there is a strong interconnection between these two elements of organisational life—our values influence our culture, and our culture in turn can shape our values. There is also relatively little formal research evidence of successful and sustained culture change in relation to specific aspects of practice and as a consequence, details of what interventions will work best in which circumstance are not well established (Parmelli et al. 2011). However, that is not to say that we do not have insights based on practice and applied research on the key elements of change management that can positively shape and build upon cultures and values (see e.g. Drumm 2014). Top-down mandated mechanisms may alter behaviour in the short term if the sanctions and rewards are strong enough, but are unlikely to result in fundamental and resilient improvement. This requires the engagement of key stakeholders and should demonstrate impact on outcomes that are seen to matter (see Text Box 15.4). In this next section, we will turn to two interventions that are thought to facilitate such positive change—teamwork and interprofessional learning. Leadership, which is covered in elsewhere in this compendium, would have been our third intervention if space allowed.

15.4.1 Teamwork

Teams are central to the delivery of most health and social care services, and there is increasing recognition of the importance of good teamwork to providing safe and quality services (see e.g. Jelphs et al. 2016). This is also true for integrated services, with the strength of good inter-professional teamwork being evidenced in acute, primary and specialist settings. For example, Prades et al. (2015) report that cancer patients who receive care from a multidisciplinary team have increased survival rates and improved experience of receiving care. Franx et al. (2008) suggest that people with severe mental health problems have reduced rates of hospitalisation and better social wellbeing when supported by inter-professional community teams. It is important to remember that whilst individuals may have a core team to which they belong, they will often also be members of other teams, and that whilst some teams may be established on a long-term basis with a degree of continuity of staff and structure, others will be more short-term and transient in nature. This includes those that are formed around service users and their families, and which may require collaboration between professionals and other practitioners that have not previously met or worked together. Conversely, poor (or as it is sometimes described 'pseudo') teamwork can provide a difficult environment for people to perform their professional roles and can lead to poorer service user experience and outcomes (West and Lyubovnikova 2013).

Teams can also be highly influential in the shaping of 'how things are done round here' through the pressure that members can feel to conform to the norms and values that are adopted by a team. This can be a positive or negative influence on the quality of care that is provided, depending on the team culture that emerges. For example, it is common for inquiries of poor and abusive practice to highlight teams that had become very inward-looking and resistant to external challenge. Such 'dysfunctions' reflect wider accounts of teams and the factors that can contribute to their success (Lencioni 2006). It is therefore vital that teams are well run and focused on improving the lives of service users and carers and work in line with the expected values and vision. The Input-Process-Output model is based on the considerable evidence base regarding team working, and depicts the core elements that need to be in place for a team to operate effectively (see Fig. 15.1).

Reeves et al. (2011) highlight that encouraging strong inter-professional team working requires both relational and processual elements to be addressed. Relational interventions seek to promote trust and communication team members and include learning opportunities (see section below), opportunities to meet on a regular basis, and to spend time getting to know each other personally and professionally. Process interventions seek to better organise the work undertaken by a team and include care pathways detailing respective contributions, and 'role-shifting' to give greater flexibility in the tasks team members undertake. Jelphs et al. (2016) provide an overview of helpful tools and frameworks to support relational and process interventions. These include—the Belbin team inventory to facilitate reflection on team roles and behaviours; 'de bono's' hat exercise to encourage creative thinking; the SBAR model (Situation: Background: Assessment: Recommendation) to provide a structure for communication; and the 'thinking environment' approach to expressing the emotions that underlie team dynamics. Reflecting the IPO model, both Reeves et al. (2011) and Jelphs et al. (2016) highlight the importance of organisational context in the nurturing of teams. For those within an integrated service this will be more complicated as it is likely to

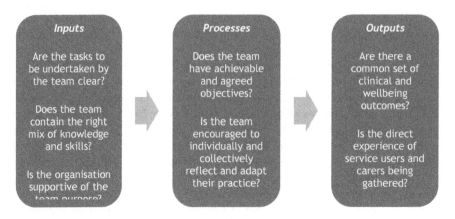

Fig. 15.1 The Input-Process-Output model of team effectiveness (based on West and Lyubovnikova 2013)

involve multiple organisations as well as the governance arrangements across the partnership.

15.4.2 Inter-professional Learning

Inter-professional learning (or education) occurs 'when two or more professionals learn with, from and about each other to improve collaboration and the quality of care' (CAIPE 2002; NES 2005). It is also described as 'an intervention where the members of more than one health or social care profession, or both, learn interactively together, for the explicit purpose of improving inter professional collaboration or the health/wellbeing of patients/clients, or both' (Reeves et al. 2013, p2). Inter-professional learning can take place amongst students, who are studying to become professionals (Gould et al. 2015), as well as amongst professionals (Reeves et al. 2013). The interactive nature of this knowledge exchange between professionals plays a crucial part in shifting organisational cultures and values (Hammick et al. 2007; Thistlethwaite 2012).

A shared organisational culture, which recognises 'a pattern of shared basic assumptions learned by a group' (Schein 2010, p18), may be facilitated by inter-professional learning by fostering an understanding and respect of the 'other' profession. As mutual understanding and respect develops, a silo-structured way of working could be overcome within an organisation (Frenk et al. 2010; Reeves et al. 2013; Thistlethwaite 2012). Inter-professional learning could, for example, address the challenges posed by professional tribalism (Braithwaite et al. 2007) and encourage team working (Billingsley and Lang 2002; Thistlethwaite 2012; Reeves et al. 2013).

An underlying learning theory for inter-professional learning is the 'intergroup contact hypothesis' introduced by Allport (Allport 1954; Barr 2015; Foster and Clark

2015). The intergroup contact hypothesis entails that contact between groups can counter prejudice, if groups have equal status, common goals, and if groups can experience successful collaboration and support is provided by authorities (Allport 1954; Dovido et al. 2005; Taylor et al. 2008; Pettigrew and Tropp 2011).

Inter-professional learning can also enhance a more comprehensive, holistic approach to care provision and understanding of the needs and abilities of patients (Billingsley and Lang 2002; Gould et al. 2015), and can therefore improve patient care and collaboration between professionals (McKimm and Brake 2010; Barwell et al. 2013; Reeves et al. 2013). Indeed, a variety of institutions including the World Health Organization, Canadian Inter-professional Health Collaborative and Inter-professional Education Collaborative Expert Panel advocate that inter-professional learning contributes to professionals working in a collaborative manner, which in turn contributes to improved patient care (CIHC 2010; WHO 2010; IECEP 2011; Reeves et al. 2013).

Inter-professional learning, conversely, may also be regarded as reductionist as it can be interpreted as devaluing the skills and knowledge of a certain profession (Billingsley and Lang 2002) thereby encouraging tribal l behaviour as professionals strive to protect their own profession (Braithwaite et al. 2007). It could be argued, however, that inter-professional learning takes into account the skills and knowledge specific to certain professions, whilst indicating the common ground of other skills and knowledge between professions (Billingsley and Lang 2002). More (applied) research and practice in this area is encouraged particularly as the integration agenda unfolds (Doel and Shardlow 2009; Gould et al. 2015; Thistlethwaite 2012; Reeves et al. 2013; Foster and Clark 2015).

Box 15.5 Example of inter-professional learning in practice (based on feedback from participants)

As part of building future leadership capacity, NHS Education Scotland (NES) provided masterclasses on various topics varying from the Ladder of Inference (the thinking process that we go through, normally without realising it, to get from a fact to a decision or action) to wicked issues (complex problems that are challenging or impossible to resolve due to partial, contrary and changing conditions), and action learning sets. These masterclasses and action learning sets were multi-disciplinary and consisted of psychologists, doctors, allied health professionals managers, nurses and staff working in finance.

There was a focus on co-production—working with the assets that already exist within teams—to encourage mutual learning and create an understanding of the challenges people from different professions are facing through health and social care integration.

Participants found the experience invaluable as it gave them insight into the practical realities encountered by other professionals, but also helped

---

(continued)

Box 15.5 (continued)

them realise that people were experiencing similar challenges mainly related to dealing and communicating with others. The exchange cultivated respect and trust between staff and their respective professions.

The group also organised a collective community challenge at a secondary school, which involved preparing posters about various NHS jobs and corresponding study requirements and presenting these to schoolchildren. This helped raise awareness of career opportunities for schoolchildren while making NHS staff more aware of other roles within the organisation.

15.5   Conclusion

This chapter has focused on the role of Culture and Values within integrated care. As Culture and Values are deeply embedded within individuals, organisations, and their ways of working, seeking to alter these in practice is unlikely to be simple or quick. The difference in the understanding and interpretation of values can result in individuals, organisations, and policy makers having different interpretations of a value and how they would see this being implemented. Simultaneously, there may be a clash between the values that underpin the different duties and responsibilities that professionals and practitioners are expected to undertake. A failure to do so will limit the impact and sustainability of any integrated care initiative. Key contributors to developing a positive culture and values include leadership style (particularly that which is more transformational), consistency in vision, the development of shared artefacts to provide a common allegiance, and a focus on collaboration between professionals and practitioners, service users and communities. Teamwork can make a positive contribution by bringing together those from shared and different professional backgrounds to achieve a common aim and in so doing enhance individual and collective contributions to better care. Inter-professional learning can contribute through creating a mutual understanding of the other profession's values and ways of working as well as the competences of collaboration. Team and learning interventions are most impactful when introduced alongside each other, with the learning supporting inter-professional team working and teams providing a reflective environment to implement the new knowledge and skills developed through training and development. Together they encourage the values and culture that will underpin the collaborative, holistic approach which enables service user to receive the support that is important to them in a coordinated way.

References

Allport, G. W. (1954). *The nature of prejudice*. Cambridge, MA: Perseus Books.
Barr, H. (2015). Toward a theoretical framework for interprofessional education. *Journal of Integrated Care, 27*, 4–9.
Barwell, J., Arnold, F., & Berry, H. (2013). How interprofessional learning improves care. *Nursing Times, 109*(21), 14–16.
BASW. (2012). *The code of ethics for social work statement of principles*. Retrieved December 2, 2015, from https://www.basw.co.uk/codeofethics/
Billingsley, R., & Lang, L. (2002). The case for interprofessional learning in health and social care. *Journal of Integrated Care, 10*(4), 31–34.
Bissell, G. (2012). *Organisational behavior for social work*. Bristol: Policy Press.
Braithwaite, J., Iedema, R. A., & Jorm, C. (2007). Trust, communication, theory of mind and the social brain hypothesis: Deep explanations for what goes wrong in health care. *Journal of Health Organization and Management, 21*(4), 353–367.
Branson, C. M. (2008). Achieving organisational change through values alignment. *Journal of Educational Administration, 46*(3), 376–395.
CAIPE. (2002). *Interprofessional education*. Retrieved November 15, 2015, from http://caipe.org.uk/about-us/the-/definition-and-principles-of-interprofessional-education//
Cameron, A. (2011). Impermeable boundaries? Developments in professional and inter-professional practice. *Journal of Interprofessional Care, 25*(1), 53–58.
Cameron, A., Lart, R., Bostock, L., & Coomber, C. (2012). *Factors that promote and hinder joint and integrated working between health and social care services*. Retrieved from www.scie.org.uk
Carroll, J. S., & Quijada, M. A. (2004). Redirecting traditional professional values to support safety: Changing organizational culture in health care. *Quality and Safety in Health Care, 13*(1), 16–21.
CIHC. (2010). *Canadian Interprofessional Health Collaboration. A national inter professional competency framework*. Retrieved from www.cihc.ca/files/CIHC_IPCompetencies_Feb1210.pd
Cummings, T., & Worley, C. (2014). *Organization development and change*. Stamford: Cengage Learning.
Department of Health. (2002). *Care trusts: Background briefing*. Retrieved from www.dh.gov.uk
Dickinson, H., Peck, E., & Davidson, D. (2007). Opportunity seized or missed? A case study of leadership and organisational change in the creation of a Care Trust. *Journal of Interprofessional Care, 21*(5), 503–513.
Doel, M., & Shardlow, S. M. (Eds.). (2009). *Educating professionals, practice learning in health and social care*. Farnham: Ashgate.
Dovido, J. F., Glick, P., & Rudman, L. A. (Eds.). (2005). *On the nature of prejudice fifty years after Allport*. Malden: Blackwell.
Drumm, M. (2014). *Culture change in the public sector*. Glasgow: IRISS.
Foster, R., & Clark, J. M. (2015). Moderating the stereotypical views of health and social care students: The role of interprofessional education. *Journal of Interprofessional Care, 29*, 34–40.
Franx, G., Kroon, H., Grimshaw, J., Drake, R., Grol, R., & Wensing, M. (2008). Organizational change to transfer knowledge and improve quality and outcomes of care for patients with severe mental illness: A systematic overview of reviews. *Canadian Journal of Psychiatry, 53*(5), 294.
Frenk, J., Chen, L., Bhutta, Z., Cohen, J., Crisp, N., Evans, T., et al. (2010). Health professionals for a new century: Transforming education to strengthen health systems in an interdependent world. *The Lancet, 376*(9756), 1923–1958.
Gale, N. K., Shapiro, J., McLeod, H. S., Redwood, S., & Hewison, A. (2014). Patients-people-place: Developing a framework for researching organizational culture during health service redesign and change. *Implementation Science, 9*(1), 106.

Gould, P. R., Lee, Y., Berkowitz, S., & Bronstein, L. (2015). Impact of collaborative interprofessional learning experience upon medical and social work students in geriatric health care. *Journal of Interprofessional Care, 29*(4), 372–373.

Hammick, M., Freeth, D., Koppel, I., Reeves, S., & Barr, H. (2007). A best evidence systematic review of interprofessional education: BEME Guide no. 9. *Medical Teacher, 29*(8), 753–751. doi:10.1080/01421590701682576.

Heginbotham, C. (2012). *Values-based commissioning of health and social care.* Cambridge: Cambridge University Press.

Interprofessional Education Collaborative Expert Panel. (2011). *Core competencies for interprofessional collaborative practice: Report of an expert panel.* Washington, DC: Interprofessional Education Collaborative. Retrieved from www.aacp.org/resource/education/Documents/10-2421PECFullReprtfinal.pdf

Jelphs, K., Dickinson, H., & Miller, R. (2016). *Working in teams.* Bristol: Policy Press.

Lencioni, P. (2006). *The five dysfunctions of a team.* Hoboken, NJ: Wiley.

Mangan, C., Miller, R., & Ward, C. (2015). Knowing me, knowing you. *Journal of Integrated Care, 23*(2), 62–73.

McKimm, J., & Brake, D.-J. (2010). Interprofessional learning. *British Journal of Hospital Medicine, 71*(10), 580–583.

Meyerson, D., & Martin, J. (1987). Cultural change: An integration of three different views. *Journal of Management Studies, 24*(6), 0022–2380.

Miller, R., Dickinson, H., & Glasby, J. (2011). The care trust pilgrims. *Journal of Integrated Care, 19*(4), 14–21.

Miller, R., Mangan, C., & Brown, H. (2016). *Integrated care in action: A practical guide for health, social care and housing support.* London: Jessica Kingsley.

Minkman, M. M. (2012). The current state of integrated care: An overview. *Journal of Integrated Care, 20*(6), 346–358.

NES. (2005). *Educational development.* http://www.nes.scot.nhs.uk/education-and-training/educational-development/

Parmelli, E., Flodgren, G., Beyer, F., Baillie, N., Schaafsma, M. E., & Eccles, M. P. (2011). The effectiveness of strategies to change organisational culture to improve healthcare performance: A systematic review. *Implementation Science, 6*(1), 33.

Perry, E., Barber, J., & England, E. (2013). *A review of values-based commissioning in mental health.* London: National Survivor User Network.

Petch, A. (2014). *Delivering integrated care and support.* Glasgow: IRISS.

Pettigrew, T. F., & Tropp, L. R. (2011). *When groups meet: The dynamics of intergroup contact.* New York: Psychology Press.

Prades, J., Remue, E., van Hoof, E., & Borras, J. M. (2015). Is it worth reorganising cancer services on the basis of multidisciplinary teams (MDTs)? A systematic review of the objectives and organisation of MDTs and their impact on patient outcomes. *Health Policy, 119*(4), 464–474.

RAND Europe, & Ernst & Young LLP. (2012). *National evaluation of the department of health's integrated care pilots.* Retrieved from http://www.dh.gov.uk/en/Publicationsandstatistics/Publications/PublicationsPolicyAndGuidance/DH_133124

Reeves, S., Lewin, S., Espin, S., & Zwarenstein, M. (2011). *Interprofessional teamwork for health and social care* (Vol. 8). Hoboken, NJ: Wiley.

Reeves, S., Perrier, L., Goldman, J., Barr, H., Freeth, D., & Zwarenstein, M. (2013). *Interprofessional education: Effects on professional practice and health care outcomes (update) (Review).* New York: The Cochrane Collaboration.

Schein, E. (2010). *Organizational culture and leadership* (4th ed.). San Francisco: Jossey Bass.

Schneider, B., & Barbera, K. M. (2014). Introduction: The oxford handbook of organizational climate and culture. In B. Schneider & K. M. Barbera (Eds.), *The Oxford handbook of organizational climate and culture* (pp. 3–20). Oxford University Press: Oxford.

Sullivan, H., & Williams, P. (2012). Whose kettle? Exploring the role of objects in managing and mediating the boundaries of integration in health and social care. *Journal of Health Organization and Management, 26*(6), 697–712.

Taylor, I., Whiting, R., & Sharland, E. (2008). *Integrated children's services in higher education project (ICS-HE): Knowledge review*. Southampton: Higher Education Academy.

Thistlethwaite, P. (2011). *Integrating health and social care in Torbay: Improving care for Mrs Smith*. London: Kings' Fund.

Thistlethwaite, J. (2012). Interprofessional education: A review of context, learning and the research agenda. *Medical Education, 46*, 58–70.

West, M. A., & Lyubovnikova, J. (2013). Illusions of team working in health care. *Journal of Health Organization and Management, 27*(1), 134–142.

WHO. (2010). *Framework for action on interprofessional education and collaborative practice*. Geneva: World Health Organization.

Woodbridge, K., & Fulford, K. W. M. (2004). *Whose values? A workbook for values-based practice in mental health care*. London: Sainsbury Centre for Mental Health.

Change Management

16

Nick Goodwin

16.1   Introduction

> "The experience of organisations that have made the transition from fragmentation to integration demonstrates that the work is long and arduous. [Managers responsible for achieving change] need to plan over an appropriate timescale (at least five years and often longer) and to base their actions on a coherent strategy" (Ham and Walsh 2013, p. 7)

Enabling health systems to become more coordinated and integrated in how they function in the delivery of care to patients is a long-term and complex task. The process of change towards integrated care requires decision-makers to take action at a number of different levels to not only ensure that the key building blocks for integrated care are in place but that they function well together to promote continuity of care and coherence in the way care is organised and delivered. Evidence points to the need for *simultaneous* action to be taken at a number of levels to support the range of changes that are necessary—for example, in supporting shared decision-making between patients and providers; in building inter-disciplinary teams of care professions; in creating effective networks between partners in care; and in engaging and promoting action to support changes that help to embed integrated care as an accepted and legitimate approach to care delivery.

However, despite recognition that the complexity of integrated care requires pro-active management support and action, there has been little guidance produced that might help to understand the various processes that are necessary to support change to happen (WHO Regional Office for Europe 2015). This chapter seeks to articulate the components of a change management strategy for taking forward integrated care policies in practice at a local and regional level.

N. Goodwin (✉)
International Foundation for Integrated Care, Wolfson College, Linton Road, Oxford OX2 6UD, UK
e-mail: nickgoodwin@integratedcarefoundation.org

© Springer International Publishing AG 2017
V. Amelung et al. (eds.), *Handbook Integrated Care*,
DOI 10.1007/978-3-319-56103-5_16

16.2   A Conceptual Understanding of Change Management

Any successful strategy for change depends on its mission, the resources and competencies it has at its disposal, and the environment in which it is operating. The strategic direction to be chosen for change must analyse these elements and identify what needs to be done to ensure the 'strategic fit' of the various organisations and stakeholders involved. It should be recognised from the beginning that in no health and social care system, given the history in the way care provision has been established, does integrated care emerge naturally as a solution. In order to achieve change towards integrated care there is strong evidence to demonstrate that systems must be effectively led, managed and nurtured (Ham and Walsh 2013).

In health and social care, leaders and managers must seek to empower people at all levels to take responsibility for an appropriate level of decision-making. This is particularly important for integrated care where evidence and experience point to the need to grow integrated care strategies from the 'bottom-up' where professionals and local communities work together with a degree of operational autonomy to lead the change process. This is why building communities of practice to support change, and investing in their ability to collaborate with each other effectively, should be seen as a core area for action within the 'change' domain. In other words, the change management process is seeking to support three core things (Goodwin 2015):

- Alignment—to support organisations to take on integrated care as part of their core business;
- Agility—to develop systems and processes that enable integration to happen
- Attitudes—through changing behaviours of key stakeholders by addressing cultural issues through good management practice

It is likely that significant variation will exist in the way integrated care is implemented, but a key lesson from policy reviews is that long-term commitment to change is necessary to enable reforms and changes to health systems to embed over time. To make change successful, the evidence suggests that a balance needs to be struck between 'top-down' management of change, with the necessary space for innovation, and emergent strategies to be created at a more local level by creating the right environment for innovation (Bengoa 2013; Montenegro et al. 2012). Hence, participation and support across all stakeholders in health and other sectors (including policy-makers, managers, professionals, community groups and patients) is a key to success (World Health Organisation 2015). The managerial challenge is to create a step-wise process through which this can be achieved.

16.3   The Evidence Base

There is a lack of evidence in the written literature that has researched and articulated the process to support change when designing, piloting, implementing, assessing and scaling-up innovations that support integrated care (Engineer et al. 2014). Indeed, as Chap. 1 outlined, most frameworks describe the process as highly 'complex' given the range of stakeholders that must necessarily be involved in working together in devising new approaches to integrate care (Edgren and Barnard 2009; Goodwin 2013a; Minkman 2012). Hence, pro-active change management is needed. Yet, there is a lack of appreciation and understanding of the complexity of this process and of the tools that can help support change (Cash-Gibson and Rosenmuller 2014; Goodwin 2013b; Valentijn et al. 2013).

A planned change management strategy represents a reasoned and deliberate set of actions for managers of the system that requires a need to identify and explore new ways of working as well as to challenge established practice (Goodwin et al. 2006; Iles and Sutherland 2001). Change management, therefore, represents the 'how' of integrated care implementation through setting out the various operational tasks that need to be undertaken to enable change to happen. The approach requires 'whole systems thinking' since it is necessary for managers to understand and capitalise on interrelationships rather than linear cause and effect chains.

Evidence from experience and research has contributed much to our understanding of the building blocks for the effective deployment of integrated care, yet the field of integrated care remains weak in terms of the implementation science to support policy-makers and managers to make effective decisions. Indeed, there is evidence to suggest that there is a lack of appreciation of the necessary change management processes and skills needed (Goodwin 2013b). In part, this lack of understanding is because achieving success through integrated care appears highly complex since it involves change at the nano- (e.g. with patients) micro- (e.g. with multi-disciplinary teams) meso- (e.g. through organisations of physician networks) and macro-scale (e.g. by alignment of government policies) (Plsek and Wilson 2001; Curry and Ham 2010; Valentijn et al. 2015a). Hence, efforts to reform complex systems like integrated care need to look at 'whole system' change with a priority in influencing the high-level behaviour of key decision-makers, the performance of individual sub-systems and—crucially—the interdependencies between different stakeholders and how these impact on outcomes.

A number of relevant frameworks to integrated care have been developed to explain these interdependencies as a means to understanding how change might be achieved—for example: the Normalisation Process Model that focuses on the importance of building relationships and skills in collaboration (May et al. 2009); the Continuity of Care Model that tracks how chronic care to populations may be achieved through adopting different strategies at different points across the life-course (Sunol et al. 1999); and the Multi-Level Framework that sought to understand how care co-ordination between provider organisations and care professionals operates in practice (McDonald et al. 2007). None of these, however, have really articulated the management strategies necessary to achieve change.

Perhaps the most famous approach to change management adopted in health care settings has been Lean Thinking (Womack and Jones 2003) and related improvement methodologies in health care that have sought to improve quality and safety in healthcare (Institute of Medicine 2001). By focusing on the effectiveness of teams and the promotion of evidence-based and cost-effective care pathways, the manager has been provided with a new suite of tools through which to transform care. The Lean approach in health care has been strongly developed with many tool-kits and support agencies advocating its use. Whilst Lean is highly relevant to the management of integrated care, the biggest criticism labelled against it is that it focuses on 'doing right things' (i.e. eliminating waste through efficiencies) rather than 'doing the right thing' (i.e. focusing on quality of outcomes and effectiveness). Lean also tends to work best for specific diseases or for predictable care processes but is perhaps less relevant for people with variable care trajectories (Allen et al. 2004).

In the field of integrated care, the most coherent approach to date that seeks to explain how the management of integrated care may be taken forward is the Development Model for Integrated Care (DMIC) (Minkman 2012). Unlike other work, the DMIC was specifically designed to help managers and leaders reflect on whether the essential elements for integrated care were in place and, in particular, established a four-phase programme for change: design, experimentation, expansion and monitoring, and then consolidation.

The DMIC is a complex evidence-based model since it includes 89 unique elements for action grouped into nine clusters. These clusters provide a basis for a model for the 'comprehensive quality management' of integrated care. In particular, in terms of change management, the model highlights the conditions necessary for effective collaboration such as commitment, clear roles and tasks and entrepreneurship. The model can be used for self-assessment and evaluation and provide inspiration and insights for further improvement. The DMIC is an important resource since it also shows that certain attributes of integrated care are more important at different phases of implementation. For example, in younger collaborations it stresses how the management of change should focus on building interprofessional teamwork and defining roles and tasks. The DMIC can also enable a situational analysis to be undertaken to examine any deficiencies in the competencies needed to achieve integrated care in practice (for example, the lack of attention on quality of care and performance management).

The DMIC was developed in the context of the policy innovation in the Dutch context of Care Groups that encouraged primary care providers to utilise new financial incentives (bundled payments) to support chronic illness care to people with specific diseases such as diabetes. Whilst the DMIC approach has been applied with some success in other settings, for example in the context of stroke care in Canada (Minkman et al. 2011), there remain some caveats to how the model might be adapted to the needs of populations with physical and mental health co-morbidities and complex health and social care needs (Fig. 16.1).

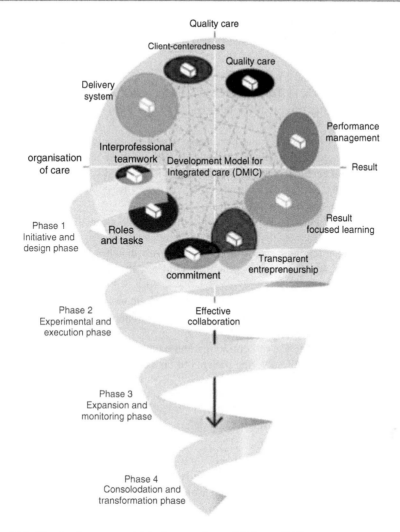

Fig. 16.1 The development model for integrated care (Minkman 2012)

16.4   Lessons from Practical Experience

The development of the evidence-base to support the uptake of integrated care remains in an early stage of development yet much can be learned from the experiences of key leaders and managers who have been at the forefront of implementing integrated care strategies at a national and regional scale. Though captured through relatively few documents and presentations, a summary of the evidence would suggest that there are a number of key managerial lessons to be learned (see Box 16.1).

Box 16.1 Key lessons for change towards integrated care from practical experience

- Finding common cause with partners;
- Developing a bold shared narrative to explain why integrated care matters, written in a way that is tailored to meet local circumstances and conditions;
- Creating a compelling and persuasive vision for change that sets out an urgent case for why 'business as usual' will not work and describes what integrated care can achieve, especially to the potential benefits of patients;
- Identifying services and user groups where the potential benefits of integrated care are the greatest;
- Understanding that there is no 'one model' of integrated care and supporting a process of discovery rather than design;
- Building integrated care from the bottom-up that has support from the top-down whilst avoiding structural solutions that over-emphasise cost-containment;
- Aligning financial incentives, or removing financial disincentives, for example through pooling resources to enable planners and purchasers to use resources flexibly;
- Innovating in the use of contracting and payment mechanisms;
- Supporting and empowering patients to take control over their health and wellbeing;
- Sharing information about patients with the support of appropriate information governance;
- Using the workforce effectively and to be open to innovations in skill mix and staff substitution;
- Restructuring care delivery assets, for example through less hospital-based care and more primary and community-based care;
- Setting specific objectives and measures to stimulate integrated care delivery, enable the evaluation of progress, and supported by a performance and quality management system;
- Establishing a strategic communications plan that enables a clearly defined message to be provided and understood across all stakeholders;
- Being realistic about the costs of integrated care;
- Integrated care is a long-term agenda and represents an ongoing system-wide transformation; and
- Acting on all these lessons together as part of a coherent strategy

Sources: WHO Regional Office for Europe (2015); Bengoa (2013); Goodwin and Shapiro (2001); Bengoa (2014); Kizer (2012); Kizer (2014); Timmins and Ham (2013); Meates (2014); Øvretveit et al. (2010)

The list of key factors in Box 16.1 is based on the lived experience of those that have led the management of strategies to support integrated care. What they reveal is a striking resemblance to Kotter's 'eight steps' model for leading change derived from an analysis on the key strategies taken by managers in making a success of transformational change (Kotter 1996). These eight steps are:

1. Create a sense of urgency
2. Form a guiding coalition
3. Create a vision
4. Communicate the vision
5. Empower others to act on the vision
6. Plan for quick wins
7. Build on the change
8. Institutionalise the change

A key observation from this work is that care systems often need to have *external* change management support to help manage the various viewpoints of different stakeholders within the various contexts for change in which integrated care will be implemented. Furthermore, since the needs for developing integrated care require an appreciation of the complexity of the task there is a need to find a balance between emergent strategies (one that adapts over time) versus approaches that seek to systematise processes. Flexibility in the management of change is therefore needed and learning networks and communities of practice need to be built to support adoption and build capabilities.

16.5   The Components of a Change Management Process Towards Integrated Care

This section examines nine core components in the management of change that, taken sequentially, sets out a sequence of actions that managers should consider when addressing the need to introduce or develop programmes that support integrated care (see Table 16.1). The nine steps represent a range of actions from the planning stages that define the priorities for action, to issues related to strategic planning, implementation and evaluation. This section draws upon work previously undertaken by the author for the WHO Regional Office for Europe (see Goodwin 2015).

16.5.1 Needs Assessment

Integrated care represents a strategy that recognises the fundamental seriousness of the challenges faced by health and care systems to meet current and future demands (WHO Regional Office for Europe 2013; Stein et al. 2013). Yet, at a local and regional level, it can often be difficult to find 'common cause' amongst local stakeholders on the priorities for action that need to be taken in local communities to overcome system fragmentations through new approaches to care integration

Table 16.1 Nine core components of a change management plan

1. Needs assessment
2. Situational analysis
3. Value case
4. Vision and mission statement
5. Strategic plan
6. Ensuring mutual gain
7. Communications strategy
8. Implementation and institutionalisation
9. Monitoring and evaluation: developing systems for continuous quality improvement

(Goodwin and Shapiro 2001). One of the core issues in the change management process is that organisations will be asked to work together and, as a result, share their sovereignty in pursuit of the greater good of the population they serve—and this is not always easy (WHO Regional Office for Europe 2015).

A first step, therefore, is for the different key stakeholders to develop an objective understanding of population health needs to support the underlying rationale for integration and to promote priority setting. This might be achieved, for example, through the development of a Joint Strategic Needs Assessment (JSNA) that looks at the wider determinants of health and needs of a local community. Though the process varies in different countries across Europe, it usually involves local health authorities with a responsibility for population health to work alongside public health departments, municipal authorities (social care), housing and other sectors to examine the current and future health needs of a local population. Such JSNAs might typically focus on a specific patient cohort (e.g. people with chronic illness or older people with frailty) and enable priority-setting by mapping the flow of financial resources spent on key priorities and/or examining gaps in care provision (NHS Confederation 2011).

16.5.2 Situational Analysis

Understanding change management towards integrated care faces a series of problems related to implementation including issues such as the legacy of existing service provision; changing environmental pressures; changing technologies; varying degrees of complexity of organisational systems; the many competing views of stakeholders; and the potentially adverse impact of unforeseen event or unintended consequences of different strategies. Managers therefore face the challenge in adopting the right tools and strategies for the circumstances they face.

The literature on change management commonly shows how achieving change rests on actions at a number of levels, for example: the *political* system where formal and informal configurations of power influence decision-making; the *technical* system of existing human, technical and financial resources available to produce more integrated service delivery; and the *cultural* system that encompasses organisational values and behaviours of those influenced by changes (Tichy 1985). In other words, managers need to recognise that change towards building the technical competencies of integrated care will be significantly influenced by economic, political and cultural forces that may be beyond their control.

One of the key methodologies to enable the change management process is the use of diagnostic tools to assess the current situation in relation to what is trying to be achieved. These situational analyses attempt to yield insights on the 'strategic fit' of new approaches like integrated care amongst key stakeholders and are often used to justify change management programmes and/or to prioritise the focus of change.

16.5.3 Value Case Development

One of the most pressing concerns in the process of developing integrated care strategies is how to convince key stakeholders, and particularly health insurance organisations or those holding the financial power, of the 'value case' for investment. A 'value case,' however, looks at more than just the potential financial returns from the development of integrated care, but looks at the benefits to patients and whole communities of the approach (e.g. from the perspective of living healthier lives through to the development of stronger local economies).

The focus on value cases is important since it helps to develop the shared vision and set of common goals across different providers or teams. Hence, value cases do not just to articulate the aims and objectives of integrated care based on the needs of local populations, but they also represent a pro-active process through which to engage partners in care and build social capital. Hence, in the design phase of an integrated care initiative, there needs to be inclusion of all relevant stakeholders in preparing the case for change and, in so doing, establishing a shared understanding, a shared vision for change, a degree of mutual respect on each other's roles in the integrated care enterprise, and the development or election of respected professional and managerial leaders whom people trust to take initiatives forward.

There are many examples internationally about how this approach has been used to create a convincing argument for change. For example, in Canterbury, New Zealand, the creation of the 'value case' and subsequent mission was supported between different provider agencies through a mantra of 'one system, one budget' (Timmins and Ham 2013). In other words, an argument was constructed in favour of an integrated health and social care system as a means to improving patient care as well as balancing the financial budget. To support this, more than 1500 managers and professionals completed learning courses—named *Xceler8* and *Collabor8*—in which staff themselves were tasked with coming up with projects for change with help from planners, funders and business developers. Rather than a full 'business case' with a cost/benefit analysis the underlying questions discussed were of the value for improving patient and staff experiences.

16.5.4 Vision and Mission Statement

Change management theory argues that it is important to articulate a vision of the future with a compelling case for change. Evidence from experience suggests that is especially true for progress on the journey towards integrated care that would otherwise be slow unless it is possible to describe an alternative and better future that motivates and inspires care providers to work differently (WHO Regional Office for Europe 2015; Goodwin 2015). This includes developing a clear understanding of what integrated care means for all those involved, including those delivering services but also for those living in the community. Important in this process is to create a sense of urgency (that business as usual will not work) but also to centre the narrative based on improvements in care and outcomes to people and for quality improvement in bold but reachable terms. The vision and mission also needs to be co-produced with key stakeholders, including patients (and perhaps even led by service users).

A common strategy has been to develop a shared narrative of the future to explain why integrated care matters to both care providers and to patients. In England, the national strategy for integrated care has been underpinned by 'the narrative' developed by National Voices, a non-profit organisation representing the views of patients and patient groups (National Voices; National Collaboration for Integrated Care and Support 2013). The purpose of the narrative has been to articulate a national vision for person-centred coordinated care and it has proven hugely influential in establishing the overarching purpose of national strategies.

16.5.5 Strategic Plan

A strategic plan is the document that is used to communicate within and between the organisations involved in the planning and delivery of integrated care the core actions and critical partnership elements necessary to achieve shared goals and outcomes. The development of a strategic plan has the advantage of committing a range of organisations involved in funding and delivering care to a collective set of objectives and actions to guide what needs to be done, by when and why. An effective strategic plan, therefore, helps to tie together networks of care professionals and otherwise separate organisations into a collective agreement, sets the terms of engagement between the different parties, their key roles and responsibilities, and the range of outcomes and performance indicators that may be used to judge whether integrated care strategies have been successful.

16.5.6 Ensuring Mutual Gain

One of the most important issues at stake in the development of effective partnership working within programmes that support integrated care is not just related to the development of a 'shared vision' that enables key stakeholders to recognise the 'inter-dependencies' that each have in working together to achieve a better outcome for patients and communities. What appears to be just as important is the ability to ensure that all partners in care fully understand and accept their roles and responsibilities to the extent that a high degree of trust and respect exists between partners in care, a trust that is built on the knowledge that each partner is contributing fully and as expected. The building of trust, therefore, requires all partners to recognise and value the level of commitment and reciprocity of actions of others. In other words, each partner recognises the 'mutual gain' that can be made through collaborative actions. Hence, it is essential that any partnership which focuses on integration recognises from the outset that a 'win-win' scenario needs to be supported otherwise there is a risk in undermining the degree to which partners in care are willing to cooperate with each other.

However, one of the core problems with integrated care is that it usually not the case that the benefits of involvement are equally shared compared to the effort or workforce that is needed to make it happen (6 et al. 2006; Leutz 2005). As a result, it can be difficult to bring partners to the table to discuss integrated care where it is perceived that some partners might gain, yet others lose. Moreover, the issue is not simply related to budgetary or financial concerns but also involves issues related to perceptions of authority, to social and professional status, to workload and effort, to intellectual property and, often, to the competitive advantage different care providers might gain in terms of gaining clients (patients) at the expense of others.

> Collaborative partnerships and networks are necessary to achieve integrated care, yet the evidence demonstrates that these can be time-consuming, resource-intensive and unstable leading to the observation that there is a high failure rate in such innovations (Goodwin 2013a; Roussos and Fawcett 2000; Weiner and Alexander 1998).

The recognition of the need to articulate 'mutual gains' and build 'tie-ins' is important since it establishes the 'baseline' that underpins the nature and expectations of the collaboration that recognises their underlying interests. A useful conceptual framework by Bell et al. (2013) can help to evaluate the strength of the collaborative process across five key themes:

1. The degree of shared ambition (the shared commitment of the involved partners)
2. Mutual gains (understanding the various interests of the involved partners)
3. Relationship dynamics (the relationships and degree of trust displayed between each partner)
4. Organisational dynamics (governance arrangements across the partners)
5. Process management (the skill with which managers help negotiate relationships between partners over time) (Bell et al. 2013)

A good example of this is recent research that looked at the comparative effectiveness of 69 Dutch Care Groups enrolled in a Ministry of Health initiative to create integrated care primary care programmes to support the management of chronic diseases such as diabetes or COPD (Valentijn et al. 2015b). The research found that difference in the perceived success of the different programmes was *not* related to issues related to shared ambition. Rather, they relied heavily on the explicit voicing of interests of the partners in determining the 'mutual gain' to be made, primarily by setting out the preconditions for what a successful partnership would look like and ensuring that managers and decision-makers 'steered' the process of integration to ensure that these partnership preconditions were maintained. Relationship dynamics between partners in care, therefore, are a key to the successful functioning of professional and organisational partnerships that in turn are reliant on the continued brokering of the 'contract' between them and the 'gains' that each expect.

16.5.7 Communications Strategy

Often missed, but important in the literature, is the need to create an effective communications strategy and plan that delivers clear and consistent messages to all key stakeholders, but specifically to organisations and professionals tasked with delivering change at the clinical and service level (e.g. doctors, nurses and patients). Lessons from managerial experience suggest that effective communication of the vision requires multiple channels is needed as a means to develop relationships (for example, the internet and social media) and therefore needs to be achieved using consistent and simple language.

As many of the proposed changes for care integration are likely to be complex and have a direct impact on vested interests as well as patients, it has been suggested that an experienced communications manager or team is likely to be essential to engaging and aligning teams and organisations. The nature of communication management might include: ensuring that all senior managers are aware of, and own, the narrative for integrated care; developing a communications and engagement strategy; establishing and managing a wide range of communication channels at a local, regional and national level (where required); and developing media releases to provide updates and briefings on progress, good news stories and case examples of best practice, and dealing with enquiries to build relationships (The Better Care Fund, p. 11)

16.5.8 Implementing and Institutionalising the Change

The next key element in the management of change involves the implementation of the change in practice, both in terms of 'system' (e.g. joint financing, governance and accountability) and 'services' (e.g. joint delivery through the development of teams). Often, the change process requires the initial piloting of options with the intention of 'institutionalising' or rolling-out the lessons learned for wider adoption afterwards. Moving from small-scale programs is important in order to deliver benefits on the scale needed to make a significant and transformational impact on the way care is delivered (Ham 2011). There are, however, very few examples of tool-kits which have sought to address the issue of scaling-up of pilots, though one is the DMIC model cited earlier in which 'phase 4' of the model supports strategies for consolidating change (Minkman 2012).

16.5.9 Monitoring and Evaluation: Developing Systems for Continuous Quality Improvement

A common weakness in approaches to integrated care is that not enough time and effort has been placed to agree the specific objectives for integrated care and how to measure and evaluate outcomes objectively. In particular, it is common that the lack of evidence for cost and impact can lead to significant problems (and programme failures) when seeking to embed programmes within wider health system funding streams (Valentijn et al. 2015b). In practice, therefore, managing change requires the ability to measure and monitor outcomes in a number of areas including: user experience, service utilisation, staff experience and the costs of delivering care. Progress towards these goals must be measured frequently to support learning and inform implementation (Table 16.2).

For health care systems it is important to adopt and use a set of measures that align with the main elements of a national, regional or local strategy for integrated care. However, the complexity and the necessary variety in how integrated care strategies need to be developed means that outcomes and measures need to be chosen to suit local and national priorities. Many countries and regions have sought to establish a set of key measures and indicators for people-centred and integrated health services as a means to monitor and manage performance (e.g. Raleigh et al. 2014; IPIF 2013) and a summary of the range of measures that have been used has been usefully summarised through work supporting WHO's Global Framework on People-Centred and Integrated Health Services (World Health Organisation 2015).

An important aspect of developing a monitoring and evaluation framework is that it can be used to bring relevant stakeholders together to define the outcomes

Table 16.2 Examples of indicators of maturity to integrated care change management

Examples dimension	Objective	Maturity indicator
Readiness for change	Compelling vision, sense of urgency, stakeholder support	Public consultations, clear strategic goals and milestones, stakeholder engagement
Structure and governance	Sustains and delivers new systems of integrated care, presence of effective change management	Funded programmes, effective communication, governance and accountability in place
Capacity building	Investment in training, skills and technologies of the workforce, including systems for continuous quality improvement	Developing of funding and availability of courses to support bottom-up innovation and workforce development

through which integrated care strategies should be judged and, as a result, promote joint ownership and collective responsibility to achieving key goals. Including key stakeholders in how care systems will be held to account supports the inclusive process of developing a vision and driving change forwards.

A final key element of a change strategy is to utilise data and information from the monitoring and evaluation process to build-in a process for continuous quality improvement. For example, to identify 'high impact' changes that would most benefit patients, or reduce variation in standards between provider teams. In essence, an 'improvement process' is needed to help clarify or re-frame objectives, redesign processes, address capabilities, integrate risks, develop performance measures, learning from performance measures and, crucially, create a feedback loop for improvement over time. Two key aspects for this include: first, the need for managers to properly engage service providers, communities and service users; and, second, the need to build in 'rapid cycles' of building and re-building strategies for change following their implementation and assessment of progress.

16.6 Building an Enabling Environment

The change process towards integrated care can take considerable time and effort to achieve but enabling the environment within which the management of change is to be taken forward is a necessary process and catalyst for change (Kotter 1996). This includes three core tasks:

- the building of *a guiding coalition* of leaders and key stakeholders to drive change forward from the top-down;
- the building of *support for change* from the 'bottom-up' within and between key professional groups and the communities of practice where integrated care is to be deployed is a core requirement for success, including the development of a shared set of norms, beliefs, values and assumptions that help to enable change to happen; and
- the development of *collaborative capacity* at a local level that enables and supports professional groups to work together effectively in multi-disciplinary or multi-agency teams that new approaches to coordinated and integrated health service delivery will require

16.6.1 Developing a Guiding Coalition

There is a significant amount of literature that describes the importance of developing a 'guiding coalition' of partners at a political and senior level in order to agree on the collective aims and mission of integrated care and so provide the mandate to people working within different parts of the health care sector to co-operate with each other and co-ordinate activities. For example, reflections on the process of development of strategies to support chronic care management in the Basque

Country emphasised the importance of taking the integrated care agenda to a 'policy level'. As a result, bottom-up approaches to innovation were supported by a regional research institute which monitored progress whilst at a national level there were regular meetings convened by the Ministry of Health which included public administration, professional associations and patient representatives to discuss the burning issues and how they may be addressed on the national and regional levels.

Pulling together a 'guiding team' of key people and organisations is also highly relevant at a local and regional level to champion integrated care and to lead change amongst key professional and patient groups. The effectiveness of such approach is often cited as a key step in change management strategies (King et al. 2008). To make such as approach effective, key issues include: choosing key managers with the position power, credibility and ability to drive the change process; and developing an inclusive and multi-disciplinary guiding team with the management skills to control the process (6 et al. 2006). Developing such front-line commitments requires the removal of barriers to integration by policy-makers, supporting the observation that creating an enabling environment for change requires both top-down and bottom-up initiatives (Ham and Walsh 2013; Bengoa 2013).

16.6.2 Building Support for Change

Evidence suggests that building support for change across networks of health and social care providers and other local stakeholders (such as patient representative groups) is complex and adaptive in nature (Goodwin 2015). A key reason for this is that each stakeholder usually will have a different perspective on the purpose of integration. Hence, politicians, managers, clinicians and patients are likely to have different priorities and different levels of understanding—integrated care will mean different things to different people. Moreover, attitudes to change are reliant on relationship-driven behaviours and inter-personal connections. Building support for integrated care between key stakeholders is thus a socio-cultural task akin to 'nation-building' through developing notions of community and citizenship.

The building of such support, then, requires being 'inclusive' at the design stage with those who would benefit or be influenced by the networks created as a result of care integration. Even so, a number of key managerial tensions will remain when building support for change including:

- Achieving a centralised position through which to wield managerial authority; yet to ensure the right balance between trust and control so as to encourage rather than alienate partners in care;
- Avoiding mandating change from the 'top-down' but to maintain it through peer-led approaches; yet there is a tendency for professional and organisational capture of activities by dominant 'elites' that need to be avoided;

- Promoting mutual interdependencies, for example through joint targets on care outcomes or quality improvement targets; yet networks need to continue to provide 'net worth' to participants to ensure their engagement;
- Driving change through senior managers, yet recognising the relationship between physician-leaders and managerial-leaders remains underdeveloped (6 et al. 2006)

The major problem in building support for change, therefore, is one of control as all activists for integrated care realise that they have relatively little direct power (e.g. hierarchical, financial, knowledge) and so suffer from a lack of authority. As a result, managers need key skills in brokering inter-personal relationships and act as 'boundary spanners' that help to connect people together or unlock barriers to partnership working.

Ultimately, overcoming the 'governance gap' requires the network members themselves to sign-up voluntarily to collective governance rules, for example through a network constitution based on the notion of dual accountabilities. Contracts across care pathways or disease-based programmes appear less easy to maintain than those which focus on population health. Harmonising incentives, targets, audit and governance are important but come after network members have provided the 'mandate to be managed' both technically and culturally.

At a more local level, even with the establishment of a guiding coalition, evidence demonstrates that there can be considerable resistance to change towards integrated care amongst professional groups and providers. This is not simply an issue related to differing funding and incentives or pre-existing professional roles and tasks, but a more deep-rooted concern related to the lack of understanding of the importance of integrated care and why change should be embraced. This demonstrates the importance that needs to be paid to pre-existing cultures, norms and values and how to potentially understand and recognise such issues when introducing change at a local level. Building support for change at a local level is thus essential and requires participants and stakeholders to be included in the design and development of solutions to ensure a collective vision and common understanding for change so that new ways of working have a greater chance of success.

In theoretical terms, the process might be termed as a 'soft systems methodology' which understands that, in the real world, a complexity of relationships exists and which need to be actively explored. Hence, understanding relationships and building social capital is an explicit activity that requires understanding the challenges of integrated care without first imposing a preconceived structure or solution to the issue. As explored above, empirical evidence suggests that avoiding 'mandated partnerships' and 'top-down' imposition of new ways of working is important for integrated care to become an accepted idea, and that inclusiveness of people in the design and development of new approaches to care is important in the process (as is the subsequent assessment of impact and ideas for continuous improvements and change).

Building support for change is therefore an explicit component that requires understanding of the challenges of integrated care to promote inclusiveness and fostering a collaborative culture that builds the commitment of local leaders, staff, managers and the community (Goodwin 2015). The experiences of key people who have led the process of health service transformation commonly cite that achieving clinical integration is fundamentally about changing the culture of health care; it's more sociological than technological (Bengoa 2014; Kizer 2014; Meates 2014). Healthcare culture, manifest in silo-based working in specific professional groups and organisations, appears to be the biggest barrier to change and requires new ways of thinking and new competencies including: systems thinking; collaboration in teams; quality management and process improvement science (Kizer 2014).

16.6.3 Developing Collaborative Capacity

The changing needs of patients with more long-term and complex problems highlight the need for care delivery to become reliant on a greater number of care professionals and organisations. Such changes clearly carry a greater risk to patients given the problems that might result from fragmentations in care. Developing effective and reliable multi- and inter-disciplinary teams and care networks is therefore important, yet the process is not always achieved with great success due to problems in team-based skills with the right skill-mix (Baker et al. 2006).

Evidence suggests that consistent efforts need to be taken in the long-term to help build the collaborative culture necessary to take integrated care forward at a local level. Creating effective teams is a change management process in its own right and the development of evidence-based approaches to supporting effective teams and team-building has become widespread across Europe (Mayer et al. 2001). Such support has been shown to be successful in breaking down silos and promoting inter-professional education and learning (Margalit et al. 2009). This task can be supported by a number of component strategies including education and training in multi-disciplinary working to support effective networks and teams.

The issue of developing a collaborative culture has often been put forward as a key ingredient to making a success of integrated care. A characteristic underpinning the success of case studies of integrated care is often the personal commitment of staff—both managers and professionals—to go that 'extra mile' by working beyond the boundaries of their job description in order to achieve the best results for their clients and in supporting colleagues to do the same. Lying behind this finding is sometimes a range of explicit strategies that promote a strong ethos amongst staff to 'do the right thing'—for example: promoting the needs of clients before themselves; supporting knowledge-sharing; and enabling role-substitution and subsidiarity through staff empowerment (Goodwin et al. 2014).

There have been concerns about the time and cost implications of this kind of approach to change management given the lack of any guarantee that stakeholders can be sufficiently motivated to support change. Hence, the problem with promoting the idea that a values-driven approach should be a pre-requisite to the successful adoption of integrated care is that the weight of both evidence and experience predicts that such a process requires considerable time and effort. Moreover, given the mismatch of motives that exists when integrating the work of professionals and organisations, such efforts often go unrewarded and/or require continual negotiation. Hence, rather than being perceived as a catalyst for change, leaders and managers tasked with applying integrated care 'at scale and pace' might instead focus on driving forward the organisational solution or introduce various financial inducements in the hope this will be more effective. Given the evidence, such an approach would be a mistake. When looking at successful implementation strategies in integrated care it is clear no short cuts exist—it takes vision and commitment over the long-term to build the collaborative capacity necessary to take integrated care forward.

16.6.4 The Facilitating Role of Managers and Decision-makers in Supporting the Process of Change

The evidence for the successful adoption of integrated care provides considerable emphasis on the role of individual managers and decision-makers in driving change forward. Lessons from evidence and experience strongly indicate that there needs to be a person, or team, with the necessary skills and responsibilities for facilitating partnerships and brokering effective networks of organisations and the development of well-functioning professional teams. Establishing collaborative practice requires hard work and effort to develop the necessary inter-dependencies between partners in care. Often, this requires challenging often well-established cultural ways of working to build-in collective values and thinking. Hence, the successful adoption of coordinated/integrated health services delivery in practice requires long-term and continuous effort to support and nurture change. As a managerial task, achieving care integration is as much about changing culture as it is about the management of resources or the application of technical processes.

Many studies have sought to examine the attributes and tasks that are needed of senior managers in this area (e.g. Ham and Walsh 2013; Bengoa 2013; Engineer et al. 2014; Kizer 2014; Meates 2014; Kotter 1996; Valentijn et al. 2015b; West et al. 2014, 2015) and these can be summarised as follows:

- Start with a coalition of the willing
- Inspire vision between partners in care—action is inspired through emotion
- Involve patients, service users and community groups from the beginning
- Build an evidence base to justify thinking
- Provide managerial decision-making 'across' the system so that it spans organisational and professional boundaries and promotes co-operation
- Develop a consensus-style of management that includes and encourages all key stakeholders to participate as equal partners
- Engage clinicians and enable them to lead efforts for change with the freedom to innovate
- Foster 'collaborative capacity'

- Encourage long-term commitments from managers and decision-makers to drive through change
- Invest time and support in training people in these roles as they require specific skills in managing across diverse organisational contexts and boundaries

16.7 Conclusions

The successful adoption and roll-out of strategies for the delivery of integrated care is to a large extent reliant on their being a receptive environment for change at both a national (political), regional and local level. Integrated care can be a highly challenging proposition to many individuals and organisations that may not value the change being advocated or feel threatened by its consequences. Moreover, in many cases, partnership working between different providers and professionals will represent an entirely new way of working, so requiring new skills to be developed and a change in outlook.

Figure 16.2, seeks to provide a visual representation of how these components fit together. On the left hand side of the figure are represented the step-wise progression of change management tasks whilst on the right are set out the need, over the timescale of implementation, the necessary 'relationship building' tasks that seek to create the enabling environment for change. It is important to recognise three key things:

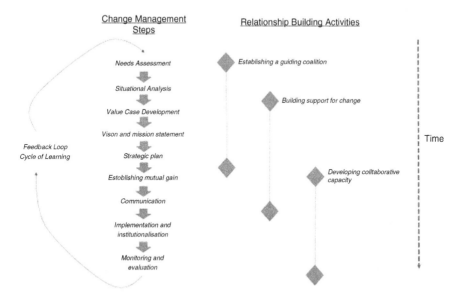

Fig. 16.2 A change management model for integrated care (adapted from Goodwin 2015)

1. the overlapping and continuous nature in how relationships are built over time;
2. the cyclical nature of the change management process itself in building and re-building strategies for change; and
3. how mangers and key decision-makers are essential in facilitating the process of implementation over time.
4. the evidence from experience in integrated care suggests that much has been achieved in different countries to establish a degree of consensus at a political level that may help to create an enabling environment through changes to financial and accountability rules. Yet, the evidence also shows that it is the professional barriers to change at a clinical and service level that remain the most persistent and most difficult to overcome.

This chapter has argued that the management of change towards integrated care requires the combination of two principle sets of processes: a step-wise progression of managerial tasks that come together to represent the core components of a change management plan ('management') and the ability to adapt these strategies for change in the context of the complex and multi-dimensional nature of practical reality ('environment'). Both tasks require key individuals with the managerial skills and both have a strong relationship-building component and are inherently inter-related.

References

6 Perri, Goodwin, N., Peck, E., & Freeman, T. (2006). *Managing networks of 21st century organizations.* Basingstoke: Palgrave-McMillan.

Allen, G., Griffiths, L., & Lyne, P. (2004). Understanding complex trajectories in health and social care provision. *Sociology of Health & Illness, 27*(7), 1008–1030.

Baker, D., et al. (2006). Teamwork as an essential component of high-reliability organisations. *Health Services Research, 41*(4), 1576–1598.

Bell, J., Kaats, E., & Opheij, W. (2013). Bridging disciplines in alliances and networks: In search for solutions for the managerial relevance gap. *International Journal of Strategic Business Alliances, 3*(1), 50–68.

Bengoa, R. (2013). Transforming health care: An approach to system-wide implementation. *International Journal of Integrated Care, 13*, e039.

Bengoa, R. (2014, April 2–4). *Achieving integrated care from a systems perspective: Key dimensions and lessons learned from the Basque Country.* Paper to ICIC14, Brussels.

Cash-Gibson, L., & Rosenmuller, M. (2014). Project INTEGRATE—A common methodological approach to understand integrated health care in Europe. *International Journal of Integrated Care, 14*, e035.

Curry, N., & Ham, C. (2010). *Clinical and service integration: The route to improve outcomes.* London: The King's Fund.

Edgren, L., & Barnard, K. (2009). Applying a complex adaptive systems approach to the management of integrated care. *International Journal of Integrated Care, 9*(Suppl), e125.

Engineer, C., Aswani, M., Bennett, S., Peters, D., & Gundlach, A.-M. (2014). *Change management across health care organisations: A structured rapid review.* Baltimore: John Hopkins Bloomberg School of Public Health.

Goodwin, N. (2013a). Understanding integrated care: A complex process, a fundamental principle. *International Journal of Integrated Care, 13*, e011.

Goodwin, N. (2013b). How do you build programmes of integrated care? The need to broaden our conceptual and empirical understanding. *International Journal of Integrated Care, 13*, e040.

Goodwin, N. (2015, November). *Managing change towards co-ordinated/integrated health services delivery, WHO regional office for Europe*. Unpublished Report.

Goodwin, N., & Shapiro, J. (2001). *The road to integrated care working*. Birmingham: Health Services Management Centre, University of Birmingham.

Goodwin, N., Gruen, R., & Iles, V. (2006). *Managing health services*. Maidenhead: Open University Press.

Goodwin, N., Sonola, L., Thiel, V., & Kodner, D. (2014). *Co-ordinated care for people with complex chronic conditions. Key lessons and markers for success*. London: The King's Fund.

Ham, C. (2011, September 22). The NHS needs to avoid the wrong kind of integration. *Health Service Journal*. Retrieved from www.hsj.co.uk/comment/opinion/the-nhs-needs-to-avoid-the-wrong-kind-of-integration/5035022

Ham, C., & Walsh, N. (2013). *Making integrated care happen at scale and pace: Lessons from experience*. London: The King's Fund.

Iles, V., & Sutherland, K. (2001). *Managing change in the NHS*. London: NCCSDO, London School of Hygiene and Tropical Medicine.

Institute of Medicine. (2001). *Crossing the quality chasm: A new health system for the 21st century*. Washington, DC: National Academy Press.

IPIF. (2013). *New Zealand health improvement and innovation resource framework. Description and outline of potential measures. Draft integrated performance and incentive framework (IPIF)*. Retrieved from http://www.hirc.org.nz/page/42610

King, H., et al. (2008). *TeamSTEPPS (^{TM}): Team strategies and tools to enhance performance and patient safety*. Rockville: Agency for Healthcare Research and Quality.

Kizer, K. (2012, May 4). *The do's and don't's of transforming a health care system*. Paper to the International Integrated Care Summit, The King's Fund. Retrieved from http://www.kingsfund.org.uk/audio-video/kenneth-kizer-achieving-integrated-care-highlights

Kizer K. (2014, April 2–4) *Achieving integrated care: Key lessons in the transformation of the Veterans Health Administration in the USA*. Paper to ICIC14, Brussels.

Kotter, J. (1996). *Leading change*. Boston: Harvard Business School Press.

Leutz, W. (2005). Reflections on integrating medical and social care: Five laws revisited. *Journal of Integrated Care, 13*(5), 3–12.

Margalit, et al. (2009). From professional silos to interprofessional education. *Quality Management in Healthcare, 18*(3), 165–173.

May, C., et al. (2009). Development of a theory of implementation and integration: Normalization process theory. *Implementation Science, 4*, 29.

Mayer, C., et al. (2001). Evaluating efforts to optimise TeamSTEPPS Implementation in surgical and pediatric intensive care units. *The Joint Commission Journal on Quality and Patient Safety, 37*(8), 365.

McDonald, K., et al. (2007). *Care coordination* (Rep. No. 7). Rockville, MD: Agency for Healthcare Research and Quality.

Meates, D. (2014, November). *Making integrated care work in Canterbury New Zealand: Lessons for leaders and policy makers*. Paper to WCIC2, Sydney. Retrieved from http://integratedcarefoundation.org/resource/questions-and-answers-plenary-2-wcic2

Minkman, M. (2012). Developing integrated care. Towards a development model for integrated care. Thesis review. *International Journal of Integrated Care, 12*, e197.

Minkman, M., Vermeulen, R., Ahaus, K., & Huijsman, R. (2011). The implementation of integrated care: The empirical validation of the development model for integrated care. *BMC Health Services Research, 11*, 177.

Montenegro, H., Ramagem, C., Kawar, R., et al. (2012). Making progress in people-centred care: Country experiences and lessons learned. *The International Journal of Person Centred Medicine, 2*(1), 64–67.

National Collaboration for Integrated Care and Support. (2013, May). Integrated care and support: Our shared commitment. Retrieved from https://www.gov.uk/government/uploads/system/uploads/attachment_data/file/287815/DEFINITIVE_FINAL_VERSION_Integrated_Care_and_Support_-_Our_Shared_Commitment_2013-05-13.pdf

National Voices. *The narrative for person-centred coordinated care developed by National Voices in England.* Retrieved from http://www.nationalvoices.org.uk/defining-integrated-care

NHS Confederation. (2011, July). *The joint strategic needs assessment: A vital tool to guide commissioning.* Briefing, issue 221. Retrieved from http://nhsconfed.org/~/media/Confederation/Files/Publications/Documents/Briefing_221_JSNAs.PDF

Øvretveit, J., Hansson, J., & Brommels, M. (2010). An integrated health and social care organisation in Sweden: Creation and structure of a unique local public health and social care system. *Health Policy, 97*, 113–121.

Plsek, P. E., & Wilson, T. (2001). *Complexity, leadership, and management in healthcare organisations. BMJ, 323*(7315), 746–749.

Raleigh, V., et al. (2014) *Integrated care and support pioneers: Indicators for measuring the quality of integrated care.* Final report. London: Policy Innovation Research Unit.

Roussos, S., & Fawcett, S. (2000). A review of collaborative partnerships as a strategy for improving community health. *Annual Review of Public Health, 21*(1), 369–402.

Stein, K., Barbazza, E., Tello, J., & Kluge, H. (2013). Towards people-centred health service delivery: A framework for action for the world health organisation (WHO) European region. *International Journal of Integrated Care, 13*, e040.

Sunol, R., et al. (1999). Towards health care integration: The proposal of an evidence-based and management system-based model. *Medicina Clínica, 112*(Suppl 1), 97–105.

The Better Care Fund. *The Better Care Fund's guide on how to lead and manage better care implementation.* Retrieved from http://www.england.nhs.uk/wp-content/uploads/2015/06/bcf-user-guide-01.pdf.pdf

Tichy, N. (1985). Strategic approaches. In E. Huse & T. Cummings (Eds.), *Organisation development and change.* St Paul: West Publishing.

Timmins, N., & Ham, C. (2013, September). *The quest for integrated health and social care. A case study in Canterbury, New Zealand.* London: The King's Fund.

Valentijn, P., et al. (2013). Understanding integrated care: A comprehensive conceptual framework based on the integrative functions of primary care. *International Journal of Integrated Care, 13*, e010.

Valentijn, P., et al. (2015a). Towards a taxonomy for integrated care: A mixed methods study. *International Journal of Integrated Care, 15*, e003.

Valentijn, P., Vrijhoef, B., Ruwaard, D., de Bont, A., Arends, R., & Bruijnzeels, M. (2015b). Exploring the success of an integrated primary care partnership: A longitudinal study of collaboration. *BMC Health Services Research, 15*(1), 32.

Weiner, B., & Alexander, J. (1998). The challenges of governing public-private community health partnerships. *Health Care Management Review, 23*(2), 39–55.

Weiss, E., Anderson, R., & Lasker, R. (2002). Making the most of collaboration: Exploring the relationship between partnership synergy and partnership functioning. *Health Education & Behavior, 29*(6), 683–698.

West, M., Steward, K., Eckert, R., & Pasmore, B. (2014, May). *Developing collective leadership for healthcare.* London: The King's Fund.

West, M., Armit, K., Loewenthal, L., Eckert, R., West, T., & Lee, A. (2015, February). *Leadership and leadership development in health care: The evidence-base.* London: Faculty of Medical Leadership and Management.

WHO Regional Office for Europe. (2013). *Roadmap "strengthening people-centred health systems in the WHO European region".* Copenhagen: WHO Regional Office for Europe.

WHO Regional Office for Europe. (2015). *Second Annual Technical Meeting on coordinated/integrated health service delivery.* Meeting Report. Copenhagen: WHO Regional Office for Europe.

Womack, J., & Jones, D. (2003). *Lean thinking: Banish waste and create wealth in your corporation*. New York: Simon & Schuster.

World Health Organisation. (2015). *People-centred and integrated health services: An overview of the evidence*. Interim report. Geneva: World Health Organisation; WHO/HIS/SDS/2015.7.

How to Make a Service Sustainable? An Active Learning Simulation Approach to Business Model Development for Integrated Care

17

Ingo Meyer, Reinhard Hammerschmidt, Lutz Kubitschke, and Sonja Müller

When developing and implementing integrated care services, decision makers need to create complex business models involving many stakeholders, both for-profit and non-profit, and rely on reimbursement from statutory health and social care bodies as well as on other revenue streams. The needs of these stakeholders have to be identified and duly balanced within the framework of what is possible. This requires the handling of a large amount of economic data, the capacity to anticipate future developments, and creativity in dealing with unintended consequences. Furthermore, the development of a business model is likely to involve stakeholders that are not economic experts. We present a combined approach to business model development that allows stakeholders to get acquainted with economic assessments through active learning and to carry out their own assessment and business model development.

17.1 Introduction

Developing business models for integrated care services means grappling with the complexities of the concept, with the needs of many different stakeholders and with the drivers and restrictions created by context. Also a large amount of data on economic and other impacts, both positive (benefits) and negative (costs), needs to be handled and brought together into one or more potential business models that can become the basis for negotiations with stakeholders. Often this will require a certain amount of "looking into the future", that is anticipating developments, testing different service deployment scenarios and seeing how they respond to changes

I. Meyer (✉)
Gesundes Kinzigtal, Eisenbahnstr. 17, Hausach 77756, Germany
e-mail: i.meyer@gesundes-kinzigtal.de

R. Hammerschmidt • L. Kubitschke • S. Müller
empirica, Oxfordstr. 2, Bonn 53119, Germany

© Springer International Publishing AG 2017
V. Amelung et al. (eds.), *Handbook Integrated Care*,
DOI 10.1007/978-3-319-56103-5_17

in patient populations, changes in reimbursement regimes and changes to other factors. There can be unintended side effects or consequences, restrictions that were not known in the beginning and other factors requiring that initial assumptions (or aspirations) are adapted.

Furthermore, the development of a business model is likely to involve stakeholders other than managerial staff and accountants. This may include social carers, nurses, doctors and other care professionals, IT staff, call centre personnel and others, but also service users (clients or patients) and other persons involved in the service, such as informal carers or volunteers. Depending on the service scenario, these stakeholders can be holders of valuable information in relation to work processes, the actual impacts of process innovation in day-to-day (working) life, as well as staff or end-user acceptance. While a narrower economic viewpoint might tend to exclude such factors from a business model, they are in reality just as crucial to success as immediately monetary factors such as revenues (see for example, Meyer et al. 2011, Goodwin and Alonso 2014 or Rigby 2014). At the same time, these stakeholders will usually not be experts in business model development or economic assessment, since this is not part of their work or they are (in the case of clients/patient or informal carers) possibly not even remotely involved in activities of this kind.

A business model development process that aims to involve these stakeholders is therefore faced with the additional challenge of communicating a complex subject matter to a non-expert audience with the aim of empowering them to make informed design suggestions or decisions.

This chapter presents an approach to these challenges that we developed over the past 7 years. The approach consists of two elements, building on each other. The first element is a method and toolkit for the assessment of socio-economic impacts in health, care and ageing, called ASSIST. The second element is a simulation tool based on real-life data that allows building an integrated care services and modelling how it responds to changes in economic factors. This second element we call the ASSIST Service Implementation Simulator. Both elements will be described in the following.

We would like to acknowledge the contributions made by partners in the two integrated care projects CommonWell (2012) and INDEPENDENT (2013) to the refinement of the original ASSIST method as well as the feedback given on their practical experiences made while going through assessment process. Thanks are also due to the partners of the current integrated care projects BeyondSilos (2014a), CareWell (2014) and in particular SmartCare (2013) for being part of the testing of the ASSIST Service Implementation Simulator and freely sharing their experience, criticism and suggestions for improvement.

17.2 ASSIST: Socio-economic Impact Assessment Using Cost-Benefit Analysis

17.2.1 Background

The full name of the approach we apply is *ASSIST—Assessment and evaluation tools for e-service deployment in health, care and ageing* (empirica 2014) and it was originally developed for use in the context of telemedicine and telehealth services, specifically to assess the economic viability of telemedicine pilot projects funded by the European Space Administration (ESA). Its core aim is to support stakeholders in taking the step from a pilot project to routine service operation and in achieving a sustainable economic model where service benefits are equal to or higher than service costs.

In summary, the ASSIST approach consists of a methodology, a service assessment model and a software toolkit. The methodology covers the basic characteristics of the framework as well as descriptions of the empirical and economic methods used. The service assessment model consists of a generic set of stakeholders that can be involved in a service (divided into service users, service provider organizations and their staff, payers and IT industry), and of a set of cost and benefit indicators for each of these stakeholders. The software toolkit supports the adaptation of the service assessment model, the collection of data, the analysis and the presentation of results. Depending on its configuration it can be used as a self-assessment tool without expert support or as part of a moderated assessment process. The whole approach revolves around cost-benefit analysis (CBA) as for instance described by (Drummond 2005). CBA is considered an appropriate tool for analysing the impact of investments and activities in domains of public interest, including social and healthcare, see for example the UK Treasury's Green Book (UK HM Treasury 2003), Germany's WiBe (Röthig 2009) and the White House Office of Management and Budget (White House Office for Management and Budget 1992). CBA enables the impacts on all stakeholders to be included in a socio-economic evaluation, over the selected timescales, and the identification of the narrower financial components within the costs and benefits, also for individual stakeholder groups. These subsets can include the data used for Cost Analysis (CA), Cost Effectiveness Analysis (CEA) and Cost Utility Analysis (CUA).

Generally speaking, an ASSIST assessment is a comparison between a given status quo (usually an existing service or an established way of doing things) and a new or strongly revised intervention. We assume that this intervention is neither a single agent nor a single point in time but a process of changing care service delivery from one status to another, thereby covering multiple agents and including different stakeholders as well as IT systems. This puts an emphasis on the implementation environment and its impact on service delivery, as well as on the task of optimizing the service configuration to work in the given environment. The assessment goes along with this process, providing data and insights allowing the responsible stakeholder(s) to work towards a service model that is:

Viable—working successfully.
Sustainable—maintaining a positive ratio of costs and benefits.
Scalable—working for all patients and not only the pilot population.

An in-depth description of the ASSIST approach, the underlying requirements and assumptions and the mathematics can be found in (Hammerschmidt and Meyer 2014). We decided not to replicate this information here since it is not pertinent to the purposes of this chapter. Based on an example case, we focus instead on the practical assessment process as it is undertaken by stakeholders involved in setting up a new integrated care service or in transforming existing service provision along new, more collaborative lines. We also describe briefly ASSIST's stakeholder and indicator model for integrated care.

17.2.2 Assessment in Four Steps

An ASSIST assessment is done in four subsequent steps (see Fig. 17.1), following an implementation and deployment cycle leading from initial idea formulation to deployment either at pilot scale or in mainstreamed service provision. Such a cycle has for instance been described by (Meyer et al. 2011), but similar models are also used in other domains such as software development and more generally in quality improvement studies (Davidoff 2008).

An overview of each of those four steps is given in the following. The next chapter contains an example case showing the practical applications of the four steps.

Step 1: Stakeholder Identification Work begins with the identification of all stakeholders *involved* in the service (i.e. playing an active role) or *affected* by the service (i.e. in a passive manner). Both cases, active and passive, are characterised by a stakeholder experiencing any kind of impact, negative or positive or both, due to the new or changed service. The main caveat at this initial stage is to be inclusive and to not neglect stakeholders, especially those that may only have a

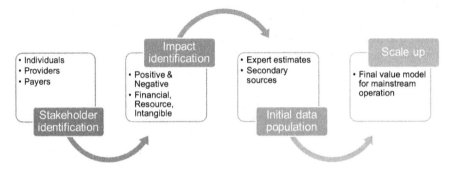

Fig. 17.1 Four steps of the assessment process

comparatively minor role. For example, this often concerns informal carers (family members, friends or neighbours), but also professionals outside the immediate care loop. Reasons for this can be simple oversight, or an unawareness of the capacities and competencies of these stakeholders, as well as factual concerns, e.g. about split of responsibility, skill levels, data security, etc. Practically, this first step in the process will usually consist of a series of meetings between project managers and stakeholders onsite.

Step 2: Impact Identification The second step is to identify all relevant positive and negative impacts for each stakeholder, as well as to define suitable indicators to measure each impact. The final shape of the impact model and indicator set depends on the local context. On the one hand, the indicators need to make sense in relation to the locally implementable service configuration, and any given framework conditions that cannot be changed. At the same time, populating the indicator set with data needs to be practically feasible under the given circumstances.

Picking up the results of Step 1, work now is more systematic, with a view to ensuring a full coverage of all relevant impacts and a correct identification of indicators for each. This can be achieved by employing a causal chain linking the outputs and outcomes of the service to its impacts (see Fig. 17.2). Indicators are then defined that allow the measuring of each impact.

Step 3: Data Collection Data to populate the indicators defined in Step 2 usually comes from different sources. Primary sources include all data collected during an evaluated pilot period, such as log data stored in ICT (Information & Communication Technology) systems, administrative data, and time sheet data specifically gathered for the purpose of the project. Also, end-user/staff related data can be gathered by means of dedicated questionnaires. Where necessary, secondary data can also be used, e.g. data derived from official statistics, published studies, or administrative databases.

Step 4: The Value Case: Strengths and Weaknesses of the Services The final step of the approach focuses on analysing the quantified costs and benefits for each stakeholder. This includes the calculation of key performance measures such as

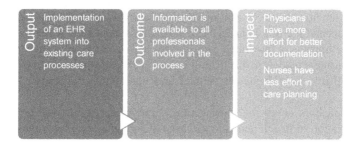

Fig. 17.2 Causal chain: From output to impacts

"socio-economic return", "economic return" and "breakeven point". A more detailed description of these performance measures and their calculation is available in Hammerschmidt and Meyer (2014) and Hammerschmidt and Jones (2012). The analysis also includes identification of the key "adjusting screws" that are available to the pilot service for further optimising the value case under the given conditions.

Overall, the analysis of the results will allow the involved stakeholders to:

Identify benefit shifts: These occur frequently when new services are being introduced or existing ones are changed. Wherever such a change is to the disadvantage of a stakeholder, that one is likely to become a veto player which will reduce the overall utility and performance of the service, especially if that stakeholder holds a powerful role.

Justify investment: The analysis of the overall performance of the service will allow responsible service managers and other decision makers to prove that the investment (both in terms of money and time) is worthwhile.

Calculate break-even: When communicating the costs and benefits to involved persons it is important to understand when the benefits surpass the costs. This will allow preparing stakeholders for a prolonged phase of investment, again both in terms of money (e.g. cost for equipment) and of time (e.g. staff time for training and adapting to the new way of working). In integrated care, as in health and care in general, services may often take a comparatively long time to arrive at break-even. Time spans between 5 and 7 years are not uncommon (Stroetmann et al. 2006).

Understand service impacts: The understanding of all impacts (including secondary and long-term effects) may offer a new perspective on the service that is led by an economic and strategic view. This is a value in its own right, because it complements a technical and organisational point of view and explains and predicts why stakeholders behave as they do.

17.2.3 A Cost-Benefit Indicator Set for Integrated Care

The assessment uses a pre-defined set of cost and benefit indicators for different potential stakeholders in a service, covering service clients/patients, informal carers, different types of health and care provider organisations as well as their staff, payers and the ICT industry. The indicator set was specifically developed to capture the impacts of integrated care services and to allow for the development of value or business models in this field. It is, however, also applicable to other service concepts that do not focus on vertical and horizontal co-operation of service providers.

The indicators cover the most common costs and benefits occurring in the implementation of health and care services, including efforts for service development, efforts for training (providing and receiving), costs for the procurement of hardware and software and other material goods, costs for the procurement of supporting services (such as installation or maintenance), different types of quality and efficiency benefits, as well as different types of revenue streams.

A core element consists of indicators covering the time spent (cost) on service provision (for providers) and service use (for clients/patients and informal carers), as well as time liberated (benefit) e.g. due to more efficient work processes, avoided hospital stays or visits to and by providers. This part of the indicator set is conceptually linked to two high-level pathways for integrated care, one covering short-term support (e.g. after hospital discharge), the other long-term support (e.g. for people with chronic conditions). Both pathways were originally developed in the SmartCare project (SmartCare 2015b) and further developed in the BeyondSilos project (BeyondSilos 2014b). Common activities defined in the pathways were used to construct the respective indicators.

17.3 Learning by Example: The Service Implementation Simulator

The *Service Implementation Simulator—Integrated eCare* was created in the framework of the SmartCare project as a tool to support the project's activities to develop sustainability models for the services being deployed. In practical terms, the Simulator can be considered an ASSIST software tool filled with exemplary data illustrating an exemplary service (see below).

The Simulator can be used to explore potential configurations of ICT-supported, integrated care services. With the Simulator, different ways of setting up a service (in terms of stakeholders involved, service processes, etc.) can be chosen. Using the tool, assumptions can be made for different types of service-related costs and benefits, ranging from direct revenue models to high-level societal goals. Both short- and long-term consequences of each design choice can be explored immediately. Furthermore, the Simulator can be used to get acquainted with the general ASSIST method.

It was created in particular for stakeholders who are not experts in economic assessments and cost-benefits analysis, but who still want or need to be involved in related activities. Following an "active learning" (Bonwell and Eison 1991) approach, the Simulator allows users to get into immediate contact with the content-related aspects of the assessment, while (initially) by-passing methodological questions and the need for data collection. Since it is filled with data already, a user can instantly delve into understanding the economic characteristics of the example case and begin modifying data to see how the sustainability model of the service reacts to changes in costs and benefits. While doing this, the user is also made acquainted with the functionalities of the ASSIST software tool and the underlying methodological assumptions. In the further course of the assessment of the user's own case, the Simulator can either be used by modifying the model data already present or by deleting all model data to start the own assessment from an empty tool.

17.3.1 Integrated eCare Example Case

The *Service Implementation Simulator—Integrated eCare* is built around a model case scenario of an ICT-supported, integrated care service. The scenario was developed as part of SmartCare. In particular, it makes use of the integrated care pathways developed in SmartCare and the cost-benefit indicator set described above. Some elements of the scenario were developed based on actual integrated eCare services implemented in the CommonWell and INDEPENDENT projects.

17.3.2 Overall Service Model

The case scenario is built on a service supporting older people suffering from COPD (Chronic Obstructive Pulmonary Disease) and possible co-morbidities, as well as their family members or friends caring for them (informal carers). As an integrated service, it amalgamates services provided to patients and their carers by different stakeholders, including healthcare providers, social care providers and third-sector providers. ICT systems are used to support service delivery.

The service is supposed to be set-up in three stages, beginning with a 6-months development and implementation stage, followed by a 12-month evaluated piloting period, after which the service began routine operation.

17.3.3 Elements of the Service

The service is conceived of as a socio-technical system bringing together elements provided by (individual and organisational) human stakeholders and different ICT systems, both working in close relationship. It consists of three core elements:

1. An early supported discharge (ESD) programme for COPD patients following an exacerbation of their condition. The ESD programme uses home telehealth to provide monitoring and guidance to the patients after their discharge from hospital. Follow-up, e.g. in case of out-of-threshold telehealth readings, is relocated from primary care (GPs) to a social care providers. Patients can be re-admitted to hospital or referred to the GP if required.
2. Eligible patients are furthermore enrolled in a video-based physiotherapy programme to improve or maintain their physical fitness. Patients can participate in guided online physio sessions at regular intervals, using a computer with webcam and headset or microphone and speakers in their home.
3. A voluntary organisation (third-sector provider) supports informal carers (family members or friends) in caring for the COPD patients, by means of counselling, self-help meetings, information provision and other offers.

For the start of the service, the provider organisations involved agreed on a general collaboration mechanism that is based on a common care pathway. The pathway foresees joint care planning as well as sharing of relevant patient or client data in a joint care record. All providers have access to that record in compliance with data protection legislation and based on informed consent given by the patient. Informal carers can be granted access to parts of the record under the same conditions.

17.3.4 Assessment of the Example Case in Four Steps

17.3.4.1 Step 1: Stakeholders

The following stakeholders are either actively involved in the service or passively affected by it:

The COPD patients will usually be 60 years old or older, diagnosed with COPD and possible co-morbidities. A considerable share of the patients will be smokers. They enter the service after hospital admission following an exacerbation of their COPD and prior to hospital discharge. They pay a monthly fee to the Telehealth Call Centre and the physiotherapy provider. An evaluation of the service showed that patients are satisfied to very satisfied with the service and how it effects life with their chronic conditions.

The informal carers are family members or friends of the patient who have taken over some or all caring responsibilities for the patient. They will usually be 50 years or older, with at least half of them in part- or full-time employment. They can but do not have to live in the same household as the patient. They pay a nominal fee to the carer support organisation. An evaluation of the service showed that informal carers are by and large satisfied to very satisfied with the service and how it affects themselves and the people they are caring for.

The Telehealth Call Centre is a private business entity providing home telehealth to the patient. It is responsible for the provision and installation of the telehealth hardware, for training of the patients as well as for technical maintenance and support. They monitor telehealth readings, including technical triaging, and pass alerts on to the social care provider, the GP or the hospital, as the situation demands. The call centre receives a service fee paid by the COPD patients. Under the current service model, this fee covers about 50% of the costs.

The primary care organisations (GP practices) are private organisations reimbursed from a public budget (held by the health and social care payer). Usually, they provide day-to-day healthcare to the COPD patients. The early supported discharge programme means that a considerable amount of care is now being provided by social care providers. The GP remains responsible only for certain types of follow-ups requiring the attention of a doctor. As a consequence, the number of consultations that the COPD patients used to have at the GP practice is being reduced. As the GP is reimbursed on a DRG (Diagnosis Related Group) basis (i.e. per treatment) the immediate effect is a loss of income.

The hospitals are public institutions financed by their own budgets which they receive from the state. They provide care to the COPD patients, especially in case of exacerbations. The early supported discharge programme and the home telehealth monitoring substantially reduces admissions due to exacerbations as well as readmissions. For the hospitals this means that a considerable amount of staff time is being saved, beds are freed and the waiting lists shortened. Since the hospitals' budgets remain unchanged, this is an immediate benefit for them.

The physiotherapy provider is part of a larger public institution providing different types of health and social services, not only to older people but also to children, people with disabilities and people receiving welfare benefits. The whole institution finances itself via a budget received from the state. For the physiotherapy team, the introduction of video training allows them to take on more clients than before. Clients pay a monthly fee for the video service, which however is not intended to cover the operational costs.

The social care providers are private business entities, financed from a state budget on a case basis. They take on the immediate follow-up of the COPD patients, based on the technical triaging done by the Telehealth Call Centre. They take over much of the work originally done by primary care organisations and receive additional reimbursement for this, allowing them to break even on the new service after about 1.5 years.

The carer support organisation is a volunteer organisation that funds itself through membership fees, fundraisers and various state aid schemes. Furthermore, informal carers receiving support pay a nominal monthly fee. A major part of the support services provided is delivered by unpaid volunteers. A small core team of employed staff deals primarily with managerial and administrative work. For the carer support organisation, the new service resulted in the wide-spread implementation of IT (mostly computers and mobile devices) into their offices and work processes. After initial problems, this has led to considerably efficiency gains in the organisation's administration.

17.3.4.2 Step 2: Impact Identification

To show how the identification of impacts is done using the example case, we focus on two stakeholders: the COPD patients receiving the service and the GP practices that, under the new service, are responsible for certain types of follow-ups. For the sake of the example case let us assume that impact identification was done by the team implementing the new service based on interviews with GPs and practice nurses as well as a focus group with patients.

Consideration of the different elements of the service as well as consultation with older people suffering from COPD in a focus group showed that the main negative impacts of the new service would be:

Inconvenience related to the time it takes patients to learn the use of the telehealth devices

Inconvenience related to the time it takes them to receive support from the social care provider and the time it takes them to do their daily telehealth readings

Furthermore, it is being considered to introduce a patient-payable fee or co-payment for the telehealth service, which would be an additional cost factor

On the positive side the following impacts were considered likely:

Intangible benefits perceived by patients, such as an increased feeling of safety, improved capacity to live with their own condition, satisfaction with a more co-ordinated way of providing care to them
Convenience related to the time saved due to avoided visits to the GP

For the GP practice, the impact identification showed that the main negative impacts were likely to be:

The time spent by the GP and the practices nurses on the development of the service, especially the definition of work processes
The extra time spent by the GP and the nurses to contribute to the joint care plan for each patients
The loss of income from practice consultations and home visits that are being relegated to the social care provider

On the positive side there are:

Time saved due to the consultations and visits relegated to the social care provider
Travel costs saved in relation to the relegated home visits

17.3.4.3 Step 3: Data Collection

Data is collected e.g. in the course of an evaluation of the service pilot and entered directly into the ASSIST tool. In the example case, data on the time spent by patients for training and for using the service, as well as on time saved due to the avoided GP visits is collected by means of a quantitative survey using a questionnaire including questions on time use. The resulting data are therefore based on patients' recollection of the time they spent or saved. The questionnaire also covered the perception of intangible impacts. In order to have an empirical basis for the co-payment amount, a willingness-to-pay questionnaire was furthermore carried out. Table 17.1 shows the data collected on the different variables making up each impact.

A Note on Data Handling The cost-benefit analysis is solely based on monetary values. This is straightforward for monetary impacts, such as the fee for service in this case. Both inconvenience related to time spent (and convenience to time saved) are intangible effects which are here approximated by the amount of time and then monetarized using the average individual income of the patient target group. The results of the survey on the perception of intangible impacts were aggregated into a standardized score and then monetarized relative to the costs the service causes to the patients, i.e. in this case the inconvenience for the time spent using the service. For a more detailed description of the approaches used see Hammerschmidt and Meyer (2014).

Table 17.1 Patient impact data

Negative impacts	Value	Unit	Time period
Fee for services			
Service fee paid by Clients/Patients 1 to Telehealth call centre	20	€	per month
Service fee paid by Clients/Patients 1 to Physiotherapy providers	10	€	per month
Inconvenience: training time			
Time spent by Clients/Patients 1 receiving training	0.5	hours	per new patient/client
Inconvenience: extra time for service use spent by Clients/Patients 1			
Average (extra) time spent by Clients/Patients 1 receiving social care, per session.	45	min	per session
Number of (extra) sessions of social care of Clients/Patients 1	6	number	per patient/client per year
Average (extra) time spent by Clients/Patients 1 receiving remote care, per session.	10	min	per session
Number of (extra) sessions of remote care of Clients/Patients 1	365	number	per patient/client per year
Positive impacts	Value	Unit	Time period
Valuation of intangible benefits by Clients/Patients 1 according to eCCIS			
Average score for specific benefits (SBS) by Clients/Patients 1	1.75	Score	
Average score for overall assessment (OAS) by Clients/Patients 1	1.34	Score	
Degree of uncertainty (DU) for assessment by Clients/Patients 1	15%	%	
Convenience: time saved for service use by Clients/Patients 1			
Average time saved by Clients/Patients 1 receiving health care, per session.	12,240	min	per session
Number of sessions of health care saved by Clients/Patients 1	2	number	per patient/client per year

Data for the GP practice were collected by means of a staff time protocol analysis for the extra staff time and time saved, and by means of an analysis of accounts for the number and costs of avoided consultations and home visits. Data on saved travel cost was gained through interview with several GPs. Table 17.2 again shows the data collected on the different variables making up each impact.

A Note on Data Handling Other than for the patients above, extra time spent and time saved at the GP practice are not intangible impacts but resource impacts. By way of labour cost (wages plus employer contributions) they are more or less direct financial impacts for the practice. Accordingly, they are monetarized using labour cost.

Table 17.2 GP practice impact data

Negative impacts	Value	Unit	Time period
Staff time spent on service development			
Time spent by General Practitioners on service development and implementation	12	hours	per month
Time spent by GP nurses on service development and implementation	6	hours	per month
Duration of development period	6	months	
Extra staff time for service provision (assessment/planning) by General Practitioners to Clients/Patients 1—actual time			
Average (extra) time spent by General Practitioners on discharge planning for Clients/Patients 1	15	min	per session
Number of (extra) discharge planning sessions of Clients/Patients 1 done by General Practitioners	1	number	per year
Extra staff time for service provision (assessment/planning) by GP nurses to Clients/Patients 1—actual time			
Average (extra) time spent by GP nurses on discharge planning for Clients/Patients 1	15	min	per session
Number of (extra) discharge planning sessions of Clients/Patients 1 done by GP nurses	1	number	per year
Forgone income from avoided practice consultations			
Reimbursement lost due to avoided practice consultations at the Primary care organisations by Clients/Patients 1	100	€	per patient/client per day
Number of practice consultations avoided for Clients/Patients 1 at the Primary care organisations	4.00	number	per year
Forgone income from avoided home visits			
Reimbursement lost due to avoided home visits at the Primary care organisations by Clients/Patients 1	120	€	per patient/client per day
Number of home visits avoided for Clients/Patients 1 at the Primary care organisations	2.00	number	per year
Positive impacts	Value	Unit	Time period
Resource liberation (intervention) for General Practitioners working with Clients/Patients 1—actual time			
Average time saved by General Practitioners on consultations with Clients/Patients 1	30	min	per session
Number of consultations with Clients/Patients 1 saved by General Practitioners	4	number	per year
Average time saved by General Practitioners on home visits to Clients/Patients 1	60	min	per visit
Number of home visits to Clients/Patients 1 saved by General Practitioners	2	number	per year
Resource liberation (intervention) for GP nurses working with Clients/Patients 1—actual time			
Average time saved by GP nurses on consultations with Clients/Patients 1	15	min	per session
Number of consultations with Clients/Patients 1 saved by GP nurses	4	number	per year

17.3.4.4 Step 4: Analysing the Value Case

Based on the data entered into it, the ASSIST tool calculates the costs and benefits for each stakeholder and for the overall service. Two important elements are added in the calculation: the first is the number of patients, staff members and other individuals involved by which the costs and benefits are multiplied as applicable. The second element is a projection of the data over time, modelling the development of the costs and benefits depending on the inclusion of patients and further individuals as the service progresses.

The result is a graph showing for example what is called the cumulative socio-economic return rate, i.e. the relation of costs and benefits over time, as shown for the COPD patients in Fig. 17.3.

The projection covers a time period of 7 years, from January 2015 (at which time the development of the model case is supposed to have started) until December 2021. With the begin of the service operation in June 2015, the socio-economic return immediately rises to somewhat more than 50%, indicating that the benefits to the patients outweigh their costs by about a factor of 0.5. This rate steadily decreases as a result of depreciation, but always remains above 0%. There is a notable dip in July 2016 when the pilot project is supposed to end and the service transferred to mainstreamed operation. At that point in time, the patient-payable fee of 30€ per patient and month is introduced, reducing the total benefits.

The grey dotted line shows an alternative scenario, by which the patient-payable fee is 50€ per patient and month instead of 30€. As the graph show, even under these conditions the benefits would be higher than the cost and the option of a higher fee would seem viable in principle. This should however be supported by

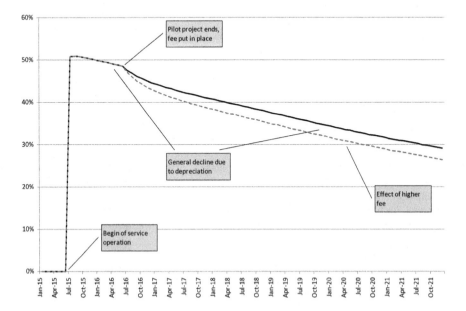

Fig. 17.3 Socio-economic return for patients

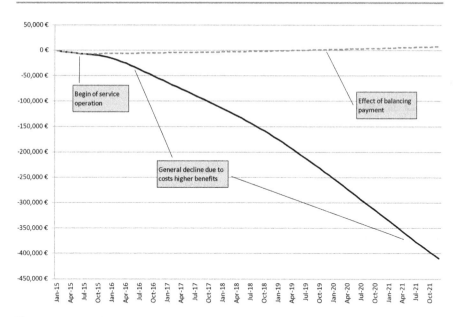

Fig. 17.4 Cumulative net-benefit for GP practice

according findings in the willingness-to-pay analysis indicating that such an amount would be acceptable.

The alternative scenario shows how results of the analysis (and the data in the Simulator respectively) can be changed to develop different scenarios and how they impact on the stakeholders in the model.

For the GP practices, Fig. 17.4 shows the cumulative net-benefit, i.e. the sum of all costs and benefits (excluding intangibles). Cumulative net-benefit is usually used as the key performance measure for for-profit stakeholders.

The picture that emerges for the GP practice is considerably different from the one for the patients. From the start of service operation, the net-benefit decreases steadily to reach a minimum of below −400,000 € towards the end of the 7 year period. This means that for the GP practice the costs of the new service are constantly higher than the benefits. This is the direct result of the follow-up visits relegated from the comparatively high-cost GP practice to the comparatively low-cost social care provider. Under these conditions there is a high probability that GP practices will not be in favour of the new service and are actually likely to actively work against its implementation.

An alternative to this scenario is again shown by the grey dotted line. In that case, what can be called a balancing payment from the healthcare payer to the GP practices is introduced, to compensate for the losses caused by the relegated consultations and home visits. This might well be acceptable to the payer, given that the service as a whole leads to considerable cost savings due to avoided hospitalizations.

Again, this shows a way of developing and testing different scenarios with the aim of achieving an overall model that satisfies the needs of most if not all stakeholders.

17.3.5 A Set of Lessons to Be Learned

The example presented above shows two ways how the Simulator can be used for business models development and the associated learning. Further to this, the Simulator comes with guidance material (SmartCare 2015a) containing a number of lessons to be learned by its users. Following the "active learning" approach these lessons are designed to make the users acquainted with the software tool and then to carry out a series of ever more complex tasks. These tasks take the user on a journey of first understanding how the service works in economic terms and second identifying and then solving a number of problems that were built into the service's sustainability model.

Currently there exist five lessons and further lessons are being developed. The first lesson addresses some basic functionalities of the ASSIST software tool, allowing the user to navigate through the tool, include or exclude stakeholders from the assessment as well as activate or deactivate indicators from the existing set, depending on whether those will be needed or not. A second lesson addresses challenges to the business model of the (profit-oriented) Telehealth Call Centre resulting from a lack of revenues. A third lessons deals with the benefit shift phenomenon already briefly described above. It confronts the user with a (potentially powerful) veto player that could jeopardize the overall service model and explores ways how this veto player could be included in the service in a sustainable manner. A fourth lesson addresses a problem that is common in economic assessments involving public bodies financed from a larger budget (such as a national health service). In such a situation it can be difficult to determine what share of the budget is being used for the new service. In practical terms this could mean that there is no immediate benefit to set against cost caused by the new service. A fifth lesson explores ways how a user can deal with uncertainties in the data to be used that might results from a lack of suitable data, the workload of the staff to be involved or other factors. Inter alia, the ASSIST tool incorporates a mechanism for sensitivity analysis using Monte Carlo simulations that can be used to address such issues.

Each lesson in the guidance begins with a description of the problem, followed by a series of ever more concrete hints as to how the problem might be solved. The lessons are generally designed to be solved by working alone, but a group setting can also be used. The latter can be considered particularly useful for those lessons where no single solution exists, but there are rather alternative options, each with its own advantaged and disadvantages. Since the ASSIST tool carries out all calculations on-the-fly, the impact of any solution on the relevant key performance measures can be checked by the user immediately and without need of feedback from a "teacher".

17.4 Conclusions and Outlook

The ASSIST approach and the Service Implementation Simulator are currently (as of spring 2016) in active use in three EU-funded projects addressing integrated care: SmartCare, BeyondSilos and CareWell. They are being used to support the economic assessment of a total of 22 pilot services, with results expected to be available towards the end of 2016 and early 2017. The Simulator was used in all three projects to make project partners acquainted with the approach. It was introduced in the course of a training workshop held during a SmartCare consortium meeting in June 2015 in Belgrade, Serbia, with about 65 attendants. Another face-to-face meeting and four webinars were held to introduce the Simulator to the partners of the BeyondSilos and CareWell projects, about 25 individuals. Feedback from those training workshops was predominantly positive, with attendants stating that they were able to follow the lessons and went away feeling that they now understood the ASSIST approach and the tool.

Conceptually and practically the Service Implementation Simulator can therefore probably be considered a useful instrument to support socio-economic impact assessments in integrated care. On the other hand there remains room for improvement, both in relation to the guidance material provided to users and in relation to the lessons covered. Further lessons are currently being developed, based on questions emerging from the ongoing assessment work in all three projects. These lessons are planned to address ways of measuring service impacts on staff time and the time of clients, patients and informal carers, the monetarisation of intangible impacts and the modelling of scale-up scenarios taking a service from a pilot population to a fully mainstreamed model.

Both the ASSIST tool and the Service Implementation Simulator are available under the GNU General Public License (GPL) and can be downloaded from (empirica 2014) and (SmartCare 2015a), respectively.

References

BeyondSilos. (2014a). *BeyondSilos—Learning from integrated eCare practice and promoting deployment in European regions* [Online]. Accessed 2015, from http://beyondsilos.eu/
BeyondSilos. (2014b). *BeyondSilos pilot level pathways and integration infrastructure* (Deliverable 1.2).
Bonwell, C., & Eison, J. (1991). *Active learning: Creating excitement in the classroom AEHE-ERIC Higher Education Report No. 1*. Washington, DC: Jossey-Bass.
CareWell. (2014). *CareWell—Delivering integrated care to frail patients through ICT* [Online]. Accessed 2015, from http://www.carewell-project.eu/
CommonWell. (2012). *CommonWell—Common platform services for ageing well in Europe* [Online]. http://www.commonwell.eu/
Davidoff, F. (2008). Publication guidelines for quality improvement in health care: Evolution of the SQUIRE project. *Quality & Safety in Health Care, 17*, i3–i9.
Drummond, M. F. (2005). *Methods for the economic evaluation of health care programmes*. Oxford: Oxford University Press.

empirica. (2014). *ASSIST—Assessment and evaluation tools for e-service deployment in health, care and ageing* [Online]. Accessed 2015, from http://assist.empirica.biz/

Goodwin, N., & Alonso, A. (2014). Understanding integrated care: The role of information and communication technology. In I. Meyer, S. Müller, & L. Kubitschke (Eds.), *Achieving effective integrated e-care beyond the silos.* IGI Global: Hershey.

Hammerschmidt, R., & Jones, T. (2012). *Telemedicine evaluation methodologies. ASSIST— Assessment and evaluation tools for telemedicine.*

Hammerschmidt, R., & Meyer, I. (2014). Socio-economic impact assessment and business models for integrated eCare. In I. Meyer, S. Müller, & L. Kubitschke (Eds.), *Achieving effective integrated e-care beyond the silos.* IGI Global: Hershey.

INDEPENDENT. (2013). *INDEPENDENT—ICT enabled service integration for independent living* [Online]. http://www.independent-project.eu/

Meyer, I., Müller, S., & Kubitschke, L. (2011). AAL markets—Knowing them, reaching them. Evidence from European research. In J. C. Augusto, M. Huch, A. Kameas, J. Maitland, P. J. Mccullagh, J. Roberts, A. Sixsmith, & R. Wichert (Eds.), *Handbook of ambient assisted living. Technology for healthcare, rehabilitation and well-being.* Amsterdam: IOS Press.

Rigby, M. (2014). The core vision of person-centred care in a modern information-based society. In I. Meyer, S. Müller, & L. Kubitschke (Eds.), *Achieving effective integrated e-care beyond the silos.* IGI Global: Hershey.

Röthig, P. (2009). *ICT Investionen begründen—Wirtschaftlichkeitsberechnungen mit dem WiBe-Konzept.* Weimar: WiBe.

SmartCare. (2013). *SmartCare—Delivering integrated eCare* [Online]. Accessed 2015, from http://pilotsmartcare.eu/

SmartCare. (2015a). *Service implementation simulator—Integrated eCare* [Online]. Accessed 2015, from http://pilotsmartcare.eu/outcomes/service-implementation-simulator/

SmartCare. (2015b). The SmartCare pathways. An initial step towards implementing integrated eCare. SmartCare White Paper No. 1. In SmartCare (Ed.), *SmartCare White Papers.* Bonn.

Stroetmann, K., Jones, T., Dobrev, A., & Stroetmann, V. N. (2006). *eHealth is worth it—The economic benefits of implemented eHealth solutions at ten European sites.* Luxembourg: Office for Official Publications of the European Communities, European Commission.

UK HM Treasury. (2003). *The green book—Appraisal and evaluation in central government.* London: TSO.

White House Office for Management and Budget. (1992). Circular No. A-94—*Guidelines and discount rates for benefit-cost analysis of federal programs.*

Part IV

Evaluation and Health Services Research

Evaluating Complex Interventions

18

Apostolos Tsiachristas and Maureen P.M.H. Rutten-van Mölken

18.1 Definition of Complex Intervention

There is an increasing interest in evaluating complex interventions. This is because epidemiological changes increasingly call for composite interventions to address patients' needs and preferences. It is also because such interventions increasingly require explicit reimbursement decisions. That was not the case in the past, when these interventions often entered the benefit package automatically, once they were considered standard medical practice. Nowadays, payers as well as care providers are intrigued to know not just if a health care intervention works but also when, for whom, how, and under which circumstances. In addition, there is broad recognition in the research community that evaluating complex interventions is a challenging task that requires adequate methods and scientific approaches. One of the main points of discussion across all interested parties is what exactly a complex intervention is.

One of the first attempts to define complex interventions was undertaken by the Medical Research Council (MRC) in UK, which issued a guidance in 2000 for developing and evaluating complex interventions (Campbell et al. 2000). The guidance was updated and extended in 2008 to overcome limitations in the earlier guidance (Craig et al. 2008). The guidance was published in response to the

A. Tsiachristas (✉)
Health Economics Research Centre, Nuffield Department of Population Health, University of Oxford, Oxford, UK
e-mail: apostolos.tsiachristas@dph.ox.ac.uk

M.P.M.H. Rutten-van Mölken
Institute of Medical Technology Assessment, Institute of Health Care Policy and Management, Erasmus University Rotterdam, Rotterdam, The Netherlands
e-mail: m.rutten@bmg.eur.nl

© Springer International Publishing AG 2017
V. Amelung et al. (eds.), *Handbook Integrated Care*,
DOI 10.1007/978-3-319-56103-5_18

challenges faced by those who develop complex interventions and evaluate their impact. MRC defines an intervention as being complex, if it includes one or more of the following characteristics: (a) various interacting components, (b) targeting groups or organizations rather than or in addition to individuals, (c) a variety of intended outcomes, (d) they are amendable to tailoring through adaptation and learning by feedback loops, and (e) effectiveness is impacted by behaviour of those delivering and receiving the intervention. In other words, the MRC argues that the greater the difficulty in defining precisely what exactly are the effective ingredients of an intervention and how they relate to each other the greater the likelihood that a researcher is dealing with a complex intervention. Examples of complex interventions are presented in Box 18.1.

Box 18.1 Examples of complex interventions

Tele-health, e-health and m-health interventions
    Online portal for diabetes patients to support self-management
    Home tele-monitoring
    Mobile phone-based system to facilitate management of heart failure
Interventions directed at individual patients:
    Cognitive behavioural therapy for depression
    Cardiac or pulmonary rehabilitation programs
    Care pathways
    Motivational interviewing and lifestyle support to improve physical activity and a healthy diet
Group interventions:
    Group psychotherapies or behavioural change strategies
    School-based interventions to reduce smoking and teenage pregnancy
Interventions directed at health professional behaviour:
    Implementation strategies to improve guideline adherence
    Computerised decision support systems
Service delivery and organization:
    Stroke units
    Hospital at home
Community and primary care interventions:
    Community-based programmes to prevent heart disease
    Multi-disciplinary GP-based team to optimize health and social care for frail elderly
Population and public health interventions
    Strategies to increase uptake of cancer screening
    Public health programs to reduce addiction to smoking, alcohol and drugs
Integrated care programs for chronic diseases
    Could include all interventions above

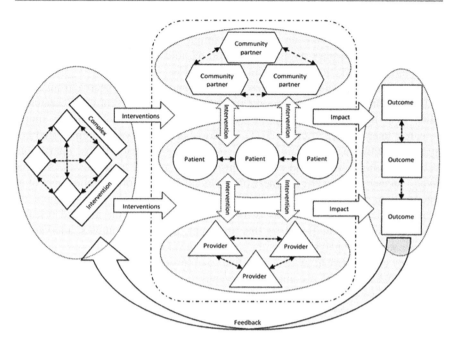

Fig. 18.1 Illustration of complex intervention

In the same line, other definitions also emphasize the degree of flexibility and non-standardization of complex interventions, which may have different forms in different contexts, while still conforming to specific theory driven processes (Hawe et al. 2004). Although there are many more definitions of complex interventions, they all tend to emphasize multiple interacting components and non-linear causal pathways. Figure 18.1 illustrates how a complex intervention is diffused to different groups of recipients, interacts, and impacts different outcomes.

In contrast, health technologies such as medicines, diagnostic tests, medical devices, and surgical procedures are considered to be simple interventions because they are usually delivered by one care provider or provider organization and have mostly linear causal pathways linking the intervention with its outcome. However, the distinction between complex and simple interventions may be not entirely clear because after all simple interventions can also have a degree of complexity. Complexity is defined as 'a scientific theory which asserts that some systems display behavioural phenomena that are completely inexplicable by any conventional analysis of the systems' constituent parts (Hawe et al. 2004). Reducing a complex system to its components amounts to irretrievable loss of what makes it a system.

In has also been suggested that complexity is not necessarily a feature of an intervention but it is the complexity of the setting in which interventions are implemented. In other words, complexity is a property of the setting in which an intervention is being implemented not an inherent feature of the intervention itself

(Shiell et al. 2008). For example, a vaccination program for tuberculosis in a low-income country may be seen as a simple intervention implemented in a complex setting because its implementation requires the interaction between primary care, hospitals, local community, and schools.

It has also been argued that the research question and the perspective from which that question is answered define the complexity of an intervention. Researchers often treat interventions as simple because it is convenient to answer simple research questions (Petticrew 2011). Addressing complexity requires studying synergies between components, phase changes and feedback loops, interactions between multiple health and non-health outcomes as well as processes. Alternatively, focusing on the effectiveness of the single most-important component of an intervention, simplifies the research question considerably. The intervention is the same but the research questions is different and therefore, the adopted research methods are different. Based on this argument, not every complex intervention requires complex analysis unless the research question demands it.

In any of the above arguments to define complex interventions, integrated care is a brilliant example of a complex intervention. The World Health Organization (WHO) defines it as "services that are managed and delivered in a way that ensures people receive a continuum of health promotion, disease prevention, diagnosis, treatment, disease management, rehabilitation and palliative care services, at the different levels and sites of care within the health system and according to their needs throughout their life course. It is an approach to care that consciously adopts the perspectives of individuals, families and communities and sees them as participants as well as beneficiaries of care" (WHO 2015). Similar definitions of integrated care can be found elsewhere (Kodner and Spreeuwenberg 2002; Nolte and McKee 2008). Based on this definition, integrated care may be considered an ultra-complex intervention or according to Shiell et al. (2008) a complex system (Shiell et al. 2008) because it is composed of multiple complex interventions (e.g. shared decision-making and self-management support), it behaves in a non-linear fashion (i.e. change in output is not proportional to change in input), the interventions interact with the context in which they are implemented, and involved decision-makers are merely interested in complex research questions.

18.2   The Rationale for Evaluation

Although research and service innovation have not been always aligned, service leaders and managers are increasingly keen to assess the effects of changes in such a way that they can be causally attributed to the complex intervention. Policy makers are also keen to ensure that they allocate scarce healthcare resources only to services that have proven value for money (i.e. to increase allocative efficiency). Some health care systems, such as Germany, do not allow process innovations without proof of efficiency. This is mainly driven by the notion that we cannot afford to make poor investments in times of tight budgets. Investing in any new interventions requires an increase in taxes, premiums, patients' co-payments or takes away budget from other interventions. As a result, there is a rationale to evaluate complex interventions already during their development and implementation. However, there are some questions to be addressed by researchers before pursuing an evaluation of a complex intervention, including (Lamont et al. 2016): (a) why is it important to address the aims of the evaluation and what is already known about the intervention, (b) who are the main stakeholders and users of research at outset, (c) how will the evaluation be performed in terms of study design and research methods, (d) what to measure and which data to be used, (e) when is the perfect timing to maximize the impact of the evaluation results.

Similar, policy makers may want to assess its evaluability to support more systematic resources allocation decisions depending on the knowledge generated by an evaluation of a complex intervention. An assessment of evaluability may include the following questions (Ogilvie et al. 2011): (a) where is a particular intervention situated in the evolutionary flowchart of an overall intervention program? (b), how will an evaluative study of this intervention affect policy decisions?, (c) what are the plausible sizes and distribution of the intervention's hypothesized impacts?, (d) how will the findings of an evaluative study add value to the existing scientific evidence?, (e) is it practical to evaluate the intervention in the time available?

18.3   Challenges in Evaluating Complex Interventions

Key challenges in the evaluation of complex interventions were identified in a recent review of 207 studies (Datta and Petticrew 2013). One of the main challenges was related to the content and standardization of interventions due to variation in the delivery of services in terms of frequency of interventions and lack of precise definition of the start of the treatment and a wide range of patients' diagnoses, stage of diseases, needs and preferences. Other challenges were related to the people (health care providers and patients) involved in the delivery of complex interventions. On the provider side, time and resource limitations may obscure data collection for evaluation purposes. Data collection may also be challenged due to issues related to patient's preferences, patient/provider interaction, and recruitment and retention to trials.

Furthermore, the organizational context of implementation, such as hierarchies, professional boundaries, staffing arrangements, social, geographical and environmental barriers, and the impact of other simultaneous organizational changes may affect the implementation of a complex intervention. A deterrent organizational context alongside with lack of support from healthcare providers pose another major challenge in evaluating complex interventions. Considering the plural, multi-dimensional (bio-psycho-social-clinical aspects), and multi-level (patient/organizational/local level) outcomes of complex interventions and their time spanning (i.e. short, medium, and long term), researchers face difficulties in establishing 'hard' outcomes that capture all effects. Combining quantitative with qualitative methods may ease part of this challenge. However, to do that sufficiently, more resources should be committed to the evaluation. Furthermore, we have seen an increase in the use of so-called composite endpoints (Hofman et al. 2014). Taking this step further, Datta and Petticrew suggested a departure from focusing on primary outcomes and a small number of secondary outcomes towards a much more multi-criteria form of assessment which acknowledges the multiple objectives of many complex interventions (Datta and Petticrew 2013).

Similar challenges were identified in a cross-national study that investigated barriers in the evaluation of chronic disease management programmes in Europe (Knai et al. 2013). The study found that lack of awareness for the need of evaluation and capacity to undertake sound evaluations, including experienced evaluators, deterred the development of an evaluation culture. Other reported barriers included the reluctance of payers to commit to evaluation in order to secure financial interests and the reluctance of providers to engage in evaluation due to perceived administrative burden and compromises their freedom. A more technical set of barriers to evaluate disease management programs was related to low quality of routinely collected data, or the lack of, inaccessibility, fragmentation, and wide variety of information and communication technology (ICT). The authors argued that these barriers lie on the complexity of the intervention and current organizational, cultural and political context.

The evaluation of a complex intervention may also be challenged at the policy-making level, where the decision to allocate substantial resources to implement and evaluate a complex intervention is often taken. Failing to convince policy-makers about the 'evaluability' of a complex intervention may hamper any action for evaluation.

18.4 Evaluation Frameworks

The increasing attention for complex interventions and urgent need to evaluate them boosted the development of evaluation frameworks in the last decade. One of these is May's rational model, which focuses on the normalization of complex interventions. Normalization is defined as the embedding of a technique, technology or organizational change as a routine and taken-for-granted element of clinical practice (May 2006). In this model, four constructs of normalizing a complex intervention are distinguished. The first is interactional workability, referring to the immediate conditions in which professionals and patients encounter each other, and in which complex interventions are operationalized. The second construct is relational integration, which is the network of relations in which clinical encounters between professionals and patients are located, and through which knowledge and practice relating to a complex intervention is defined and mediated. Skill-set workability is the third construct and includes the formal and informal divisions of labour in health care settings, and to the mechanisms by which knowledge and practice about complex interventions are distributed. Finally, the fourth construct is the contextual integration and refers to the capacity of an organization to understand and agree on the allocation of control and infrastructure resources to implementing a complex intervention, and to negotiating its integration into existing patterns of activity. The model is argued to have face validity in assessing the potential of a complex intervention to be 'normalized' and evaluating the factors of its success of failure in practice.

The multiphase optimization strategy (MOST) is another framework for optimizing and evaluating complex interventions (Collins et al. 2005). It consists of the following three phases: (a) screening; in which randomized experimentation closely guided by theory is used to assess an array of program and/or delivery components in order to select the components that merit further investigation; (b) refining; in which interactions among the identified set of components and their interrelationships with covariates are investigated in detail, again via randomized experiments. Optimal dosage levels and combinations of components are identified; and (c) confirming; in which the resulting optimized intervention is evaluated by means of a standard randomized intervention trial. To make the best use of available resources, MOST relies on design and analysis tools that help maximize efficiency, such as fractional factorial designs.

The MRC guidance is probably the most influential framework in developing and evaluating complex interventions. It is based on the following key elements (Craig et al. 2008): (a) development including the identification of evidence bases and theory as well as modelling of processes and outcome, (b) feasibility/piloting incorporating testing procedures, estimating recruitment and determining sample size, (c) evaluation by assessing the effectiveness and cost-effectiveness as well as understanding the change processes, and (d) implementation including dissemination, surveillance and monitoring and long-term follow-up. Regarding evaluation, the MRC guidance is supportive of using experimental study designs when possible and combining process evaluation to understand process changes with formative and summative evaluation to estimate (cost-) effectiveness.

18.5   Process Evaluation

Process evaluation is as important as outcome evaluation, which can provide valuable insight not only within feasibility and pilot studies, but also within definitive evaluation studies and scale-up implementation studies. Process evaluations can examine how interventions are planned, delivered, and received by assessing fidelity and quality of implementation, clarifying causal mechanisms and identifying contextual factors associated with variation in outcomes (Craig et al. 2008). It is particularly important in multi-site studies, where the 'same' intervention may be implemented and received in different ways (Datta and Petticrew 2013). The recognition that the MRC guidance elaborated poorly on guiding process evaluation (Moore et al. 2014), resulted in to a separate MRC guidance on the process evaluation of complex interventions (Moore et al. 2015). This guidance provides key recommendations for planning, designing and conducting, analysing, and reporting process evaluations. Figure 18.2 shows the functions of process evaluation and relations among them as identified in the MRC guidance.

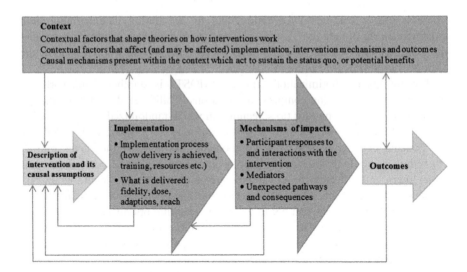

Fig. 18.2 Elements and relations of process evaluation. Source: Moore et al. (2015)

Following the MRC guidance and the earlier work of Steckler et al. (2002), the following subsections provide more details on the implementation, context, and causal mechanisms of complex interventions as the main components of their process evaluation. This is in accordance with an early case study of treating integrated care as complex intervention, Bradley et al. (1999) who suggested three levels of defining the intervention, including theory and evidence which inform the intervention, tasks and processes involved in applying the theoretical principles, and people with whom and context within which the intervention is operationalized (Bradley et al. 1999).

18.5.1 Fidelity and Quality of Implementation

A complex intervention may be less effective as initially thought because of weak or incomplete implementation (Boland et al. 2015). This is because they often go through adaptations depending on the context, which might undermine intervention fidelity. Standardizing all components of an intervention to be the same in different sites would treat complex interventions as being simple interventions. According to Hawe et al. (2004), the function and process of a complex intervention should be standardized not the components themselves. This allows the intervention to be tailored to local conditions and could improve effectiveness. Intervention integrity would be defined as evidence of fit with the theory or principles of the hypothesized change process. However, others may argue otherwise and propose the standardization of the components, while allowing flexible operationalization of these components based on the context.

Hence, the first stage in process evaluation focuses on the fidelity (the extent to which the intervention is delivered as intended), reach (whether an intervention is received by all those it targeted), dose delivered (the amount or number of units of intervention offered to participants, and dose received (the extent of participants' active engagement in the scheme). Steckler and Linnan conceive of evaluating intervention reach and dose, and participants' responses to an intervention largely in quantitative terms (Steckler et al. 2002). Reach and dose are commonly examined quantitatively using methods such as questionnaire surveys exploring participants' exposure to and satisfaction with an intervention. However, receipt can also be seen in qualitative terms as exploring participants' reports of an intervention in their own terms. Qualitative research can be useful in examining how participants perceive an intervention in unexpected ways which may not be fully captured by researcher-developed quantitative constructs. Qualitative research can also explore how providers or participants exert 'agency' (willed action) in engaging with the intervention rather than merely receiving it passively.

At this stage of the process evaluation, the RE-AIM framework developed by Glasgow et al. (1999) may be used to assess the reach, efficacy, adoption, implementation and maintenance of a complex intervention at individual and organizational level. This framework provides also specific metrics on each of these five dimensions (Glasgow et al. 2006a) and has been used in the process evaluation of many complex interventions including diabetes self-management interventions (Glasgow et al. 2006b) and community-based interventions for people with dementia (Altpeter et al. 2015).

18.5.2 Context

Context is a critical aspect of process evaluation. Although there is no consistent definition, context refers to the social, political, and/or organizational setting in which an intervention is implemented (Rychetnik et al. 2002). In broader terms, this could include factors such as the needs of participants, the infrastructure within which interventions will be delivered, the skills and attitudes of providers, and the attitudes and cultural norms of potential participants. The context in which a complex intervention is implemented usually influences the intervention's implementation by supporting or hindering it (Steckler et al. 2002). For example, an intervention may be delivered poorly in some areas, but well in others, because of better provider capacity or more receptive community norms in some areas. Context can be measured quantitatively in order to inform 'moderator' analyses but this occurs rarely and inconsistently between studies (Bonell et al. 2012). Qualitative research allows for a different understanding of the importance of context, for example, examining how intervention providers or recipients describe the interaction between their context and their own agency in explaining their actions (Oakley et al. 2006).

Moreover, the context interacts with complex interventions and therefore influences outcomes. The interaction of context and interventions has two major implications (Rychetnik et al. 2002). Firstly, it is likely to affect the transferability of a complex intervention. Secondly, interactions greatly complicate attempts to pool the results of different interventions. Distinguishing between components of interventions that are highly context dependent (for example, a self-management support programme) and those that may be less so (for example, wearable health devices that support self-management) may be a way of scaling down these implications. A process evaluation should therefore determine whether interactions between the context and intervention have been sought, understood and explained. Where such interactions seem to be strong, it may be preferred to explore and explain their effects, rather than pooling the findings. To do this, a combination of different qualitative methods, including interviews, focus groups, observations and tick descriptions should be used. Qualitative research can also enrich the understanding of intervention effects and guide systematic reviews. Standards for conducting qualitative investigations are widely available (Taylor et al. 2013).

18.5.3 Causal Mechanisms

Assessing an intervention's mechanisms of effects involves assessing whether the validity of the theory of change does indeed explain its operation. Such analysis can explain why an intervention is found to be effective or ineffective within an outcome evaluation. This might be critically important in refining an intervention found to be ineffective or in understanding the potential generalizability of interventions found to be effective. Quantitative data can be used to undertake mediator analyses to assess whether intervention outputs or intermediate outcomes appear to explain intervention effects on health outcomes (Rickles 2009). Qualitative data can be used to examine such pathways and this is particularly useful when the pathways in question have not been comprehensively examined using quantitative data, as well as when pathways are too complex (e.g. using multiple steps or feedback loops) to be assessed adequately using quantitative analyses. However, such analyses can be challenging. First, quantitative analyses require evaluators to have correctly anticipated what data is needed to examine causal pathways and to have collected these. A second challenge involves using qualitative alongside quantitative data to understand causal pathways. If qualitative data are analysed in order to explain quantitative findings, this may introduce confirmation bias. This may occur because the qualitative analysis will be used to confirm hypothesis of the quantitative analysis and focus disproportionally less to alternative possibilities. Furthermore, quantitative and qualitative methods originate from different research paradigms. Qualitative research is inductive and generalizations are made from particular circumstances making the external validity of the findings somewhat uncertain.

18.6 Formative and Summative Evaluation

In a formative evaluation, complex interventions are typically assessed during their development or early implementation to provide information about how best to revise and modify for improvement. For these purposes, a pilot study can be designed to test that both the intervention and the evaluation can be implemented as intended. If the pilot is successful and no changes are made then data from it can be incorporated into the main study. Moreover, a feasibility study can be used to indicate whether or not a definitive study is feasible and to examine important areas of uncertainty such as possibility and willingness for randomization, response rates to questionnaires collecting outcome data, or the standard deviation of the primary outcome measure required for the sample size calculation.

In summative evaluation, complex interventions are assessed for their definitive effectiveness and cost-effectiveness to support decisions-making of whether an intervention should be adopted, continued, or modified for improvement. The key statistical design issues alongside formative and summative evaluations of complex interventions are related to the study design and outcomes (Lancaster et al. 2010).

18.6.1 Study Design

The MRC guidance advocates the adoption of an experimental study design when evaluating complex interventions because it is the most robust method of preventing selection bias (Craig et al. 2008). Experimental designs include randomized controlled trials where individuals are randomly allocated to an intervention or a control group. These trials are sometimes considered to be inapplicable to complex interventions, but there are many flexible variants that can overcome technical and ethical issues associated with randomization such as randomised stepped wedge designs (Brown and Lilford 2006), preference trials (Brewin and Bradley 1989) and randomised consent designs (Zelen 1979; Torgerson and Sibbald 1998), and N-of-1 designs (Guyatt et al. 1990). When there is a risk of contamination (i.e. the control group is affected by the intervention), cluster randomised trials, in which groups of individuals (e.g. patients in a GP practice) are randomized instead of single individuals, are preferred.

Realist-RCTs have also been suggested as adequate design in evaluating complex intervention because they emphasize the understanding of the individual and combined effects of intervention components and examination of change mechanisms (Bonell et al. 2012). Realist-RCTs should be based on 'logic models' that define the components and mechanisms of specific interventions and combine qualitative and quantitative research methods. However, Marchal et al. (2013) objected the 'realist' nature of RCTs and proposed that the term 'realist RCT' should be replaced by 'theory informed RCT', which could include the use of logic model and mediation analysis that are entirely consistent with a positivist philosophy of science. Such an approach would be based on theory based impact evaluations for complex interventions and would be aligned with the approach suggested in the MRC guidelines. Irrespective of the terminology, both studies agree that experimental designs should be based on theories and incorporate methods adequate to evaluate complex interventions.

If an experimental approach is not feasible, for example because the intervention is irreversible, necessarily applies to the whole population, or because large-scale implementation is already under way, non-experimental alternatives should be considered. Quasi-experimental designs or natural experiments may be the best alternatives when evaluating complex interventions because they involve the application of experimental thinking to non-experimental situations. They widen the range of interventions beyond those that are amendable to planned experimentation and they encourage a rigorous approach to use observational data (Craig et al. 2012). Natural experiments are applicable when control groups are identifiable or when groups are exposed to different levels of intervention. Regression adjustment and propensity-score matching could reduce observed confounding between the comparators while, difference-in-differences, instrumental variables, and regression discontinuity could reduce the unobserved confounding between the comparators. A combination of these techniques is also possible in the evaluation (Stuart et al. 2014).

The selection of the study design could be informed by primary studies, literature reviews, and qualitative studies (Lancaster et al. 2010) and decided based on size and timing of the expected effects, the likelihood of the selection bias, the feasibility and acceptability of randomization and the underlying costs (see Box 18.2).

Box 18.2 Choosing between randomised and non-randomised designs

Size and timing of effects: randomisation may be unnecessary if the effects of the intervention are so large or immediate that confounding or underlying trends are unlikely to explain differences in outcomes before and after exposure. Randomization may be inappropriate if the changes are very small, or take a very long time to appear. In these circumstances a non-randomised design may be the only feasible option, in which case firm conclusions about the impact of the intervention may be unattainable.

Likelihood of selection bias: randomisation is needed if exposure to the intervention is likely to be associated with other factors that influence outcomes. Post-hoc adjustment is a second-best solution, because it can only deal with known and measured confounders and its efficiency is limited by errors in the measurement of the confounding variables.

Feasibility and acceptability of experimentation: randomisation may be impractical if the intervention is already in widespread use, or if key decisions about how it will be implemented have already been taken, as is often the case with policy changes and interventions whose impact on health is secondary to their main purpose.

(continued)

> **Box 18.2** (continued)
>
> *Cost*: if an experimental study is feasible, and would provide more reliable information than an observational study, you need then to consider whether the additional cost would be justified by having better information.
>
> *Source*: Craig et al. (2008)

18.6.2 Outcomes

Given the nature of complex interventions, an appraisal of evidence should determine whether the outcome variables cover the interests of all the important stakeholders, not just those who conduct or appraise evaluative research. Important stakeholders include those with responsibility for implementation decisions as well as those affected by the intervention. Identification of the appropriate range of outcomes that should be included in a formative/summative evaluation requires a priori agreement about the relevant outcomes of an intervention from important stakeholders' perspectives, including agreement on the types of evidence deemed to be adequate to reach a conclusion on the value of an intervention, and the questions to be asked in evaluating the intervention (Rychetnik et al. 2002).

Outcomes can be measured using qualitative and quantitative research methods. Qualitative studies can also be used as a preliminary to a quantitative study to establish for example meaningful wording for a questionnaire. The selection of the outcome measures can be based on recommendations and evidence form the literature as well as practical issues in collecting or gathering the necessary data. The outcomes measures should extent over different dimensions (for example dimensions of quality of life), time scales (for example short, medium and long term) and levels (for example, patient, organizational and local). For this reason, there is need for a multi-criteria form of assessment which acknowledges the multiple objectives of many complex interventions (Datta and Petticrew 2013).

Costs should be included in an evaluation to make the results far more useful for decision-makers. Ideally, economic considerations should be taken fully into account in the design of the evaluation, to ensure that the cost of the study is justified by the potential benefit of the evidence it will generate, appropriate outcomes are measured, and the study has enough power to detect economically important differences.

18.7 Reporting and Reviewing Evaluation Results

It is of crucial importance to provide detailed reporting of the results from the process, formative and summative evaluations for several reasons. First, information on the design, development and delivery of interventions as well as its context is required to overcome the challenges of evaluating complex interventions (Datta and Petticrew 2013) and enable the transferability of the interventions to other settings (Rychetnik et al. 2002). Second, well reported outcomes, knowledge of factors that influence the intervention's sustainability and dissemination, and information on the characteristics of people for whom the intervention was effective or less effective supports evidence based decision-making and practice. Third, poor reporting limits the ability to replicate interventions and synthesize evidence in systematic reviews.

The availability of such information from an evaluation study is a marker of the quality of evidence on a complex intervention. High quality evidence should refer to evaluative research that was matched to the stage of development of the intervention; was able to detect important intervention effects; provided adequate process measures and contextual information, which are required for interpreting the findings; and addressed the needs of important stakeholders (Rychetnik et al. 2002).

Several instruments have been developed and reported in the literature to systematize the reporting of evaluation studies of complex interventions. Some of them are mentioned in the MRC guidance for developing and evaluating complex interventions (Craig et al. 2008) and included generic statements (i.e. not specifically applicable to complex interventions) such as the CONSORT statement for reporting clinical trials (Moher et al. 2010) and the STROBE statement for observational studies (von Elm et al. 2007). Extended versions of the CONSORT statement for cluster randomised trials (Campbell et al. 2012), pragmatic trial (Zwarenstein et al. 2008) and complex social and psychological interventions have been issued (Montgomery et al. 2013a). Similar, the Criteria for reporting the Development and Evaluation of Complex Interventions in healthcare (CReDECI 2) is a checklist based on the CONSORT statement and EQUATOR network to report 17 items related to the development, feasibility and piloting, and evaluation of complex interventions (Mohler et al. 2015).

Authors of systematic reviews are increasingly being asked to integrate assessments of the complexity of interventions into their reviews. The challenges involved are well recognized (Shepperd et al. 2009). Some studies attempted to contribute in overcoming these challenges by systematically classifying and describing complex interventions for a specific medical area (Lamb et al. 2011). A more comprehensive attempt towards that direction was the Oxford Implementation Index. This tool was developed to incorporate information in systematic literature reviews and meta-analyses about the intervention characteristics with regards to their design, delivery and uptake as well as information about the contextual factors (Montgomery et al. 2013b). Furthermore, the Cochrane collaboration has published a series of methodological articles on how to consider complexity of interventions in systematic reviews (Anderson et al. 2013).

References

Altpeter, M., Gwyther, L. P., Kennedy, S. R., Patterson, T. R., & Derence, K. (2015). From evidence to practice: Using the RE-AIM framework to adapt the REACHII caregiver intervention to the community. *Dementia (London), 14*, 104–113.

Anderson, L. M., Petticrew, M., Chandler, J., Grimshaw, J., Tugwell, P., O'Neill, J., Welch, V., Squires, J., Churchill, R., & Shemilt, I. (2013). Introducing a series of methodological articles on considering complexity in systematic reviews of interventions. *Journal of Clinical Epidemiology, 66*, 1205–1208.

Boland, M. R., Kruis, A. L., Huygens, S. A., Tsiachristas, A., Assendelft, W. J., Gussekloo, J., Blom, C. M., Chavannes, N. H., & Rutten-Van Molken, M. P. (2015). Exploring the variation in implementation of a COPD disease management programme and its impact on health outcomes: A post hoc analysis of the RECODE cluster randomised trial. *NPJ Primary Care Respiratory Medicine, 25*, 15071.

Bonell, C., Fletcher, A., Morton, M., Lorenc, T., & Moore, L. (2012). Realist randomised controlled trials: A new approach to evaluating complex public health interventions. *Social Science & Medicine, 75*, 2299–2306.

Bradley, F., Wiles, R., Kinmonth, A. L., Mant, D., & Gantley, M. (1999). Development and evaluation of complex interventions in health services research: Case study of the Southampton heart integrated care project (SHIP). The SHIP Collaborative Group. *BMJ, 318*, 711–715.

Brewin, C. R., & Bradley, C. (1989). Patient preferences and randomised clinical trials. *BMJ, 299*, 313–315.

Brown, C. A., & Lilford, R. J. (2006). The stepped wedge trial design: A systematic review. *BMC Medical Research Methodology, 6*, 54.

Campbell, M., Fitzpatrick, R., Haines, A., Kinmonth, A. L., Sandercock, P., Spiegelhalter, D., & Tyrer, P. (2000). Framework for design and evaluation of complex interventions to improve health. *BMJ, 321*, 694–696.

Campbell, M. K., Piaggio, G., Elbourne, D. R., Altman, D. G., & Group, C. (2012). Consort 2010 statement: Extension to cluster randomised trials. *BMJ, 345*, e5661.

Collins, L. M., Murphy, S. A., Nair, V. N., & Strecher, V. J. (2005). A strategy for optimizing and evaluating behavioral interventions. *Annals of Behavioral Medicine, 30*, 65–73.

Craig, P., Dieppe, P., Macintyre, S., Michie, S., Nazareth, I., Petticrew, M., & Medical Research Council Guidance. (2008). Developing and evaluating complex interventions: The new Medical Research Council guidance. *BMJ, 337*, a1655.

Craig, P., Cooper, C., Gunnell, D., Haw, S., Lawson, K., Macintyre, S., Ogilvie, D., Petticrew, M., Reeves, B., Sutton, M., & Thompson, S. (2012). Using natural experiments to evaluate population health interventions: New medical research council guidance. *Journal of Epidemiology and Community Health, 66*, 1182–1186.

Datta, J., & Petticrew, M. (2013). Challenges to evaluating complex interventions: A content analysis of published papers. *BMC Public Health, 13*, 568.

Glasgow, R. E., Vogt, T. M., & Boles, S. M. (1999). Evaluating the public health impact of health promotion interventions: The RE-AIM framework. *American Journal of Public Health, 89*, 1322–1327.

Glasgow, R. E., Klesges, L. M., Dzewaltowski, D. A., Estabrooks, P. A., & Vogt, T. M. (2006a). Evaluating the impact of health promotion programs: Using the RE-AIM framework to form summary measures for decision making involving complex issues. *Health Education Research, 21*, 688–694.

Glasgow, R. E., Nelson, C. C., Strycker, L. A., & King, D. K. (2006b). Using RE-AIM metrics to evaluate diabetes self-management support interventions. *American Journal of Preventive Medicine, 30*, 67–73.

Guyatt, G. H., Keller, J. L., Jaeschke, R., Rosenbloom, D., Adachi, J. D., & Newhouse, M. T. (1990). The n-of-1 randomized controlled trial: Clinical usefulness. Our three-year experience. *Annals of Internal Medicine, 112*, 293–299.

Hawe, P., Shiell, A., & Riley, T. (2004). Complex interventions: How "out of control" can a randomised controlled trial be? *BMJ, 328*, 1561–1563.

Hofman, C. S., Makai, P., Boter, H., Buurman, B. M., De Craen, A. J., Olde Rikkert, M. G., Donders, R. A., & Melis, R. J. (2014). Establishing a composite endpoint for measuring the effectiveness of geriatric interventions based on older persons' and informal caregivers' preference weights: A vignette study. *BMC Geriatrics, 14*, 51.

Knai, C., Nolte, E., Brunn, M., Elissen, A., Conklin, A., Pedersen, J. P., Brereton, L., Erler, A., Frolich, A., Flamm, M., Fullerton, B., Jacobsen, R., Krohn, R., Saz-Parkinson, Z., Vrijhoef, B., Chevreul, K., Durand-Zaleski, I., Farsi, F., Sarria-Santamera, A., & Soennichsen, A. (2013). Reported barriers to evaluation in chronic care: Experiences in six European countries. *Health Policy (Amsterdam), 110*, 220–228.

Kodner, D. L., & Spreeuwenberg, C. (2002). Integrated care: Meaning, logic, applications, and implications – a discussion paper. *International Journal of Integrated Care, 2*, e12.

Lamb, S. E., Becker, C., Gillespie, L. D., Smith, J. L., Finnegan, S., Potter, R., Pfeiffer, K., & Taxonomy, I. (2011). Reporting of complex interventions in clinical trials: Development of a taxonomy to classify and describe fall-prevention interventions. *Trials, 12*, 125.

Lamont, T., Barber, N., Pury, J., Fulop, N., Garfield-Birkbeck, S., Lilford, R., Mear, L., Raine, R., & Fitzpatrick, R. (2016). New approaches to evaluating complex health and care systems. *BMJ, 352*, i154.

Lancaster, G. A., Campbell, M. J., Eldridge, S., Farrin, A., Marchant, M., Muller, S., Perera, R., Peters, T. J., Prevost, A. T., & Rait, G. (2010). Trials in primary care: Statistical issues in the design, conduct and evaluation of complex interventions. *Statistical Methods in Medical Research, 19*, 349–377.

Marchal, B., Westhorp, G., Wong, G., Van Belle, S., Greenhalgh, T., Kegels, G., & Pawson, R. (2013). Realist RCTs of complex interventions – an oxymoron. *Social Science & Medicine, 94*, 124–128.

May, C. (2006). A rational model for assessing and evaluating complex interventions in health care. *BMC Health Services Research, 6*, 86.

Moher, D., Hopewell, S., Schulz, K. F., Montori, V., Gotzsche, P. C., Devereaux, P. J., Elbourne, D., Egger, M., & Altman, D. G. (2010). CONSORT 2010 explanation and elaboration: Updated guidelines for reporting parallel group randomised trials. *BMJ, 340*, c869.

Mohler, R., Kopke, S., & Meyer, G. (2015). Criteria for reporting the development and evaluation of complex interventions in healthcare: Revised guideline (CReDECI 2). *Trials, 16*, 204.

Montgomery, P., Grant, S., Hopewell, S., Macdonald, G., Moher, D., Michie, S., & Mayo-Wilson, E. (2013a). Protocol for CONSORT-SPI: An extension for social and psychological interventions. *Implementation Science, 8*, 99.

Montgomery, P., Underhill, K., Gardner, F., Operario, D., & Mayo-Wilson, E. (2013b). The oxford implementation index: A new tool for incorporating implementation data into systematic reviews and meta-analyses. *Journal of Clinical Epidemiology, 66*, 874–882.

Moore, G., Audrey, S., Barker, M., Bond, L., Bonell, C., Cooper, C., Hardeman, W., Moore, L., O'Cathain, A., Tinati, T., Wight, D., & Baird, J. (2014). Process evaluation in complex public health intervention studies: The need for guidance. *Journal of Epidemiology and Community Health, 68*, 101–102.

Moore, G. F., Audrey, S., Barker, M., Bond, L., Bonell, C., Hardeman, W., Moore, L., O'Cathain, A., Tinati, T., Wight, D., & Baird, J. (2015). Process evaluation of complex interventions: Medical research council guidance. *BMJ, 350*, h1258.

Nolte, E., & Mckee, M. (2008). In E. Nolte & M. McKee (Eds.), *Caring for people with chronic conditions: A health system perspective* (p. 259). Maidenhead: Open University Press/ McGraw-Hill, (European observatory on health systems and policies series), isbn: 978 0 335 23370 0.

Oakley, A., Strange, V., Bonell, C., Allen, E., Stephenson, J., & Team, R. S. (2006). Process evaluation in randomised controlled trials of complex interventions. *BMJ, 332*, 413–416.

Ogilvie, D., Cummins, S., Petticrew, M., White, M., Jones, A., & Wheeler, K. (2011). Assessing the evaluability of complex public health interventions: Five questions for researchers, funders, and policymakers. *The Milbank Quarterly, 89*, 206–225.

Petticrew, M. (2011). When are complex interventions 'complex'? When are simple interventions 'simple'? *European Journal of Public Health, 21*, 397–398.

Rickles, D. (2009). Causality in complex interventions. *Medicine, Health Care, and Philosophy, 12*, 77–790.

Rychetnik, L., Frommer, M., Hawe, P., & Shiell, A. (2002). Criteria for evaluating evidence on public health interventions. *Journal of Epidemiology and Community Health, 56*, 119–127.

Shepperd, S., Lewin, S., Straus, S., Clarke, M., Eccles, M. P., Fitzpatrick, R., Wong, G., & Sheikh, A. (2009). Can we systematically review studies that evaluate complex interventions? *PLoS Medicine, 6*, e1000086.

Shiell, A., Hawe, P., & Gold, L. (2008). Complex interventions or complex systems? Implications for health economic evaluation. *BMJ, 336*, 1281–1283.

Steckler, A. B., Linnan, L., & Israel, B. A. (2002). *Process evaluation for public health interventions and research*. San Francisco, CA: Jossey-Bass.

Stuart, E. A., Huskamp, H. A., Duckworth, K., Simmons, J., Song, Z., Chernew, M., & Barry, C. L. (2014). Using propensity scores in difference-in-differences models to estimate the effects of a policy change. *Health Services & Outcomes Research Methodology, 14*, 166–182.

Taylor, B. J., Francis, K., & Hegney, D. (2013). *Qualitative research in the health sciences, Methodologies methods and processes*. London: Routledge.

Torgerson, D. J., & Sibbald, B. (1998). Understanding controlled trials. What is a patient preference trial? *BMJ, 316*, 360.

von Elm, E., Altman, D. G., Egger, M., Pocock, S. J., Gotzsche, P. C., Vandenbroucke, J. P., & Initiative, S. (2007). The strengthening the reporting of observational studies in epidemiology (STROBE) statement: Guidelines for reporting observational studies. *Lancet, 370*, 1453–1457.

WHO. (2015). *WHO global strategy on people-centred and integrated health services: Interim report*. Geneva: World Health Organization.

Zelen, M. (1979). A new design for randomized clinical trials. *The New England Journal of Medicine, 300*, 1242–1245.

Zwarenstein, M., Treweek, S., Gagnier, J. J., Altman, D. G., Tunis, S., Haynes, B., Oxman, A. D., Moher, D., Group, C., & Pragmatic Trials In Healthcare, Group. (2008). Improving the reporting of pragmatic trials: An extension of the CONSORT statement. *BMJ, 337*, a2390.

Economic Evaluation of Integrated Care

19

Apostolos Tsiachristas and Maureen P.M.H. Rutten-van Mölken

19.1 Need for Economic Evaluation of Integrated Care

Health economists are increasingly interested in integrated care for chronic diseases. This is because the rapidly increasing prevalence of chronic diseases reduces population's health, increases the demand for health and social care (WHO 2011) and has macroeconomic consequences for consumption, capital accumulation, labour productivity and labour supply (Busse et al. 2010). Health economists support healthcare decision makers with evidence in finding an adequate response to these challenges by investigating the efficiency of health care interventions, studying their financing mechanisms, and advocating the efficient allocation of scarce resources. The findings of health economics support decision-makers to define the right mixture of health technologies to maximise the health and well-being of society as well as to meet the preferences and needs of patients.

One of these responses is the provision of integrated care, which refers to initiatives that seek to improve outcomes for those with (complex) chronic health problems and needs by overcoming issues of fragmentation through linkage or coordination of services of different providers along the continuum of care (Nolte and Pitchforth 2014). It puts the patients and their individual needs and preferences in the centre and organizes care around them. Integrated care is seen as a promising

A. Tsiachristas (✉)
Health Economics Research Centre, Nuffield Department of Population Health,
University of Oxford, Oxford, UK
e-mail: apostolos.tsiachristas@dph.ox.ac.uk

M.P.M.H. Rutten-van Mölken
Institute of Medical Technology Assessment, Institute of Health Care Policy and Management,
Erasmus University Rotterdam, Rotterdam, The Netherlands
e-mail: m.rutten@bmg.eur.nl

© Springer International Publishing AG 2017   315
V. Amelung et al. (eds.), *Handbook Integrated Care*,
DOI 10.1007/978-3-319-56103-5_19

means to increase productive efficiency in care for people with chronic conditions (Epping-Jordan et al. 2004). According to the triple aim framework, as advocated by the Institute for Healthcare Improvement, integrated care aims to (1) improve population health, (2) improve patient experience with care, and (3) reduce costs (Berwick et al. 2008).

Economic evaluation in integrated care is still in its early years, facing several difficulties. Difficulties come from the fact that integrated care is a complex package of interventions with varying definition, composition, and application, which deviates substantially from simple technologies and health care interventions that are traditionally subject to health economic analysis. However, the urge for a wider implementation of integrated care to address the needs of people with chronic diseases and improve efficiency calls for more evidence-based decision-making based on thorough economic evaluations. The existing evidence about the economic impact of integrated care available in the thin scientific literature is inconclusive (Nolte and Pitchforth 2014). The main reasons are the great variation in interventions, and the relatively weak methodological approaches to evaluate integrated care (Conklin et al. 2013). Many studies have called for more reliable and replicable economic evaluation of integrated care (Nolte et al. 2014) and recognised that current evaluative frameworks may not be sufficient to address complex interventions (Payne et al. 2013), because these interventions require a wider range of costs to be included and their outcomes extend beyond Quality Adjusted Life Years (QALYs). Therefore, a modified framework with extended costing methods and outcome metrics that include the non-health benefits of integrated care may be needed.

19.2   Current Economic Evaluation Frameworks

The foundations of economic evaluation in health care lay in welfare economics, an area which is concerned with the analysis of conditions under which policies may be said to have improved societal wellbeing relative to alternative courses of action. Thus, economic evaluations should be comparative in nature, societal in scope and concerned with the resulting wellbeing of the individuals involved. In addition, economists have a preference for quantitative techniques and scientifically robust study designs that produce unbiased estimated of costs and effects.

Economic evaluations of health interventions have been defined as "the comparative analysis of alternative courses of action in terms of both their costs and their consequences" (Drummond et al. 2005). All economic evaluations assess costs, but approaches to measuring and valuing the consequences of health care interventions differ (see Box 19.1). Economic evaluations often rely on mathematical modelling to synthesize information from different sources, compare different treatment comparisons that have not been compared head to head empirically, and extrapolate the time horizon of the analyses beyond the time horizon of empirical studies (Husereau et al. 2013). Economic evaluations are important because resources (i.e. people, time, facilities, equipment and knowledge) are scarce.

Box 19.1 Forms of economic evaluation
Specific forms of analysis reflect different approaches to evaluating the consequences of health interventions.

Cost-consequences analyses (CCA) examine costs and consequences, without attempting to isolate a single consequence or aggregate consequences into a single measure.

Cost minimization analysis (CMA) compare costs only as the consequences are demonstrated to be equal.

Cost-effectiveness analysis (CEA) describes consequences in natural units, such as clinical cases detected, or life-years (LYs) gained.

Cost-utility analysis (CUA) measures consequences in terms of preference-based measures of health, such as disability adjusted life years (DALYs) or quality-adjusted life-years (QALYs).

Cost-benefit analysis (CBA) describes consequences in monetary units.

Although analysts may choose to use one or more forms of these analyses in their study, they should be aware that each form of analysis might have unique advantages or disadvantages for decision making.

The terms "cost-effectiveness", "cost-benefit" "economic evaluation" are often used interchangeably and, therefore, the term "economic evaluation" is preferred to avoid confusion.

Adapted from Drummond et al. (2005) and Husereau et al. (2013)

They allow those charged with managing resources to either anticipate the potential impact or measure the real impact of any change to the delivery of health care. In the context of health research, they can aid researchers in demonstrating the potential or real economic impact on the health system of a new intervention that can in turn promote its uptake and adoption. For example, one review of telemedicine applications suggested "The absence of a cohesive body of rigorous economic evaluation studies is a key obstacle to the widespread adoption, proliferation, and funding of telemedicine programs" (Davalos et al. 2009). However, the need to make decisions based on economic evaluations may extend beyond the health system. The effects of public health interventions, for example, may extend into the justice and education systems and require different forms of analysis used in those sectors (e.g., such as cost benefit analysis). Similarly, the effects of integrated care may extend into the informal care sector and the welfare sector. Economic evaluations may be also useful for private sector developers of technology, who must make research and development decisions based on an assumed return on investment (Ijzerman and Steuten 2011). Health system researchers may have to consider the various private and public sector actors that will use an economic evaluation for future decision-making.

There are several handbooks describing the methods of economic evaluation (Drummond et al. 2005; Gray et al. 2011) and some of them focus on how to perform economic evaluation methods in complex interventions, mainly public health interventions (Parkin et al. 2015; Griffin et al. 2009). Several methodological challenges in the economic evaluation of public health intervention are discussed in the literature (Weatherly et al. 2009; Edwards et al. 2013; Goldie et al. 2006). However, researchers that perform economic evaluation of integrated care may face different challenges than evaluators of public health interventions and may need different solutions to overcome them.

19.3   Challenges and Recommendations in Economic Evaluation of Integrated Care

Integrated care, as being a complex intervention, requires complex economic evaluation (Byford and Sefton 2003). Therefore, current economic evaluation methods may need to be adjusted or extended to address the challenges in performing economic evaluation of integrated care (Shiell et al. 2008). To do this methodological challenges in the economic evaluation of integrated care should be thoroughly identified and supplemented with recommendations to overcome them. A description of such challenges and recommendations is presented in the next sections.

19.3.1 Defining the Intervention

For an intervention to be appropriately costed and evaluated, it should be accurately and comprehensively described (Drummond et al. 2005). This definition should include information on the setting where the intervention is delivered, the target population, the time frame, the intervention components, the actors involved, the frequency and duration of intervention delivery and the extent of coverage of the target population. For a package of care interventions such as integrated care, the details of the components and the relative intensities of their implementation often vary with every implementation site. That is because such an intervention needs to be tailored to the specific context in which it is implemented. Moreover, at one particular site, the interventions do not remain constant but are often continuously improved as more experience is gained. Contextual characteristics of intervention and/or control settings are also rarely static (Barasa and English 2011). Therefore, economic evaluation of integrated care should be accompanied with a process evaluation as described in Chap. 18.

19.3.2 Comparator

Economic evaluation is a comparative analysis. Even if it is not possible to identify control groups, the relative efficiency of integrated care still needs to be assessed. In general, comparators used in economic evaluations frequently include active comparators such as current practice, best available alternative, or alternative levels of treatment intensity, different variations of similar programs etc. Identifying an appropriate comparator for integrated care is challenging. Standard practice, frequently called "usual care", is often an appropriate control but it can be at least as complex as the intervention being evaluated and may change over time by national or regional policy reforms that stimulate the evolution of usual care for an individual with one or more chronic diseases towards integrated care. As a result, usual care may have become a low intensity integrated care. Comparing integrated care models that differ in terms of their intensity or comprehensiveness may be a good alternative when appropriate control groups without integrated care are difficult to identify (Tsiachristas et al. 2014a, 2015). However, the room for improvement when comparing a more intense or comprehensive programme with a less intense or comprehensive alternative may be reduced. Summarizing, the competing alternatives to be considered in an economic evaluation include: (a) integrated care (complex intervention) to simple interventions delivered in current clinical practice, (b) integrated care to usual care (considered also as complex intervention), (c) various components of integrated care to each other or the sequence in which they were introduced, or (d) all the above. Although, it is not straightforward which pair of competing alternatives to choose and each option has pros and cons, evaluation guidelines suggest that the evaluation of a complex health intervention is accompanied by a detailed description of the components rather than disentangling the effects of the individual components (Craig et al. 2008; NICE 2007). Arguably, the interdependence of the interventions creates synergy effects. As a result the total cost-effectiveness of integrated care is not a linear summation of the partial cost-effectiveness of the interventions provided. For example, a thorough diagnostic assessment, which is not followed by a mutually agreed treatment package based on a patient's personal goals is unlikely to be of benefit to the patient (Bodenheimer and Handley 2009). However, the benefits of the latter are likely to be greater when based on a broad assessment of impairments, symptoms, functional limitations, disease perceptions, health behaviour and quality of life.

19.3.3 Study Design

For economic evaluations that are conducted alongside clinical studies, the clinical study design is an important issue. Most evaluation studies of integrated care are observational studies and very often lack a control group (Conklin et al. 2013). Besides the difficulty of creating an appropriate control group, other reasons for adopting an observational design include financial considerations, difficulties in identifying suitable participants, concerns about the generalizability of the results, and ethical considerations (Conklin and Nolte 2010). However, observational studies raise major concerns about the potential sources of bias and confounding factors that may jeopardize attribution of effect (or causality). Experimental designs such as randomised clinical trials (RCTs) are considered as the most robust designs to infer causality. Since integrated care includes interventions on organizational level and the risk of contamination (i.e. the control group is affected by the intervention) is high, cluster-RCTs could be considered as an adequate study design. In a stepped-wedge randomized trial the order in which the clusters receive the intervention is randomized, so that at the end of the entire time period all sites have received (Hussey and Hughes 2007). Even in those cases, experimental designs may face similar problems as observational studies in inferring causality when evaluating complex interventions such as integrated care. This is due to hidden differences in the context with which the treatment and control groups and periods interact that may critically affect the results (Rickles 2009). Standardization of interventions would be a solution to replicate the results in other settings but in the case of integrated care, it would preclude its adaptability to the local context and would treat it as a simple intervention (Hawe et al. 2004). Moreover, it is recognised that health interventions that are observed to be efficacious and cost-effective in the context of highly structured randomized trials may not be effective or cost-effective once they are made available in practice, under less controlled conditions (Boaz et al. 2011).

Quasi-experimental designs or natural experiments may be an alternative when evaluating integrated care because they involve the application of experimental thinking to non-experimental situations. They widen the range of interventions beyond those that are amendable to planned experimentation and they encourage a rigorous approach to use observational data (Craig et al. 2012). Natural experiments are applicable when control groups are identifiable and when groups are exposed to different levels of intervention. Natural experiments using regression adjustment and propensity-score matching could reduce observed confounding between the comparators while, difference-in-differences, instrumental variables, and regression discontinuity could reduce the unobserved confounding between the comparators (Craig et al. 2012). A combination of these techniques is also possible in the evaluation (Stuart et al. 2014). Figure 19.1 provides an overview of study designs to be considered in the evaluation depending on the availability of a control group and degree of experimenting.

Data availability and quality is another important factor to be considered when choosing a study design. Routine data from electronic medical records, existing patient registries, and payers might be of good quality and comprehensiveness but it can be costly or time consuming to access it and lengthy procedures involving 'trusted third parties' may be needed to merge data from different sources as confidentiality should be secured. In addition researchers have lack of control of the type of outcome measures included in the routinely collected data. In the absence or inadequacy of routine data, survey data could be used in the economic evaluation. However, the quality of survey data depends on the validity of the questionnaire, the response rate, the amount of missing observations, and data comprehensiveness (consider that lengthy surveys with many measures lead to low response rates). Ideally, routine data would be combined with survey data in the evaluation of integrated care and would be interpreted with the support of data collected from qualitative research. However, a complete economic evaluation based on different data sources requires substantial financial and human resources. Even when

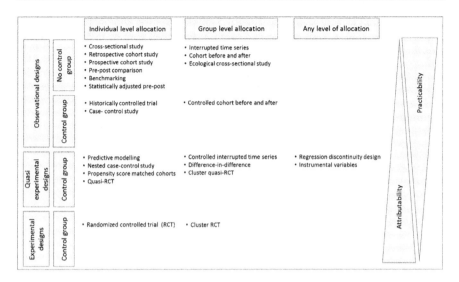

Fig. 19.1 Study designs by type and level of allocation. Source: Adapted from a series of RAND reports (Mattke et al. 2006; Conklin and Nolte 2010; Nolte et al. 2012)

resources are not an issue, lack of evaluation culture, and reluctance of payers or providers to engage in evaluation might challenge the evaluation of integrated care (Knai et al. 2013).

19.3.4 Evaluation Period

Most economic evaluation guidelines issued by health technology assessment agencies worldwide suggest to adopt a lifetime horizon in economic evaluation of medical innovations (Mathes et al. 2013). However, most evaluation studies of integrated care had an evaluation period of a year and some were extended up to 3 years (Conklin et al. 2013). This short to medium-term evaluation period may fail to capture the full effect of integrated care. This is because it takes at least 3–5 years for health management initiatives to identify "true" programme effectiveness due to lags in full implementation (Serxner et al. 2006). This may not even be long enough to study the effects of the preventive interventions in the integrated care package. However, adopting a follow-up period longer than 5 years would be problematic in attributing effects to integrated care because in the long-term, the intervention and eventually control groups are contaminated with other interventions and health policy reforms (Steuten et al. 2006b). Common sense would suggest to consider the start and end points of integrated care to determine an adequate evaluation period but none of these points is clear-cut in integrated care. An exact baseline measurement for evaluation is often hard to determine because the preparation and development of some integrated care interventions may have occurred way before that point. Failing to capture these efforts would underestimate the development costs of integrated care (Tsiachristas et al. 2014b). Determining the end point of integrated care is challenging as well. Integrated care interventions may be delivered one-off (e.g. eight sessions of self-management support), repeatedly or continuously in case of a permanent change in the way care is delivered (e.g. monitoring of high risk patients, establishment of multi-disciplinary teams, and development of integrated ICT system). Thus, the (partial) effects of integrated care are expected to be recurrent in time.

One way to extend the evaluation period is to set up a continuous monitoring system that tracks a core set of outcomes over time, not as part of the research but as part of routine practice. This can guide managers, healthcare providers, and payers, and may even be used to motivate patients when they have access to their own outcome data via patient portals. The challenge is to choose this core set and to adequately adjust for differences in case-mix when these data are used to compare groups.

19.3.5 Outcome Measures

Integrated care, as being a complex intervention, impacts many outcomes on different levels. These outcomes could be categorised in process indicators of the organization and delivery of care, patient's satisfaction with care, access to care, informal caregivers' satisfaction and quality of life, patients' lifestyle and risk factors, patients' ability to self-manage and cope with disease, clinical outcomes, functional status, quality of life, wellbeing, and mortality (Nolte and Pitchforth 2014; Tsiachristas et al. 2013a; Steuten et al. 2006a). These outcomes encompass the argument of Huber et al. (2011), that health should be defined more dynamically and more positively, based on the resilience or capacity to cope and maintain and restore one's integrity, equilibrium, and sense of wellbeing (Huber et al. 2011), as well as the capabilities approach of Amartya Sen including 'empowerment' which can be viewed as a type of capability that measures the 'ability of a person to function' (Coast et al. 2008a, b). Even advocates of QALYs as outcomes to support decision-making would argue that all of these outcomes cannot be captured in a single unit of measurement. Moreover, literature suggests that the QALY may not be relevant for decision-making at the level of provider organisations and insurers, when decisions to include an intervention in the benefit package at national or regional level have already been made (Kind et al. 2009). In that case, the decision that needs to be taken is not whether to fund integrated care but which type of programme should be provided, to whom and how in day-to-day practice. Thus, a QALY is not a relevant measurement to be used in clinical decision support systems, which are primarily informed by changes in clinical outcomes, health risk factors, care processes, and behaviour. To fully understand the impact of integrated care, multiple outcome measures, measured at multiple levels (e.g. patient, GP practice, and community) and eventually from different perspectives (e.g. providers and patient) should be employed to assess whether the triple aim of integrated care has been reached.

Some of these outcome measures could be used to inform performance indicators to facilitate the provision of financial incentives for integrating care. This would go beyond the performance indicators currently used in pay-for-performance schemes (e.g. in England (Downing et al. 2007)) by informing integrated care specific indicators and group specific indicators (e.g. disadvantaged people or people with multi-morbidity). Examples of such measures have been issued by WHO and include for example care planning and coordination, shared decision making, and medication review in older adults (WHO 2015). Looking at the care continuum, performance indicators could be assigned with different importance in time. For example indicators of physical improvements may be more important in the short term and indicators of psychological and social improvements in the long term for a patient who had a stroke. Furthermore, absolute and relative performance indicators could be combined to stimulate high-performing providers to maintain their performance levels and motivate low-performing providers to achieve relatively high performance (Tsiachristas 2015; van Herck et al. 2011).

19.3.6 Measurement and Valuation of Costs

Similar to outcomes, integrated care also impacts a broad range of costs, inside and outside the health care system. As a result, the societal perspective (i.e. considering all costs at societal level) is preferred to the narrower health care perspective when estimating the costs of integrated care. A full societal perspective would include the impact of integrated care on all sectors of the society (e.g. social care, workforce, education, security and justice). However, such a perspective would demand complex, time-consuming, and costly data collection and cost calculation. Thus, health economists may want to restrict the societal perspective to include only those societal costs that are expected to be most impacted by the integrated care programme under evaluation. For example, costs in the education and justice sectors might be relevant for inclusion in an economic evaluation of integrated care programmes for adolescents with mental conditions but not for a programme targeting adults with diabetes. Costs of informal care are commonly important to include in an economic evaluation of integrated care for frail elderly or individuals with severe or multiple conditions that require a lot of support. Furthermore, integrate care programmes require substantial development costs (including but not limited to training costs, ICT costs, and costs of redesigning the care delivery process) and implementation and operating costs (such as multidisciplinary team meetings, the costs of coordination between care-givers, the costs of monitoring and feedback). These costs are commonly carried by the organization that implements the programme and should be included in the economic evaluation.

A "minimum" set of cost categories relevant in the evaluation of integrated care may include (Vondeling 2004; Tsiachristas et al. 2013a): (1) the development costs of integrated care, (2) the implementation costs of integrated care, including process oriented costs, (3) the costs of health and social care utilization (including long-term care), (4) the costs borne by the patient (and the informal caregiver), such as home adaptations, specific diets, particular assistive devices, travelling to receive care, and (5) the costs of productivity loss due to absence from paid work or reduced productivity while at work. But again, the selection or relevant cost categories depends on the context. For example, if an already developed integrated care programme was implemented in another setting, then the development costs would not be relevant for inclusion in the analysis.

Development and implementation costs of integrated care could be collected via surveys or interviews with managers or financial controllers of integrated care programmes. A study systematically collected these costs by using a template based on the CostIt instrument of the World Health Organisation (WHO) (Tsiachristas et al. 2014b; Johns et al. 2003). This study could provide inspiration on how to treat overhead and capital costs as well as how to amortize development costs of integrated care.

Measuring and valuing the various cost categories could follow current practices and guidelines in health economic literature. The costs of health and social care utilization could be measured retrospectively by standardised questionnaires like the Client Service Receipt Inventory (CSRI) (Beecham and Knapp 1992) or based on routine or claims data. The CSRI also includes questions for residential care, criminal justice service and state benefits. Patient travelling costs and productivity costs could also be collected via standardized surveys (Bouwmans et al. 2015). Information to calculate costs of informal care could be collected with the *i*MTA Valuation of Informal Care Questionnaire (*i*VICQ) (Hoefman et al. 2011). Developing and applying questionnaires to measure resource use customized to a study would be an alternative for using existing questionnaires but this would require additional research time to validate them (Thorn et al. 2013). Unit costs could be gathered similar to traditional economic evaluations (Gray et al. 2011). When national average unit cost prices are not available or not precise enough, activity-based costing may be a useful alternative in estimating service costs of integrated care (Paulus et al. 2002, 2008). However, this approach is very costly and in many cases impractical to be performed in large scale economic evaluations (Mogyorosy and Smith 2005).

19.3.7 Broader Economic Evaluation

Considering the broad range of health and non-health outcomes for inclusion in the evaluation of integrated care, the adoption of cost-benefit analysis (CBA)—in which all benefits are expressed in monetary terms- and cost-effectiveness analysis (CEA)—in which the effects are measured in natural units (e.g. life years gained)— is precluded because these methods have a single measure of outcome (Gray et al. 2011; Drummond et al. 2005). Even if all outcomes of integrated care could be expressed in monetary terms and included in CBA (Evers 2010), it would be very time-consuming and costly to do so and the objections against assigning monetary values to health would still remain (Coast et al. 2008b). Performing a cost-utility analysis (CUA), which is the most widely used evaluation method and believed to have a comprehensive outcome measure, might be problematic in the case of integrated care because as mentioned earlier, a QALY does not capture the non-health benefits of integrated care (e.g. patient satisfaction with the process of care delivery). Therefore, a cost-consequence analysis (CCA) seems an adequate alternative because it presents a range of outcomes alongside costs. CCA probably fits better with real-world decision-making, in which decisions are made based on other criteria besides cost-effectiveness but it does not support a systematic ranking of alternative interventions based on their cost-effectiveness (Baltussen and Niessen 2006). Multi-Criteria Decision Analysis (MCDA) could overcome this limitation of CCA by supporting a systematic comparison of different alternatives based on their performance on various pre-specified criteria (i.e. a range of outcomes and costs) (Baltussen and Niessen 2006). In this process, different criteria are weighted according to their relative importance to the decision by different stakeholders, including patients, allowing an aggregation of the performance on multiple criteria into an overall composite score. Hence, MCDA is a sophisticated method for comparing complex interventions, such as different types of integrated care programs, incorporating all relevant categories of outcomes and costs (Goetghebeur et al. 2012; Bots and Hulshof 2000).

A framework to evaluate integrated care based on MCDA is reported in the literature (Tsiachristas et al. 2013a). The challenge for performing MCDA in this context is to determine a set of criteria relevant for decision-making and assign weights based on the preferences of stakeholders in integrated care. Whether the new composite measure that results from a MCDA can include other criteria than health and non-health benefits (e.g. costs) is debated (Baltussen 2015; Claxton 2015). If the new composite measure only includes benefits, then a new incremental cost-effectiveness ratio (ICER) threshold value for one unit of additional benefit on this composite measure may need to be determined to support reimbursement decisions. However, MCDA may also be used alongside and as a supplement to the existing deliberate process, serving to structure the discussions and feed back to decision makers the weights implicit in their decisions (Thokala et al. 2016). This may particularly apply when other criteria than benefits are included in the composite measure. Inter-sectoral costs and consequences may also be addressed by combining CCA and MCDA (Weatherly et al. 2009).

19.3.8 Determinants of Cost-Effectiveness

Whether a particular intervention is cost-effective depends on key contextual variables involving place and time. Sculpher et al. (2004) identified 26 such factors that may cause variability in cost-effectiveness across locations, including case mix, culture/attitudes, demography, and health professional's skillsets and experience. Welte et al. (2004) offer a similar list of 14 "transferability factors" to be considered when transferring economic evaluation results across country contexts. In some instances, interventions that are found to be presently cost-effective or cost-saving in a particular setting may not remain so if expanded or delivered under different circumstances. The "transferability" of economic evaluation results is highly challenging when integrated care is regarded because it interacts with the context in which it is provided. Thus, standardizing reporting of methods and results is necessary (see respective subsection below for further details).

Similar to many complex interventions, the cost-effectiveness of integrated care also depends on the provided interventions and their combination. There is evidence about the (cost-) effectiveness of most interventions included in integrated care (Tsai et al. 2005; Ouwens et al. 2005; Zwar et al. 2006; Weingarten et al. 2002; WHO 2015b). However, theoretical and conceptual studies on integrated care strongly suggest that the value of integrated care is in the combination of interventions. This is because integrated care "is not a discrete and immediately replicable intervention and its elements should be treated as a totality" (Coleman et al. 2009). Ham (2010) argues that the tenth characteristic of a high performing chronic care system is the link between individual interventions that transforms them into a coherent whole and has an additional effect (Ham 2010). It is unclear whether this effect of combining different interventions is additive or multiplicative but it surely is the synergy and interaction between interventions that contributes to the overall effect. Therefore, the evaluation of integrated care should be undertaken at an aggregated level (Hawe et al. 2004). Moreover, the complexity of integrated care in terms of intervention intensity (Nolte et al. 2012) and comprehensiveness (Tsiachristas et al. 2015) as well as its uptake and successful implementation (Boland et al. 2015) may impact outcomes and costs. Especially the development and implementation costs would increase with complexity (Tsiachristas et al. 2014b). The target population is another determinant of integrated care cost-effectiveness (Tsiachristas et al. 2014a). This may largely be explained by the fact that integrated care involves behavioural aspects. Literature shows that behaviour interventions are highly cost-effective but not for everyone (McDaid et al. 2014). This notion is also shared by the National Institute for Health and Care Excellence (NICE) in England where thorough subgroup analysis is recommended when evaluating behavioural change interventions (NICE 2007). Finally, the existence of economies of scale and economies of scope may influence development and implementation costs of integrated care and therefore its cost-effectiveness (Tsiachristas et al. 2014b).

19.3.9 Policy Evaluation and Implementation Analysis

The implementation of integrated care in many countries was supported by new forms of financing and payments (Nolte et al. 2014; Tsiachristas et al. 2013b; Busse and Mays 2008). This is because adequate funding and payment systems with financial incentives that steer behaviour towards collaboration between professionals are prerequisites for the successful implementation of integrated care (Busse et al. 2010; Scheller-Kreinsen et al. 2009). Examples include the reduction in co-payments for patients participating in disease management programmes in France, the performance based payment system in England that stimulates GP adherence to clinical guidelines, the bundled payment in The Netherlands where care groups receive a single annual payment for a patient to cover the (mostly primary) care for a particular chronic disease. Positive evidence from the implementation of such financial incentives and payment schemes is reported in the literature (Eijkenaar et al. 2013; Song et al. 2014; Rosenthal et al. 2004; de Bakker et al. 2012; Tsiachristas et al. 2016).

These incentives may either be considered as behavioural interventions that are part of an integrated care programme or they may be seen as part of the local context with which the integrated care programme interacts. In the former case, a broad policy evaluation may accommodate the implementation of integrated care and accompanying payment reforms simultaneously. In the latter case, payment reforms could be seen as strategies to successfully implement integrated care. As a result, the application of Value of Implementation analysis (Hoomans et al. 2009; Mason et al. 2001) may be employed to provide the overall cost-effectiveness of implementing integrated care with the support of financial incentives. However, it would be hard to disentangle the impact of the payment reform from the effect of the care reform on health care expenditure and care quality.

19.3.10 Standardised Reporting

Reporting of methods and results should be systematised to allow traceability and transferability of the health economic evidence in integrated care. A thorough description of the interventions provided as part of integrated care, and eventually in the control group, including their timing and intensity and the involved providers should provide a clear understanding of "what" was evaluated. The methods employed and the assumptions made in the economic evaluation should also be clearly stated regarding the "how" was it evaluated and the results of subgroup analysis should highlight "for whom" it was cost-effective. Existing statements such as the CHEERS statement (Husereau et al. 2013), the STROBE statement for observational studies (von Elm et al. 2007), and the disease management quality assessment instrument developed by Steuten et al. (2004) could be used to standardize reporting. Including a periodic evaluation and detailed documentation of the provided interventions (including the control group, if available) in the stream of integrated care interventions, could provide meaningful information about the full and sustainable cost-effectiveness of integrated care.

19.4 Conclusion

The complexity of integrated care and the substantial resources needed to collect reliable data appears to have challenged health economists to evaluate the cost-effectiveness of integrated care to date. Economic evaluations published in health economic journals mostly focus on single elements of integrated care (Gandjour 2010; Scott et al. 2009; Cuellar and Gertler 2006; Dusheiko et al. 2011;

McCullough and Snir 2010). There is need for that to change and health economists to understand the peculiarities of integrated care as intervention under evaluation. On the health services research side, health economists were not involved in many evaluation studies so far, which presumably resulted in low quality evidence on cost-effectiveness. Economic evaluations are frequently piggy back tailed in the effectiveness evaluation of integrated care but this needs to be changed because there is a clear need for better understanding and communication between health economists, researchers from other disciplines, clinicians, payers and decision-makers during the set-up of an evaluation study.

References

Baltussen, R. (2015). Question is not whether but how to use MCDA. *Value and Outcomes Spotlight, Jan–Feb*, 14–16.

Baltussen, R., & Niessen, L. (2006). Priority setting of health interventions: The need for multi-criteria decision analysis. *Cost Effectiveness and Resource Allocation: C/E, 4*, 14.

Barasa, E. W., & English, M. (2011). Viewpoint: Economic evaluation of package of care interventions employing clinical guidelines. *Tropical Medicine & International Health, 16*, 97–104.

Beecham, J., & Knapp, M. (1992). Costing psychiatric interventions. In G. Thornicroft, C. Brewin, & J. Wing (Eds.), *Measuring mental health needs*. London: Gaskell.

Berwick, D. M., Nolan, T. W., & Whittington, J. (2008). The triple aim: Care, health, and cost. *Health Affairs (Project Hope), 27*, 759–769.

Boaz, A., Baeza, J., Fraser, A., & European Implementation Score Collaborative, G. (2011). Effective implementation of research into practice: An overview of systematic reviews of the health literature. *BMC Research Notes, 4*, 212.

Bodenheimer, T., & Handley, M. A. (2009). Goal-setting for behavior change in primary care: An exploration and status report. *Patient Education and Counseling, 76*, 174–180.

Boland, M. R., Kruis, A. L., Huygens, S. A., Tsiachristas, A., Assendelft, W. J., Gussekloo, J., Blom, C. M., Chavannes, N. H., & Rutten-Van Molken, M. P. (2015). Exploring the variation in implementation of a COPD disease management programme and its impact on health outcomes: A post hoc analysis of the RECODE cluster randomised trial. *NPJ Primary Care Respiratory Medicine, 25*, 15071.

Bots, P. W. G., & Hulshof, J. A. M. (2000). Designing multi-criteria decision analysis processes for priority setting in health care. *Journal of Multi-Criteria Decision Analysis, 9*, 56–75.

Bouwmans, C., Krol, M., Severens, H., Koopmanschap, M., Brouwer, W., & Hakkaart-Van Roijen, L. (2015). The iMTA productivity cost questionnaire: A standardized instrument for measuring and valuing health-related productivity losses. *Value in Health, 18*, 753–758.

Busse, R., & Mays, N. (2008). Paying for chronic disease care. In E. Nolte & M. Mckee (Eds.), *Caring for people with chronic conditions: A health system perspective*. Maidenhead: Open University Press.

Busse, R., Blümel, M., Scheller-Kreinsen, D., & Zentner, A. (2010). *Tackling chronic disease in Europe: Strategies, interventions and challenges*. Copenhagen: European Observatory on Health Systems and Policies.

Byford, S., & Sefton, T. (2003). Economic evaluation of complex health and social care interventions. *National Institute Economic Review, 186*, 98–108.

Claxton, K. (2015). Three questions to ask when examining MCDA. *Value and Outcomes Spotlight, 1((1))*, 18–20. Jan–Feb.

Coast, J., Smith, R., & Lorgelly, P. (2008a). Should the capability approach be applied in health economics? *Health Economics, 17*, 667–670.

Coast, J., Smith, R. D., & Lorgelly, P. (2008b). Welfarism, extra-welfarism and capability: The spread of ideas in health economics. *Social Science & Medicine, 67*, 1190–1198.

Coleman, K., Austin, B. T., Brach, C., & Wagner, E. H. (2009). Evidence on the chronic care model in the new millennium. *Health Affairs (Project Hope), 28*, 75–85.

Conklin, A., & Nolte, E. (2010). *Disease management evaluation: A comprehensive review of current state of the art*. Cambridge: RAND Europe.

Conklin, A., Nolte, E., & Vrijhoef, H. (2013). Approaches to chronic disease management evaluation in use in Europe: A review of current methods and performance measures. *International Journal of Technology Assessment in Health Care, 29*, 61–70.

Craig, P., Dieppe, P., Macintyre, S., Michie, S., Nazareth, I., Petticrew, M., & Medical Research Council Guidance. (2008). Developing and evaluating complex interventions: The new Medical Research Council guidance. *BMJ, 337*, a1655.

Craig, P., Cooper, C., Gunnell, D., Haw, S., Lawson, K., Macintyre, S., Ogilvie, D., Petticrew, M., Reeves, B., Sutton, M., & Thompson, S. (2012). Using natural experiments to evaluate population health interventions: New medical research council guidance. *Journal of Epidemiology and Community Health, 66*, 1182–1186.

Cuellar, A. E., & Gertler, P. J. (2006). Strategic integration of hospitals and physicians. *Journal of Health Economics, 25*, 1–28.

Davalos, M. E., French, M. T., Burdick, A. E., & Simmons, S. C. (2009). Economic evaluation of telemedicine: Review of the literature and research guidelines for benefit-cost analysis. *Telemedicine Journal and E-Health, 15*, 933–948.

de Bakker, D. H., Struijs, J. N., Baan, C. B., Raams, J., de Wildt, J. E., Vrijhoef, H. J., & Schut, F. T. (2012). Early results from adoption of bundled payment for diabetes care in the Netherlands show improvement in care coordination. *Health Affairs (Project Hope), 31*, 426–433.

Downing, A., Rudge, G., Cheng, Y., Tu, Y. K., Keen, J., & Gilthorpe, M. S. (2007). Do the UK government's new Quality and Outcomes Framework (QOF) scores adequately measure primary care performance? A cross-sectional survey of routine healthcare data. *BMC Health Services Research, 7*, 166.

Drummond, M. F., Sculpher, M. J., Torrance, G. W., O'Brien, B. J., & Stoddart, G. L. (2005). *Methods for the economic evaluation of health care programmes*. Oxford: Oxford University Press.

Dusheiko, M., Gravelle, H., Martin, S., Rice, N., & Smith, P. C. (2011). Does better disease management in primary care reduce hospital costs? Evidence from English primary care. *Journal of Health Economics, 30*, 919–932.

Edwards, R. T., Charles, J. M., & Lloyd-Williams, H. (2013). Public health economics: A systematic review of guidance for the economic evaluation of public health interventions and discussion of key methodological issues. *BMC Public Health, 13*, 1001.

Eijkenaar, F., Emmert, M., Scheppach, M., & Schoffski, O. (2013). Effects of pay for performance in health care: A systematic review of systematic reviews. *Health Policy, 110*, 115–130.

Epping-Jordan, J. E., Pruitt, S. D., Bengoa, R., & Wagner, E. H. (2004). Improving the quality of health care for chronic conditions. *Quality & Safety in Health Care, 13*, 299–305.

Evers, S. M. (2010). Value of integrated care: Revival of the monetary valuation of health care benefits. *International Journal of Integrated Care, 10*, e045.

Gandjour, A. (2010). A model to predict the cost-effectiveness of disease management programs. *Health Economics, 19*, 697–715.

Goetghebeur, M. M., Wagner, M., Khoury, H., Levitt, R. J., Erickson, L. J., & Rindress, D. (2012). Bridging health technology assessment (HTA) and efficient health care decision making with multicriteria decision analysis (MCDA): Applying the EVIDEM framework to medicines appraisal. *Medical Decision Making: An International Journal of the Society for Medical Decision Making, 32*, 376–388.

Goldie, S. J., Goldhaber-Fiebert, J. D., & Garnett, G. P. (2006). Chapter 18: Public health policy for cervical cancer prevention: The role of decision science, economic evaluation, and mathematical modeling. *Vaccine, 24*(Suppl. 3), S3/155–S3/163.

Gray, A. M., Clarke, P. M., Wolstenholme, J. L., & Wordsworth, S. (2011). *Applied methods of cost-effectiveness analysis in health care*. Oxford: Oxford University Press.

Griffin, S., Rice, N., & Sculpher, M. (2009). Economic evaluation of public health interventions. In A. Killoran & M. P. Kelly (Eds.), *Evidence-based public health: Effectiveness and efficieny*. Oxford: Oxford University Press.

Ham, C. (2010). The ten characteristics of the high-performing chronic care system. *Health Economics, Policy, and Law, 5*, 71–90.

Hawe, P., Shiell, A., & Riley, T. (2004). Complex interventions: How "out of control" can a randomised controlled trial be? *BMJ, 328*, 1561–1563.

Hoefman, R. J., van Exel, N. J. A., & Brouwer, W. B. F. (2011). *iMTA valuation of informal care questionnaire: Version 1.0*. Rotterdam: Institute for Medical Technology Assessment.

Hoomans, T., Fenwick, E. A., Palmer, S., & Claxton, K. (2009). Value of information and value of implementation: Application of an analytic framework to inform resource allocation decisions in metastatic hormone-refractory prostate cancer. *Value in Health, 12*, 315–324.

Huber, M., Knottnerus, J. A., Green, L., van der Horst, H., Jadad, A. R., Kromhout, D., Leonard, B., Lorig, K., Loureiro, M. I., van der Meer, J. W., Schnabel, P., Smith, R., van Weel, C., & Smid, H. (2011). How should we define health? *BMJ, 343*, d4163.

Husereau, D., Drummond, M., Petrou, S., Carswell, C., Moher, D., Greenberg, D., Augustovski, F., Briggs, A. H., Mauskopf, J., Loder, E., & Force, C. T. (2013). Consolidated Health Economic Evaluation Reporting Standards (CHEERS) statement. *BMJ, 346*, f1049.

Hussey, M. A., & Hughes, J. P. (2007). Design and analysis of stepped wedge cluster randomized trials. *Contemporary Clinical Trials, 28*, 182–191.

Ijzerman, M. J., & Steuten, L. M. (2011). Early assessment of medical technologies to inform product development and market access: A review of methods and applications. *Applied Health Economics and Health Policy, 9*, 331–347.

Johns, B., Baltussen, R., & Hutubessy, R. (2003). Programme costs in the economic evaluation of health interventions. *Cost Effectiveness and Resource Allocation: C/E, 1*, 1.

Kind, P., Lafata, J. E., Matuszewski, K., & Raisch, D. (2009). The use of QALYs in clinical and patient decision-making: Issues and prospects. *Value in Health, 12*(Suppl. 1), S27–S30.

Knai, C., Nolte, E., Brunn, M., Elissen, A., Conklin, A., Pedersen, J. P., Brereton, L., Erler, A., Frolich, A., Flamm, M., Fullerton, B., Jacobsen, R., Krohn, R., Saz-Parkinson, Z., Vrijhoef, B., Chevreul, K., Durand-Zaleski, I., Farsi, F., Sarria-Santamera, A., & Soennichsen, A. (2013). Reported barriers to evaluation in chronic care: Experiences in six European countries. *Health Policy, 110*, 220–228.

Mason, J., Freemantle, N., Nazareth, I., Eccles, M., Haines, A., & Drummond, M. (2001). When is it cost-effective to change the behavior of health professionals? *JAMA: The Journal of the American Medical Association, 286*, 2988–2992.

Mathes, T., Jacobs, E., Morfeld, J. C., & Pieper, D. (2013). Methods of international health technology assessment agencies for economic evaluations–a comparative analysis. *BMC Health Services Research, 13*, 371.

Mattke, S., Bergamo, G., Balakrishnan, A., Martino, S., & Vakkur, N. (2006). *Measuring and reporting the performance of disease management programs*. Santa Monica, CA: RAND Health.

McCullough, J. S., & Snir, E. M. (2010). Monitoring technology and firm boundaries: Physician-hospital integration and technology utilization. *Journal of Health Economics, 29*, 457–467.

McDaid, D., Oliver, A., & Merkur, S. (2014). *What do we know about the strengths and weakness of different policy mechanisms to influence health behaviour in the population?* Copenhagen: European Observatory on Health Systems and Policies.

Mogyorosy, Z., & Smith, P. (2005). *The main methodological issues in costing health care services: A literature review*. York: Centre for Health Economics, University of York.

NICE. (2007, October). *National institute for health and care excellence, behaviour change: The principles for effective interventions*. guidance.nice.org.uk/ph6. Manchester: NICE public health guidance 6.

Nolte, E., & Pitchforth, E. (2014). *What is the evidence on the economic impacts of integrated care?* Copenhagen: European Observatory on Health Systems and Policies.

Nolte, E., Conklin, A., Adams, J., Brunn, M., Cadier, M., Chevreul, K., Durand-Zaleski, I., Elissen, A., Erler, A., Flamm, M., Frølich, A., Fullerton, B., Jacobsen, R., Knai, C., Krohn, R., Pöhlmann, B., Saz Parkinson, Z., Sarria Santamera, A., Sönnichsen, A., & Vrijhoef, H. (2012). *Evaluating chronic disease management: Recommendations for funders and users.* Cambridge: RAND Europe.

Nolte, E., Knai, C., & Saltman, R. B. (2014). *Assesing chronic disease management in European health systems: Concepts and approaches, Observatory Studies Series.* Copenhagen: European Observatory on Health Systems and Policies.

Ouwens, M., Wollersheim, H., Hermens, R., Hulscher, M., & Grol, R. (2005). Integrated care programmes for chronically ill patients: A review of systematic reviews. *International Journal for Quality in Health Care: Journal of the International Society for Quality in Health Care/Isqua, 17,* 141–146.

Parkin, D., Morris, S., & Devlin, N. (2015). Economic appraisal in public healthcare: Assessing efficiency and equity. In R. Detels, M. Gulliford, Q. A. Karim, & C. C. Tan (Eds.), *Oxford textbook of global public health* (6th ed.). Oxford: Oxford University Press.

Paulus, A., van Raak, A., & Keijzer, F. (2002). ABC: The pathway to comparison of the costs of integrated care. *Public Money And Management, Jul–Sep,* 25–32.

Paulus, A. T., van Raak, A. J., & Maarse, H. J. (2008). Is integrated nursing home care cheaper than traditional care? A cost comparison. *International Journal of Nursing Studies, 45,* 1764–1777.

Payne, K., Mcallister, M., & Davies, L. M. (2013). Valuing the economic benefits of complex interventions: When maximising health is not sufficient. *Health Economics, 22,* 258–271.

Rickles, D. (2009). Causality in complex interventions. *Medicine, Health Care, and Philosophy, 12,* 77–790.

Rosenthal, M. B., Fernandopulle, R., Song, H. R., & Landon, B. (2004). Paying for quality: Providers' incentives for quality improvement. *Health Affairs (Project Hope), 23,* 127–141.

Scheller-Kreinsen, D., Blümel, M., & Busse, R. (2009). Chronic disease management in Europe. *Eurohealth, 15,* 1–4.

Scott, A., Schurer, S., Jensen, P. H., & Sivey, P. (2009). The effects of an incentive program on quality of care in diabetes management. *Health Economics, 18,* 1091–1108.

Sculpher, M. J., Pang, F. S., Manca, A., Drummond, M. F., Golder, S., Urdahl, H., Davies, L. M., & Eastwood, A. (2004). Generalisability in economic evaluation studies in healthcare: A review and case studies. *Health Technology Assessment, 8*(III–IV), 1–192.

Serxner, S., Baker, K., & Gold, D. (2006). Guidelines for analysis of economic return from health management programs. *American Journal of Health Promotion, 20*(Suppl), 1–17.

Shiell, A., Hawe, P., & Gold, L. (2008). Complex interventions or complex systems? Implications for health economic evaluation. *BMJ, 336,* 1281–1283.

Song, Z., Rose, S., Safran, D. G., Landon, B. E., Day, M. P., & Chernew, M. E. (2014). Changes in health care spending and quality 4 years into global payment. *The New England Journal of Medicine, 371,* 1704–1714.

Steuten, L. M., Vrijhoef, H. J., van Merode, G. G., Severens, J. L., & Spreeuwenberg, C. (2004). The health technology assessment-disease management instrument reliably measured methodologic quality of health technology assessments of disease management. *Journal of Clinical Epidemiology, 57,* 881–888.

Steuten, L., Vrijhoef, B., Severens, H., van Merode, F., & Spreeuwenberg, C. (2006a). Are we measuring what matters in health technology assessment of disease management? Systematic literature review. *International Journal of Technology Assessment in Health Care, 22,* 47–57.

Steuten, L., Vrijhoef, B., van Merode, F., Wesseling, G. J., & Spreeuwenberg, C. (2006b). Evaluation of a regional disease management programme for patients with asthma or chronic obstructive pulmonary disease. *International Journal for Quality in Health Care: Journal of The International Society for Quality in Health Care/Isqua, 18,* 429–436.

Stuart, E. A., Huskamp, H. A., Duckworth, K., Simmons, J., Song, Z., Chernew, M., & Barry, C. L. (2014). Using propensity scores in difference-in-differences models to estimate the effects of a policy change. *Health Services & Outcomes Research Methodology, 14,* 166–182.

Thokala, P., Devlin, N., Marsh, K., Baltussen, R., Boysen, M., Kalo, Z., Longrenn, T., Mussen, F., Peacock, S., Watkins, J., & Ijzerman, M. (2016). Multiple criteria decision analysis for health care decision making-an introduction: Report 1 of the ISPOR MCDA emerging good practices task force. *Value in Health, 19*, 1–13.

Thorn, J. C., Coast, J., Cohen, D., Hollingworth, W., Knapp, M., Noble, S. M., Ridyard, C., Wordsworth, S., & Hughes, D. (2013). Resource-use measurement based on patient recall: Issues and challenges for economic evaluation. *Applied Health Economics and Health Policy, 11*, 155–161.

Tsai, A. C., Morton, S. C., Mangione, C. M., & Keeler, E. B. (2005). A meta-analysis of interventions to improve care for chronic illnesses. *American Journal of Managed Care, 11*, 478–488.

Tsiachristas, A. (2015). *Payment and economic evaluation of integrated care*. PhD Dissertation, Erasmus University Rotterdam.

Tsiachristas, A., Cramm, J. M., Nieboer, A., & Rutten-Van Molken, M. (2013a). Broader economic evaluation of disease management programs using multi-criteria decision analysis. *International Journal of Technology Assessment in Health Care, 29*, 301–308.

Tsiachristas, A., Dikkers, C., Boland, M. R., & Rutten-Van Molken, M. P. (2013b). Exploring payment schemes used to promote integrated chronic care in Europe. *Health Policy, 113*, 296–304.

Tsiachristas, A., Cramm, J. M., Nieboer, A. P., & Rutten-Van Molken, M. P. (2014a). Changes in costs and effects after the implementation of disease management programs in The Netherlands: Variability and determinants. *Cost Effectiveness and Resource Allocation*. doi:10.1186/1478-7547-12-17. eCollection 2014.

Tsiachristas, A., Hipple Waters, B., Adams, S. A., & Rutten-Van Mölken, M. P. M. H. (2014b). Identifying and explaining the variability in development and implementation costs of disease management programs in The Netherlands. *BMC Health Services Research, 14*, 518.

Tsiachristas, A., Burgers, L., & Rutten-Van Mölken, M. P. M. H. (2015). Cost-effectiveness of disease management programs for cardiovascular risk and COPD in The Netherlands. *Value in Health, 18*, 977–986.

Tsiachristas, A., Dikkers, C., Boland, M., & Rutten Van Molken, M. (2016). Impact of financial agreements in European chronic care on health care expenditure growth. *Health Policy, 120*, 420–430.

van Herck, P., Annemans, L., de Smedt, D., Remmen, R., & Sermeus, W. (2011). Pay-for-performance step-by-step: Introduction to the MIMIQ model. *Health Policy, 102*, 8–17.

von Elm, E., Altman, D. G., Egger, M., Pocock, S. J., Gotzsche, P. C., Vandenbroucke, J. P., & Initiative, S. (2007). The strengthening the reporting of observational studies in epidemiology (STROBE) statement: Guidelines for reporting observational studies. *Lancet, 370*, 1453–1457.

Vondeling, H. (2004). Economic evaluation of integrated care: An introduction. *International Journal of Integrated Care, 4*, e20.

Weatherly, H., Drummond, M., Claxton, K., Cookson, R., Ferguson, B., Godfrey, C., Rice, N., Sculpher, M., & Sowden, A. (2009). Methods for assessing the cost-effectiveness of public health interventions: Key challenges and recommendations. *Health Policy, 93*, 85–92.

Weingarten, S. R., Henning, J. M., Badamgarav, E., Knight, K., Hasselblad, V., Gano Jr., A., & Ofman, J. J. (2002). Interventions used in disease management programmes for patients with chronic illness-which ones work? Meta-analysis of published reports. *BMJ, 325*, 925.

Welte, R., Feenstra, T., Jager, H., & Leidl, R. (2004). A decision chart for assessing and improving the transferability of economic evaluation results between countries. *PharmacoEconomics, 22*, 857–876.

WHO. (2011). *Global status report on noncommunicable diseases: 2010*. Geneva: World Health Organization.

WHO. (2015). *People-centred and integrated health services: An overview of the evidence (Interim Report)*. Geneva: World Health Organization.

Zwar, N., Harris, M., Griffiths, R., Roland, M., Dennis, S., Davies, G. P., & Hasan, H. (2006). *A systematic review of chronic disease management*. Canberra: Australian Primary Health Care Research Institute.

Claims Data for Evaluation

20

Enno Swart

20.1 Background

Integrated care aims at reorganizing and/or continuously enhancing care structures and processes to improve patient-related outcomes and economic results in standard every-day care. It also aims to boost patients' and care providers' satisfaction with and acceptance of medical care. The question is therefore to what extent we may use data generated in standard care when it comes to evaluating integrated care.

Contrary to traditional clinical research which relies on randomized studies to explore the efficiency of new approaches in therapy in a standardized defined clinical setting with typically closely defined inclusion and exclusion criteria of study participants, claims data offers opportunities for a higher external validity (often at the expense of a lower internal validity) without narrowing down the patients involved in advance.

This paper will examine if claims data generated in standard medical care is suitable for evaluating integrated care. To do so, we need to describe the structure and contents of relevant data and explain its advantages as well as the methodological challenges of using such data for evaluation research. Selected short examples will illustrate how to use the data and the conclusions drawn from the results for practical application. This paper ends with a description of the potential of the data in addition to approaches pursued in clinical research. In order to do so we will examine to what extent the conclusions drawn for Germany can be applied to other countries based on a number of examples.

E. Swart (✉)
Medical Faculty, Institute für Social Medicine and Health Economics (ISMHE),
Otto-von-Guericke-University Magdeburg, Magdeburg, Germany
e-mail: enno.swart@med.ovgu.de

© Springer International Publishing AG 2017
V. Amelung et al. (eds.), *Handbook Integrated Care*,
DOI 10.1007/978-3-319-56103-5_20

20.2   Claims Data

In 2014, approximately 70 million people, i.e. about 85% of the German population, had statutory health insurance. Civil servants, members of the police and armed forces, freelancers and self-employed people are not required to have statutory health insurance. They must or can take out private health insurance. Employees subject to statutory health insurance whose income exceeds the income threshold have the right to opt for either statutory or private health insurance. Family members (spouses that do not work and children) are covered by the insurance plan (family insurance) of the income earner (Bormann and Swart 2014).

A catalog binding for all currently existing 110-plus statutory health insurers (as of spring 2017) lists the mandatory services covered by statutory health insurance plans. It comprises medical, dental and psychotherapeutic services provided in inpatient and outpatient care (including prevention measures such as vaccinations or screening), drug prescriptions and prescriptions of remedies and medical aids (e.g., physical therapy and ergotherapy or wheelchairs, optical aids) as well as medical rehabilitation if not covered by other social welfare services (e.g., the statutory pension insurance fund) and expenses for sick pay for people with a long-term work incapacity. The services mentioned make up about 90% of the total expenditure of more than €200 billion (2015; see www.gkv-spitzenverband.de).

Services are provided as non-cash benefits. That means that the statutory health insurers or self-governing bodies directly or indirectly pay doctors and non-medical service providers for their services. Insured people only pay for services not listed in the statutory health insurance service catalog or for over-the-counter drugs. This does not apply to limited contributions paid by the insurant for drug prescriptions and prescriptions of remedies and medical aids, dental prostheses or hospitalization.

All services covered by statutory health insurance are subject to standardized documentation, which the German Social Code (Book V) regulates specifically for each care sector (Swart 2014) (see Table 20.1), and are thus available for scientific use under certain conditions. Due to the system, statutory health insurers do not document services paid for by the insurant.

In summary, the data comprises socio-demographic information about the insured person (age, gender, place of residence, to a limited extent social attributes such as education and income, insurance periods, in case of death the day of death (but not the cause of death)), diagnoses documented by outpatient health care providers and hospitals (ICD coded). However, collected data not only includes the diagnosis to be treated but also secondary diagnoses, outpatient medical services as well as diagnostic, operative (surgical) and therapeutic services provided by hospitals (coded according to OPS), the type and quantity of drug given out by pharmacies (ATC coded), the type and quantities of remedies and medical aids provided. The information also includes the date of the services provided, the duration of work incapacity and the diagnosis justifying it. A precise description of the structure and content of claims data is contained in Swart et al. (2014).

Table 20.1 Provisions in the Social Code Book V on the transmission of routine data from the statutory health insurance

	Health care sector	Case-related contents (among others)[a]
§295	Outpatient care	Type of case (e.g., direct contact, referral, emergency), specialties of the treating physician and any referring physician, diagnoses (ICD), services (uniform value scale ['Einheitlicher Bewertungsmaßstab'; EBM], German procedure classification ['Operationen- und Prozedurenschlüssel'; OPS])
§295	Incapacity to work	Diagnosis (ICD) that justifies the incapacity to work, initial versus follow-up certificate
§300	Pharmaceutical prescriptions	Proprietary medicinal products; central pharmaceutical number (PZN) indicates active ingredient, price, and quantity of the pharmaceutical (anatomic-therapeutic-chemical-[ATC]-Code); prescription date
§301	Inpatient care	Admitting hospital, diagnoses at admission and discharge, secondary diagnoses (ICD), procedures and diagnostics (OPS), reimbursement (DRG), reason for admission and discharge, date of admission and discharge
§302	Prescriptions of non-pharmaceutical therapies and technical aids	Rendered services by type, quantity, and price, as well as medical diagnosis

[a]Member-related data (age, sex, etc.) are available for every sector. Source: Swart (2014)

This paper will only examine the use of claims data provided by statutory health insurers and not look at administrative data collected by other social security providers that may also be used for scientific purposes under certain conditions (Swart et al. 2014).

The paper primarily focuses on the situation in Germany where specific (strict) general conditions exist pertaining to the scientific use of health insurance claims data. The methodological considerations of the strengths and weaknesses of the data also apply to claims data from other countries. At the end of this paper, we will list a number of general criteria that may be used to assess the usability of claims data for evaluation purposes.

20.3 Methodological Aspects of Using Claims Data

The administrative data collected by statutory health insurers primarily serves to pay for medical services. This primary purpose of use defines the provisions, the variables to be transmitted and the type of coding. This circumstance must always be taken into consideration when discussing the advantages and drawbacks of the scientific use of claims data (also referred to as "secondary data" in Germany because of this secondary use) particularly in the context of evaluating integrated care. The characteristics of the data determine its validity and later processing as central steps prior to the actual analysis of the data. What follows is a short description of the strengths illustrating why the data is suited for research.

- *As it relates to population*: With the help of the data it is possible to calculate epidemiological parameters that are typically calculated as the rate of an absolute number of target events as the numerator and a definable and quantifiable population denominator. This makes it possible to show treatment frequency (e.g., the number of diabetic patients per 1000 insured people) or identifiable events (e.g., the number of hospital stays of patients diagnosed with diabetes as their principle diagnosis). It can be further differentiated by age, gender and other insurance or disease-related characteristics. Incidences (new diseases or more precisely the first documentation of a diagnosis) and prevalence (number of patients treated or documented with a certain diagnosis) can be determined accurately using standard statutory health insurance data based on the number of insured persons at a certain date or within an observation period (so-called population at risk). For instance, this makes it possible to determine the number of insurants in a defined integrated care project. Typically, information about the use of medical services obtained from primary surveys as well as from other secondary data (from doctor's offices, hospitals or disease registers) does not relate to the population to the same precise extent (Grobe and Ihle 2014).
- *As it relates to individual persons*: Claims data collected by statutory health insurers is so important for evaluating specific care options and structures because care processes pertaining to individual insured persons (for example within an integrated care project) can be mapped both retrospectively and prospectively over a longer period of time for that person. With the help of a person's health insurance number, pseudonymized for scientific use, all contacts of that patient can be combined across sectors and irrespective of the service provided and the place of service provision (Grobe and Ihle 2014). However, statistics relating only to incidents and sectors lack this feature and cannot be differentiated by individual insurants. For instance, it is not possible to derive from official German diagnosis statistics how many patients account for the more than 19 million hospitalizations in Germany (2013; see www.gbe-bund. de).
- *As relating to place of residence and location*: Based on the postal code of the insurant's place of residence, it is possible to map epidemiological data on a regional level. No other care data currently has the ability to depict the care context with a clear population reference on a small-scale regional level. By adhering to data protection regulations, it is also possible to perform local care analyses with regard to service providers (Swart et al. 2008). Below we will describe how this feature is used to evaluate an integrated care project in a control group design.
- *Completeness*: Since the data is used for payment purposes we can assume that most claims data is nearly 100% complete and thus the danger of a selective reporting bias, which is always a problem with primary surveys, is very low. However, the data is only complete with regards to services covered by statutory

health insurance. By definition, it does not include information on privately paid services (see above) such as over-the-counter medicine. This information is not systematically documented. Short-term sick leave of no more than 3 days is also underrepresented in the data on work incapacity because employees are obliged by law to furnish a certificate of incapacity for work starting on the fourth day of sick absence (Meyer 2014).

- *Data quality*: In view of its primary use, standard claims data is assessed for completeness and correctness, e.g., with regard to the consistency of information on diagnoses and surgery relevant for compensation. At the same time one should keep in mind that the data owner must separately assess the validity of data variables not assessed for quality, such as information on departments or the reason for hospital admission. One should also take note of the fact that the diagnoses entered must first be understood as diagnoses eligible for compensation that must be validated internally and possibly externally in a disease-specific analysis (Schubert et al. 2010; Schubert and Köster 2014).
- *Expenses*: Claims data is generated in a standardized way as part of standard care procedures. In terms of costs, the care researcher is particularly interested in expenses incurred by the data owner for data processing, provision and transmission. Normally the data is available in a form easily suitable for further computer-assisted processing. However, the financial and personnel costs arising in connection with providing claims data may oppose the intended scientific use in light of the standard responsibilities of the data owner (Reis 2005; Holle et al. 2005).

More in-depth insights regarding the content and methodological aspects of analyzing and processing claims data can be found in Swart (2014) and the monograph by Swart et al. (2014) and the individual descriptions of sector-specific data in these works.

20.4 Methods

In the 1990s, the science community first published several basic fundamental publications on the chances and perspectives of using health and social data (von Ferber and Behrens 1997). However, the concrete use and development of specific approaches and methods for analyzing and processing this data was limited to a few working groups, until at the beginning of this century when a larger group of researchers discovered the opportunities the data offers as a result of the establishment of care research and its linkage with clinical subjects. The memoranda of the German Network of Care Research (Deutsches Netzwerk Versorgungsforschung; see www.netzwerk-versorgungsforschung.de) expressly talk about the equal usage of secondary data and primary data (Glaeske et al. 2009; Neugebauer et al. 2010).

This development called for transparency beyond the data itself as a prerequisite for scientific use and validated methods for processing and analysis. To this end, researchers could rely on existing standards of statistics and epidemiology only to a limited extent. Good epidemiologic practice insufficiently accounted/accounts for the specific general conditions and preconditions of methodologically grounded secondary data analysis (Hoffmann et al. 2005). This encouraged the work group on secondary data collection and usage ("Arbeitsgruppe Erhebung und Nutzung von Sekundärdaten" (AGENS)) of the German Society of Social Medicine and Prevention (Deutsche Gesellschaft für Sozialmedizin und Prävention; DGSMP) and the German Society for Epidemiology (DGEpi) to develop a good practice of secondary data analysis based on the standards of good epidemiologic practice which was published for the first time in 2005 and has been revised twice since (Swart et al. 2015; available both in German and English online at www.dgepi.de).

At the same time, the use of this data became easier and was fostered by the fact that the handbooks (Swart and Ihle 2005; Swart et al. 2014) not only described the contents of claims data in great detail but that they contained numerous descriptive examples of application as well as a description of the relevant specific processes such as (diagnosis) validation, risk adjustment or matching (Horenkamp-Sonntag et al. 2014; Mostardt et al. 2014; Lux et al. 2014).

In light of the specific German context, AGENS currently works on modifying the well-known STROBE statement (Vandenbroucke et al. 2007) since this reporting standard does not address a large number of important aspects of secondary data analysis required for a critical assessment. After publication of a first draft of the so-called STROSA checklist (STandardized Reporting of Secondary Data Analyses; Swart and Schmitt 2014) a working group of AGENS revised this checklist and presented a new version recently (Swart et al. 2016). Parallel, an international initiative published a similar reporting format named "RECORD (Reporting of studies Conducted using Observational Routinely-collected Health Data)" on the basis of STROBE (Nichols et al. 2015; Benchimol et al. 2015; see www.record-statement.org).

20.5 Prerequisites for Data Usage

In Germany, the scientific use of claims data is subject to strict legal requirements. As data owners, health insurers may use this primarily administrative data only within the scope of their responsibilities pursuant to their by laws, defined in the German Social Code, Book V [online available on the website of the German Federal Ministry of Health; http://www.bundesgesundheitsministerium.de/].

The further use of the data by third parties is also limited by its special character as "social data". It is not only protected by German data protection law (Bundesdatenschutzgesetz; available on the website of the German Federal Commissioner of Data Protection and Freedom of Information (http://www.bfdi.bund.de/) but also by the restrictions stipulated by the German Social Code, Book X, which makes usage subject to meeting strict requirements. It permits, however data utilization for research if it is necessary for reaching the research objective and if the public interest in the research considerably outweighs the private interests of those concerned with keeping their data private. If the researcher can reasonably be expected to obtain the informed consent of the participants in the study, s/he is obliged to do so (March et al. 2014b). The supervisory authorities of the relevant data owners will assess in a specific application process if the prerequisites have been fulfilled. In addition, researchers and data owners are obliged to conclude an agreement regulating their collaboration pursuant to the requirements of good practice of secondary data analysis (Swart et al. 2015).

In view of the research process, the large number of regulations that need to be adhered to regarding the use of claims data means that from the very beginning and at the time of determining the study design it is essential to take data protection, technical, legal and organizational aspects into consideration and to calculate expenses in terms of time as well as personnel and financial costs.

For other countries, the technical and legal requirements of using claims data for evaluating integrated care must be assessed specifically. It is no secret that researchers in Germany face particularly high legal hurdles.

20.6 Examples

Two briefly described evaluation approaches to complex integrated care programs aimed primarily at chronically sick people and older insurants in Germany serve to illustrate the usability of claims data for care and evaluation research and the resulting insights and methodological further developments. For more details about these programs we suggest further reading. We will briefly shed light on the data used, the design on which the evaluation is based and its results.

20.6.1 Evaluating Disease Management Programs

Implemented since 2002 for defined chronic diseases (diabetes mellitus type 1 and 2, breast cancer, asthma or coronary obstructive pulmonary disease, coronary heart disease), disease management programs (DMP) are structured treatment programs for chronically ill patients covered by statutory health insurance. They aim to provide coordinated care by general practitioners (GPs) and specialists in the outpatient sector and hospitals in line with applicable guidelines. By actively involving patients and individually determining care objectives, DMP strive to improve the quality of mid- and long-term care and to make it more effective. In Germany, disease management programs require accreditation by the responsible supervisory body (German Federal Insurance Authority; Bundesversicherungsamt) and are subject to the standardized documentation of all patients enrolled and mandatory evaluation. Participation in DMPs is free for registered doctors and patients (Stock et al. 2010).

Since participation is voluntary and there is no control group design, fundamental methodological difficulties arise when it comes to performing a scientifically sound evaluation of the programs and comparing the mid- and long-term outcomes with regard to enrolled and non-enrolled insurants. The sole pre-post comparison of care outcomes based on the standard documentation of insurants enrolled in the program only cannot be used as valid proof of the program's success due to assumed selection effects (Birnbaum and Braun 2010).

With the help of claims data provided by statutory health insurers it is possible to differentiate between enrolled and non-enrolled insurants. At the same time it is possible to map hard endpoints of care, e.g., in case of diabetes mellitus hospital stays due to a derailed metabolism or obvious complications or long-term damage. Therefore, it should not come as a surprise that claims data has been used several times for the controlled evaluation of disease management programs.

So far, most studies available based on claims data have examined DMPs for diabetes mellitus. Following a survival period approach, Miksch et al. (2010) hint at the fact that the overall mortality of enrolled patients may be lower compared with a control group of non-enrolled diabetics that is formed based on age, gender, pension status, federal state, medicine provision costs, and diagnostic groups. A study by Stock et al. (2010) where a propensity-score technique was applied to guarantee the structural equality of the intervention and control group came to similar conclusions. Linder et al. (2011) provide complex results because DMP patients had fewer emergency hospital stays and less hospital costs but the intensity of outpatient care and pharmacotherapy increased.

It can be said that beyond all similarities and differences, claims data is generally suited for complex controlled evaluation designs facilitating a validated comparison of patients in different care regimes by controlling a number of confounders. However, structural equivalence can only be guaranteed with regard to features that the claims data depicts. "Soft" patient-related qualities such as health-related behaviour or health models that fundamentally impact participation in a DMP but that cannot be operationalized in the claims data, can't be excluded as further determinants of the differences observed. This could explain why the three groups of researchers are hesitant in interpreting the effectiveness of DMPs.

20.6.2 Gesundes Kinzigtal

The triple aim evaluation of the "Gesundes Kinzigtal" project is an outstanding example of the use of secondary data to evaluate integrated care (IC). Running since 2005, the project has aimed at establishing new regional care structures involving and coordinating medical and non-medical service providers from all health care sectors plus other service partners such as sports clubs, etc. The integrated care concept strives to (a) improve the health of the target population, (b) optimize individual care for individual patients, and (c) make health care more resource-efficient in general.

The evaluation of the project rests on several qualitative and quantitative modules comprising; surveys of service providers and patients as well as the scientific supervision of individual projects (Mnich et al. 2013). However, the focus is on using claims data provided by the two statutory health insurers involved (AOK Baden-Württemberg and LKK Baden-Württemberg). The data is used for a comprehensive evaluation of the overall project and to identify and reduce excessive, insufficient and wrong care provision. The data serves to explain the development of care quality in the Kinzigtal valley for selected frequent, primarily chronic diseases by applying parameters based on medical care guidelines (Hildebrand et al. 2015).

The use of claims data for insured persons who voluntarily enrolled in the IC project is based on a permission given at the time of enrollment (Swart et al. 2011). Moreover, the service data of all insurants living in the Kinzigtal valley may be used to compare developments in the Kinzigtal valley with a representative sample of insurants living outside the valley. The evaluation is based on a quasi-experimental controlled prospective study design (Hildebrand et al. 2012) using standard claims data and the deduction of validated raw and standardized outcome parameters. This includes, for example, the percentage of insured persons taking medication in accordance with guidelines or prescription costs incurred by the insurant.

In detail, service data from all care sectors is used with the contents described above. Target diseases may be: chronic coronary heart disease, heart failure, diabetes mellitus, psychiatric conditions (incl. depression), dementia, chronic back pain. According to preliminary analyses, the evaluation shows in case of the indications mentioned for twelve out of a total of 36 process and structural indicators a significantly better development for all people insured in the Kinzigtal valley compared to a comparative age and gender-standardized population. For ten indicators they found a slight, insignificant improvement or an analogous development, and only with regard to four indicators developments in the Kinzigtal valley were not as positive as in the comparative region. Except for the supply with remedies, the Kinzigtal valley exhibits a relative reduction of health care costs (Hildebrand et al. 2015).

The strength of this evaluative approach based on claims data is that because of the intention-to-treat approach we may exclude selective distortions due to the preferred registration of so-called "good risks". This makes it more difficult to evaluate other intervention programs such as the DMPs described (Siegel et al. 2014). By deriving indicators based on guidelines, it becomes clear that claims data can be used in a clinical care context closing the gap to clinical subjects. Finally, the individual permission given by the insured persons enrolled in the model makes it possible to individually link primary and secondary data in the scope of specific evaluation studies (Swart et al. 2011).

This paper cannot further detail the large number of other examples of using claims data for evaluating standard care provision. In a review published in 2009, Hoffmann (2009) already identified 70 publications from Germany alone in the field of pharmaco-epidemiology. The scientific use of this data has further increased. As an example of the opportunities, which is by no means exhaustive, we would like to mention the evaluation of complications following (screening) colonoscopies (Stock et al. 2013), the determination of expenses for (standard) diabetes care (Köster et al. 2014), the effectiveness of various forms of geriatric rehabilitation (Abbas et al. 2015), guideline-based heart attack care (Egen-Lappe et al. 2013), the extent of contra-indicated drug supply (Schubert et al. 2013) or mapping the mid- and long-term quality of hospital care (Klauber et al. 2014).

Other examples illustrating the usage of claims data for transparency purposes are included in the annual sector-specific reports issued by large statutory health insurers and their umbrella organizations, e.g., report on medicine, absence, care, hospitals or remedies and medical aids published by the AOK Bundesverband (www.bv.aok.de) or the dentist, physician or care report by BARMER (www. barmer.de).

20.7 Limitations

The specific characteristics of standard statutory health insurance data and the short examples indicate the wide range of opportunities for use in evaluation research. This was already clear 30 years ago in the context of assessing the quality of surgical therapies: "Insurance claims data are population based, covering all services provided to a defined population regardless of where the care is obtained. [...] Their low cost and routine availability facilitate their use for monitoring outcomes over long periods. They are free of the reporting bias and inadequate follow-up that afflict case series studies and avoid the high costs required when special registries are organized." (Wennberg et al. 1987).

Nonetheless, we should not overlook the limitations of this claims data. In this context, two issues need to be stressed, i.e., the validity of diagnostic information and the transferability of the results of such studies to other populations when the analysis is based on claims data pertaining to a single or a small number of health insurers. A patient-related comparison of diagnostic information contained in GP patient records and diagnostic information contained in claims data found a considerable amount of underreporting in standard health insurance data (in 30% of the cases) mainly pertaining to frequent, less serious GP diagnoses and chronic diseases not treated with medication. At the same time it revealed the over-reporting (in 19% of the cases) of currently not treated permanent diagnoses (Erler et al. 2009). Another study using claims data only revealed deficits in the continuous documentation of chronic diseases and inconsistencies between diagnostic coding and prescriptions of specific medication (Giersiepen et al. 2007).

The possibilities of using outpatient claims data since 2004 in connection with the coding of diagnostic safety introduced bindingly have increased the validity of diagnosis-related incidence and prevalence estimates. Nethertheless, overall diagnostic information requires a specific validation beyond the health insurer's error checks without considering information contained in patient records or hospital information systems a gold standard in the first place. Depending on the clinical symptoms, reliable outpatient and hospital-based diagnoses and if applicable specific prescriptions and services are used to validate and identify so-called epidemiologically clear cases. In case of a chronic disease, a singular documentation is typically not sufficient (Schubert et al. 2010).

If the observation period is short, it becomes a problem to differentiate between incidental and prevalent cases of chronic diseases because lighter versions that do not necessarily require medication or intervention treatment may not necessarily be documented in the claims data. In such cases, claims data should be available for a longer period of time to avoid an overestimation of incidences (Abbas et al. 2012).

Normally, the external validity of secondary data analyses must be examined separately. Since the body of data used often comes from a single health insurer, results may not be automatically applied to people covered by other statutory health insurance plans. Incidence and prevalence estimates particularly depend on the insurer's insurant structure (Hoffmann and Icks 2012).

Nevertheless, in consideration of their strengths and weaknesses, claims data offers a great potential for evaluating models of integrated care, not only as an alternative to clinical studies based on randomized controlled designs but rather to supplement them while implementing principles and methods of clinical research and epidemiology as best as possible in the new research field of routine care and by applying its specific methods.

20.8 Perspective: Data Linkage

The lack of information on an individual's health-related behaviour and concrete risk factors may be overcome by linking that person's primary and secondary data. Allegedly, this would be the best of two worlds in epidemiology as well as in evaluation research but the approach does present a number of legal, technical and organization challenges (March et al. 2014a). Current studies (March et al. 2012; Swart et al. 2011) demonstrate that it is technically feasible and legally permitted to link primary data but at a steep logistical price. The opportunity to gain new insights has encouraged the 'NAKO Health Study' (German National Cohort; GNC Consortium 2014), the largest German epidemiological cohort study so far, to strive to link primary data with a wide range of secondary data (Jacobs et al. 2015).

Depending on whether (1) secondary data is individually linked with primary data or whether (2) - the other way around - primary data is enriched by secondary data, individual data linkage offers a chance to overcome the limitations of the bodies of data concerned. In case (1), secondary data can be supplemented by individual socio-demographic features or risk profiles that facilitate a risk adjustment or an estimate of selection effects when comparing IC-participants and non-participants as well as an assessment of new care concepts for the insurant. Case (2) makes it possible to overcome the methodological limitations of primary data as regards information on the utilization of services (e.g. recall bias; Swart 2012) and problems of longitudinal study designs (e.g. drop outs).

20.9 Conclusions

The German examples presented and the conclusions drawn specifically apply to Germany. It goes without saying that claims data is also used in other countries to evaluate integrated care projects. Although structures and contents as well as access and usage requirements vary from country to country, the operationalized process and outcome indicators derived from the data are similar. Consequently, a brief glimpse across the German border suffices. A London-based pilot project on integrated care for diabetics and patients 75 years or older used information [not specified in detail] generated from administrative data on the utilization of inpatient services in a mixed-methods evaluation (Curry et al. 2013). In the scope of an evaluation of several IC projects in Great Britain, data from Hospital Episode Statistics (HES; http://www.hscic.gov.uk/hes) was used in addition to questionnaires for patients and staff of the IC projects in order to compare the number of hospitalizations and outpatient contacts in hospitals of the NHS and outpatient and inpatient care costs incurred by patients in IC projects and non-enrolled standard care control patients in a certain design (Roland et al. 2012). Hser and Evans (2008) describe a very complex approach to evaluating care programs for addicts in California. Patient-related data was not only used to utilize the health care system for mentally ill people but also linked individually and with other government databases to obtain information on road accidents or driving under the influence of alcohol or drugs or convictions and detentions, for example. Linkage was based on matching variables identifying the person such as name, social security number, and date of birth.

What follows is a list of internationally applicable criteria and key questions that help structure the evaluation of potential claims data or its suitability for evaluating integrated care projects:

- Do you have sufficient knowledge about how the data was generated, its inclusion and exclusion criteria and possibilities to precisely determine the reference population?
- Are all or at least all essential services used by patients participating in IC projects included in the claims data?
- Is a longitudinal patient-related analysis of the services provided possible so that pre and post-periods can be mapped?
- Are suitable matching methods available in order to make a valid comparison between the intervention and the comparison group in a controlled design?
- Is it possible to operationalize parameters needed for the evaluation (independent and dependent variables, confounders, moderating and mediating variables) and if necessary to validate them internally/externally?
- Is there sufficient knowledge about the strengths and weaknesses of the data in question in order to handle possible limitations?
- Is it possible to stratify the claims data in a valid way according to socio-demographic and socio-economic variables?
- Is the claims data available in a comparable quality for the entire evaluation period?

If you can answer these questions with YES, the claims data presents a valuable data source for the evaluation of integrated care whose validity may be even increased by linking it with primary data. Therefore programmes of integrated care should be outlined from the beginning to use claims data for evaluation. No other data source delivers more and broader objective information on utilization of health care in terms of diagnoses, diagnostic, surgical or pharmacological interventions as well as costs. Also, specific methods of claims data analysis were developed enabling advanced epidemiologic study designs like case-control or cohort studies with a potentially high degree of external validity.

On the other hand, as mentioned above, evaluation of integrated care should keep in mind limitations of claims data and therefore look for alternatives or supplements of claims data analysis in terms of an observational/intervention study or data linkage of primary and claims data. An evaluation of integrated bases solely on primary data of participants will always be prone to different kinds of bias, for example selection bias.

Al least, from the German point of view, it would be helpful if the legal limitations of using claims data for scientific purposes could be overcome by actual initiatives to change the respective paragraphs of social code, books V and X.

References

Abbas, S., Ihle, P., Köster, I., & Schubert, I. (2012). Estimation of disease incidence in claims data dependent on the length of follow-up: A methodological approach. *Health Services Research, 47*, 746–755. doi:10.1111/j.1475-6773.2011.01325.x.

Abbas, S., Ihle, P., Hein, R., & Schubert, I. (2015). Vergleich der geriatrischen frührehabilitativen Komplexbehandlung und der geriatrischen Anschlussrehabilitation. [Comparison of rehabilitation between in-hospital geriatric departments and geriatric out-of-hospital rehabilitation facilities]. *Zeitschrift für Gerontologie und Geriatrie, 48*, 41–48. doi:10.1007/s00391-013-0542-4.

Benchimol, E. I., Smeeth, L., Guttmann, A., Harron, K., Moher, D., Petersen, I., Sørensen, H. T., von Elm, E., Langan, S. M., & RECORD Working Committee. (2015). The reporting of studies conducted using observational routinely-collected health data (RECORD) statement. *PLoS Medicine, 12*(10), e1001885. doi:10.1371/journal.pmed.1001885.

Birnbaum, D. S., & Braun, S. (2010). Evaluation von Disease Management Programmen – Bewertung der Methodik und der ersten Ergebnisse aus gesundheitsökonomischer Sicht. [Evaluation of disease management programmes – assessing methods and initial outcomes from a health economic perspective]. *Zeitschrift für Evidenz, Fortbildung und Qualität im Gesundheitswesen, 104*, 85–91. doi:10.1016/j.zefq.2009.07.002.

Bormann, C., & Swart, E. (2014). Utilization of medical services in Germany – outline of statutory health insurance system (SHI). In C. Janssen, E. Swart, & T. von Lengerke (Eds.), *Health care utilization in Germany. Theory, methodology and results* (pp. 29–41). New York: Springer Science Business Media. doi:10.1007/978-1-4614-9191-0.

Curry, N., Harris, M., Gunn, L. H., Pappas, Y., Blunt, I., Soljak, M., Mastellos, N., Holder, H., Smith, J., Majeed, A., Ignatowicz, A., Greaves, F., Belsi, A., Costin-Davis, N., Jones Nielsen, J. D., Greenfield, G., Cecil, E., Patterson, S., Car, J., & Bardsley, M. (2013). Integrated care pilot in north west London: A mixed methods evaluation. *International Journal of Integrated Care, 13*. URN:NBN:NL:UI:10-1-114735.

Egen-Lappe, V., Köster, I., & Schubert, I. (2013). Incidence estimate and guideline-oriented treatment for post-stroke spasticity: An analysis based on German statutory health insurance data. *International Journal of General Medicine, 6*, 135–144. doi:10.2147/IJGM.S36030.

Erler, A., Beyer, M., Muth, C., Gerlach, F. M., & Brennecke, R. (2009). Garbage in – Garbage out? Validität von Abrechnungsdiagnosen in hausärztlichen Praxen. [Garbage in – garbage out?

Validity of coded diagnoses from GP claims records]. *Gesundheitswesen, 71*, 823–831. doi:10.1055/s-0029-1214399.

German National Cohort (GNC) Consortium. (2014). The German national cohort: Aims, study design, and organization. *European Journal of Epidemiology, 29*, 371–382. doi:10.1007/s10654-014-9890-7.

Giersiepen, K., Pohlabeln, H., Egidi, G., & Pigeot, I. (2007). Die ICD-Kodierqualität für Diagnosen in der ambulanten Versorgung. [Quality of diagnostic ICD coding for outpatients in Germany]. *Bundesgesundheitsblatt, 50*, 1028–1038. doi:10.1007/s00103-007-0297-4.

Glaeske, G., Augustin, M., Abholz, H., Banik, N., Brüggenjürgen, B., Hasford, J., Hoffmann, W., Kruse, J., Lange, S., Schäfer, T., Schubert, I., Trampisch, H.-J., & Windeler, J. (2009). Epidemiologische Methoden für die Versorgungsforschung. [Epidemiological methods for health services research]. *Gesundheitswesen, 71*, 685–693. doi:10.1055/s-0029-1239517.

Grobe, T. G., & Ihle, P. (2014). Stammdaten und Versichertenhistorien. In E. Swart, P. Ihle, H. Gothe, & D. Matusiewicz (Eds.), *Routinedaten im Gesundheitswesen: Handbuch Sekundärdatenanalyse: Grundlagen, Methoden und Perspektiven* (2nd ed., pp. 28–37). Bern: Hans Huber.

Hildebrand, H., Schulte, T., & Stunder, B. (2012). Triple aim in Kinzigtal, Germany. Improving population health, integrating health care and reducing costs of care – lessons for the UK? *Journal of Integrated Care, 20*, 205–222. doi:10.1108/14769011211255249.

Hildebrand, H., Pimperl, A., Schulte, T., Hermann, C., Riedel, H., Schubert, I., Köster, I., & Wetzel, M. (2015). Triple Aim-Evaluation der Integrierten Versorgung Gesundes Kinzigtal – Gesundheitszustand, Versorgungserleben und Wirtschaftlichkeit. [Pursuing the triple aim: Evaluation of the integrated care system Gesundes Kinzigtal: Population health, patient experience and cost-effectiveness]. *Bundesgesundheitsblatt, 58*, 383–392. doi:10.1007/s00103-015-2120-y.

Hoffmann, F. (2009). Review on use of German health insurance medication claims data for epidemiological research. *Pharmacoepidemiology and Drug Safety, 18*, 349–356. doi:10.1002/pds.1721.

Hoffmann, F., & Icks, A. (2012). Unterschiede in der Versichertenstruktur von Krankenkassen und deren Auswirkungen für die Versorgungsforschung: Ergebnisse des Bertelsmann-Gesundheitsmonitors. [Structural differences between health insurance funds and their impact on health services research: Results from the Bertelsmann health-care monitor]. *Gesundheitswesen, 74*, 291–297. doi:10.1055/s-0031-1275711.

Hoffmann, W., Latza, U., & Terschüren, C. (2005). Leitlinien und Empfehlungen zur Sicherung Guter Epidemiologischer Praxis (GEP) – überarbeitete Fassung nach Revision. [Guidelines and recommendations for ensuring good epidemiological practice (GEP) – revised version after evaluation]. *Gesundheitswesen, 67*, 217–225. doi:10.1055/s-2004-813850.

Holle, R., Behrend, C., Reitmeier, P., & John, J. (2005). Methodenfragen der Nutzung von GKV-Routinedaten für Kostenanalysen. In E. Swart & P. Ihle (Eds.), *Routinedaten im Gesundheitswesen. Handbuch Sekundärdatenanalyse: Grundlagen, Methoden und Perspektiven* (pp. 310–318). Bern: Huber.

Horenkamp-Sonntag, D., Linder, R., Wenzel, F., Gerste, B., Schubert, I., & Ihle, P. (2014). Prüfung der Datenqualität und Validität von Routinedaten. In E. Swart, P. Ihle, H. Gothe, & D. Matusiewicz (Eds.), *Routinedaten im Gesundhgealyse: Grundlagen, Methoden und Perspektiven* (2nd ed., pp. 314–330). Bern: Hans Huber.

Hser, Y.-I., & Evans, E. (2008). Cross-system data linkage for treatment outcome evaluation: Lessons learned from the California treatment outcome project. *Evaluation and Program Planning, 31*, 125–135. doi:10.1016/j.evalprogplan.2008.02.003.

Jacobs, S., Stallmann, C., & Pigeot, I. (2015). Verknüpfung großer Sekundär- und Registerdatenquellen mit Daten aus Kohortenstudien. Doppeltes Potenzial nutzen. [Linkage of large secondary and registry data sources with data of cohort studies. Usage of a dual potential]. *Bundesgesundheitsblatt, 58*(8), 822–828. doi:10.1007/s00103- 015-2184-8.

Klauber, J., Günster, C., & Biermann, A. (2014). Verbesserung der Versorgungsqualität durch sektorenübergreifende Qualitätsmessung. In: C. Fuchs, B.-M. Kurth, P.C. Scriba (Eds.), Report Versorgungsforschung (pp. 97–108). Köln: Deutscher Ärzte-Verlag.

Köster, I., Huppertz, E., Hauner, H., & Schubert, I. (2014). Costs of diabetes mellitus (CoDiM) in Germany, direct per-capita costs of managing hyperglycaemia and diabetes complications in 2010 compared to 2001. *Experimental and Clinical Endocrinology & Diabetes, 122*, 510–516. doi:10.1055/s-0034-1375675.

Linder, R., Ahrens, S., Köppel, D., Heilmann, V., & Verheyen, F. (2011). The benefit and efficiency of the disease management program for type 2 diabetes. *Deutsches Ärzteblatt International, 108*, 155–162. doi:10.3238/arztebl.2011.0155.

Lux, G., Biermann, J., Dahl, H., Matusiewicz, D., Mostardt, S., Nimptsch, U., & Walendzik, A. (2014). Risikoadjustierung und Komorbidität. In E. Swart, P. Ihle, H. Gothe, & D. Matusiewicz (Eds.), *Routinedaten im Gesundheitswesen: Handbuch Sekundärdatenanalyse: Grundlagen, Methoden und Perspektiven* (2nd ed., pp. 411–423). Bern: Hans Huber.

March, S., Rauch, A., Thomas, D., Bender, S., & Swart, E. (2012). Datenschutzrechtliche Vorgehensweise bei der Verknüpfung von Primär- und Sekundärdaten in einer Kohortenstudie: die lidA-Studie. [Procedures according to data protection laws for coupling primary and secondary data in a cohort study: The lidA study]. *Gesundheitswesen, 74*, e122–e129. doi:10.1055/s-0031-1301276.

March, S., Rauch, A., Bender, S., & Ihle, P. (2014a). Datenschutzrechtliche Aspekte bei der Nutzung von Routinedaten. In E. Swart, P. Ihle, H. Gothe, & D. Matusiewicz (Eds.), *Routinedaten im Gesundheitswesen: Handbuch Sekundärdatenanalyse: Grundlagen, Methoden und Perspektiven* (2nd ed., pp. 291–303). Bern: Hans Huber.

March, S., Stallmann, C., & Swart, E. (2014b). Datenlinkage. In: E. Swart, P. Ihle, H. Gothe, & D. Matusiewicz (Hrsg.), *Routinedaten im Gesundheitswesen: Handbuch Sekundärdatenanalyse: Grundlagen, Methoden und Perspektiven* (2nd edn, pp. 347–356) Bern: Huber.

Meyer, M. (2014). Arbeitsunfähigkeit. In E. Swart, P. Ihle, H. Gothe, & D. Matusiewicz (Eds.), *Routinedaten im Gesundheitswesen: Handbuch Sekundärdatenanalyse: Grundlagen, Methoden und Perspektiven* (2nd ed., pp. 146–160). Bern: Hans Huber.

Miksch, A., Laux, G., Ose, D., Joos, S., Campbell, S., Riens, B., & Szecsenyi, J. (2010). Is there a survival benefit within a German primary-care based disease management programm? *American Journal of Managed Care, 16*, 49–54.

Mnich, E., Hofreuter-Gätgens, K., Salomon, T., Swart, E., & von dem Knesebeck, O. (2013). Ergebnis-Evaluation einer Gesundheitsförderungsmaßnahme für ältere Menschen. [Outcome evaluation of a health promotion among the elderly]. *Gesundheitswesen, 75*, e5–e10. doi:10. 1055/s-0032-1311617.

Mostardt, S., Lux, G., Dahl, H., Matusiewicz, D., & Biermann, J. (2014). Matching-Verfahren. In E. Swart, P. Ihle, H. Gothe, & D. Matusiewicz (Eds.), *Routinedaten im Gesundheitswesen: Handbuch Sekundärdatenanalyse: Grundlagen, Methoden und Perspektiven* (2nd ed., pp. 402–410). Bern: Hans Huber.

Neugebauer, E. A. M., Icks, A., & Schrappe, M. (2010). Memorandum III: Methoden für die Versorgungsforschung (Teil 2). [Memorandum III: Methods for health services research (part 2)]. *Gesundheitswesen, 72*, 739–748. doi:10.1055/s-0030-1262858.

Nichols, S. G., Quach, P., von Elm, E., Guttmann, A., Moher, D., Petersen, I., Sorensen, H. T., Smeeth, L., Langan, S. M., & Benchimol, E. I. (2015). The reporting of studies conducted using observational routinely-collected health data (RECORD) statement: Methods for arriving at consensus and developing reporting guidelines. *PLoS One, 10*(5), e0125620. doi:10. 1371/journal.pone.0125620.

Reis, A. (2005). Krankheitskostenanalysen. In E. Swart & P. Ihle (Eds.), *Routinedaten im Gesundheitswesen. Handbuch Sekundärdatenanalyse: Grundlagen, Methoden und Perspektiven* (pp. 291–300). Bern: Huber.

Roland, M., Lewis, R., Steventon, A., Abel, G., Adams, J., Bardsley, M., Brereton, L., Chitnis, X., Conklin, A., Steaetsky, L., Tunkel, S., & Ling, T. (2012). Case management for at-risk elderly patients in the english integrated care pilots: Observational study of staff and patient experience and secondary care utilization. *International Journal of Integrated Care, 12*. URN:NBN: NL:UI:10-1-113731/ijic2012-130.

Schubert, I., & Köster, I. (2014). Krankheitsereignis: Falldefinition und Operationalisierung. In E. Swart, P. Ihle, H. Gothe, & D. Matusiewicz (Eds.), *Routinedaten im Gesundheitswesen: Handbuch Sekundärdatenanalyse: Grundlagen, Methoden und Perspektiven* (2nd ed., pp. 358–368). Bern: Hans Huber.

Schubert, I., Ihle, P., & Köster, I. (2010). Interne Validierung von Diagnosen in GKV-Routinedaten: Konzeption mit Beispielen und Falldefinition. [Internal confirmation of diagnoses in routine statutory health insurance data: Concept with examples and case definitions]. *Gesundheitswesen, 72*, 316–322. doi:10.1055/s-0030-1249688.

Schubert, I., Küpper-Nybelen, J., Ihle, P., & Thürmann, P. (2013). Prescribing potentially inappropriate medication (PIM) in Germany's elderly as indicated by the PRISCUS list. An analysis based on regional claims data. *Pharmacoepidemiology and Drug Safety, 22*, 719–727. doi:10.1002/pds.3429.

Siegel, A., Köster, I., Schubert, I., & Stößel, U. (2014). Utilization dynamics of an integrated care system in Germany: Morbidity, age, and sex distribution of Gesundes Kinzigtal integrated care's membership in 2006–2008. In: Janssen, C., Swart, E., & von Lengerke, T. (Eds.), Health care utilization in Germany. Theory, methodology, and results. Foreword by Ronald M. Anderson (pp. 321–335). New York: Springer.

Stock, S., Drabik, A., Büscher, G., Graf, C., Ulrich, W., Gerber, A., Lauterbach, K. W., & Lüngen, M. (2010). German diabetes management programs improve quality of care and curb costs. *Health Affairs, 29*, 2197–2205. doi:10.1377/hlthaff.2009.0799.

Stock, C., Ihle, P., Sieg, A., Schubert, I., Hoffmeister, M., & Brenner, H. (2013). Adverse events requiring hospitalization within 30 days after outpatient screening and nonscreening colonoscopie. *Gastrointestinal Endoscopy, 77*, 419–429. doi:10.1016/j.gie.2012.10.028.

Swart, E. (2012). The prevalence of medical services use. How comparable are the results of large-scale population surveys in Germany? *GMS Psycho-Social-Medicine, 9*, Doc10. doi:10.3205/psm000088.

Swart, E. (2014). Health care utilization research using secondary data. In C. Janssen, E. Swart, & T. von Lengerke (Eds.), *Health care utilization in Germany. Theory, methodology and results* (pp. 63–86). New York: Springer Science Business Media.

Swart, E., & Ihle, P. (Eds.). (2005). Routinedaten im Gesundheitswesen: Handbuch Sekundärdatenanalyse: Grundlagen, Methoden und Perspektiven. Bern: Hans Huber.

Swart, E., & Schmitt, J. (2014). STROSA – Vorschlag für ein Berichtsformat für Sekundärdatenanalysen. [STandardized reporting of secondary data analyses (STROSA) – a recommendation]. *Zeitschrift für Evidenz, Fortbildung und Qualität im Gesundheitswesen, 108*, 511–516. doi:10.1016/j.zefq.2014.08.022.

Swart, E., Deh, U., & Robra, B.-P. (2008). Die Nutzung der GKV-Daten für die kleinräumige Analyse und Steuerung der stationären Versorgung [Using claims data for small area analysis and controlling of hospital care]. *Bundesgesundheitsblatt, 51*, 1183–1192. doi:10.1007/s00103-008-0653-z.

Swart, E., Thomas, D., March, S., Salomon, T., & von dem Knesebeck, O. (2011). Erfahrungen mit der Datenverknüpfung von Primär- und Sekundärdaten in einer Interventionsstudie. [Experience with the linkage of primary and secondary claims data in an intervention trial]. *Gesundheitswesen, 73*, e126–e132. doi:10.1055/s-0031-1280754.

Swart, E., Ihle, P., Gothe, H., & Matusiewicz, D. (Eds.). (2014). *Routinedaten im Gesundheitswesen: Handbuch Sekundärdatenanalyse: Grundlagen, Methoden und Perspektiven* (2nd ed.). Bern: Hans Huber.

Swart, E., Gothe, H., Geyer, S., Jaunzeme, J., Maier, B., Grobe, T., & Ihle, P. (2015). Gute Praxis Sekundärdatenanalyse (GPS): Leitlinien und Empfehlung, 3. Revision, Fassung 2012/2014;

[Good practice of secondary data analysis (GPS): Guidelines and recommendations, third revision 2012/2014]. *Gesundheitswesen, 77*, 120–126. doi:10.1055/s-0034-1396815.

Swart, E., Bitzer, E.M., Gothe, H., Harling, M., Hoffmann, F., Horenkamp-Sonntag, D., Maier, B., March, S., Petzold, T., Röhrig, R., Rommel, A., Schink, T., Wagner, C., Wobbe, S., & Schmitt, J. (2016). STandardisierte BerichtsROutine für SekundärdatenAnalysen (STROSA) – ein konsentierter Berichtsstandard für Deutschland, Version 2. *Gesundheitswesen, 78 (suppl 1)*, e145-e160. doi: 10.1055/s-0042-108647.

Vandenbroucke, J. P., von Elm, E., Altman, D. G., Gøtzsche, P. C., Mulrow, C. D., Pocock, S. J., Poole, C., Schlesselmann, J. J., & Egger, M. (2007). Strenghtening the reporting of observational studies in epidemiological (STROBE-) statement. Explanation and elaboration. *Annals of Internal Medicine, 147*, W163–W194. doi:10.7326/0003-4819-147-8-200710160-00010-w1.

von Ferber, L., & Behrens, J. (Eds.). (1997). Public Health Forschung mit Gesundheits- und Sozialdaten. Stand und perspektiven. St. Augustin: Asgard-Verlag.

Wennberg, J. E., Roos, N., Sola, L., Schori, A., & Jaffe, R. (1987). Use of claims data systems to evaluate health care outcomes. *JAMA, 257*, 933–936. doi:10.1001/jama.1987. 03390070053022.

Children

21

Ingrid Wolfe

21.1 Challenges in Providing Care for Infants, Children and Young People

The epidemiological transition towards chronic conditions applies to children[1] just as it does to adults and the elderly. Health systems need to adapt to provide more and better quality planned care, health promotion, disease prevention, and health policies that address the upstream determinants of chronic disease. Yet countries struggle to shift the focus of healthcare away from acute and urgent reactive care, so the hospital-centric health model continues to dominate. A wide variety of government and non-governmental strategies are focused on developing integrated care services as a way for health systems to adapt to meet current and evolving needs more effectively and efficiently. However, the majority of these initiatives are tailored to the needs of adults or the elderly, with scarce consideration for the distinct needs of children and young people.

There is convincing evidence that the greatest long term population health gains come from improving health at the earliest stages of the life course (Marmot 2012; Waldfogel 2004). Child health differs in important and sometimes subtle ways from the rest of the population. The relative importance of health, education, political, and economic systems varies with age and developmental stage and they also interact to shape and influence health differently across the stages of the life course.

---

[1]The term children will be used for brevity and convenience, but all the stages of early years from birth, including infants, children, and young people, should be understood unless otherwise specified.

I. Wolfe (✉)
Public Health, King's College London, London, UK

Paediatric Public Health, Evelina London Children's Healthcare, Guy's and St Thomas' NHS Foundation Trust, London, UK
e-mail: Ingrid.wolfe@kcl.ac.uk

© Springer International Publishing AG 2017
V. Amelung et al. (eds.), *Handbook Integrated Care*,
DOI 10.1007/978-3-319-56103-5_21

More narrowly, paediatric medicine, which was once considered a subset of adult medicine, has evolved into a sophisticated specialty with different knowledge and skills required for different stages. Preterm and term newborns, infants and toddlers, children, adolescents, and young people are increasingly recognized as having distinct and often different health needs (Forrest et al. 1997). There are specific diseases of childhood, and in addition children may manifest illness symptoms and signs differently from older children and adults. The trajectory of acute illness often differs too, rapid decline and recovery being common features. While older adults and the elderly population frequently suffer from multiple co-morbidities and may be dependent on social care, these are rare circumstances among children (Wolfe et al. 2016a). The demography of early life differs from later years too. For example, children are especially sensitive to the effects of social and economic conditions and in many countries more children live in poverty and social disadvantage than adults and the elderly (Eurostat 2013). Children, especially at younger ages, are dependent on their parents or care-givers to seek healthcare, to communicate their health needs and experience of care, and to administer medicines and other interventions. Finally, all the factors described here differ according to developmental stage.

The distinct health and healthcare needs of children merit different service, system, and policy responses. For example, a good balance between access and expertise in primary care may require different conditions for children reflecting the different skills required by generalists and specialists in caring for children. Furthermore, while the policy drivers for integrated care among the elderly reflects the interdependence between health and social care, most children do not require social care support so their integration needs are different. A child-centred approach to integrated care is needed.

21.2 Goals of Integrated Care for Children

Children's health needs are changing as a result of the transition to chronic disease. These changes are reflected in trend data showing that an increasingly large proportion of deaths and the majority of the burden of disease in early years are caused by chronic and non-communicable conditions (Wolfe et al. 2013). This is similar to what is happening in the rest of the population, but there are important differences that mean different policy responses are needed. Most children are healthy and well, and have occasional acute illnesses and simple chronic conditions; so cure or support to enable the best possible quality of life and development are the goals. Therefore, integration between primary and secondary care, and between health and education services, including services that promote early childhood development, are important to the majority of children and young people. By contrast, integration between health and social care services which is an important need for older adults, is required by only a small proportion of children who have complex conditions as most children are dependent on their families for care, as illustrated in Fig. 21.1 (Wolfe et al. 2016a).

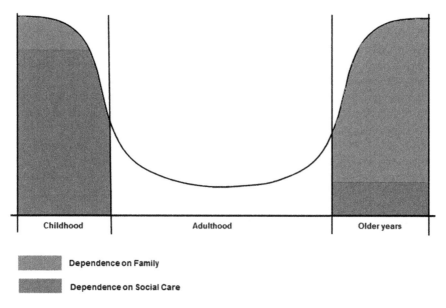

Dependence on Family

Dependence on Social Care

Fig. 21.1 The differences in integrated service needs and policy drivers between children and older people (Wolfe et al. 2016b)

Family-friendly services are important in the early years, to ensure the context of care is appropriate to need (British Association for Child and Adolescent Public Health and British Association for Community Child Health 2014). But there are similarities between the young and the old too. Children's health is shaped partly by healthcare, but wider social and economic factors are very important determinants. Therefore, integrated healthcare in the context of a strong health system and healthy policy is important for the early years population.

21.3 Value Proposition of Integrated Care for Children

The United Nations Convention on the Rights of the Child (UNCRC) specifies the right to the highest standard of healthcare, and to a standard of living and social security that enables their physical, mental, and social development (United Nations Convention on the Rights of the Child 1990). The value of integrated care for children and young people lies in securing some of the conditions towards realising the rights articulated in the UNCRC. The ultimate goal of integrated care should be about improved health and care services to ensure optimal health development for each child, and delivering maximal health gain at the population level. From the child and family's perspective this simply means the right care, at the right time, and in the right place (British Association for Child and Adolescent Public Health and British Association for Community Child Health 2014). The value proposition of integrated care can be more specifically articulated by considering how children and their families need and use services in the real world: when they are well, have acute illnesses, or chronic conditions. Moreover, children at each life stage within the early years will have different requirements for each scenario, and vulnerable children need special consideration towards achieving equity of access and outcome.

Children who are well need services that help keep them well, promote health and development and prevent disease. Integrated care for this group of children means population and individual level public health services delivered as conveniently as possible in school, home, and community settings where healthy children spend their lives. It also means healthy public policy and a strong health system. A life course approach to planning and providing holistic and integrated services for children to keep children well is important. For example, promoting social, emotional, and speech and language development for infants is quite a different service from youth worker support for adolescents who may be engaging in excessively risky health-harming behaviour. Integrated services for well children means population health and policies providing a strong foundation for health and development, in concert with health systems and services when needed.

All children develop acute illnesses from time to time. While most illnesses are minor and self-limiting, universal access to urgent care delivered by professionals who are competent in differentiating between minor and serious illness in children is important. Children's acute healthcare is often considered especially challenging, partly because of the differences between adults and children described previously, but also because the changing family structures in many cultures mean fewer children are raised in extended families, so parents may lack the close support of experienced relatives to help them manage minor childhood illness. These factors, together with the rising public expectations of medicine and an increasingly risk-averse society, may help explain why normal childhood conditions and complaints are increasingly often medicalised, reflected in more frequent care-seeking behaviour for minor problems.

Integrated care for children with acute illnesses means achieving a balance in first contact care between access and expertise in child health. In practice this means primary and secondary care (or generalists and specialists) working well together in community and hospital settings. Because first-contact care performs a gate-keeping role in health services, effective integration between primary and secondary care for children is also important for enabling the rest of the health service to function optimally. This is an example of vertical integration, between tiers of healthcare providers. Different professionals will need to work in integrated child health teams depending on the developmental stage. Nurses and doctors who provide care for infants, may require different skills from those looking after children in their middle years, and different again in adolescence and early adulthood.

Children with usually simple chronic conditions, such as asthma and diabetes, need preventive, proactive, and coordinated healthcare, and accessible urgent care to manage problems and exacerbations if they occur. School staff should be able to assist with administering daily medicines. Children with complex and multiple chronic conditions form a small part of the child population, but they have high needs. For example, a child with epilepsy who has neuro-developmental delay and difficulties with feeding and toileting, may need several medical and therapeutic specialties to be involved, and may need extra help at school. Multiple agencies, organisations, and professionals may be involved in providing care for children with complex needs, and coordinating services can be a major undertaking, described by many parents as a full time occupation. Integrated care for children with chronic conditions means vertical integration between healthcare providers, and horizontal integration between health and education for many children, and for those with complex conditions, horizontal integration with social care too.

The health and care needs of children with chronic conditions may evolve as the child develops, and adolescents who may be used to child-centred care suddenly find that there are different expectations in adults' healthcare. The transition between children's and adults' services for adolescents with chronic conditions is a particularly a vulnerable time. For example, older adolescents with diabetes may develop complications of their disease reflecting less effective management during the transition to adulthood and adult healthcare. Children with chronic conditions need integration in a longitudinal dimension, across stages of the life course so that services are coordinated and evolve according to the child's development (Halfon et al. 2007).

Integration is truly comprehensive when it links public health, population-based and patient-centred approaches to children's health care, when it serves the needs of whole populations. Integrated care for children is complex; indeed four dimensions of integrated care may be described, as shown in Fig. 21.2: vertical, between tiers of healthcare; horizontal, between health and education or social care sectors; longitudinal, across the life course; and population integration between health, public health, and wider policy. The diagram shows also the different ways these four dimensions might be needed at different stages within the early years of life.

Comprehensive integration would require policy coherence to produce an integrated delivery system, alignment of functions and activities including payment and incentive systems, information technology, and regulatory systems, and cultural change among professionals and families (Nolte and McKee 2008; Curry and Ham 2010). Whole systems thinking underpins such a comprehensive approach to integrating care (de Savigny and Adam 2009).

Achieving an appropriate balance between all four dimensions of integrated care for children begins by considering health at the population level. Child health can be described along a normal distribution curve. The middle part of the bell-shaped curve describes the majority of children, who are healthy and well most of the time and have occasional acute illnesses. Increasing numbers of children in this group also have chronic conditions. The two tail ends of the curve describe the smaller proportions of children who are either very healthy, or very unhealthy. This distribution of child population health is different from elderly people who often have multiple chronic conditions and high social care dependence. A population health curve for older people would be skewed to the right, since a larger proportion of the population has ongoing illnesses, and fewer people are healthy and well. The

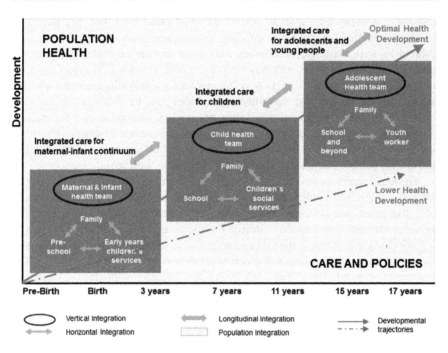

Fig. 21.2 Four dimensions of integration for a comprehensive approach towards strengthening health systems for children to achieve optimal health development. (Wolfe et al. 2016b)

need for integrated care between young and older populations varies, as described earlier, and not surprisingly the policy drivers are different too. Integrated care for the elderly is much more about cooperation between health and social care than it is for children. If social and health care fail to work smoothly together, elderly people end up staying in hospital longer than necessary waiting for social care interventions to be put in place so they can safely go home. Hospitals therefore have a strong incentive to ensure social care services are efficient and effective and that care packages are planned together. A similar scenario applies only to a small proportion of children with complex conditions. Minor acute illnesses are common in children, but it can be challenging to distinguish between minor and serious illness. Unscheduled care services necessarily take precedence over planned proactive care because of the risks involved in caring for acutely and potentially seriously ill children. However if first contact primary care is not as effective and efficient as it should be, and if primary and secondary care services do not cooperate closely, the inevitable consequences are excessive and avoidable use of hospital and secondary care services through high referral rates or parents bypassing primary care, resulting in unnecessary expense, and suboptimal quality and experience of care. With limited resources, the ineluctable result of excessive use of unscheduled care for children is that human and financial resources are directed away from planned proactive care. This failure-demand cycle is one reason why health systems are struggling to adapt to the epidemiological transition to chronic conditions. For the majority of children, the value proposition of integrated care for children is different from the elderly population; integrated primary and secondary health care, and effective integration with education are the key features to achieve for improving healthcare for children.

Comprehensive integrated services for children should improve care compared with the traditional service models, solving problems of imbalances between access and expertise in first contact care to improve effectiveness and efficiency and redirect resources to planned proactive care for children with chronic conditions. Fully integrated care should improve population and individual level services and ultimately improve child health.

21.4 The Integrated Treatment Path: Examples and Outcomes

The policy drivers for integrating children's care are different from the elderly, and gain much less attention from policy-makers, researchers, and the public. This makes achieving integrated care for children particularly challenging. However, there are commonalities between the young and the elderly. For example, primary care staff shortages, increasing demand, and pressure to reduce hospital-use in many countries have increased interest in developing new models of care that cross the boundaries between generalism and specialism, enhancing the best features of primary care and increasing the access to specialist expertise in the community. Several countries have made progress in developing integrated care services that are appropriate for children's needs and there are numerous examples that illustrate interesting and useful points about integrated care for children. However health systems, services, and policy research for children and young people is less advanced than for the adult and elderly population, and there has been little evaluation of the impact of integrated care for children. However there are useful lessons to be learned through examining the breadth of experience.

The Medical Home model in the USA is an integrated healthcare model for children. The aim is to deliver coordinated personalised and high-quality care (Cooley et al. 2009). The key features are that each child has a personal physician or other key worker who provides first-contact, continuous and comprehensive care, backed up by comprehensive teams including primary care and specialist doctors, nurses, and other professionals. Importantly, the Medical Home model incorporates preventive care, ambulatory and inpatient care for acute illnesses, coordinated continuity of care for chronic conditions, and access to specialists when needed (American Academy of Pediatrics 1992). A study of medical home services for children with chronic conditions including asthma, diabetes, attention-deficit-hyperactivity disorder, cerebral palsy, and epilepsy, reported a significant association between a strong medical home model (measured by an index of implementation) and reduced hospital admissions but a non-significant association with reduced emergency department visits (Cooley et al. 2009). There are a few individual studies that suggest beneficial outcomes for specific diseases in children. For example, a pre- and post-intervention comparison of patients receiving integrated asthma services, with matched controls at non-participating sites, found that clinically important processes of care, health-related quality of life, and asthma-specific quality of life improved significantly in the intervention group (Mangione-Smith et al. 2005). A US study comparing quality of care between specialists and generalists for children with asthma found significantly more compliance with national guidelines for children looked after by specialists (Diette et al. 2001). These are important, if indicative, results since under-treatment is an important element in poor outcomes for children with asthma (Asthma 2007). Children and young people who receive multi-professional and intensive medical management together with psychosocial support, and whose families receive tailored education, have improved glycaemic control and diabetes outcomes (Diabetes Control and Complications Trial Research Group 1994; White et al. 2001). Additionally, there is weak evidence that medical homes may achieve improved health outcomes, timeliness of care, family-centred care, and better family functioning among children with special health care needs (Cooley 2004; Homer et al. 2008).

Australia has a reputation for improving care through innovative new models of services. However primary care in Australia is a mix of public and private provision, and efforts to integrate care have been variable. Although there have been policy changes to enable supportive financing for coordinated chronic condition care and integration is viewed as important to enable the coordinating role of primary care, there are significant reported challenges including fragmented policy and responsibility for primary and community care, incompatible funding and accountability mechanisms, and difficulties in planning and accessing coordinated multidisciplinary care (Davies et al. 2009). Integrated primary care centres are being developed across the country, and Australia's version of integrated care for children is a broadly comprehensive rights-based approach to child and family services with a stated focus on health and wellbeing, learning and development. Services vary across the country but typically encompass education, day care, maternal and child health services, early childhood intervention, parenting, play groups and community activity space, and occasionally include other social services such as housing support services and employment advice (Press et al. 2012). The governance and organisational structures of Australia's integrated child health centres and services range from independent single or multiple employing organisations to government backed non-profit organisations managed by a governing council. Primary Care Partnerships are considered the most well established integrated care systems, and they include primary and community health, local government, hospitals, and voluntary sector organisations. Service innovations are fostered through such partnerships, which are voluntary and based on memoranda of understanding (Davies et al. 2009; Department of Health 2010).

Sweden's multiprofessional primary care and child health centres have GPs, paediatricians, and children's nurses working closely together, supplementing chains of care designed to improve integration of services and quality of care for children with chronic conditions. Children's health centres are staffed by general practitioners and children's nurses working closely together with paediatricians. Preventing disease and promoting health and development are the aims of children's health centres. Acute and minor illnesses are managed through primary care centres where GPs and children's nurses manage most problems, while paediatricians are close on hand if needed. A system called Chains of Care was developed for integrating services for chronic conditions as a response to the increasingly fragmented uncoordinated care that happened concurrent with growing decentralisation of service planning. Implementation was improved by involving patients as active participants in developing care, devising supportive financing and other policy tools, and fostering culture change through maintaining focus on quality improvement as the aim to the change process (Åhgren 2003). Specific aspects of services for children with chronic conditions include having a named physician who coordinates care, and specialist nurses who provide a point of contact for urgent problems. In addition, there are family education programmes to encourage supported self-management. A complementary system of integration in Sweden is known as Local Health Care, a system of primary and community care that incorporates some specialist services (Åhgren 2010). Although there has been a deal written about the implementation of integrated healthcare in Sweden, there are as yet insufficient reports of measurable outcomes for children (Åhgren and Axelsson 2011).

France has a general practitioner system, with mandated registration, providing gatekeeping and navigation roles (Nolte and McKee 2008). However parents are entitled to choose any doctor for acute illnesses, and it is usual for parents to seek specialist care for young children. Routine care for children with chronic conditions is provided by specialists, such as paediatric pneumologists. The system for coordinating and integrating care for children with specified chronic conditions, or affections de longue dureé, is intended to ensure that children receive personal treatment plans. There are lists of investigations and interventions covered by health insurance for specific conditions, and a system of financial incentives for using evidence-based guidelines and national standards for management of chronic conditions. Coordinated planned care is achieved through multidisciplinary appointments in specialist centres. This system focuses on specialist aspects of the child's health and development, and is not thought to integrate care between generalists and specialists (Wolfe 2013).

The Netherlands has a General Practitioner based primary care system supplemented by a youth-only primary and preventive healthcare system. The Trans-Mural system is a series of policies and practices to promote integration between primary and secondary care and between multiple insurers and providers of care. Health professionals have defined responsibilities at the individual and team level. Specialist nurses have a central role in organising and coordinating care. GPs and nurses provide everyday management for chronic conditions such as asthma, and paediatricians in hospitals provide care for children with complex conditions or where management is particularly challenging. Urgent advice is available through either the primary care or hospital system depending on the severity of the child's needs. Guidelines are shared between primary and secondary care, designed to reinforce shared practice and teamwork (van der Linden et al. 2001; Zwar et al. 2006). Evaluations of transmural care have demonstrated persistent discontinuity between primary and secondary care, emphasising the point that organisational integration did not necessarily produce clinical and service integration (van der Linden 2001). The Netherlands' provision of mental health care is divided between sectors, and there has been a small scale attempt to test an integrated approach to delivering mental healthcare in primary care settings. The Eureka project comprised an incentive payment to GPs to perform a comprehensive assessment of children and parents with possible mental health problems, consult with specialists as needed, and deliver treatment in primary care. A study evaluating outcomes using a before-after design suggested some increase in the number of children identified as having mental health problems, but this effect seems not to have been sustained (Verhaak et al. 2015).

The United Kingdom's universal primary care system is led by GPs, with a strong role in gatekeeping and navigation. However there is a national drive towards developing new models of integrated health care, albeit with little or no emphasis on the distinct needs of children and young people in national policy to date (NHS 2014). Various aspects of an integrated or chronic care model have been implemented or are being developed in the UK, but the emphasis on integrated care for children thus far has been largely about education and other children's services but without mainstream primary, community, and hospital-based services. The Sure Start programme was developed in the late 1990s to improve and promote health and development for children under 5 years and their families, particularly in disadvantaged areas (Eisenstadt 2011). The intention originally was to bring together local services and integrate staffing and management to include early learning and child care, family support, child and family health services, and advice and information on children's services and parental employment, to improve health and development outcomes. Sure Start evaluations demonstrated variable success in delivering its aims (SQW 2005). The programme evolved and became a national network of Children's Centres, but has more recently contracted with the financial crisis. Children's Centres have, however, enabled co-location of some services for children under 5 years, for example community and family support workers, and some health workers such as health visitors. Although there is a statutory requirement for partnership working between Children's Centres and the health sector, in practice this has been variable, with little involvement by GPs (Government UK 2009). The Every Child Matters (ECM) policy was introduced in 2003 following the death of a vulnerable child. ECM described fve key outcomes for children: being healthy, staying safe, enjoying and achieving, making a positive contribution, and economic wellbeing. It aimed to bring together many children's services within the local government and education sectors and included some specific health services but excluded primary healthcare and other mainstream health services. Similarly, the Team around the Child concept is about fostering horizontal integration and is particularly suited for children with additional needs, usually complex social and educational needs, and there is relatively little health sector input (Jones 2006). Getting it Right for Every Child, introduced in Scotland in 2004 and enshrined in law in 2014, is a rights-based approach to care which emphasises an integrated approach to care for children with multiple needs. There are some encouraging signs of changing practice associated with GIRFEC, and some indication of changes in outcomes (Stradling et al. 2009). Children with chronic illnesses in the UK may not have a specific professional who coordinates care and this function is often the responsibility of the parents. A variety of formal and informal integrated health care services and networks have been or are being set up. Although there is generally limited evaluation of outcomes to date, some implementation evaluation has been attempted. Difficulties in establishing coordinated services and networks include cultural resistance to change; lack of evidence to demonstrate benefits; financial disincentives to cooperate (promoting competition instead of collaboration); and organisational boundaries preventing cooperation between providers (Royal College of Paediatrics and Child Health 2012). New models of care that focus more on medical aspects of child health are being developed in several centres throughout the UK (Nuffield Foundation 2015). Four types of services have been described that attempt to integrate primary and secondary care: multidisciplinary teams with telephone links, hospital at home, GP outreach clinics, and decision support or advice and guidance (Woodman et al. 2015). Specific aspects of integrated care have been implemented to varying degrees, though not all of them have been described by the term. For example, an RCT investigating the effects of a Hospital at Home service for children with acute asthma found that home care was as effective as hospital care, and more acceptable to parents and children (Sartain et al. 2002). A randomised controlled trial of a clinical pathway for asthma in general practice in New Zealand (which has a similar system to the UK) achieved reduced numbers of hospital admissions and emergency department attendances, however the positive results were demonstrated in both intervention and control groups (Mitchell et al. 2005).

In Italy children's health care is delivered nearly exclusively by paediatricians who are the first point of access for urgent advice and consultations and assume responsibility for monitoring and managing children with long-term conditions. Children with very severe or complex conditions who require specialist paediatric management are often followed up in hospitals rather than by primary care paediatricians in community settings. Assistenza Domiciliare Pediatrica is a system joining specialist health centres with primary care paediatricians and other community services. The aim is to provide as much care as possible at home for children with complex chronic conditions who need specific interventions such as parenteral nutrition, oxygen therapy, physiotherapy, or frequent blood sampling, for example, rather than on integrating primary and secondary for the population (Tamburlini 2012).

Germany has primary care paediatricians, and paediatricians with a particular expertise in chronic conditions, for example pneumologists, working in community based offices and hospitals. Specialised paediatricians act as care coordinators working in teams with nurses and therapists. Coordinated multidisciplinary care in Germany is facilitated by funding packages of care with a single provider organisation rather than the usual fee for service model (Strassburg 2011). In addition, for children with complex chronic conditions such as neurodevelopmental disorders, there is a specific location-based multidisciplinary service known as

Social Paediatric Centres *(SPZ)* supplemented with a teaching programme, ModuS, to foster self-management for children with chronic conditions, and their families (Szczepanski 2010). SPZs are usually co-located with hospitals.

Norway's health system has a strong universal primary care focus. Children with chronic illnesses have a local key health worker who acts as coordinator, guiding care according to individualised written plans which describe roles and responsibilities for all professionals involved. Hospital-based paediatricians provide most of the specialist medical care, and parents are able to telephone them directly for advice. All hospitals have educational centres that provide information and training for families after their child has been diagnosed with a chronic disorder, also providing a connecting function with other families who have similar problems. Mental health care services for children in Norway are beset by similar problems as in other countries, fragmented and complex services that often fail to deliver coordinated care (Manikam 2002; Walker 2001; Hudson 2005). There has been a national drive towards improving care and developing new services, backed by a ten year national mental health escalation plan (Ådnanes and Halsteinli 2008). Fostering interprofessional collaboration between health and social care has been an important feature of Norway's mental health care improvement plan (Odegard 2006).

21.5 Lessons Learned and Outlook

Integrated care for children is in early stages in most countries, but there are promising signs that children's distinctive health needs are beginning to be recognised. Policy translation is the next goal in realising integrated care for children, and it is helpful to look again at the ultimate goals.

> Comprehensive integrated services for children should improve care compared with the traditional service models, solving problems such imbalances between access and expertise in first contact care to improve effectiveness and efficiency and redirect resources to planned proactive care for children with chronic conditions. Child health services evaluation research will be needed to establish the evidence to support new and integrated models of care.
>
> *Fully integrated care should improve population and individual level services and ultimately improve child health.*

Optimising child health requires health system strengthening, and integrated care is one aspect of this endeavour. It is widely accepted that we should now be evolving towards an era of health systems, having progressed through earlier periods dominated by medical and public health models, and more recently healthcare systems. A new era of health systems responds to the understanding that a life course health development approach to optimising health of individuals and populations is needed. Integrating care will be one important aspect of strengthening health systems for children. To achieve these things will require community-based organisations that are accountable to the communities they serve, flexible financing instruments that promote cooperation, and families as active participants and co-designers of health.

A community integrated health system aims to optimise health across the life course. Services and networks between healthcare organisations and public health and other community services are needed to prevent risk factors, promote health, treat disease and manage conditions. Care processes will focus also on optimising health and wellbeing and promoting development. Sophisticated payment systems and information connectivity will be needed. Embedding a community integrated health system for children in a learning healthcare system ensures continuous improvement of quality of care, and services that respond to population need. Finally, population level health improvement will come from a comprehensive approach ensuring that vertical, horizontal, longitudinal, and population integration are part of an overall programme of health systems strengthening.

References

Ådnanes, M., & Halsteinli, V. (2008). Improving child and adolescent mental health services in Norway: Policy and results 1999-2008. *EuroHealth*.

Åhgren, B. (2003). Chain of care development in Sweden: Results of a national study. *International Journal of Integrated Care, 3*, e01.

Åhgren, B. (2010). Competition and integration in Swedish health care. *Health Policy, 96*(2), 91–97.

Åhgren, B., & Axelsson, R. (2011). A decade of integration and collaboration: The development of integrated health care in Sweden 2000-2010. *International Journal of Integrated Care, 11 Spec Ed*, e007.

American Academy of Pediatrics. (1992). Ad hoc task force on definition of the medical home: The medical home. *Pediatrics, 90*(5), 774.

Asthma UK. (2007). *The asthma divide: Inequalities in emergency care for people with asthma in England*. London: Asthma UK.

British Association for Child and Adolescent Public Health and British Association for Community Child Health. (2014). http://www.bacch.org.uk/policy/BACCH%20Family%20Friendly%20Framework%20final.pdf

Cooley, W. C. (2004). Redefining primary pediatric care for children with special health care needs: The primary care medical home. *Current Opinion in Pediatrics, 16*(6), 689–692.

Cooley, W. C., et al. (2009). Improved outcomes associated with medical home implementation in pediatric primary care. *Pediatrics, 124*(1), 358–364.

Curry, N., & Ham, C. (2010). *Clinical and service integration: The route to improved outcomes*. London: King's Fund.

Davies, G. P., et al. (2009). Integrated primary health care in Australia. *International Journal of Integrated Care, 9*, e95.

de Savigny, D., & Adam, T. (Eds.). (2009). *Systems thinking for health systems strengthening*. Geneva: Alliance for Health Policy and Systems Research.

Department of Health. (2010). *Primary care partnerships: Achievements 2000-2010*. Australia: Victoria State Government. https://www2.health.vic.gov.au/primary-and-community-health/primary-care/primary-carepartnerships/pcp-achievements

Diabetes Control and Complications Trial Research Group. (1994). Effect of intensive diabetes treatment on the development and progression of long-term complications in adolescents with insulin-dependent diabetes mellitus: Diabetes Control and Complications Trial. *The Journal of Pediatrics, 125*(2), 177–188.

Diette, G. B., et al. (2001). Comparison of quality of care by specialist and generalist physicians as usual source of asthma care for children. *Pediatrics, 108*(2), 432–437.

Eisenstadt, N. (2011). *Providing a sure start: How government discovered early childhood.* Bristol: Policy Press.

Eurostat. (2013). *Children at risk of poverty or social exclusion. Statistics in focus 4/2013.* European Commission: Eurostat.

Forrest, C., Simpson, L., & Clancy, C. (1997). Child health services research: Challenges and opportunities. *JAMA, 277*, 1787–1793.

Government UK. (2009). *Sure start children's centres—Children, schools and families committee* (Report by UK Government's Department of Children, Schools, and Families). DCSF.

Halfon, N., Plessis, H. D., & Inkelas, M. (2007). Transforming the US child health system. *Health Affairs, 26*(2), 315–330.

Homer, C. J., et al. (2008). A review of the evidence for the medical home for children with special health care needs. *Pediatrics, 122*(4), e922–e937.

Hudson, B. (2005). Information sharing and children's services reform in England: Can legislation change practice? *Journal of Interprofessional Care, 19*(6), 537–546.

Jones, J. (2006). *Parents' views about 'Team around the Child' How your feedback is helping to shape 'Team around the Child' in the future.* Telford: Mindful Practice, Telford and Wreckin Council, Shropshire County Council.

Mangione-Smith, R., et al. (2005). Measuring the effectiveness of a collaborative for quality improvement in pediatric asthma care: Does implementing the chronic care model improve processes and outcomes of care? *Ambulatory Pediatrics: The Official Journal of the Ambulatory Pediatric Association, 5*(2), 75–82.

Manikam, R. (2002). Mental health of children and adolescents. In N. Singh, T. H. Ollendick, & A. Singh (Eds.), *International perspectives on child and adolescent mental health care.* Amsterdam: Elsevier.

Marmot, M. (2012). WHO European review of social determinants of health and the health divide. *The Lancet, 380*, 1011–1029.

Mitchell, E. A., et al. (2005). A randomized controlled trial of an asthma clinical pathway for children in general practice. *Acta Paediatrica, 94*(2), 226–233.

NHS. (2014). *Five year forward view.* https://www.england.nhs.uk/wpcontent/uploads/2014/10/5yfv-web.pdf

Nolte, E., & McKee, M. (2008). *Caring for people with chronic conditions. A health system perspective.* Maidenhead: Open University Press.

Nuffield Foundation. (2015). *Five year forward view: What about children?* Nuffield Foundation.

Odegard, A. (2006). Exploring perceptions of interprofessional collaboration in child mental health care. *International Journal of Integrated Care, 6*, e25.

Press, F., Sumsion, J., & Wong, S. 2012. *Integrated early years provision in Australia .* Professional Support Coordinators Alliance (PSCA).

Royal College of Paediatrics and Child Health. (2012). *Bringing networks to life—An RCPCH guide to implementing clinical networks.* London: RCPCH.

Sartain, S. A., et al. (2002). Randomised controlled trial comparing an acute paediatric hospital at home scheme with conventional hospital care. *Archives of Disease in Childhood, 87*(5), 371–375.

SQW. (2005). *Research to inform the management and governance of children's centres.* DfES.

Stradling, B., MacNeil, M., & Berry, H. (2009). *An evaluation of the development and early implementation phases of Getting it Right for Every Child in Highland: 2006-2009.* Scottish Government.

Strassburg, H.M. (2011). Sozialpaediatrische Versorgung in Deutschland. In: R. Kerbl, et al. (Eds.) *Kinder und Jugendliche im besten Gesundheitssystem der Welt.* Springer: Wien. p. 91-102.

Szczepanski, R. (2010). Schulungen bei chronischen Erkrankungen. Editoral. *Kinder- und Jugendarzt, 41*, 361.

Tamburlini, G. (2012). Child health and child health services in Italy. *Medico e Bambino, 31*, 178–184.

United Nations Convention on the Rights of the Child. (1990). http://www.ohchr.org/EN/ProfessionalInterest/Pages/CRC.aspx

van der Linden, B. A. (2001). *The birth of integration; Explorative studies on the development and implementation of transmural care in the Netherlands 1994-2000*. Utrecht: Universiteit Utrecht.

van der Linden, B. A., Spreeuwenberg, C., & Schrijvers, A. J. (2001). Integration of care in The Netherlands: The development of transmural care since 1994. *Health Policy, 55*(2), 111–120.

Verhaak, P. F., et al. (2015). A new approach to child mental healthcare within general practice. *BMC Family Practice, 16*(1), 132.

Waldfogel, J. 2004. *Social mobility, life chances, and the early years* (CASE Paper 88). London School of Economics, Centre for the Analysis of Social Exclusion London.

Walker, S. (2001). Developing child and adolescent mental health services. *Journal of Child Health Care, 5*(2), 71–76.

White, N. H., et al. (2001). Beneficial effects of intensive therapy of diabetes during adolescence: Outcomes after the conclusion of the Diabetes Control and Complications Trial (DCCT). *The Journal of Pediatrics, 139*(6), 804–812.

Wolfe, I. (2013). Health services for children wtih long-term conditions and non-communicable diseases. In I. Wolfe & M. McKee (Eds.), *European Child Health Services and Systems: Lessons without borders* (pp. 63–93). Maidenhead: Open University Press.

Wolfe, I., Lemer, L., & Cass, H. (2016a). Integrated care: A solution for improving children's health? *Archives of Disease in Childhood, 101*(11), 992–997.

Wolfe, I., Lemer, C., & Cass, H. (2016b). Integrated care: A solution for improving children's health? *Archives of Disease in Childhood, 101*(11), 992–997.

Wolfe, I., et al. (2013). Health services for children in western Europe. *Lancet, 381*(9873), 1224–1234.

Woodman, J. et al. (2015). Integrating primary and secondary care for children and young people: Sharing practice. *Archives of Disease in Childhood*. Published Online First: 20 October 2015. doi:10.1136/archdischild-2015-30855.

Zwar, N., et al. (2006). *A systematic review of chronic disease management*. Sydney: Australian Primary Health Care Institute.

Integrated Care for Frail Older People Suffering from Dementia and Multi-morbidity

22

Henk Nies, Mirella Minkman, and Corine van Maar

22.1 The Challenge

Due to improved living conditions and better health care, life expectancy is expanding very rapidly in many countries (Colombo et al. 2011). Overall, we consider this as a blessing. But this blessing is to some extent ambiguous. Many people also extend their life with years in which they suffer from multiple chronic diseases, disabilities or frailty. One could wonder, whether quality of care has improved quality of life and whether the solution—better treatment and decreased

H. Nies (✉)
Executive Board, Vilans, National Centre of Expertise for Long-Term Care, P.O. Box 8228, Catharijnesingel 47, Utrecht 3503, RE, The Netherlands

Organization Sciences, Vrije Universiteit, De Boelelaan 1081, Amsterdam 1081, HV, The Netherlands
e-mail: h.nies@vilans.nl; h.nies@vu.nl

M. Minkman
Executive Board, Vilans, National Centre of Expertise for Long-Term Care, P.O. Box 8228, Catharijnesingel 47, Utrecht 3503, RE, The Netherlands

Department Innovation and Research, Vilans, National Centre of Expertise for Long-Term Care, P.O. Box 8228, Catharijnesingel 47, Utrecht 3503, RE, The Netherlands

Innovation of the Organization and Governance of Integrated Long Term Care, University of Tilburg/TIAS School for Business and Society, Tilburg, The Netherlands
e-mail: m.minkman@vilans.nl; m.minkman@tias.edu

C. van Maar
Executive Board, Vilans, National Centre of Expertise for Long-Term Care, P.O. Box 8228, Catharijnesingel 47, Utrecht 3503, RE, The Netherlands

Department Innovation and Research, Vilans, National Centre of Expertise for Long-Term Care, P.O. Box 8228, Catharijnesingel 47, Utrecht 3503, RE, The Netherlands
e-mail: Corine@vanmaaradvies.nl

© Springer International Publishing AG 2017
V. Amelung et al. (eds.), *Handbook Integrated Care*,
DOI 10.1007/978-3-319-56103-5_22

mortality—has become a problem. It is a challenge to add life to years, instead of adding years to life.

This requires reconsideration of what we see as 'good health'. The concept of health as defined by the World Health Organisation dating from 1948 -a state of complete physical, mental and social well-being and not merely the absence of disease or infirmity'—appears to be outdated (WHO, 2006). According to this conceptualization, everyone who is not completely successful in life, could be seen as unhealthy (Nordenfelt 2009). Also, the WHO definition is a rather static conceptualisation of health, recognising that being healthy is ambiguous and a dynamic process.

It can be argued that this conceptualization of health contributes to an over-medicalization of society. Machteld Huber and colleagues (2011, 2016) recently proposed a new concept of health: the "ability to adapt and self-manage in the face of social, physical, and emotional challenges" (Huber et al. 2011: 235). Resilience and self-management are key to achieving as good as possible quality of life and wellbeing. The challenge for care professionals, organizations and to society is to support older people in living a meaningful life in dignity, in spite of the 'social, physical, and emotional challenges' they are faced with.

In this chapter we will explore avenues to meeting the multiple health challenges for frail older people, in particular people suffering from dementia and multi-morbidity. We will take their needs as the point of departure for our analysis. Secondly, we will address how integrated care for these people can be organized. We will use the Dutch so called Care Standard Dementia as an example of a framework for service integration at regional level. Thirdly, we will discuss how the implementation can be monitored in regional networks on dementia care by using indicators of integration. Then, we will address our view on future developments in integrated care by applying principles of person centred care and personalized care. Generic standards need to be translated to individuals, as frail older people require tailored care and support. Finally, we will discuss how the organisation of integrated care for frail older people suffering from dementia and/or multiple problems may be built up of similar elements. Adequate diagnostics and multiple interventions by care professionals and organizations will not suffice. A community approach combined with a holistic point of view is also required to improve healthy life styles, as well as adapting the environment.

22.2   Service Users' Needs for Integrating Services

Before thinking about (multiple ways towards) solutions, the needs of the service users are to be explored. Frailty, dementia and multi-morbidity are frequent among the older population.

Frailty is often used to describe the high vulnerability of older people. It manifests itself in adverse health outcomes such as falls leading to immobility, disability and dependency, and other negative health outcomes, which may on their turn lead to increased institutionalization and mortality. Frailty represents an imbalance of the person's homeostatic reserve, with a weakened resistance to harmful agents (Fried et al. 2004; Puts et al. 2005; Gobbens et al. 2011; Castell et al. 2013). The phenotype has been reported to include sarcopenia, loss of endurance, decreased balance and mobility, slowed performance, inactivity, and often decreased cognitive function (Fried et al. 2004; Wick 2011). It is a condition of increased risk caused by functional decline and manifested by three or more core "frailty" elements like weakness, poor endurance, weight loss, low physical activity, and slow gait speed (Fried et al. 2004). In other words, frailty is a multidimensional condition. It is estimated that a large proportion of the older population are frail, ranging from around 5% among people aged 65–70, to more than 15% in persons aged 80 and over, with significant differences among various subpopulations (Fried et al. 2004; Castell et al. 2013).

Dementia occurs relatively often in old age. The term 'dementia' refers to a syndrome and **describes a wide range of symptoms** associated with a decline in memory. According to the World Health Organisation (2015) 'It affects memory, thinking, orientation, comprehension, calculation, learning capacity, language, and judgement. Consciousness is not affected. The impairment in cognitive function is commonly accompanied, and occasionally preceded, by deterioration in emotional control, social behaviour, or motivation.' Alzheimer's disease is the most prevalent and best known form of dementia. It accounts for 60–70% of all cases of people with dementia (WHO 2015). The second most common type of dementia is vascular dementia, accounting for about 10%. Other types are Dementia with Lewy Bodies, mixed dementias, dementia as a manifestation of Parkinson's disease, Frontotemporal Dementia and Creutzfeldt-Jacob Disease. There are also reversible conditions that can cause symptoms of dementia, such as thyroid problems, and vitamin deficiencies (Alzheimer's Association 2015).

Dementia primarily occurs in the 'oldest old'. After the age of 80 the prevalence increases rapidly from around 15% in the age group 80–84 to almost 50% among the 95+ population (OECD 2015). It is expected that worldwide the number of people suffering from dementia will rise from 47.5 million at present to 75.6 million in 2030 and 135.5 million in 2050 (WHO 2015). In the Netherlands dementia is in the top 5 of diseases with the highest mortality among women, it accounts for 5.3% of total health spending in the Netherlands, being the second most expensive disease (Nationaal Kompas Volksgezondheid 2014).

Comorbidity can be conceived as the presence of additional diseases in relation to an index disease in one individual, when the nature of conditions, the time span and sequence of conditions are considered (Valderas et al. 2009). This assumes one disease taking a central place (for instance Alzheimer's disease), in terms of being dominant in terms of the care and well-being of the individual. *Multimorbidity* is defined as the 'co-existence of two or more chronic conditions, where one is not necessarily more central than the others' (Boyd and Fortin 2010: 453). This implies that differentiating the nature of conditions is critical to the conceptualization of comorbidity (Valderas et al. 2009).

Data on incidence and prevalence of multimorbidity are complex to aggregate. Studies vary in the populations being studied, sources of data, data collection methods, age groups and diagnoses that are included (Boyd and Fortin 2010). Data from The Netherlands suggest that around two thirds of the Dutch seniors (65+) have more than one chronic condition. In the 85+ population this is around

85% (Van Oostrom et al. 2011). However, multimorbidity is not only a phenomenon in the older population. An Australian cohort study found more than 40% of the people with multimorbidity are younger than 60 years of age (Boyd and Fortin 2010). The bad news is that prevalence of multimorbidity is rapidly increasing; the good news is that most older people with multimorbidity remain independent and self-supporting, and most people don't feel limited in daily functioning. However, this is different in the oldest age group. Of the Dutch 85+ population, 28% of the men and 46% of the women did envisage serious impairments (Deeg 2012).

Studies into the comorbidities of dementia are scarce. From the few studies that exist, it is known that people with dementia have on average two to eight additional chronic diseases or comorbidities. One of the larger studies among nearly 73,000 people aged 65 and over in Spanish primary care centres, showed that 12% of the people suffering from dementia had dementia as the only diagnosis, almost 70% had at least two comorbidities, nearly 50% had three or more. These figures are around 50% higher than in the total older population. Like in the general population, hypertension and diabetes were most often observed among people with dementia. However, the conditions that were most strongly associated with dementia are Parkinson's disease, congestive heart failure, cerebrovascular disease, anemia, cardiac arrhythmia, chronic skin ulcers, osteoporosis, thyroid disease, retinal disorders, prostatic hypertrophy, insomnia and anxiety and neurosis. Some of these can be considered as risk factors, others as complications and others just as comorbidities (Poblador-Plou et al. 2014). What these studies show, is that dementia often doesn't come 'alone' and that, also related to ageing, more health challenges have to be faced.

Frailty, dementia, co- and multimorbidity are multi-faceted conditions, which require multi-faceted interventions. These multiple, mental and physical problems are often associated with (psycho-) social problems, such as limited participation in society, loneliness or weak social relations, restricted mobility, feelings of meaninglessness or uselessness, anxiety, depression and loss of dignity. From a traditional point of view of health care—being compartmentalised and organized according to medical, paramedical, psychosocial and social disciplines and organizational entities—these needs cannot be met by simply adding up single interventions. On the contrary, coherent multiple interventions are required from professionals, but also from non-professional carers, such as next of kin and neighbours, as well as by the community at large (Nies 2014). In our view, the perspective should be oriented to the new—above depicted—concept of health, in strengthening self-management and resilience. Thus, an integrated approach for these groups of people is needed which goes beyond connecting medical and social care. The new paradigm of health needs focuses on domains such as bodily functions, mental functions, perception, spiritual/existential issues, quality of life, social and societal participation and daily functioning (Huber et al. 2016). To put it in simple wordings: it is about 'living your day-to-day life in a satisfactory way'.

In practice of care delivery this means that while drafting an individual care/support plan with a person suffering from dementia, one needs first to discuss what matters for this person. Before thinking in solutions for care and support, a deeper insight in to what is important for a satisfactory, meaningful way of living is necessary to guide interventions that do not only address the physical and mental condition. It is about how the household can be run, how social contacts can be maintained, what the person can do or mean for his or her relatives, what role intimacy and sexuality plays, whether membership of activities such as a choir or a lunch club, whether spiritual needs are being met and so on. It requires professionals to have attention beyond traditional professional domains. It requires care providing organisations to operate in collaboration in networks of relevant professional and non-professional organisations (volunteers, citizens' initiatives). It requires dementia friendly communities, in which public (police, clubs, public transport etc.) and private services (shops, restaurants, museums etc.) and infrastructure (signage, ramps, housing etc.) are attuned to people with dementia (Davis et al., 2009).

22.3   Inter-organisational Collaboration by Care Standards

In order to organise care and support for older people with complex needs, new coherent inter-professional and inter-organizational arrangements are required. As in many countries, in the Netherlands care and support for people with dementia could and can be improved. Although GP services, diagnostic clinics and home care are available for all persons in the Netherlands, the quality of dementia care is subject to multiple shortcomings and inter-regional differences. Areas for improvement include early detection of the disease, support after medical diagnosis, and under-diagnosis of patient and caregiver depression. Lack of care coordination, timely referrals and information flows between health professionals and informal carers are other improvement areas (Minkman et al. 2009).

To improve dementia care, a number of incentives were initiated in the last decade. In 2008 the National Dementia Program was launched sponsored by the Ministry of Health, Welfare and Sports. This four-year program was coordinated by the knowledge centres Vilans and CBO and the patients' federation Alzheimer Nederland. The latter ensured the users' perspective. Besides implementing improvements in the care delivery process for persons with dementia, a result was also the forming of regional networks of regional care providers. Encouraged and facilitated by the National Program these networks were initiated and further developed by the local care and welfare providers, often in close collaboration with the local users' organisations. At this moment there are about 85 dementia care networks in the Netherlands. In these networks professionals and managers of different organisations (e.g. mental health care, home care, long term care, municipalities) and local Alzheimer users' organisations work together for more coherent dementia care. The needs as defined by users and their informal carers, formulated in their language, were taken as the point of departure for the regional plans (Nies et al. 2009; Minkman et al. 2009).

To prevent that every region had to figure out their own way of setting up inter-organizational arrangements, for this purpose a so-called Care Standard can be helpful. A Care Standard is a document developed multidisciplinarily, which describes what the important ingredients are for dementia care and support, based on the most state-of-the-art (evidence based) knowledge and guidelines. Based on this national standard, solutions can be contextualised to adapt to the specific needs of the local communities.

The emergence of the dementia care networks and the needed collaboration between a wide range of professionals showed that for providing the best care and support guidelines from one perspective or profession were not sufficient. Therefore, a national Care Standard for dementia was developed, led by Alzheimer Nederland, supported by Vilans, and launched in 2013 (Alzheimer Nederland, Vilans 2013). The instrument resembles to a certain extent the NICE guideline on *Dementia, disability and frailty in old age* (NICE 2015), but is more specific in term of what in these services should be organised. The process of developing this standard was time consuming, as all relevant professionals and stakeholders were involved. In the end, the care standard was authorised by all these parties, a current requirement for being acknowledged by the National Quality Institute. In this authorization process different points of view between professional groups became apparent. However, eventually the care standard was established.

The standard focusses on six domains:

1. Early recognition and prevention
2. Diagnostics
3. Case management
4. Treatment, counselling and support
5. Delivery of care and services
6. Organisation of integrated services/care

These domains describe what 'good' care should be, based on—for as far as possible—established guidelines and consensus, and how it should be organised. The sixth domain is of a different order, in the sense that it describes how the interconnections of the services along the process should be structured and managed; it is about the integration of service delivery. The standard does not define *which* professional (group) is eligible for providing care, this is held to the professional organisations and the local context.

Since 2013 a large number of dementia networks started to implement the care standard. However, there is a gap between the (total) standard and the actual delivery of individual person centred dementia care. To bridge this gap a number of networks started to describe a regional or local standard or pathway, which translated the 'national standard' into a regional version. This is a necessary step, because the standard gives a functional description of what should be considered or arranged, not whose task this is or how it looks like in practice. Translating the national standard into a regional version, facilitates implementation and guides steps that can be taken.

Benchmark Dutch dementia networks 2011 and 2013

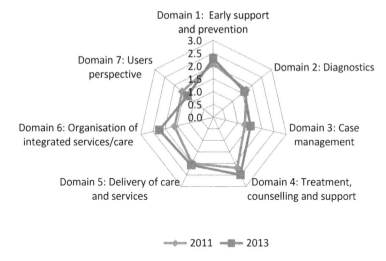

Fig. 22.1 Progress of implementation of dementia care networks in the Netherlands 2011–2013

22.4   Implementation

In order to monitor progress of regional dementia care networks and the implementation of the care standard, the quality of regional collaboration is measured bi-annually by a set of indicators based on the care standard. The above-mentioned domains are measured by a number of operationalised indicators, which are solicited from each dementia network through a digital questionnaire. The user perspective is added as the seventh domain. Figure 22.1 gives an overview of the average scores per domain of the care standard for the years 2011 and 2013. During these years respectively 55 (2011) and 65 (2013) integrated dementia networks participated in the benchmark study (Van Maar et al. 2014).

These results highlight a number of areas for improvement:

1. There are significant differences between regional networks, also with respect to the collaboration with municipalities (which have a role in social support and prevention);
2. Commitments on diagnostics and follow up activities exist, but are not always followed in day-to-day practice;
3. Often, there is no structural funding for case management;
4. Inter-organizational collaboration is not fully implemented;
5. Network partners can further develop what the network has to offer;
6. Structural funding of the networks is still a challenge;

7. Commitments regarding quality of life of people with dementia and their informal cares can be improved.
8. Progress was monitored on the majority of domains, however attention for the client perspective was lagging behind.

In spite of these critical remarks, the networks are realising also progress. They report to work more according to the principles of the Care Standard. Moreover, the coordinators are more connected to other networks in the region, in particular generic networks for care for older people and networks for palliative care. Some of the networks are focusing on one of the domains of dementia care, such as case management, others are focusing on the full range of services.

The Care Standard provides an external framework for inter-organisational collaboration. It is also used as a basis for commissioning services by health care insurers, although not very strictly. Health care insurers are working on process and outcome indicators to make quality and progress visible. The aforementioned network indicators will be used to monitor progress, next to indicators that measure quality of life of service users. Experiences are now being collected, to combine both process and outcome measures on network and client level. Outcome indicators are for instance quality of life of the person with dementia as rated by the principle professional caregiver. Also quality of life of the informal carer is rated, as well as the time he or she thinks he can endure further care tasks.

The example demonstrates that a care standard provides a national framework based on (inter)nationally agreed evidence and consensus which is to be translated at regional level as a basis for—in the terminology of Valentijn et al. (2013)—normative and functional integration of services. It needs regional or local contextualisation to make collaboration work.

22.5 Personalization

The term 'Care Standard' suggests that care is standardized and that personalized care is not feasible. However, the instrument of a Care Standard does recognize individual needs and requires tailoring services to needs. There are two ways of tailoring service provision to needs: one is to apply methodical principles of person centred care in interacting with the service user and his or her informal carers and that are applicable across various groups of service users. The other is to develop more evidence on which interventions work for particular groups of users and—more specifically—for which persons and under which conditions.

For person-centred care a number of main ingredients can be defined. *The key is putting the person and the family at the heart of every decision and empowering them to be genuine partners in their care.* The focus shifts to new models of care that change the conversation from "What's the matter?" to "What matters to you?" Initiatives that focus on person-centreed care are trying to demonstrate that engagement, co-design and co-production with individuals and families improves health, quality and value. A starting point of person-centreed care is that people's care preferences are understood and honored, including at the end of life. In providing care, collaborating with partners on programs designed to improve engagement, shared decision-making and compassionate, empathic care is important (Barry and Edgman-Levitan 2012). In this scope it is not only about care, but a much broader perspective on daily living is captured, in line with the aforementioned new paradigm of health (Huber et al. 2011; Huber et al., 2016). Working with partners to ensure that communities are supported to stay healthy and to provide care for their loved ones closer to home is the leading societal perspective.

On a more detailed level personalized care requires evidence on 'what works for whom?' Most studies on interventions in frail older people and people with dementia are generic. They do not make distinctions between the characteristics of the subgroups, the circumstances in which they are effective and the specific outcomes. However, effects of interventions, also in multi-problem target groups can be enhanced by tailoring services to the idiosyncrasies of the person and his or her social network. A review by van Mierlo et al. (2010) analysed the effectiveness for people with Alzheimer's disease and non-specified types of dementia. Furthermore, a distinction was made in people living in an institutionalized setting, or living in the community. Within these categories distinctions were made such as severity of dementia (mild, moderate, severe), behavioural problems (general, agitation, aggression, disruptive wandering behaviour, repetitive disruptive vocalisations), mental health problems (withdrawn behaviour, depression, bipolar disorders, sleep disorders, irregular sleep-wake rhythm), ADL dependency, living circumstances, gender, and the intervention taking place in a small group or a large group. The outcomes were categorized in factors such as quality of life, behavioural functioning, cognitive functioning, mental health and physical health. Interventions such as reminiscence therapy, behavioural therapy, progressive muscle relaxation, cognitive stimulation, meeting centres support, dementia special care units, were assessed according to these categories. The wide array of interventions demonstrates differentiated effects for different types of dementia for people in different circumstances. The study provided first evidence for referrals and interventions that are more tailored to subgroups of people suffering from dementia. It yielded information which can be implemented and translated by professionals (with a particular specialisation).

A similar review was carried out on the effectiveness of support to informal carers of people with dementia (Van Mierlo et al. 2012). The key message of these studies is that we need to tailor interventions to specific characteristics of frail older people and that a 'one size fits all' policy is not the most effective in dementia care. This personalized knowledge can underpin care standards and the included professional and non-professional interventions, even—or maybe just—in integrated settings. Reality is, that we have a long time to go before there is a sound body of knowledge on personalized interventions.

22.6 Future Perspectives

The current state of play is that dementia is a syndrome that with some exceptions cannot be cured, is multifaceted and asks for person-centreed integrated care. The same holds for frailty and to a large extent for the accompanying complex multi-morbidities. The symptoms can be alleviated and people can be supported in their self-management and resilience. At macro-level the best strategy is prevention of diseases and disability. Recent research shows that the prevalence of dementia is substantially decreasing in some countries if corrected for age, sex, area and deprivation status. Although there are various factors that could have increased dementia prevalence at specific ages, associated with diabetes, survival after stroke, and vascular incidents, it appears that other factors such as improved prevention of vascular disease and higher levels of education appear to have a greater effect (Matthews et al. 2013; Larson et al. 2013). This implies that preventive measures, improvements in treatment and care, and disease modifying interventions combined will be the most effective strategy for the future (Prince et al. 2013).

In a recent report, the OECD (2015) describes the key elements of such a strategy. Generic lifestyles recommendations such as non-smoking, physical activity, healthy diets, cognitive training and formal education are linked to reduced risk of dementia. Treatment of medical conditions such as brain injury, diabetes, mid-life obesity, mid-life hypertension and depression are a second line of reducing the risk of dementia. What at present cannot be influenced are hereditary factors and age.

Following this analysis of risk factors, the OECD defines ten elements of dementia policy:

1. Risk reduction by healthy ageing strategies targeting generic risk factors;
2. Selective early diagnostics (standardized needs assessment) for people who are concerned about symptoms and post-diagnostic support to people;
3. Safer communities for and more acceptance of people with dementia by awareness raising, dementia education at schools, training of people who get in contact with people with dementia in the community;
4. Support of relatives and friends who care for people with dementia respite services, peer to peer support networks, training to informal carers etc.;
5. Safe and appropriate environments including alternatives to institutional care for living with dementia in dignity, making houses suitable for living with dementia and communities safer and more accessible for people with dementia (dementia friendly communities);
6. Access to safe and high quality long-term care services by recruiting and training a dementia care workforce, systematic attention to behavioural symptoms, including the use of antipsychotics and physical restraints, and promoting independence and self-determination through user-directed support;
7. Health services recognizing and dealing with people with dementia effectively, supported by registries or electronic health records, trained, dedicated and specialized staff in hospitals;

8. Increasing opportunities for dying in dignity in the place of people's choosing, trained home care staff in palliative care;
9. Coordinated, proactive and closer to home delivered primary care, multidisciplinary management of comorbidities;
10. Applying the potential of technology to support dementia care.

The OECD translates user-directed support also in financial terms for users and informal carers. It signals that financial systems should support independence and give control to service users and their families. This can be strengthened by appropriate benefits in the form of cash benefits, vouchers or personal care budgets, instead of services in kind. This allows people with dementia to choose the type of services they prefer, which may go well beyond traditional care and across financial, legislative and professional barriers.

Changes in funding and legislation, in roles between stakeholders and in collaboration also have consequences for governance. Governance of (traditional) organisations need reframing, because inter-organisational collaboration becomes more important and asks for new dynamics and governance which is linked to the community (Nies and Minkman 2015).

Lastly, it can be argued that most of the above mentioned elements for dementia policy are also relevant for frail older people and people with multi-morbidities. Hence, one of the key elements is safe and supportive living at home, be it in the community or in a care facility supported by—when useful—technology and by informal caregivers and people in the community. These elements relate to the earlier described new concept of health of Huber (Huber et al. 2016) in which 'whole person thinking' is key.

22.7 Conclusions

The challenges of care for frail older people with dementia and multi-morbidity are increasing, partly due to our improved health care services and increased life expectancy. This challenge is not an easy one. It requires innovative approaches in order to face these challenges and to reduce current and future burden of service users, their families and society. It is a challenge that requires new care paradigms and new organizational paradigms. Working towards the principles of a new concept of health, working towards personalized and person-centreed care in networks, based on shared normative and functional frameworks needs full attention of policy makers and care providing organisations. But the challenge of an ageing population is not merely a professional task in the field of health, long-term and social care. The solution also lies in the community. It has to get tuned to a changing demography, supporting people with limited functioning and supporting healthy behaviour at all ages. Communities need to get acquainted with a changing population, where people sometimes behave 'differently'. Therefore, health and long-term care professionals and services should not limit their focus of integrated care to their peers or care partners; it is a challenge to society and to local communities.

New questions need to be addressed such as how to create adoptive and resilient communities and organisations? What are effective approaches and which preconditions are necessary? How do we improve collaboration between the public sector in a broad sense such as schools, clubs, welfare services, public transport, police on the one hand, and the private sector and private life of citizens, such as housing, shops, banks, neighbours' support, volunteers and the dementia care sector? Examples such as Dementia Friends (see: https://www.dementiafriends. org.uk/) and dementia Friendly Communities (see: http://www.alzheimers.net/ 2013-12-12/building-dementia-friendly-communities/) (Scharlach and Lehning 2013) are promising, but ambitious. Turning population ageing into a blessing requires high ambition on a wide variety of societal actors, integrating their strengths to meet the challenging social and individual needs of frail older people suffering from dementia and accompanying problems.

References

Alzheimer Nederland, Vilans. (2013). *Zorgstandaard Dementie*. Utrecht: Alzheimer Nederland, Vilans.

Alzheimer's Association. (2015). *What is dementia?* Accessed October 14, 2015, from http://www.alz.org/what-is-dementia.asp

Barry, M. J., & Edgman-Levitan, S. (2012). Shared decision making—The pinnacle of patient-centered care. *New England Journal of Medicine, 366*, 780–781.

Boyd, C. M., & Fortin, M. (2010). Future of multimorbidity research: How should understanding of multimorbidity inform health system design? *Public Health Reviews, 32*(2), 451–474.

Castell, M.-V., Sánchez, M., Julián, R., Queipo, R., Martín, S., & Otero, A. (2013). Frailty prevalence and slow walking speed in persons age 65 and older: Implications for primary care. *BMC Family Practice, 14*, 86. doi:10.1186/1471-2296-14-86.

Colombo, F., Llena-Nozal, A., Mercier, J., & Tjadens, F. (2011). *Help wanted? Providing and paying for long-term care*. Paris: OECD Health Policy Studies.

Davis, S., Byers, S., Nay, R., & Koch, S. (2009). Guiding design of dementia friendly environments in residential care settings: Considering the living experiences. *Dementia, 8* (2), 185–203. doi:10.1177/1471301209103250.

Deeg, D. (2012). Veroudering en ouderenzorg. In M. Adriaansen, P. Hermsen, & R. van der Sande (Eds.), *Langdurige zorg. Thema's en perspectieven* (pp. 133–155). Deventer: Van Tricht Uitgeverij.

Fried, L. P., Ferrucci, L., Darer, J., Williamson, J. D., & Anderson, G. (2004). Untangling the concepts of disability, frailty, and comorbidity: Implications for improved targeting and care. *Journal of Gerontology: Medical Sciences, 59*(3), 255–263.

Gobbens, R., Luijkx, K., Wijnen-Sponselee, R., Assen, M. v., & Schols, J. (2011). Wetenschappelijke definities en metingen van kwetsbaarheid. In C. v. Campen (Ed.), *Kwetsbare ouderen* (pp. 39–50). Den Haag: Sociaal en Cultureel Planbureau.

Huber, M., Knotnerus, J. A., Green, L., van der Horst, H., Jadad, A. R., Kromhout, D., et al. (2011). How should we define health? *British Medical Journal, BMJ, 343*, d4163.

Huber, M., van Vliet, M., Giezenberg, M., Winkens, B., Heerkens, Y., Dagnelie, P. C., & Knotnerus, J. A. (2016). Towards a 'patient-centred' operationalisation of the new dynamic concept of health: A mixed methods study. *BMJ Open, 6*, e010091. doi:10.1136/bmjopen-2015-010091.

Larson, E. B., Kristine Yaffe, M. P. H., & Langa, K. M. (2013). New insights into the dementia epidemic. *New England Journal of Medicine, 369*, 2275–2277. doi:10.1056/NEJMp1311405.

Matthews, F. E., Arthur, A., Barnes, L. A., Bond, J., Jagger, C., Robinson, L., & Brayne, C. (2013). A two-decade comparison of prevalence of dementia in individuals aged 65 years and older from three geographical areas of England: Results of the cognitive function and ageing study I and II. *The Lancet, 382*(9902), 1405–1412.

Minkman, M. M. N., Ligthart, S. A., & Huijsman, R. (2009). Integrated dementia care in the Netherlands: A multiple case study of case management programmes. *Health and Social Care in the Community, 17*(5), 485–494.

Nationaal Kompas Volksgezondheid. (2014). *Dementie.* Accessed October 14, 2015, from http://www.nationaalkompas.nl/gezondheid-en-ziekte/ziekten-en-aandoeningen/psychische-stoornissen/dementie/

NICE. (2015). Dementia, disability and frailty in later life—Mid-life approaches to delay or prevent onset. *NICE Guidelines [NG16].* Accessed January 7, 2016, from http://www.nice.org.uk/guidance/ng16

Nies, H. (2014). Communities as co-producers in integrated care. *International Journal of Integrated Care.* ISSN 1568-4156.

Nies, H., Meerveld, J., & Denis, R. (2009). Dementia care: Linear links and networks. *Healthcare Papers, 10*(1), 34–43.

Nies, H., & Minkman, M. (2015). Innovatie in governance. Eigenaarschap van het publieke belang in een participatiesamenleving. In H. Den Uyl, T. van Zonneveld (red.), *Zorg voor toezicht. De maatschappelijke betekenis van governance in de zorg* (pp. 74–82). Amsterdam: Mediawerf.

Nordenfelt, L. (2009). Health, autonomy and quality of life: Some basic concepts in the theory of health care and the care of older people. In L. Nordenfelt (Ed.), *Dignity in care for older people* (pp. 3–25). Chichester: Wiley.

OECD. (2015). *Addressing dementia: The OECD response.* Paris: OECD Health Policy Studies, OECD Publishing.

Poblador-Plou, B., Calderón-Larrañaga, A., Marta-Moreno, J., Hancco-Saavedra, J., Sicras-Mainar, A., Soljak, M., & Prados-Torres, A. (2014). Comorbidity of dementia: A cross-sectional study of primary care older patients. *BMC Psychiatry, 14*, 84. doi:10.1186/1471-244X-14-84.

Prince, M., Bryce, R., Albanese, E., Wome, A., Ribeiro, W., & Ferri, C. P. (2013). The global prevalence of dementia: A systematic review and metaanalysis. *Alzheimer's and Dementia, 9* (1), 63–75.

Puts, M. T. E., Lips, P., & Deeg, D. H. J. (2005). Static and dynamic measures of frailty predicted decline in performance-based and self-reported physical functioning. *Journal of Clinical Epidemiology, 58*, 1188–1198.

Scharlach, A. E., & Lehning, A. J. (2013). Age-friendly communities and social inclusion in the United States of America. *Ageing and Society, 33*, 110–136. doi:10.1017/S0144686X12000578.

Valderas, J. M., Starfield, B., Sibbald, B., Salisbury, C., & Roland, M. (2009). Defining comorbidity: Implications for understanding health and health services. *The Annals of Family Medicine, 7*(4), 357–363.

Valentijn, P., Schepman, S., Opheij, W., & Bruijnzeels, M. (2013). Understanding integrated care: A comprehensive conceptual framework based on the integrative function of primary care. *International Journal of Integrated Care, 13* (Jan–Mar), URN:NBN:NL:UI:10-1-114415.

Van Mierlo, L. D., Van der Roest, H. G., Meiland, F. J. M., & Dröes, R. M. (2010). Personalized dementia care: Proven effectiveness of psychosocial interventions in subgroups (review). *Ageing Research Reviews, 9*, 163–183.

Van Mierlo, L. D., Meiland, F. J. M., Van der Roest, H. G., & Dröes, R. M. (2012). Personalized caregiver support: Effectiveness of psychosocial interventions in subgroups of caregivers of people with dementia (Review). *International Journal of Geriatric Psychiatry, 27*, 1–14.

Van Maar, C. E., Wijenberg, E., Stapersma, E., & Siegerink, E. (2014). *Ketens dementie goed op koers met de Zorgstandaard Dementie als kompas.* Utrecht: Vilans.

Van Oostrom, S. H., Picavet, H. S. J., van Gelder, B. M., Lemmens, L. C., Hoeymans, N., Verheij, R. A., Schellevis, F. G., & Baan, C. A. (2011). Multimorbiditeit en comorbiditeit in de Nederlandse bevolking—gegevens van huisartsenpraktijken. *Nederlands Tijdschrift voor Geneeskunde, 155*, A3193.

Wick, J. Y. (2011). Understanding frailty in the geriatric population. *The Consultant Pharmacist, 26*(9), 634–645.

WHO. (2006). *Constitution of the World Health Organization.* www.who.int/governance/eb/who_ constitution_en.pdf

World Health Organization. (2015, March). *Dementia* (Fact sheet N°362).

Physical and Mental Health

23

Chris Naylor

Physical and mental health are closely dependent on each other. Evidence reviewed in this chapter demonstrates that having a physical health condition significantly increases the risk of developing a mental health problem, and vice versa. More broadly, mental health is a vital component of health and well-being and is influenced by the activities of all parts of the health care system. It is for this reason that the World Health Organisation has long argued that there is "no health without mental health" (Herrman et al. 2005).

Despite this interdependency, it often remains the case that the institutional architecture of health systems, the design of reimbursement systems, and the training and education of professionals, all tend to reinforce structural and cultural barriers between mental and physical health care. As described below, these barriers mean that mental and physical health are often treated as if existing in isolation of each other.

When thinking about this dimension of integrated care, there are three separate but closely related issues that require consideration:

1. Comorbidity between long-term physical health conditions and mental health problems is highly common and has a significant effect on outcomes
2. Psychological distress is frequently expressed in the form of physical symptoms—so-called 'medically unexplained symptoms' that lack an organic cause and are often challenging to manage
3. All physical illness can have an important psychological or emotional component, regardless of whether or not a diagnosable mental health problem is present

The first two of these issues relate to defined client groups, whereas the third is a cross-cutting issue applicable to any form of healthcare. All three have profound

C. Naylor (✉)
Health Policy, The King's Fund, London, UK
e-mail: c.naylor@kingsfund.org.uk

© Springer International Publishing AG 2017   383
V. Amelung et al. (eds.), *Handbook Integrated Care*,
DOI 10.1007/978-3-319-56103-5_23

implications for integrated care. In this section we will focus largely on the specific needs of people with comorbid conditions and/or medically unexplained symptoms. However, many of the principles discussed are also relevant to the wider issue of the psychological and emotional aspects of health.

The prevalence of comorbid mental and physical health problems is high. A review of the literature suggested that overall, around 45% of people with mental health problems also have a long-term physical health problem. Similarly, people with cardiovascular diseases, chronic respiratory diseases, diabetes or chronic musculoskeletal disorders are around two to three times more likely to experience a mental health problem than the general population (Naylor et al. 2012). The strength of this interaction is exacerbated significantly by social deprivation—among those with multiple physical disorders living in the lowest socio-economic groups, the prevalence of mental ill health is almost 50% (Barnett et al. 2012). Medically unexplained symptoms are also highly common, accounting for an estimated 15–30% of all primary care consultations (Kirmayer et al. 2004) and, in one study, over 20% of all outpatient consultations among the most frequent attenders (Reid et al. 2001).

Physical health outcomes are poor among people with co-morbid mental health problems. Mortality rates among people with cardiovascular diseases or diabetes are significantly higher for those who also have depression (Blumenthal et al. 2003; Junger et al. 2005; Lesperance et al. 2002; Park et al. 2013). Outcomes are particularly poor for people with schizophrenia or other psychoses, for whom excess mortality largely attributable to poorer physical health leads to a life expectancy 15–20 years below the general population (Laursen et al. 2014). The presence of mental health problems can lead to reduced access to care for physical health problems—for example, in a Canadian study revascularisation rates among people with ischaemic heart disease were found to be significantly lower for those who also had dementia or psychosis, after adjusting for clinical need (Kisely et al. 2007).

The interaction between physical and mental health has significant consequences in terms of resource utilisation and costs. In an analysis conducted in the UK, emergency department attendance rates were three times higher and unplanned hospital admissions were five times higher among people with mental health problems, compared to a matched control group drawn from the general population, with most of these attendances and admissions being for physical health care (Dorning et al. 2015). A large number of other studies have confirmed that conditions such as depression significantly increase the risk of unplanned hospitalisation for ambulatory care sensitive conditions (Davydow et al. 2013). Overall, by interacting with and exacerbating physical health problems comorbid mental health problems are estimated to increase the costs of long-term conditions by at least 45% per affected person. This suggests that at least 12% of all expenditure on chronic diseases in high-income countries is linked to poor mental health and well-being (Naylor et al. 2012). In addition to this, a conservative estimate of the cost of medically unexplained symptoms is around 3% of the entire health budget in the UK (Bermingham et al. 2010).

Prevention / public health	1. Incorporating mental health into public health programmes
	2. Health promotion and prevention of physical ill health among people with severe mental illnesses
General practice	3. Improving management of 'medically unexplained symptoms' in primary care
	4. Strengthening primary care for people with severe mental illnesses
Chronic disease management	5. Supporting the mental health of people with long term conditions
	6. Supporting the mental health of carers
Hospital care	7. Mental health liaison in acute general hospitals
	8. Physical health liaison in mental health inpatient facilities
Community / social care	9. Integrated support for perinatal mental health
	10. Supporting the mental health needs of people in residential homes

Fig. 23.1 Key areas where integration of physical and mental health is needed (Source: Naylor et al. 2016)

These and other findings suggest there is a strong case for integrating physical and mental health care more closely. Figure 23.1 lists 10 areas where the opportunities to achieve better integration are particularly striking (Naylor et al. 2016). People with comorbid mental and physical health problems, as well as those with medically unexplained symptoms, should be seen as priority target group for integrated care. The rest of this section outlines some of the challenges involved in providing integrated care to these client groups, and describes the evidence-based interventions available for doing so.

23.1 Challenges Involved in Integrating Physical and Mental Health Care

23.1.1 Disease Factors

Integrating mental and physical health care is not one challenge, but rather a whole set of related challenges. This follows from the fact that underneath the umbrella term 'mental health problems' sits a wide array of very different conditions. This includes various kinds of depressive and anxiety disorders, psychoses such as schizophrenia, eating disorders, personality disorders, neurocognitive disorders such as dementias or delirium, and substance abuse disorders. Forms of integration that may be successful for one of these will not necessarily translate to another. However, there is enough commonality for a discussion of generic approaches and issues to be meaningful.

A distinctive feature of mental health is the degree to which needs are not currently met. For many mental health problems this far exceeds levels of unmet needs observed in physical health—for example, even in high-income countries it is typical for less than half of those with depressive or anxiety disorders to be receiving any form of formal treatment, and in the case of alcohol and other substance abuse disorders the proportion is smaller still (Kohn et al. 2004). In this context, it is important to recognise that integration of mental health care into general health systems may lead to identification of previously unmet needs. This improvement in access to care is one of the potential benefits that a more integrated approach offers. However, it does also highlight the need to ensure that sufficient capacity exists to deal with new demand.

A significant issue in mental health is the paucity of high quality data. In many countries prevalence data is limited, and the nature of many mental health diagnoses and interventions makes outcomes measurement intrinsically difficult. This lack of reliable data adds to the challenges involved in planning new, integrated approaches to care. It is no coincidence that some of the most successful examples of integrated mental and physical health care have made significant investments in building robust, shared data systems.

23.1.2 Patient Factors

One of the most important clinical consequences of comorbid mental health problems is the impact on self-care and self-management. A cornerstone of integrated care is the principle that chronic diseases are managed most effectively when patients take an active role in this themselves. Comorbid mental health problems can significantly reduce a person's ability and motivation to manage their physical health. For example, diabetic self-care, medication adherence and health behaviours (e.g. diet, exercise, smoking) are significantly poorer among people who also have depression (Lin et al. 2004; Egede et al. 2009). Clinicians may need to adopt different consultation techniques to help motivate and support people with mental health problems to look after their physical health. However, there is evidence that self-management programs and lifestyle interventions can be effective for this group, particularly when adapted to the specific needs of people with mental health problems (Cimo et al. 2012).

A challenge for clinicians working in this area is the multiple and diverse understandings that patients may have of the relationship between their mental and physical health. The sensitivities around this require particular skill in the case of medically unexplained symptoms. People experiencing physical symptoms which may be highly painful and debilitating should not be given the impression that a clinician believes their symptoms are 'all in the head'. Introducing the notion that physical symptoms and mental health are closely intertwined takes a high level of clinical skill and sensitivity, and professionals may require training in specific techniques that can be used to discuss the psychological aspects of health without undermining the physical reality of symptoms.

23.1.3 Professional Factors

The trend for increasing sub-specialisation in medical education reinforces the notion that some clinicians are responsible for the body, while others are responsible for the mind. In most countries there is little or no mandatory mental health training in the core educational curricula for general practitioners, acute physicians or nurses. Where mental health rotations are available, these are often in acute psychiatric facilities, and fail to provide trainees with exposure to mental health in a form that will be relevant to general health care settings. Similarly, many mental health professionals report feeling under-confident in relation to even basic aspects of physical health care, such as measuring blood pressure.

While the issue of skills is important, a more fundamental challenge is the existence of deeply engrained attitudinal barriers, and a restrictive understanding of the boundaries of professional responsibility. Integrating physical and mental health care requires that professionals on either side of the 'divide' see themselves as being responsible for health, in the fullest sense of the word. This does not mean that all professionals need to become mental health experts, but it does mean that the culture of seeing mental health as something distinct and separate from the rest of health care needs to change. Part of the challenge here will involve acknowledging and confronting the stigma that still exists around mental health, and related issues regarding the relative status of mental health professionals.

23.1.4 Institutional and Systems Factors

Physical and mental health care are often, although not always, provided by separate organisations. While integration at the organisational level is neither necessary nor sufficient for integration at the clinical or service level (Curry and Ham 2010), this institutional separation does create some specific barriers. For example, the impact of some attempts to deliver more integrated services has been reduced as a result of separate and incompatible IT systems being used in physical and mental health care providers. A specific example of this is that liaison psychiatrists working in acute hospital settings (but employed by a separate mental health provider) are not always able to access the medical records used by other staff in the hospital.

Separate reimbursement systems can also create a barrier to integration. For example, in the UK most physical health care is reimbursed through activity-based payment, whereas mental health providers are paid largely through a single block contract covering the full set of services they provide. Financial incentives to integrate physical and mental health care more closely are often weak, with the costs and benefits of integration accruing to different budget-holders.

New provider models such as accountable care organisations potentially offer a way of overcoming this institutional separation, and creating financial incentives to manage physical and mental health together. However, it appears that in the USA this opportunity has not yet been widely embraced, with few accountable care organisations pursuing innovative service models that integrate mental health care with general health systems (Lewis et al. 2014).

23.2   Goals of Integrated Physical and Mental Health Care

As discussed in the introduction, the rationale for integrating physical and mental health care is founded on evidence demonstrating that treating physical and mental health separately leads to poor outcomes for patients and unnecessary expense for health systems. The overall goal of integrated physical and mental health care should be to overcome this separation in such a way that there is improvement in terms of both outcomes and costs. Figure 23.2 provides a more detailed analysis of what some of the specific goals might be, in terms of clinical practice, health outcomes, professional skills and attitudes, and health care utilisation.

Clinical practice

- Routine exploration of the psychological and mental health aspects of physical health, including through routine screening for mental health problems among people with long-term physical health conditions
- Routine physical health checks for people with mental illnesses
- More effective management of medically unexplained symptoms in primary care
- Closer working between mental health specialists and other professionals, with collaborative care protocols and clear referral pathways

Health outcomes

- Improved clinical outcomes for people with comorbid physical and mental health conditions
- Reduction in all-cause mortality rates among people with mental health problems
- Improved self-management and self-efficacy among people with comorbid physical and mental health conditions
- Lower rates of smoking among people with mental health problems and improvements in other health behaviours e.g. diet, exercise

Professional skills and attitudes

- All health and social care professionals see physical and mental health as part of their job
- Physical and mental health included in core educational curricula and ongoing training for all professionals
- Greater confidence among physical health professionals to discuss mental health and well-being with patients – and vice versa
- Eradication of stigmatising beliefs in the health and social care workforce about mental illness

Health service utilisation

- Reduction in unplanned hospital admission for ambulatory care sensitive conditions among people with mental health problems
- Reduction in emergency transfers from mental health inpatient facilities to acute general hospitals
- Reduction in unnecessary tests and investigations among people with medically unexplained symptoms

Fig. 23.2 Goals of integrated physical and mental health care

23.3   Key Components of Integrated Physical and Mental Health Care

23.3.1 Collaborative Care

Improving support for the mental health and psychological aspects of physical illness cannot mean treating a large number of additional people within specialist mental health services; an expansion along these lines would be both unaffordable and undesirable. Instead, a primary care-based approach is needed. The best-developed model available for this is collaborative care.

Collaborative care is a model for managing patients with chronic conditions in primary care that has been extensively tested in a number of countries. A major focus has been on using collaborative care to improve support for people with comorbid physical and mental health problems. The core components of collaborative care are:

- Proactive management of physical and mental health conditions by a non-medical case manager, working closely with a GP and/or other primary care staff
- Regular supervision meetings involving the case manager, primary care staff and a mental health specialist, in which new cases and progress made by existing patients is reviewed
- Use of standardised treatment protocols by the case manager
- Active exploration of the interaction between mental well-being and physical conditions by the case manager
- In some cases, case managers may also be trained to deliver brief psychological interventions
- A focus on education and skills transfer among the different professionals involved in the collaborative care process

Collaborative care is often delivered within a stepped care framework, with escalation to more specialist support where required. For example, NICE recommends the use of collaborative care for people with moderate to severe depression alongside a chronic physical health condition, particularly in cases where the depression has not responded to initial psychological or pharmacological treatment, but is not considered sufficiently severe to warrant a referral to specialist mental health services (NICE 2009).

The collaborative care model has been used both in multi-provider systems, and within the context of integrated delivery systems. In the USA the principles of collaborative care have been used by organisations such as Intermountain Healthcare (see Box 23.1), the Veterans Health Administration, and Kaiser Permanente as part of major integrated care programmes seeking to integrate mental health services into primary care. Collaborative care approaches have also been used in Europe, for example in the UK (Coventry et al. 2015), Italy (Rucci et al. 2012) and the Netherlands (Goorden et al. 2015), and in some lower- and middle-income countries, for example through the 'PRIME' and 'Emerald' research programmes (see http://www.prime.uct.ac.za/ and http://www.emerald-project.eu/).

The principles of collaborative care have been adapted for use in other settings outside of primary care. For example, there is some evidence indicating that collaborative care can be successfully used in obstetrics and gynaecology clinics for managing depression during the perinatal period (Katon et al. 2015).

Box 23.1 Case Study: Mental Health Integration in Intermountain Healthcare
In the early 2000s, primary care practitioners in Intermountain Healthcare, a non-profit health system operating in Utah and Idaho, USA, identified a need for a more effective way of supporting the large number of people presenting with mental health needs, often alongside a mixture of physical illness, substance abuse problems and complex social circumstances. In response to this, Intermountain developed a mental health integration (MHI) programme, which has now been rolled out in the majority of primary care clinics.

The MHI programme involves primary care practitioners accepting an increased responsibility for providing mental health, with the support of an enhanced multi-disciplinary team embedded in primary care. Key elements of the model include:

- Team-based care with mental health professionals embedded in the primary care team, including input from psychiatry, psychology, psychiatric nursing and social work
- A nurse care manager to coordinate medical, psychological and social support
- Significant investments in training practice staff (including physicians, nurses, receptionists and others) in mental health awareness, empathic communication skills, and shared-decision making
- Shared electronic medical records accessible by all team members
- Proactive screening for mental health problems among high-risk groups in the population
- Supported self-management of physical and mental health
- Making use of extended community resources and peer support
- Using disease registries and evidence-based guidelines
- Exploiting new technologies e.g. telehealth and telecare

Under MHI, mental healthcare is delivered through a stepped care approach, with the balance of responsibilities between primary and specialist care depending on the level of complexity. Overall, around 80% of mental healthcare is delivered by non-specialists. Evaluations of the model have found significant improvements in both physical and mental health outcomes, better self-management and lower per patient medical costs (Reiss-Brennan et al. 2010).

23.3.2 Multidisciplinary Case Management

Community-based multidisciplinary teams are a key mechanism for coordinating the care provided to people with multiple or complex chronic diseases. Successful integration of physical and mental health care requires that mental health is fully embedded within these teams. A number of different approaches towards this have been tried, some of which are disease-specific whereas others cut across multiple diseases.

Disease-specific approaches include multidisciplinary teams established to respond to the physical and mental health needs of people with diabetes. For example, as part of an integrated care programme in North West London, liaison psychiatrists attend a regular multidisciplinary case conference at which the needs of people who are struggling to manage their diabetes are discussed. An evaluation found that mental health issues were discussed in over 80% of all cases brought to these meetings, with the impact of mental well-being on self-management being a particularly common theme (Sachar 2012). Another successful example of multi-disciplinary care for the physical and mental aspects of long-term conditions is the 'three dimensions for diabetes' service (see case study in Box 23.2 below).

An alternative to the disease-specific approach is to use multidisciplinary team meetings to discuss patients identified as being at greatest risk of unplanned hospital admission (generally through the use of a risk prediction algorithm). Again, it is important that input from mental health specialists is an integral part of this approach. An example is the 'extensive care' model. In this, a dedicated primary care clinic exists (often virtually) to provide intensive, multidisciplinary case management to the highest need patients in a defined locality. This model has so far been used largely for frail older people, but its applicability to other multi-morbid patients, including those with co-occurring physical and mental health problems, is now being tested. For example, as part of the 'vanguard' integrated care program in England, an extensive care service has recently been established in Blackpool focusing on people with complex mental health problems, substance abuse issues and other problems including co-morbid physical health conditions. The effectiveness of these approaches still requires evaluation.

Box 23.2 Case Study: Three Dimension of Care for Diabetes

'Three dimension of care for diabetes' (3DFD) was an award-winning service in an inner-city area of London, UK, which provided integrated care for the physical, mental and social aspects of diabetes. The service was specifically targeted at people with poor glycaemic control, and served a highly mixed population, including many people with multiple complex co-morbid conditions and high levels of social deprivation. More recently, the 3DFD service has evolved into a broader service aimed at people with other conditions beyond diabetes, and is now known as 'three dimensions for long-term conditions'.

(continued)

Box 23.2 (continued)

While inclusion of a mental health professional in multidisciplinary team meetings is increasingly common in diabetes care, the 3DFD model went further than most by having a wider range of mental health professionals fully integrated in the team and including the social dimension of support. Alongside diabetologists and diabetes nurses, the team included a psychiatrist, psychologists and social support workers. This allowed the team to provide support to people with a wider range of mental health problems—not only mild-to-moderate depression or anxiety, but also severe depression, psychosis, eating disorders or dementia.

The team provided brief psychological therapies as well as interventions targeting social problems, such as issues with housing, debt management, carer support or domestic violence. In addition to seeing patients directly, an important part of the role of mental health staff in the 3DFD team was to provide formal and informal training to diabetes physicians and nurses, for example in motivational interviewing techniques, basic principles of cognitive behavioural therapy, and general training in mental health.

An evaluation of 3DFD found significant improvements in glycaemic control, reduced psychological distress and a reduction in emergency attendances and unscheduled admissions.

23.3.3 Liaison Mental Health

Liaison psychiatrists, and related professionals such as liaison nurses and clinical health psychologists, are experts in the interface between mental and physical health. These professionals are most commonly employed in acute hospital settings, often as part of liaison psychiatry or psychological medicine teams. These teams perform a vital function in identifying mental health needs among people attending emergency departments, outpatient clinics or using inpatient services, and ensuring that appropriate support is then available to meet these needs.

Mental health problems are highly prevalent in hospital settings, and the need for high-quality liaison mental health services is clear. It is therefore regrettable that the provision of these services is often highly variable. Guidance for commissioners of liaison mental health services suggests that the following standards should be met (JCPMH 2013):

- Liaison services should be comprehensive, with clear and explicit responsibility for all patients in acute hospital settings
- Liaison services should cover all ages, including children, adults and older people
- Part of the role of liaison clinicians should be to build capacity within the wider hospital workforce, for example by improving the mental health skills of nurses
- There should be a single integrated set of healthcare notes

- Integrated governance arrangements should exist to allow the liaison team to work closely with the acute hospital
- There should be capability for providing a range of interventions including brief psychological therapy
- Liaison teams should have strong links with specialist mental health services in the community, and good knowledge of local resources
- Liaison clinicians should be able to assess physical health as well as mental health

In some cases, liaison mental health services have extended their focus beyond acute hospitals, becoming involved in supervisory and direct clinical activities in primary care and other community settings (including through collaborative care models and multi-disciplinary locality teams, as described above). This is a promising development and particularly relevant to the care of people with ongoing needs likely to continue beyond their hospital stay, such as those with long-term conditions or medically unexplained symptoms.

23.3.4 Managing Medically Unexplained Symptoms in Primary Care

A critical aspect of effective care for people with medically unexplained symptoms is the quality and style of communication between professionals and patients. Clinicians need to strike a delicate balance, introducing people to new ways of understanding their symptoms without challenging the reality of their experience. Techniques such as motivational interviewing can provide a useful framework for consultations.

Some psychological therapies, in particular cognitive behavioural therapy, have been shown to be effective and cost-effective interventions for people with medically unexplained symptoms (van Dessel et al. 2014; Konnopka et al. 2012). One benefit is that these can have the effect of improving the patient's 'psychological literacy' such that their readiness to engage in discussions with their GP about the psychological aspects of their symptoms is subsequently improved. Psychological therapies and other interventions for medically unexplained symptoms can be delivered in primary care through stepped-care approaches (Guthrie 2008).

The challenges of working with people experiencing medically unexplained symptoms means that educational interventions aimed at GPs and other primary care staff are often particularly valuable. A 'primary care psychotherapy consultation service' provided to GPs in the City and Hackney area of London is one example of an innovative service that combines an educational function with direct clinical work. An evaluation suggested the service has both delivered results for patients and been positively received by the local GP community (Parsonage et al. 2014)—see Naylor et al. (2016) for a detailed case study.

23.4   Results of Integrated Care Approaches

Integration of physical and mental health is a new frontier for integrated care, and is an area where further evaluative studies are needed. However, in some areas a significant body of research already exists, and the evidence that is available suggests that there are significant opportunities both for quality improvement and potentially for improving the cost-effectiveness of care.

Collaborative care is one area where the evidence base is relatively well-established. Studies such as the TEAMcare trial in the USA (Rosenberg et al. 2014) and the COINCIDE trial in the UK (Coventry et al. 2015) have found that collaborative care interventions can improve recovery from depression among people with diabetes and/or coronary heart disease, at the same time as improving self-management of physical health. This was also the conclusion of a systematic review conducted by Huang et al. (2013). Collaborative care also appears to be highly cost-effective and potentially cost-reducing (Katon et al. 2008, 2012; Simon et al. 2007).

Liaison psychiatry has received significant recent interest in the UK, partly in response to the impressive findings of an economic evaluation of a 'rapid assessment interface discharge' (RAID) service in Birmingham. Parsonage and Fossey (2011) found that by facilitating early discharge from hospital and reducing rates of readmission (particularly among older people), the value of reduced bed use within the acute hospital exceeded the costs of the RAID service by a factor of more than 4 to 1.

Similarly, there is evidence of significant potential benefits to both patients and the system stemming from embedding mental health specialists within chronic disease management programs. There is particularly good evidence of the benefits of including a psychological component within pulmonary and cardiac rehabilitation programmes. For example, a systematic review found that psychological interventions for people with coronary heart disease led to improvements in depression and anxiety, and also a small reduction in cardiac mortality. However, it also concluded that more research is needed to establish which patient groups benefit most and what the core components of effective interventions should be (Whalley et al. 2014). There is some evidence that integrated psychological support can reduce costs related to conditions such as COPD (Howard et al. 2010) and angina (Moore et al. 2007).

23.5   Lessons Learned

It is clear that in the absence of integrated care, the interaction between physical and mental ill health can lead to significantly poorer health outcomes, reduced quality of life, and increased costs to the health care system. The prevailing approach to dealing with chronic disease is at risk of failing unless it is recognised that many of the people most in need of integrated care have comorbid psychological or mental health problems that can impair their ability and motivation to self-manage. Care for large numbers of people could be improved by better integrating mental health support within primary care, acute hospital care and chronic disease management programmes.

Fundamentally, integrating physical and mental health care involves re-drawing professional boundaries, such that all practitioners working in health and social care accept their role as de facto mental health professionals. Similarly, mental health specialists should see physical health and well-being as part of their responsibility. For many, this poses a significant cultural change as well as a technical one. It will therefore require skilled and committed leadership, and new forms of integrated training and education.

Naylor et al. (2016) discuss the practical lessons learned from the process of implementing integrated service models for physical and mental health in the UK. A key finding is that innovation has often been driven by individual clinical champions working, at least initially, in relative isolation from the rest of the system. To be sustainable, the work of these clinical innovators needs to receive support from senior leaders within local organisations, and must be reinforced by consistent messages from this leadership. Without this, there is little hope of widespread cultural change taking place. A powerful catalyst for cultural change is direct contact between professionals working in different parts of the system—specifically, those traditionally responsible for physical health and those specialising in mental health. Given this, the service models which have the greatest potential may be those which combine direct clinical work with joint supervision and educational functions, creating opportunities (formal and informal) for skills transfer between mental and physical health care professionals.

Integration of physical and mental health care should be seen as a core component of any integrated care programme. This important aspect of integrated care has often received insufficient attention in the past, and should be a priority for research and service improvement in future.

References

Barnett, K., Mercer, S. W., Norbury, M., Watt, G., Wyke, S., & Guthrie, B. (2012). Epidemiology of multimorbidity and implications for health care, research, and medical education: A cross-sectional study. *The Lancet, 380*(9836), 37–43.

Bermingham, S. L., Cohen, A., Hague, J., & Parsonage, M. (2010). The cost of somatisation among the working-age population in England for the year 2008-2009. *Mental Health in Family Medicine, 7*(2), 71–84.

Blumenthal, J. A., Lett, H. S., Babyak, M. A., White, W., Smith, P. K., Mark, D. B., Jones, R., Matthew, J. P., Newman, M. F., & NORG Investigators. (2003). Depression as a risk factor for mortality after coronary bypass surgery. *The Lancet, 362*(9384), 604–609.

Cimo, A., Stergiopoulos, E., Cheng, C., Bonato, S., & Dewa, C. S. (2012). Effective lifestyle interventions to improve type II diabetes self-management for those with schizophrenia or schizoaffective disorder: A systematic review. *BMC Psychiatry, 12*, 24.

Coventry, P., Lovell, K., Dickens, C., Bower, P., Chew-Graham, C., McElvenny, D., Hann, M., Cherrington, A., Garrett, C., Gibbons, C. J., Baguley, C., Roughley, K., Adeyemi, I., Reeves, D., Waheed, W., & Gask, L. (2015). Integrated primary care for patients with mental and physical multimorbidity: Cluster randomised controlled trial of collaborative care for patients with depression comorbid with diabetes or cardiovascular disease. *British Medical Journal, 350*, h638.

Curry, N., & Ham, C. (2010). *Clinical and service integration. The route to improved outcomes.* London: The King's Fund.

Davydow, D. S., Katon, W. J., Lin, E. H., Ciechanowski, P., Ludman, E., Oliver, M., & Von Korff, M. (2013). Depression and risk of hospitalizations for ambulatory care-sensitive conditions in patients with diabetes. *Journal of General Internal Medicine, 28*(7), 921–929.

Dorning, H., Davies, A., & Blunt, I. (2015). *Focus on: People with mental ill health and hospital use. Exploring disparities in hospital use for physical healthcare. Research summary.* London: The Health Foundation and Nuffield Trust.

Egede, L. E., Ellis, C., & Grubaugh, A. L. (2009). The effect of depression on self-care behaviors and quality of care in a national sample of adults with diabetes. *General Hospital Psychiatry, 31*(5), 422–427.

Goorden M, Huijbregts KM, van Marwijk HW, Beekman AT, van der Feltz-Cornelis CM, Hakkaart-van Roijen L. (2015). Cost-utility of collaborative care for major depressive disorder in primary care in the Netherlands. *Journal of Psychosomatic Research.* 79(4):316–323. pii: S0022-3999(15)00469-9.

Guthrie, E. (2008). Medically unexplained symptoms in primary care. *Advances in Psychiatric Treatment, 14*(6), 432–440.

Herrman, H., Saxena, S., & Moodie, R. (2005). *Promoting mental health. Concepts, emerging evidence, practice.* Geneva: World Health Organisation.

Howard, C., Dupont, S., Haselden, B., Lynch, J., & Wills, P. (2010). The effectiveness of a group cognitive-behavioural breathlessness intervention on health status, mood and hospital admissions in elderly patients with chronic obstructive pulmonary disease. *Psychology, Health and Medicine, 15*(4), 371–385.

Huang, Y., Wei, X., Wu, T., Chen, R., & Guo, A. (2013). Collaborative care for patients with depression and diabetes mellitus: A systematic review and meta-analysis. *BMC Psychiatry, 13*, 260.

Joint Commissioning Panel for Mental Health. (2013). *Guidance for commissioners of liaison mental health services to acute hospitals.* London: Joint Commissioning Panel for Mental Health.

Junger, J., Schellberg, D., Muller-Tasch, T., Raupp, G., Zugck, C., Haunstetter, A., Zipfela, S., Herzog, W., & Haass, M. (2005). Depression increasingly predicts mortality in the course of congestive heart failure. *European Journal of Heart Failure, 7*(2), 261–267.

Katon, W., Russo, J., Lin, E. H., Schmittdiel, J., Ciechanowski, P., Ludman, E., Peterson, D., Young, B., & Von Korff, M. (2012). Cost-effectiveness of a multicondition collaborative care intervention: A randomized controlled trial. *Archives of General Psychiatry, 69*(5), 506–514.

Katon, W., Russo, J., Reed, S. D., Croicu, C. A., Ludman, E., LaRocco, A., & Melville, J. L. (2015). A randomized trial of collaborative depression care in obstetrics and gynecology clinics: Socioeconomic disadvantage and treatment response. *The American Journal of Psychiatry, 172*(1), 32–40.

Katon, W. J., Russo, J. E., Von Korff, M., Lin, E. H. B., Ludman, E., & Ciechanowski, P. S. (2008). Long-term effects on medical costs of improving depression outcomes in patients with depression and diabetes. *Diabetes Care, 31*(6), 1155–1159.

Kirmayer, L. J., Groleau, D., Looper, K. J., & Dao, M. D. (2004). Explaining medically unexplained symptoms. *Canadian Journal of Psychiatry, 49*(10), 663–672.

Kisely, S., Smith, M., Lawrence, D., Cox, M., Campbell, L. A., & Maaten, S. (2007 Mar 13). Inequitable access for mentally ill patients to some medically necessary procedures. *Canadian Medical Association Journal, 176*(6), 779–784.

Kohn, R., Saxena, S., Levav, I., & Saraceno, B. (2004). The treatment gap in mental health care. *Bulletin of the World Health Organization, 82*(11), 858–866.

Konnopka, A., Schaefert, R., Heinrich, S., Kaufmann, C., Luppa, M., Herzog, W., & König, H. H. (2012). Economics of medically unexplained symptoms: A systematic review of the literature. *Psychotherapy and Psychosomatics, 81*(5), 265–275.

Laursen, T. M., Nordentoft, M., & Mortensen, P. B. (2014). Excess early mortality in schizophrenia. *Annual Review of Clinical Psychology, 10*, 425–448.

Lesperance, F., Frasure-Smith, N., Talajic, M., & Bourassa, M. G. (2002). Five-year risk of cardiac mortality in relation to initial severity and one year changes in depression symptoms after myocardial infarction. *Circulation, 105*(9), 1049–1053.

Lewis, V. A., Colla, C. H., Tierney, K., Van Citters, A. D., Fisher, E. S., & Meara, E. (2014). Few ACOs pursue innovative models that integrate care for mental illness and substance abuse with primary care. *Health Affairs (Millwood), 33*(10), 1808–1816.

Lin, E. H., Katon, W., Von Korff, M., Rutter, C., Simon, G. E., Oliver, M., Ciechanowski, P., Ludman, E. J., Bush, T., & Young, B. (2004). Relationship of depression and diabetes self-care, medication adherence, and preventive care. *Diabetes Care, 27*(9), 2154–2160.

Moore, R. K., Groves, D. G., Bridson, J. D., Grayson, A. D., Wong, H., Leach, A., Lewin, R. J., & Chester, M. R. (2007). A brief cognitive-behavioural intervention reduces admission in refractory angina patients. *Journal of Pain and Symptom Management, 33*(3), 310–316.

National Institute for Health and Clinical Excellence (NICE). (2009). *Depression in adults with chronic physical health problems: Treatment and management* (Clinical Guideline 91). London: National Clinical Guideline Centre.

Naylor, C., Das, P., Ross, S., Honeyman, M., Thompson, J., & Gilburt, H. (2016). *Bringing together mental and physical health: A new frontier for integrated care*. London: The King's Fund.

Naylor, C., Parsonage, M., McDaid, D., Knapp, M., Fossey, M., & Galea, A. (2012). *Long-term conditions and mental health: The cost of co-morbidities*. London: The King's Fund.

Park, M., Katon, W. J., & Wolf, F. M. (2013). Depression and risk of mortality in individuals with diabetes: A meta-analysis and systematic review. *General Hospital Psychiatry, 35*(3), 217–225.

Parsonage, M., & Fossey, M. (2011). *Economic evaluation of a liaison psychiatry service*. London: Centre for Mental Health.

Parsonage, M., Hard, E., & Rock, B. (2014). *Managing patients with complex needs*. London: Centre for Mental Health.

Reid, S., Wessely, S., Crayford, T., & Hotopf, M. (2001). Medically unexplained symptoms in frequent attenders of secondary health care: Retrospective cohort study. *British Medical Journal, 322*(7289), 767.

Reiss-Brennan, B., Briot, P. C., Savitz, L. A., Cannon, W., & Staheli, R. (2010). Cost and quality impact of Intermountain's mental health integration program. *Journal of Healthcare Management, 5*(2), 97–113.

Rosenberg, D., Lin, E., Peterson, D., Ludman, E., Von Korff, M., & Katon, W. (2014). Integrated medical care management and behavioral risk factor reduction for multicondition patients: Behavioral outcomes of the TEAMcare trial. *General Hospital Psychiatry, 36*(2), 129–134.

Rucci, P., Piazza, A., Menchetti, M., Berardi, D., Fioritti, A., Mimmi, S., & Fantini, M. P. (2012). Integration between primary care and mental health services in Italy: Determinants of referral and stepped care. *International Journal of Family Medicine, 2012*, 507464.

Sachar, A. (2012). How important is mental health involvement in integrated diabetes care? The Inner North West London experience. *London Journal Primary Care, 5*(1), 63–67.

Simon, G. E., Katon, W. J., Lin, E. H. B., Rutter, C., Manning, W. G., Von Kroff, M., Ciechanowski, P., Ludman, E. J., & Ypung, B. A. (2007). Cost-effectiveness of systematic depression treatment among people with diabetes mellitus. *Archives of General Psychiatry, 64*(1), 65–72.

van Dessel, N., den Boeft, M., van der Wouden, J. C., Kleinstäuber, M., Leone, S. S., Terluin, B., Numans, M. E., van der Horst, H. E., & van Marwijk, H. (2014). Non-pharmacological interventions for somatoform disorders and medically unexplained physical symptoms (MUPS) in adults. *Cochrane Database of Systematic Reviews, 11*, CD011142.

Whalley, B., Thompson, D. R., & Taylor, R. S. (2014). Psychological interventions for coronary heart disease: Cochrane systematic review and meta-analysis. *International Journal of Behavioral Medicine, 21*(1), 109–121.

Integrated Palliative and End-of-Life Care

24

Health and Social Care and Compassionate Communities to Provide Integrated Palliative Care

Emilio Herrera Molina, Arturo Álvarez Rosete, Silvia Librada Flores, and Tania Pastrana Uruena

24.1 Introduction

The work of Dr. Cicely Saunders, founder of the modern hospice movement in the 1960s, is considered the key milestone in the development of palliative care services (Saunders 2005). In contrast to the focus on curing in the contemporary medicalized paradigm, palliative care aims at alleviating the suffering of people with advanced diseases and who are at the end of their lives, supporting them, their families and caregivers with dignified, sensitive and patient-centred care (Hall et al. 2011).

Over 29 million (29,063,194) people worldwide died from diseases requiring palliative care in 2011. The estimated annual number of people in need of palliative care at the end of life is 20.4 million. The biggest proportion, 94%, corresponds to adults of which 69% are over 60 years old and 25% are 15–59 years old. Only 6% of all people in need of palliative care are children (WHO 2014a, b). Europe may count as many as 7000 patients per year per million inhabitants requiring palliative care at the end of life. Of these, 60% would require palliative care provided by a specialized palliative care team (Centeno et al. 2013).

Data on palliative care need to be set within the context of the growing chronic care challenge to contemporary health systems, as the chronic patient of today will very possibly become candidate to palliative care as the disease progresses. Furthermore, due to the fact that 40% of the total health care expenditure of a chronic

E.H. Molina • A. Álvarez Rosete (✉) • S.L. Flores
NewHealth Foundation, Sevilla, Spain
e-mail: emilio.herrera@newhealthfoundation.org; arturo.alvarez@newhealthfoundation.org; silvia.librada@newhealthfoundation.org

T.P. Uruena
Uniklinik RWTH Aachen, Aachen, Germany
e-mail: tpastrana@ukaachen.de

© Springer International Publishing AG 2017
V. Amelung et al. (eds.), *Handbook Integrated Care*,
DOI 10.1007/978-3-319-56103-5_24

patient concentrates at the end-of-life, palliative care becomes an obvious key element in any chronic care strategy.

There are, however, better quality and more cost-efficient ways of treating people at the later stages of their chronic diseases and end-of-life than treating them in acute hospitals. As this chapter will show new innovative models of people-centred integrated palliative care, involving health and social care staff working together with sensitized community networks, which are flourishing around the world.

24.2 Defining Palliative Care and End-of-Life Care

The World Health Organization (WHO) has defined palliative care as "an approach that improves the quality of life of patients and their families facing the problem associated with life-threatening illness, through the prevention and relief of suffering by means of early identification, impeccable assessment and treatment of pain and other problems, physical, psychosocial and spiritual" (WHO 2010).

Through the consideration of pain as well as other problems, the 2004 WHO definition of palliative care is itself a call for integrated person-centred care. Recent conceptual developments have added further explanation to the WHO definition to highlight the comprehensive nature of palliative care and in particular, care not limited to the moment of dying. The Worldwide Palliative Care Alliance (WPCA) policy statement on defining palliative care supports palliative care earlier in illness, so that it is provided "alongside disease-modifying treatment such as anticancer therapy or anti-retroviral therapy, for people with significant symptoms or who require other support" (WPCA 2009). The WPCA policy statement includes the following key points:

- palliative care is needed in chronic as well as life threatening/limiting-conditions
- there is no time or prognostic limit on the delivery of palliative care: it should be delivered on the basis of need, not diagnosis or prognosis
- palliative care is not limited to specialist palliative care services but includes primary and secondary level care.
- palliative care is not limited to one care setting: it is provided wherever a person's care takes place, whether this is the patient's own home, a care facility, hospice inpatient unit, hospital, or outpatient or day care service.

In the English context, the term 'end-of-life care' has been used to refer to the care that takes place at a specific period of time preceding death. However, more contemporary uses avoid such meaning and instead refer to "the care and support needs of patients and carers regardless of diagnosis and regardless of the estimated period of time before death" (Addicott 2010).

The traditional service model conceptualised palliative care as replacing curative care once the latter were no longer effective. Instead, as Fig. 24.1 shows, the modern model (Ferris et al. 2009; Hui and Bruera 2015) sees palliative care as being

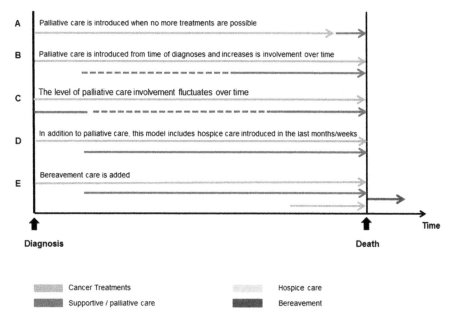

A Palliative care is introduced when no more treatments are possible

B Palliative care is introduced from time of diagnoses and increases is involvement over time

C The level of palliative care involvement fluctuates over time

D In addition to palliative care, this model includes hospice care introduced in the last months/weeks

E Bereavement care is added

Time

Diagnosis   Death

Cancer Treatments   Hospice care

Supportive / palliative care   Bereavement

Fig. 24.1 Time based model. Source: Adapted from Hui and Bruera (2015)

provided at early stages of the disease to control symptoms to alleviate pain while the disease(s) progresses. This is concurrent with other curative health care treatments—hence the term 'time based model' (Hui and Bruera 2015). Such approach requires the inclusion of supportive care, palliative care, hospice care and bereavement as part of a continuum of care.

24.3 Challenges for Providing Care to Palliative and End-of-Life Patients

As the end-of-life approaches, symptoms prevalent become gradually intense, physical deterioration advances rapidly and the level of dependency grows to be complete. The risk of catastrophic impact on the household economy increases, and thus the consequences of the illness are experienced, alongside emotional suffering and spiritual crises, not only by the patient but by his/her family and carers experience as well (Librada et al. 2015).

At a system level, the ageing of the population and the chronic disease epidemic are changing how people suffer and what they die from. "Increasingly, more people die as a result of serious chronic disease, and older people in particular are more likely to suffer from multi-organ failure towards the end of life" (Davies and Higginson 2004). While traditionally, palliative care programmes have been narrowly offered mostly to cancer patients, it is now being increasingly recognised as useful to people with advanced chronic conditions who are at risk of deteriorating and dying (Nuño 2014).

Healthcare systems however, are not ready to cope with these changing dynamics. Where they exist, services for end-of-life multimorbid patients tend to remain fragmented and uncoordinated. True, many contemporary health systems have set up high-quality palliative care services, either at hospital, hospices or at home. As "most people prefer to remain in their home at the end of their life, various models of home-based end of life care exist, ranging from those that primarily offer nursing and personal care, to others that involve multidisciplinary teams" (Gomes and Higginson 2008; Nuño 2014). This however poses additional challenges to care systems, among other reasons, due to the progressive decrease in availability of family support networks at home. A retrospective study conducted in the region of Extremadura (Spain) in 2003 with 944 patients who had died, showed that the risk of hospital admission (odds ratio) was 50% higher for patients who did not have a social support network at home. The reason for admission to a hospital was related to the lack of social support rather than to difficulties of symptom control. Patients with a Karnofsky index <50% (highly dependent) and lack of social support network, had a chance of 65% versus 45% of those who possessed social support network (Herrera et al. 2006a, b).

If it is not addressed as a cornerstone in the reorganization of the health and social care systems, it will result in their failure in the coming years. The lack of a supportive network increases the demand for more formal or informal social care, but the solution is not to compensate it by super specialized physicians and increased hospital-based services.

24.4 Goal of Integrated Care

24.4.1 What Needs Do End-of-Life Patients Have?

The complexity of each situation at end of life and the variety of psychosocial factors lead to a wide range of needs with different grade of severity, all of which need to be addressed. For example:

- Care needs regarding the patients' dependency: Assistance to perform daily activities, reduction of loss of sensory capabilities and compensating deterioration, training habits for improving personal autonomy, safety and protection measures as well as environmental adaptation.
- Caregivers' needs and social support network: Information about available support services, training of professionals and/or informal care givers, development of communication skills, psychosocial support of family members, balance of care activities/tasks and working life, prevention of family collapse, sharing experiences with other caregivers.

• Protection of the social role of the patient: Autonomy in decision making and communication of last wills, spiritual expression, leisure and entertainment, privacy vs. intimacy, interpersonal and social relationships.

From the health care perspective, the palliative care range of support should not only be limited to provide specially trained medical and nursing services, but also seek to provide emotional support (psychotherapy, counseling, support services and caregiver relief). It should also support dependency care (support in home work/task/activities, support by personal care and occupational therapy) (Librada et al. 2015).

24.4.2 Health and Social Integrated Care Based on Empathy and Compassion

As the discipline of palliative care has been evolving, practitioners have gradually realized that palliative care cannot be considered solely from the health perspective (Juvero 2000; Georghiou et al. 2012). Health and social needs of the patient at the end of life and his/her family are closely related and have mutual influence. If any of these aspects is not well addressed, it can result in misuse of resources and overcharge. The lack of adequate social support causes increased consumption of healthcare resources. Although it is still necessary to improve specialized palliative care health teams, it is also relevant to meet the needs of social support for patients and their families (Herrera et al. 2013).

The call for coordination and integration of health and social care services patients at the end of life has featured strongly in recent declarations of international organisations. For example, the 2014 European Declaration on Palliative Care has called for

> a paradigm shift in health and social care towards basic palliative care skills for all health care professionals, to empower them to deliver patient-centreed family-focused care for all people with a life-limiting illness, based on personalized or tailored care plans, with attention to all needs of the patient and his or her family (European Declaration on Palliative Care 2014; WHO 2014a, b).

Health and social care staff need to work in interdisciplinary teams, using empathy as the basis for analyzing the needs of patients and their families. The 2014 European Declaration on Palliative Care understands empathy as the cognitive ability to perceive in a common context, what another individual may feel. Also it is described as a feeling of emotional involvement of a person in the reality that affects another with the aim to identify individual patients' and family caregivers' unique combination of needs (European Declaration on Palliative Care 2014). While empathy is a cognitive ability, compassion is the attitude towards others in trying to alleviate other's suffering, "an evolutionary construct that compels us to be concerned about the welfare and suffering of others" (Busek 2014). In sum, quality in palliative care requires people to have both empathy and compassion, forming interdisciplinary teams who are able to work together in a coordinated manner.

24.5   The Integrated Care Path

The specialist literature on integrated care has referred to a number of key elements that make possible integrated care at the service-delivery level, including the existence a single point of entry to holistic care assessments and joint care planning, delivered by multidisciplinary teams where one professional in particular act as care coordinator for patients (Goodwin et al. 2014). The home or the homely setting within the community are "the hub of care" (Ham et al. 2012), the preferred locations, alternative to hospitals, to provide palliative care services. Home is also the "preferred place of death" (Addicott 2010). Thus, the integrated palliative care path is built around these elements and has the home as the primary location of care.

These elements are embodied in the number of international innovative experiences that are providing high-quality integrated palliative care to end-of-life patients (Hall et al. 2011). For example, the Midhurst Macmillan Community Specialist Palliative Care Service in England is a community-based, consultant-led, specialist palliative care programme (UK) "which covers approximately 150,000 people in a largely rural area" (Thiel et al. 2013: 7). A multidisciplinary team of nurses (who act as care coordinators), palliative care consultants, occupational therapists and physioterapists work along side Macmillan Cancer Support volunters to enable patients to be cared for at home. The team liaise with other health care providers, including general practitioners (GPs), district nurses and continuing care teams (Thiel et al. 2013).

The Marie Curie Nursing Service (MCNS) provides home-based care to around 28,000 people at the end of life annually in the UK. Although it initially focused on caring for people with cancer, it has increasingly provided care to people with other conditions. Staffed by registered nurses and senior healthcare assistants, the MCNS offers a number of different models of care, ranging from overnight nursing care booked in advance to urgent support in response to crises.

Similarly, in Andalusia, Spain, the Home and Ambulatory Care programme of the Cudeca Foundation embodies these same key elements (OMIS 2015). Care to oncology patients is delivered at home by multidisciplinary teams of nurses, physicians, psychologists and social carers. Coordinated by the nurses, the team meets weekly to discuss, evaluate and monitor patients and adjust treatments if needed. Volunteers also have a role in the programme by providing support and helping to transport patients from and to their home. Public patients are referred from the regional health service. While at the Cudeca programme, there is intense liaising with the primary and hospital care levels, with whom they are aligned through agreed protocols.

The Milford Care Centre (Milford Care Centre 2015) is a voluntary not-for-profit organisation which provides specialist palliative care and older person's services in the Mid-West of Ireland. Services include: 47-bed voluntary nursing home; a Day Care Centre for Older Persons; 30-bed Specialist Palliative Care Inpatient Unit; Palliative Care Day Care Centre (Specialist Palliative Care Day Unit); Community based, multi-disciplinary Specialist Palliative Care Team; and an Education, Research and Quality Unit.

Referral to specialist palliative care is made through the GP or hospital consultant. Patients living at home remain under the care of their GP, but they get the support from the Specialist Palliative Care team, which comprises a nurses (Clinical Nurse Specialists; Registered Nurses, Care Assistants), physiotherapists, occupational therapists, social workers. Then, the Palliative Day Care Centre bridges the interface between homecare services and Specialist Palliative Care Inpatient unit, so that patients can be referred smoothly from one to the other as required. In addition to the professionals above mentioned, the Day Unit multi-disciplinary team comprises dieticians, speech and language therapists, music and art therapists, etc. Referral to the inpatient unit can be also be made through the Specialist Palliative Care Day Unit or Hospice at Home services. Patients are accepted based on an overall assessment of their needs (e.g. medical needs, social circumstances, support required, etc.).

Weekly multidisciplinary care planning meetings are held in each area of care (Inpatient Unit, Hospice at Home service and SPC Day Unit). New patients are reviewed and care plans discussed and agreed; care plans for existing patients are also reviewed and updated as appropriate. Decisions about discharge of patients are discussed and agreed. Also, all deaths that had taken place since the previous meeting are reviewed and decisions made as to what level of immediate bereavement support may be required by particular family members.

In eastern Canada, the Nova Scotia Integrated Palliative Care strategy (Nova Scotia 2015) embodies the philosophy that care is delivered in a seamless manner by the various health care providers and services that function in the community. It is person- and family-centreed rather than system-centreed. There is integration between primary, secondary and tertiary care with a shared responsibility among all care providers along the continuum. Support to patients and families is available early in the disease process, and adapts as one's condition advances and changes. Support to families also continues on during the bereavement stage.

To meet the goal of keeping patients at home as much as possible, continuous and 24/7 support is very much needed, especially at night time and weekends. This can be delivered though telephone service or similar. In the United Kingdom, the Partnership for Excellence in Palliative Support (PEPS) (Sue Ryder 2015) service provides 24-h support to patients in the last year of life and coordination of palliative care between 15 organisations across the county of Bedfordshire in England. A telephone number held at the PEPS centre offers a single point of contact to provide a seamless service for patients, their carers and care professionals from qualified nurses when advice and support are needed. In Spain, the regional government of the Basque Country launched a specialized palliative home care program in 2014 termed SAIATU ("to try" in Basque language) (Herrera et al. 2013; Millas et al. 2015; Nuño 2014). The programme provided in-home social support services rendered by specially-trained caregivers, to complement the palliative clinical services offered by the public system as well as 24/7 telephone support. Initiated as a pilot in the Basque province of Guipuzcoa, lack of funding has prevented the experience to be sustained and scaled-up, however.

Integrated palliative care is not however exclusive of Western developed countries. The Hong Kong Special Administrative Region of China, for example, has introduced integrated palliative care pathways (Lo et al. 2009).

Colombia is taking promising steps towards the setting up of high-quality integrated palliative care programs and teams, applying the NEWPALEX® method developed by NewHealth Foundation (NewHealth Foundation 2015). This method sets up integrated care pathways and establishes specific programmes and resources at the service-delivery level and offers basic and intermediate training for palliative care specialists. At present (Feb 2016), one third of Colombia's population (around 16 million people) are registered with health insurance companies that, having applied the NEWPALEX® method, have included integrated palliative care in the basket of services to their insured members. For example, the model of palliative care included in basket of services of the health insurance company SURA is delivered by a multidisciplinary team who care for the physical, social, emotional, spiritual and psychological needs of patients (EPS SURA 2016).

At the core of the Colombian experience is the reorganization of the funding models by which health insurers pay health care providers for the existence and quality of palliative care services. These insurers are contracting with more than ten healthcare providers who have set up high-quality palliative care resources and programs.

24.6   Results of Integrated Palliative Care

There is growing research evidence that confirms that in-home palliative care achieves better quality of care, higher satisfaction rates and with lower costs than traditional models of hospital-based care (Brumley et al. 2007; Gomes et al. 2013). Results from the innovative experiences described above come to strengthen the case for integrated palliative care for patients and their families.

According to research, home-based palliative care provided under the Marie Curie Cancer Care MCNS model reduces the demand for costly and often undesirable hospital care, and allowing more people to die at home (Chitnis et al. 2012). 76.7% of those who received care under the MCNS model died at home, while only 7.7% died in hospital. In contrast, 35.0% of the controls died at home, while 41.6% died in hospital.

The SAIATU program has shown how resources developed from a social care perspective and with an emphasis on care integration can be cost-effective and efficient for a healthcare system and increase the satisfaction of families. Thus, comparison of SAIATU with traditional care (primary and specialized health care) and advanced care (primary and specialized health care and home care) resulted in a reduction in the intensity of external specialized care services utilization, emergency room visits, hospital admissions and length of hospital stays. Moreover, SAIATU favored the community intervention of primary health care professionals by increasing calls and interaction with caregivers trained by the family physician and community nurse. In consequence, it avoided diversions to unnecessary emergency services or inadequate early intervention of unnecessary specialized means (Herrera et al. 2013).

These results support other studies confirming that the activity of palliative care teams at home improves the performance of primary care professionals (Herrera 2006). This suggests that a more specialized palliative support, both medically and socially, does not antagonize with a strong primary care, rather on the contrary, it promotes synergies between levels of care and offers alternatives to unnecessary hospital admission. SAIATU's caregivers helped to detect problems in the patient early, liaising with primary care staff to visit patients when necessary. Finally, the results of the SAIATU also favored the possibility of dying at home when that was the preference of the patient. These data show that the integration of social status and health at the end of life enhances the overall efficiency of two subsystems: the health and social sectors.

In Colombia, first preliminary results of the country-wide transformative programme explained above is showing reductions of approximately 10–15% in the costs of care at the end-of-life compared to standard treatments (mainly provided at hospital) (Montoya et al. 2014).

24.7   A New Paradigm: Compassionate Communities

In the context of the new paradigm of people-centred integrated care models, true integrated palliative care does not stop at the integration of health and social care services, regardless of how crucially important this is. Community-centreed models for end of life care have been proposed, such as the "circles of care" model by Abel et al. (2013) "which appreciates the persons with illness in their everyday context of living within their communities, not separate individuals with needs that have to be met" (Abel et al. 2013: 3). The "circles of care" around the person cannot be fulfilled just by interdisciplinary health care teams, even if supplemented by trained social services. The care system will not be able to provide the care needed. It also requires the involvement of society through awareness and the raising of community networks. The real social change must come from the sensitized community, caring for their loved ones. Thus, the keystone of the new paradigm of people-centred integrated palliative care lies in the existence of networks of care (Herrera 2015).

At the international level, the "compassionate communities for end-of-life care" movement seeks to promote and integrate palliative care socially into everyday life (Kellehear 2005). People are trained to care for people at the end of life. But this does not stop at creating and managing volunteers' teams. The concept goes much further: the aim is to enable society to accept and be involved in the accompaniment and care at the end of life as a natural act of compassion.

The movement is quickly spreading worldwide. In Kerala (India), the Institute of Palliative Medicine has been working for over 20 years in training community members and in promoting awareness of palliative care, and is now a World Health Organization (WHO) Collaborating Center for community participation in Palliative Care and Long Term Care. One of the key projects of the Institute, the "Neighborhood Network in Palliative Care" project has more than 60 units covering a population of more than 12 million people of Kerala, and is probably the largest community-owned palliative care network in the world (Kumar and Numpeli 2005; Kumar 2013).

In Ireland, the Milford Care Centre is also urging forward the movement of Compassionate Communities through awareness and leadership experiences (Milford Care Centre 2015). In Spain, the non-for-profit organisation, the NewHealth Foundation promotes the development of care networks between organizations and associations under the slogan 'A Global Community United by the Vocation to Care' (NewHealth Foundation 2015). Through the leadership of the NewHealth Foundation, similar initiatives are beginning to evolve in Argentina and Colombia as well.

24.8 Conclusion

Over the past 40 years, palliative care programmes around the world have aimed at alleviating the suffering of people with advanced diseases who are at the end of life, supporting them, their families and caregivers with dignified, sensitive and patient-centred care. As the discipline of palliative care has been evolving, practitioners have gradually realized that palliative care cannot be considered solely from the health perspective, but needs to incorporate social care and the involvement of the community as well.

The integrated palliative care model proposed in this chapter involves a set of professional health and social care services, which envelop the support and assistance of family and volunteers from an empowered community capable of caring for their families and neighbours.

In the context of the growing chronic care challenge to contemporary health systems, palliative care provides better quality, more cost-efficient ways of treating people at the later stages of their chronic diseases and end-of-life than treating them in acute hospitals. Thus, as a key element in any chronic care strategy, palliative care shows the way forward in the design of a service delivery model truly embedded in the emerging integrated care paradigm.

References

Abel, J., Walter, T., Carey, L. B., et al. (2013). Circles of care: Should community development redefine the practice of palliative care? *BMJ Supportive & Palliative Care, 3*, 383–388.

Addicott, R. (2010). *End-of-life care*. London: The King's Fund. Accessed February 22, 2016, from http://www.kingsfund.org.uk/sites/files/kf/field/field_document/end-of-life-care-gp-inquiry-research-paper-mar11.pdf

Brumley, R., Enguidanos, S., Jamison, P., et al. (2007). Increased satisfaction with care and lower costs: Results of a randomized trial on in-home palliative care. *Journal of the American Geriatrics Society, 55*(7), 993–1000.

Busek, A. (2014). *Compassion as a biological imperative*. Stanford's Center for Compassion and Altruism Research and Education. Accessed March 15, 2016, from http://ccare.stanford.edu/press_posts/compassion-as-a-biological-imperative/

Centeno, C., Lynch, T., Donea, O., et al. (2013). *EAPC atlas of palliative care in Europe*. Milan: IAHPC Press.

Chitnis, X., Georghiou, T., Steventon, A., & Bardsley, M. (2012). *The impact of the Marie Curie nursing service on place of death and hospital use at the end of life*. London: Nuffield Trust. Accessed February 21, 2016, from http://www.nuffieldtrust.org.uk/sites/files/nuffield/marie_curie_full_report_final.pdf

Davies and Higginson. (Eds.). (2004). *Palliative care: The solid facts*. WHO. Accessed October 6, 2015, from http://www.euro.who.int/__data/assets/pdf_file/0003/98418/E82931.pdf

EPS SURA. (2016). *Colombia*. Accessed February 22, 2016, from https://www.epssura.com/index.php

European Declaration on Palliative Care. (2014). Brussels. Accessed February 21, from http://www.palliativecare2020.eu/declaration/

Ferris, F. D., Bruera, E., Cherny, N., et al. (2009). Palliative cancer care a decade later: Accomplishments, the need, next steps—From the American Society of Clinical Oncology. *Journal of Clinical Oncology, 27*, 3052–3058.

Georghiou, T., Davies, S., Davies, A., & Bardsley, M. (2012). *Understanding patterns of health and social care at the end of life*. London: Nuffield Trust. Accessed February 21, 2016, from http://www.nuffieldtrust.org.uk/sites/files/nuffield/121016_understanding_patterns_of_health_and_social_care_full_report_final.pdf

Gomes, B., Calanzani, N., Curiale, V., McCrone, P., & Higginson, I. J. (2013). Effectiveness and cost-effectiveness of home palliative care services for adults with advanced illness and their caregivers. *The Cochrane Database of Systematic Reviews, 6*, CD007760.

Gomes, B., & Higginson, I. (2008). Where people die (1974—2030): Past trends, future projections and implications for care. *Palliative Medicine, 22*(1), 33–41.

Goodwin, N., Dixon, A., Anderson, G., & Wodchis, W. (2014). *Providing integrated care for older people with complex needs. Lessons from seven international case studies*. London: The King's Fund. Accessed February 21, 2016, from http://www.kingsfund.org.uk/sites/files/kf/field/field_related_document/providing-integrated-care-for-older-people-with-complex-needs-background-to-case-studies-kingsfund-jan14.pdf

Hall, S., Petkova, H., Tsouros, A. D., Costantini, M., & Higginson, J. (Eds.). (2011). *Palliative care for older people: Better practices*. Accessed February 21, 2016, from http://www.euro.who.int/__data/assets/pdf_file/0017/143153/e95052.pdf

Ham, C., Dixon, A., & Brooke, B. (2012). *Transforming the delivery of health and social care*. London: The King's Fund. Accessed February 22, 2016, from http://www.kingsfund.org.uk/sites/files/kf/field/field_publication_file/transforming-the-delivery-of-health-and-social-care-the-kings-fund-sep-2012.pdf

Herrera, E. (2006). *Palliative care as a component of public policy: The regional program in Extremadura Spain*. Washington: World Cancer Congress.

Herrera, E. (2015). European Journal of Palliative Care (EJPC) Palliative Care Policy Development Award: An interview with the 2015 winner. *European Journal of Palliative Care.* Accessed February 21, 2016, from http://www.eapcnet.eu/Home/tabid/38/ctl/Details/ArticleID/1223/mid/878/EJPC-Palliative-Care-Policy-Development-Award-an-interview-with-the-2015-winner-Emilio-Herrera.aspx

Herrera, E., Campón Durán, J. C., Fernández Bermejo, F., et al. (2006a). *Plan marco de atención sociosanitaria de Extremadura. Modelo Marco. Plan director 2005-2010.* Accessed February 21, 2016, from http://www.mad.es/serviciosadicionales/ficheros/jext-plan-marco.pdf

Herrera, E., Nuño, R., Espiau, G., et al. (2013). Impact of a home-based social welfare program on care for palliative patients in the Basque Country (SAIATU Program). *BMC Palliative Care, 12,* 3.

Herrera, E., Rocafort, J., Cuervo, M. A., & Redondo, M. (2006b). Primer nivel asistencial en cuidados paliativos: evolución del contenido de la cartera de servicios de atención primaria y criterios de derivación al nivel de soporte. *Atencion Primaria, 38,* 85–92.

Hui, D., & Bruera, E. (2015). Models of integration of oncology and palliative care. *Annals of Palliative Medicine, 4*(3), 89–98.

Juvero, M. (2000). Reflexión sobre el trabajo social en Cuidados Paliativos. *Medicina Paliativa, 12,* 185–186.

Kellehear, A. (2005). *Compassionate cities: Public health and end-of-life care.* Milton Park, Oxfordshire: Routledge.

Kumar, S. (2013). Models of delivering palliative and end-of-life care in India. *Current Opinion in Supportive and Palliative Care, 7*(2), 216–222.

Kumar, S., & Numpeli, M. (2005). Neighborhood network in palliative care. *Indian Journal of Palliative Care, 11,* 6–9.

Librada, S., Herrera, E., & Pastrana, T. (2015). Atención Centrada en la Persona al Final de la Vida: Atención Sociosanitaria Integrada en Cuidados Paliativos. *Actas de Coordinación Sociosanitaria, 13,* 67–94.

Lo, S. H., et al. (2009). The implementation of an end-of-life integrated care pathway in a Chinese population. *International Journal of Palliative Nursing, 15,* 384–388.

Milford Care Centre. (2015). *Compassionate communities.* Limerick, Ireland. Accessed October 14, 2015, from http://www.compassionatecommunities.ie/

Millas, J., Hasson, N., Aguiló, M., Lasagabaster, I., Muro, E., & Romero, O. (2015). Programa de atención social domiciliaria sobre la atención a los cuidados paliativos en el País Vasco. Experiencia Saiatu. *Palliative Medicine, 22*(1).

Montoya Jaramillo, Y. M., Yepes Naranjo, M. M., Navales Cardona, E. S., Otero Ramón, P. F., Herrera Molina, E., Librada Flores, S., et al. (2014). *46,6 Millones de dólares al año en el último año de vida: la oportunidad de incorporar cuidados paliativos para 1.8M de afiliados al sistema de salud en Colombia.* X Congress of the Spanish Society of Palliative Care (Sociedad Española de Cuidados Paliativos, SECPAL). Madrid, 13–15 November.

NewHealth Foundation. (2015). *Todos Contigo.* Seville, Spain. Accessed October 14, 2015, from http://www.newhealthfoundation.org/index.php/es/

Nova Scotia. (2015). *Nova Scotia Government.* Canada. Accessed October 22, 2015, from http://novascotia.ca/dhw/palliativecare/

Nuño, R. (2014). Integrated end of life care: The role of social services. *International Journal of Integrated Care, 14,* 1–2.

OMIS (Spanish Observatory on Integrated Care). (2015). *Fundación Cudeca. Cuidados Paliativos. Programa de Atención a Domicilio.* Accessed March 15, 2016, from http://www.newhealthfoundation.org/web/wp-content/uploads/2015/12/cudeca-pdf.pdf

Saunders, C. (2005). The founder of the Modern Hospice movement. *British Medical Journal, 331,* 23.

Sue Ryder. (2015). *PEPS*. Sue Ryder Organization. Accessed October 22, 2015, from http://www. sueryder.org/how-we-help/care-services/PEPS

Thiel, V., Sonola, L., Goodwin, N., & Kodner, D. L. (2013). *Midhurst Macmillan Community Specialist Palliative Care Services. Delivering end of live care in the community*. London: The King's Fund. Accessed February 21, 2016, from http://www.kingsfund.org.uk/sites/files/kf/ field/field_publication_file/midhurst-macmillan-coordinated-care-case-study-kings-fund-aug13.pdf

World Health Organization (WHO). (2010). *WHO definition of palliative care*. Accessed February 21, 2016, from http://www.who.int/cancer/palliative/definition/en/

World Health Organization (WHO). (2014a). *Global atlas of palliative care at the end of life*. Accessed February 21, 2016, from http://www.who.int/nmh/Global_Atlas_of_Palliative_Care. pdf

World Health Organization (WHO). (2014b). *Strengthening of palliative care as a component of comprehensive care throughout the life course. 67th World Health Assembly*. Accessed February 21, 2016, from http://apps.who.int/medicinedocs/documents/s21454en/s21454en.pdf

Worldwide Palliative Care Alliance (WPCA). (2009). *WPCA policy statement on defining palliative care*. Accessed February 21, 2016, from http://www.thewhpca.org/resources/item/ definging-palliative-care

Rare Diseases

25

Raquel Castro, Juliette Senecat, Myriam de Chalendar, Ildikó Vajda, Silvia van Breukelen, Maria Montefusco, Stephanie Jøker Nielsen, and Dorica Dan

25.1 Challenges Faced When Providing Care to People Living with a Rare Disease

The following chapter focuses on presenting rare diseases and the needs of people affected by these, as well as providing context on the provision of integrated care to this client group in Europe.

25.1.1 Background on Rare Diseases

"When you have a rare disease it feels like you are so alone and no one cares", Janet, mid 50s, living with Alkaptonuria (EUCERD Joint Action 2012)

R. Castro (✉) • J. Senecat
European Organisation for Rare Diseases, Paris, France
e-mail: raquel.castro@eurordis.org

M. de Chalendar
Rare Disease Network—Filière de Santé Maladies Rares TETECOU, Hôpital Necker—Enfants Malades, Paris, France

I. Vajda • S. van Breukelen
Dutch Genetic Alliance VSOP—Vereniging Samenwerkende Ouder-en Patiëntenorganisaties, Soest, Netherlands

M. Montefusco
Council of Nordic Cooperation on Disability, Nordic Centre for Welfare and Social Issues, Stockholm, Sweden

S.J. Nielsen
Rare Diseases Denmark—Sjældne Diagnoser, Taastrup, Denmark

D. Dan
Romanian National Alliance for Rare Diseases RONARD—Alianta Nationala Pentru Boli Rare Romania, Zalau, Romania

© Springer International Publishing AG 2017
V. Amelung et al. (eds.), *Handbook Integrated Care*,
DOI 10.1007/978-3-319-56103-5_25

Rare diseases (RDs) affect a small number of people relative to the general population. A disease is defined as rare when it affects less than 1 in 2000 people in Europe (Orphanet 2012) and less than one in 1250 people in the United States of America (Schieppati et al. 2008). Definitions vary in different countries/world regions according to population sizes. The World Health Organisation suggests a frequency of less than 6.5–10 in 10,000 (Aronson 2006).

There are 6000–7000 RDs (Orphanet 2012). Although each RD is characterised by a low prevalence, they affect 30 million people in Europe and 400 million people worldwide (World Health Organisation 2013). Most patients suffer from less frequent diseases affecting 1 in 100,000 people or less and are consequently particularly isolated and vulnerable (Council of the European Union 2009).

The cause remains unknown for many RDs. Most of them are genetic, but there are also very rare forms of infectious diseases, auto-immune diseases and cancers (Orphanet 2012). Rare disorders may affect patients in different ways and are often multisystem disorders, affecting various organs and tissues.

Rare diseases are heterogeneous in terms of prevalence, age of onset, clinical severity and outcome. However, they share various common features: they are serious, often chronic, progressive, degenerative and associated with comorbidities (Orphanet 2012). As a result, they substantially affect life expectancy and altogether account for a considerable rate of the early-life deaths and life-long disabilities in the European population (Rare Diseases Task Force 2008).

Rare diseases are the cause of various severe impairments and a high percentage of people with a RD is affected by motor or intellectual impairments, which can occur simultaneously (Guillem et al. 2008; Tozzi et al. 2013).

There are currently no treatments available for 4000–5000 RDs (Orphanet 2015). Scientific knowledge is growing rapidly but not translating into therapies quickly enough. Patients are facing major hurdles to access approved new therapies. About one third of patients do not have access to the orphan medicine they need. Another third have access only after waiting several years, as medicines are introduced first in the main markets and then progressively over 6 years in the other markets. More recently, approved breakthrough orphan medicines are not made available to patients because of their price. The sustainability of provide an increasing number of rare disease therapies is an issue for national healthcare budgets that are already under high pressure (Le Cam 2015).

Additionally, existing and accessible treatments are not always able to minimise all the complex impairments generated by the disease, highlighting the need for integrated care provision to alleviate the impact of RDs in patients' and families' daily life.

25.1.2 Unmet Needs of People Living with a Rare Disease

"MP has so many medical appointments, and therapy sessions that I had to stop working. I have only 4 hours free to come back home, do the cleaning, cook, go to supermarket, deal with the infinite bureaucratic processes to get a special school, special social wealth assistance and ask for budget support. Then, I pick him up, come back home and accompany him in all the exercises his therapist has given him. I go to bed exhausted and I don't get a lot of help at home. I loved my work and I miss it a lot! At this moment, it is impossible for me to find a job", Sandra, mother of MP, living with Congenital Disorder of Glycosylation (EUCERD Joint Action 2012)

The unmet needs of people with a RD and their families affect their dignity, autonomy and other fundamental human rights expressed in the Universal Declaration of Human Rights and in the United Nations Convention on the Rights of Persons with Disabilities.

The cumulative effects of illness and disability generated by RDs amplify the social exclusion experienced by patients and their relatives. People living with a RD face significant challenges accessing school, employment, leisure, transport, adapted housing and bank credit to name a few. Patients and families are therefore psychologically, socially, economically and culturally vulnerable.

The social challenges faced by RD patients and families include; for instance, the necessity to reduce or stop professional activity, the need to relocate to another home adapted to their health needs and difficulties in meeting with a social worker (EURORDIS 2009).[1] RD patients and families also face challenges regarding domestic tasks, transport and mobility, leisure activities, educational and professional activities, self-care, financial burden and feelings of discrimination in the labour market (FEDER 2009).[2]

Family members—often the main carers—frequently find themselves in burn out situations, unable to cope physically and psychologically with the situation.

RDs generate a considerable moral suffering (French Social and Economic Council 2001) and it has been recognised that these diseases result in reduced quality of life and affect individuals' potential for education and learning abilities (Schieppati et al. 2008).

Compared to more prevalent chronic disorders, people living with a RD have a worse quality of life and experience higher losses in terms of medical care and social and economic activities (Van Nispen et al. 2003).

---

[1]EURORDISCare Survey to 12,000 patients from 23 countries (2002–2008) - 1/3 of the respondents reported that a patient in their family had to reduce or stop professional activities due to the disease; an additional 1/3 reported that one member in the family had to reduce or stop professional activities to take care of a relative with a RD; almost 1/3 of the respondents required assistance from a social worker in the 12 months preceding the survey. More than 1/3 of those reported they met the social work with difficulties or did not meet one at all; 1/5 of the respondents had to move house, usually to relocate to a home better adapted to their health needs.

[2]Study performed in Spain (2009) - patients mentioned that they generally need support for: domestic life (46%), transport (42%), personal mobility (40%), leisure activities (37%), educational/professional activities (39%) and self-care (32%). Only 1 in 10 did not need any sort of assistance in daily life; 27% spend income in adapted transport, 23% in personal assistance and 9% in adapting their house;, patients reported to feel discriminated in: leisure activities (32%), education (30%) and daily activities (29%); labour market (32%) either when searching for a job (17%) or at their current job (15%).

25.1.3 Challenges in Care Provision

"Only the strong survive", mother of rare disease patient while navigating the welfare system (Byskov Holm and Jensen 2014)

"It is not possible to get a 'check list' of all the people you need to talk with. Also, service providers differ in the amount of interest they show", Denis Ryan, husband of Anne, living with Huntington Disease (EUCERD Joint Action 2012)

"If anyone would coordinate my daughter's care it would be wonderful as I've been doing it for years", parent of patient with 1q21.1 micro deletion (Brains for Brain Foundation 2014).

A patient with a RD is seldom a standard beneficiary. The combination of the rarity, complexity and lack of treatment creates a particular set of hurdles in the provision of holistic care:

- Expertise and information on RDs and their consequences are scarce and difficult to access and therefore professionals lack knowledge on RDs;
- RD patients and families need multidisciplinary care, including medical and paramedical care as well as social, psychological or educational aspects. They need to be followed simultaneously by a set of national, regional and local health, social and support services which are often managed by different authorities;
- People living with a RD often need continuous and lifelong support;
- The scarcity of expertise forces many RD patients to seek care abroad.

Adding to these challenges, people with RDs experience barriers when accessing health and welfare services (Grut and Kvam 2013):

- Care systems are usually designed around common diseases and mainstream services are not flexible enough to take into consideration unprecedented health needs (EURORDIS 2009);
- Care systems are extremely difficult to navigate for patients and families who struggle to make the most of their potential throughout their life course;
- Care pathways are fragmented and obtaining the correct diagnosis, the needed social care and support to manage the transitions between hospital and home and between childhood and adulthood remain a challenge (Brains for Brain Foundation 2014);
- There is a lack of communication and coordination within and between the health and social care sectors, as well as between national and local services (Byskov Holm and Jensen 2014);
- Medical and social care professionals are insufficiently informed and trained to care for people living with a RD and tend to be reluctant to treat patients due to the complexity of their disease (EURORDIS 2009);
- Cross border health care remains a challenge due to the fragmentation of legal systems, different access to and reimbursement of services, lack of information

on how and when to access it, as well as burdensome administrative requirements;

- In most cases, the management and coordination of care has to be done by patients and families, which places a heavy burden on family life (Dammann 2015).

These issues are of particular importance given that patients and families perceive that their quality of life of is more closely linked to the quality of care provided than to the gravity of their illness, or the degree of the associated disabilities (EURORDIS 2009).

25.2 Goal of Integrated Care for Rare Diseases

When considering RD patients as a whole, the need to integrate social and medical services becomes obvious (EURORDIS 2009) and recent studies show that integrated care is especially beneficial for people with complex needs (Klinga et al. 2015).

The low prevalence and complexity of RDs, as well as the significant unmet needs of RD patients, highlight the need for the implementation of holistic, integrated and patient-centred care pathways, which respond to the complexity of RD challenges through an interdisciplinary approach.

Integrated care for RDs ensures:

- The transfer of scarce information and expertise on RDs;
- Coordination and communication between health, social and local care providers;
- Optimisation of care pathways and resources, increasing patients'/families' quality of life and reducing health care expenditure and economic burden for society (Reich et al. 2012);
- Integration of RD specificities into mainstream services;
- An answer to some of the main challenges of RDs, such as diagnostic delays, transitions from child to adult services and from hospital to home, access to social and community services;
- Reduction of the burden on patients and families who will no longer be responsible for coordinating care and will be supported in navigating the care system.

25.3   The Integrated Care Pathway for Rare Diseases

25.3.1 Proposals for the Provision of Integrated Care to Rare Disease Patients

Care for people living with a RD needs to be holistic, multidisciplinary and specifically tailored to patients' unique needs (McGarvey and Har 2008). This implies the provision of a set of health, social and support services, including rehabilitation, day-care, home care, personal assistants, respite services, adapted schools and work place, psychological support and social prescribing, among others.

There is agreement in Europe upon the necessity of coordinating RD patients' care nationally and internationally. The recommendations of the European Union Committee of Experts on Rare Diseases (EUCERD)[3] to the European Commission (EC) and Member States (MS) promote a set of important measures and quality criteria,[4] supporting the development of health care pathways at national level and European networks at international level.

The development of National Plans[5] for RDs is encouraged, alongside the organisation of national care pathways embedded into the health system, including Centres of Expertise[6] and national networks for a RD/cluster of RDs. On the other hand, the development of European Reference Networks[7] for RDs is regarded as essential to facilitate the provision of cross border health care[8] and to reduce the burdens associated with seeking care abroad.

In regards to access to treatment, society, patients, experts, healthcare systems and the pharma industry need to think outside the box to address new challenges facing the rare disease community. There is an urgent need for a seamless approach

---

[3]The EUCERD was charged with aiding the EC with the preparation and implementation of Community activities in the field of RDs, in cooperation and consultation with the specialised bodies in MS, the relevant European authorities and other relevant stakeholders. In 2014, the EUCERD was replaced by the European Commission Expert Group on Rare Diseases. More information available at: http://www.eucerd.eu/.

[4]EUCERD recommendations available at: http://www.eucerd.eu/?page_id=13.

[5]More information available at: http://www.europlanproject.eu/Content?folder=1.

[6]Centres of Expertise (CEs) are physical expert structures for the management and care of RD patients. Each CE is specialised in a single RD or group of RDs and share the mission of providing patients with the highest standards of care to deliver timely diagnosis, appropriate treatments and follow up. More information available at http://www.eurordis.org/sites/default/files/publications/factsheet_Centres_Expertise.pdf.

[7]European Reference Networks (ERNs) for RDs should serve as research and knowledge centres, updating and contributing to the latest scientific findings, treating patients from other MS and ensuring the availability of subsequent treatment facilities where necessary. More information available at: http://ec.europa.eu/health/rare_diseases/european_reference_networks/erf/index_en.htm.

[8]More information available at: http://eur-lex.europa.eu/LexUriServ/LexUriServ.do?uri=OJ:L:2011:088:0045:0065:EN:PDF.

to European cooperation on medicines development to bridge the gap between EU regulatory decisions and fragmented national/local pricing and reimbursement decisions. And patients need to be engaged in these processes (Le Cam 2015).

The European Commission Expert Group on Rare Diseases (CEGRD),[9] a multi-stakeholder group including RD experts, MS and patient representatives, is currently developing recommendations to support the integration of RDs into social services and policies.[10] The group proposes various approaches to facilitate integrated and continuous patient-centred care provision to people living with a RD through: Centres of Expertise; individual care plans; care pathways and standards of care; case managers; one-stop-shop services; networking and training programmes for service providers; and the integration of RDs into national functionality assessment systems. Additionally, eHealth can also be an asset for integrated care in RDs. These approaches are explained below.

25.3.1.1 Centres of Expertise

Centres of Expertise, as health structures specialised in RDs, have a key role in sharing information and knowledge and building networks to facilitate integrated patient-centred care provision to people living with a RD and their families.

According to the EUCERD (2011) Recommendations on Quality Criteria for Centres of Expertise on Rare Diseases, these centres should: bring together or coordinate multidisciplinary competences/skills, including paramedical skills and social services; contribute to building healthcare pathways and to the elaboration and dissemination of good practice guidelines; provide education and training to non-healthcare professionals; and produce information adapted to the specific needs of patients/families and of health and social professionals.

25.3.1.2 Individual Care Plans

Simple, holistic and flexible individual care plans which can be implemented by central, regional and local services would be of great use in the context of RDs. Based on the assessment of individual needs, including health and social dimensions of care, these plans should be developed and implemented in collaboration between care providers, patients and families. Ideally, a coordinator should be assigned to manage and follow up the individual care plan.

25.3.1.3 Care Pathways and Standards of Care

Care pathways and standards of care are multidisciplinary care management tools which define the different tasks to be undertaken by professionals involved in

---

[9]The CEGRD replaced the EUCERD in 2014 in supporting the EC with the preparation and implementation of Community activities in the field of RDs. More information available at: http://ec.europa.eu/health/rare_diseases/expert_group/index_en.htm.

[10]Final document to be published in 2016 at http://ec.europa.eu/health/rare_diseases/publications/index_en.htm#anchor0.

patient care and are essential to create equality in the level of care and services provided to people with a RD.

In Sweden, for example, the care pathway for RDs is organised through the Act on Support and Service for Persons with certain Functional Impairments,[11] an entitlement law that guarantees good living conditions for people with extensive and permanent functional impairment, ensuring that they receive the help they need in daily life and that they can influence the support and services they receive. The Swedish care pathway ensures a permanent contact in health, responsible for interactions within healthcare and for coordination of stakeholders, treatments and services in line with an individual coordinating plan. The Centres of Expertise ensure interactions between medical and non-medical issues and there is ongoing work on national treatment and care programs, within a holistic and lifelong approach.[12]

Other EU MS are currently developing care pathways for RD patients using standards of care. For example, France and the Netherlands are establishing standards of care, in which the organisation of care within the national health network is described for a certain RD.

In France, by 2012, 50 national good practice guidelines for diagnosis, treatment and follow-up of patients with RDs were developed by expert health centres with the support of the French National Authority for Health (HAS). In 2012, the HAS published a new simplified method to develop these guidelines, aiming to boost the production to 200 protocols in 4 years (EUCERD 2014).

In the Netherlands, there has been important progress concerning RDs and integrated care, with the development of standards of care for 16 diseases, some of which are already implemented (Vajda et al. 2012).[13] The Dutch Genetic Alliance has been an important stakeholder in this process and keeps developing standards of care and other quality standards, according to a new national guideline.[14]

25.3.1.4 Case Managers

Case managers are essential for integrated care in RDs. They can ensure coordination between centralised and local care and alleviate the care coordination burden faced by patients and families.

Case managers have an instrumental role in adapting the existing care system to patients' individual needs and in supporting holistic and continuous care by establishing networks of care providers, providing information and support to

---

[11]More information available at: http://www.socialstyrelsen.se/Lists/Artikelkatalog/attachments/8407/2009-126-188_2009126188.pdf.

[12]More information available at: http://bit.ly/1M2noBZ.

[13]A national network of expertise is being set up for some RDs to provide integrated care. Moreover, the Dutch Genetic Alliance hosts a website to disseminate RD quality standards. More information available at: www.zorgstandaarden.net.

[14]More information available at: http://bit.ly/1WPmhgt [Dutch].

local professionals, patients and families coordinating individual care plans and providing information on cross border care when needed.

Ideally, case managers should be trained and employed by or work in connection with Centres of Expertise. Case managers should be located at regional/local level in order to facilitate local care provision, and should remain the same for as long as possible in order to ensure stability during transition periods.

A pilot implemented in France, PRIOR-RH, shows how case management can be organised by a regional centre of expertise for RDs. Implemented at regional level, PRIOR-RH employs a multidisciplinary mobile team—health manager, genetic counsellor, social worker, psychologist, occupational therapist—which undertakes the role of case management for people living with RDs in the region, thus improving their care pathways. PRIOR-RH has built a regional network of competence both in health and social care involving 23 partners. Additionally, PRIOR-RH provides information on RDs, draws-up an inventory of regional expertise, directs patients towards social and medical care services, provides social follow up to support patients in their life course, and organises stakeholders meetings.[15]

25.3.1.5 One-Stop-Shop Services for Rare Diseases

Resource Centres for RDs[16] are a one-stop-shop style of service, specifically designed for people living with a RD, often functioning in partnership with Centres of Expertise. Resource centres commonly create a bridge between patients/families and various stakeholders involved in patient care (EURORDIS 2013a, b) and can coordinate with regional/local case managers.

Resource Centres empower patients, families, carers and professionals at various levels and undertake an essential role in integrated care provision to people living with a RD. Resource Centres' services include information and guidance, training courses, respite care, therapeutic education, information on social benefits and research. Sometimes daily therapies, medical/psychological consultations and therapeutic recreation are also provided.

The EUCERD Joint Action (2012–2015)[17] mapped existing Resource Centres for RDs, identifying 21 services in 12 European countries.[18] Among these are NoRo (Romania), Frambu (Norway) and Ågrenska (Sweden).

The NoRo Pilot Reference Centre for Rare Diseases is a Resource Centre accredited both as a social service and a medical service which provides holistic care based on a multidisciplinary and complementary approach and on the

---

[15]More information at: http://download.eurordis.org.s3.amazonaws.com/emm2015/ws4/5.DOMI NIQUE_FRANCE_Prior%20Eurordis%20Madrid.pdf.

[16]More information at:http://www.eurordis.org/sites/default/files/publications/fact-sheet-resource-centres.pdf

[17]The EUCERD Joint Action: Working for Rare Diseases, co-funded by the EC, supported the activities and mandate of the EUCERD until the end of 2013 and the activities of the CEGRD, from 2014. More information available at: http://www.eucerd.eu/?page_id=54.

[18]Map and list of services available at: http://www.eurordis.org/specialised-social-services.

individual assessment of patients' needs. The centre ensures continuity of care through collaboration with other services in the community and by establishing networks with medical universities.[19] NoRo runs a help line for RDs, organises training for patients, volunteers and professionals,[20] support groups, therapeutic weekends for families and therapeutic camps for children.

Frambu's multidisciplinary team provides services to people affected by over 120 different RDs as well as to carers and service providers. The centre complements the services provided by the Norwegian health system and works in connection with university hospitals. Frambu is a meeting place for families and professionals providing competence, knowledge, documentation and guidance and organising residential courses, summer camps, research projects and outreach activities in local communities.

Ågrenska's main objective is to gather, develop and spread knowledge on RDs and their consequences. The centre provides family programmes, adult programmes, respite care services, summer camps, a family support unit, courses for professionals and social research. The centre aims at supporting and empowering people to cope with everyday life and to be as independent as possible.[21]

25.3.1.6 Networking and Training Programmes for Service Providers

Coordination and networking between all parties involved in care provision is essential to supporting the transfer of the scarce expertise on RDs from central structures to regional and local services.

National authorities should allocate funding to support the creation of multidisciplinary teams composed by health (including Centres of Expertise), social and local care providers. Networking at an international level could be facilitated via the European Reference Network for RDs.

Training health and non-health professionals is essential to support the integration of RDs specificities into mainstream services. Centres of Expertise should take the lead in developing training and networking programmes/tools for social and local support service professionals involved in the different stages of the care pathway. The EUCERD Joint Action has developed guiding principles and case study documents essential to support the design of training programmes for social care providers (EUCERD Joint Action 2014a, b).

---

[19] NoRo has organised a network of videoconference facilities with 7 Romanian medical universities which aims at facilitating direct access to information/good practices and meetings between patients and professionals.

[20] More information at: www.edubolirare.ro.

[21] More information available at: http://download.eurordis.org/documents/pdf/sss/3-RCS-Agrenska-Gunilla-Jaeger.pdf.

25.3.1.7 Integration of Rare Diseases into National Functionality Assessment Systems

The integration of RDs into functioning and disability assessment systems, in line with the United Nations Convention on the Rights of Persons with Disabilities, is a way to ensure that health care and welfare systems take into account the complexity of RDs. A fair assessment of patients' functionality will support medical and social services to develop integrated care plans.

To ensure an adequate evaluation, the assessment system should be flexible to adapt to people with a RD affected by complex combinations of several impairments, less visible impairments, degenerative conditions or acute disease periods. The Orphanet Disability Project[22] (de Chalendar et al. 2014) which develops RD disability core sets derived from and compatible with the International Classification of Functioning, Disability and Health (ICF) is an important tool that can support national authorities to improve the assessment of functionality and disability of people living with a RD.

25.3.1.8 eHealth to Facilitate Data Sharing and Interoperability

Integrated care for RDs can also be supported by the use of eHealth solutions which can improve the quality of treatment, broaden access to medical care, improve health outcomes and quality of life, get the most out of technologies and new services and reduce pressures on public healthcare budgets.

Additionally, eHealth can help address a major issue for the RD community: data protection and interoperability. A priority for any eHealth service should be to enable the integration of (possibly-disparate) sources of data, based on unambiguous electronic identification of patients, across countries and across databases.

25.3.2 An Innovative Patient-Centred Approach for Integrated Care for People with Rare Diseases

INNOVCare (2015–2018),[23] a new project co-funded by the EU, addresses the issue of integrated care for people affected by RDs by developing, testing and promoting a holistic, personalised care pathway.

The innovative approach brings together national one-stop-shop services for RDs and regional case managers, in partnership with public bodies. In addition, the project establishes a European Network of Resource Centres to collate good practices vital to improve quality of care, in line with the Voluntary European Quality Framework for Social Services.[24]

---

[22]More information available at: http://www.rare-diseases.eu/wp-content/uploads/2014/05/0602_Myriam_de_CHALENDAR.pdf.

[23]More information at: www.innovcare.eu.

[24]More information at: http://www.ec.europa.eu/social/BlobServlet?docId=6140&langId=en.

The care pathway of INNOVCare proposes that the case handlers at a regional level should rely on the national resource centre to gather expertise by concentrating patients with the same RDs and good practices. In addition, national centres should rely on the expertise of centres in other countries and on the patient outreach capacity of the regional case handlers.

The new care model will be implemented and evaluated in a pilot in Romania. INNOVCare will also conduct robust data collection on the cost-benefit of the proposed care model.

25.4   Results of Integrated Care Approaches to Care Delivery

Regardless of the scarcity of data and studies on integrated care provision to people living with RDs, models of care which take into account integrated care methods have proven to be effective in optimising health outcomes and quality of life of RD patients.

An example of integrated care provision for Cystic Fibrosis patients in Europe shows that the establishment of a centre providing multidisciplinary care for this RD—including consultants, nurse, microbiologist, physiotherapist, dietician, pharmacist, psychologist, social worker, geneticist and allied healthcare professionals experienced in cystic fibrosis care—results in a significant increase in life expectancy for patients (Conway et al. 2014).

A study conducted by Ågrenska's one-stop-shop service for RDs, revealed that this resource centre is perceived as an improvement relative to patients' experience within the healthcare system in terms of treatment, outlook for the future, socioeconomic support, peer support and consideration by professionals and by the institution. Additionally, this type of holistic approach is cost-effective and leads to a nearly three-fold decrease in costs to society (Olauson 2002).[25]

Various pilots of integrated care provision for RD patients and families are currently ongoing throughout Europe. In the upcoming years, the results of the evaluation of these pilots and the outcomes of the INNOVCare project are expected to provide further insight into the health, social and economic benefits of integrated care provision to people living with a RD, as well as data on the cost-effectiveness of these services and on their impact on the optimisation of resources for national care systems.

---

[25]Study done by the Department of Economics of the University of Gothenburg on Ågrenska: the approach offered by the centre saves money compared to ordinary programmes for disabled children. Moreover, a family requires less support from social services when having access to the centre. There is a nearly three-fold decrease in costs when the child is correctly diagnosed and accesses proper treatment, compared to a child who is improperly diagnosed and treated through ordinary programmes. The savings appear to result from the reduction of costs with seeking emergency help, visiting specialists and sick leaves.

25.5   Lessons Learned and Outlook

The rarity, complexity and lack of treatment of RDs lead to significant unmet medical and social needs and create particular obstacles to the provision of integrated care.

The provision of integrated care is essential for RD patients to ensure the transfer of the scarce expertise and information available, to support the coordination and communication between care providers, to optimise resources, to integrate RD specificities into mainstream services, to improve care and care pathways, and to reduce the burden for families consequently increasing their quality of life.

Health services have a key role in facilitating integrated care for RD patients and in facilitating the integration of RD specificities into social and local services in line with the upcoming CEGRD recommendations to support the integration of RDs into social policies and services.

Various methods can be used to promote integrated care for RDs including: Centres of Expertise and one-stop-shop services for RDs; case managers; care pathways and standards of care; individual care plans; networking and training programmes for service providers; the integration of RDs into national functionality assessment systems; and eHealth.

Studies conducted so far have shown that integrated holistic care provision in RDs increases patients' life expectancy and quality of life while being cost-effective and decreasing costs for society.

INNOVCare, a new project co-funded by the EU, will conduct a pilot for an innovative model of integrated care provision in RDs and will collect important data on the social impact and on the cost-effectiveness of the innovative care pathway. The results of INNOVCare and of various ongoing pilots are expected to provide further insight into the health, social and economic benefits of integrated care provision to people living with a RD.

References

Aronson, J. K. (2006). Rare diseases and orphan drugs. *British Journal of Clinical Pharmacology*, *61*(3), 243–245. doi:10.1111/j.1365-2125.2006.02617.x. Accessed October 7, 2015, from http://www.ncbi.nlm.nih.gov/pmc/articles/PMC1885017/

Brains for Brain Foundation. (2014). *Dr Horst Schmidt Klinik. Healthcare transition of adolescent rare disease patients* (Position Paper 2014). Accessed September 18, 2015, from http://www.innermed.eu/uploads/assets/6_BfB_Transition_Paper_Final_03022015.pdf

Byskov Holm, B., & Jensen, L. (2014). Only the strong survive—Said by a mother navigating the welfare systems. *Rare Diseases Denmark*. Accessed September 18, 2015, from http://www.rare-diseases.eu/wp-content/uploads/2013/08/12_t1.pdf

de Chalendar, M., Bee, S., Olry, A., & Rath, A. (2014). Appraisal of disability in rare diseases with the ICF-CY: The Orphanet disability project. *Archives of Disease in Childhood 99*(Suppl 2), A14–A15.

Conway, S. et al. (2014). European cystic fibrosis society standards of care: Framework for the cystic fibrosis centre. *Journal of Cystic Fibrosis, 13*(1):3–22. doi: 10.1016/j.jcf.2014.03.009. Accessed September 22, 2015, from http://www.cysticfibrosisjournal.com/article/S1569-1993%2814%2900084-8/pdf

Council of the European Union. (2009). *Council recommendation of 8 June 2009 on an action in the field of rare diseases* (2009/C 151/02). Accessed September 18, 2015, from http://eur-lex.europa.eu/LexUriServ/LexUriServ.do?uri=OJ:C:2009:151:0007:0010:EN:PDF

Dammann, B. (2015). Does an individual plan make better services for children with rare disorders? *International Journal of Integrated Care* (Annual Conf Suppl. URN:NBN:NL: UI:10-1-117075). Accessed September 18, 2015, from http://www.ijic.org/index.php/ijic/article/view/2067/2864

EUCERD (European Union Committee of Expert on Rare Diseases). (2011, October 24). *EUCERD recommendations on quality criteria for centres of expertise for rare diseases in member states.* Accessed September 21, 2015, from http://ec.europa.eu/health/rare_diseases/docs/eucerd_centresexpertise_en.pdf

EUCERD (European Union Committee of Expert on Rare Diseases). (2013, January 31). *EUCERD recommendations rare disease European reference networks (RD ERNs).* Accessed September 21, 2015, from http://www.eucerd.eu/?post_type=document&p=2207

EUCERD Joint Action. (2012). *Rare diseases: Addressing the need for specialised social services and integration into social policies.* Accessed October 7, 2015, from http://www.eurordis.org/sites/default/files/paper-social-policies-services-eja-wp6.pdf

EUCERD Joint Action. (2014a). *Guiding principles on training for social services providers—Examples of training programmes.* Accessed October 7, 2015, from http://www.eurordis.org/sites/default/files/examples-training-for-social-services-providers.pdf

EUCERD Joint Action. (2014b). *Report of the EUCERD joint action workshop on guiding principles for social care in rare diseases.* Accessed October 7, 2015, from http://www.eurordis.org/sites/default/files/eja-wp6-workshop-report-guiding-principles-social-care.pdf

EURORDIS. (2009). *The voice of 12000 patients. Experiences and expectations of rare disease patients on diagnosis and care in Europe.* Paris: EURORDIS. Accessed October 7, 2015, from http://www.eurordis.org/IMG/pdf/voice_12000_patients/EURORDISCARE_FULLBOOKr.pdf

EURORDIS. (2013a). *Policy fact sheet—Centres of expertise.* Accessed October 7, 2015, from http://www.eurordis.org/sites/default/files/publications/factsheet_Centres_Expertise.pdf

EURORDIS. (2013b). *Policy fact sheet—Resource centres for rare diseases.* Accessed September 21, 2015, from http://www.eurordis.org/sites/default/files/publications/fact-sheet-resource-centres.pdf

FEDER (Federación Española de Enfermedades Raras). (2009). *Study on the situation of social-sanitary needs of people with rare diseases in Spain—ENSERio.*

French Social & Economic Council. (2001). Cinq mille maladies rares, le choc de la génétique : constat, perspectives et possibilités d'évolution. Avis et rapports du Conseil économique et social. *Journal officiel de la République française.* Accessed September 18, 2015, from http://www.lecese.fr/sites/default/files/pdf/Avis/2001/01092516.pdf

Grut, L., & Kvam, M. H. (2013). Facing ignorance: People with rare disorders and their experiences with public health and welfare services. *Scandinavian Journal of Disability Research, 15*(1). doi:10.1080/15017419.2011.645870.

Guillem, P., Cans, C., Robert-Gnansia, E., Aymé, S., & Jouk, P. S. (2008). Rare diseases in disabled children: An epidemiological survey. *Archives of Disease in Childhood, 93*(2), 115–118. doi:10.1136/adc.2006.104455. Published Online on 17 October 2007.

INNOVCare. (2015). *Project funded by the European Commission, DG employment, social affairs and inclusion, under grant agreement VS/2015/0249.* http://www.innovcare.eu/

Klinga, C. M., Hansson, J., Hasson, H., & Andreen-Sachs, M. (2015). Collective leadership as a management arrangement of integrated health and social care. *International Journal of Integrated Care.* Annual Conf Suppl. URN:NBN:NL:UI:10-1-117016. Accessed September 18, 2015, from http://www.ijic.org/index.php/ijic/article/view/2091/2888

Le Cam, Y. (2015). Patients need faster, cheaper treatment. *The Financial Times*. Retrieved January 15, 2016, from http://www.ft.com/intl/cms/s/0/6a298724-2951-11e5-acfbcbd2e1c81cca.html#axzz3xKRjSaF1

McGarvey, B., & Har, C. (2008). An investigation into the social support needs of families who experience rare disorders on the island of Ireland. *RehabCare*. Accessed September 21, 2015, from http://www.rehab.ie/about/PDFS/July2008/RehabCare_RD_Report.pdf

Olauson, A. (2002). The Agrenska centre. A socioeconomic case study of rare diseases. *PharmacoEconomics, 20*(Suppl 3), 73–75.

Orphanet. (2015, May). *List of rare diseases and synonyms listed in alphabetical order*. Orphanet Report Series, Rare Diseases Collection. Accessed September 18, 2015, from http://www.orpha.net/orphacom/cahiers/docs/GB/List_of_rare_diseases_in_alphabetical_order.pdf

Orphanet: An Online Database of Rare Diseases and Orphan Drugs. Copyright, INSERM 1997. Last update October 2015. *What is an orphan drug?* Accessed September 18, 2015, from http://www.orpha.net/consor/cgi-bin/Education_AboutOrphanDrugs.php?lng=EN

Rare Diseases Task Force. (2008). *Health indicators for Rare diseases: State of the art and Future directions*. Accessed September 18, 2015, from http://www.eucerd.eu/?post_type=document&p=1207

Reich, O., Rapold, R., & Flatscher-Toni, M. (2012). An empirical investigation of the efficiency effects of integrated care models in Switzerland. *International Journal of Integrated Care, 12*. Accessed September 18, 2015, from http://www.ijic.org/index.php/ijic/article/view/685

Schieppati, A., Henter, J. I., Daina, E., & Aperia, A. (2008). Why rare diseases are an important medical and social issue. *Lancet, 371*, 2039–2041. doi:10.1016/S0140-6736(08)60872-7.

Tozzi, A. E., Mingarelli, A., Agricola, E., Gonfiantini, M., Pandolfi, E., Carloni, E., Gesualdo, F., & Dallapiccola, B. (2013). The internet user profile of Italian families of patients with rare diseases: A web survey. *Orphanet Journal of Rare Diseases* ; 8:76. doi:10.1186/1750-1172-8-76. Accessed October 7, 2015, from http://www.ojrd.com/content/8/1/76

United Nations Convention on the Rights of Persons with Disabilities. Adopted in December 2016. Accessed October 7, 2015, from http://www.un.org/disabilities/convention/conventionfull.shtml

Vajda, I., Hendriks, S., & Oosterwijk, C. (2012). Standards of care for rare diseases: A Dutch case of patient involvement. Poster Presentation. In: *European Conference on Rare Diseases & Orphan Products*.

Van Nispen, R. M. A., Rijken, P. M., & Heijmans, M. J. W. M. (2003, May). *Leven met een zeldzame chronische aandoening: Ervaringen van patiënten in de zorg en het dagelijks leven*. NIVEL—Nederlands Instituut voor onderzoek van de gezondheidszorg. ISBN 90-69056-14-3. Accessed September 18, 2015, from http://www.nivel.nl/sites/default/files/bestanden/zeldzame-aandoeningen.pdf

World Health Organisation.(2013). *Priority medicines for Europe and the World 2013 Update*. Accessed October 9, 2015, from http://www.who.int/medicines/areas/priority_medicines/Ch6_19Rare.pdf

Pathways in Transplantation Medicine: Challenges in Overcoming Interfaces Between Cross-Sectoral Care Structures

26

Lena Harries, Harald Schrem, Christian Krauth, and Volker Amelung

26.1 Introduction

Organ transplantation is a particularly sensitive area of medicine in which chronically severely ill patients are treated in an extremely complex care setting. Due to the nature of the underlying disorder, transplant surgery and postsurgical care, the transplantation process involves a variety of different healthcare institutions and sectors. Thus, outpatient and inpatient physicians of different specializations as well as various rehabilitation, nursing and mental care service providers must deal with the various treatment and ethical issues associated with transplantation in an integrated manner. The decline in the number of donors due to the transplantation scandal in Germany has demonstrated just how vulnerable the area of organ transplantation (Tx) and donation is: only 864 organs were donated in 2014

L. Harries (✉)
Institute for Epidemiology, Social Medicine and Health Systems Research, Hannover Medical School, Hannover, Germany

Core Facility Quality Management & Health Technology Assessment in Transplantation, Integrated Research and Treatment Center Transplantation (IFB-Tx), Hannover Medical School, Hannover, Germany
e-mail: harries.lena@mh-hannover.de

H. Schrem
Core Facility Quality Management & Health Technology Assessment in Transplantation, Integrated Research and Treatment Center Transplantation (IFB-Tx), Hannover Medical School, Hannover, Germany

Department of General, Visceral and Transplantation Surgery, Hannover Medical School, Hannover, Germany
e-mail: schrem.harald@mh-hannover.de

C. Krauth • V. Amelung
Institute for Epidemiology, Social Medicine and Health Systems Research, Hannover Medical School, Hannover, Germany
e-mail: krauth.christian@mh-hannover.de; amelung@inav-berlin.de

© Springer International Publishing AG 2017
V. Amelung et al. (eds.), *Handbook Integrated Care*,
DOI 10.1007/978-3-319-56103-5_26

compared to 1200 in 2011 (DSO 2014; Pondrom 2013; Schrem and Kaltenborn 2013).

Organ allocation is influenced by several independent variables, such as the time on the waiting list. Patients who need a liver transplant, for example, generally wait for approximately 5–13 months for a transplant, depending on their blood group and urgency (Samuel 2015; Jung et al. 2008; Schlitt et al. 2011). The situation regarding kidney transplantation is even more complicated. Once ultimate kidney failure has occurred and dialysis is necessary, the median waiting time for a donor transplant is about 43 months (Samuel 2015). As recent statistics point out, the time on the waiting list can be extremely long—up to 15 years in some cases (DSO 2015). Furthermore, because patients require continuous maintenance therapy while waiting for transplantation, all possible drug interactions must be taken into account throughout the entire waiting period (Schrem et al. 2009).

26.2   Structures of Care

26.2.1 Outpatient and Inpatient Care

During the organ donation and transplantation process, various stakeholders register patients in need of transplantation, allocate and deliver donor organs, perform transplant surgery and provide follow-up care. Additional institutions are involved in the organization, coordination, examination and quality assurance of this process (Veit et al. 2014). For the patients, this decentralized organization means many separate and individual treatment steps between the sectors as well as parallel treatments by in- and outpatient physicians (Fig. 26.1). Considering the continuous deterioration of the patient's organ function and the likelihood of organ failure, this situation is precarious for the patient.

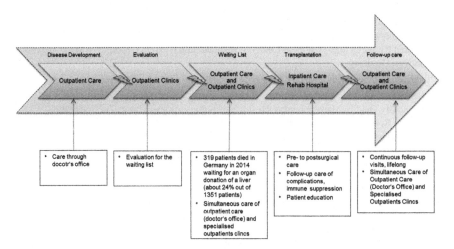

Fig. 26.1 Inpatient and outpatient treatment pathways within the process of transplantation. Source: Own presentation

Depending on the individual patient characteristics (underlying disease, multimorbidity, etc.), outpatient care may require further medical specialists besides the General Practitioner (GP). In case of chronic liver disease, those may include gastroenterologists, hepatologists and/or oncologists. Parallel to outpatient treatment, the patients need to visit the transplant outpatient clinic regularly, as the transplant centre must always be aware of the patient's health status (Niedermeyer et al. 2001; IFB-Tx 2015).

The evaluation for inclusion on the waiting list requires certain clinical assessments. For example, cardiological, pneumological, urological, gastroenterological, endocrinological, vascular and/or hematologic examinations are needed for kidney transplantation. This places enormous stress on the patient as the evaluation process is time-consuming and involves a large number of physicians (Kumar 2015).

Moreover, the patient's medical data has to be updated regularly for the waiting list, as changes can have an impact on one's position on the waiting list. Therefore, it is essential that all information about medical events involving a patient be passed on quickly and completely to the physicians in charge.

Furthermore, especially close cooperation between the several outpatient physicians, the outpatient clinics and the rehabilitation clinics is needed for optimal aftercare of organ transplant recipients. Long-term success in terms of the overall goals of complete restoration of health as well as social and professional re-integration largely depends on the quality of interdisciplinary care and aftercare. Regardless of the complexity of the original transplantation supply chain, close control is a high-priority success factor for a "good" outcome after transplantation. Close control includes continuous monitoring of the compliance of the patient and enables the early diagnosis and treatment of complications. Both aspects play a crucial role.

The fact that there is no obligatory system for the tracking of Tx patients is a critical issue in Germany. Some patients do not visit the outpatient clinic regularly, so strict monitoring is not possible (Mayr 2005; Bundesärztekammer 2015). In contrast, other countries have a transplant registry. The UK or USA, for example, have such a mandatory registry for the centralized collection of data on organ donation and transplantation. Therefore, each stakeholder (e.g., hospital staff, National Organ Retrieval Service, and recipient transplant coordinators in the UK) must report follow-up data in the registry (NHS Blood and Transplant). Besides the aforementioned aspects, all possible drug interactions and relevant drug safety issues also have to be considered at all times, for instance, even when prescribing medication for a flu. Thus, the aftercare of transplant patients requires a high quality of coordination and communication between the different actors (Schrem et al. 2009).

In addition to the transplant physicians and surgeons, even more institutions are involved in the context of organ donation. In Germany, these include the German Foundation for Organ Transplantation (DSO), Eurotransplant (ET), and the hospital administration. A practical map for visualization of this comprehensive process has been developed by the Integrated Research and Treatment Center for Transplantation (IFB-Tx) and the Core Facility for Quality Management and Health

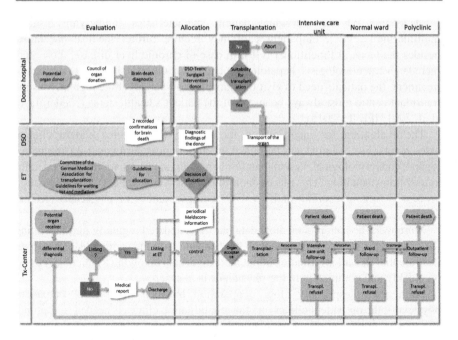

Fig. 26.2 Process map liver transplantation (post mortal). Source: Own presentation based on the process map of the Core Facility Qualitymanagement and HTA Transplantation of the IFB-Tx (Authors: Carola Stumpp, Torsten Kirsch, Harald Schrem)

Technology Assessment (HTA)—Transplantation at Hanover Medical School (MHH) (Fig. 26.2). It clearly depicts the variety of horizontal and vertical interfaces in the clinical workflow and identifies highly sensitive and vulnerable areas while clarifying the simultaneous responsibilities of the various institutions involved during each step (evaluation, allocation, etc.). The mapped actions in the transplantation centre alone illustrate the parallel course of several steps and the complexity of the clinical processes involved in transplantation medicine. The process map also highlights the need to prepare patients for a care process carried out by a team of various physicians, in addition to the challenges concerning their inpatient stay. The fact that there are further interfaces to the social sector as well as to psychological care throughout the clinical process further increases the complexity of the treatment process.

26.2.2 Living Donations

Like the complex healthcare paths for transplant recipients, the pathway for living donors is challenging in several respects as well. People who decide to make a living donation do so for altruistic reasons, to save a loved one or even a total stranger (Davis 2011). However, in some countries, it is not possible to donate an organ to someone unknown for altruistic reasons. In Germany, for example, a living donation is only permitted between individuals who are first or second-degree relatives, married or engaged, or otherwise apparently close to the donor (Bundesärztekammer 2000). Other countries such as the UK and the USA have a solidarity approach to altruistic donors (Davis 2011; NHS Choices 2014).

Other barriers to living donation include remaining risks related to insurance law. It is the responsibility of the state to provide health insurance coverage for a living donor, not just during the pre- and perioperative period, but lifelong coverage for all risks associated with a living donation. Issues like the capacity to work, safety and medical care in the event of accident or illness are important factors affecting the willingness to make a living donation (Davis 2011; Gold et al. 2001).

Furthermore, the expenses associated with a donation must be taken into account. This includes not only medical costs, but also living expenses, lost salary, and travel expenses. Moreover, it is also necessary to have a supportive employer who is willing to approve the employee's request for paid or unpaid leave required for the donation process. The system must offer assistance to potential donors to enhance access to donation (Davis 2011).

Further evidence is required to support new approaches to living donation. This includes collecting data on the results of newer practices, such as accepting organs from donors not traditionally accepted due, for instance, to obesity or higher risk genetic backgrounds. Furthermore, it is important to conduct more studies on donor outcomes, including potential harm to the donor, risks modifications and post-donation interventions (Davis 2011). High-quality data is necessary for quality assurance and improved performance (Living Kidney Donor Follow-Up Conference Writing Group et al. 2011).

26.3   General Key Elements for the Future

More strongly integrated cross-sectoral and cross-professional models of care are needed to build a more patient-centreed and multidisciplinary approach to transplant medicine. Several key success factors are described below.

26.3.1 Communication

In transplantation medicine, it is of particular importance that interfaces concerning the continuity of a cross-sectoral treatment be supported through a process and information technology link. An integrated exchange of information between decentralized actors and institutions is essential to avoid ambiguity and prevent information loss. The necessary unifying and merging of transplant data is best achieved in terms of a national transplant register. Important aims of establishing such a register include improved documentation, harmonized data flow, and increased efficiency in the documentation and integration of data from different sources. The prerequisite for this is the large-scale use of structured information and communication tools. A key element of such a system is the use of electronic health cards or electronic medical records. This expedites and simplifies the exchange of information between stakeholders, which is particularly important in case of medical emergencies (Veit et al. 2014; Amelung and Wolf 2012).

26.3.2 Forms of Compensation

Different forms of remuneration of doctors, such as a fixed monthly salary, case rates or diagnosis related groups (DRGs), can also inhibit intersectional collaboration between the involved stakeholders. Resource allocation between the interfaces of the different care sectors is in need of improvement. Some of the existing payment practices generate incentives for the stakeholders of one sector to act to the disadvantage of those of another sector in order to ensure their own financial benefit. A form of compensation designed to overcome the organizational separation of the sectors is the so-called bundled payments system. Here, payments are based on a defined package of services generated in the context of a specific episode of care and are paid in lump sum and prospectively. This compensation strategy includes not only the separate care sectors, but also all stages of the supply chain. This form of remuneration could help to overcome the separation of the sectors as well as to promote the cooperation between service providers.

An essential prerequisite for bundled payments is adequate representation of the required resources. On the basis of evidence-based guidelines, it is recommended to determine the resource utilization for a treatment period, from which the corresponding amount of compensation can be derived. To avoid the problem that individual actors offer more lucrative services than less financially attractive services, the distribution can also be regulated by guidelines. Further disincentives, such as risk selection of patients or diminished service quality, can be counteracted by adding various modifications as needed. Risk selection of certain patients can be minimized, for example, by performing risk adjustment according to age or gender. In order to integrate a quality assurance measure, this can be carried out in combination with additional compensation. Therefore, bundled payments could be increased by a percentage, which is subject to certain conditions.

In the field of transplantation, it could be possible to demand a lump sum payment for outpatient and inpatient care as well as for medications. This remuneration could cover the time on the waiting list, for instance. After transplantation a further lump sum payment would then be required for the aftercare, including outpatient, inpatient and rehabilitative services, as well as drug prescriptions. This system supports a better interexchange between the involved actors, as each actor has an incentive to balance their service in combination with the individual fee, as this is part of a service and compensation package (Amelung 2013). A unified system of payment would support a more frictionless care process and help to achieve a reduction of costs in transplant medicine.

It is also important to consider that the costs of transplantation vary greatly, depending on disease severity or complications. In Germany, for example, the average cost of an inpatient stay for liver transplantation is about 52,570 €, but the range is from 18,330 € to 397,450 € (Lock et al. 2010). The results of a meta-analysis by van der Hilst et al. (2009) underline the great variability of costs for transplantation: the mean cost in the USA was US$163,438 compared to US$103,438 in the other OECD countries evaluated.[1]

26.3.3 Leadership

The complex and vulnerable care structures for transplant patients as well as the important role of the public trust require holistic management of the process besides the established management structures. It is the responsibility of management to develop and communicate effective strategies and involve all stakeholders. In healthcare, this appears to be a particularly difficult task because the focus is on the whole organization. The creation of such structures is more extensive than for a classical organization. Concerning the transplantation process, which has a variety of cross-sectoral and -institutional interfaces, this task is even more complex. The implementation of a comprehensive management approach also requires a disruption of previous traditional role patterns and structures, which can mean intrusion into previously autonomous areas. Therefore, it is equally important to integrate the various professions, cultures and corporate structures. The leadership should be focused on isolation from the existing structures and should be implemented accordingly (Sydow et al. 2011; Reinertsen et al. 2008; den Hertog et al. 2005; Schmitz and Berchthold 2009).

Although the medical profession within the treatment process is not to be disposed of by substitution, it is important to delegate medical tasks. One strategy is to integrate a case management system. Case managers supervise the treatment process across the different care sectors. They plan, judge, implement, coordinate, assess and evaluate each step. Their tasks include obtaining medical and psychological assessments and providing guidance on financial issues or occupational difficulties. These highly ambitious functions can be performed by specially trained nurses. Such further education enables them to provide evidence-based management and to support the self-care of the patient (Amelung 2013; Harries et al. 2015).

26.4   Conclusions

The structures of care in the field of transplantation present a variety of complicated paths and hurdles for the patient. Besides challenges concerning the involvement of different sectors of care and multiple institutions, there is no so-called owner of the process for the patients. Since the treatment path includes contacts with a variety of specialists from various fields, it is important that GPs assist in organization and help patients get their bearings. Though it all, the patients need to consolidate all information and organize their own treatment process along with the different

---

[1]This was a meta-analysis with a random effects model, which included nine U.S. articles and five OECD articles (van der Hilst et al. 2009).

physicians. As local physicians generally do not have much experience in handling specific issues of transplantation, the patient is kind of left to deal with it alone. Considering the fact that transplant patients have to cope with a severe illness, this can be an overwhelming and additional stress for the patient. Moreover, organ transplantation is a particularly sensitive area of medicine. The failure of an organizational structure can have a strong impact on the survival of transplantation patients. For example, it has been shown that the transplant scandal in Germany resulted in a sharp decline in the willingness to donate; this, in turn, reduced the total number of organs available for transplantation (BT-Drs. 18/3566 2014).

In this context, the World Health Organization (WHO) published a report with a "Global Strategy on People-Centered and Integrated Health Service" (WHO 2015). For the field of transplantation medicine, in particular, this might influence efforts in terms of optimizing the integration of different professions and ensuring better cooperation between the different institutions and care sectors. The extremely complex supply chain of transplant medicine is a burden for patients and a challenge to providing high-quality care in terms of continuous treatment. There is an urgent need to improve the problems at the interface between the sectors, eliminate the existing breaks in the supply chain, and stop the breakdown of information flows in transplantation medicine. These efforts should be focused on supporting a holistic course of treatment with a patient-oriented approach to the coordination of healthcare delivery.

References

Amelung, V. E. (2013). *Healthcare management. Managed care organisations and instruments.* Heidelberg u.a.: Springer.

Amelung, V. E., & Wolf, S. (2012). Integrierte Versorgung—Vom Hoffnungsträger zum Ladenhüter der deutschen Gesundheitspolitik? *G&S Gesundheits- und Sozialpolitik, 1,* 13–19.

BT-Drs. 18/3566. (2014). *Unterrichtung durch die Bundesregierung. Bericht der Bundesregierung über den Fortgang der eingeleiteten Reformprozesse, mögliche Missstände und sonstige aktuelle Entwicklungen in der Transplantationsmedizin.* Drucksache 18/3566 ed.: Deutscher Bundestag 18. Wahlperiode.

Bundesärztekammer. (2000). Empfehlung zur Lebendorganspende. *Deutsches Ärzteblatt, 97*(48), A3287–A3288.

Bundesärztekammer. (2015). Richtlinien zur Organtransplantation gem. § 16TPG. Richtlinie gemäß § 16 Abs. 1 S. 1 Nrn. 2 u. 5 TPG für die Wartelistenführung und Organvermittlung zur Lebertransplantation.

Davis, C. L. (2011). How to increase living donation. *Transplant International, 24*(4), 344–349.

Den Hertog, F., Groen, M., & Weehuizen, R. (2005). *Mapping health care innovation: Tracing walls and ceilings.* Maastrich: Maastricht Economic Research Institute on Innovation and Technology (MERIT), International Institute of Infonomics.

DSO. (2014). Organspende und Transplantation in Deutschland. *Jahresbericht.* Accessed February 22, 2016, from http://www.dso.de/uploads/tx_dsodl/JB_2014_Web_1.pdf

DSO. (2015). *Niere—Warteliste und Vermittlung.* Accessed March 3, 2016, from http://www.dso.de/organspende-und-transplantation/warteliste-und-vermittlung/niere.html

Gold, S. M., Schulz, K., & Koch, U. (2001). *Der Organspendeprozess: Ursachen des Organmangels und mögliche Lösungsansätze: Inhaltliche und methodenkritische Analyse vorliegender Studien.* BZgA: Köln.

Harries, L., Tangermann, U., & Amelung, V. E. (2015). Arztentlastende Konzepte in schwer zu versorgenden Regionen in Deutschland: Ein Vergleich mit England und den Niederlanden. *G&S Gesundheits- und Sozialpolitik, 69*(3–4), 62–69.

IFB-Tx. (2015). *Patienteninformation—Lebertransplantation*. Accessed March 13, 2016, from http://www.ifb-tx.de/patienteninformation/lebertransplantation/

Jung, G. E., Encke, J., Schmidt, J., & Rahmel, A. (2008). Model for end-stage liver disease. New basis of allocation for liver transplantations. *Chirurg, 79*(2), 157–163.

Kumar, V. (2015). Current status on the evaluation and management of the highly sensitized kidney transplant recipient. *Current Opinion in Nephrology and Hypertension, 24*(6), 570–575.

Living Kidney Donor Follow-Up Conference Writing Group, Leichtman, A., Abecassis, M., Barr, M., Charlton, M., Cohen, D., et al. (2011). Living kidney donor follow-up: State-of-the-art and future directions, conference summary and recommendations. *American Journal of Transplantation, 11*(12), 2561–2568.

Lock, J., Reinhold, T., Bloch, A., Malinowski, M., Schmidt, S. C., Neuhaus, P., et al. (2010). The cost of graft failure and other severe complications after liver transplantation—Experience from a German Transplant Center. *Annals of Transplantation, 15*(3), 11–18.

Mayr, M. (2005). Management after transplantation. *Ther Umsch, 62*(7), 487–501.

NHS Blood and Transplant. *Organ donation and transplantation, data*. Accessed March 30, 2016, from http://www.odt.nhs.uk/uk-transplant-registry/data/

NHS Choices. (2014). *Organ donation—Living donation*. Accessed 16 March 2016, from http://www.nhs.uk/Conditions/Organ-donation/Pages/Recommendations.aspx

Niedermeyer, J., Bewig, B., Bickhardt, T., Ewert, R., Fischer, P., Hamm, M., et al. (2001). Lungen-und Herz-Lungen-Transplantation. *Pneumologie, 55*(08), 396–400.

Pondrom, S. (2013). Trust is everything. *American Journal of Transplantation, 13*(5), 1115–1116.

Reinertsen, J. L., Bisognano, M., & Pugh, M. D. (2008). *Seven leadership leverage points for organization—Level improvement in health care. IHI innovation series white paper* (2nd ed.). Cambridge, MA: Institute for Healthcare Improvement.

Samuel U. (2015). *Annual report 2014*. Eurotransplant International Foundation.

Schlitt, H. J., Loss, M., Scherer, M. N., Becker, T., Jauch, K. W., Nashan, B., et al. (2011). Current developments in liver transplantation in Germany: MELD-based organ allocation and incentives for transplant centres. *Zeitschrift fur Gastroenterologie, 49*(1), 30–38.

Schmitz, C., & Berchthold, P. (2009). Managing professionals—Führung im Krankenhaus. In V. E. Amelung, J. Sydow, & A. Windeler (Eds.), *Vernetzung im Gesundheitswesen Wettbewerb und Kooperation* (pp. 167–180). Stuttgart: W. Kohlhammer Druckerei GmbH + Co. KG.

Schrem, H., Barg-Hock, H., Strassburg, C. P., Schwarz, A., & Klempnauer, J. (2009). Aftercare for patients with transplanted organs. *Deutsches Ärzteblatt International, 106*(9), 148–156.

Schrem, H., & Kaltenborn, A. (2013). Germany: Avoid more organ transplant scandals. *Nature, 498*(7452), 37.

Sydow, J., Lerch, F., Huxham, C., & Hibbert, P. (2011). A silent cry for leadership: Organizing for leading (in) clusters. *The Leadership Quarterly, 22*(2), 328–343.

van der Hilst, C. S., Ijtsma, A. J., Slooff, M. J., & Tenvergert, E. M. (2009). Cost of liver transplantation: A systematic review and meta-analysis comparing the United States with other OECD countries. *Medical Care Research and Review, 66*(1), 3–22.

Veit, C., Bungard, D., Eichwald, D., Schillhorn, K., & Trümner, A. (2014). *Fachgutachten zu einem nationalen Transplantationsregister*. Sachstandsbericht zur Datenerfassung und Vorschläge für die Gestaltung eines Transplantationsregisters im Auftrag des Bundesministeriums für Gesundheit. Accessed 13 March 2016, from https://www.bundesgesundheitsministerium.de/fileadmin/dateien/Publikationen/Gesundheit/Bericht/BMG-TxReg-Gutachten_140808c.pdf

WHO. (2015). *Global strategy on people-centred and integrated health services*. Accessed February 25, 2016, from http://www.who.int/servicedeliverysafety/areas/people-centred-care/en/

Integrated Care Concerning Mass Casualty Incidents/Disasters: Lessons Learned from Implementation in Israel

27

Bruria Adini and Kobi Peleg

27.1 Introduction

Mass casualty incidents (MCIs) of all types tax the immediately available resources of the healthcare system and impact on the capacity to provide optimal treatment to all casualties and patients needing medical services (Schenk et al. 2014). At times, especially during and following natural or manmade MCIs and/or large-scale disasters, the medical providers themselves may be impacted by the event, and their resources become even more dwindled (Ardagh et al. 2012). Provision of integrated care and business continuity, that are crucial in such events, necessitate pre-planning and implementation of actions targeted to assure stability and continuous operation of vital, life-saving services (Wen et al. 2014).

The aim of this sub-chapter is to describe the methodology adopted in Israel to assure an integrated care approach before, during and following mass casualty incidents and disasters.

27.2 Basic Assumptions

- Actions well versed in routine will work efficiently during MCIs and disasters.
- As MCIs are frequently characterized by chaos, confusion, contradictory or unclear information, an automatic response should be in place.
- The emergency response system and the personnel need to be acquainted, educated and trained concerning what is expected of them in advance.

B. Adini (✉) • K. Peleg
Disaster Management & Injury Prevention Department, School of Public Health, Sackler Faculty of Medicine, Tel Aviv University, Tel Aviv, Israel
e-mail: adini@netvision.net.il; kobi.peleg@gmail.com

© Springer International Publishing AG 2017
V. Amelung et al. (eds.), *Handbook Integrated Care*,
DOI 10.1007/978-3-319-56103-5_27

439

- A prepared healthcare system-based national doctrine, replenishment, order of operations, method, trust and training is the key for an effective response to MCIs.
- Clear and structured modes of authority and responsibility are needed in order to assure a coordinated response.

27.3   Main Components of Integrated Care

27.3.1 The Preparatory Phase

Why is it important that the healthcare systems be prepared to MCIs and disasters? The answer can be found in the statistics of damages inflicted by these events. Despite the fact that in the year 2014, the annual average of disaster frequency (324) was lower than that observed in the former decade (384 average frequency of events between 2004 and 2013), natural disasters still killed 7823 people and victimized 140.8 million people worldwide (Guha-Sapir et al. 2014).

The responsibility of the national authority charged with assuring emergency preparedness consists of three main functions, including the establishment of national policies, creation of standards and criteria for the implementation of the policies, and control as well as monitoring the actual application of the policies and standards. Accordingly, ensuring efficient preparedness to provide integrated care is based on five main preparatory measures: (1) development of national multi-sectorial, multi-organizational guidelines and institutional Standard Operating Procedures (SOPs) for emergency response (Peleg and Rozenfeld 2015); (2) instigating training programs to assure knowledge and competencies of personnel (Leow et al. 2012); (3) implementing ongoing monitoring systems to assure effectiveness and validity of the readiness of each institution (Adini et al. 2012); (4) operating information systems to collect and distribute crucial data in all phases of emergency management (Bar-El et al. 2013); and (5) procuring and installing vital equipment and infrastructure (Duncan et al. 2014).

27.3.1.1 Development of Integrated Guidelines and SOPs

The Israeli Ministry of Health (MOH) has the overall responsibility to assure an effective emergency preparedness and response of the healthcare system to all types and scopes of MCIs and disasters (Adini and Peleg 2013). The responsibility and authority of the MOH concerning emergency management encompasses all health institutions regardless of their ownership, thus including all governmental, public and private hospitals. Aligned with this responsibility, the MOH adopted an integrated centralized approach, thus all activities are directed and monitored by the national level. Accordingly, risk assessment procedures are in place and implemented continuously in order to identify the emergency scenarios that may occur in the region (Adini and Peleg 2013). Based on the results of the risk assessment, national guidelines for emergency response are developed, encompassing the expected mechanisms and modes of operation that must be adopted by the different stakeholders, including the emergency medical services

(EMS), hospitals, health district officials, and health maintenance organizations (HMOs). Though the guidelines are prepared by the national level, representatives from the different stakeholders and various professional sectors are involved in the development process, consisting of the most senior experts from each entity/ profession. Resulting from this process, the guidelines are characterized by cross-sectoral and multi-professional coordination, taking into consideration the various needs and challenges. Following the approval of the guidelines by the Supreme Health Authority (the highest authority in the healthcare system, headed by the director-general of the MOH), they are disseminated to all entities, as obligatory policies. Each medical organization is then committed to preparing an institutional SOP, based on the building blocks that are delineated in the guidelines, modified according to the organizational infrastructure and available resources. The SOPs are reviewed by the MOH and the Home Front Command (HFC) to ensure their applicability to the national doctrines and policy. Accordingly, as all SOPs are based on the same policy and guidelines, there is great similarity between them, and during emergency response, coordination of actions and intra-organizational collaborations are easily attained.

27.3.1.2 Training and Exercise Programs

Cross-sector multidisciplinary joint training programs are implemented in order to achieve the development and ongoing use of a common "disaster language". The training materials are centrally developed by the MOH which also conducts training programs for "nucleus knowledge teams" from the different entities, designated to provide them with the capacity to further implement the materials in their respective organizations. Using a "snowballing technique", the trainings are then implemented in the different entities, encompassing the various sectors, emergency sites/wards and levels of responsibility. The effectiveness of the training programs and the knowledge and competencies of the personnel is reviewed in a series of exercises, commencing in institutional local drills and completed by national exercises that are initiated and conducted by the MOH and the HFC. Each entity participates in at least one exercise annually, designated to assure a continuous maintenance of competencies (Adini et al. 2010a).

27.3.1.3 Ongoing Monitoring Systems

Similar to the development of guidelines and initiation of training and exercise programs, the continuous monitoring system is also enacted centrally and nationally by the MOH (Adini et al. 2012). The monitoring is designated to assure an ongoing continuous level of emergency preparedness of all entities involved in the response to MCIs and disasters. It is based on objective evaluation measures that were developed and disseminated to all entities, serving as benchmarks that must be implemented in each organization to maintain a continuous high level of emergency preparedness to all scenarios that were identified in the risk assessment process as potential in the region. Once every two years, an extensive evaluation is conducted in each institution, based on expert evaluators from the MOH and the HFC, in which all aspects of emergency preparedness including the SOPs, the equipment and infrastructure, knowledge and competencies of personnel, implementation of policies, etc. are reviewed. Upon the completion of the evaluation, the organization, as well as the senior managers of the MOH, receives a comprehensive report delineating strengths and gaps and an overall summation of the level of emergency preparedness. The specific organization is compelled to submit a plan to correct gaps in a short period of time and the implementation of such steps is monitored by the MOH.

27.3.1.4 Information Systems

Accurate and timely situation awareness is crucial to apply an efficient response to MCIs and disasters. In order to achieve availability of and accessibility to needed data at times of emergency, the information needs to be collected and disseminated routinely, otherwise at the time of need, it will not be attainable. The optimal mechanism to access data is through online continuous stream of information from the source entities, such as from the hospitals, to the agencies responsible for the evacuation of casualties (the EMS) and for defining the policies of emergency response (the MOH). In order to assure the availability of the needed information, two types of data are continuously transferred by all acute-care hospitals to the MOH: admissions to the emergency departments and admissions to the different hospitals' wards. The data is streamed online from the computerized information systems of each hospital to the MOH and is thus available at any point of time, displaying the relative load that characterizes each entity, including crucial sites/departments such as intensive care units, upon the occurrence of an MCI (Adini and Peleg 2013). Nonetheless, additional information is needed concerning the load in the respective organizations, such as in the operating rooms, availability of vital equipment such as ventilation machines, presence of personnel, for example surgeons, anesthesiologists etc. In order to access such data in the needed time-frames, a web-based computerized program was developed. During routine, the hospitals report to this system once daily, in order to accustom them to utilize the system. During a MCI, the frequency of reporting may be accelerated, according to the specific needs.

27.3.1.5 Equipment and Infrastructure

Assuring an effective response to MCIs and disasters necessitates the utilization of designated infrastructure (such as decontamination sites) and expanded inventories of vital equipment (such as ventilation machines, monitors, or unique drugs). Significant resources are needed in order to procure these equipment and infrastructure over time and maintain their validity over time (Duncan et al. 2014). This is achieved in Israel through a joint effort of the MOH and the respective institutions. The initial procurement of equipment is performed by the MOH which then distributes part of the inventories to each respective institution. Each institution is then required to implement the needed maintenance steps designated to assure the ongoing validity and readiness of the equipment for immediate use during MCIs. Similarly, vital infrastructure such as helipads, decontamination sites, generatores etc. are installed in the various entities by the MOH, and the administrations of all respective organizations are then required to assure their proper state at any given point of time.

27.3.2 The Response Phase

The implementation of integrated care during the response phase is constituted on five major components: (1) an automatic response; (2) central control and coordination; (3) collaboration and connectivity between all the emergency and the response agencies (4) collaboration between military and civilian entities; and, (5) coordinated risk communication.

27.3.2.1 Implementation of an Automatic Response

The SOPs for MCIs of all emergency responders, including the emergency medical services and the acute-care hospitals, all constitute an automatic response that is initiated upon such an occurrence, aimed to ensure an effective and coordinated response, decrease confusion, stress and inefficiency. The Israeli EMS is a national service operated by Magen David Adom (MDA), divided into 11 main districts. Upon a notification that an MCI occurred or is suspected, an automatic response is initiated, according to which the adjacent MDA regions dispatch two basic life support and one advanced life support ambulances to the scene, to reinforce the resources dispatched by the local operation centre. The hospitals in the vicinity of the event are all prepared to admit casualties in the scope of 20% of their routine bed capacity (Peleg and Rozenfeld 2015). As most hospitals are characterized by nearly 100% occupancy levels, they implement the SOPs which delineate which sites can be immediately deployed to expand surge capacity. Equipment that is stored in the immediate vicinity of the emergency department is rolled in, and the staff that is on alert reports to the admitting sites. Direct communication is immediately formed between the MDA operation centre and the control rooms of the various hospitals in the region in order to share information concerning the event and the capacities of each entity. Nonetheless, based on lessons learnt from former MCIs, liaison officers from the MDA are immediately sent to the emergency departments of each admitting hospital, in order to facilitate a face-to-face connectivity. These officers relay information to the MDA operation centre concerning the capacity of the hospital to admit and treat casualties, and report to the hospitals the scope and type of casualties that are being evacuated from the scene and their destinations.

27.3.2.2 Central Control and Coordination

The scene of an MCI is frequently characterized by the presence of massive emergency resources, operated by both formal and informal entities, as well as well-meaning bystanders. Lack of coordination between these different entities may increase the chaos that is characteristic of such events. In order to mitigate confusion and uncoordinated operations, the lines of authority were very clearly defined and integrated in the laws and regulations. The police force has the overall responsibility to direct all on-site operations, and as such is authorized to control and command the operations of all entities, including the MDA (Peleg and Rozenfeld 2015). Under the jurisdiction of the overall responsibility of the police, and in coordination with the MOH, the national MDA was authorized to direct all medical on-site operations (Adini and Peleg 2013). Accordingly, the senior, experienced MDA officer is appointed as the on-site commander of medical operations. All ambulance services that are present at the scene act under and according to the directives of this commander and abide to his orders. The local MDA operation centre maintains direct communication with this commander, provides him with crucial information concerning the capacities of the admitting hospitals and relays his directives concerning evacuation destinations to the relevant medical facilities. In order to ascertain effective coordination and sharing of information throughout the response phase of the event, several operation centres are activated: an on-site front command unit is deployed, which consists of representatives from the different first responders that are active on the scene of the MCI; operation centres are also immediately activated by the MOH, the HFC and the various admitting hospitals. The information concerning the event as well as the admitting capacities of all entities is shared by these operation centres, through the computerized information systems as well as through direct communication. Overall coordination is thus maintained throughout the event and facilitates sharing of information and effective communication and coordination with all relevant stakeholders (Peleg and Rozenfeld 2015). If needed, teams from one entity can easily assist other entities, as the work is based on similar guidelines and milestones.

Central control and coordination is also maintained concerning the hospitals' resources. The MOH, through the operation of the Supreme Health Authority, directs all activities aimed to maximize the surge capacity including limiting internal beds while expanding trauma capabilities, expanding surge capacities of geriatric and psychiatric hospitals so that patients may be transferred from acute-care facilities to these institutions, thus vacating additional beds to treat trauma casualties. As abovementioned, the MOH directs the operation of all hospitals, both public and private, and thus maximum optimization of crucial resources may be achieved.

27.3.2.3 Connectivity Between Response Agencies

Connectivity between the various first responders and additional emergency authorities is achieved through the implementation of three major elements. The first is the sharing of information, which is crucial in the emergency response (Bar-El et al. 2013). Direct communication lines are installed between the MDA and the emergency departments of all acute-care hospitals. These systems are utilized to transmit information concerning the occurrence of a MCI, the extent of incurred casualties, evacuation destinations and any other relevant information, throughout the event. Direct communication lines are also operated between the various first responders, such as the police force, the fire and rescue commission, and the MDA. The operation centres of these organizations maintain an open line during the event, to ensure joint sharing of information and ongoing updates. The HFC can access the civilian computerized information systems, which facilitates the coordination between the two systems. The second step to assure connectivity is the allocation of liaison officers. For example, upon the activation of an operation centre in the MOH, a liaison officer from the HFC is appointed to that centre, in order to facilitate a coordinated response, concerning both policy and decision-making as well as to monitor the implementation of all directives in the field. The third step is initiation and ongoing maintenance of direct dialogues between all stakeholders. Considering the importance of maintaining close communication with the response agencies, in prolonged scenarios (continuing for over a day, such as following major natural disasters or during periods of conflicts), forums for daily consultations and coordination are implemented, based on tele-conference lines. These daily discussions are used to share information concerning the events, debate over potential solutions to various challenges, consult concerning different needs and achieve consensus regarding modes of operation. All hospitals, MDA and other involved stakeholders participate in these coordination meetings (Adini et al. 2010a).

27.3.2.4 Collaboration Between Military and Civilian Entities

A very close collaboration is maintained between the military and civilian entities, in all phases of the emergency preparedness and response. The Surgeon-General of the Israeli Defense Forces' Medical Corps is a member of the Supreme Health Authority, thus is part of the highest mechanism that is responsible for both policy and decision-making concerning emergency management. The chief medical officer of the HFC participates in all physical and virtual meetings of this Authority, and thus is also involved in all facets of emergency management of all events. The military medical resources can be immediately deployed to assist the civilian forces in all emergency events. The aerial medical evacuation resources, including helicopters and planes are frequently deployed to provide reinforcement to the civilian limited means. Thus, the military and civilian personnel are well versed in working together during MCIs, and their joint work is characterized by extensive acquaintance of their respective capacities, competencies and abilities (Adini et al. 2010a).

27.3.2.5 Coordinated Risk Communication

Similar to routine operations, during emergencies all first responders and emergency authorities have their respective spokespersons, responsible for dissemination of information to the public. Nonetheless, considering the impact of each message to the population, during emergencies, coordination of messaging is employed. Through close collaboration of both the managers and the spokespersons of all major stakeholders, the coordination is implemented, and coordination mechanisms are at place targeted to jointly decide upon and disseminate accurate and applicable information. The great challenge in the last few years is the rapid dissemination of information, both accurate and false rumors, through the social media (Simon et al. 2015). As there is no control over the information that is published by any person through Facebook, Twitter, WhatsApp or other channels of the new media, the emergency responders must very quickly relay accurate and reliable information to the public. The public's trust in the formal entities can be significantly damaged if this is not done. This need of urgency proves to be very challenging to all formal responders, and thus steps are at present being implemented with the aim of strengthening the capacity to effectively provide risk communication to the population during MCIs and large-scale disasters. During prolonged emergencies, such as during conflict situations, central spokespersons are allocated by the HFC to all major TV channels. These representatives relay information to the public and answer questions, several times daily, thus a two-directional communication is being attained, and crucial, rapid information is accessible to the public. More so, a central information centre is operated by the HFC, which is accessible 24/7 to the population.

Another facet of crucial information that the public searches for during MCIs is the location of a relative that may have been involved in the event. In order to provide this data, the MOH developed a designated computerized system (called "ADAM") which interconnects the admission systems of all acute-care hospitals with each other, as well as with the MOH and the HFC (Adini et al. 2010b). This information is immediately available to the public upon the onset of a MCI, by approaching (by phone or physically) any information centre that is operated (all hospitals, police, and local municipalities operate such operation centres in all MCIs). Due to personal data protection, the only information that is provided upon approach is where the person that is being searched for is located (i.e. in which hospital).

27.3.3 The Post-Response Phase (Return to Normalcy)

Learning lessons from each training program and real MCI is crucial in order to assure continuous improvement of the capacity to provide integrated care during any type of emergency scenario (Wen et al. 2014). Aligned with this need, following each training session and/or MCI, a structured After Action Review (AAR) is implemented. This is a multi-disciplinary, multi-organizational process, based on a series of debriefing meetings that are conducted, initially at the site/sector level, through an institutional AAR, and up to a regional AAR, organized and directed by the MOH. Each of these meetings is designated to identify strengths and weaknesses, elements that should be maintained or improved, and potential mechanisms to achieve a better preparedness and response modes of operation (Tami et al. 2013).

The AAR meetings are conducted in a non-judgmental atmosphere, aimed at identifying elements for improvement without laying blame to any of the participants. This medico-legal balance must be very carefully maintained otherwise the various involved parties will be reluctant to share actual experiences that may not represent best-practices. It should be stressed that lack of fear from being liable or prosecuted for any potential (non-negligent) wrong-doing is crucial not only in the AAR phase, but also during the response phase; thus, complete insurance and coverage for any liability, for both employees and volunteers, is integral in the emergency response system.

It should be stressed that in large-scale disasters, the recovery phase may take many years and necessitate the investment of significant resources. An effective response should consider the implementation of an early recovery stage, in parallel to the response phase. Thus, care for ongoing humanitarian needs such as food, shelter, routine medical and public health care (including immunization programs) should be instituted at the same time as the emergency response actions.

27.4 Conclusions

The challenge in attaining delivery of integrated care during MCIs or large-scale disasters is achieving optimal coordination and collaboration among the various stakeholders. This crucial element is implemented in Israel routinely, and thus it is more easily attained also during emergency scenarios. The different involved medical entities, including the EMS, hospitals, other health providers, as well as the additional first responders such as the police, interact continuously in developing plans and guidelines and conducting integrated training programs. These joint collaborations facilitate an efficient coordinated response during MCIs. More so, adopting automatic responses to MCIs enable to overcome the initial chaos and confusion that characterize emergency scenarios. When each entity and every member of the responding entities are well acquainted with what is expected of them, they can more easily and efficiently react to the situation, and collaborate more smoothly with all involved parties. Accordingly, the needs and expectations of the public can be met and optimal care can be provided. The Israeli emergency management system has established a clear and structured mode of authority and responsibility, which facilitates the provision of an effective and coordinated response to the needs of the affected population, while maintaining flexibility to modify the response to the specific characteristics of each event.

References

Adini, B., Laor, D., Hornik-Lurie, T., Schwartz, D., & Aharonson-Daniel, L. (2012). Improving hospital mass casualty preparedness through ongoing readiness evaluation. *American Journal of Medical Quality, 27*(5), 426–433.

Adini, B., Laor, D., Lev, B., & Israeli, A. (2010a). The five commandments for preparing the Israeli healthcare system for emergencies. *Harefuah, 149*(7), 445–450. Hebrew.

Adini, B., & Peleg, K. (2013). On constant alert: Lessons to be learned from Israel's emergency response to mass casualty terrorism incidents. *Health Affairs, 32*(12), 2179–2185.

Adini, B., Peleg, K., Cohen, R., & Laor, D. (2010b). A national system for information dissemination on victims during Mass Casualty Incidents and Emergencies. *Disasters, 34*(2), 542–551.

Ardagh, M. W., Richardson, S. K., Robinson, V., Than, M., Gee, P., Henderson, S., Khodaverdi, L., Mckie, J., Robertson, G., Schroeder, P. P., & Deely, J. M. (2012). The initial health-system response to the earthquake in Christchurch, New Zealand in February, 2011. *Lancet, 379* (9831), 2109–2115.

Bar-El, Y., Tzafrir, S., Tzipori, I., Utitz, L., Halberthal, M., Beyar, R., & Reisner, S. (2013). Decision-support information system to manage mass casualty incidents at a Level 1 Trauma Center. *Disaster Medicine and Public Health Preparedness, 7*(6), 549–554.

Duncan, E. A. S., Colver, K., Dougall, N., Swingler, K., Stephenson, J., & Abhyankar, P. (2014). Consensus on items and quantities of clinical equipment required to deal with a mass casualties big bang incident: A national Delphi study. *BMC Emergency Medicine, 14*(1), 2–21.

Guha-Sapir, D., Hoyois, P., & Below, R. (2014). *Annual disaster statistical. Review 2014: The numbers and trends.* Brussels, Belgium: Centre for Research on the Epidemiology of Disasters (CRED), Institute of Health and Society (IRSS) Université catholique de Louvain.

Leow, J. J., Brundage, S. I., Kushner, A. L., Kamara, T. B., Hanciles, E., Muana, A., Kamara, M. M., Daoh, K. S., & Kingham, T. P. (2012). Mass casualty incident training in a resource-limited environment. *The British Journal of Surgery, 99*(3), 356–361.

Peleg, K., & Rozenfeld, M. (2015). Dealing with terror-related mass casualty events: Principles and lessons learned. *Notfall Rettungsmed, 18*, 285–292.

Schenk, E., Wijetunge, G., Mann, N. C., Lerner, E. B., Longthorne, A., & Dawson, D. (2014). Epidemiology of mass casualty incidents in the United States. *Prehospital Emergency Care, 18* (3), 408–416.

Simon, T., Goldberg, A., & Adini, B. (2015). Socializing in emergencies—A review of the use of social media in emergency situations. *International Journal of Information Management, 35* (5), 609–619.

Tami, G., Bruria, A., Fabiana, E., Tami, C., Tali, A., & Limor, A. D. (2013). An after-action review tool for EDs: Learning from mass casualty incidents. *The American Journal of Emergency Medicine, 31*(5), 798–802.

Wen, J. C., Tsai, C. C., Chen, M. H., & Chang, W. T. (2014). Operation of emergency operating centers during mass casualty incidents in Taiwan: A disaster management perspective. *Disaster Medicine and Public Health Preparedness, 8*(5), 426–431.

Integrated Care for People with Intellectual Disability 28

Marco O. Bertelli, Luana Salerno, Elisa Rondini, and Luis Salvador-Carulla

28.1 Definition and Classification of Intellectual Disability (Intellectual Developmental Disorder)

Intellectual Disability (ID) is not a disease or a disability, but a syndrome grouping similar to that of dementia, characterised by a pervasive cognitive impairment occurring in the early developmental period. It includes a heterogeneous group of conditions with considerable differences in the nature, ranging from genetic to environmental factors. The prevalence rate of ID for Northern European countries is reportedly around 0.7%, but it may rise to 4% in low and middle-income countries (LAMIC) (Durkin 2002; Maulik et al. 2011; Girimaji and Srinath 2010; Jeevanandam 2009). In these regions the excess rate of ID appears to be associated to fully preventable aetiologies such as teratogens, diet deficiencies, pregnancy and birth-related conditions (Persha et al. 2007; Bertelli et al. 2009). However, the cause remains not identified in 60% of persons with ID.

Besides a few genetic and congenital problems, international agencies have not given enough attention to the causes of ID (Salvador-Carulla et al. 2000). In their review, Bertelli et al. (2009) identified five major factors contributing to this lack of visibility. First, the ID field suffers from the lack of both a reliable construct of intelligence and a commonly agreed and freely available tool for IQ measuring. Second, comprehensive epidemiological data are still not available, particularly in relation to the different levels of severity of these conditions. Third, ID is an underfunded field, and this is a consequence of not being a key topic in many

M.O. Bertelli • L. Salerno (✉) • E. Rondini
CREA (Research and Clinical Centre), San Sebastiano Foundation, Florence, Italy
e-mail: mbertelli@crea-sansebastiano.org; luanasalerno@alice.it

L. Salvador-Carulla
Mental Health Policy Unit, Brain and Mind Centre, Faculty of Health Sciences, University of Sydney, Camperdown, NSW, Australia
e-mail: luis.salvador-carulla@sydney.edu.au

© Springer International Publishing AG 2017
V. Amelung et al. (eds.), *Handbook Integrated Care*,
DOI 10.1007/978-3-319-56103-5_28

national health research programmes. In many countries, ID management is not included within the health department but it is considered matter of the social or educational area. As a result, the attention given to ID from the health sector is constrained. Finally, the case of ID is particularly challenging due to an on-going debate on whether it should be classified in the International Classification of Diseases (ICD) as a health condition or in the International Classification of Functioning (ICF) as a disability. The lack of agreement on such a basic question reflects the complexity of this construct. As a matter of fact, many national agencies follow the approach of the American Association of Intellectual and Developmental Disabilities (AAIDD) that defines "Intellectual disability" as "a disability characterized by significant limitations both in intellectual functioning [IQ < 70] and in adaptive behaviour, which covers many everyday social and practical skills". The timeframe for age of onset is defined from birth to 18 years. This has oriented the recommendations made by this group for naming and conceptualising this condition at ICD (Tassé et al. 2013; Wehmeyer et al. 2008). Other organisations such as the World Psychiatric Association (WPA) have defined it as a group of health conditions, namely developmental conditions, characterized by a significant impairment of cognitive functions associated with limitations of learning, adaptive behaviour and skills (Salvador-Carulla and Bertelli 2008).

The latter conceptualisation was adopted by the ICD Working Group in 2011 which coined the term "Intellectual Developmental Disorders" (IDD) to define this group of aetiologically diverse conditions, present from birth or occurring during the developmental period, characterized by a marked impairment of those cognitive functions that are necessary for the development of knowledge, reasoning, and symbolic representation in comparison to typically developing peers. IDD has been also defined as a life span condition requiring attention and support during all developmental stages and life transitions (Salvador-Carulla et al. 2011; Bertelli et al. 2014).

In the attempt to develop a better definition of ID, the ICD Working Group proposed revised diagnostic criteria for ICD-11 on the basis of an articulated model of cognitive impairment. The proposed approach aimed to assess cognitive skills in the most comprehensive way, using tests, semi-structured observations, and direct clinical examination. Such tests should combine measurement of IQ with measures of the complex aspects of executive functioning, e.g. perceptual reasoning, processing speed, verbal comprehension, and of more specific aspects, such as attention maintenance, attention switch, visual-spatial perception, working memory, or short-term memory, along with contextualised description of the consequent adaptive and learning difficulties. Such evaluation will allow the identification of the specific cognitive dysfunctions that have the greatest negative impact on the person's lifespan, not only in the cognitive domain but also in the domains of behaviour, ability, adjustment, autonomy, and others that rely on person-centered health (Salvador-Carulla et al. 2011; Bertelli et al. 2014).

28.2   General Health Issues

People with ID may present a wide range of co-morbid physical problems and poor health related habits (Bertelli et al. 2009; Perry et al. 2010). To date, epidemiological studies deal with a 2.5-fold greater prevalence of physical illnesses in this group than in the general population (Van Schrojenstein Lantman-De Valk et al. 2000; Dixon-Ibarra and Horner-Johnson 2014). The most observed medical states are obesity, metabolic disorders, osteoporosis (Center et al. 1994; Dreyfus et al. 2014), thyroid and cardiac diseases, sensory impairments (Kapell et al. 1998), and dementia (Janicki and Dalton 2000). Furthermore, people with severe or profound ID present a prevalence of eating problems and epilepsy (Robertson et al. 2015).

Specific physical alterations and diseases can appear both in developmental age and at a later time. For example, in Down Syndrome some clinically relevant anatomical and functional disorders appear after birth, others arise in infancy, in adolescence and youth (Pueschel and Pueschel 1992), or in late adulthood, such as epilepsy (McVicker et al. 1994) and dementia (Devenny et al. 1996). The vulnerability of persons with ID results also in frequent visits to the emergency room and in hospitalization. Persons with ID present a twofold greater prevalence of hospital admissions rather than the general population (14% vs. 26%) (Mencap 2004), including emergencies (50% vs 31%) (Emerson et al. 2012).

Physical vulnerability associated with ID is also shown in the causes of death. Persons with ID present an increased risk of early death in comparison with the general population (Hollins et al. 1998; McGuigan et al. 1995; Hosking et al. 2016). In a recent study conducted in the state of New South Wales (Australia), the population with ID was found to have a standardized mortality ratio (SMR) of 2.48 for all ages and an SMR of 3.15 for those aged 5–69 years; higher for females (4.26) (Florio and Trollor 2015). The age standardized death rates (ASDR) for the ID cohort was 4.04 (deaths per 1000) whilst the ASDR for the rest of the population was 1.58, with a comparative mortality ratio of 2.55.

In a study conducted by Hollins and colleagues at the end of last century, the risk of dying before the age of 50 was 58 times higher than in the English general population (Hollins et al. 1998).

The list of causes of death in persons with ID also differs from the general population. In the former the main death causes are cardiovascular diseases, respiratory disorders and neoplasms whilst main causes of death in the latter are neoplasms, ischaemic heart disease and cerebrovascular diseases (Janicki et al. 1999; Tait 1983). Significantly, other relatively frequent causes of death in ID include epilepsy, asphyxia, and gastrointestinal disorders (Robertson et al. 2015; Ouellette-Kuntz et al. 2015; Puri et al. 1995; Eyman and Call 1991; Raitasuo et al. 1997; O'Brien et al. 1991). Hollins et al. (1998) found that early death was significantly associated with cerebral palsy, incontinence, and institutionalisation.

In the last two decades, the average life expectancy for persons with ID living in high-income countries has increased, due to the improvement of life conditions and healthcare practices, although it remains lower than in the general population (Janicki et al. 1999; Bittles et al. 2002; Reppermund and Trollor 2016).

Simultaneously, a rise of ageing-related diseases has been recorded (McCallion and McCarron 2004). Nevertheless, ageing-related diseases and life conditions in persons with ID have not yet received the attention they deserve and the few available studies on these issues present several limitations, such as sampling errors, distortions of clinical characteristics (Evenhuis 1997; Bittles et al. 2002), unreliable admission practices and policies (Carter and Jancar 1983), lack of control for concurrent illnesses and related health interventions (Edgerton et al. 1994; Beange et al. 1995).

28.3 Mental Health Issues

In persons with ID, mental health problems are even more frequent than physical ones. In fact, a third of this population has comorbid psychiatric disorders, and another 10–20% has behavioural problems not related to psychiatric illness, but to psychological, environmental or physical conditions. As a consequence, nearly one half (0.75–2% of the total population) of individuals with ID need psychiatric care, exceeding those with any other major psychiatric disorder in the general population (Salvador-Carulla et al. 2000; Cooper et al. 2007; Salvador-Carulla and Bertelli 2008).

There are various causes underlying the high psychological and physical vulnerability of persons with ID. Some biological factors are linked to genetic or infectious alterations that outline a complex syndromic framework. Other bio-psychological factors are represented by alterations of the central nervous system, chronic physical disabilities, hygiene problems, inappropriate eating habits, pharmacological side effects, hypoactivity and communication difficulties (Van Schrojenstein Lantman-De Valk et al. 2000). Most frequently reported psychological factors are difficulties in coping, self-determination, and environmental mastery. Social-environmental factors are also implicated, such as traumatic experiences, negative life events, repeated failures, lack of satisfying relationships, lack of interests, variable or inadequate housing conditions (Eyman and Call 1991; Raitasuo et al. 1997; Carter and Jancar 1983).

Diagnosing psychiatric symptoms in persons with ID entails several complications, including the hardness to recognize the impact of symptoms on daily functioning and personal distress. Assessment, diagnosis and treatment of mental problems in this population demand particular adjustments due to the cognitive dysfunctions, communication limitations, sensory impairments, skill deficits, difficulties in adaptation and other disabilities that are often present in ID (Bertelli et al. 2015). A frequent problem is the diagnostic overshadowing between psychiatric symptoms and behavioural alterations or expressive ways that could be both typical for ID in general or for certain phenotypes in particular.

The prevalence of problem behaviours (PBs) in ID ranges between 5% and 60% (Smiley 2005) with several limitations on the social functioning and the rehabilitative processes. It is difficult to prove whether PBs are the outcome of organic conditions, psychiatric disorders, environmental influences, or a combination of these factors (Bertelli et al. 2015). Nevertheless, some studies support the existence of a relationship between PBs and psychiatric disorders (Emerson et al. 1999; Felce et al. 2009; Kishore et al. 2005), with a particular strength in people with limitations in functioning (Felce et al. 2009). Furthermore, some behavioural equivalents have been recognized for specific psychiatric symptoms (Hurley 2006).

The difficulty in the identification of symptoms relies also on communication problems. These persons may have poor verbal expression abilities, be inclined to acquiescence and show deviations from the norm in the attribution of meaning to communicative contents. In addition, some individuals present a limited introspection capacity, having difficulties in defining their own life experiences and in communicating states of uneasiness or suffering. Furthermore, sources of information other than the individuals themselves may be limited, heterogeneous, and contradictory. Family members are often in difficulty in finding answers aimed at detecting the presence of further mental functioning disorders or problem behaviours (Salvador-Carulla et al. 1998). First-line support personnel do not have appropriate tools for discriminating the observed behaviours and are not able to attribute a possible pathological meaning to these behaviours. Also for therapy outcome, self-assessment can be challenging or impossible for most persons with moderate-to-severe ID and there is some agreement on that it could be integrated with proxy-assessments.

Generally, ID produces a considerable burden on families and caregivers throughout the life span (Salvador-Carulla and Bertelli 2008), which becomes even higher in case of co-occurrence of psychiatric disorders (Martorell et al. 2011; Irazábal et al. 2012). Moreover, psychiatric problems and behavioural disorders are the main causes of isolation and stigmatisation associated with ID (McIntyre et al. 2002). In spite of its global burden, which surpasses the burden of dementia, ID is regarded as a second-level condition within health care, particularly in psychiatry. This lack of attention is evident in the limited clinical and practice guidelines on identification, assessment and intervention for mental health needs. Many reasons have been identified for this misconsideration, including the above mentioned peculiarities in the presentation of symptoms and the diagnostic overshadowing with the manifestations of the neurodevelopmental disorder itself. However, the most relevant cause is probably the assumption that the early neurodevelopmental impairment represents an untreatable neurological condition which significantly and definitely compromises the overall psychic functioning, so that there is not even the possibility to have any psychiatric suffering or at least to use any of the psychopathological knowledge acquired with the general population.

In order to get attention from the medical sector, public health planners, and other health organisations, these issues should be thoroughly reviewed. Results from several studies report a lack of appropriate resources available for persons with ID and their carers, in spite of the difficulties and health-related problems they experience. Thus, more support should be provided to this population, especially in the field of primary and mental health care where vertical integration across the different levels of specialisation and horizontal integration with social services are needed.

28.4   Access to Care

To date, there is a significant gap between the health related needs of persons with ID and the provision of care (Van Schrojenstein Lantman-De Valk et al. 2000; Perry et al. 2010). As regards to the health status, the European POMONA study, which included 13 countries, revealed that 65% of the sample of persons with ID used one or more forms of medication, 28% had a diagnosis of epilepsy, two thirds were either underweight, overweight or obese, 52% reported a sedentary life (Perry et al. 2010).

Failings in healthcare provision represent a significant problem for this vulnerable group of patients that requires well-timed, adequate, and sensitive care interventions. Actually, in several European countries, healthcare does not succeed in providing adequate services. Gaps include access to primary care, to medical prescriptions, to the disclosure of useful information, to actual treatment for serious mental illnesses, and to the communication between health and social services (O'Hara 2006). According to Tuffrey-Wijne et al. (2014) the major barriers to care provision in this population include the detection of persons with ID, the lack of clear lines of responsibility and accountability for implementing care, and in the shortage of financial supports and resources.

Other difficulties concern the communication of the consumer with professionals (Ali et al. 2013; Wilson and Haire 1990) and the lack of general practitioners (GPs) adequately trained to manage and treat these patients (Lennox et al. 1997). This is further compounded by the lack of an adequate and rigorous training of mental health professionals in the field. In Norway, a recent study examined the experience and aptitude of ten GPs providing health care for persons with ID and co-occurring mental health and/or behavioural problems. It revealed training problems and difficulties in patient management. GPs admitted to have a poor knowledge about communication manners and clinical peculiarities of this population (Fredheim et al. 2013). Their knowledge came from daily clinical practice (medical examinations and pharmacological treatment), and individual educational paths. Training in ID is not included in the psychiatric curriculum of professionals in many countries and the majority of psychiatrists are not prepared to deal with the specific health needs and demands of persons with these conditions (Salvador-Carulla et al. 2015).

Similar trends and needs have been described in other countries (Kwok and Chui 2008; Jeevanandam 2009; Werner and Stawski 2012), suggesting that problems of manpower and service delivery may be considered as a universal phenomenon. Usually, information coming from rigorous research trials helps the clinicians in any field of health to take appropriate decision on intervention, and this applies also to psychiatry. Nevertheless, an extensive search of databases spanning over 16 years performed by Balogh et al. (2008) indicated that there were only six randomised controlled trials in the field, and virtually none on organisational interventions, and a few more were in need of corroboration. Obviously, more clinical training opportunities are mandatory for psychiatrists to gain the knowledge, competence and attitudes that are necessary to improve specialist clinical services.

A wide disparity between high-income countries (HIC) and LAMIC with regard to the mental health care of ID has been reported. In HIC there is no dearth of manpower and advanced mental health facilities for the general public as well as for people with special needs, including those with ID. Conversely, in LAMIC even the general population struggles for basic, accessible health facilities, and therefore the particular needs of people with ID receive less attention. However, it is not possible to affirm with certainty that ID uniformly figures at the bottom of health care across LAMIC. For example, in countries like India, there are some advanced facilities for ID, mainly located at national and regional centres, and a few in the private sector, which are usually located at urban settings. On the other hand, basic health or rehabilitation facilities are abysmally poor in the rural settings where a majority of the disabled population lives.

Hence, there is a greater need for high quality, holistic mental health services to cater to mental health needs. Moreover, there is an urgent need for a multi-level health care system that should be accessible, equitable but more importantly with a monitoring system. In absence of such facilities, benefits might be obtained by a system providing cost-effective screening methods and referral processes by community based workers or caregivers.

Taking all these issues into account, it is hoped that once the psychiatry training is systematized, and information on intervention research is available to professionals, quality services can be provided even through general settings. As it is, there is no clear evidence in favour of general or special settings to provide mental health services (Chaplin 2004).

28.5 Specialized Services for ID Associated to Other Mental Disorders

Specific services for ID associated to other mental disorders (ID-MD), mainly non-acute hospital care, are lacking across many of the European Countries and very few areas have more than two different service types available for this particular population. With the exception of few Northern Countries, The Netherlands and the UK, the majority of European region lacks a full range of specialised services including hospital care, community residential care, day care and outpatient care for ID-MD. There is a generalised indifference towards the ID-MD care needs in the mental health policy plans. In those places where services have recently expanded, hospital care originally intended for acute patients have been transformed in non-acute hospital facilities and there is still a lack of residential care in the community for this specific population group. Similar problems have been identified in other World regions. The care gaps in integrated care have been recently reported in New South Wales (Australia) (Howlett et al. 2015) and Ontario, the latter through the Health Care Access Research and Developmental Disabilities (H-CARDD) program. H-CARDD is a partnership of scientists, policymakers and clinicians which uses administrative data to provide information on the health of a cohort of adults with developmental disabilities in respect to other adults in Ontario (Lunsky et al. 2014). The key findings of H-CARDD have been published in the Atlas of the Primary care of Developmental Disabilities in Ontario (Lunsky et al. 2013).

Taking into account all the available data, a European expert group estimated that 50% of the persons with ID-MD have not been offered a minimum clinical assessment and that 95% did not received adequate clinical support (Salvador-Carulla et al. 2013). In order to overcome this, the expert group prepared a model of minimum standards required for basic ID-MD care. According to the plan, agreed minimum care needs included an outpatient ID-MD unit and 6.5 beds per 1 million population. Specialised outpatient ID services required at least one multidisciplinary team per 1 million inhabitants. These facilities should include at least one ID psychiatrist, one clinical psychologist, a nurse and a social worker, plus administrative personnel. This minimum mobile team should provide support and be an intermediary between over 10 community mental health centres in its catchment area and around 30 primary care centres in the same area. It should also ensure on-site care to complex cases and set a continuity of care programme with hospital and non-hospital community care.

As next step, care needs for the different regions in Spain were estimated. The minimum estimate of outpatient specialized mobile services (preferably within an already existing mental health centre) was 44, and one psychiatrist and one psychologist should be present in each team. For this project, at least 277 new beds were needed in over 20 units with 10–15 beds each. These in-patient units should be designed for medium stay patients, usually over 6 weeks. They should give support to the non-hospital residential care subsystem, but also to the community care subsystem in order to support acute and sub-acute care needs for persons with ID-MD. The services aforementioned required at least 46 new trained psychiatrists and psychologists in Spain. In all a minimum of 134 specialized psychiatrists and psychologists were necessary to fit the basic ID-MD services in Spain, apart from nurses, social workers and other support staff.

Additionally, the expert group suggested to develop complementary residential community services for this specific group, a bridging strategy that would necessitate share funding and management strategies from the health and social sectors, and recommended five centres of excellence for integrative evaluation of ID (one per every 7 million inhabitants). These supra-regional integrative diagnosis services should promote person-centred bio-psycho-social screening, assessment, intervention planning, counselling and liaison in ID, including mental health. Finally, in consideration of the mentioned problems regarding the information databases and the existence of other care needs in ID-MD, it was recommended to develop a national observatory on ID-MD. Table 28.1 summarizes why ID patients need special attention in psychiatric care.

Table 28.1 Factors explaining why ID patients need attention in psychiatric care

Factors		
General health issues	Presence of a wide range of co-occurrent physical problems and poor health habits	Bertelli et al. (2009), Perry et al. (2010), Van Schrojenstein Lantman-De Valk et al. (2000) and Dixon-Ibarra and Horner-Johnson (2014)
	Higher rate of hospitalizations	Mencap (2004) and Emerson et al. (2012)
	Increased risk of early death	Hollins et al. (1998), McGuigan et al. (1995) and Florio and Trollor 2015
	Paucity of studies on ageing-related diseases in IDD and interventions	Evenhuis (1997), Bittles et al. (2002), Carter and Jancar (1993), Edgerton et al. (1994) and Beange et al. (1995)
Mental health issues	Higher rates of co-morbid psychiatric disorders	Salvador-Carulla et al. (2000), Cooper et al. (2007) and Salvador-Carulla and Bertelli (2008)
	Assessment challenged by cognitive and communication deficits and sensory impairments	Bertelli et al. (2015)
	Co-occurrence of problem behaviours (PBs)	Smiley (2005), Emerson et al. (1999), Felce et al. (2009), Kishore et al. (2005) and Hurley (2006)
	Higher burden on families and caregivers throughout the life span	Salvador-Carulla and Bertelli (2008), Martorell et al. (2011) and Irazábal et al. (2012)
	Higher risk for isolation and stigmatisation	McIntyre et al. (2002)
	Lack of specific assessment tools, clinical guidelines and expertise for interventions	Bertelli et al. (2015) and Salvador-Carulla et al. (2011)
Access to care	Limited access to primary care and shortage of adequate services	Van Schrojenstein Lantman-De Valk et al. (2000), Center et al. (1998), Perry et al. (2010) and O'Hara (2006)
	Poor knowledge regarding IDD patients because of the lack of an adequate training for practictioners	Lennox et al. (1997), Fredheim et al. (2013) and Salvador-Carulla et al. (2015)
	Wide disparity in IDD mental health care between high-income and low-income countries	Maulik et al. (2011) and Salvador-Carulla et al. (2011)
Specialized services for ID-MD	Dearth of hospital care, community residential care, day care and outpatient care	Howlett et al. (2015)

28.6   Integrated Care and Person-Centred Approaches

Person-centred care as a model of care provision, care individualisation and life-style support was first developed in the ID sector long before other areas of health and social care picked it up. However, and although some agencies have actually implemented person-centred care (PCC) over decades in the US, Australia and Europe, the claims of adherence to the PCC goals are larger than its actual application (Balogh et al. 2008; Kendrick 2012). Leutz (1999) defines "integrated care" as a broad inter-sectorial system approach that aims to connect the health care system with other human service systems in order to improve outcomes (clinical, satisfaction and efficiency). Even though these two models, PCC and integrated care, have evolved jointly in the field of ID, and are widely supported for improving accessibility and quality of health care, a comprehensive shared knowledge base about issues related to integrated care and PCC is lacking and its full implementation is slow due to barriers in the philosophy or culture of care, power and funding structures, high levels of staff turnover and lack of training, inexperience among service management, inadequate staff supervision, and ambiguity among some stakeholders (Dowling et al. 2007). From a clinical point of view, integration requires the adoption of a person-focused perspective. This is an essential aspect to improve an individual's overall well-being and to take into account their needs.

The main characteristic of person-focused care is defined by a bio-psycho-social approach applied to health. From this point of view diseases are simultaneously a medical, psychological and social problem (Valentijn et al. 2013). Comprehending the personal meaning of a disease is at the base of person-focused care that attempts to comply with individual needs and preferences. Conversely, focusing on the illness reveals a clinical perspective that connects the needs of an individual to separated biological entities (Starfield 2011; Pulvirenti et al. 2014).

Generally, Western health systems adopt a disease-focused approach which often overlooks the implicit reasons of health or illness, but this perspective is inappropriate in a population where more and more patients present chronic and overlapping diseases (Nolte and McKee 2008). Therefore, adopting a person-focused view seems to be more functional, particularly in the context of integrated care. Actually, in this holistic vision most health and social issues are interrelated and its adoption allows to identify the links between the different systems. Integration is also required from an organizational point of view to ensure a continuing and comprehensive supply of services matched to the necessities of the users. The major challenge is to convert general understandings about integrated care into practical terms to make available more effective health services able to improving quality of care and quality of life for the individuals.

A significant contribution has been provided by the International College of Person-centred Medicine (ICPCM) and the Person-centred Integrative Diagnosis (PID) multidimensional matrix (Mezzich et al. 2010), which takes into account not only the health condition and the disability but also the positive aspects defined as wellbeing and good functioning. IDD/ID may not be an exception in health but a prototypical example of how the holistic and comprehensive approach recommended by ICPCM is useful for understand these complex constructs in health care.

28.6.1 Integrating Care of Somatic Illnesses

Up until now, people with ID continue to experience disparities in health care provision. Integrated care approach should be addressed to those factors which have been identified as obstacles to their access to services and proper treatment provision. Therefore, greater efforts should be made in providing adequate training in ID for all health professionals, in order to improve knowledge regarding the identification and treatment for chronic health conditions which affect this population. This will also to promote a better understanding of how to monitor health conditions among those who are ageing. Increasing evidence shows that in the general population adopting healthy lifestyles in old age can yield health benefits (Kenfield and Stampfer 2013), but indications for better health habits have not been provided and supported for persons with ID. It would be necessary to promote adequate strategies for including this population in health and wellness prevention programs, through an early identification of such problems, and to develop and use structured assessment tools, coupled with tailored interventions.

According to some recent studies, mental and physical problems relate to each other to a greater extent and in a more direct way in ID than in the general population (Kwok and Chui 2008; Cooper et al. 2015). This suggests a collaboration between psychiatrists and other specialists, such as GPs, neurologists, dental practitioners, orthopedists, or otolaryngologists to be particularly advisable (Galli-Carminati et al. 2006; Patja et al. 2001; Gimbel 2000; Bohmer et al. 2000).

28.6.2 Integrating Care of Psychiatric Disorders

It is important to note that the ID construct presents also several positive implications for psychiatry. A review conducted by Salvador-Carulla and Bertelli (2008) highlights several dimensions for which ID deserves more attention. First, ID provides genetic models for scores of psychiatric disorders. It also provides models for the assessment, support system and diagnostic frameworks (for example, provision for incorporating a developmental/ideographic approach) in severe mental and cognitive disorders. It is worth to note that models of care—such as residential care, respite care and multidisciplinary approach to care—as well social issues of health—such as stigma and labelling and self-advocacy—were developed first in the ID field, and now they are widely used in general psychiatry. Similarly, the need for close interaction between various agencies related to social, education, legal and health sectors for the integration of services to form a holistic management of the individual, originated in the ID field. Therefore, the mainstream mental health organization can benefit from the field of ID regarding successful models of identification, assessment, care and support system. In spite of all, ID is still a disregarded topic in psychiatry, not to say in medicine.

It is clear that ID requires full attention with regard to both general health and mental health needs. This attention is of particular importance to face other issues that are intricately related to the nature of ID and the settings of evaluation. First, there will always be an overlap between the symptoms of mental health disorders and features of the developmental problems of ID and thus mental health services are not sought or extended (Szymanski and King 1999; Ailey 2003). Sometimes diagnostic decisions tend either in favour of psychiatric disorders or maladaptive behaviours depending on the setting in which evaluations are conducted, and on the professionals involved in the examination (Nezu 1994; Einfeld and Aman 1995). Even after accurate diagnosis, people with both ID and mental health problems slip through the service delivery system as in many countries the services are dichotomized into hospital-based services predominantly utilized by the non-ID population and the rehabilitation centres and special education centres meant for persons with disabilities, including those with ID. Furthermore, many countries lack appropriate policies to bridge this gap and cater to the mental health needs of people with ID within the mainstream health delivery system. As a result, unmet mental health needs are common across the lifespan of ID, and the challenges arise accordingly with increased severity levels of ID (Allerton et al. 2011). But the real challenge is to both provide interventions to reduce these health inequalities and support a structure that systematically monitors the impact of the interventions over time. The interactions between early age-onset and older age-onset conditions may have relevant negative effects on functional impairment in PwID, physical and mental morbidity, and even mortality. For this reason, it seems to be particularly useful to adopt a dynamic life-span approach since it may contribute to the identification of improvements or consequences of specific diseases and interventions (Hogg et al. 2000).

The Person-centred Integrative Diagnosis highlights the importance of engagement, empathy and partnership in the clinical care process, and sustains the patients' autonomy, responsibility and dignity while advancing the recovery and promotion of wellbeing. To assess the domain of person's experience and values PID uses descriptive categories, dimensions, and narratives, to cultivate patient-family-clinician partnerships for achieving shared diagnostic understanding and shared commitment to care. The application of this model to the assessment of personal well-being, experiences, satisfaction and aspirations of persons with IDD faces significant challenges in persons with IDD as the self-reported assessment of these complex concepts is limited due to the cognitive and communication impairments (Bertelli and Brown 2006).

The conceptualisation of ID should shift the traditional over-reliance on the intelligence (IQ) score in favour of the daily life expression of specific cognitive functions and the determination of the levels of severity of intellectual functioning, that was previously based on the person's IQ score, should be reached through a system that is predicated on the person's satisfaction attainment towards life (Bertelli et al. 2014).

28.6.3 Integrating Specialised or Secondary Mental Health Care

The usefulness of an integrated psychiatric assessment results from the consideration of several factors, most of which have been already mentioned. Considering the high vulnerability of PwID and the significant prevalence of psychiatric disorders (PDs) in this group, it is important to adopt an approach that comprehends as many points of views as possible in their assessment.

Also PBs may be an example of usefulness of the participatory paradigm. Generally, PBs in PwID are pharmacologically treated and the search for a therapy which takes into account the individual specific conditions and the improvement of quality of life is disregarded. Actually, clinical practice suggests that an effective intervention on PBs should be characterized by a simultaneous consideration of organic, psychiatric, and socio-functional aspects and their pathogenetic contribution, on the basis of a multimodal analytical approach. This indication is confirmed by recent evidence from scientific literature that support the effectiveness of therapeutic processes developed starting from specific clinical and environmental information related to each patient. Such procedures can also be helpful in providing effective models for the assessment of PwID' adaptive skills with positive effects on their life.

An integrative assessment which consists of contributions from various disciplines might also allow the identification of problems in the classification systems, strictly linked to clinical practices. It can be useful also in providing genetic models for psychiatric disorders commonly experienced by PwID, with potential benefits for their early identification, and identifying more and more sensitive diagnostic tools, instead of starting from very generic symptoms in assessing skills and performances. In fact, more than any other mental health condition, ID provides enough opportunities to explore the clinical expression of the body-mind link. In order to have a clear understanding of it, all parameters of a quality mental health management such as holistic consideration of individual, sensitive diagnostic methods including skills and tools are highly relevant (Bertelli and Brown 2006).

Multiple perspectives may lead to the development of new intervention models based on person-oriented approaches so as to address individual preferences. For that reason, the usefulness of Patient-Reported Outcomes (PROs) is more and more emphasized. The adoption of PROs is widely encouraged as a method to assess the patients and to improve the quality of healthcare. The term covers a set of potential types of measurement which can play a significant role in assessing patients' performances and evaluating the efficacy of the treatments. These measures include the model of Quality of Life (QoL), widely applied with reference to PwID. The assessment of QoL should take aim at identifying priorities and interests of each person in order to increase satisfaction in these aspects, improving the general satisfaction towards life.

Thus, a contextualized multimodal assessment and a multidisciplinary integrated intervention, involving different professionals, family, and life environments seems to be a more useful solution, with several positive implications. The aim should be

Table 28.2 Reasons for integrated secondary care in persons with ID experiencing mental disorders

Higher prevalence rate of PD than in the general population
Identification of problems in the classification systems (i.e. ICD)
New understanding for intelligence
Models for the assessment of behavioural problems in severe mental disorders and cognitive deficit
Genetic models for PD
Direct clinical expression of the body-mind link
Changes and adaptation of diagnostic criteria and diagnostic process for PD
Sensitive diagnostic skills and tools (one often has to start from very generic symptoms, like behavioural changes or problems)
Models for the assessment of adaptive skills as well as supports
Life-span approach
Holistic consideration of the patient and requires multi-disciplinary intervention
Model for high vulnerability to distress
Person-related outcome measures, like generic quality of life

to achieve a holistic consideration of physical, behavioural, and mental health issues related to PwID, involving in their care a range of disciplines and health professionals.

Traditionally, healthcare for individuals with ID has been parsed out to multiple providers and/or agencies along disparate funding lines. Physical health, mental health, and behavioural providers often have separate allocations and are managed by different entities. Bringing together those disciplines who have traditionally served individuals with ID, as to make them aligned with the person-centred approach, challenges the status quo and implies a drastic renewal of the current system of service provision in many countries across the world.

The main factors supporting the relevance of an integrated care in psychiatry for ID is summarised in Table 28.2.

28.7 Conclusion

Intellectual disability is a very interesting area to explore and to understand the design and implementation of person-centred integrated care due to its complexity in the classification and assessment, interventions, care delivery and policy planning. There is a significant ambiguity in the conceptualisation and classification of this health condition and disparities emerge between the health sector and the social and education sectors on this condition and these disparities have significant implications for service planning and delivery.

The early development of strategies of both person-centred care and integrated care in this field may contribute to a better knowledge of the challenges of developing integrated care both in the interaction between primary care and secondary care and in the integration of health and social care. There is an urgent need to encompass the existing developments and models in this specific areas of care with the general models developed in the integrated care sector, particularly in relation to the WHO strategy on people-centred integrated care for all (WHO 2015) and the international taxonomy of integrated care (Valentijn et al. 2015).

References

Ailey, S. H. (2003). Beyond the disability: Recognizing mental health issues among persons with intellectual and developmental disabilities. *Nursing Clinics of North America, 38*(2), 313–329.

Ali, A., Scior, K., Ratti, V., Strydom, A., King, M., & Hassiotis, A. (2013). Discrimination and other barriers to accessing health care: Perspectives of patients with mild and moderate intellectual disability and their carers. *PLoS One, 8*(8), e70855.

Allerton, L. A., Welch, V., & Emerson, E. (2011). Health inequalities experienced by children and young people with intellectual disabilities: A review of literature from the United Kingdom. *Journal of Intellectual Disabilities, 15*(4), 269–278.

Balogh, R., Ouellette-Kuntz, H., Bourne, L., Lunsky, Y., & Colantonio, A. (2008). Organising health care services for persons with an intellectual disability. *Cochrane Database of Systematic Reviews, 8*(4), CD007492.

Beange, H., McElduff, A., & Baker, W. (1995). Medical disorders of adults with mental retardation: A population study. *American Journal of Mental Retardation, 99*(6), 595–604.

Bertelli, M., & Brown, I. (2006). Quality of life with intellectual disabilities. *Current Opinion in Psychiatry, 19*(15), 508–513.

Bertelli, M., Hassiotis, A., Deb, S., & Salvador-Carulla, L. (2009). New contributions of psychiatric research in the field of intellectual disability. In G. N. Christodoulou, M. Jorge, & J. E. Mezzich (Eds.), *Advances in psychiatry* (pp. 37–43). Athens: Beta Medical Publishers.

Bertelli, M., Rossi, M., Scuticchio, D., & Bianco, A. (2015). Diagnosing psychiatric disorders in people with intellectual disabilities: Issues and achievements. *Advances in Mental Health and Intellectual Disabilities, 9*(5), 230–242.

Bertelli, M., Salvador-Carulla, L., Scuticchio, D., Varrucciu, N., Martinez-Leal, R., Cooper, S. A., Simeonsson, R. J., Deb, S., Weber, G., Jung, R., Munir, K., Adnams, C., Akoury-Dirani, L., Girimaji, S. C., Katz, G., Kwok, H., & Walsh, C. (2014). Moving beyond intelligence in the revision of Icd-10: Specific cognitive functions in intellectual developmental disorders. *World Psychiatry, 13*(1), 93–94.

Bittles, A. H., Petterson, B. A., Sullivan, S. G., Hussain, R., Glasson, E. J., & Montgomery, P. D. (2002). The influence of intellectual disability on life expectancy. *Journals of Gerontology Series A: Biological Sciences and Medical Sciences, 57*(7), 470–472.

Bohmer, C. J., Klinkenberg-Knol, E. C., Niezen-de Boer, M. C., & Meuwissen, S. G. (2000). Gastroesophageal reflux disease in intellectually disabled individuals: How often, how serious, how manageable? *American Journal of Gastroenterology, 95*, 1868–1872.

Carter, G., & Jancar, J. (1983). Mortality in the mentally-handicapped: A 50 year survey at the Stoke-Park Group of Hospitals (1930-1980). *Journal of Mental Deficiency Research, 27*(2), 143–156.

Center, J. R., McElduff, A., & Beange, H. (1994). Osteoporosis in groups with intellectual disability. *Journal of Intellectual and Developmental Disability, 19*, 251–258.

Chaplin, R. (2004). General psychiatric services for adults with intellectual disability and mental illness. *Journal of Intellectual Disability Research, 48*(1), 1–10.

Cooper, S. A., McLean, G., Guthrie, B., McConnachie, A., Mercer, S., Sullivan, F., & Morrison, J. (2015). Multiple physical and mental health comorbidity in adults with intellectual disabilities: Population-based cross-sectional analysis. *BMC Family Practice, 27*(16), 110.

Cooper, S. A., Smiley, E., Morrison, J., Williamson, A., & Allan, L. (2007). Mental ill-health in adults with intellectual disabilities: Prevalence and associated factors. *British Journal of Psychiatry, 190*, 27–35.

Devenny, D. A., Silverman, W. P., Hill, A. L., Jenkins, E., Sersen, E. A., & Wisniewski, K. E. (1996). Normal ageing in adults with Down's syndrome: A longitudinal study. *Journal of Intellectual Disability Research, 40*(3), 208–221.

Dixon-Ibarra, A., & Horner-Johnson, W. (2014). Disability status as an antecedent to chronic conditions: National Health Interview Survey, 2006-2012. *Preventing Chronic Disease, 11*, 130251. doi:10.5888/pcd11.130251.

Dowling, S., Manthorpe, J., & Cowley, S. (2007). Working on person-centred planning: From amber to green light? *Journal of Intellectual Disability Research, 11*(1), 65–82.

Dreyfus, D., Lauer, E., & Wilkinson, J. (2014). Characteristics associated with bone mineral density screening in adults with intellectual disabilities. *Journal of American Board of Family Medicine, 27*(1), 104–114.

Durkin, M. (2002). The epidemiology of developmental disabilities in low-income countries. *Mental Retardation and Developmental Disabilities Research Reviews, 8*, 206–211.

Edgerton, R. B., Gaston, M. A., Kelly, H., & Ward, T. W. (1994). Health care for aging people with mental retardation. *Mental Retardation, 32*(2), 146–150.

Einfeld, S. L., & Aman, M. (1995). Issues in the taxonomy of psychopathology in mental retardation. *Journal of Autism and Developmental Disorders, 25*(2), 143–167.

Emerson, E., Baines, S., Allerton, L., & Welch, V. (2012). *Health inequalities and people with learning disabilities in the UK: 2012*. Learning Disabilities Observatory, Department of Health, 2011-09: IHAL.

Emerson, E., Moss, S., & Kiernan, C. K. (1999). The relationship between challenging behaviour and psychiatric disorders in people with severe intellectual disabilities. In N. Bouras (Ed.), *Psychiatric and behavioral disorders in mental retardation* (pp. 33–48). Cambridge: Cambridge University.

Evenhuis, H. M. (1997). Medical aspects of ageing in a population with intellectual disability: III. Mobility, internal conditions and cancer. *Journal of Intellectual Disability Research, 41*(1), 8–18.

Eyman, R. K., & Call, T. L. (1991). Life expectancy of persons with Down syndrome. *American Journal of Mental Retardation, 95*(6), 603–612.

Felce, D., Kerr, M., & Hastings, R. P. (2009). A general practice-based study of the relationship between indicators of mental illness and challenging behaviour among adults with intellectual disabilities. *Journal of Intellectual Disability Research, 53*(3), 243–254.

Florio, T., & Trollor, J. (2015). Mortality among a cohort of persons with an intellectual disability in New South Wales, Australia. *Journal of Applied Research in Intellectual Disability, 28*(5), 383–393.

Fredheim, T., Haavet, O. R., Danbolt, L. J., Kjønsberg, K., & Lien, L. (2013). Intellectual disability and mental health problems: A qualitative study of general practitioners' views. *BMJ Open, 3*(3). pii: e002283. doi:10.1136/bmjopen-2012-002283

Galli-Carminati, G., Chauvet, I., & Deriaz, N. (2006). Prevalence of gastro-intestinal disorders in adult clients with pervasive developmental disorders. *Journal of Intellectual Disability Research, 50*, 711–718.

Gimbel, H. (2000). Diagnosis and treatment of gastrooesophageal reflux disease in the mentally retarded: Guidelines of aì multidisciplinary consensus work group. Dutch Association of Physicians in Care of Mentally Handicapped. *Ned Tijdschr Geneeskd, 144*, 1161–1165.

Girimaji, S. C., & Srinath, S. (2010). Perspectives of intellectual disability in India: Epidemiology, policy, services for children and adults. *Current Opinion in Psychiatry, 23*(5), 441–446.

Hogg, J., Lucchino, R., Wang, K., Janicki, M. P., & Working Group. (2000). *Healthy ageing—Adults with intellectual disabilities: Ageing and social policy*. Geneva, Switzerland: World Health Organization.

Hollins, S., Attard, M. T., von Fraunhofer, N., McGuigan, S., & Sedgwick, P. (1998). Mortality in people with learning disability: risks, causes, and death certification findings in London. *Developmental Medicine and Child Neurology, 40*(1), 50–56.

Hosking, F. J., Carey, I. M., Shah, S. M., Harris, T., DeWilde, S., Beighton, C., & Cook, D. G. (2016). Mortality among adults with intellectual disability in England: Comparisons with the general population. *American Journal of Public Health, 106*(8), 1483–1490.

Howlett, S., Florio, T., Xu, H., & Trollor, J. (2015). Ambulatory mental health data demonstrates the high needs of people with an intellectual disability: Results from the New South Wales intellectual disability and mental health data linkage project. *Australian and New Zealand Journal of Psychiatry, 49*(2), 137–144.

Hurley, A. (2006). Mood disorders in intellectual disability. *Current Opinion in Psychiatry, 19*(5), 465–469.

Irazábal, M., Marsá, F., García, M., Gutiérrez-Recacha, P., Martorell, A., Salvador-Carulla, L., & Ochoa, S. (2012). Family burden related to clinical and functional variables of people with intellectual disability with and without a mental disorder. *Research in Developmental Disabilities, 33*(3), 796–803.

Janicki, M. P., & Dalton, A. J. (2000). Prevalence of dementia and impact on intellectual disability services. *Mental Retardation, 38*(3), 276–288.

Janicki, M. P., Dalton, A. J., Henderson, C. M., & Davidson, P. W. (1999). Mortality and morbidity among older adults with intellectual disability: Health services considerations. *Disability and Rehabilitation, 21*(5–6), 284–294.

Jeevanandam, L. (2009). Perspectives of intellectual disability in Asia: Epidemiology, policy, and services for children and adults. *Current Opinion in Psychiatry, 22*(3), 462–468.

Kapell, D., Nightingale, B., Rodriguez, A., Lee, J. H., Zigman, W. B., & Schupf, N. (1998). Prevalence of chronic medical conditions in adults with mental retardation: comparison with the general population. *Mental Retardation, 36*(4), 269–279.

Kendrick, M. J. (2012). Getting a good life: The challenges for agency transformation so that they are more person centered. *International Journal of Disability, Community and Rehabilitation* [online], *11*(1). Accessed February 6, 2015, from http://www.ijdcr.ca

Kenfield, S., & Stampfer, M. (2013). Healthy behaviours yield major benefits in ageing: Poor diet, smoking, and physical inactivity predict disability in previously non-disabled people. *British Medical Journal, 347*, f5156.

Kishore, M. T., Nizamie, S. H., & Nizamie, A. (2005). The behavioural profile of psychiatric disorder in persons with intellectual disability. *Journal of Intellectual Disability Research, 49*(11), 852–857.

Kwok, H. W. M., & Chui, E. M. C. (2008). A survey on mental health care for adults with intellectual disabilities in Asia. *Journal of Intellectual Disability Research, 52*, 996–1002.

Lennox, N. G., Diggens, J. N., & Ugoni, A. M. (1997). The general practice care of people with intellectual disability: Barriers and solutions. *Journal of Intellectual Disability Research, 41*(5), 380–390.

Leutz, W. N. (1999). Five laws for integrating medical and social services: Lessons from the United States and the United Kingdom. *Milbank Quarterly, 77*(1), 77–110.

Lunsky, Y., Balogh, R. S., Cobigo, V., Barry, I., Lin, E., & Oulette-Kuntz, H. M. J. (2014). ICES report primary care of adults with developmental disabilities in Ontario. *Healthcare Quarterly, 17*(3), 11–13.

Lunsky, Y., Klein-Geltink, J. E., & Yates, E. A. (Eds.). (2013). *Atlas on the primary care of adults with developmental disabilities in Ontario*. Toronto, ON: Institute for Clinical Evaluative Sciences.

Martorell, A., Gutiérrez-Recacha, P., Irazábal, M., Marsà, F., & García, M. (2011). Family impact in intellectual disability, severe mental health disorders and mental health disorders in ID. *A comparison. Research in Developmental Disabilities, 32*(6), 2847–2852.

Maulik, P. K., Mascarenhas, M. N., Mathers, C. D., Dua, T., & Saxena, S. (2011). Prevalence of intellectual disability: A meta-analysis of population-based studies. *Research in Developmental Disabilities, 32*(2), 419–436.

McCallion, P., & McCarron, M. (2004). Aging and intellectual disabilities: A review of recent literature. *Current Opinion in Psychiatry, 17*(5), 349–352.

McGuigan, S. M., Hollins, S., & Attard, M. (1995). Age-specific standardized mortality rates in people with learning disability. *Journal of Intellectual Disability Research, 39*, 527–531.

McIntyre, L. L., Blacher, J., & Backer, B. L. (2002). Behaviour/mental health problems in young adults with intellectual disability: The impact on families. *Journal of Intellectual Disability Research, 46*, 239–249.

McVicker, R. W., Shanks, O. E., & McClelland, R. J. (1994). Prevalence and associated features of epilepsy in adults with Down's syndrome. *British Journal of Psychiatry, 164*(4), 528–532.

Mencap. (2004). *Treat me right*. London: Mencap. Accessed November 2009, from https://www.mencap.org.uk/gettingitright

Mezzich, J. E., Salloum, I. M., Cloninger, C. R., Salvador-Carulla, L., Kirmayer, L. J., Banzato, C. E., Wallcraft, J., & Botbol, M. (2010). Person-centred integrative diagnosis: Conceptual bases and structural model. *Canadian Journal of Psychiatry, 55*(11), 701–708.

Nezu, A. M. (1994). Introduction to special section: Mental retardation and mental illness. *Journal of Consulting and Clinical Psychology, 62*(1), 4–5.

Nolte, E., & McKee, M. (2008). *Caring for people with chronic conditions: A health system perspective*. Maidenhead: Open University Press.

O'Brien, K. F., Tate, K., & Zaharia, E. S. (1991). Mortality in a large Southeastern facility for persons with mental retardation. *American Journal of Mental Deficiency, 95*, 397–403.

O'Hara, J. (2006). Standards and quality measures for services for people with intellectual disabilities. *Current Opinion in Psychiatry, 19*(5), 497–501.

Ouellette-Kuntz, H., Shooshtari, S., Balogh, R., & Martens, P. (2015). Understanding information about mortality among people with intellectual and developmental disabilities in Canada. *Journal of Applied Research in Intellectual Disabilities, 28*(5), 423–435.

Patja, K., Eero, P., & Iivanainen, M. (2001). Cancer incidence among persons with intellectual disabilities. *Journal of Intellectual Disability Research, 45*, 300–307.

Perry, J., Linehan, C., Kerr, M., Salvador-Carulla, L., Zeilinger, E., Weber, G., Walsh, P., van Schrojenstein Lantman-de-Valk, H., Haveman, M., Azema, B., Buono, S., Câra, A. C., Germanavicius, A., Van Hove, G., Määttä, T., Berger, D. M., & Tossebro, J. (2010). The P15—A multinational assessment battery for collecting data on health indicators relevant to adults with intellectual disabilities. *Journal of Intellectual Disability Research, 54*(11), 981–991.

Persha, A., Arya, S., Nagar, R. K., Behera, P., Verma, R. K., & Kishore, M. T. (2007). Biological and psychosocial predictors of developmental delay in persons with intellectual disability: Retrospective case-file study. *Asia Pacific Disability Rehabilitation Journal, 18*, 93–100.

Pueschel, S. M., & Pueschel, J. K. (1992). *Biomedical concerns in persons with Down syndrome*. Baltimore: Paul Brookes.

Pulvirenti, M., Hons, B. A., McMillan, J., & Lawn, S. (2014). Empowerment, patient centred care and self management. *Health Expectations, 17*(3), 303–310.

Puri, B. K., Lekh, S. K., Langa, A., Zaman, R., & Singh, I. (1995). Mortality in a hospitalized mentally handicapped population: a 10-year survey. *Journal of Intellectual Disability Research, 39*(5), 442–446.

Raitasuo, J., Mölsä, S., Raitasuo, S., & Mattila, K. (1997). Deaths among the intellectually disabled. *Journal of Applied Intellectual Disability Research, 10*, 280–288.

Reppermund, S., & Trollor, J. N. (2016). Successful ageing for people with an intellectual disability. *Current Opinion in Psychiatry, 29*(2), 149–154.

Robertson, J., Hatton, C., Emerson, E., & Baines, S. (2015). Prevalence of epilepsy among people with intellectual disabilities: A systematic review. *Seizure, 29*, 46–62.

Salvador-Carulla, L., & Bertelli, M. (2008). "Mental retardation" or "intellectual disability": Time for a conceptual change. *Psychopathology, 41*(1), 10–16.

Salvador-Carulla, L., Garcia-Mellado, M. J., Velazquez, R., Romero, C., & Alonso, F. (1998). A reliability study of the Spanish version of the social behaviour schedule (SBS) in a population of adults with learning disabilities. *Journal of Intellectual Disability Research, 42*(1), 22–28.

Salvador-Carulla, L., Martinez-Leal, R., Heyler, C., Alvarez-Galvez, J., Veenstra, M. Y., García-Ibáñez, J., Carpenter, S., Bertelli, M., Munir, K., Torr, J., & van Schrojenstein Lantman-De Valk (2015). Training on intellectual disability in health sciences. The European perspective. *International Journal of Developmental Disabilities, 61*(1), 20–31.

Salvador-Carulla, L., Martinez-Leal, R., Poole, M., Salinas-Perez, J. A., Tamarit, J., Garcia-Ibanez, J., Almenara-Barrios, J., & Alvarez-Galvez, J. (2013). Perspectives: The mental health care gap in intellectual disabilities in Spain: Impact analysis and knowledge-to-action plan. *Journal of Mental Health Policy and Economics, 16*(3), 131–141.

Salvador-Carulla, L., Reed, G. M., Vaez-Azizi, L. M., Cooper, S. A., Martinez-Leal, R., Bertelli, M., Adnams, C., Cooray, S., Deb, S., Akoury-Dirani, L., Girimaji, S. C., Katz, G., Kwok, H., Luckasson, R., Simeonsson, R., Walsh, C., Munir, K., & Saxena, S. (2011). Intellectual developmental disorders: Towards a new name, definition and framework for "mental retardation/intellectual disability" In Icd-11. *World Psychiatry, 10*(3), 175–180.

Salvador-Carulla, L., Rodríguez-Blázquez, C., Rodrìguez de Molina, M., Pérez-Marín, J., & Velázquez, R. (2000). Hidden psychiatric morbidity in a vocational programme for people with intellectual disability. *Journal of Intellectual Disability Research, 44*(2), 147–154.

Smiley, E. (2005). Epidemiology of mental health problems in adults with learning disability: An update. *Advances in Psychiatric Treatment, 11*, 214–222.

Starfield, B. (2011). Is patient-centered care the same as person-focused care? *The Permanente Journal, 15*(2), 63.

Szymanski, L., & King, B. H. (1999). Practice parameters for the assessment and treatment of children, adolescents, and adults with mental retardation and comorbid mental disorders. American Academy of Child and Adolescent Psychiatry Working Group on Quality Issues. *Journal of American Academy of Child and Adolescent Psychiatry, 38*(12 Suppl), 5S–31S.

Tait, D. (1983). Mortality and dementia among ageing defectives. *Journal of Mental Deficiency Research, 27*(2), 133–142.

Tassé, M. J., Luckasson, R., & Nygren, M. (2013). Aaidd proposed recommendations for Icd-11 and the condition previously known as mental retardation. *Intellectual And Developmental Disabilities, 51*(2), 127–131.

Tuffrey-Wijne, I., Goulding, L., Giatras, N., Abraham, E., Gillard, S., White, S., Edwards, C., & Hollins, S. (2014). The barriers to and enablers of providing reasonably adjusted health services to people with intellectual disabilities in acute hospitals: Evidence from a mixed-methods study. *BMJ Open, 4*, e004606. doi:10.1136/bmjopen-2013-004606.

Valentijn, P. P., Schepman, S. M., Opheij, W., & Bruijnzeels, M. A. (2013). Understanding integrated care: A comprehensive conceptual framework based on the integrative functions of primary care. *International Journal of Integrated Care, 13*, e010.

Valentijn, P. P., Vrijhoef, H. J., Ruwaard, D., Boesveld, I., Arends, R. Y., & Bruijnzeels, M. A. (2015). Towards an international taxonomy of integrated primary care: A Delphi consensus approach. *BMC Family Practice, 16*, 64.

Van Schrojenstein Lantman-De Valk, H. M., Metsemakers, J. F., Haveman, M. J., & Crebolder, H. F. (2000). Health problems in people with intellectual disability in general practice: A comparative study. *Family Practice, 17*(5), 405–407.

Wehmeyer, M. L., Buntinx, W. H., Lachapelle, Y., Luckasson, R. A., Schalock, R. L., Verdugo, M. A., Borthwick-Duffy, S., Bradley, V., Craig, E. M., Coulter, D. L., Gomez, S. C., Reeve, A., Shogren, K. A., Snell, M. E., Spreat, S., Tassé, M. J., Thompson, J. R., & Yeager, M. H. (2008). The intellectual disability construct and its relation to human functioning. *Intellectual and Developmental Disabilities, 46*(4), 311–318.

Werner, S., & Stawski, M. (2012). Mental health: Knowledge, attitudes and training of professionals on dual diagnosis of intellectual disability and psychiatric disorder. *Journal of Intellectual Disability Research, 56*(3), 291–304.

Wilson, D. N., & Haire, A. (1990). Health care screening for people with mental handicap living in the community. *BMJ, 301*(6765), 1379–1381.

World Health Organization (WHO). (2015). *WHO global strategy on people- centered and integrated health services: Interim report.* Geneva: WHO.

Integrated Care for Older Patients: Geriatrics

29

Sofia Duque, Elisa Giaccardi, and Tischa J.M. van der Cammen

29.1 Introduction

For our contribution "Integrated Care for the Geriatric Patient", we have used the WHO definition of Integrated Care: 'Integrated care is a concept bringing together inputs, delivery, management and organization of services related to diagnosis, treatment, care, rehabilitation and health promotion. Integration is a means to improve services in relation to access, quality, user satisfaction and efficiency" (Gröne and Garcia-Barbero 2002). An overall working definition of integrated service delivery is "The management and delivery of health services so that clients receive a continuum of preventive and curative services, according to their needs over time and across different levels of the health system." (Waddington and Egger 2008).

S. Duque
Internal Medicine and Geriatrics, Faculty of Medicine of Lisbon, Beatriz Ângelo Hospital, Loures, Portugal
e-mail: sofia.b.duque@gmail.com

E. Giaccardi
Interactive Media Design, Faculty of Industrial Design Engineering, Department of Industrial Design, Delft University of Technology, Delft, The Netherlands
e-mail: E.Giaccardi@tudelft.nl

T.J.M. van der Cammen (✉)
Autonomous Ageing, Faculty of Industrial Design Engineering, Department of Applied Ergonomics and Design, Delft University of Technology, Delft, The Netherlands

Section of Geriatric Medicine, Department of Internal Medicine, Erasmus University Medical Center, Rotterdam, The Netherlands
e-mail: T.J.M.vanderCammen@tudelft.nl

© Springer International Publishing AG 2017
V. Amelung et al. (eds.), *Handbook Integrated Care*,
DOI 10.1007/978-3-319-56103-5_29

29.2   Challenges for Providing Care for the Geriatric Patient

In humans, ageing refers to a multidimensional process of physical, psychological, and social change, leading to functional decline. However, we must keep in mind that ageing is not a uniform process, and that there is a large inter-individual variety.

In old age, usually defined as from age 75 onwards, there is an accumulation of diseases and risk factors, the so-called "cumulative complexity" (Inouye et al. 2007), and an age-related increase in functional decline (Hebert 1997).

This complexity makes the care of the geriatric patient a challenge (Table 29.1).

29.2.1 Multimorbidity and Geriatric Syndromes

Multimorbidity, the co-occurrence of two or more chronic medical conditions in one person, correlates with age, and currently represents the most common "disease pattern" found among the elderly (Barnett et al. 2012).

Multimorbidity is characterized by complex interactions of co-existing diseases where a medical approach focused on a single disease does not suffice. New models of care for these patients are needed (Roland and Paddison 2013).

Usually, the geriatric patient presents with several age-related chronic diseases and geriatric syndromes simultaneously. Geriatric syndromes are common clinical presentations that do not fit into specific disease categories but have substantial implications for functionality and life satisfaction in older adults. Examples of geriatric syndromes are immobility, instability, falls, impaired cognition, incontinence, as well as sensorial impairments and dependency in activities of daily living (Tinetti et al. 1995). Heart failure, cerebrovascular disease, chronic obstructive pulmonary disease, osteoarthritis, dementia, diabetes and cancer are amongst the most prevalent chronic and disabling diseases in older people.

Table 29.1 Factors of older patient complexity

Multiple chronic diseases (synergistic or antagonistic interaction)
Multiple healthcare providers and facilities
Geriatric syndromes
Polypharmacy (adverse drug reactions and events, drug-drug interactions)
Functional impairment
Cognitive impairment
Loneliness, homeboundness
Lack of caregivers
Poor social support
Poverty
Lack of knowledge and training about older patient specificities among healthcare providers
Inter-individual heterogeneity

Table 29.2 Geriatric syndromes

Instability
Falls
Immobility
Impaired cognition (Delirium, Mild Cognitive Impairment, Dementia)
Urinary incontinence
Urinary retention
Faecal incontinence
Constipation and faecal impaction
Sensorial impairments (hearing and vision)
Dependency in activities of daily living
Anorexia
Malnutrition/failure to thrive
Poor oral health
Pain
Insomnia
Depression
Iatrogeny
Social isolation
Poverty

Consequently, commonly there are interactions between diseases, modulating the clinical presentation of diseases, precipitating the decompensation of chronic diseases and limiting the treatment efficacy or increasing the risk of side effects. Also, interactions between treatments, pharmacological or non-pharmacological, must be considered as they can lead to undesirable side effects, new symptoms and diseases or even compromise the treatment efficacy.

Concerning Geriatric syndromes, the definition is still not consensual, nor are the conditions that are considered geriatric syndromes (Table 29.2). Nevertheless, it is fairly consensual that geriatric syndromes are highly prevalent conditions in vulnerable older persons, multifactorial in nature, which can be precipitated or decompensated by acute insults. Different geriatric syndromes can result from the same aetiological factor and can be the atypical presentation of a chronic or acute condition. Globally geriatric syndromes lead to disability and poor quality of life. Complexity of geriatric syndromes aetiology makes its management a hard task which is usually underestimated, as geriatric syndromes are frequently still considered as inevitable consequences of ageing. Geriatricians are trained in the assessment and treatment of geriatric syndromes, focusing on their multifactorial basis. Nevertheless, appropriate management of geriatric syndromes usually involves a step-by-step approach that requires plenty of time, human capital, time and continuity of care.

Appropriate management of all these chronic conditions requires a long term care plan, in which continuity of care is regarded. Decompensations of chronic conditions should not be fragmentarily addressed; instead management of acute decompensations should be directed according to the basal status of chronic conditions and goals previously established. Although there is considerable evidence-based knowledge about management of single chronic diseases, little to no evidence exists about the management of the same chronic conditions in multimorbid geriatric patients. Not rarely, recommendations for single diseases are contraindicated in the management of other conditions. Management of the older patient consequently relies more on wisdom and experience than on evidence-based medicine.

Chronic diseases and age-related conditions are highly associated with functional decline, like gait impairment or inability to perform basic or instrumental activities of daily living. Some chronic diseases may be stronger or earlier associated with functional impairment than others. A higher number of chronic conditions seems to be associated with a greater functional impairment, higher than the sum of disabilities for each chronic condition. Some studies suggest that disability results from clustering of specific conditions, with interaction between diseases a keyword in the development of functional impairment. Functional impairment not only decreases patient autonomy, quality of life and sense of well-being, but also can prevent access to healthcare facilities and compliance to medical recommendations. In this scenario formal and informal caregivers are crucial to achieve treatment goals and preserve the quality of life of the older patient. They should be involved and empowered in the planning of care according to the best interest of the patient.

29.2.2 Fragmentation of Care

Typically, several healthcare professionals of different levels of medical care participate in the management of the multimorbid geriatric patient. For instance, a single patient can be assisted by the general practitioner, the medical or surgical specialists and the nursing home physician at the same time. When communication between them is not effective, there is fragmentation of care, and the risk of complications due to interactions between treatments and diseases is potentially increased. Some geriatric syndromes and decompensation of previous chronic diseases may result in fragmentation of care and treatment of single diseases separately. Fragmentation of care and its negative consequences are more pronounced when there is no general physician (geriatrician, general practitioner or internal medicine specialist) or other healthcare professional to manage and coordinate care delivered by different providers and facilities. Such a professional can play the role of case manager optimizing care and building one single plan of care that summarizes all the recommendations and goals of all the providers involved in care. In a fragmented system of care several factors contribute to inappropriate care of the geriatric patient, namely the lack of knowledge of healthcare professionals about the specificities of the older patient, unawareness of the importance of reconciliation of care and underestimation of the role of a coordinator with training in Geriatrics (case manager).

Social isolation is another common problem of older people. This could be a result from death of family members and friends of the same age group, professional and family commitments of younger family members, homeboundness due to physical inability precluding maintenance of social relationships, and cognitive or mental diseases. Social isolation not only affects well-being and quality of life but can also have an impact on the access to healthcare and on the quality of care. Nevertheless, social isolation is frequently undetected by healthcare systems and direct intervention is usually lacking.

Financial problems also play an important role in the health status of the older patient. Financial status of the older person depends on the reimbursement policy of healthcare systems, the individual levels of financial capability (income, savings and charity) and the cognitive ability of the older person to manage finances appropriately, and to protect oneself against financial abuse. Poor financial status can limit access to healthcare facilities, diagnostic and treatment procedures. Older persons may not be able to financially support a formal caregiver, home care, other social and community services (e.g. meals on wheels, mobile care teams), or even medication acquisition.

Indeed, social and financial problems can have a great impact on the health status and quality of life of the older patient. Therefore, care of the geriatric patient should not be restricted to management of medical conditions but also special attention should be given to social and financial issues. Depending on national health and social systems, older people may not be able to afford their medical assistance, and social and community services, especially when reimbursement policies are too restricted. Healthcare, social and community services providers as well as policy makers must be aware of those limitations in order to hierarchize priorities and set goals. Coordination between providers at a local level may enable optimal allocation of financial resources and delivery of high standard medical, social and community care.

29.2.3 Place of Living: From Community to Institutions

The place of living of the geriatric patient depends not only on the health status, functional and cognitive status, and medical needs, but also on the patient preferences and community and social resources available in a specific place or society.

Older people tend to prefer to continue living at home as long as they can, even if they have some limitation that impairs their ability to live alone, rather than transit to residential care or nursing homes. This requires comprehensive social and community services, training in geriatrics for health and social care professionals working in the community, and promoting an increased awareness of ageing in the local community.

Maintenance of quality of life of older people that remain living at home requires a global assessment of several aspects that interfere with daily living, and not only a purely medical assessment.

The concept of *Ageing in place* is defined as "the ability to live in one's own home and community safely, independently, and comfortably, regardless of age, income, or ability level" (Centers_for_Disease_Control_and_Prevention 2013). Older people usually see *Ageing in place* as an advantage in terms of a sense of attachment or connection and feelings of security and familiarity in relation to their homes as well as their communities. "Ageing in place" is seen to promote maintenance of independence, autonomy, social relationships and therefore higher satisfaction and quality of life (Wiles et al. 2012). In general, institutionalization is significantly more expensive than maintaining older people living at their own home. Indeed, OECD data published in 2011, revealed that while 70% of long-term care users from OECD countries received home care, 62% of total cost resulted from institutional care (Colombo et al. 2011). Therefore, *ageing in place* is usually supported by policy makers, which have been more focused in building age-friendly cities and communities. This challenging goal requires several interventions at home, as well as in the environment, community and at different healthcare levels (Kochera et al. 2005).

Home modifications might be necessary to compensate physical disability and to avoid accidents, increasing safety of homes and facilitating performance of daily living activities; however, older people may not be able to decide home adjustments that should be made, and to manage bureaucratic and financial implications alone. Counselling and orientation by social workers may be useful to accomplish these goals. Also, urban environment must be adjusted to disabled older citizens, making available appropriate and safe urban equipment (for example sidewalks and public transports stops), building easily accessible social and healthcare facilities and providing suitable and affordable public transports. Physical, occupational therapists, ergonomists, designers and urban architects may have a key role in home and environment adaptations.

Community services for older people may be developed to meet the diverse needs of older people, to make them available at nearby facilities or even at home by mobile teams. The services provided may include supervision or assistance in personal hygiene, deliverance of meals at home, house cleaning, assistance in medication management and chronic diseases monitoring (for instance glucose and arterial hypertension control), assistance in shopping and managing administrative and financial issues. Social workers can play an important role in organizing and handling these services but the participation of volunteers and informal support by neighbours and friends might be considered, not only to save financial resources but also to raise awareness of the importance of the civic engagement in an ageing society.

Socialization, practice of leisure and recreational activities, intellectual stimulation and physical activity are essential to maintain happiness, self-esteem, sense of well-being, cognitive and physical performance. These processes must be promoted to ensure a successful ageing. Whenever possible older people must remain active in the society and contribute to the community as it reinforces social ties and the sense of identity, satisfaction and usefulness. Regarding patients with highly impaired mobility, home based initiatives must be established to warrant socialization, and intellectual and physical stimulation, so that cognitive and functional decline are delayed.

Healthcare facilities should be redesigned and reorganized to care for community-dwelling patients with different grades of disability, including easily accessible outpatient facilities, geriatric day care centres and rehabilitation clinics.

To achieve an age-friendly liveable community a robust network must be established between all the healthcare, social and community providers. National political stakeholders must be engaged and face development of a liveable community as a major priority to achieve successful ageing. Local stakeholders should lead the establishment of a network of providers adjusted to local geographic and social specificities of the population, as solutions needed for city environment are not the same as for countryside.

More physical and cognitively impaired older persons can remain living at homes relying on the presence of formal caregivers. Assistance may be needed 24 h/day, increasing the cost of home-based care. Ideally formal caregivers should be trained for dealing with the older person and efficiently handle their problems and should be integrated in the local medical and social network, to ensure continuity of care but also to support them when needed. Geographic isolation of countryside small villages can be a barrier to *Ageing in place* due to the reduced offer of social and community services and may precipitate institutionalization.

The ability to continue living at home will depend on the availability of informal caregivers, and on the older person's income, but also on the financial support assured by the national social and health policies. Individually, some persons may not be able to afford expenses related to healthcare, home adjustments, regular house maintenance, delivery of meals, house cleaning and personal hygiene assistance, or services or formal caregivers, for example. These older persons turn out to be institutionalized, if nursing homes are available and still affordable. Indeed, sociodemographic characteristics seem to be better predictors of admission in long term care facilities than health status and physical functioning (Shapiro and Tate 1985).

Qualification, reimbursement policy and availability of nursing homes is widely variable worldwide; in some communities nursing homes may not be available at all or too expensive to be afforded by poorer older persons. Indeed, reimbursement of nursing home costs is heterogeneous worldwide and individual older persons may have inadequate incomes to pay for nursing home costs, ending up living at home even without basic care guaranteed. National and local governments must work to promote a successful and dignified ageing, respecting the basic human rights.

If older people cannot live at home anymore, other residential alternatives exist that avoid or delay admission to traditional nursing homes such as assisted living residences and continuing care retirement communities (Rogers 2011), which can promote autonomy, independency and cognitive function more than nursing homes.

Overall, there is now evidence that home care is less expensive than residential care, even taking into account the indirect costs relative to the time spent by the informal caregiver (Chappell et al. 2004; Ostbye and Crosse 1994; Hux et al. 1998; Weissert et al. 1997; Hollander 2001). This data favours reallocation of resources from residential services to community and home-based services within Continuing Care.

Previously, in the 70s and 80s, evidence revealed that enhanced home based and community care programs were not cost-effective and did not prevent admission to long term care institutions. Interpretation of cost-effectiveness of services may depend on social and health policies practised at country/regional level concerning reimbursement and how much older people rely on informal care (for instance, in Canada, family is expected to support older people while in USA older people usually depend on formal care). Informal caregivers can play an important role in frail older patients care, enabling patients to stay at own homes and promoting a sense of well-being that formal caregivers cannot meet, despite their professionalism (Byrne et al. 2009). Informal care can reduce financial direct costs and delay institutionalization. Nevertheless, informal caregiving represents an economic value that should be measured and taken into account in calculation of total costs of care (Langa et al. 2001; Van Houtven et al. 2013). Therefore, informal caregivers must be reimbursed for that commitment, namely when their professional activity and resulting income is undermined. Caregivers burden can result when patients require a full psychological and physical engagement of informal carers, which can prevent effective care and feasibility of informal care (Capistrant 2016; Schulz and Sherwood 2008; Ranmuthugala et al. 2009; Okamoto et al. 2007). Social and health policies must address caregiver burden, developing strategies to prevent it. Several ways to make informal caregiving sustainable have been described such as implementation of financial support for carers, flexible work conditions that allow caregivers to combine work and eldercare, support services for the carer (Colombo et al. 2011), such as respite care services, group support and information and communication technology (Lopez-Hartmann et al. 2012; Scott et al. 2015).

Possible strategies to improve cost-effectiveness of home care are to implement a needs-based screening to identify the best care model (home-care or residential care) for individual patients (Weissert 1991) and case-management approach (You et al. 2013).

As mentioned above, institutionalization occurs when older people are not able to live alone and home care, community and social services are not able to meet the older person's basic needs or are not available or affordable. Some studies have identified several predictors of institutionalization, namely older age, physical impairment, medical burden, frequent falling, low and high body mass index, cognitive impairment, depressive symptoms, behavioural problems, difficulty and lack of assistance in daily living activities, lack of informal support and socio-economic resources, living alone and limited contact with the relatives, usage of community services, low education and lack of engagement in social activities (Salminen et al. 2017; von Bonsdorff et al. 2006; Woo et al. 2000; Metzger et al. 1997; Luppa et al. 2010; Bharucha et al. 2004; Chau et al. 2012; Gnjidic et al. 2012; Gaugler et al. 2007). Delay of institutionalization by home care based services is controversial (Gaugler et al. 2007; Sarma et al. 2009; Yamada et al. 2012; Cohen-Mansfield and Wirtz 2011).

Institutionalization has also been associated with poorer health outcomes such as early mortality, cognitive decline, dependency in activities of daily living, depression and malnutrition (Gonzalez-Colaco Harmand et al. 2014; Smoliner et al. 2009; McConnell et al. 2002). Institutionalization is commonly linked to psychological and emotional dissatisfaction of the patient and caregivers, feelings of loneliness and marginalization, development of psychiatric symptoms and poorer health-related quality of life (Schulz et al. 2004; Scocco et al. 2006; Drageset et al. 2008).

To sum up, the geriatric patient is very complex and heterogeneous. The medical and basic needs depend on the individual consequences of physiological ageing, the presence of chronic diseases and geriatric syndromes, the functional and cognitive abilities, the social and financial support, the healthcare system, the place of living, etc. Interdisciplinary teams, including professionals of different domains and diverse levels of care can be the keyword to establish a geriatric integrated care network; able to cope with the multifaceted and complex needs of the older person. Some authors have stated that care of frail elderly requires health professionals with skills and knowledge in 3 core competencies: geriatrics, interprofessional practice, and interorganizational collaboration (Ryan et al. 2013). The ability to plan individually tailored interventions must be developed as each older person is a single one, with specific needs, disabilities and functional limitations.

29.3 Goals of Integrated Care

Comprehensive integration of care of the older patient should articulate medical, social, community and family resources. Goals for a single patient should be defined and shared by all the care providers and also by the patient and their family. The geriatric patient and their needs, as well as their interests and wishes, ought to be in the centre of the care plan, also when the patient has a legal guardian due to cognitive or mental disability. The patient's opinion on their quality of life must also be taken into account. This holistic approach is the standard methodology used by geriatricians and other professionals with training in Geriatrics and Gerontology, but other providers delivering care services to older patients, who may not be aware of the importance of integration of care, constitute important barriers to reconciliation and unification of care. A holistic and multimorbidity-focused approach is a basic principle of a successful geriatric integrated care network, in which there is effective communication between all the providers from the various fields, sharing a single care plan and intervention. In order for such a care plan to succeed, a main coordinator of care (case manager) should be appointed and accepted by all partners participating in the care plan. A recent systematic review about the impact of case management in the care of community-dwelling older patients revealed improvement of psychological health or well-being and decline of unmet service needs (You et al. 2012).

Management of multimorbid older patients represents a large financial expense. Potentially, expenses are higher when: healthcare resources and providers are not coordinated, incurring in unnecessary repetition of diagnostic procedures, overprescription of drugs, duplication of medical consultations, unnecessary hospital or nursing home admissions, avoidable travels between the place of living and health-care facilities, underuse of financial reimbursement policies or free services. Integration of care may reduce some of this unnecessary spending (Beland et al. 2006; Counsell et al. 2007; Bird et al. 2007; Eklund and Wilhelmson 2009) and saved amounts can be invested in useful healthcare interventions, making healthcare more cost-effective (Bernabei et al. 1998; Landi et al. 2001; Wiley-Exley et al. 2009; Bird et al. 2007).

Integrated Care of the Geriatric patient is not only intended to improve financial resources utilization and to streamline administrative procedures, but likewise to improve clinical outcomes. Effective control of chronic diseases in multimorbid patients is one of the major outcomes, with the aim to prevent acute decompensations of chronic conditions, and to reduce hospitalization and mortality. To successfully tackle chronic diseases in multimorbidity, patients are managed through a single comprehensive approach rather than through several single disease-focused approaches, which decreases antagonistic interactions between diseases and interventions. Integration of care is crucial to implement this single and holistic plan of care in clinical practice and across the overall network of healthcare providers. Different services, institutions and organizations that provide care must be coordinated, cooperate and integrate in a network centred approach around the patient and their environment, avoiding fragmentation of care and disruptive transitions of care. Interventions of healthcare providers working outside this network in a fragmented pattern can result in failure of previous interventions and reverse improvements that have already been achieved, jeopardizing the sustainability of integrated care.

Another important aim of health care provision in the geriatric setting is to preserve the older person's quality of life. The great subjectivity of such outcome is a major challenge to healthcare providers and to standardisation of procedures and policies. Quality of life is a multidimensional outcome depending not only on the health status but also on social and financial support. Quality of life usually relies on maintaining self-autonomy in activities of daily living, reducing disability and mobility limitations and preventing further functional decline. Therefore, these are significant goals which always should be taken into account by healthcare providers of older patients. Integration of care plays a key role in the achievement of quality of life by joining together and coordinating the interventions of providers of different fields such as healthcare and social services.

Older persons usually prefer to continue living at home and institutionalization usually bears negative consequences, like further functional decline, cognitive impairment, disruption of previous social relationships, depression and malnutrition. To allow older persons to continue living at home and to maintain their daily routine, some social support and home-based health care might be needed. These community-based providers must be included in the global network of care providers and their services must also be considered in the care plan.

Prevention of functional decline is a core objective of geriatric medicine, playing an important role in autonomy and quality of life of older people. Integrated care models based on case-management revealed to be effective in prevention of function decline (Hutt et al. 2004; Mukamel et al. 2007).

Control of chronic diseases might be quite difficult, requiring complex therapeutic regimens, strict monitoring and ability to recognize early signs of poor control or decompensations, which enable timely intervention to reverse acute complications or progression of chronic diseases. Patients and caregivers must be educated so that they can actively participate in the management of chronic diseases (self-management). Caregivers of physically disabled or cognitively impaired patients may even have a more active role. Empowerment of patients and caregivers can improve awareness about the severity of chronic disease complications and the importance of treatment (Shearer et al. 2012; Jones et al. 2011, Lyttle and Ryan 2010). This leads to increased adherence to healthy lifestyle behaviours, increased adherence to pharmacological therapy and follow up directives (Wendt 1998, Crawford Shearer et al. 2010; Jones et al. 2011; Tannenbaum et al. 2014; Rabiei et al. 2013; Boonyasopun et al. 2008; DeCostera and Georgea 2005; Figar et al. 2006). To ensure that patients and caregivers are performing monitoring and therapeutic procedures appropriately they should be considered active participants in establishing a care plan and given the necessary tools to effectively communicate within the care network.

To achieve the above goals (Table 29.3), new models of care must be designed for the multimorbid geriatric patient, not focusing on single chronic diseases but instead on clustering of chronic diseases and age related conditions, including geriatric syndromes.

Goals of care must include not only the control of the chronic diseases but also functional outcomes and geriatric syndromes. Outcomes concerning chronic diseases should be established according to the physiological reserve of the older patient, and their previous functional and cognitive status. Some authors have suggested that new models of care of the geriatric patient should replace the central concept of chronic diseases by the concept of geriatric syndromes.

Table 29.3 Goals of integrated care for the geriatric patient

Reduce expenses, be cost-effective
Effective chronic diseases management, prevent decompensation and hospitalization or death
Provide continuity of care/effective transitions of care
Improve quality of life
Reduce disability
Prevent function decline
Reduce institutionalization
Reduce risk of death
Self-empowerment (patients and caregivers)
Self-management (patients and caregivers)

29.4   The Integrated Treatment Plan

Recognizing the importance of integration of care in Geriatrics some projects have been developed and below examples are presented.

Telehealth and other technology based systems may facilitate coordination of care and cooperation between providers as information and communication may be available immediately. Telehealth services may be used to monitor symptoms and to improve communication between healthcare professionals but some uncertainty may exist concerning older people as they are usually still not so engaged with new technologies.

The K4CARE (Riano et al. 2012) launched in 2006 following an European call under the auspice the program "Digital Agenda for Europe" intended to define a new health care model for care of elderly people grounded in an integrated knowledge-based intelligent technology to be available to help in the management and provision of health care services to chronically ill patients anytime and anywhere through the Web. The final product implemented the health care model as a web platform and intended to optimise the safe management of the care of chronically ill patients at home. All the different kinds of professionals involved are considered in the K4Care model and the system adapts automatically to the personal profile of each professional, allowing only the performance of specific actions related to the user's role. In a practical point of view through K4CARE web platform the family doctor, at the patient's home, consults a shared electronic health record. During the examination, guidelines are automatically presented, standardized procedures proposed and the individual set of diseases is examined. The physician can immediately modify treatment and the electronic health record is updated in real time from different sources, following the evolution of the patient. Integration of medical and social information allows comprehensive interventions (e.g. nurse reporting side effects of therapy). Shared access allows optimization of interventions (e.g. relatives or social worker asking information on management of feeding).

The Integrated Telehealth Education and Activation of Mood (I-TEAM) (Gellis et al. 2014) is another technology based integrated care system of which the goal is to improve chronic illness (heart failure, chronic obstructive pulmonary disease) and comorbid depression in the home healthcare setting. I-TEAM intervention comprises self-management and decision support, implementation of evidence-based protocols for chronic disease and depression management, collaboration with primary care for medication management and electronic medical record. Care is mainly delivered by a trained telehealth nurse who monitors symptoms, body weight and medication use daily as well as runs sessions of problem-solving treatment focused on depressive symptoms and mediates communication with the primary care physician. Evidence suggests that this kind of telehealth system can be used in older patients, with positive outcomes (see below).

In 2008–2009 a Canadian program of integration of healthcare in Primary Care, called Seniors Collaborative Care Program (SCCP) (Moore et al. 2012), was developed in Ontario to improve the quality, efficiency and coordination of care for the frail community-dwelling older people and to enhance geriatric and interprofessional skills of healthcare providers. The SCCP used an interprofessional, shared-care, geriatric model. The interdisciplinary team comprised a nurse practitioner, a family physician, a pharmacist, a dietitian, a social worker and a visiting geriatrician. A case-finding strategy by telephone was used to identify seniors at risk of falling or for cognitive impairment. In a first contact patients were screened for several geriatric conditions followed by comprehensive geriatric assessment. Assessment was made in outpatient clinic or in patient's home for housebound patients. Patient and caregiver preferences were also taken into account. Case-based team meetings were held monthly. Twenty five patients were included in this pilot project and selected patients were assessed by a geriatrician in five weeks, which was a great improvement considering a 6-month delay for non-urgent referrals to geriatricians in that region. It was considered an advantageous model because care remained in the primary care setting and coordination of care was easier and facilitated by effective communication through electronic medical records and a messaging tool. Educational advantages were also mentioned by the team, which recognized the importance of the expertise of the geriatrician in teaching the other providers and solving geriatric clinical issues. One of the barriers previously recognized by the team to provide adequate geriatric care was the inability to offer geriatric specialized care to all the seniors due to the shortage of geriatricians. Inclusion of a geriatrician in a multidisciplinary team can be an effective method to improve individual patient care, to select candidates for specialized assessment and to train other healthcare providers. On the other hand, geriatricians learn about the challenges that primary care providers usually face treating frail older patients.

The American GRACE Team Care model (Indianapolis) (Counsell et al. 2006) is another primary care based project, developed to overcome limitation of time and resources in provision of comprehensive care to older patients in primary care setting. The acronym GRACE stands for Geriatric Resources for Assessment and Care of Elders. GRACE relies on Geriatric Assessment to improve diagnosis of geriatric syndromes and guide management of care. GRACE project includes patients' in-home assessment by the nurse provider and the social worker, specific care protocols to manage common geriatric conditions, integrated electronic medical records, web-based care management tracking and integration of outpatient clinical services with hospital, pharmacy, mental health, home health and community-based services. An individualized care plan is established, according to individualized goals. GRACE provides caregiver support and held a weekly interdisciplinary team conference, with participation of a geriatrician. The major goal of GRACE is to ensure continuity and coordination of care and smooth care transitions between different levels of care (in-hospital and outpatient services). The GRACE team receives hospital and emergency department alerts notifying older patients discharge to timely plan delivery of transitional care, which comprised a home visit. The home visit is intended to offer proactive support to the patient and caregivers, to reconcile medications, to ensure implementation of post-discharge arrangements and to inform the primary care physician about the hospitalization and discharge.

Hospital-based geriatricians have also been involved in secondary, primary and community care settings in European countries (Robertson et al. 2014), with the major goal of avoiding hospital admission. This collaboration between community and hospital healthcare professionals enables timely specialized geriatric assessment when needed for high risk patients identified by the primary care provider and promotes multidisciplinary team meetings for case-management. Primary care providers are also able to refer patients to a medical acute setting and interface where geriatricians collaborate in emergency department assessment to streamline discharges.

Another attempt to reduce unneeded prolonged hospitalization of older people took place in the United Kingdom (Challis et al. 1991). Case–managers were integrated in geriatric multidisciplinary teams and were supposed to arrange social services to meet the patients' needs at home. Institutionalization rate and functional disability decreased and the intervention was cost-effective, highlighting the importance of multidisciplinary management and coordination with outpatient providers.

Some integrated care systems are mainly focused on social services, which can play a key role in health status and quality of life of older people. In San Francisco a daycare centre-based integrated care model (On Lok) (Kane et al. 1992; Bodenheimer 1999) was developed for frail older Chinese people who were eligible for nursing home admission. Each frail older person was assessed by a multidisciplinary team, which established a care plan and coordinated provision of health and social care according the individual needs. Patients receiving more community-based care were less likely to be placed in nursing homes and had lower costs than patients not assigned to the program. This innovative project led to the national PACE program (Program for All-Inclusive Care for the Elderly) (Mukamel et al. 2007; Borgenicht et al. 1997) in the USA, financially funded by Medicare and Medicaid. PACE addresses the needs of disabled frail older people who are candidates for long-term care. Its major goal is to enable patients to live independently in the community as long as possible. Social services such as day care centre, home care, meals-on-wheels and transportation service, are tailored to each unique patient by an interdisciplinary team. PACE programs were shown to improve functional status of enrolled patients.

The PACE project was replicated in Canada (Montreal, Quebec) named Integrated System for Frail Elderly Persons (French acronym SIPA). SIPA was a community-based primary care system based on a patient-focused model designed for frail elderly. SIPA goals were to assure comprehensive care, integration of all available services and continuity of care by all professionals and institutions involved, including primary and secondary medical services, social services, rehabilitation, medication and technical aids provision and long-term care (Bergman et al. 1997). Eligible patients were those presenting moderate - severe disability, including functional disability, mobility problems, cognitive impairment or incontinence. A multidisciplinary team selected health care and social support needed and managed its provision. Despite favourable health outcomes (see below), SIPA was interrupted because of no consensus about health outcomes benefit (Kodner 2006).

The PRISMA model (Program of Research to Integrate Services for the Maintenance of Autonomy) is another integration of care system focused on frail older people which established a network including all the social and healthcare providers in the geographic region of Quebec, irrespective of the source of funding (Hebert et al. 2003). A major goal is to integrate service delivery and to ensure continuity of care, in order to preserve patients' functional autonomy. Eligible participants are elderly with moderate to severe disability, able to stay at home and needing two or more health or social services. Case-management process, a single assessment instrument, individualized plans and computerized clinical records shared by different providers are important components of the PRISMA program. First three years' results (1997–2000) were favourable to PRISMA model, showing lower functional decline in PRISMA participants compared to control, as well as reduction of the desire to be institutionalized, decrease of caregivers' burden and decline of the risk of readmission in 10 days after emergency department visit or after hospitalization in acute ward.

Other integrated care models are more geriatrics based, focusing in integration of community-based healthcare resources and social resources by Geriatric Units, namely by a case-manager, who coordinates an intervention plan. Two trials were performed in Italy in the 1990s.

The first one was a randomized controlled trial, performed in Northern Italy to evaluate the impact of a programme of integrated social and medical care among frail elderly people living in the community (Bernabei et al. 1998). 200 patients were included and randomized for intervention or control group. The intervention group patients received case management and care planning by the community geriatric evaluation unit and general practitioners. The control group patients received the conventional and fragmented primary and community care. Hospitalization, nursing home admission and home visits by general practitioners were higher in the control group. Improvement of functional status was higher in the intervention group and cognitive decline and healthcare costs were lower. This Italian integrated care programme with case management approach showed to be effective.

The second trial was performed in 4 distant sites of Italy which were engaged in a national Home Care programme. A medical and social home care programme based on comprehensive geriatric assessment and case management was delivered to Italian frail elderly individuals. Pre-intervention and post-intervention outcomes were compared, and hospitalization rates and length of stay decreased, supporting efficiency and cost-effectiveness of comprehensive geriatric assessment (Landi et al. 2001).

An integrated care model was also developed and tested in Australia. Eligible participants were older people with complex health care needs, who had presented to the emergency department three or more times in the last 12 months or who were identified as high-risk patients for hospital admission. A "care facilitator" was provided who was responsible for identifying and making accessible medical services needed. 231 elderly were enrolled and after 12 months of follow up there was a decline of emergency department admissions, hospitalization and length of stay (Bird et al. 2007).

The Walcheren Integrated Care Model (Fabbricotti et al. 2013), recently implemented in the southwest of Netherlands, focuses on frail elderly—living independently in their homes or in a specific type of assisted living facility—, and especially on the informal caregivers. It consists of an umbrella organizational structure and frailty screening and assessment of patients' needs are the first step of the intervention, performed by a multidisciplinary team. General practitioner is the single entry point of the patient in the system. Case management approach and multidisciplinary team meetings area also included. Caregivers are also assessed, regarding their potential role and needs to accomplish it.

Another novel integrated elderly care model was developed in the Netherlands in the "Embrace" project (Spoorenberg et al. 2013). Central features of "Embrace" are: (1) self-management support; (2) multidisciplinary care teams including the general practitioner, a geriatrician, a nurse and a social worker, focused not only on disease treatment but also on primary and secondary prevention; social and medical resources are provided by the nurse or the social worker; (3) decision support, addressed through multiple decision support tools; (4) clinical information systems, represented by an online electronic record system. Stratification tools enable characterization of patients according to three profiles (robust, frail, complex care needs). A trial to test "Embrace" effectiveness is now ongoing. Primary outcomes are complexity of care needs, frailty, health status, and self-management ability and caregiver burden. Preliminary results from a qualitative study based on participants interviews indicate that Embrace has positive effects on patients, increasing the sense of safety and security (Spoorenberg et al. 2015). Results of the randomized control trial will soon be available (Wynia et al. 2014).

29.5   Results of Integrated Care Approaches to Care Delivery

Most literature about integrated care models in Geriatrics only reports local and small scale experiences, mainly centred in Primary Care. Although its efficacy is usually reported, there is not enough statistically valid evidence to support a specific model and to disseminate it to other settings and countries.

I-TEAM technology (Gellis et al. 2014), above mentioned, was tested in frail older homebound patients in a randomized controlled trial. Patients (n = 102) were included and telehealth-managed patients revealed lower prevalence of depression, fewer admissions to the emergency department and improved problem-solving skills and self-management ability.

The effectiveness of the GRACE model, described in the previous section, was tested in a controlled clinical trial (Counsell et al. 2007, 2009), which included 951 adults 65 years or older with low-income. Patients were randomized to participate in the GRACE intervention or to receive usual care in community-based health centres during 2 years. The intervention group revealed improved quality of care and reduced acute care utilization among patients with high-risk of hospitalization, ie emergency department admissions, hospitalizations and readmissions. Overall mean 2-year total costs for intervention patients were not significantly different from those who received usual care but in high-risk subgroup there was a saving of $1,500 per. patient (Bielaszka-DuVernay 2011). Patients with high risk of hospitalization and randomized for GRACE intervention revealed higher chronic and preventive care costs, which however were offset by reductions in acute care costs. Mean 2-year total costs were higher in the low-risk group. Collaboration of geriatrics, primary care and community-based organizations, integration with community resources and social services, focus on geriatric conditions, incorporation of care transitions strategies and home based management, were considered by the providers important key factors for the success of GRACE program. GRACE model has been further implemented in other settings with similar results.

The previously described American PACE programme is still ongoing, and the On Lock model has been replicated in more than 100 sites and in more than 30 states (Poku 2015). Continued outcomes analyses showed consumer satisfaction, reduction in use of institutional care and medical services, and cost savings to public and private payers of care (Eng et al. 1997; Friedman et al. 2005; Meret-Hanke 2011; Segelman et al. 2014; Wieland et al. 2013). Short term hospitalization was lower in PACE participants compared to other older and disabled elders (Wieland et al. 2000). Nevertheless, Mukamel et al. (2006) considered that health outcomes of PACE participants could even be enhanced by improving the care team performance.

The Canadian SIPA model contributed to increasing accessibility and utilization of health and social home care and reduction of length of stay in acute hospitals for patients who inappropriately were not discharged ("bed blockers"). The utilization and costs of emergency department, hospital acute inpatient, and nursing home stays did not change significantly (Beland et al. 2006).

The Canadian PRISMA model effectiveness was also assessed comparing delivery of PRISMA with standard care delivered in other geographic areas of Canada during 4 years (Hebert et al. 2010). A quasi-experimental study including about 1500 patients was undertaken and revealed that PRISMA model reduced functional decline incidence, reduced health services utilization (lower emergency department admissions and hospitalization) and increased patient satisfaction and empowerment. Hebert (2009) concluded that the PRISMA model improved the efficacy of the health care system for frail older people, without extra cost. Stewart et al. (2013) reviewed all the PRISMA evidence published since 1988 and concluded that creation of partnerships between policy-makers, project implementers, and academic teams has an important role in establishing integrated care models for older persons. The importance of information technology supporting integration of services is also highlighted by the authors. Recently, MacAdam (2015) stressed that PRISMA is one of the few, if not the only, integrated care model to have been adopted at the system level by policy-makers.

The Walcheren Integrated Care Model study was mainly envisioned to assess quality of life of patients and informal caregivers and burden of caregivers. It was a quasi-experimental study. Frail older patients were included and randomized to the integrated care model or to usual care. In the short term integrated care model had positive impact on patients' quality of life. The intervention also contributed to the increased participation of informal caregivers in household tasks and reduced subjective caregiver burden (Janse et al. 2014).

A systematic literature review by Mirella Minkman et al. (2007) on performance improvement based on integrated quality management models [i.e. the Malcolm Baldrige Quality Award (MBQA) criteria, the European Foundation Quality Management (EFQM) Excellence model (Excellence award models) and the Chronic Care Model] found some evidence that implementing interventions based on the 'evidence-based developed' Chronic Care Model may improve process or outcome performances. The Chronic Care Model describes six elements–the community, the health system within it and four elements within the health system: self-management support, delivery system design, decision support and clinical information systems. The authors state that successful implementation of interventions based on the six elements may result in productive interactions between informed and activated patients and prepared and proactive care teams and in better functional and clinical outcomes. The Chronic Care Model is not specifically aimed at geriatric patient but rather describes the organisations and institutions involved in the model.

The evidence for performance improvement by interventions based on the 'expert-based developed' MBQA criteria and the EFQM Excellence model was more limited. The authors conclude that only a few studies included balanced measures on multiple performance dimensions. Considering the need for integrated care and chronic care improvement, the further development of these models for guiding improvements in integrated care settings and their specific context factors is suggested.

29.6 Matters of Integration in Technology Design for Ageing People

The demographic trend of an ageing society has triggered a range of new products and services. The Ambient Assisted Living program alone (2008–2013) had a budget of 700 million €, half of which was public funding (European-Comission 2015). A number of areas spanning the fields of engineering, information technology and Human-Computer Interaction (HCI) have developed various assisted living technologies and care systems targeted at the 'elderly'.

However, the 'fool proof' designs currently developed for ageing people—or better their stereotypes—do not match the everyday lives, creative capital and identities of ageing people. These constitute a group that spans from the 'young old' still physically and mentally capable of living independently to the 'old old' with failing health and no longer able to conduct an independent life (Laslett 1991). This group is far from being homogeneous (Peine and Neven 2011). Not only is there great variety in the everyday lives, needs and motivations of ageing people, these needs and motivations are also continuously changing with the changing capabilities and routines of an ageing body, which is the characteristic that unites them.

In a study of the literature in both gerontology and Human Computer Interaction (HCI) about the social relationships of older adults, (Lindley et al. 2008) found the shared tendency to ignore heterogeneity. As emphasized in (Durick et al. 2013), despite one of the central tenets of HCI being 'know your user', HCI research into technologies for ageing people prioritizes technology over users: "the outcome is that ageing people are subsequently defined in relation to their use of the selected technology, which is then adapted to their supposed 'specific needs'" (e.g. Östlund (2005); cited in Durick et al. (2013)).

Gerontechnology specifically, often underlies the assumption that without a technological intervention, users are somehow incapable of engaging in cognitive or physical activity (Östlund 2005; Rogers and Marsden 2013). As a study of the relationship between the 'elderly' and technological products and services, gerontechnology emphasizes the need for "compensation" (of declining cognitive and physical abilities) and "prevention" (of the consequences of such declining abilities). While existing technological solutions informed by these principles offer potential, they are unlikely to apply to all users or to remain appropriate in the long term.

Fozard acknowledges the transitional quality of old age and suggests that designing for an ageing body means that designs cannot stop with the use of a designed solution (Fozard 2002). It must continue through its use: "gerontechnology significantly expands the philosophy of human factors engineering and consumer oriented product design because the interaction between individual aging and secular changes in the environment over time is not static" (Fozard 2002), cited in (Durick et al. 2013). This position is echoed in engineering by (McBryan et al. 2008) with a proposition for how to design complex and dynamic home care systems, and by (Durick et al. 2013) in HCI. Similarly in ICT, (Winthereik and Jørgen 2007) advocate the need of developing ICT infrastructures in support of integrated care that acknowledge that organizational practices, roles and identities are mutually transformed and entirely new practices are created simultaneously.

With this *variety* and *ongoing change*, the solution cannot lie in simply 'matching better' at the drawing table. As noted by (Hernandez-Encuentra et al. 2009) in their survey on older, frequent users of technology, 'avoiding' one's loss of ability by introducing a technology to support or augment one's declining abilities may lead to technology "assimilation" (when not rejection) and this is not necessarily conducive to wellbeing.

We argue that empowering elderly people to resourcefully address the challenges of ageing, such as skills and self-images that are continuously changing, requires new forms of openness in the materiality and functionality of designs. It requires designs that can adapt and remain appropriate for the wide variety of situations they may end up in.

Countering stereotypes of elderly people and addressing the problem of inflexible technologies designed on the basis of 'ageing myths' (Durick et al. 2013) requires a design disposition that views ageing as something positive and places emphasis on active and healthy ageing (including facilitating autonomous living and integrated care). In line with this view, technology design for ageing people should consider elderly people not as technologically illiterate, but technologically differently skilled, and incorporate the idea of technology generations (Docampo Rama et al. 2001). In this idea, elderly people are certainly very well capable of creatively finding solutions to challenges they encounter as they age (such as deteriorating skills and changing self-images).

From a societal standpoint, such an approach promotes a view on ageing to technology developers at large that does not see ageing as a problem but an achievement, and that sees elderly people not just as 'old old' but as a broader category of people that are differently skilled (Neven 2011) but certainly resourceful, and very much capable of creatively finding solutions to the wide variety of challenges they encounter as they age. The impact of this approach can be significant, as it has the potential to empower a larger, growing group of ageing population and support them to negotiate their changing bodily and mental skills while remaining in control of their own lives.

From an economic standpoint, the approach has impact in several ways. It has the potential to open up a new market targeted to the 'young old', or Third Age people, which will broaden the potential base of users of products and services for ageing people, and possibly generate ideas and innovations for resourceful living that can be rewarding and fulfilling for all ages. It also introduces new ways of using technology for design and innovation that enable to avoid the waste of investment and lack of adoption of existing products and services for ageing people conceived for single-use scenarios and single functionalities.

An application of this approach is the project *Resourceful Ageing* at Delft University of Technology in the Netherlands (Giaccardi et al. 2016). This interdisciplinary project focuses on how to empower elderly people to live longer and more resilient lives. It steps away from the stereotype of ageing people as frail, passive and technologically incompetent. Ageing people are very well capable of creatively dealing with the high variety of challenges they encounter as they age, and use the everyday things that surround them as resources. However, the 'foolproof' designs currently developed for them do not allow for such resourcefulness. Think of how a walking cane is used 'in practice' also to reach things, push a button or call the neighbour upstairs (Forchhammer 2006). The project researches how to design products and services *for* and *with* elderly people that can adapt and be improvised with while in use. The approach is facilitated via a 'research-through-design' process that enlists as participants a community of both Third Age people and the things they ordinarily use and 'mis-use' (from mundane objects to everyday technologies) across a living lab of sixteen households. Together with the elderly community, this community of familiar objects is instrumented with small wireless sensors, and data on their daily lives and interactions with their ageing owners are gathered and analysed in support of design ideation and conceptualization of novel products and services for older adults.

We believe the understandings that underpin this project are fundamental and can be useful also to the development of integrated care systems.

29.7 Lessons Learned and Outlook

Most models of chronic care that have been planned usually focus on a single disease, a single healthcare provider or a single standard transition. Given the clustering of conditions and complexity of geriatric patients these models are unsuitable in geriatric care, leading to undertreatment, overtreatment or mistreating.

Comprehensive and coordinated systems of care focusing on the older patient with several chronic diseases, several providers and different kinds of transitions are lacking.

Not only are new models of care of the geriatric patient needed but also models must be individualized according to national and regional specificities of the population, and the health and social policies. Moreover, research is needed about the effectiveness of those models, comparing outcomes related to chronic diseases, function, cognition, quality of life, life expectancy, mortality and costs. Nevertheless, the heterogeneity of the geriatric patient makes that an effective model applied in a specific population is not suitable for other groups/populations of patients.

Effective communication across all the healthcare providers involved might be a key factor in efficiency of integrated care models. New information technologies may help organizing, summarizing and integrating clinical and social data delivered by different healthcare providers, so that a case manager can establish a single care plan prioritizing demands and goals, that is shared with all the partners providing care. Ideally, clinical informatics systems must allow continuous interaction with the patient and caregivers, who can report their feedback about interventions or present new problems and ask for advice. Distance technologies for patient monitoring allow early identification of decompensations, medication error and ineffective treatment, triggering prompt interventions, with less time and human resources spent than in standard consultations. However, it is also important to acknowledge that in the design of such technologies, older people must be considered more holistically, not just as patients. For such technologies to be effective, societally relevant and economically sustainable, designs must allow for some sort of resourcefulness on the part of the elderly. Older people must be able to incorporate technologies for integrated care systems in the uniqueness and variety of their own lives. Therefore, systems and technologies must be designed with this principle in mind.

References

Barnett, K., Mercer, S. W., Norbury, M., Watt, G., Wyke, S., & Guthrie, B. (2012). Epidemiology of multimorbidity and implications for health care, research, and medical education: A cross-sectional study. *Lancet, 380*, 37–43.

Beland, F., Bergman, H., Lebel, P., Clarfield, A. M., Tousignant, P., Contandriopoulos, A. P., & Dallaire, L. (2006). A system of integrated care for older persons with disabilities in Canada: Results from a randomized controlled trial. *The Journals of Gerontology. Series A, Biological Sciences and Medical Sciences, 61*, 367–373.

Bergman, H., Beland, F., Lebel, P., Contandriopoulos, A. P., Tousignant, P., Brunelle, Y., Kaufman, T., Leibovich, E., Rodriguez, R., & Clarfield, M. (1997). Care for Canada's frail elderly population: fragmentation or integration? *CMAJ, 157*, 1116–1121.

Bernabei, R., Landi, F., Gambassi, G., Sgadari, A., Zuccala, G., Mor, V., Rubenstein, L. Z., & Carbonin, P. (1998). Randomised trial of impact of model of integrated care and case management for older people living in the community. *British Medical Journal, 316*, 1348–1351.

Bharucha, A. J., Pandav, R., Shen, C., Dodge, H. H., & Ganguli, M. (2004). Predictors of nursing facility admission: A 12-year epidemiological study in the United States. *Journal of the American Geriatrics Society, 52*, 434–439.

Bielaszka-Duvernay, C. (2011). The 'Grace' model: In-home assessments lead to better care for dual eligibles. *Health Affairs (Millwood), 30*, 431–434.

Bird, S. R., Kurowski, W., Dickman, G. K. & Kronborg, I. 2007. Integrated care facilitation for older patients with complex health care needs reduces hospital demand. *Australian Health Review, 31*, 451–461. Discussion 449–450.

Bodenheimer, T. (1999). Long-term care for frail elderly people—The On Lok model. *The New England Journal of Medicine, 341*, 1324–1328.

Boonyasopun, U., Aree, P., & Avant, K. C. (2008). Effect of an empowerment-based nutrition promotion program on food consumption and serum lipid levels in hyperlipidemic thai elderly. *Nursing & Health Sciences, 10*, 93–100.

Borgenicht, K., Carty, E., & Feigenbaum, L. Z. (1997). Community resources for frail older patients. *The Western Journal of Medicine, 167*, 291–294.

Byrne, D., Goeree, M. S., Hiedemann, B., & Stern, S. (2009). Formal home health care, informal care, and family decision making. *International Economic Review, 50*, 1205–1242.

Capistrant, B. D. (2016). Caregiving for older adults and the caregivers' health: An epidemiologic review. *Current Epidemiology Reports, 3*, 72. doi:10.1007/s40471-016-0064-x.

Centers_For_Disease_Control_And_Prevention. (2013). *Healthy places terminology* [Online]. Accessed February 22, 2016, from http://www.cdc.gov/healthyplaces/terminology.htm

Challis, D., Darton, R., Johnson, L., Stone, M., & Traske, K. (1991). An evaluation of an alternative to long-stay hospital care for frail elderly patients: II. Costs and effectiveness. *Age and Ageing, 20*, 245–254.

Chappell, N. L., Dlitt, B. H., Hollander, M. J., Miller, J. A., & Mcwilliam, C. (2004). Comparative costs of home care and residential care. *Gerontologist, 44*, 389–400.

Chau, P. H., Woo, J., Kwok, T., Chan, F., Hui, E., & Chan, K. C. (2012). Usage of community services and domestic helpers predicted institutionalization of elders having functional or cognitive impairments: A 12-month longitudinal study in Hong Kong. *Journal of the American Medical Directors Association, 13*, 169–175.

Cohen-Mansfield, J., & Wirtz, P. W. (2011). Predictors of entry to the nursing home: Does length of follow-up matter? *Archives of Gerontology and Geriatrics, 53*, 309–315.

Colombo, F., Llena-Nozal, A., Mercier, J., & Tjadens, F. (2011). *Help wanted? Providing and paying for long-term Care.* OECD.

Counsell, S. R., Callahan, C. M., Buttar, A. B., Clark, D. O., & Frank, K. I. (2006). Geriatric resources for assessment and care of elders (Grace): A new model of primary care for low-income seniors. *Journal of the American Geriatrics Society, 54*, 1136–1141.

Counsell, S. R., Callahan, C. M., Clark, D. O., Tu, W., Buttar, A. B., Stump, T. E., & Ricketts, G. D. (2007). Geriatric care management for low-income seniors: A randomized controlled trial. *JAMA, 298*, 2623–2633.

Counsell, S. R., Callahan, C. M., Tu, W., Stump, T. E., & Arling, G. W. (2009). Cost analysis of the geriatric resources for assessment and care of elders care management intervention. *Journal of the American Geriatrics Society, 57*, 1420–1426.

Crawford Shearer, N. B., Fleury, J. D., & Belyea, M. (2010). Randomized control trial of the health empowerment intervention: Feasibility and impact. *Nursing Research, 59*, 203–211.

Decostera, V. A., & Georgea, L. (2005). An empowerment approach for elders living with diabetes: A pilot study of a community-based self-help Group—The diabetes club. *Journal of Educational Gerontology, 31*(9).

Docampo Rama, M., Ridder, H. D., & Bouma, H. (2001). Technology generation and age in using layered user interfaces. *Gerontotechnology, 1*, 25–40.

Drageset, J., Natvig, G. K., Eide, G. E., Clipp, E. C., Bondevik, M., Nortvedt, M. W., & Nygaard, H. A. (2008). Differences in health-related quality of life between older nursing home residents without cognitive impairment and the general population of Norway. *Journal of Clinical Nursing, 17*, 1227–1236.

Durick, J., Robertson, T., Brereton, M., Vetere, F., & Nansen, B. (2013). Dispelling ageing myths in technology design. In H. Shen, R. Smith, J. Paay, P. Calder, & T. Wyeld (Eds.), *Ozchi '13 Proceedings of the 25th Australian Computer-Human Interaction Conference: Augmentation, Application, Innovation, Collaboration*. ACM: Flinders University, Adelaide, Australia.

Eklund, K., & Wilhelmson, K. (2009). Outcomes of coordinated and integrated interventions targeting frail elderly people: A systematic review of randomised controlled trials. *Health and Social Care in the Community, 17*, 447–458.

Eng, C., Pedulla, J., Eleazer, G. P., Mccann, R., & Fox, N. (1997). Program of all-inclusive care for the elderly (Pace): An innovative model of integrated geriatric care and financing. *Journal of the American Geriatrics Society, 45*, 223–232.

European_Comission. (2015). *The active and assisted living joint programme* [Online]. https://ec.europa.eu/digital-agenda/en/active-and-assisted-living-joint-programme-aal-jp

Fabbricotti, I. N., Janse, B., Looman, W. M., De Kuijper, R., Van Wijngaarden, J. D., & Reiffers, A. (2013). Integrated care for frail elderly compared to usual care: A study protocol of a quasi-experiment on the effects on the frail elderly, their caregivers, health professionals and health care costs. *BMC Geriatrics, 13*, 31.

Figar, S., Galarza, C., Petrlik, E., Hornstein, L., Rodriguez Loria, G., Waisman, G., Rada, M., Soriano, E. R., & De Quiros, F. G. (2006). Effect of education on blood pressure control in elderly persons: A randomized controlled trial. *American Journal of Hypertension, 19*, 737–743.

Forchhammer, H. G. (2006). The woman who used her walking stick as a telefone: The use of utilities in praxis. In A. C. O. Dreier (Ed.), *Doing things with things: The design and use of everyday objects*. Ashgate.

Fozard, J. L. (2002). Gerontechnology-beyond ergonomics and universal design. *Gerontechnology, 1*, 137–139.

Friedman, S. M., Steinwachs, D. M., Rathouz, P. J., Burton, L. C., & Mukamel, D. B. (2005). Characteristics predicting nursing home admission in the program of all-inclusive care for elderly people. *Gerontologist, 45*, 157–166.

Gaugler, J. E., Duval, S., Anderson, K. A., & Kane, R. L. (2007). Predicting nursing home admission in the U.S: A meta-analysis. *BMC Geriatrics, 7*, 13.

Gellis, Z. D., Kenaley, B. L., & Ten Have, T. (2014). Integrated telehealth care for chronic illness and depression in geriatric home care patients: The integrated telehealth education and activation of mood (I-Team) study. *Journal of the American Geriatrics Society, 62*, 889–895.

Giaccardi, E., Kuijer, L., & Neven, L. (2016). Design for resourceful ageing: Intervening in the ethics of gerontechnology. In *Proceedings of the 50th Design Research Society (DRS) Conference 2016*. Brighton: Uk.

Gnjidic, D., Stanaway, F. F., Cumming, R., Waite, L., Blyth, F., Naganathan, V., Handelsman, D. J., & Le Couteur, D. G. (2012). Mild cognitive impairment predicts institutionalization among older men: A population-based cohort study. *PLoS One, 7*, E46061.

Gonzalez-Colaco Harmand, M., Meillon, C., Rullier, L., Avila-Funes, J. A., Bergua, V., Dartigues, J. F., & Amieva, H. (2014). Cognitive decline after entering a nursing home: A 22-year follow-up study of institutionalized and noninstitutionalized elderly people. *Journal of the American Medical Directors Association, 15*, 504–508.

Gröne, O. & Garcia-Barbero, M. 2002. *Trends in integrated care–Reflections on conceptual issues* (Eur/02/5037864). Copenhagen: World Health Organization.

Hebert, R. (1997). Functional decline in old age. *Canadian Medical Association Journal, 157*, 1037–1045.

Hebert, R. (2009). Home care: From adequate funding to integration of services. *Healthcare Papers, 10*, 58–64. Discussion 79–83.

Hebert, R., Durand, P. J., Dubuc, N., Tourigny, A., & Group, P. (2003). Frail elderly patients. New model for integrated service delivery. *Canadian Family Physician, 49*, 992–997.

Hebert, R., Raiche, M., Dubois, M. F., Gueye, N. R., Dubuc, N., Tousignant, M., & Group, P. (2010). Impact of prisma, a coordination-type integrated service delivery system for frail older people in Quebec (Canada): A quasi-experimental study. *Journal of Gerontology. Series B Psychological Sciences and Social Sciences, 65b*, 107–118.

Hernandez-Encuentra, E., Pousada, M., & Gomez-Zuniga, B. (2009). ICT and older people: Beyond usability. *Educational Gerontology, 35*, 226–245.

Hollander, M. J. (2001). *Final report of the study on the comparative cost analysis of home care and residential care services.* Victoria, BC: Health Transition Fund, Health Canada.

Hutt, R., Rosen, R., & Mccauley, J. (2004). *Case-managing long-term conditions: What impact does it have in the treatment of older people?* London: King's Fund.

Hux, M. J., O'brien, B. J., Iskedjian, M., Goeree, R., Gagnon, M., & Gauthier, S. (1998). Relation between severity of Alzheimer's disease and costs of caring. *CMAJ, 159*, 457–465.

Inouye, S. K., Studenski, S., Tinetti, M. E., & Kuchel, G. A. (2007). Geriatric syndromes: Clinical, research, and policy implications of a core geriatric concept. *Journal of the American Geriatrics Society, 55*, 780–791.

Janse, B., Huijsman, R., De Kuyper, R. D., & Fabbricotti, I. N. (2014). The effects of an integrated care intervention for the frail elderly on informal caregivers: A quasi-experimental study. *BMC Geriatrics, 14*, 58.

Jones, P. S., Winslow, B. W., Lee, J. W., Burns, M., & Zhang, X. E. (2011). Development of a caregiver empowerment model to promote positive outcomes. *Journal of Family Nursing, 17*, 11–28.

Kane, R. L., Illston, L. H., & Miller, N. A. (1992). Qualitative analysis of the program of all-inclusive care for the elderly (Pace). *Gerontologist, 32*, 771–780.

Kochera, A., Straight, A., & Guterbock, T. (2005). *Beyond 50.05: A report to the nation on livable communities: Creating environments for successful aging.* Washington: American Association of Retired Persons, Public Policy Institute.

Kodner, D. L. (2006). Whole-system approaches to health and social care partnerships for the frail elderly: An exploration of North American models and lessons. *Health and Social Care in the Community, 14*, 384–390.

Landi, F., Onder, G., Russo, A., Tabaccanti, S., Rollo, R., Federici, S., Tua, E., Cesari, M., & Bernabei, R. (2001). A new model of integrated home care for the elderly: Impact on hospital use. *Journal of Clinical Epidemiology, 54*, 968–970.

Langa, K. M., Chernew, M. E., Kabeto, M. U., Herzog, A. R., Ofstedal, M. B., Willis, R. J., Wallace, R. B., Mucha, L. M., Straus, W. L., & Fendrick, A. M. (2001). National estimates of the quantity and cost of informal caregiving for the elderly with dementia. *Journal of General Internal Medicine, 16*, 770–778.

Laslett, P. (1991). *A fresh map of life: The emergence of the third age.* Cambridge, MA: Harvard University Press.

Lindley, S. E., Harper, R. & Sellen, A. 2008. Designing for elders: Exploring the complexity of relationships in later life. In *Proceedings of the 22nd British HCI Group Annual Conference on People and Computers: Culture, Creativity, Interaction.*

Lopez-Hartmann, M., Wens, J., Verhoeven, V. & Remmen, R. 2012. The effect of caregiver support interventions for informal caregivers of community-dwelling frail elderly: A systematic review. *International Journal of Integrated Care, 12.*

Luppa, M., Luck, T., Weyerer, S., Konig, H. H., Brahler, E., & Riedel-Heller, S. G. (2010). Prediction of institutionalization in the elderly. A systematic review. *Age and Ageing, 39,* 31–38.

Lyttle, D. J., & Ryan, A. (2010). Factors influencing older patients' participation in care: A review of the literature. *International Journal of Older People Nursing, 5,* 274–282.

Macadam, M. (2015). Prisma: Program of research to integrate the services for the maintenance of autonomy. A system-level integration model in Quebec. *International Journal of Integrated Care, 15,* E018.

Mcbryan, T., Mcgee-Lennon, M. R. & Gray, P. (2008). An integrated approach to supporting interaction evolution in home care systems. In *Proceedings of the First International Conference on Pervasive Technologies Related to Assistive Environments.* Athens, Greece: ACM.

Mcconnell, E. S., Pieper, C. F., Sloane, R. J., & Branch, L. G. (2002). Effects of cognitive performance on change in physical function in long-stay nursing home residents. *The Journals of Gerontology. Series A, Biological Sciences and Medical Sciences, 57,* M778–M784.

Meret-Hanke, L. A. (2011). Effects of the program of all-inclusive care for the elderly on hospital use. *Gerontologist, 51,* 774–785.

Metzger, M. H., Barberger-Gateau, P., Dartigues, J. F., Letenneur, L., & Commenges, D. (1997). Predictive factors for institutionalization in the context of geriatric planning in the Gironde Department (France). *Revue d'Épidémiologie et de Santé Publique, 45,* 203–213.

Minkman, M., Ahaus, K., & Huijsman, R. (2007). Performance improvement based on integrated quality management models: What evidence do we have? A systematic literature review. *International Journal for Quality in Health Care, 19,* 90–104.

Moore, A., Patterson, C., White, J., House, S. T., Riva, J. J., Nair, K., Brown, A., Kadhim-Saleh, A., & Mccann, D. (2012). Interprofessional and integrated care of the elderly in a family health team. *Canadian Family Physician, 58,* E436–E441.

Mukamel, D. B., Peterson, D. R., Temkin-Greener, H., Delavan, R., Gross, D., Kunitz, S. J., & Williams, T. F. (2007). Program characteristics and enrollees' outcomes in the program of all-inclusive care for the elderly (pace). *The Milbank Quarterly, 85,* 499–531.

Mukamel, D. B., Temkin-Greener, H., Delavan, R., Peterson, D. R., Gross, D., Kunitz, S., & Williams, T. F. (2006). Team performance and risk-adjusted health outcomes in the program of all-inclusive care for the elderly (pace). *Gerontologist, 46,* 227–237.

Neven, L. B. M. 2011. *Representations of the old and ageing in the design of the new and emerging: Assessing the design of ambient intelligence technologies for older people.* PhD Thesis. University Of Twente, Netherlands.

Okamoto, K., Hasebe, Y., & Harasawa, Y. (2007). Caregiver psychological characteristics predict discontinuation of care for disabled elderly at home. *International Journal of Geriatric Psychiatry, 22,* 1110–1114.

Ostbye, T., & Crosse, E. (1994). Net economic costs of dementia in Canada. *Canadian Medical Association Journal, 151,* 1457–1464.

Östlund, B. (2005). Design paradigms and misunderstood technology: The case of older users. In B. Jæger (Ed.), *Young technologies in old hands: An international view on senior citizen's utilization of Ict.* Djøf Forlag: Copenhagen.

Peine, A., & Neven, L. (2011). *Social-structural lag revisited. Gerontechnology, 10*(3), 129–139.

Poku, M. (2015). The program of all-inclusive care for the elderly model: Lessons for the medicare-medicaid coordination office. *Journal of the American Geriatrics Society, 63,* 2223–2224.

Rabiei, L., Mostafavi, F., Masoudi, R., & Hassanzadeh, A. (2013). The effect of family-based intervention on empowerment of the elders. *Journal of Education and Health Promotion, 2,* 24.

Ranmuthugala, G., Nepal, B., Brown, L., & Percival, R. (2009). Impact of home based long term care on informal carers. *Australian Family Physician, 38,* 618–620.

Riano, D., Real, F., Lopez-Vallverdu, J. A., Campana, F., Ercolani, S., Mecocci, P., Annicchiarico, R., & Caltagirone, C. (2012). An ontology-based personalization of health-care knowledge to support clinical decisions for chronically ill patients. *Journal of Biomedical Informatics, 45,* 429–446.

Robertson, R., Sonola, L., Honeyman, M., Brooke, B., & Kothari, S. (2014). *Specialists in out-of-hospital settings findings from six case studies.* London: The King's Fund.

Rogers, R. (2011). *Planning and delivering continuing care retirement communities.* Bristol: Tetlow King Planning.

Rogers, Y., & Marsden, G. (2013). Does he take sugar?: Moving beyond the rhetoric of compassion. *Interactions, 20,* 48–57.

Roland, M., & Paddison, C. (2013). Better management of patients with multimorbidity. *British Medical Journal, 346,* F2510.

Ryan, D., Barnett, R., Cott, C., Dalziel, W., Gutmanis, I., Jewell, D., Kelley, M. L., Liu, B., & Puxty, J. (2013). Geriatrics, interprofessional practice, and interorganizational collaboration: A knowledge-to-practice intervention for primary care teams. *The Journal of Continuing Education in the Health Professions, 33,* 180–189.

Salminen, M., Vire, J., Viikari, L., Vahlberg, T., Isoaho, H., Lehtonen, A., Viitanen, M., Arve, S., & Eloranta, S. (2017, February 17). Predictors of institutionalization among home-dwelling older Finnish people: A 22-year follow-up study. *Aging Clinical and Experimental Research.* doi:10.1007/s40520-016-0722-3 [Epub ahead of print].

Sarma, S., Hawley, G., & Basu, K. (2009). Transitions in living arrangements of Canadian seniors: Findings from the nphs longitudinal data. *Social Science & Medicine, 68,* 1106–1113.

Schulz, R., Belle, S. H., Czaja, S. J., Mcginnis, K. A., Stevens, A., & Zhang, S. (2004). Long-term care placement of dementia patients and caregiver health and well-being. *Journal of American Medical Association, 292,* 961–967.

Schulz, R., & Sherwood, P. R. (2008). Physical and mental health effects of family caregiving. *The American Journal of Nursing, 108,* 23–27. Quiz 27.

Scocco, P., Rapattoni, M., & Fantoni, G. (2006). Nursing home institutionalization: A source of eustress or distress for the elderly? *International Journal of Geriatric Psychiatry, 21,* 281–287.

Scott, J. L., Dawkins, S., Quinn, M. G., Sanderson, K., Elliott, K. E., Stirling, C., Schüz, B., & Robinson, A. (2016, August). Caring for the carer: a systematic review of pure technology-based cognitive behavioral therapy (TB-CBT) interventions for dementia carers. *Aging and Mental Health, 20*(8), 793–803. doi:10.1080/13607863.2015.1040724. Epub 2015 May 15.

Segelman, M., Szydlowski, J., Kinosian, B., Mcnabney, M., Raziano, D. B., Eng, C., Van Reenen, C., & Temkin-Greener, H. (2014). Hospitalizations in the program of all-inclusive care for the elderly. *Journal of the American Geriatrics Society, 62,* 320–324.

Shapiro, E., & Tate, R. B. (1985). Predictors of long term care facility use among the elderly. *Canadian Journal on Aging, 4,* 11–19.

Shearer, N. B., Fleury, J., Ward, K. A., & O'brien, A. M. (2012). Empowerment interventions for older adults. *Western Journal of Nursing Research, 34,* 24–51.

Smoliner, C., Norman, K., Wagner, K. H., Hartig, W., Lochs, H., & Pirlich, M. (2009). Malnutrition and depression in the institutionalised elderly. *The British Journal of Nutrition, 102,* 1663–1667.

Spoorenberg, S. L., Uittenbroek, R. J., Middel, B., Kremer, B. P., Reijneveld, S. A., & Wynia, K. (2013). Embrace, a model for integrated elderly care: Study protocol of a randomized controlled trial on the effectiveness regarding patient outcomes, service use, costs, and quality of care. *BMC Geriatrics, 13,* 62.

Spoorenberg, S. L., Wynia, K., Fokkens, A. S., Slotman, K., Kremer, H. P., & Reijneveld, S. A. (2015). Experiences of community-living older adults receiving integrated care based on the chronic care model: A qualitative study. *PLoS One, 10,* E0137803.

Stewart, M. J., Georgiou, A., & Westbrook, J. I. (2013). Successfully integrating aged care services: A review of the evidence and tools emerging from a long-term care program. *International Journal of Integrated Care, 13*, E003.

Tannenbaum, C., Martin, P., Tamblyn, R., Benedetti, A., & Ahmed, S. (2014). Reduction of inappropriate benzodiazepine prescriptions among older adults through direct patient education: The empower cluster randomized trial. *Journal of American Medical Association Internal Medicine, 174*, 890–898.

Tinetti, M. E., Inouye, S. K., Gill, T. M., & Doucette, J. T. (1995). Shared risk factors for falls, incontinence, and functional dependence. Unifying the approach to geriatric syndromes. *Journal of American Medical Association, 273*, 1348–1353.

Van Houtven, C. H., Coe, N. B., & Skira, M. M. (2013). The effect of informal care on work and wages. *Journal of Health Economics, 32*, 240–252.

Von Bonsdorff, M., Rantanen, T., Laukkanen, P., Suutama, T., & Heikkinen, E. (2006). Mobility limitations and cognitive deficits as predictors of institutionalization among community-dwelling older people. *Gerontology, 52*, 359–365.

Waddington, C. & Egger, D. 2008. *Integrated health services—What and why?* [Online]. World Health Organization. Accessed September 30, 2015, from http://www.who.int/healthsystems/service_delivery_techbrief1.pdf

Weissert, W. G. (1991). A new policy agenda for home care. *Health Affairs (Millwood), 10*, 67–77.

Weissert, W. G., Lesnick, T., Musliner, M., & Foley, K. A. (1997). Cost savings from home and community-based services: Arizona's capitated medicaid long-term care program. *Journal of Health Politics, Policy and Law, 22*, 1329–1357.

Wendt, D. A. (1998). Evaluation of medication management interventions for the elderly. *Home Healthcare Nurse, 16*, 612–617.

Wieland, D., Kinosian, B., Stallard, E., & Boland, R. (2013). Does medicaid pay more to a program of all-inclusive care for the elderly (pace) than for fee-for-service long-term care? *The Journals of Gerontology: Series A, 68*, 47–55.

Wieland, D., Lamb, V. L., Sutton, S. R., Boland, R., Clark, M., Friedman, S., Brummel-Smith, K., & Eleazer, G. P. (2000). Hospitalization in the program of all-inclusive care for the elderly (pace): Rates, concomitants, and predictors. *Journal of the American Geriatrics Society, 48*, 1373–1380.

Wiles, J. L., Leibing, A., Guberman, N., Reeve, J., & Allen, R. E. (2012). The meaning of "aging in place" to older people. *Gerontologist, 52*, 357–366.

Wiley-Exley, E., Domino, M. E., Maxwell, J., & Levkoff, S. E. (2009). Cost-effectiveness of integrated care for elderly depressed patients in the Prism-E study. *The Journal of Mental Health Policy and Economics, 12*, 205–213.

Winthereik, B. R. B., & Jørgen, P. (2007). Connecting practices: Ict infrastructures to support integrated care. *International Journal of Integrated Care, 7*, E16.

Woo, J., Ho, S. C., Yu, A. L., & Lau, J. (2000). An estimate of long-term care needs and identification of risk factors for institutionalization among Hong Kong Chinese aged 70 years and over. *The Journals of Gerontology. Series A, Biological Sciences and Medical Sciences, 55*, M64–M69.

Wynia, K., Kremer, B., Spoorenberg, S., Uittenbroek, R., & Reijneveld, S. (2014). *European Journal of Public Health, 24*, 206.

Yamada, Y., Siersma, V., Avlund, K., & Vass, M. (2012). Formal home help services and institutionalization. *Archives of Gerontology and Geriatrics, 54*, E52–E56.

You, E. C., Dunt, D. R., & Doyle, C. (2013). Case managed community aged care: What is the evidence for effects on service use and costs? *Journal of Aging and Health, 25*, 1204–1242.

You, E. C., Dunt, D., Doyle, C., & Hsueh, A. (2012). Effects of case management in community aged care on client and carer outcomes: A systematic review of randomized trials and comparative observational studies. *BMC Health Services Research, 12*, 395.

Part VI

Case Studies

Canada: Application of a Coordinated-Type Integration Model for Vulnerable Older People in Québec: The PRISMA Project

30

Réjean Hébert

30.1 Integrated Care in Québec and Canada

Canada is a confederation of ten provinces and three territories. In the province of Québec, the population is mostly French speaking. The health care system in Canada was developed in the sixties, based on a Beveridgian model of universal, public, tax-funded coverage of hospital and physician services. Under the Canadian constitution, health care is the responsibility of the provinces and territories. However, in 1966, the federal government set out four principles for implementing a national health care system: public administration, comprehensiveness (all "medically necessary" services), universality, and portability (between provinces). The Canada Health Act (1984) consolidated the four original principles and added a fifth: accessibility (without any financial barriers). Although not responsible for delivery of health care, the federal government used its spending power to introduce the public health care system and committed to partially fund provinces that complied with those principles. Originally, the federal share was 50%; now it is around 25%. The health care system in Canada covers hospital and physician services ("medically necessary"). Dental care, professional services (other than from physicians) provided outside hospitals, and drugs are not included, except in the province of Québec which introduced a universal mixed pharma care program in 1997. Hospital services are delivered through public or not-for-profit organizations. Physicians work mostly in private clinics and are paid directly by the government without overbilling.

The province of Québec set up its system in 1971 (Act Respecting Health and Social Services) with full integration of health and social services at the local, regional and provincial level. There was a Ministry of Health and Social Services, Regional Authorities for health and social services, and local institutions that

R. Hébert (✉)
Department of Management, Evaluation and Health Policy, School of Public Health, Université de Montréal, Montréal, QC, Canada
e-mail: Rejean.Hebert@UMontreal.ca

© Springer International Publishing AG 2017
V. Amelung et al. (eds.), *Handbook Integrated Care*,
DOI 10.1007/978-3-319-56103-5_30

integrate those services. Québec is still the only province in Canada to integrate health and social services. The Ministry sets policy, pays for physician services and allocates budgets to the 18 Regional Authorities. Regional authorities were responsible for adapting services to their particular population and allocating budgets to the local institutions. Locally, services are provided via hospitals, rehabilitation centres, youth centres, and nursing homes. In addition, Local Community Services Centres (Centres locaux de services communautaires, CLSC) were designed to be the primary care portal for health and social services in the community.

Private for-profit operations are virtually non-existent in the Québec health care system, except for residential facilities for older people. Voluntary agencies are well developed, particularly for home services. Social economy agencies (not-for-profit) are also very active in providing support for domestic tasks and personal care.

30.2 Integrated Care in Practice

30.2.1 Problem Definition

The population of Canada and Québec is aging quickly. In 2014, 17% of the population in Québec (1.4 million people) was over 65 years old. Since the baby boom in the fifties, particularly in the French-speaking Québec population, it is expected that older people will make up over 25% of the population by 2031 (Azeredo and Payeur 2015). Despite the integration of health and social services, delivering services to a growing vulnerable older population was a challenge. Prior to 2003, many public organizations (hospitals, nursing homes, rehabilitation centres, CLSCs), together with social economy and voluntary agencies, delivered care, without coordination. Multiple assessments, delays, redundant services, gaps in services and multiple providers created inefficiencies, compromised service quality and increased costs probably unduly. There was a pressing need to integrate those services (Hébert 2010).

To address these challenges, two large experiments were carried out simultaneously from 1997 to 2001. First, the SIPA (Integrated Services for Older People: Services intégrés pour les personnes âgées) project in Montreal was an attempt to test a fully integrated model in the Québec context. Experimental implementation took place from 1999 to 2001 across two sites in Montréal, The SIPA team of professionals (case managers, nurses, physicians, physiotherapists, social workers) was responsible for the care of frail older people at home, with some services outsourced to the usual health care organizations. An evaluation of SIPA using a prospective randomized controlled trial demonstrated its efficacy in improving the use of home services instead of institutions (Béland et al. 2006). However, the capitation funding that was part of the model was never implemented in the experiment. Since the SIPA organization operated in parallel with the usual health care system, generalization of such a model was deemed difficult within the universal health care system in Québec. The SIPA model was abandoned after the experiment.

PRISMA (Program of Research to Integrate Services for the Maintenance of Autonomy) was the second large project designed to better fit the health care system in developing a coordinated-type integration model. PRISMA was developed by a steering committee including policy-makers at the provincial and regional levels, health care managers, clinicians and researchers. The coordination level of integration was originally suggested by Leutz (1999) as one of three types of integration (in addition to liaison and full integration), but at that time there was no model developed to operationalize it. Unlike fully integrated systems such as SIPA, this model includes all public, private and voluntary health and social service organizations involved in caring for older people in a given area. Each organization keeps its own structure but agrees to participate under an umbrella system and to adapt its operations and resources to the agreed requirements and processes. At this level, the integrated service delivery system is not just nested in the health care and social services system (like fully integrated models); it is embedded within it.

30.2.2 Description of the PRISMA Model

The PRISMA model comprises six components: (1) coordination between decision-makers and managers at the regional and local levels, (2) single entry point, (3) case management, (4) individualized service plans, (5) single assessment instrument coupled with a case-mix management system, and (6) computerized clinical chart.

Coordination between institutions is at the core of the PRISMA model. Coordination must be established at every level of the organizations. First, at the strategic level (governance), a Joint Governing Board (JGB) is created involving all health care and social services organizations and community agencies (public, private and voluntary) and the decision-makers agree on policies and orientations and what resources to allocate to the integrated system. Second, at the tactical level (management), a service coordination committee, mandated by the JGB and comprising public and community service representatives together with older people, monitors the service coordination mechanism and facilitates adaptation of the service continuum. Finally, at the operational level (clinical), a multidisciplinary team of practitioners surrounding the case manager evaluates patients' needs and delivers the required care and services.

The **single entry point** is the mechanism for accessing the services of all health care institutions and community organizations in the area for a frail senior with complex needs. It serves as a unique portal that older people, family caregivers and professionals can access by phone or written referral. A link is established with the Health Information Line available 24/7 to the general public in Québec. Callers are screened using a brief 7-item questionnaire (PRISMA-7) (Raîche et al. 2008) that has shown good levels of sensitivity and specificity in identifying older people with significant disabilities. PRISMA-7 is also used by health professionals in physicians' offices, emergency rooms, and flu shut clinics to screen older people. A detailed assessment of disabilities is then undertaken for those screened positive; individuals deemed eligible for the integrated service delivery are referred to a

case manager. The eligibility criteria are to be over 65 years old and present
significant disabilities as defined by a SMAF score over 15 or an Iso-SMAF Profile
over 4 (see Box 30.1).

**Box 30.1 Functional Autonomy Measurement System: SMAF (Système de
mesure de l'autonomie fonctionnelle)**

The SMAF (Hébert et al. 1988, 2001; McDowell 2006) measures functional
ability in five areas:

- Activities of daily living (ADL) (seven items)
- Mobility (six items)
- Communication (three items)
- Mental functions (five items)
- Instrumental activities of daily living (IADL) (eight items).

For each item, the disability is scored on a 5-point scale:

- 0: independent
- −0.5: with difficulty
- −1: needs supervision
- −2: needs help
- −3: dependent

The resources available to compensate for the disability are evaluated and
a handicap score is calculated. The stability of the resources is also assessed.
A disability score (out of −87) can be calculated, together with sub-scores for
each dimension.

A case-mix classification system based on the SMAF has been developed
(Dubuc et al. 2006). Fourteen Iso-SMAF profiles were generated using
cluster analysis techniques in order to define groups that are homogeneous
with regard to their profile.

- Profiles 1–3: slight disabilities in instrumental activities of daily
  living only.
- Profiles 4, 6 and 9: moderate disabilities predominantly in motor functions.
- Profiles 5, 7, 8 and 10: moderate disabilities predominantly in
  mental functions.
- Profiles 11–14: severe disabilities (those people are usually cared for in
  nursing homes).

The Iso-SMAF profiles are used to establish eligibility criteria for different
services and to calculate the organizations' required budget, based on the
disabilities of their patient groups (Tousignant et al. 2003, 2007).

The **Case Manager** (CM) model included in PRISMA draws directly from those described as a Clinical CM (Scharlach et al. 2001), Neighborhood Team (Eggert et al. 1990), or Basic CM (Phillips et al. 1988). The case manager is responsible for conducting a thorough assessment of the patient's needs, planning the required services, arranging patient access to these services, organizing and coordinating support, directing the multidisciplinary team of practitioners involved in the case, advocating for, monitoring and reassessing the patient. The CM is legitimate by the JGB for working in all institutions and services. The CM can be a nurse, social worker or other health professional and should be specifically trained. An ideal caseload is around 40 patients per CM. Figure 30.1 summarizes the flow of patients through the coordinated PRISMA model.

The **Individualized Service Plan** (ISP) results from the patient's overall assessment and summarizes the prescribed services and target objectives (Somme et al. 2009). The ISP is led by the CM and established at a meeting of the multidisciplinary team including all the main practitioners involved in caring for the older person. The ISP should be confirmed with the patient and informal caregivers so that they are empowered in the decision-making process.

The **single assessment instrument** is used to evaluate the needs of clients in all organizations and by all professionals working in home care organizations or in hospitals and institutions. The instrument implemented in the PRISMA model is the SMAF (French acronym for Functional Autonomy Measurement System),

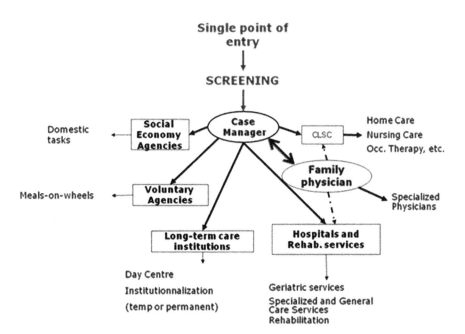

Fig. 30.1 Flow of patients through the coordinated PRISMA model (reproduced with permission from the Journal of Integrated Care—Emerald Group)

a 29-item scale developed according to the WHO classification of disabilities (see Box 30.1) (Hébert et al. 1988, 2001).

Finally, the PRISMA model includes a **Computerized Clinical Chart** (CCC) to facilitate communication between organizations and professionals. This shareable clinical chart specific to the care of elderly people uses the Québec Ministry of Health and Social Services Internet network and is interconnected to other clinical electronic records (hospitals, physicians' offices).

30.3   Experimental Implementation and Impact

After being pretested in the Bois-Francs area with promising results (Tourigny et al. 2004), the PRISMA model was implemented in July 2001 in three regions of the Eastern Townships in the province of Québec: (1) the city of Sherbrooke, an urban area (population: 144,000 of which 18,500 were over 65 years of age) with many institutions (university regional hospital, university geriatric institute, regional rehabilitation institution, and many nursing homes); (2) the rural Coaticook region (population: 16,500 of which 2300 were over 65) with no local hospital; and (3) the Granit region a rural area (population: 22,000of which 3300 were over 65) with a local hospital.

The PRISMA model was subject to rigorous evaluation, including an implementation study that sought to monitor the degree and the process of implementation, and an outcome study, using a population-based quasi-experimental design.

The implementation evaluation study was carried out using an embedded multiple case method (Yin 1994), with each region being a case. Mixed methods, quantitative and qualitative, were applied using multiple sources of evidence (policymakers, managers, clinicians, patients, caregivers, and administrative data). Multiple data collection methods were used: documentation analysis (minutes, charts, CCC data), individual interviews (policymakers, managers, clients, caregivers), focus groups (CM, clinicians), postal questionnaires (physicians), and standardized questionnaires. Detailed results from these studies can be found elsewhere (Hébert et al. 2005, 2008a, b). Postal questionnaires were used to measure the opinion of family physicians regarding the integrated service delivery network and CMs. The response was very positive, with CMs being perceived as very useful by family physicians (Milette et al. 2005).

A method was developed for monitoring the degree of implementation, based on specific indicators for each of the six elements of the PRISMA model (Hébert and Veil 2004). The indicators were weighted according to their importance and the different elements of the model were also weighted to obtain a score out of 100. Overall, the degree of implementation reached 70% after 2 years. This was the a priori threshold set for defining a significant degree of implementation. After 4 years of implementation, the rate reached 85% in Sherbrooke, 78% in Granit and 69% in Coaticook (Hébert et al. 2008a).

To evaluate the impact of the PRISMA model on health, satisfaction, empowerment and services utilization of frail older people, a population-based, quasi-experimental study was conducted with the three experimental and three comparison areas. From a random selection of people 75 years and over, 1501 persons identified as at risk for functional decline were recruited (728 experimental, 773 comparison). Over 4 years, participants were measured for disabilities (SMAF), unmet needs, satisfaction with services and empowerment. Information on utilization of health and social services was collected via bi-monthly telephone questionnaires (Hébert et al. 2010).

Over the last 2 years (when the implementation rate was over 70%), there was a 6% reduction of functional decline (62 fewer cases per 1000 individuals) in the experimental group ($p < 0.05$). In the fourth year of the study, the annual incidence of functional decline dropped by 14% in the experimental group (137 cases per 1000; $p < 0.001$), while the prevalence of unmet needs in the comparison region was nearly double the prevalence observed in the experimental region ($p < 0.001$). Satisfaction and empowerment were significantly higher in the experimental group ($p < 0.001$). For health services utilization, fewer visits to emergency rooms ($p < 0.001$) and hospitalizations ($p = 0.11$) than expected were observed in the experimental cohort (Hébert et al. 2010). Using growth-curve analysis, Dubuc et al. (2011) showed that the needs of elders living in the area where PRISMA was implemented were better met over time. An economic analysis comparing the cost of care in the experimental group, including the cost of the PRISMA component, to the comparison group showed that the costs were similar. This means that the PRISMA model was more efficient than the usual care.[1]

30.3.1 Dissemination and Replication

During the study in 2003, the Québec Minister of Health was convinced that the model would be successful (even before the results were formally published) and decided to undertake the major health care reform merging the different public organizations involved in caring for older people within a local area (hospitals, nursing homes and CLSCs) in the CSSSs (Health and Social Services Centres) (Levine 2007). This structural integration was seen by the Minister as providing strong support for improving the coordination of services. However, as demonstrated in other contexts, structural integration does not necessarily foster functional integration (Demers 2013). The reverse was actually observed in Québec over the first 4 years of the reform. According to the Québec Ministry of Health, the implementation rate of the PRISMA model, based on the same indicators developed in the experiment, was only on average 38% in 2008, although wider roll-out of the PRISMA model was included in the Ministry's 2005–2010 action plan (Gouvernement du Québec 2005). It was noted that the newly created CSSSs (health and social service centres) struggled to implement the strategic planning

---

[1] All the publications on the PRISMA model and experiments, in both French and English are available on the following website: http://www.prisma-qc.ca/cgi-cs/cs.waframe.index?lang=2

process and the reorganization of services. The roll-out of the PRISMA model was slowed considerably and even stopped momentarily in many regions because, first, the CSSSs' different programs continued to work in silos and, second, this new big organization in the system (the CSSS) no longer prioritized coordination committees and collaboration with the voluntary agencies, social economy enterprises and private providers also involved in delivering services for frail older people (INSPQ 2014).

This natural experiment showed that it is not always desirable or necessary to structurally integrate different providers into a common organization in order to implement a functional integration model like PRISMA. Nevertheless, after 10 years, implementation of the PRISMA model reached 70% across the province in 2014 (Fig. 30.2). Implementation of the computerized clinical chart, the sixth element of the PRISMA model, was delayed because the Ministry wanted to develop new, more powerful Web-based software. This allowed for the utilization of the management tool (Iso-SMAF Profiles) and completed the implementation of the fifth element of the PRISMA model. In 2014, a module to support the elaboration of the Individualized Service Plan and the allocation of services was added to the software, boosting the implementation of this element.

In 2015, a new structural reform was implemented in Québec, merging all the public institutions in a region, including rehabilitation and youth centres this time. These new Integrated Health and Social Services Centres (CISSSs) replaced also the regional authorities. From a three-tiered system (provincial, regional, local), Quebec moved toward a two-tiered system by abolishing the regional level. In each region, only one public institution provides all the health care and social services to the population. Although improving integrated services was one of the reasons for the reform, this new structural integration will likely have negative impacts on functional integration as it was the case in the 2003 reform.

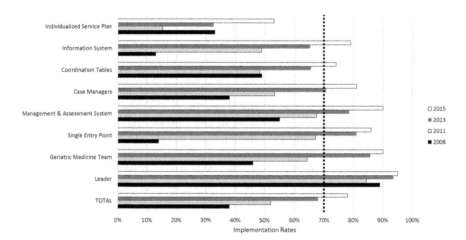

Fig. 30.2 Implementation rates of the PRISMA model in Québec, Canada from 2008 to 2015

The experience of the PRISMA model influenced integrated care models beyond Quebec. For example, in France, where the comparatively high number of actors involved in funding and delivering care to older people was seen to be a challenge for coordination, the PRISMA model was adapted in three experimental implementations (Somme et al. 2008). Following this experiment, the model was applied to people with dementia in the so-called MAIA model of care (Maison pour l'autonomie et l'intégration des malades d'Alzheimer) as part of the 2008–2012 Alzheimer Plan (République française 2008). In 2013, the MAIA model was extended to cover all frail older people, and over 350 MAIA homes were set up across France. The acronym MAIA was then used for Méthode d'Action pour l'Intégration des services d'aide et de soin dans le champ de l'Autonomie. The PRISMA model is also being implemented in several areas in Spain.

30.3.2 Lessons Learned and What's Ahead

The PRISMA model can be seen to be a good illustration of an effective transfer of scientific knowledge to public policy. The continuous presence, right from the beginning, of representatives from the Ministry of Health and Social Services and regional authorities on the PRISMA steering committee was one of the factors that led to this success.

However, wider dissemination of the model following the experimental phase was not optimal. Implementation has been very slow, due mainly to the structural reforms, delays in designing the new computerized clinical chart, and budget restrictions that slowed the recruitment of case managers. Additional financial resources to hire case managers were spread over a long period of time. One of Leutz's laws (1999) was confirmed: "Integration costs before it benefits". Despite the experiment showing that PRISMA was cost-efficient, implementation requires investments upfront to generate the expected benefits.

The role description and training requirements for case managers were not precise enough; in many areas, case managers received only minimal training. This was not sufficient to induce a real role change away from that taught by previous professional education. In some areas, there are still waiting lists to get access to case managers and the waiting time can be very long, with inevitable consequences for frail older people. The Joint Governing Boards are no longer active in many areas, not only because of the recent structural reform but also because this mechanism is not considered critical by new managers coming on board. Contrary to the experimental setup, administrative collection of data to generate indicators is not verified independently. There is also evidence that, when completing the instrument measuring implementation, some areas reported false results. In one area, we observed that the official rate was more than 10% over the actual one.

Institutionalization of an innovation is a challenge and there is a real risk of the system returning to its previous state without sustainable change. Although the PRISMA model is not very prescriptive and elements of the model can be adapted to the local context, it should be acknowledged that it is being implemented within complex organizations and networks in which self-regulation mechanisms can prevent any significant change (Begun 2003).

In PRISMA, a necessary seventh component was not included in the model, namely financing which is usually one component of integrated models (Kodner 2006). This was not possible since the Québec health care system is a universal, publicly funded, Beveridge-type system. Long-term care is included in the overall funding of health and social services. This arrangement makes it impossible to prioritize long-term care and home care, especially during a period of budget restrictions since with global funding, hospital care drives most of the budget. In the new CSSSs (and more so in the CISSSs) most of the funding is directed to hospitals and nursing homes, which leaves home care programs with insufficient funds to really make a difference in the way care is provided to frail older people with multiple care needs. Improving the efficacy of the PRISMA model and case managers' actions would require a specific funding scheme for long-term care modelled on the public long-time care insurance programs which are in place in many European and Asian countries (DaRoit and LeBihan 2010; Ikegami 2007). Following the needs assessment by the case manager, an allowance corresponding to the disability level of the frail older person could then be managed in order to outsource the appropriate services to the client. Such a financial incentive could give the case manager real power to obtain the necessary services from providers. Québec and Canada will have to move towards this type of funding scheme, coupled with the integration of services, in order to cope with the rapid aging of the population (Hébert 2011). An attempt to implement an autonomy insurance plan in Québec was unfortunately stopped for political reasons in 2014 (Hébert 2016).

PRISMA-type integration needs the funding model to be adapted in a Beveridgian context for long-term care by borrowing characteristics of social insurance systems. This type of integration can be facilitated in Bismarkian systems, where such funding is already in place. This was the case in France.

The PRISMA model has been adapted to other populations. In Québec, it is used for young patients with mental and physical disabilities. It could be used to meet the needs of patients with mental health problems.

Integrating services for a given population (e.g. frail older people) may conflict with disease-oriented integration (e.g. diabetes, cancer). According to another Leutz law (1999): "Your integration is my fragmentation". An older patient with diabetes, cardiovascular disease and cancer may have three different disease-oriented case managers and another from the frail older network. In such cases meta-integration mechanisms are necessary. With an elderly population with comorbidities, only the case manager from the frail older people network should get in touch with the patient and communicate with the other case managers, who would not deal directly with the patient.

The PRISMA model shows that it is feasible and efficacious to improve integration functionally without—or in spite of—structural integration and merging of organizations. Implementation of the innovation should be closely monitored and adequate resources should be allocated to support the implementation and training for professionals and managers. Funding is a key issue in integration, and budget incentives and mechanisms should be adapted to the integration model. The most difficult challenge is to institutionalize the innovation, given the complexity of health care systems.

References

Azeredo, A. C., & Payeur, F. F. (2015). Vieillissement démographique au Québec: comparaison avec les pays de l'OCDE. *Données statistiques en bref, 19*(3), 1–10.

Begun, J. W. (2003). Health care organizations as complex adaptive systems. In S. M. Mick & M. Wyttenbach (Eds.), *Advances in health care organization theory* (pp. 253–288). San Francisco: Jossey-Bass.

Béland, F., Bergman, H., Lebel, P., Clarfield, A. M., Tousignant, P., Contandriopoulos, A. P., et al. (2006). A system of integrated care for older persons with disabilities in Canada: Results from a randomized controlled trial. *Journals of Gerontology Series A: Biological Sciences and Medical Sciences, 61*, 367–373.

DaRoit, B., & LeBihan, B. (2010). Similar and yet so different: Cash-for-care in six European countries' long-term care policies. *Milbank Quarterly, 88*(3), 286–309.

Demers, L. (2013). Mergers and integrated care: The Quebec experience. *International Journal of Integrated Care*, Jan–Mar, URN:NBN:NL:UI:10-1-114229.

Dubuc, N., Hébert, R., Desrosiers, J., Buteau, M., & Trottier, L. (2006). Disability-based classification system for older people in integrated long-term care services: The Iso-SMAF profiles. *Archives of Gerontology and Geriatrics, 42*, 191–206.

Dubuc, N., Dubois, M. F., Gueye, R. N., Raîche, M., & Hébert, R.. (2011). Meeting the home care needs of disabled older persons living in the community: Do integrated services delivery make a difference? *BMC Geriatrics*, 11, 67. http://www.biomedcentral.com/1471-2/11/67

Eggert, G. M., Friedman, B., & Zimmer, J. G. (1990). Models of intensive case management. *Journal of Gerontological Social Work, 15*(3), 75–101.

Gouvernement du Québec. (2005). Un défi de solidarité: Les services aux aînés en perte d'autonomie. Plan d'action 2005–2010. Québec.

Hébert, R. (2010). Home care: From adequate funding to integration of services. *Healthcare Papers, 10*(1), 58–69.

Hébert, R. (2011). Public long-term care insurance: A way to ensure sustainable continuity of care for frail older people. *Healthcare Papers, 11*(1), 69–75.

Hébert, R. (2016). Still-born autonomy insurance plan in Quebec: Example of a public long-term care insurance system in Canada. *Healthcare Papers, 15*(4), 45–50.

Hébert, R., & Veil, A. (2004). Monitoring the degree of implementation of an integrated delivery system. *International Journal of Integrated Care, 4*, e1–e11.

Hébert, R., Carrier, R., & Bilodeau, A. (1988). The functional autonomy measurement system (SMAF): Description and validation of an instrument for the measurement of handicaps. *Age and Ageing, 17*, 293–302.

Hébert, R., Guilbault, J., Desrosiers, J., & Dubuc, N. (2001). The functional autonomy measurement system (SMAF): A clinical-based instrument for measuring disabilities and handicaps in older people. *Geriatrics Today: Journal of Canadian Geriatrics Society, 4*(3), 141–147.

Hébert, R., Tourigny, A., & Gagnon, M. (2005). *Integrated service delivery to ensure persons' functional autonomy* (323 p). St-Hyacinthe: Edisem.

Hébert, R., Dubois, M. F., Dubuc, N., Tousignant, M., Raîche, M., & Veil, A. (2008a). Evaluation of the implementation of PRISMA, a coordination-type integrated service delivery system for frail older people in Quebec. *Journal of Integrated Care, 16*(6), 4–14.

Hébert, R., Tourigny, A., & Raîche, M. (2008b). *Integration of services for disabled people: Research leading to action* (542 p). St-Hyacinthe: Edisem.

Hébert, R., Raîche, M., Dubois, M. F., Gueye, N. R., Dubuc, N., Tousignant, M., & The PRISMA Group. (2010). Impact of PRISMA, a coordination-type integrated service delivery system for frail older people in Quebec (Canada): A quasi-experimental study. *Journal of Gerontology Series B: Social Sciences, 65*(B), 107–118.

Ikegami, N. (2007). Rationale, design and sustainability of long-term care insurance in Japan—in retrospect. *Social Policy and Society, 6*(3), 423–434.

INSPQ. (2014). *Synthèse des connaissances sur les conditions de mise en œuvre des réseaux de services intégrés aux personnes âgées*. Québec: Institut national de santé publique du Québec.

Kodner, D. L. (2006). Whole-system approaches to health and social care partnerships for the frail elderly: An exploration of North American models and lessons. *Health & Social Care in the Community, 14*, 384–390.

Leutz, W. N. (1999). Five laws for integrating medical and social services: Lessons from the United States and the United Kingdom. *Milbank Quarterly, 77*, 77–110.

Levine, D. (2007). The reform of health and social services in Quebec. *Healthcare Papers, 8*(special issue), 46–54.

McDowell, I. (2006). *Measuring health: A guide to rating scales and Questionnaires*. New York: Oxford University Press.

Milette, L., Hébert, R., & Veil, A. (2005). Early perceptions of family physicians regarding the introduction of integrated service delivery networks for older people. *Canadian Family Physician Journal, 51*, 1104–1105.

Phillips, B. R., Kemper, P., & Applebaum, R. A. (1988). The evaluation of the national long term care demonstration. Chap. 4. Case management under channeling. *Health Services Research, 23*(1), 67–81.

Raîche, M., Hébert, R., & Dubois, M. F. (2008). PRISMA-7: A case-finding tool to identify older adults with moderate to severe disabilities. *Archives of Gerontology and Geriatrics, 47*(1), 9–18.

République française. (2008). Quality labelling throughout the country for "single points of contact", the "Maisons pour l'Autonomie et l'Intégration des malades Alzheimer" (MAIA). http://www.plan-alzheimer.gouv.fr/measure-no4.html

Scharlach, A. E., Giunta, N., & Mills-Dick, K. (2001). *Case management in long-term care integration: An overview of current programs and evaluations*. Paper written for California Center for Long-Term Care Integration, 84 p.

Somme, D., Trouvé, H., Couturier, Y., Carrier, S., Gagnon, D., Lavallart, B., Hébert, R., Cretin, C., & Saint-Jean, O. (2008). Prisma France: Implementation program of an innovation in health and services system for disabled people. Adaptation of a case-management based integration model. *Revue d'épidémiologie et de santé publique, 56*, 54–62.

Somme, D., Bonin, L., Lebel, P., Hébert, R., & Blanchard, F. (2009). Development of an individualized service plan tool and rules for case management in Québec. *Care Management Journals, 10*(3), 89–99.

Tourigny, A., Durand, P., Bonin, L., Hébert, R., & Rochette, L. (2004). Quasi-experimental study of the effectiveness of an integrated service delivery network for the frail elderly. *Canadian Journal on Aging, 23*, 231–246.

Tousignant, M., Hébert, R., Dubuc, N., Simoneau, F., & Dieleman, L. (2003). Application of a case-mix classification based on the functional autonomy of the residents for funding long-term care facilities. *Age and Ageing, 32*, 60–66.

Tousignant, M., Dubuc, N., Hébert, R., & Coulombe, C. (2007). Home-care programmes for older adults with disabilities in Canada: How can we assess the adequacy of services provided compared with the needs of users? *Health & Social Care in the Community, 15*, 1–7.

Yin, R. K. (1994). Case study research: Design and methods. In *Applied Social Research Methods Series* (Vol. 5). Thousand Oaks, CA: Sage.

Germany: Evolution and Scaling Up of the Population-Based Integrated Health Care System "Healthy Kinzigtal"

31

Oliver Groene and Helmut Hildebrandt

31.1 Integrated Care in Germany

Germany's health system is based on social health insurance (SHI) contributions and provides universal access to a comprehensive basket of services. Residents can freely choose their social health insurance fund. A risk-compensation mechanism balances differences in the age and morbidity structure of the pool of insured between the insurance funds in order to prevent excessive risk selection (Busse and Blümel 2014).

Ambulatory care is mainly delivered by office-based primary and specialist care physicians who are paid via a combined capitation and fee-for-service basis. Patients have the freedom to choose any provider in the ambulatory care sector and some choice of hospital upon referral (Kringos et al. 2015a, b). Hospitals receive activity based reimbursement of services based on a diagnosis-related group (DRG) system (Busse et al. 2011). International comparisons demonstrate that the system provides high quality health services independent of income, and has low access barriers (Riesberg and Wörz 2008). However, the German health system is also among the most expensive in the OECD (national health expenditure was 11.0% of GDP in 2013, compared to the OECD average of 8.9%) but the system only performs averagely on overall population health indicators status compared to similar high income countries (OECD 2015). The reasons are largely seen in the disincentives embedded in the organisation of health services that are not fit to cater to the needs of chronically ill patients (OECD 2015).

The strict separation of primary and secondary care with insufficient care coordination is widely seen to be at the core of the problem, shown to lead to unnecessary duplication of services, poor care coordination and suboptimal health outcomes, despite the high level of funding for health care in Germany (OECD 2015).

O. Groene (✉) • H. Hildebrandt
OptiMedis AG, Hamburg, Germany
e-mail: o.groene@optimedis.de; h.hildebrandt@optimedis.de

© Springer International Publishing AG 2017
V. Amelung et al. (eds.), *Handbook Integrated Care*,
DOI 10.1007/978-3-319-56103-5_31

Various solutions have been proposed to overcome care fragmentation towards the development of more integrated care approaches and population-oriented care provision (SVR 2007, 2009, 2012). However, these have yet to be implemented at large scale, partly because of the continued complexity of a system that is characterised by incentives that reward acute care rather than health promotion and disease prevention, along with a lack of alignment of budgets, and payment systems across multiple SHI funds, hospitals and ambulatory care providers (Amelung 2011).

Reforms since 2000 have given purchasers and providers more options to develop contracts to overcome fragmentation, and to improve the quality of care. These included the 2000 Health Care Reform act, which introduced provisions for the delivery of more integrated care, the 2001 Risk Structure Compensation Reform Act, which introduced disease management programmes, the 2004 Social Health Insurance Modernisation Act, which introduced a legal framework for integrated care provision and strengthened primary care, and the 2008 Long-term Care Act, which introduced provisions that permit delegation of tasks that were traditionally performed by doctors to non-medically trained staff. More recently, the 2012 Health Care Reform Act and the 2015 Act to Strengthen Care Provision within SHI sought to strengthen primary care further, with the 2015 reform additionally establishing an Innovation Fund to support the scaling-up of innovative forms of care delivery. Of these, the 2000 and 2004 reforms can be seen to be pivotal to introducing integrated care approaches in Germany. Specifically, the 2004 reform required SHI funds to allocate 1% of their total income to selective contracts with GP-centred or integrated care networks, and to thus facilitate establishing such networks (Amelung et al. 2012).

Between 2004 and 2008 some 6400 integrated care contracts were set up under this scheme, covering approximately 4 million insured, with a health care expenditure of 811 million euros (Grothaus 2009). The participation in such schemes was voluntary for both patients and providers. The majority of contracts addressed specific target populations in the field of cardiology, neuro-surgery or emergency orthopaedic care, for example introducing surgery in the ambulatory setting or other interventions that were previously performed as inpatient care. Only a small number of contracts sought to introduce more sector-wide approaches across the patients´ pathway and even among these, the majority only targeted parts of the pathway (e.g. integrating hospital and post-hospital rehabilitation services). Moreover, a large number of contracts were terminated when the start-up financing ran out after 2008. We here report on one model of integrated care, the 'Healthy Kinzigtal (HK)', in operation since 2005 can be seen to be the sole population-based integrated care contract in Germany that provides care across all sectors and disease areas and has been subject to rigorous external evaluation.

31.2 Case Study: Healthy Kinzigtal (HK)

The integrated care contract HK sought to systematically address fragmented service delivery, which was seen to place patients at particular risk of suboptimal outcomes, in particular those with chronic conditions and frail older people. There was a particular perception that care delivery was overly focused on (cost-intensive) services to treat disease and its sequelae, rather than incentivising more cost-effective approaches to prevent them.

The Healthy Kinzigtal model seeks to address these inefficiencies. It is based on the Triple-Aim approach, which seeks to simultaneously pursue three aims: (1) improving the patient's experience of care (including quality and satisfaction), (2) improving the health of the population; and (3) reducing the per capita cost of health care (Berwick et al. 2008). The triple aim approach posits that the three dimensions are not independent of each other and need to be balanced in order to ensure sustainable achievements at the health system level. In line with the triple aim approach, the principal components are (a) the identification of a specific population that is covered by the integrated care system (b) minimising the risk of adverse selection (ideally by a total budget for the population served) and (c) the establishment of an "integrator" who has the know-how and competences to guide the development and implementation of health improvement programs (McCarthy and Klein 2012). For HK, the triple aim approach was seen to provide a valid conceptual model to guide the design of the interventions targeted at patients, populations and providers, but also to provide a framework for the evaluation studies of the initiative.

31.2.1 Governance and Participation

The population-based integrated care health system is coordinated by Healthy Kinzigtal Ltd, a regional integrated care management company founded in 2005 by the then existing physician network 'Medizinisches Qualitätsnetz Kinzigtal' (MQNK) and OptiMedis AG, a German health care management company. OptiMedis AG provides the management know-how, investment capacity, public health and health economics knowledge, and state-of-the art data-warehouse and health analytics. Healthy Kinzigtal Ltd is owned two-thirds by MQNK and one third by OptiMedis AG. Cooperating organizations of Healthy Kinzigtal currently (2015) include 27 general practitioners, 24 specialists, 1 paediatrician, 5 psychotherapists, 6 hospitals, 10 physiotherapists, 11 nursing homes, 5 home care services, 16 pharmacies, 38 sports clubs and associations and 6 gyms. Recently, eight small and medium sized companies have joined this network in order to offer classes in health promotion to their 3500 employees and to reorganise their structure towards a healthy company approach.

31.2.2 The Business Model of Healthy Kinzigtal

The business model of HK has some distinctive characteristics: at its core is a value-oriented population-based shared savings contract (Hildebrandt et al. 2010). This model maintains existing reimbursement schemes and financial flows, but the integrator (Healthy Kinzigtal Ltd) assumes virtual responsibility for the development of the so called contribution margin. The contribution margin is the difference between the amount the social health insurance company receives from the central health care fund for the expected (risk-adjusted) mean costs of care of all SHI insured and the costs that were actually incurred by their population, adjusted for baseline differences before the start of the intervention. A positive contribution margin is then shared between the insurance companies and the integrator. Another key characteristic of the model is that Healthy Kinzigtal Ltd is financially accountable for all people in the population served, not just for those that are registered members or receive care from physicians that form part of the network. HK thus serves a clearly defined population, works on a global budget and draws on the support of Healthy Kinzigtal Ltd, who—with the support of OptiMedis AG—acts as the regional integrator. The financial goal is thus to increase the insurer's contribution margin which will provide the stimuli to integrate care delivery and engage all partners in working towards the Triple-Aim (via 'shared-savings', see Fig. 31.1).

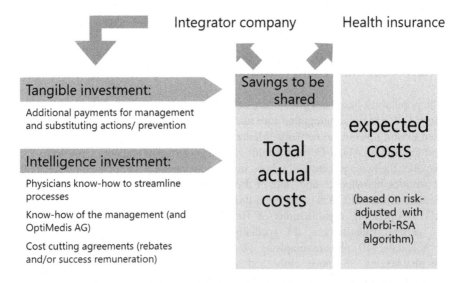

Fig. 31.1 Business model of Healthy Kinzigtal: the shared savings approach. Adapted from: Hildebrandt et al., Gesundes Kinzigtal Integrated Care (2010, p. 6)

31.2.3 Coverage and Programmes

The valley of Kinzigtal has about 71,000 inhabitants; of these about 33,000 are members of the regional SHI (AOK-BW), a SHI fund that traditionally insured blue-collar workers and has a less favourable risk pool, while about 1700 are members of the LKK-BW, a SHI fund for farmers, farm workers and their dependents, which has a similar risk pool as the AOK-BW. By 2015, of those insured by AOK-BW and LKK-BW nearly 10,500 were registered members of Healthy Kinzigtal.

In order to reach the Triple Aim, a set of activities and programmes were established, which all draw on a common set of underlying features: (a) individual treatment plans and goal-setting agreements between doctors and patients, (b) enhancing patients' self-management and shared decision-making, (c) care planning based on the Chronic-Care Model (Barr et al. 2003), patient coaching and follow up care, (d) providing the right care at the right time, and (e) overarching support through the introduction of a system-wide electronic patient record (18). A list of current prevention and health promotion programmes is shown in Box 31.1.

Box 31.1 Prevention and Health Promotion Programmes that have been developed so far:
- Strong heart (programme targeting heart failure)
- Healthy weight (for metabolic syndrome, including diabetes)
- Good prospects (care services for children)
- In balance (blood pressure)
- Strong muscles—solid bones (osteoporosis)
- Staying mobile (treating early stage rheumatism)
- Strong support—healthy back (chronic back pain)
- Better mood (depression)
- Good counselling (help, advice and support in critical times)
- Psycho Acute (acute psychological issues)
- Disease management programmes
- Smoke-free Kinzigtal (including pre-surgery smoking cessation)
- Social support (to reduce stress where patients are in critical situations)
- Liberating sounds (in tune with music) and,
- New: a self-management training programme (based on the Stanford Chronic Disease Self-Management Programme).

While the local planning and implementation of the disease prevention and health promotion programmes is conducted by Healthy Kinzigtal Ltd, OptiMedis AG provides the overarching management support, business intelligence and health data analytics, whereby the data driven health analytics propel both the planning of health programmes and guide local practice improvements via feedback reports to participating physicians.

An example of the latter is shown in Fig. 31.2, which illustrates a quarterly performance feedback report (dashboard) (Pimperl et al. 2013). These reports are based on a balanced scorecard approach, which uses structure, process and outcome indicators and is designed to be interactive in that it allows users to select indicators to retrieve more detailed information. Some indicators are supported by targeted improvement activities. For example, the dashboard indicates problematic

Quality indicators and key figures		Your Practice	Ø-LP- GP's (n=17)	Ø-NLP- GP's (n=22)	Min/ Max GP (n=39)
3. Outcomes: Which impacts have interventions on medical and financial outcomes and patient satisfaction?					
3.1 Economical outcomes	Allocation (Morbi-RSA) per patient	845,45 →	765,33	687,81	937,79
-	Total costs per patient	841,81	764,78	677,81	251,72
=	Contribution margin per patient	3,64	0,55	10,00	326,69
3.2 Health outcomes	Hospital cases per 1.000 patients (risk-adj.)	82,91	87,42	98,55	42,35
	Decedents % (risk-adj. mortality)	0,51%	0,57%	0,60%	0,00%
	Patients with osteoporosis & fracture %	3,64%	8,49%	12,98%	0,00%
3.3 Patient satisfaction	Impression of practice very good - exc. %	66,7%	61,0%	79,9%*	83,3%
Weisse Liste / GeKiM 2012/13	Med. treatment very good - exc. %	52,8%	53,0%	75,1%*	79,2%
*Ø-NLP here = Ø-Germany	Recommendation likely - certain %	85,2%	84,6%	88,1%*	95,6%
2. Process - Where do we have to be excellent?		↑		↑	
2.1 Diagnostic quality	Unspecified diagnoses %	20,4%	20,1%	24,1%	12,5%
	Suspected diagnoses %	1,6%	1,3%	1,6%	0,6%
2.2 Utilization	Patients >= 35 with health-check-up %	7,5%	7,8%	7,1%	17,1%
	Patients incapable of working %	39,0%	41,7%	43,8%	33,8%
	Length of incapacity for work	5,52	5,93	6,37	3,87
2.3 Improvement of Medication	Generic quota	93,0% →	88,6%	87,2%	93,0%
	Pat. with heart-fail. & guideline prescr. %	79,9%	75,4%	72,9%	100,0%
	Patients >= 65 with pot. inad. med. (PRISCUS)	14,3%	13,2%	12,5%	4,2%
	Patients >=65 with inad. prescr. (FORTA D) %	4,0%	4,8%	4,3%	0,6%
1. Structure - What ist the target population? Where can we improve structure elements to generate better outcomes?		↑		↑	
1.1 Patient stucture					
1.1.1 Age, gender, etc.	Ø-Number of patients	509,0	485,3	338,9	931,0
	Ø-Age	57,1	54,6	52,5	53,5
	Female %	56,8%	56,5%	55,8%	65,2%
	Patients capable of work %	55,2%	58,5%	60,5%	72,7%
	Patients dependent on care %	6,7%	7,7%	7,0%	13,0%
1.1.2 Morbidity	Ø-Charlson-comorbidity-score	1,85 →	1,26	1,14	1,99
	Regional GP-risk-score (Morbi-RSA)	1,16 →	1,05	0,94	1,29
1.1.3 Enrollment	IC-participants %	88,8%	61,1%	10,2%	88,8%
	DMP-participants %	67,4%	53,9%	32,0%	81,9%
1.2 Learning & innovation	Participation in quality circles (Ø = 1,0)	1,3	1,0	-	2,1

Fig. 31.2 Health services dashboard for a GP practice. Adapted from Pimperl et al., Case Study Gesundes Kinzigtal (2013, p. 27)

prescription behaviour (e.g. a high proportion of drug prescription according to the PRISCUS or FORTA D classification models for potentially hazardous prescriptions for older people) (Holt et al. 2010; Kuhn-Thiel et al. 2014). This indicator is supported by two-monthly geronto-pharmaceutical consultation meetings for which physicians prepare a patient case report and which discusses potential problems jointly with a pharmacologist to optimise medication regimes. The infrastructure utilised to produce the dashboards has the capacity to integrate and transform multiple data sources (such as claims data, health records, patient survey), to analyse the potential effectiveness of a programme or identify high-risk patients, and provide automated benchmark reports to participating physicians. This business intelligence solution was awarded with the Best Practice Award Business Intelligence by the German Business Application Research Center (BARC).

31.2.4 A Cross-Cutting Theme: People Involvement/Service User Perspective

The patient-centred care approach is paramount to the success of HK and embedded at three levels: at the structural level, in the planning of interventions, and in the interactions between physicians and patients. At the structural level, patients are represented in patient advisory boards, which elect their representatives on a biannual basis and are given the opportunity to contribute to identifying and developing new programmes. At the level of intervention planning there is a strong focus on shared-decision making and self-management support, which is embedded in design and development. At the level of individual interactions of patients with health professionals, patients joining HK first undergo a comprehensive health-check (including a self-assessment questionnaire) based on which they may be offered to participate in any of the health promotion and disease prevention programmes offered by HK. Patients are also given the opportunity to develop health-related goals (such as engaging in more exercise, quitting smoking, reducing alcohol consumption, or losing weight), which are discussed with the doctor and then monitored over time, accompanied by individual support and participation in patient education and self-care programmes as needed. In order to support the patient-centred care approach, physicians, other health professionals and practice staff are offered training. Underlying all these efforts is an understanding of the patient as a co-producer of their health (Batalden et al. 2015).

31.2.5 Impact

The HK has been subject to rigorous evaluation in order to assess its impacts focusing, in line with the triple aim approach, on improving patient experience, improving population health and reducing per capita costs of care. External evaluations are conducted by independent research institutions, which are coordinated by the 'Evaluation-Coordination Function Integrated Care' at the University of Freiburg and includes two main evaluation studies: First, a survey of a representative random sample of HK members assessing their perceived health and satisfaction, along with self-reported changes in health behaviours, health-related quality-of-life and levels of activation, conducted every second year (Siegel and Stößel 2013). Second, an analysis of over-, under- and misuse of health services using routine SHI claims data., This analysis is conducted as a controlled quasi-experimental study comparing the intervention population to a random sample of about 500,000 members of AOK-BW and LKK-BW not resident in the Kinzigtal region (Hildebrandt et al. 2015). These evaluation studies are complemented by further research studies, including European Union funded research projects. In addition, the AOK-BW and OptiMedis AG each conduct internal evaluations of the impact of the HK integrated care system. The financial results are assessed in relation to the development of the contribution margin described above. Key findings of the range of evaluation studies that have been carried out thus far are summarised in Table 31.1.

31.2.6 Dissemination and Replication

The Health Kinzigtal integrated care contract was initially negotiated for a period of 10 years (2005–2015). Renewed in 2016, it now runs, based on the positive evaluations, as an unrestricted contract, thus providing a stable context to pursue long-term health interventions in the region. In addition, an expansion of the model to various other regions in Baden-Württemberg and other parts of Germany is being discussed. Key questions that remain to be answered include the extent to which the positive results of the HK can be attributed to the specifics of the HK region or their population, and how can similar results be achieved elsewhere (Kringos et al. 2015a, b)? While all regions will have their idiosyncratic features and particularities, we argue that the general model, interventions and evaluation frameworks are widely applicable. For example, all key aspects of the model are deeply rooted in the scientific literature and in models that have shown to be effective elsewhere, such as the triple aim approach (Whittington et al. 2015), the chronic care model (Barr et al. 2003), audit and feedback strategies (Ivers et al. 2012), the focus on patient activation (Hibbard et al. 2015), or pharmacological consultations to improve the safety of drug prescriptions (Phatak et al. 2015). The results of HK are based on and consistent with the scientific literature.

In order to successfully transferred and scale-up this model elsewhere, a number of experiences should be taken into consideration. Their relevance may differ depending on the health system context and the organizational model applied, but in HK the following issues proved relevant

- First, a key component of the triple aim model is the role of the "integrator". In our experience, this should be a regionally-based organisation, partly owned by local providers, which is familiar with local (health) services issues, plans and

Table 31.1 Selected evaluation findings of impacts of the Health Kinzigtal integrated care system

Triple aim	Method	Result
Improving the patients' experience of care	– Random, postal survey amongst the insured – Questionnaire with items regarding perceived health, patient satisfaction, changes in health behaviour, health-related quality-of-life and levels of activation – Participants: 3038 GK members, response rate 23.6% – First assessment in 2012, since then biannual trend study	– Very high levels of overall satisfaction: 92.1% state they would recommend joining Healthy Kinzigtal – Health-related goal setting: 25.1% of risk patients voluntarily agree a goal with their physician in a consultation (which will be tracked in subsequent consultations with the patient) – Positive change in health behaviour: 19.7% state that, overall, they live a healthier life than before joining Healthy Kinzigtal (with 0.4% stating the contrary and 79.9% stating no change) • Amongst insured with an agreed health-related goal 45.4% state they live a healthier life (compared to 0.6% stating the contrary and 54% stating no change, $p > 0.001$)

Improving the health of the population	– Analysis of routinely available claims data
	– Controlled quasi-experimental study comparing the intervention population to a random sample of ca 500,000 members of the same SHI, but that are not from the Kinzigtal region
	– Six indicators of overuse and ten indicators of underuse of health services
		– Overuse of health services:
		    • Five out of the six indicators demonstrate an improvement compared to control group (prescription of anxiolytics, antibiotics for higher respiratory tract infections, non-steroidal anti-rheumatics, non-recommended prescription for vascular dementia, non- recommended prescription for Alzheimer dementia), one no difference (% avoidable hospitalization)
		– Underuse of health services:
		    • Four indicators demonstrated an improvement compared to the control group (patients with chronic coronary heart disease (CHD) on antiplatelet drugs, CHD patients on statins, acute myocardial infarct (AMI) patients on statins, heart insufficiency patients with cardiology contact), four indicators suggests no difference (CHD patients on beta blockers, heart insufficiency patients with indicated medication, diabetes patients with

(continued)

Table 31.1 (continued)

Triple aim	Method	Result
		ophthalmologist contact, diabetes patients with CHD and statins), and two indicators suggest a deterioration (AMI patients on beta blockers, osteoporosis patients with indicated therapy)
Reducing the per capita cost of health care	– Calculation of the contribution margin: the differences between the risk-adjusted expected costs for the insured, compared to the actual incurred costs (high-cost cases are winsorized) – Note: the calculation is based on all inhabitants of the region (based on the postcode of residence), and not restricted to GK members from that region	– Positive development of the contribution margin • i.e. the costs for the AOK + LKK insured in the GK post codes lie 5.613 million euros under the morbidity-adjusted expected costs of 75.353 million euros • i.e. for every AOK/LKK insured person living in the region, the costs are on average 150€ lower than expected – The incurred costs amongst AOK-BW and LKK-BW insured in Kinzigtal consistently lay below the risk-adjusted expected costs. This difference is expected to further increase in the coming years as some of the health programmes will only start paying off years after the initial intervention

delivers local intervention and maintains the communications with all stake-holders. The "integrator" needs to be supported by an organisation capable of providing investments, engaging in negotiations with high-level decision-makers, and of providing advanced health data analytics while at the same time (supported by shareholders) pursuing long-reaching value-development instead of short-term profits.

- Second, during the first years, considerable start-up investment is needed to set up the organisational structures, integrate stakeholders, and to design interventions, which in turn means that appropriate funding has to be ensured for at least 3 years until income can generate a return-on-investment. This is because of two types of delay: (a) the time lag between intervention onset and successful health improvements (at least 1 year) (b) the time lag in obtaining the data reflecting such improvements (which often amounts to another year).
- Third, a vision to go beyond traditional institutional boundaries in the planning of health interventions is needed, in particular in the form of interventions that place a focus on improving population health. This competence may not be readily available a priori in existing structures.

- Fourth, the size of the population needs to be appropriate to ensure networking among providers, the identification of local solutions and the exchange of ideas amongst all stakeholders. Population sizes smaller than 100,000 appear ideal (assuming the number of stakeholders that can be managed should not exceed 100). While it may be tempting to establish much larger regions, it is unlikely that the local "kit" (a common culture, mental models, mutual understanding of local issues, and trust) needed to motivate stakeholders towards a common goal can be easily established.
- Fifth, a comprehensive information-technology package (including shared patient records) and competencies for advanced health data analytics to inform intervention planning, feedback reports to providers, and internal evaluation are crucial in order to ensure seamless care and monitor performance.
- Sixth, an approach focusing on ´coopetition´ (a portmanteau of cooperation and competition) through transparency and benchmarking and based on management theory is needed to support the continuous strive towards improvement and to facilitate effective knowledge sharing in cross-functional teams (Ghobadi 2012).
- Seventh, a balanced payment system oriented towards achieving the triple aim which is incorporated in the shared savings approach is needed. This level of accountability which allows providers to make decisions on how cost savings are (re-)invested is an important governing factor supporting regional autonomy. In HK, the majority of these savings are used to reinvest in the population health management strategy, for example; by constructing a new comprehensive health centre (partly supported by the cost savings), by distributing tokens to citizens that can be used to support local entities (such as schools, sports club or church entities), or by providing some additional financial incentives for good performance.
- Eight, in order to have long-term success, both an innovative culture and friendly interactions are essential to harness value from the relationships with all stakeholders.
- And finally, a long-term (10 year) contract with the purchasers is required to provide stability for the planning of health interventions.

Bearing in mind the scientific evidence-base underlying the HK experience and considering the nine implementation prerequisites above, we argue that the results from the HK can be successfully transferred and achieved elsewhere, including in regions that are different in population structure and health service organisation. The existence of a stable physician network previous to the set-up of Healthy Kinzigtal Ltd was certainly a factor that facilitated the implementation. Likewise, purchasers willing to share long-term savings and a robust method to monitor costs and quality over time are a qualifying condition. However, of greater importance is that the conditions reflected in the nine prerequisite can (to some extent) be created by the integrator.

Programme expansions are currently being discussed with various regions in Germany (and abroad), taking into consideration the lessons learned in HK. We anticipate a much faster learning curve in new regions, bearing in mind that various prerequisites and interventions are ready to scale-up, such as quality indicators, evaluation protocols, programme outlines, incentive systems, management guidelines, data warehouse and reporting systems etc. Ideally, if multiple regions could be set up and implemented simultaneously, that would generate a unique source of data for advanced health analytics to further evaluate the impact of integrated, population health management systems, and moreover, to allow a systematic process evaluation of how the model could be further scaled up nationally and abroad (Ovretveit and Klazinga 2012). The decision of the German government to provide 1.2 billion € funding over 4 years (2016–2019) to support innovative forms of care delivery and health services research provides a promising context to pursue these questions. Hopefully, at the end of this 4-year period, not only will relevant integrated health systems in Germany have undergone the necessary evaluation, but actionable knowledge will have been generated to scale up innovations at national level in order to overcome the health systems challenges that have been documented in Germany over the last 15 years (Busse 2014).

References

Advisory Council on the Assessment of Developments in the Healthcare System. (2007). Cooperation and responsibility prerequisites for target-oriented health care. Retrieved July 7, 2016, from http://www.svr-gesundheit.de/fileadmin/user_upload/Gutachten/2007/KF2007-engl.pdf

Advisory Council on the Assessment of Developments in the Healthcare System. (2009). Coordination and integration – Health care in an ageing society. Retrieved July 7, 2016, from http://www.svr-gesundheit.de/fileadmin/user_upload/Gutachten/2009/KF_engl_final.pdf

Advisory Council on the Assessment of Developments in the Healthcare System. (2012). Competition at the interfaces between inpatient and outpatient healthcare. Retrieved July 7, 2016, from http://www.svr-gesundheit.de/fileadmin/user_upload/Gutachten/2012/Kurzfassung-eng_formatiert.pdf

Amelung, V. (2011). Neue Versorgungsformen auf dem Prüfstand. In *Innovatives Versorgungsmanagement*. Berlin: Medizinische Wissenschaftliche Verlagsgesellschaft.

Amelung, V., Wolf, S., & Hildebrandt, H. (2012). Integrated care in Germany—a stony but necessary road! *International Journal of Integrated Care*. Retrieved July 7, 2016, from http://www.ijic.org/index.php/ijic/article/view/URN%3ANBN%3ANL%3AUI%3A10-1-112901

Barr, V. J., Robinson, S., Marin-Link, B., Underhill, L., Dotts, A., Ravensdale, D., & Salivaras, S. (2003). The expanded chronic care model: An integration of concepts and strategies from population health promotion and the chronic care model. In *Hospital Quarterly*. Retrieved July 7, 2016, from http://www.area-c54.it/public/the%20expanded%20chronic%20care%20model.pdf

Batalden, M., Batalden, P., Margolis, P., Seid, M., Armstrong, G., Opipari-Arrigan, L., & Hartung, H. (2015). Coproduction of healthcare service. *BMJ Quality and Safety*. doi:10.1136/bmjqs-2015-004315.

Berwick, D. M., Nolan, T. W., & Whittington, J. (2008). The triple aim: Care, health, and cost. *Health Affairs, 27*, 759–769. doi:10.1377/hlthaff.27.3.759.

Busse, R. (2014). Integrated care experiences and outcomes in Germany, The Netherlands, and England. *Health Affairs, 33*(9), 1549–1558.

Busse, R., & Blümel, M. (2014). Germany: Health system review. *Health Systems in Transition, 16*(2), 1–296.

Busse, R., Geisler, A., Quentin, W., & Wiley, M. (2011). Diagnosis-related groups in Europe. Moving towards transparency, efficiency and quality in hospitals. WHO European Observatory on Health Care Systems. Retrieved July 7, 2016, from http://www.euro.who.int/__data/assets/pdf_file/0004/162265/e96538.pdf

Hibbard, J. H., Greene, J., Shi, Y., Mittler, J., & Scanlon, D. (2015). Taking the long view: How well do patient activation scores predict outcomes four years later? *Medical Care Research and Review, 72*(3), 324–337. doi:10.1177/1077558715573871.

Hildebrandt, H., Hermann, C., Knittel, R., Richter-Reichhelm, M., Siegel, A., & Witzenrath, W. (2010). Gesundes Kinzigtal integrated care: Improving population health by a shared health gain approach and a shared savings contract. *International Journal of Integrated Care, 10*, 1–14.

Hildebrandt, H., Pimperl, A., Schulte, T., Hermann, C., Riedel, H., Schubert, I., Köster, I., Siegel, A., & Wetzel, M. (2015). Triple-Aim-Evaluation in der Integrierten Versorgung Gesundes Kinzigtal – Gesundheitszustand, Versorgungserleben und Wirtschaftlichkeit. *Bundesgesundheitsblatt, 58*, 383–392.

Ghobadi, S. (2012). Knowledge sharing in cross-functional teams: A competitive model. *Journal of Knowledge Management., 16*(2), 285–301.

Grothaus, F. J. (2009). Entwicklung der integrierten Versorgung in der Bundesrepublik Deutschland 2004–2008. Bericht gemäß § 140d SGB V auf der Grundlage der Meldungen von Verträgen zur integrierten Versorgung. Retrieved July 7, 2016, from http://www.bqs-register140d.de/dokumente/bericht-140d.pdf

Holt, S., Schmiedl, S., & Thürmann, P. A. (2010). Potentially inappropriate medication in the elderly: PRISCUS list. *Deutsches Ärzteblatt International, 107*, 543–551.

Ivers, N., Jamtvedt, G., Flottorp, S., Young, J. M., Odgaard-Jensen, J., French, S. D., et al. (2012). Audit and feedback: Effects on professional practice and healthcare outcomes. *Cochrane Database of Systematic Reviews, 6*, CD000259.

Kringos, D. S., Boerma, W. G. W., & Hutchinson, A., & Saltman, R. D. (2015a). Building primary care in a changing Europe. WHO European Observatory on Health Care Systems. Retrieved July 7, 2016, from http://www.euro.who.int/__data/assets/pdf_file/0018/271170/BuildingPrimaryCareChangingEurope.pdf

Kringos, D. S., Sunol, R., Wagner, C., Mannion, R., Michel, P., Klazinga, N. S., Groene, O., & DUQuE Consortium. (2015b). The influence of context on the effectiveness of hospital quality improvement strategies: a review of systematic reviews. *BMC Health Services Research, 15*, 277. doi:10.1186/s12913-015-0906-0.

Kuhn-Thiel, A. M., Weiß, C., & Wehling, M. (2014). Consensus validation of the FORTA (Fit fOR The Aged) list: A clinical tool for increasing the appropriateness of Pharmacotherapy in the elderly. *Drugs & Aging, 31*, 131. doi:10.1007/s40266-013-0146-0.

McCarthy, D., & Klein, S. (2012). The triple aim journey: Improving population health and patients' experience of care, while reducing costs. Retrieved July 7, 2016, from http://www.commonwealthfund.org/~/media/files/publications/case-study/2010/jul/triple-aim-v2/1421_mccarthy_triple_aim_journey_overview.pdf

Organization for Economic Cooperation and Development. (2015). Health at a glance 2015: OECD indicators. Retrieved July 7, 2016, from http://www.oecd.org/berlin/publikationen/health-at-a-glance-2015.htm

Ovretveit, J., & Klazinga, N. (2012). Learning from large-scale quality improvement through comparisons. *International Journal for Quality in Health Care, 24*(5), 463–469. doi:10.1093/intqhc/mzs046.

Phatak, A., Prusi, R., Ward, B., Hansen, L. O., Williams, M. V., Vetter, E., Chapman, N., & Postelnick, M. (2015). Impact of pharmacist involvement in the transitional care of high-risk patients through medication reconciliation, medication education, and postdischarge call-backs (IPITCH Study). *Journal of Hospital Medicine.* doi:10.1002/jhm.2493.

Pimperl, A., Schulte, T., Daxer, C., Roth, M., & Hildebrandt, H. (2013). Balanced Scorecard-Ansatz: Case Study Gesundes Kinzigtal. *Monitor Versorgungsforschung, 6*, 26–30.

Riesberg, A., & Wörz, M. (2008). Quality in and equality of access to healthcare services – Country report for Germany. European Community Programme for employment and social solidarity (2007–2013), Directorate-General for Employment, Social Affairs and Equal Opportunities of the European Commission. ec.europa.eu/social/BlobServlet? docId=5085&langId=en

Siegel, A., & Stößel, U. (2013). Evaluation der Integrierten Versorgung Gesundes Kinzigtal: Bisherige Ergebnisse. *Public Health Forum, 21*, 13–15.

Whittington, J. W., Nolan, K., Lewis, N., & Torres, T. (2015). Pursuing the triple aim: The first 7 years. *The Milbank Quarterly, 93*(2), 263–300. doi:10.1111/1468-0009.12122.31.

Scotland

32

Elaine Mead

32.1 Introduction

Scotland is part of the United Kingdom (UK) and covers the northern third of Great Britain and shares a border with England to the south[1]. At the last census (2011) the population was 5.3 million, the highest ever recorded (Scotland's Census 2014).

Population density is low in comparison with the rest of the UK due to large remote and rural areas, particularly in the Highlands and Islands. While the population has remained stable over the past 50 years, the proportion of people aged 65 and over has grown and is projected to increase by around two-thirds over the next 20 years (Ham et al. 2013).

Healthcare in Scotland is mainly provided by National Health Service (NHS) Scotland, the country's public healthcare system. The NHS was founded by the National Health Service (Scotland) Act 1947 and took effect on 5th July 1948 to coincide with the launch of the NHS in England and Wales.

Over the past two decades, there have been some significant changes in how Scotland is governed. Following political devolution that took effect in 1999, the Scottish Parliament was set up with powers to make laws across a wide range of areas including health (Taylor 2015; Mooney and Scott 2012; Keating 2010; Mcfadden and Lazareswich 1999). These new arrangements also saw a move to Scottish parliamentary elections being held every 5 years.

Since 2001, NHS Scotland has been organised into 14 regional-based health boards, 7 national or special boards and one public health body. Regional boards have overall responsibility for the health of their populations and they plan and commission secondary care (which is generally provided by medical specialists in

---

[1]No passport or ID checks are required to cross the border.

E. Mead (✉)
NHS Highland, Inverness, UK
e-mail: emead@nhs.net

© Springer International Publishing AG 2017
V. Amelung et al. (eds.), *Handbook Integrated Care*,
DOI 10.1007/978-3-319-56103-5_32

acute hospitals) and community health and primary care (which is provided in the community for people making an initial approach to a medical practitioner or clinic for advice or treatment including GPs, pharmacists, dentists and optometrists).

Healthcare funding and policy is the responsibility of the Scottish Government. Each NHS board is accountable to Scottish ministers reporting to the Cabinet Secretary for Health, Wellbeing and Sport. This is supported by the executive functions of the Scottish Government's Health and Social Care Directorates. NHS Scotland operates with an annual budget of around £12 billion (Scottish Government 2014)[2] and there is a national formula that deals with the allocation of funding for each regional board.

Adult social care and social work is the responsibility of 32 local authorities (councils). While 85% of their funding comes from central government in the form of a block grant, councils are autonomous bodies, independent of central government and accountable to their electorates for the delivery of services. The remainder of their funding is raised from local taxation ('council tax') and discretionary funds.

Integrating health and social care has been on the policy agenda in Scotland for the past 20 years or so (Taylor 2015). Of particular relevance is the Community Care and Health (Scotland) Act 2002, which enabled health boards and local authorities to delegate some of their functions and resources. The subsequent NHS Reform (Scotland) Act 2004 required boards to establish one or more community health partnership (CHPs) with local authorities in their area. These were seen as a focus for integrating health promotion, primary and specialist health services at a local level (Ham et al. 2013; Taylor 2015).

In 2011, the Scottish Government's 2020 Vision articulated a clear aim that "everyone is able to live longer at home or in a homely setting". It included a plan for achieving sustainable quality in the delivery of health and social care (Scottish Government 2011). The subsequent Public Bodies (Joint Working) (Scotland) Act 2014 set out the most recent legislative framework for integrating health and social care.

Under the Act, statutory responsibility for social care functions remains with local authorities but with the provisions that allow for the delegation of some of these functions. This is either through the formation of an integration joint board that is responsible for planning and resourcing service provision for adult health and social care services (Option 1); or alternatively, the health board or the local authority takes the lead responsibility for planning, resourcing and delivering integrated adult health and social care services; known as the 'lead agency' model (Option 2) (Taylor 2015; Bruce and Parry 2015).

Health boards and local authorities were required to put in place their local plans by April 2015 with the full integration of services expected by April 2016. Notably, 31 of the 32 local authorities are implementing Option 1. The Highland Council is

---

[2]£3.9 billion was also spent on social care services (Expenditure on Adult Social Care Services, Scotland, 2013–2014).

the only local authority that is implementing the lead agency model, and in the following sections, we focus on this specific model of integrated care in Scotland.

32.2   Integrated Care in Practice

32.2.1 Problem Definition

NHS Highland health board[3] was established in October 2001 and since then has undergone a number of re-organisations, including the establishment of community health partnerships in 2004 (The Highland Council area), and in 2006 the taking on the responsibility for part of the former NHS Argyll and Clyde region. In doing so, NHS Highland became responsible for the largest health board area in Scotland. It includes some of the most remote and rural parts of the country including 36 populated islands (see Map in Fig. 32.1) (Box 32.1; NHS Highland 2015a).

Box 32.1 NHS Highland at a glance
- Co-terminus with two local authorities (The Highland Council and Argyll & Bute)
- Covering an area of 32,500 km^2 = 41% of the landmass of Scotland
- 36 populated Islands
- Population of 320,760 (National Records 2014)
- 10,088 employees (8000 whole time equivalent)
- Annual revenue budget 2015/16 c£789 m
- 100 GP practices
- 25 hospitals, made up of the following:
  - 1 district general hospital
  - 2 dedicated mental health units
  - 3 rural general hospitals
  - 19 community hospitals
- 15 care homes (The Highland Council area)
- 39,000 attendances Raigmore Hospital Emergency Department per annum

---

Arguably, however, the biggest re-organisation for the health board came in April 2012 with the signing of a partnership agreement between NHS Highland and The Highland Council.

---

[3]NHS Highland is managed by a board of directors and is accountable for the performance of NHS Highland. It is underpinned by committees, including: Clinical Governance, Area Clinical Forum, Highland Health and Social Care Committee.

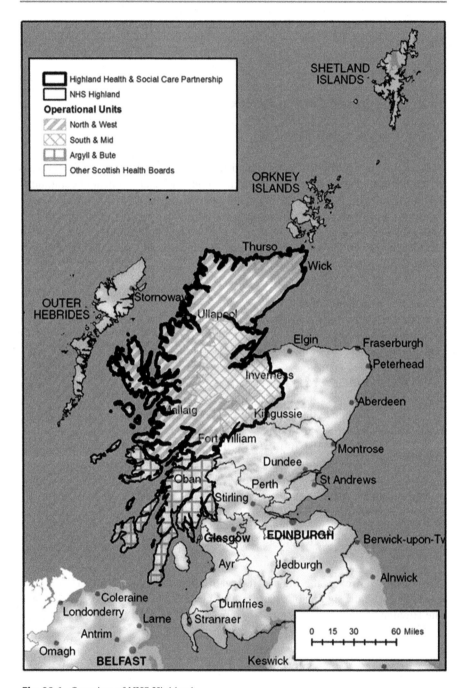

Fig. 32.1 Overview of NHS Highland

With an ageing population, particularly for those aged over 75 years, and the expectation that public expenditure would fall in real terms, while pressures on health and social spending would increase, the status quo was not seen as a viable option (NHS Highland 2011, 2012a, b).

Furthermore, the Highland Council and NHS Highland recognised that the way some services were organised was not delivering the best outcomes for people. This was despite efforts by frontline staff and managers to overcome day-to-day barriers. Delayed decision-making, conflicts over budgets and accountability, and at times a blame culture, were all considered to be barriers with some significant impacts including:

- Lack of alternatives to emergency hospital admissions
- Limited care-at-home
- Lack of 'joined-up' responses and delivery of services
- Early (young) admissions to care homes
- Limited collaboration with third and independent sector

Against this background, there was a perception that more radical reform was needed. A number of fact-finding visits were carried out and various models were considered, including Torbay in England (Thistlethwaite 2011). Following on from this a joint meeting of The Council and the Health Board was held in December 2010 and a joint statement of intent was issued:

> We will improve the quality and reduce the cost of services through the creation of new, simpler, organisational arrangements that are designed to maximise outcomes, and through the streamlining of service delivery to ensure it is faster, more efficient and more effective.

A joint board was created to deliver a 15-month programme of work to establish new arrangements to fully integrate services, particularly in relation to adult and children. Some 2 years later, on 21 March 2012, The Highland Council and NHS Highland signed a formal partnership agreement to establish the first lead agency model in Scotland.

32.2.2 Description of the Lead Agency Model

Under the lead agency model all adult social care services were transferred to NHS Highland from the Highland Council in April 2012, and in a reciprocal arrangement, The Highland Council took on responsibility for the delivery of community children's services (Mead 2015; Baird et al. 2014; Brown 2013; Highland Partnership 2012).

For NHS Highland this meant taking on new responsibilities including the management of 15 care homes, the in-house care-at-home service, day care services, tele-care services and a wide range of contracts with the third and independent sectors.

It also involved 1400 adult care staff transferring under Transfer of Undertakings (Protection of Employment)[4] from Highland Council to NHS Highland while maintaining their terms and conditions. Alongside this 200 NHS Highland staff transferred across to the Highland Council. Some of the other practical implications are summarised in Box 32.2 and set out in more detail in Mead (2015) and Highland Partnership (2012).

Box 32.2 Legal, financial and management implications of lead agency model
Legal Arrangements
- Changes to the Adult Support and Protection Act (Scotland) 2007 were necessary and were approved by the Scottish Parliament
- A legal partnership agreement (detailing legal, professional leadership, governance and performance arrangements) was required
- Some staff contracts had to be transferred across employers (NHS Highland, Highland Council)
- Change was required to pension's legislation to permit staff that were transferred to remain in their existing pension scheme.

Financial Arrangements
- New single budgets had to be prepared along with requisite resource transfer
  - £89 million annual budget was transferred from the Council to NHS Highland
  - £8 million annual budget was transferred from NHS Highland to the Council
- Different VAT reporting mechanism for each organisation had to be reconciled

Management and Governance Structures
- Existing management and governance structures, such as community health partnerships, had to be reorganised
- Outcomes had to be agreed along with associated performance management frameworks

---

32.2.3 Governance

At the point of integration (1st April 2012), new governance and management arrangements were put in place for the lead agency model which followed legis-

---

[4]Transfer of Undertakings (Protection of Employment) Regulations (TUPE) provide rights to employees when their employment changes when a business is transferred to a new owner.

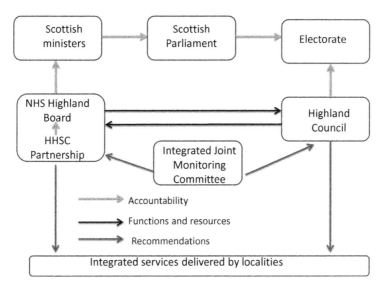

Fig. 32.2 How the lead agency model is structured

lative requirements (Fig. 32.2). These confirm that in terms of adult services the Council remains accountable but NHS Highland is responsible for the delivery of the service. Reciprocal arrangements are in place for children's services.

To make this change, three community health partnerships (north, mid and south east) were dissolved. These were replaced by a new Highland Health and Social Care (HHSC) Partnership which was established as a committee of the board. The Partnership directly oversees the governance but report into the board via the chair who is a non-executive director of the board (Fig. 32.2). A monitoring framework is also in place.

32.2.4 New Ways of Working

There have been many examples, some small and some bigger, of the positive benefits of integration (Highland Council 2015) and some of these are summarised here.

Co-ordination and Professional Communication More effective integrated district teams have been created. Each of the nine integrated district teams within The Highland Council area has a core team of key health and social care professionals representing, for example, care homes, care at home, occupational therapy, GP practices and community nursing.

By working together in a co-ordinated way, a group of key professionals are now more able to ensure clients' and patients' health and social care needs are met. Each part of the team is linked to a care co-ordinator who ensures that each patient and client gets fully co-ordinated care in a timely and efficient manner (NHS Highland 2013).

Commissioning Arrangements and Partnership Working An adult services commissioning group has been established so as to involve as many sectors and representatives as possible, in the making of strategic decisions about investment in adult social care.

In effect, The Highland Council commission services from NHS Highland, while it remains accountable for the delivery of the services. The transaction is delivered through a five-year plan which is reviewed annually and monitored in terms of delivery of agreed outcomes.

Since integration there has been evidence of much closer working with third and independent sector, with a number of documented benefits.

One example is the introduction of the living wage for the independent care-at-home sector. Contracts are in place between NHS Highland and independent sector care at home providers. The Living wage was implemented in April 2014 and since this time, providers have been required to pay their staff the living wage, and provide evidence of having done so, in order to receive an increased fee.

NHS Highland has also been successful in the innovative application of The Social Care Self-Directed Support (SDS) (Scotland) Act which was implemented in April 2014. This supports the vision that care should be based around the citizen, not the service or the service provider. It provides a means through which all clients are given a choice as to how they wish to receive their services and support. This Act places a statutory duty on Local Authorities and integrated partnerships to offer four choices as to how people are assessed as requiring care and to how they received their care or support.

Self-Directed Support option two is known as an Individual Service Fund (ISF) and enables a service provider of the individual's choice to manage their budget. Given the shortage of care at home provision in many remote and rural locations in parts of the Highlands, NHS Highland worked in partnership with independent providers and local communities to put in local solutions to provide care at home. This has proved successful in delivering a care at home service where previously traditional models of care at home could not be sustained (NHS Highland 2015c).

Service and Quality Improvement The appointment of a NHS Highland service improvement lead for care homes has brought a more consistent and multi-disciplinary approach to training, and closer working across all professionals.

A new service was introduced to ensure the safer use of medicines in the care homes managed by NHS Highland. This is because medicines are frequently prescribed for residents of care homes and carry risks, such as adverse drug reactions, which are increased in frail populations. The service involves a pharmacist providing a medication review for every care home resident within 2 weeks of admission and every 6 months thereafter.

In order to ensure adequate staffing, in particular in social care, where recruitment to social worker posts has been challenging in some areas, NHS Highland has taken steps to 'grow our own' by introducing a trainee social work scheme which got underway in 2015 (Highland Council 2015).

Furthermore, additional community geriatricians have been recruited to provide in-reach to community hospitals and care homes, and primary care. This has supported a much more multi-disciplinary and joined up approach to ensure care provision to people outside of acute hospitals.

This has built on work over many years carried out by NHS Highland to improve anticipatory care planning[5] (Baker et al. 2012), poly-pharmacy reviews (NHS Scotland 2015) and virtual wards[6] all designed to take a pro-active approach to reducing hospital admissions (Ham et al. 2013; Somerville 2012; NHS Highland 2011).

Major Service Re-design Under the new integrated arrangements NHS Highland has been able to plan new service models at district level across all health and social care resources. This has included proposals for developing community and care-at-home capacity and which will allow community hospitals beds to be reduced (Blackhurst et al. 2015; Thompson et al. 2015).

32.2.5 People Involvement/Service User Perspective (Value)

There was significant public engagement in order to inform the development and shape of the lead agency model. During the early discussions, NHS Highland held meetings with various stakeholder groups and every community care service user or carer group was contacted by letter to invite them to feed-back on their experiences. Focus groups were also undertaken by NHS Highland staff with people who used particular services and public meetings were held across the region (Highland Partnership 2012).

The vast majority of the feed-back confirmed the support for change. Those who had direct experience of accessing services expressed frustration about the often disjointed approach. Overall the feed-back provided a strong mandate to continue with integrating services. Qualitative research conducted subsequently pointed to a common theme: generally, public respondents were surprised that NHS Highland and The Highland Council did not already work in a highly co-ordinated way (Beswick 2013).

In Scotland, there is national guidance around how NHS Boards should inform, engage and consult with their local communities, service users, staff and partner agencies about proposed major service change (Scottish Health Council 2010). In

---

[5]In 2010 NHS Highland introduced an Anticipatory Care Patient Alert (ACPA) form. This is completed for patients who have one or more pre-existing conditions which may have resulted in them being admitted to hospital as an emergency on several previous occasions.

[6]The Virtual Wards work just like a hospital ward, using the same staffing, systems and daily routines, except that the people being cared for stay in their own homes throughout.

the case of major service redesign as described above, this included having a steering group made up of service users, public members, elected members, staff and partner agencies. This culminated in a formal 3 month consultation with the public (Blackhurst et al. 2015; NHS Highland 2015b; Thompson et al. 2015).

The public consultation is a requirement and feed-back was considered by the board of NHS Highland and ultimately the Cabinet Secretary. The feed-back from the public endorsed the proposed new models of care, as well as highlighting areas of concern to be addressed. A tangible example of how consultation shaped redesign proposals was the requirement to develop an integrated transport plan and for it to be in place before closing any hospitals. Another was to develop capacity in care home to provide for flexible use of beds to avoid hospital stays or support end of life care.

Two major service re-designs in Highland were the first to be approved by the Scottish Government since 2007. Arguably working in an integrated way has fostered more collaborative ways of working on moving away from a focus on buildings and beds to investing more in community services (NHS Highland 2015c).

Recently, NHS Highland made a commitment to 'My Home Life'. This is a UK-wide initiative to promote the quality of life for individuals who live, die, visit and work in care homes for older people (Help the Aged 2007). This is achieved by engaging with the community using various approaches to discover what they are prepared to contribute to help develop services.

This approach has led to improvements in community involvement. For example, several homes now hold community events, supported by residents. Other managers of care homes have used the listening tree for residents, relatives, and community as a way of facilitating feed-back. As an example, one care home now hosts a monthly dementia cafe, and another hosts monthly coffee mornings. Overall, there is increased voluntary input. This builds on work since 2012 to strive to make care homes part of their communities (NHS Highland 2013).

32.2.6 Impacts

Delivering integration and necessary organisational change was a significant challenge, and there was a risk that any effort devoted to integration could have led to deterioration in service delivery. However, during the year following integration (2013), there was no documented evidence of any adverse effects on key performance indicators (Westbrook 2017).

There has been an overall steady improvement in Inspectorate Grades for Care Homes operated by NHS Highland. While there is no reporting mechanism that allows this to be compared across Scotland within Highland, a general improvement was not similarly reflected in care homes run by other providers. Furthermore, the age of people being admitted to any care home has increased by around 2 years since integration.

In addition, NHS Highland continues to perform better than most mainland boards on the performance of the 4-hour emergency target: 98% of patients wait less than 4 hours from arrival to admission, discharge or transfer for accident and emergency treatment. This has been sustained 3 years after integration (Scottish Government 2015a, b, c).

A one-year pilot on medicines management in North Highland demonstrated that the new service made medicines safer and more effective for care home residents. This service is now provided permanently to all care homes in North and West Highland and elements of the service are also being rolled out to care-at-home service users (Claire Morrison, personal communication).

A Medicine Sick Day Rules card was also developed. The card promotes better management of long-term conditions through the safer, more effective use of medicines. Hospital admissions data were collected for 9 months and showed a small fall in admissions since the cards were introduced. This was set against a trend of increasing admissions in previous years, indicating that the cards are effective. No increase in admissions for heart failure was observed, highlighting that use of the cards are also safe (Morrison and Wilson 2015).

Considerable challenges remain to further optimise integrated service delivery. Moreover, there is a need to better understand the complex relationships between services and 'flow' and any possible unintended consequences. For example, in 2014/15, only 63% of privately-run care home places were available to admissions; five homes were subject to temporary closures and some were permanently closed due to poor quality. However, this created a shortage of care home places and increased demand on acute and community hospitals increasing the number of people who had delayed discharges—one of the key drivers to integrate health and social care services.

The University of Highlands and Islands has been commissioned to conduct an independent review of performance against the original aims of the Partnership Agreement. Initial (unpublished) results suggest that a majority of indicators show improvements with the exception of delayed discharges.

Since integration NHS Highland has shifted significant resources from health across to social care. An additional £9 million (recurring) was invested in 2015/16 to develop services to support people to live independently at home including to deliver the living wage. Whether this would have happened prior to integration is debateable but what is clear is that given single budgets, single management and single governance this was a decision that NHS Highland could take more readily and rapidly compared to other NHS boards in Scotland. This has allowed a clear understanding of the direct consequences of one part of the system on another and now with the direct authority and oversight to act.

New ways of integrated working have also been a catalyst for wider reform within NHS Highland. The only District General Hospital in the area (Raigmore in Inverness) has merged with community and primary care services to become one operational unit. Now with single management, single budgets and single governance the aim is to facilitate greater integration of health services.

32.2.7 Dissemination and Replication of the Case Study

The lead agency model, as established with Highland Council in Scotland, can be seen to constitute a very specific model of integrated care, with its focus on a largely rural area of Scotland. However, the lessons on joint working that can be learned from this model appear to be entirely transferrable to other health and care partnerships. At the same time it is important to reiterate that the Highland Council was the only council in Scotland that adopted this model, while all other councils are setting up Integrated Joint Boards from April 2016 boards (Bruce and Parry 2015).

Many of the service interventions that have been introduced since integration have been or are being rolled out across all districts and in some cases across Scotland. For instance, the Medicine Sick Day Rules card, developed, tested and evaluated in Highland (Morrison and Wilson 2015) has now been made available nationally. This was to complement the publication of the updated NHS Scotland Polypharmacy Guidance (March 2015).

32.2.8 Lessons Learned and Outlook

The lead agency model as established with Highland Council in Scotland has clarified governance and maximised the expertise of individual professionals. Nothing prevented these changes from taking place prior to 2012, but perceived barriers and different cultures and management structures appear to have had the effect of not enabling effective change in Highland and indeed across Scotland. Some of the key lessons learned and outlook may be summarised as follows:

- Leadership and management capacity are required to ensure that changes get embedded, sustained and rolled out across all relevant areas. In some cases, there have been practical challenges to overcome inevitable competing priorities.
- Senior leaders across both organisations demonstrated a 'can-do' attitude and knocked down organisational barriers to change.
- A formal project management approach was not adhered to. Given that integration is a complex, multi-faceted process, leaders accepted a degree of uncertainty.
- Support for integration was garnered by avoiding a focus on cost-savings. Respondents were convinced by the argument that, in the long term, integrated services would be more cost-effective because they would involve less duplication and allow greater support for care at home (cf hospital care).
- Practitioners pointed to the importance of leaders recognising professional identities. Professional leadership was put in place outside of line management structures, and was significant in allaying some professional mistrust and concerns.

- Partnership working (i.e. mutual trust and decision-making between staff and employers) was also significant in resolving terms and conditions issues arising from the staff transfers.
- There are inherent difficulties in trying to measure and interpret the impact of integration both at the macro and micro level and in particular at points of time especially over short time scales. A 2014 review of reviews on the economic impacts of integrated care found that evaluative information was scant, and that its scale, complexity and lack of agreed definition made this a very difficult undertaking (Nolte and Pitchforth 2014). They also pointed to a number of reasons why there is a lack of evidence around integration including evaluation not being prioritised.
- There is no doubt this has been a challenging area for this study but data has been collected pre and post integration which will hopefully contribute to the evidence base (Westbrook 2017).
- Some things may appear to, or actually, do get worse before they improve. Fully realising some of the benefits may take many years and indeed this has been the experience of others (Goodwin et al. 2014). The significance of taking a long-term view is therefore highlighted, and there needs to be recognition that there will inevitably be some ups and downs.
- For what was one of the biggest reforms in Highland, and indeed Scotland for over a decade, integration received remarkably little media attention and minimal interest from communities or groups. This is in stark contrast to how changes to service models or changes in practice have generally been reported in Highland.
- Overall, the one key lesson has to be to focus on the needs of the local population and to reconfigure services around this need rather than the organisational boundaries and limitations of institutions. As this case study has illustrated, however, this is anything but as simple as it sounds.

References

Baird, J., Mead, E., & Stark, C. (2014). Implementing health and social care integration in rural Scotland. *International Journal of Integrated Care*. Annual Conference Supplement, URN:NBN:NL:UI:10-1-116199.

Baker, A., Leak, P., Ritchie, L. D., Lee, A. J., & Fielding, S. (2012). Anticipatory care planning and integration: A primary care pilot study aimed at reducing unplanned hospitalisation. *British Journal of General Practise, 62*(595), e113–e120.

Beswick, E. (2013). What are the leadership lessons to be learned from the integration of health and social care in North Highland? Msc dissertation University of Stirling.

Blackhurst, S., Bogle, J., Peters, B., Rodgers, K., Small, N., & Thompson, M. (2015). *We started by sharing the problem: A grass root re-design of health and social care services in Badenoch and Strathspey.* Poster submission to NHS Scotland 2015 event. Retrieved September 27, 2015, from http://nhsscotlandevent.com/sites/default/files/2015%20-%20NHSScotland%20Event%20-%20Posters%20-%20PDF%20-%20VF11%20-%20Maimie%20Thomson.pdf

Brown, C. (2013). A remarkable journey, an historic transition and a new beginning. Scott-Moncrieff. Retrieved September 27, 2015, from http://www.scott-moncrieff.com/news/news-updates/a-remarkable-journey-an-historic-transition-and-a-new-beginning

Bruce, D., & Parry, B. (2015). Integrated care in Scotland. *London Journal of Primary Care (Abingdon), 7*(3), 44–48. Retrieved October 6, 2015, from http://www.ncbi.nlm.nih.gov/pmc/articles/PMC4494465/

Goodwin, N., Dixon, A., Anderson, G., & Wodchis, W. (2014). *Providing integrated care for older people with complex needs. Lessons from seven international case studies.* London: The King's Fund. Retrieved October 6, 2015, from http://www.kingsfund.org.uk/publications/providing-integrated-care-older-people-complex-needs

Ham, C., Heenan, D., Longley, M., & Steel, D. R. (2013). *Integrated care in Northern Ireland, Scotland and Wales: Lessons for England.* London: King's Fund.

Help the Aged. (2007). *My home life promoting quality of life in care homes. A review of literature.* Prepared for Help the Aged by the National Care Home research and Development Forum (London). Retrieved October 6, 2015, from http://www.scie.org.uk/publications/guides/guide15/files/myhomelife-litreview.pdf?res=true

Highland Council. (2015). Highland partnership: Chief social work officer report 2014/15. Retrieved October 6, 2015, from http://www.highland.gov.uk/meetings/meeting/3578/education_children_and_adult_services_committee

Highland Partnership. (2012). Planning for integration, integrating care in the highlands: Programme report. Retrieved September 27, 2015, from http://highlandlife.net/content/download/38033/151050/file/P4I%20End%20of%20Programme%20Report%20July12%20pdf.pdf

Keating, M. (2010). *The government of Scotland: Public policy making after devolution* (2nd ed.). Edinburgh: Edinburgh University Press.

Mcfadden, J., & Lazareswich, M. (1999). *The Scottish parliament.* Edinburgh: T & T Clark.

Mead, E. (2015). Integration in action in the highlands. *International Journal of Integrated Care.* Annual Conference Supplement. URN:NBN:NL:UI:10-1-116995

Mooney, G., & Scott, G. (2012) Devolution, social justice and social policy: The Scottish context. In G. Mooney, & G. Scott (Eds.), *Social justice and social policy in Scotland* (pp. 1–24). Bristol: Policy Press.

Morrison, C., & Wilson, M. (2015). Medicine sick day rules: A safe and effective tool to improve medicines safety in NHS Highland. *International Journal of Pharmacy Practice, 23*(S2), 92–93.

NHS Highland. (2011). *NHS Highland News.* Retrieved October 6, 2015, from http://www.nhshighland.scot.nhs.uk/News/Documents/NHS%20Highland%20News%20-%20Health%20Check.pdf

NHS Highland. (2012a). *Planning for integration – partnership agreement.* Highland NHS Board special board meeting 21 March 2012. Retrieved September 27, 2015, from http://www.nhshighland.scot.nhs.uk/Meetings/BoardsMeetings/Documents/Special%20Board%20Meeting%2021%20March%202012/3.1%20HC%20NHSH%20Lead%20Agency%20Agreement%20only%20NO%20Schedules.pdf

NHS Highland. (2012b). Leading the way: Integrating care in the highlands, video presentation. Retrieved October 6, 2015, from http://highlandlife.net/integrating_care

NHS Highland. (2013). *NHS Highland News Autumn.* Retrieved October 6, 2015, from http://edition.pagesuite-professional.co.uk//launch.aspx?eid=c4e62b46-c9aa-4fe2-b479-ca03e797257e

NHS Scotland. (2015). *Polypharmacy guidance.* Edinburgh: Scottish government health and social care directorates.

NHS Highland. (2015a). *NHS Highland 10 year operational.* Assynt House, Inverness: NHS Highland Board.

NHS Highland. (2015b). Initial agreement for modernisation of community and hospital services in Badenoch and Strathspey. Retrieved September 27, 2015, from http://www.nhshighland.

scot.nhs.uk/Meetings/BoardsMeetings/Documents/Board%20meeting%202%20June%202015/
Item%204.3(2)%20Proposed%20Redesign%20Badenoch%20and%20Strathspey.pdf

NHS Highland. (2015c). Care at home Boleskine style video presentation. Retrieved October
6, 2015, from https://www.youtube.com/watch?v=LEi6A0xfMXk

Nolte, E. & Pitchforth, E. (2014). *What is the evidence on the economic impacts of integrated care?*
Copenhagen: European Observatory on health systems and policy: A partnership hosted by the
World Health Organisation. Available at http://www.euro.who.int/__data/assets/pdf_file/0019/
251434/What-is-the-evidence-on-the-economic-impacts-of-integrated-care.pdf

Scottish Government. (2011). *Achieving sustainable quality in Scotland's Healthcare: A '20:20'
vision*. Edinburgh: Scottish Government. Retrieved October 6, 2015, from http://www.gov.
scot/Topics/Health/Policy/2020-Vision/Strategic-Narrative

Scottish Government. (2014). Scottish budget. Draft Budget 2015–16. Edinburgh. Retrieved
September 27, 2015, from http://onlinelibrary.wiley.com/doi/10.1111/ijpp.2015.23.issue-s2/
issuetoc

Scottish Government. (2015a). Polypharmacy guidance, March 2015. Retrieved October 6, 2015,
from http://www.sign.ac.uk/pdf/polypharmacy_guidance.pdf

Scottish Government. (2015b). Website. Retrieved October 6, 2015, from http://www.gov.scot/
About/Performance/scotPerforms/partnerstories/NHSScotlandperformance/4hrAEStandard

Scottish Government. (2015c). Scotland's Census 2011. Retrieved September 29, 2015, from
http://www.scotlandscensus.gov.uk/

Scottish Health Council. (2010). Guidance report: Involving patients, carers and the public in
options appraisal for major health service change. Accessed 27 Sept 2015.

Somerville, M. (2012). The annual report of the Director of Public Health Report Health and
Wellbeing of Older Adults. Retrieved October 6, 2015, from http://www.nhshighland.scot.nhs.
uk/Meetings/BoardsMeetings/Documents/Board%20Meeting%202%20October%202012/4.4%
20DPH%20Annual%20Report-APP.pdf

Taylor, A. (2015). New act new opportunity for integration in Scotland. *Journal of Integrated Care,
23*(1), 3–9.

Thistlethwaite, P. (2011). Integrating health and social care in Torbay: Improving care for
Mrs Smith, The King's Fund. Retrieved September 29, 2015, from http://www.kingsfund.org.
uk/publications/integrating-health-and-social-care-torbay

Thompson, M., Peters, B., Small, N., & Rodgers, K. (2015). A problem shared. International Journal of
Integrated Care. Annual Conference Supplement. URN:NBN:NL:UI:10-1-116970.

Westbrook, S. (2017). A comparison of NHS Highland key performance indicators pre and post
integration. University of the Highlands and Islands.

USA: Innovative Payment and Care Delivery Models—Accountable Care Organizations

33

Andreas Schmid

33.1 Integrated Care in the United States of America

Examining the past and current state of health insurance and care provision helps in understanding recent attempts to foster integrated healthcare delivery in the United States. Most strikingly, high fragmentation among payers characterizes the U.S. healthcare system. A number of different, and only partly complementary, insurance systems exist. Most citizens under age 65 are covered by private insurance, which comes in two ways. Employer-sponsored group contracts predominate among workers in larger firms and their families, while direct-purchase insurance covers individuals who are not offered insurance through their employers. The first option is community rated, but the second was traditionally subject to risk rating and medical underwriting. The latter has been changed by the Patient Protection and Affordable Care Act (ACA) in 2010, which introduced a third option, the so-called health insurance marketplaces. The marketplaces offer more standardized insurance products, partial community rating, and public subsidies for low-income individuals. In Fig. 33.1, both the second and the third option are summarized in the category of direct-purchase. The figure illustrates the percentage of people in each category as well as the dynamics triggered by the ACA (Smith and Medalia 2015).

The United States also has public payers in the form of Medicaid and Medicare. Medicaid is run by the states and covers low-income individuals who meet certain requirements—in context of the ACA, the coverage has been expanded to more of the population. Medicare is run by the federal government and primarily covers people of 65 years and older. While Medicare's beneficiaries account for a little less than 20% of the U.S. population, the program's expenditure is the second largest item of the federal budget, adding up to $600 billion a year. Medicare on average

A. Schmid (✉)
Health Management, University of Bayreuth, Bayreuth, Germany
e-mail: andreas.schmid@uni-bayreuth.de

© Springer International Publishing AG 2017
V. Amelung et al. (eds.), *Handbook Integrated Care*,
DOI 10.1007/978-3-319-56103-5_33

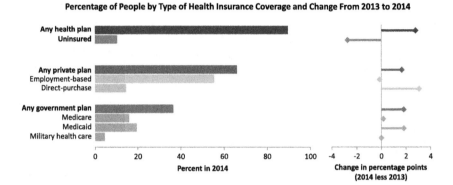

Fig. 33.1 Health insurance coverage in the U.S. Source: Smith and Medalia (2015)

contributes more than 40% to providers' total gross revenue (Aspen Publishers 2015); for many providers, it accounts for more than 50% of their business volume.

The U.S. healthcare system has a history of continuous organizational change (Bazzoli et al. 2004). Cracks in the system and fragmentation have spurred both large-scale health reforms and individual entrepreneurial initiatives. The result is by no means a perfect healthcare system. From 1980 to 2010, national health expenditure as percentage of U.S. GDP almost doubled, from 8.9 to 17.4% (CDC 2015), with access and quality still being criticized as mediocre (Squires 2012). Fragmentation also still prevails, and issues that were already discussed 30 years ago, such as community accountability or patient outcomes, remain subjects of debate. A byproduct of this history is a large number of experiments, making the U.S. probably the largest laboratory for healthcare delivery reform in the world. Many of these attempts have failed, while others endured longer than anyone would have predicted and adapted to the changing environment. Kaiser Permanente, Mayo Health System, and Geisingers Health System are just three of the largest and best-known examples of innovative healthcare delivery but not the only ones from which we can learn. The many failures can teach valuable lessons, too.

The era of managed care began in 1973 with the U.S. Congress passing the Health Maintenance Organization Act. This act popularized the term "health maintenance organization" (HMO), removed many state restrictions, and mandated that employers with more than 25 employees that provided health insurance include at least one HMO option. Over the following two and a half decades, various forms of managed healthcare delivery prospered. They proved, among many other things, two facts. First, capitation is a powerful incentive to make organizations more efficient, as it reduces care volume and eliminates unnecessary services—and occasionally more than just the unnecessary ones. Second, health reform cannot succeed without patient acceptance. Patients value the freedom to choose their providers and rank care quality higher than cost containment. Thus a consumer backlash—triggered also by patient opposition to reduced formularies, red tape, and patient-endangering pre-authorization requirements—brought the managed care movement to a halt by the mid-1990s. As a result, the term "managed care" was stigmatized and remains basically taboo in health reform. This being said, today almost all the care delivered in the U.S. has some elements of managed care, though these elements are not pushed as aggressively as they were by the original HMOs.

Today, the structure of the provider market illustrates, to some extent, outcomes of this history. The boom of managed care fostered the consolidation of services providers. To provide service along the full continuum of care for populations in defined areas and create countervailing power against large insurers, providers merged. In 2014, most of the roughly 5000 community hospitals were part of fully integrated hospital systems (more than 3200) or part of more loosely organized networks (about 1600). There is a mix of public (20%), private not-for-profit (58%), and private for-profit hospitals (21%) (AHA 2016). Physicians are mostly organized in groups with varying degrees of economic and legal integration. They contract with both hospitals and insurers. As hospitals still rely mostly on attending physicians—hospitalists have gained popularity but are not common—physician groups are important players in the market. The past also saw waves of vertical integration, such as hospitals buying physician groups, followed by waves of disintegration.

33.2   Integrated Care in Practice: Accountable Care Organizations

33.2.1 Problem Definition

Both quality and costs are pressing issues for U.S. healthcare reform. Efforts to address these issues by means of integrated care delivery and innovative payment models are mostly driven by the Centers for Medicare and Medicaid Services (CMS), an agency within the U.S. Department of Health and Human Services (HHS). CMS administers the Medicare program and the federal part of the Medicaid program. The high relevance of Medicare spending makes providers very sensitive to CMS's policy changes. And with the baby boomers hitting retirement age, the importance of Medicare looms ever larger. Many of CMS's reform efforts can be linked to goals that are known as the Triple Aim: improving the experience of care and the health of populations while reducing per-capita costs (Berwick et al. 2008). These aims conflict with traditional, fragmented delivery structures and fee-for-service (FFS) payments, which are still the norm for reimbursing providers.

In early 2015, HHS made a bold announcement, stating that it would drastically reduce traditional FFS spending (HHS 2015). While in 2011 almost all traditional[1] Medicare spending was FFS, the agency's goal is to reduce the share to 70% in 2016 and 50% by 2018, replacing FFS with alternative payment models. In 2018, the agency says 90% of the remaining traditional Medicare payments will be tied to

---

[1]That is, spending outside of Medicare Part C.

value and quality measures. CMS's goal is broader than just reforming the Medicare payment scheme; it aims also to incentivize private players in the market to foster patient-centred insurance and care delivery. While just a declaration of intent, this policy statement received considerable attention from providers.

33.2.2 Description of the ACO Model

One of the most discussed alternative payment models is the accountable care organization (ACO).[2] According to CMS's definition, ACOs "are groups of doctors, hospitals, and other health care providers, who come together voluntarily to give coordinated high quality care to their Medicare patients" (CMS 2015b). ACOs have been conceived as a means for achieving the Triple Aim of improving population health and the experience of care while containing costs while focusing on defined patient populations. Their payment system creates the corresponding incentives. The FFS scheme remains in place, but providers are evaluated financially with regard to the performance of a benchmark population and must meet quality standards. In the Medicare Shared Savings Program, savings (one-sided option) or savings and risks (two-sided option) are shared to varying degrees between providers and Medicare, mimicking incentives of a capitation-like system. Payments depend on quality targets.

ACOs can also serve patients from the private (non-Medicare) insurance market, but the largest push fostering this model came through the ACA and CMS's subsequent targeting the Medicare population. While private insurers can steer their enrollees towards their dedicated ACO—for example, by charging higher co-pays for physician visits outside of the preferred network—Medicare does not impose such restrictions. An algorithm assigns patients to a specific ACO if the data suggest that this is their primary care provider. The ACO is then accountable for the patient's care quality and costs, but the patient may also choose providers outside of the ACO. There is no requirement for an ACO to be a fully integrated company. In addition, purely contractual arrangements between participating providers to coordinate care processes and share risks and benefits are possible.

In consequence, a broad range of institutional arrangements has emerged. Muhlestein et al. (2014) have sketched out a taxonomy of ACOs, identifying at least six different setups characterized by their degree of integration across outpatient and inpatient care, the complexity of services covered, and the degree of centralization. On a general level, ACOs are either led by hospitals, physician groups, or fully integrated health systems.

Besides the Medicare Shared Saving Programs, CMS also offered the Pioneer ACO Model, a two-sided option, putting providers on a faster track for taking on

---

[2]Other concepts are, for example, bundled payments or patient centred medical homes (Jackson et al. 2013; Schmid and Himmler 2015). Predecessors of the ACO programs were the Medicare Physician Group Practice Demonstration projects from 2005 to 2010 (Wilensky 2011).

larger risks and cutting down on the relevance of the standard FFS share of their revenues. But by the end of 2015, 16 of the 32 organizations that had signed up in 2012 had left the program, mostly converting to the less ambitious Medicare Shared Savings Program. CMS thus has closed enrollment for this type of ACO. Reasons for the high dropout rate are its considerable financial uncertainty, implementation challenges, new information technology, etc. This matches with the trend in the Medicare Shared Savings Program. In April 2015, a bit more than 3 years after the start of the program, 401 ACOs operated under the one-sided regime, and only three under the two-sided regime.

A more recent alternative arose as an add-on to the Medicare Shared Savings program. The ACO Investment Model[3] addresses difficulties faced especially by smaller ACOs, particularly those in rural and underserved areas, which had struggled to come up with the investment budget to implement required changes of processes and information technology. This model pre-pays shared savings and thus tries to solve the problem of front-end investments with delayed payoffs. But CMS remains active in trying to promote new and ambitious ACO approaches. Building on the lessons from the Pioneer ACO Models, a new two-sided option is being promoted under the label Next Generation ACO Model, starting in 2016 with 21 participants. A key goal is to provide participants with better predictability of financial outcomes (CMS 2016).

33.2.3 Impact

A much-debated issue is the benchmarks used to establish savings or losses. As Douven et al. (2015) point out, the original version of the Medicare Shared Savings Program had created unintended incentives. The financial benchmark was defined for a full three-year contract cycle and referred to a weighted cost average of the attributed population over the preceding 3 years, giving the highest weight to the most recent year. This created situations in which inflating costs pre-enrollment paid off heavily during enrollment periods. What's more, very successful ACOs ended up being punished, as their benchmarks became the more challenging the more they had saved. With each new version of ACO models, the benchmarking, as well as the risk-adjustment schemes, have become more sophisticated to minimize these drawbacks. The weights have been adjusted to capture more of the long-term cost structure, and past savings are taken into account to avoid unintended penalties.

It is still too early for a judgment on success or failure based on financial or quality indicators. The experience is too recent and brief. Too many different models have emerged. High shares of new entrants and drop-outs obfuscated the results. And only a few providers and Medicare beneficiaries have participated. However, preliminary assessments can be made. The high turnover rate from the

---

[3]The Medicare Advance Payment Model can be seen as a predecessor to this model featuring 35 participating organizations in 2015.

Pioneer ACO model indicates that, while many ACOs can realize savings, not all providers are successful in this respect (Casalino 2014). In 2015, CMS announced that the net savings of Medicare amounted to $411 million for the year 2014 (CMS 2015c). This accounts for all realized savings minus savings shared with providers ($422 million), plus losses shared by ACOs in two-sided models ($9 million dollars). A closer look at the ACOs in the Medicare Shared Savings Program by Introcaso and Berger (2015) shows a mixed picture. Among the 333 ACOs, only 86 received shared savings payments, that is, realized savings above a pre-set minimum savings rate while at the same time providing complete quality information. These ACOs saved $777 million and received $341 million. An additional $41 million of payments would have been issued, if ACOs had performed better on quality criteria. However, the most successful ACOs in financial terms were also the ones with the highest benchmark—the highest pre-ACO cost level. Furthermore, among the 86 successful ACOs, payoffs were highly concentrated, with a few contributing most to the overall savings. Another notable aspect is that physician-based organizations performed better than hospital-led ACOs. This dovetails with earlier results on Pioneer ACOs (McWilliams et al. 2015).

To qualify for shared savings, ACOs must meet quality standards. CMS established 33 measures, covering four domains: patient experience, care coordination, preventive health, and at-risk population. Performance is captured through a mix of surveys, claims data and other data sources (CMS 2015a). Early findings indicate that participating institutions do improve on these indicators. As McClellan et al. (2015) point out, the data do not suggest that there is a correlation between financial and quality performance. Furthermore, all results must be considered in the context of overall Medicare volume. Total savings in 2014 were just about 1/1000 of the total Medicare budget. While the number of covered individuals has grown considerably, the 477 ACOs nationwide still serve less than 9 million Medicare beneficiaries. Provider participation is also still voluntary, suggesting that selection effects may confound some of the successes. Difficulties, for example experienced by Kaiser Permanente, have shown that transferring models that work in some regions to others can present severe challenges (Gitterman et al. 2003).

33.2.4 Dissemination

The ACA brought large momentum on various levels, changing the landscape for insurers as well as for providers. One should not underestimate the impact that the Medicare ACO programs also brought to the private market (Berenson and Burton 2012). While fragmentation continues to be a key challenge for healthcare delivery and for the health system in general, reforms such as the ACO programs give reason for optimism. The CMS-led programs have shown that ACOs can improve quality and contain costs. Even so, no ACO template has emerged; successful models still need to be identified and scaled up, and knowledge needs to be shared. At this point, too little is known about the actual changes successful (and unsuccessful) ACOs made in their care for patient populations. CMS needs to continue improving its benchmarking and incentivizing providers to embrace new approaches while not overtaxing their ability to implement them. At the same time, unintended side effects, such as growing market power on the provider side, must be addressed.

33.2.5 Lessons Learned and Challenges Ahead

Critics dismiss ACOs as repackaged HMOs, but there are key differences. CMS has taken a strong stance in favor of patients having free choice of providers; they are not limited to providers within their ACO and can leave if they are unhappy with their ACO. Furthermore, HMOs tried to reduce utilization through restrictive formularies and strict control of access. Today's approach aims at more patient-centred care, especially in primary care, while also paying attention to population health. There is at least some hope that this will live up to expectations and show that concepts like the Triple Aim and ACOs are more than just buzzwords. What may make a big difference, in contrast to the situation 20–30 years ago, is the ability to create and analyze large data sets. These can help to identify patients at risk and effective preventive services and then measure the quality of the care patients receive. "Big Data" is a buzzword itself, and many providers grumble about feeling the pain of these new technologies while receiving few of the promised rewards. But the promise in this field is enormous, so optimism seems appropriate. Still, there are concerns, especially with regard to the considerable investments required to take advantage of big data, which may overburden smaller providers, thus again driving even more consolidation of services.

Further consolidation among providers would be worrisome, as the U.S. have produced strong evidence that regional markets dominated by few large health systems tend to result in higher prices due to market power (Gaynor and Town 2012a, b; Cutler and Scott Morton 2013). Various forces are driving consolidation in the wake of the ACA. Providers need to leverage large investments and need to cover a share of the population sufficiently large to enable them to operate efficiently. As more risk is passed on to them, they need more patients to spread this risk among. Several provisions of the ACA favor the formation of large local and regional entities and have triggered a new wave of mergers and acquisitions in the U.S. hospital market (Pope 2014), adding up to 457 deals affecting 999 hospitals between 2010 and 2014 (AHA 2015).

High administrative costs are another concern. Driven, among other things, by extensive contract management and billing needs, they are one of the causes of the high healthcare costs in the U.S. (Himmler and Jugl 2016). It is unlikely that ACOs can damp this. These sorts of concerns, along with the worry that inertia will triumph and healthcare delivery will change much less than expected, can lead to skepticism about ACOs' long-term potential (Marmor and Oberlander 2012). As Casalino (2014) puts it: "The fledgling ACO movement involves two large risks. The first is that it will fail. The second is that it will succeed, but for the wrong reasons." (p. 1750) ACOs, in other words, may endure not because they provide better quality or lower costs but because they have become dominant players in the market.

Another aspect of ACOs likely to receive attention is that physician-led ACOs seem to be more successful in reducing costs than their hospital-led counterparts (Introcaso and Berger 2015). This may indicate a dilemma for providers. Hospitals still run a largely volume-driven business model. For them, the incentives to reduce admissions are mixed, especially if they cannot adjust capacity and thus reduce costs on the same scale.

ACOs are unlikely to be a panacea. However, together with many other reform initiatives that have been proposed—such as the patient-centreed medical homes or linking payments to value—they highlight both the relevance and the potential of integrated approaches to healthcare delivery in the U.S. and beyond.

References

AHA. (2015). *Trendwatch chartbook 2015: Trends affecting hospitals and health systems.* Washington. Retrieved March 1, 2016, from http://www.aha.org/research/reports/tw/chartbook/2015/15chartbook.pdf

AHA. (2016). Fast facts on US hospitals, AHA hospital statistics 2016 edition. Retrieved February 29, 2016, from http://www.aha.org/research/rc/stat-studies/101207fastfacts.pdf

Aspen Publishers. (2015). Medicare, managed care, & other sources of revenue. In *Hospital accounts receivable analysis* (Vol. 29, No. 1, pp. 20–21).

Bazzoli, G. J., Dynan, L., Burns, L. R., & Yap, C. (2004). Two decades of organizational change in health care: What have we learned? *Medical Care Research and Review, 61*(3), 247–331.

Berenson, R. A., & Burton, R. A. (2012, January 31). *Next steps for ACOs: Health Policy Brief.* Health Affairs.

Berwick, D. M., Nolan, T. W., & Whittington, J. (2008). The triple aim. care, health, and cost. *Health Affairs, 27*(3), 759–769.

Casalino, L. P. (2014). Accountable care organizations—the risk of failure and the risks of success. *The New England Journal of Medicine, 371*(18), 1750–1751.

CDC. (2015). *Health, United States, 2014: Trend tables, health care expenditures and payors, Table 102.* Retrieved February 29, 2015, from http://www.cdc.gov/nchs/hus/contents2014.htm#102

CMS. (2015a). *Accountable Care Organization 2015. Program analysis quality performance standards narrative measure specifications.* Prepared by RTI International. Retrieved February 29, 2016, from https://www.cms.gov/Medicare/Medicare-Fee-for-Service-Payment/sharedsavingsprogram/Downloads/ACO-NarrativeMeasures-Specs.pdf

CMS. (2015b). Accountable Care Organizations (ACO). Retrieved February 29, 2016, from https://www.cms.gov/Medicare/Medicare-Fee-for-Service-Payment/ACO/index.html?redirect=/Aco

CMS. (2015c). *Medicare ACOs provide improved care while slowing cost growth in 2014.* 2015 fact sheets, media release, 25 August 2015. Retrieved March 1, 2016, from https://www.cms.gov/Newsroom/MediaReleaseDatabase/Fact-sheets/2015-Fact-sheets-items/2015-08-25.html

CMS. (2016). Innovation center, next generation ACO model. Retrieved February 29, 2016, from https://innovation.cms.gov/initiatives/Next-Generation-ACO-Model/

Cutler, D. M., & Scott Morton, F. (2013). Hospitals, market share, and consolidation. *JAMA, 310* (18), 1964–1970.

Douven, R., McGuire, T. G., & McWilliams, J. M. (2015). Avoiding unintended incentives in ACO payment models. *Health Affairs, 34*(1), 143–149.

Gaynor, M., & Town, R. (2012a). *The impact of hospital consolidation – Update: The synthesis project*. Policy Brief, No. 9.

Gaynor, M., & Town, R. J. (2012b). Competition in health care markets. In M. V. Pauly, P. P. Barros, & T. G. McGuire (Eds.), *Handbook of health economics: Volume 2, Handbooks in economics* (1st ed., pp. 499–637). Amsterdam/Boston: Elsevier/North Holland.

Gitterman, D. P., Weiner, B. J., Domino, M. E., Mckethan, A. N., & Enthoven, A. C. (2003). The rise and fall of a Kaiser Permanente expansion region. *Milbank Quarterly, 81*(4), 567–601.

HHS. (2015, January 26). *Better, smarter, healthier: In historic announcement, HHS sets clear goals and timeline for shifting Medicare reimbursements from volume to value*. HHS press release. Retrieved February 29, 2016, from http://www.hhs.gov/about/news/2015/01/26/better-smarter-healthier-in-historic-announcement-hhs-sets-clear-goals-and-timeline-for-shifting-medicare-reimbursements-from-volume-to-value.html

Himmler, S. & Jugl, M. (2016). Hospital costs in the U.S. and Germany. In A. Schmid & B. Fried (Eds.), *Crossing borders – Health reform in the U.S., Schriften zur Gesundheitsökonomie* (pp. 41–55). Bayreuth: P.C.O.-Verlag.

Introcaso, D., & Berger, G. (2015). MSSP year two: Medicare ACOs show muted success. HealthAffairsBlog. Retrieved March 1, 2016, from http://healthaffairs.org/blog/2015/09/24/mssp-year-two-medicare-acos-show-muted-success/

Jackson, G. L., Powers, B. J., Chatterjee, R., Prvu Bettger, J., Kemper, A. R., Hasselblad, V., Dolor, R. J., Irvine, R. J., Heidenfelder, B. L., Kendrick, A. S., Gray, R., & Williams, J. W. (2013). The patient-centered medical home. *Annals of Internal Medicine, 158*(3), 169.

Marmor, T., & Oberlander, J. (2012). From HMOs to ACOs: The quest for the Holy Grail in U.S. health policy. *Journal of General Internal Medicine, 27*(9), 1215–1218.

McClellan, M., Kocot, L. S., & White, R. (2015). Medicare ACOs continue to show care improvements—And more savings are possible. HealthAffairsBlog. Retrieved March 1, 2016, from http://healthaffairs.org/blog/2015/11/04/medicare-acos-continue-to-show-care-improvements-and-more-savings-are-possible/

McWilliams, J. M., Chernew, M. E., Landon, B. E., & Schwartz, A. L. (2015). Performance differences in Year 1 of pioneer accountable care organizations. *The New England Journal of Medicine, 372*, 1927–1936.

Muhlestein, D., Gardner, P., Merrill, T., Petersen, M., & Tu, T. (2014). A taxonomy of accountable care organizations: Different approaches to achieve the triple aim. Retrieved June 1, 2015, from http://leavittpartners.com/wp-content/uploads/2014/06/A-Taxonomy-of-Accountable-Care-Organizations.pdf

Pope, C. M. (2014). How Obamacare fuels health care market consolidation: The Heritage Foundation, Backgrounder, No. 2928. Retrieved March 1, 2016, from http://thf_media.s3.amazonaws.com/2014/pdf/BG2928.pdf

Schmid, A., & Himmler, S. (2015). *Netzwerkmedizin – Impulse für Deutschland aus den USA: Stiftung Münch*, Projektbericht, München.

Smith, J. C., & Medalia, C. (2015). *Health insurance coverage in the United States: 2014: Current population reports, P60-253*. Washington, DC: U.S. Census Bureau.

Squires, D. A. (2012). Explaining high health care spending in the United States: An international comparison of supply, utilization, prices, and quality. *Issues in International Health Policy, 10*, 1–14.

Wilensky, G. R. (2011). Lessons from the physician group practice demonstration—A Sobering reflection. *New England Journal of Medicine, 365*(18), 1659–1661.

Switzerland

34

Isabelle Peytremann-Bridevaux, Peter Berchtold, and Isabelle Hagon-Traub

34.1 Integrated Care in Switzerland

Switzerland, which includes three main linguistic regions (German, French and Italian) and comprises a population of about 8 million in 26 cantons, is a democratic state in which government responsibilities are divided among three levels: the federal level, the 26 cantons and the over 2500 municipalities. The Swiss healthcare system is highly decentralised, with each of the 26 cantons responsible for securing healthcare provision for their populations. Cantons finance about half of hospital and are in charge of issuing and implementing the majority of federal health-related legislation; they also carry out prevention and health promotion activities (De Pietro et al. 2015; OECD/WHO 2011).

The 1996 Health Insurance Law and its subsequent revisions were of great importance to the Swiss healthcare system. It sought to strengthen social solidarity, guarantee equal access to healthcare and reduce healthcare expenditures, building on the principles of universal health insurance coverage (compulsory for all residents), risk compensation among health insurers (protection of small insurers and vulnerable categories of patients), obligation to conclude contracts (insurers must refund all providers), insurance contributions that are independent of income and that are subsidised if they exceed 8% of taxable income, cost sharing (annual deductible in ambulatory care, with additional co-payments for hospital stays over

I. Peytremann-Bridevaux (✉)
Institute of Social and Preventive Medicine, Lausanne University Hospital and University of Lausanne, 10 route de la Corniche, 1010, Lausanne, Switzerland
e-mail: Isabelle.Peytremann-Bridevaux@chuv.ch

P. Berchtold
Forum Managed Care, Zugerstrasse 193, 6314 Unterägeri, Switzerland

I. Hagon-Traub
Programme cantonal Diabète, Service de la Santé Publique du canton de Vaud, avenue des Casernes 2, 1014, Lausanne, Switzerland

© Springer International Publishing AG 2017
V. Amelung et al. (eds.), *Handbook Integrated Care*,
DOI 10.1007/978-3-319-56103-5_34

and above the deductible) and a comprehensive basket of health benefits (De Pietro et al. 2015; OECD/WHO 2011).

Healthcare coverage, defined by the Federal Department of Home Affairs, includes inpatient services, general practitioner and specialist outpatient services, pharmaceuticals, home healthcare service, non-medical services if prescribed, medical devices and some preventive or screening measures. Outpatient services are financed through social health insurance (above deductible and patients' 10% participation), which also covers half of the expenditure on inpatient services, using diagnosis-related group (DRG), with cantons covering the remainder. In 2012, total (public and private) healthcare expenditures were mainly devoted to inpatient hospital and long term care (46.2%), ambulatory (30.6%) and pharmaceutical (11%) care (De Pietro et al. 2015). Healthcare expenses are financed by mandatory health insurance and social insurance (46.5%), households (33.2%, e.g. out-of-pocket payments such as co-payments, deductibles, uninsured services and drugs, complementary private insurance), and direct spending by government (20.3%) (De Pietro et al. 2015).

Ambulatory care is provided by primary care physicians and specialists working mostly independently in private practice, but also in small group practices, in networks of physicians and sometimes in health maintenance organisations that work on the principles of managed care; hospitals also provide regular general and specialised ambulatory care. Residents principally have direct and unrestricted access to primary care physicians and specialists. The only exception are those who have opted for an alternative health insurance plan (approximately two thirds of insured residents of Switzerland) (De Pietro et al. 2015), which offers lower premiums for those signing up to voluntary gatekeeping. Inpatient care is provided by public and private hospitals that receive financial subsidies from the state if they are considered of "public interest."

Because of the high level of decentralisation, governance of the system at the national level is weak. Several reform initiatives were undertaken that aimed to strengthen system governance and to build a national consensus on healthcare in Switzerland, but this has remained challenging (Cheng 2010). While consensus building has been successful with regard to hospital care financing, involving a shift from a daily-tariff system to a national DRG system ("SwissDRG") in 2012 (De Pietro et al. 2015), this has been difficult to achieve in other areas. One example is a recent reform proposal that aimed to develop integration of care, introduce population-oriented services and strengthen efficiency and cost containment (the 'Managed Care' proposition of 2012). This reform, which would have established a national framework for integrated care into the Swiss Health Insurance Law, was, however, rejected by three quarters of the voters in a national referendum in 2012 (Swiss Federal Office of Public Health 2012). Likewise, a health promotion and prevention law was developed but rejected in parliament in 2012 because parties were unable to reconcile views on the targets, modes of governance and financing of health promotion and prevention.

In January 2013, the Federal Council approved the comprehensive strategy Health 2020 (Swiss Federal Office of Public Health 2016), which may be the first overarching national health policy Switzerland has ever had. It focuses on four domains (maintaining quality of life, increasing equal opportunities, raising quality of care and improving transparency) that are complemented by 12 objectives and includes a total of 36 measures that will be implemented over the coming years with the involvement of all key stakeholders. The overall objective is to prepare the Swiss health system for the challenges ahead, at affordable costs.

Integrated care in Switzerland can be traced to general practitioners' networks that were first initiated in 1992 (Réseau Delta in Geneva, Schaller 2008) and amounts now approximately 75 networks including approximately 50% of all general practitioners in Switzerland (Berchtold and Peytremann-Bridevaux 2011; Forum Managed Care, n.d.). Networks work on the principle of GP gatekeeping and almost all have entered into contract with social health insurance funds in which they assume budgetary co-responsibility. More recently, there has been increasing interest towards programmes to strengthen coordination of care for patients with one or more chronic diseases (Berchtold and Peytremann-Bridevaux 2011; Peytremann-Bridevaux and Burnand 2009) with a 2013 survey identifying 44 small-scale programmes targeting chronic diseases or multimorbidity in 14 of the 26 cantons (Peytremann-Bridevaux et al. 2015; Ebert et al. 2015).

34.2   Integrated Care in Practice

34.2.1 Problem Definition

The Swiss healthcare system is considered to be among the best performing healthcare systems among countries that are members of the Organisation for Economic Co-operation and Development (OECD) (OECD/WHO 2011; Commonwealth Fund 2014). Its citizens are highly satisfied with the health system (Interpharma, n.d.), mainly because of an almost unconstrained freedom of choice and overall large supply of healthcare providers and hospitals. However, a 2011 analysis of the Swiss healthcare system identified fragmented provision of services, along with lack of coordination and integration as major deficits and suggested that the relatively high healthcare expenditures were not being used efficiently. Whether Switzerland "receives value for money for its major financial investment in healthcare" (OECD/WHO 2011) is being questioned.

In this section, we focus on one cantonal programme, the "Programme cantonal Diabète" (PcD, Hagon-Traub et al. 2010), which was launched in 2010 in the canton of Vaud, a Swiss canton with a population of approximately 720,000 (about 10% of the Swiss population). The programme aimed to reduce the impact of diabetes, which affects about 7% of the population in the canton (Firmann et al. 2008) and which has been associated with a total cost of 500 million CHF to the system in 2009 (Jeanrenaud and Gay 2013), through limiting the increase in the incidence of diabetes and improving the quality of diabetes care. It further seeks to address a projected shortage of healthcare professionals, quality of care gaps and fragmentation inherent in the current structure of the Swiss healthcare system. Following both a top-down and bottom-up approach, the PcD has integrated, since its inception, all stakeholders, including patients' representatives and health-care professionals involved in the provision of diabetes care. Based on a previous smaller scale project (Arditi and Burnand 2011), the PcD emphasises a population-based perspective, and was seen as the solution that allowed the integration of all healthcare professionals and all levels of care delivery of the canton.

34.2.2 Description of the "Programme cantonal Diabète"

Intended for the whole canton of Vaud, projects developed within the PcD initially followed four main targets: people with diabetes (children and adults), practicing healthcare professionals, the healthcare system and the general population (Hagon-Traub et al. 2010). Regarding the latter, it was left to individual organisations and institutions to develop projects on health promotion and disease prevention although the PcD retained oversight, through for example, the promotion and reiter-ation of health promotion and disease prevention messages when appropriate.

Between 2010 and 2015, a wide range of complementary projects have been considered, with more than 85 single projects implemented across the following axes (Table 34.1) (Programme cantonal Diabète 2011, 2012, 2013, 2014):

- Self-management education and support: to strengthen empowerment, self-efficacy and support of patients with diabetes. This axis aims at helping patients with the daily management of their life with diabetes.
- Diabetes care and management: to improve diabetes care and management through the development of care that is evidence-based, considers interdisciplin-arity and is better integrated, coordinated and continuous. This involves the consideration of structural and organisational changes, as well as the develop-ment of documents and care pathways for specific clinical situations, for the community and for ambulatory and inpatient care sectors. It is accompanied by the development of an electronic patient record and a shared care plan. While stretching from prevention to tertiary prevention, the PcD does not currently specifically consider social and palliative care. It should, however, help patients navigate the healthcare system and have access to appropriate care in any region of the canton of Vaud.
- Information and communication: to provide information and practical tools on diabetes (broad spectrum of topics) and the PcD for the general population, people with diabetes and healthcare professionals, as well as to improve com-munication between care providers and between care providers and patients.
- Training of healthcare professionals: to give access to and encourage the use of evidence-based practice guidelines, to propose various multidisciplinary training and conferences, and to reinforce coordination between healthcare providers
- Monitoring and evaluation: to assess the way the PcD is being implemented and how single projects should be monitored, to evaluate whether the PcD has any impact on the health of patients with diabetes in the canton of Vaud, and to explore fields necessitating more attention in the future.

Table 34.1 Summary of *main* projects of the Programme cantonal Diabète (2011, 2012, 2013, 2014)

Target	Axis	Project	Period
Patients with diabetes	Self-management education & support	• DIAFIT (3-month intensive physical activity programme for patients with type 2 diabetes)	2010–
		• EVIVO (6-week Stanford Chronic Disease Self-Management course)	2010–
		• Adaptation and dissemination of the Diabetes Passport	2011–
		• Physical activity for children with diabetes	2011–
		• Expert patient programmes	2015–
		• Common diabetes documents and information sheets for patients and healthcare professionals throughout the canton (DocsDiab)	2015–
		• Patient guidelines (developed by patients)	2015
	Diabetes care & management	• Regional diabetes coordinator position	2010–
		• Care transition for children and adolescent patients	2011–
		• Gestational diabetes pathway	2012–
		• Diabetic nephropathy pathway	2014–
		• Diabetes schemes or arrangements in each of the four health regions	2013–
		• Paediatric diabetes pathway (in the eastern health region)	2013–
		• Development of tools and documents for appropriate inpatient diabetes care	2014–
		• Development of regional structures offering specific services (e.g. nurses follow-up, podiatric care, coordination activities) not remunerated under the current pricing systems	2015–
Healthcare professionals	Information & communication	• Various campaigns and publications during diabetes world day and other times of the year (diabetes screening in pharmacies, web-based diabetes screening tool, free foot consultations, Diabetes Barometer, availability of a list of accredited healthcare professionals caring for patients with diabetes)	2010–
		• Status report and web dissemination on available "diabetes-specific" healthcare professionals and courses	2011–
		• Electronic diabetes patient record (e-diab) and shared care plan	2014–
		• Common diabetes documents and information sheets for patients and healthcare professionals throughout the canton (DocsDiab)	2015–

(continued)

Table 34.1 (continued)

Target	Axis	Project	Period
	Training of healthcare professionals	• Adaptation and dissemination of diabetes-specific guidelines for the Swiss setting	2011–
		• Awareness-raising 3-day course for healthcare professionals on patient education and self-management	2010–
		• Multidisciplinary meetings and conferences	2010–
Healthcare system	Monitoring & evaluation	• Cohort of patients with diabetes residing in the canton of Vaud (CoDiab-VD)	2011–
		• Evaluation of the PcD	2014–

The development of the PcD and its individual projects followed several steps. First, preliminary work was undertaken between 2008 and 2010 by groups of experts in collaboration with healthcare professionals, their professional associations and institutions, as well as patients and their associations, and academic institutions. It was followed by a qualitative project evaluating the experiences and needs of both patients with diabetes and healthcare professionals regarding the management of diabetes in the canton of Vaud (Peytremann-Bridevaux et al. 2012). From this preliminary work, further informed by the Chronic Care Model (Epping-Jordan et al. 2004) and a logic model specifically designed for the PcD. The PcD, which is continuously being developed and adapted to the field and the needs and expectations of all stakeholders, offers a framework and a variety of tools to be used by patients and healthcare professionals. This framework aims at facilitating care adapted to the patients' complex needs. On the basis of risk-stratification and evidence-based recommendations, patients are cared for by regional healthcare professionals and regional specialised structures and hospitals. This perspective needs strong and sustained coordination between individual providers and provider organisations.

Financed by the Department of Public Health, which oversees the development and implementation of the PcD, the projects are steered by the PcD and are mainly conducted by public institutions (e.g. university and regional hospitals, the Institute of social and preventive medicine of Lausanne) or non-for-profit organisations (e.g. patients' and healthcare professionals' associations). In 2013, the steering committee, the grouping of projects within the PcD and the funding of the canton relating to diabetes were reorganised. In addition, the association of the PcD with the not-for-profit patients' diabetes association of the canton of Vaud (Association Vaudois du Diabète), was decided. Linking with the patients' association was seen to strengthen the PcD's legitimacy for patients and their families, who might perceive the programme as a 'state' project; it also makes it possible for PcD and the association to develop common projects because of the patients' association administrative and geographical embeddedness.

34.2.3 People Involvement/Service User's Perspective (Value)

Patients or their representatives (patients' association—Association Vaudoise du Diabète) were actively involved in the initial phases of development of the PcD through their participation in the expert groups and the focus groups that explored the experiences and needs of patients and healthcare professionals. In 2016, patients' representatives were still active in the PcD steering group. In addition, patients who attend the 6-week chronic disease self-management course or the 3-month physical activity course for patients with type 2 diabetes meet regularly and are supported by peers. Across the canton, patients have been trained as 'expert patients' in order to enable the sharing of experiences and help other patients cope with diabetes in their daily life. In addition, on the basis of clinical guidelines developed for healthcare professionals, patients developed their own version of diabetic foot prevention and care recommendations. Finally, patients with diabetes who are included in the CoDiab-VD cohort annually complete the follow-up questionnaire, which targets their health and care as well as specific topics of interest for the development of the PcD, that need to be investigated. The CoDiab-VD follow-up questionnaire also considers questions on awareness of, and participation in, projects proposed by the PcD. Additionally, satisfaction and opinion questionnaires are often included in the self-evaluation of PcD projects.

34.2.4 Impact

The development and implementation of the PcD was complemented by an external evaluation process that targeted both the overall implementation of the PcD and the individual projects. To date, an evaluability assessment in 2011 (Dubois-Arber and Bize 2012) and a formative evaluation in 2012 (Bize et al. 2012) have been conducted. Evaluability assessments usually precede full evaluations and are conducted to make sure that the future evaluation is apt to provide appropriate and useful information for the programme. In the case of the PcD, two evaluability assessment objectives were targeted, one at the project level to evaluate the projects' self-assessment capacities, and one at the programme level to assess overarching evaluation possibilities of the PcD and suggest solutions to meet the second objective. The analyses of the 11 projects implemented during 2010 and 2011 showed that although all projects collected data on their activities, coverage and impact (intermediary outcomes) data were almost non-existent (Dubois-Arber and Bize 2012). At the level of the programme, the evaluability assessment helped draft a first version of the programme's logic model and confirmed the need to conduct a full evaluation. More specifically, the necessity both to collect a minimum set of common data across projects and to repeat population-based measures to assess the impact of the PcD on the whole population was highlighted. The formative evaluation that followed in 2012 (Bize et al. 2012) aimed at conducting a qualitative assessment of the PcD by using semi-structured interviews with main stakeholders, at updating of the logic model, and at synthesising data collected during the first

2 years of the programme. This formative evaluation confirmed previous findings and highlighted the ability of the PcD to bring together a wide range of healthcare professionals aiming at better coordinating diabetes care and management as its main strength. At the same time, it also pointed to weaknesses in the organisation and functioning of the programme, which then led to the proposition of a structural reorganisation of the programme in 2013. The evaluation process described above will be complemented by an assessment of the impact of the PcD on the population of patients with diabetes. The latter will use data that are being collected among participants in the CoDiab-VD cohort described above (Zuercher et al. 2015), as well as by data collected among newly recruited patients with diabetes in 2017. The evaluation will include both longitudinal analyses of patients recruited in 2011–2012, as well as a comparison of cross-sectional analysis of data collected from 2011–2012 (baseline) and 2017 while recognising that it will be difficult to establish robust links between processes or outcomes of care improvements and the activities of the PcD using this approach. These comparisons will include the following primary outcomes: processes-of-care indicators (annual checks of feet, eye, microalbuninuria and HbA1C and yearly influenza immunisation) and outcomes of care such as HbA1C values, (health-related) quality-of-life measures (Short Form-12 Health Survey—SF-12, Audit of Diabetes-Dependent Quality of Life 19—ADDQoL) and Patient Assessment of Chronic Illness Care (PACIC). Data on diabetes, health status, healthcare utilisation, health behaviour, self-management activities and support, self-efficacy, knowledge of, or participation in campaigns or activities proposed by the PcD, and socio-demographic data will also be collected.

34.2.5 Dissemination and Replication

Based on the Chronic Care Model (Epping-Jordan et al. 2004), the PcD has been implemented from the perspective of a case study that could then form the basis for future extensions to other chronic diseases. Even though replication in other settings (i.e. cantons) per se seems difficult because such healthcare developments depend so much on the cantonal context, tools and experiences could be built upon. The evaluation of single projects of the PcD, and of the PcD itself and its elements, will help stakeholders to identify their appropriateness for other contexts or domains as well.

34.2.6 Lessons Learned and Outlook

The political will and support for this innovative programme, at the level of an entire canton, is unique in Switzerland. Although the programme built on a partnership with healthcare providers of the canton of Vaud, the PcD has faced resistance from these partners around issues of modifying the tasks and roles of the healthcare providers. Yet, implementation of integrated care requires not only systemic changes in terms of organisation and communication (for example, patients' electronic medical records), as well as additional budgets for facilitating and implementing coordination activities, but also a clear definition of tasks and roles of healthcare providers, which need to be adapted to integrated care and its underlying elements. However, the provision of financial resources, although key, is not enough. Healthcare authorities must show clear and firm political will that includes participative leadership, as much as they must develop an unequivocal vision about integrated care and the future of healthcare, as well as addressing related communication. Such a course will allow a progressive but positive change in the cantonal healthcare system and its delivery.

References

Arditi, C., & Burnand, B. (2011). *Evaluation de la filière coordonnée de prise en charge des patients diabétiques "Diabaide": période 2004–2006* (Raisons de santé, 179). Lausanne: Institut universitaire de médecine sociale et préventive. Retrieved October 31, 2016, from https://www.iumsp.ch/Publications/pdf/rds179_fr.pdf

Association Vaudoise du Diabète. Retrieved October 31, 2016, from http://diabete-vaud.ch/

Berchtold, P., & Peytremann-Bridevaux, I. (2011). Ten years of integrated care in Switzerland. *International Journal of Integrated Care, 11*(Spec Ed), e010.

Bize, R., Koutaissoff, D., & Dubois-Arber, F. (2012). *Programme cantonal diabète : Bilan de la première phase du programme (2010–2011) et construction d'une théorie d'action* (Raisons de santé, 207). Lausanne: Institut universitaire de médecine sociale et préventive. Retrieved October 31, 2016, from http://www.iumsp.ch/Publications/pdf/rds207_fr.pdf

Cheng, T. M. (2010). Understanding the "Swiss Swatch" function of Switzerland's health system. *Health Affairs, 29*, 1442–1452.

Commonwealth Fund. (2014). *Mirror, mirror on the wall, 2014 update: How the U.S. health care system compares internationally*. Retrieved October 31, 2016, from http://www.common wealthfund.org/publications/fund-reports/2014/jun/mirror-mirror

De Pietro, C., Camenzind, P., Sturny, I., Crivelli, L., Edwards-Garavoglia, S., Spranger, A., Wittenbecher, F., & Quentin, W. (2015). Switzerland: Health system review. *Health Systems in Transition, 17*(4), 1–288.

Dubois-Arber, F., & Bize, R. (2012). *Programme diabète: Evaluation de l'évaluabilité (evaluability assessment) des différents projets inclus dans le programme en 2010 et 2011* (Raisons de santé, 190). Lausanne: Institut universitaire de médecine sociale et préventive. http://www.iumsp.ch/Publications/pdf/rds190_fr.pdf

Ebert, S., Peytremann-Bridevaux, I., & Senn, N. (2015). *Les programmes de prise en charge des maladies chroniques et de la multimorbidité en Suisse* (Obsan Dossier 44). Neuchâtel: Observatoire suisse de la santé.

Epping-Jordan, J. E., Pruitt, S. D., Bengoa, R., & Wagner, E. H. (2004). Improving the quality of health care for chronic conditions. *Quality Safety Health Care, 13*(4), 299–305.

Firmann, M., Mayor, V., Vidal, P. M., Bochud, M., Pecoud, A., Hayoz, D., et al. (2008). The CoLaus study: A population-based study to investigate the epidemiology and genetic determinants of cardiovascular risk factors and metabolic syndrome. *BMC Cardiovascular Disorders, 8*, 6.

Forum Managed Care. *Enquête de réseaux de soins*. Retrieved October 31, 2016, from http://fmc.ch/fr/infotheque/enquete-de-reseaux-de-soins/

Hagon-Traub, I., Hirsiger, P., Bovet, P., Ruiz, J., Peytremann-Bridevaux, I., Noth, C., et al. (2010). *Programme cantonal Diabète, présentation du programme*. Lausanne: Service de la Santé Publique du canton de Vaud.

Interpharma. *High degree of satisfaction with the health system.* Retrieved October 31, 2016, from http://www.interpharma.ch/fr/faits-et-statistiques/6324-high-degree-satisfaction-health-system

Jeanrenaud, C., & Gay, M. (2013). *Coût indirect et pertes de qualité de vie attribuables au diabète Une estimation pour le canton de Vaud.* Retrieved October 31, 2016, from http://pcd.diabete-vaud.ch/fileadmin/files/regionalgesellschaften/vaud/pcd/rapport_couts_indirects_9_sept_2013_final.pdf

OECD/WHO. (2011). *OECD reviews of health systems: Switzerland 2011.* OECD Publishing. Retrieved October 31, 2016, from http://dx.doi.org/10.1787/9789264120914-en

Peytremann-Bridevaux, I., & Burnand, B. (2009). Inventory and perspectives of disease management programs in Switzerland. *International Journal of Integrated Care, 9,* e93.

Peytremann-Bridevaux, I., Lauvergeon, S., Mettler, D., & Burnand, B. (2012). Diabetes care: Opinions, needs and proposed solutions of Swiss patients and healthcare professionals: A qualitative study. *Diabetes Research and Clinical Practice, 97,* 242–250.

Peytremann-Bridevaux, I., Ebert, S., & Senn, N. (2015). Involvement of family physicians in structured programs for chronic diseases or multi-morbidity in Switzerland. *European Journal of Internal Medicine, 26,* 150–151.

Programme cantonal Diabète. (2011). *Rapport d'activités.* Retrieved October 31, 2016, from http://pcd.diabete-vaud.ch/fileadmin/files/regionalgesellschaften/vaud/pcd/PcD_Rapport_activite_2011.pdf

Programme cantonal Diabète. (2012). *Rapport d'activités.* Retrieved October 31, 2016, from http://pcd.diabete-vaud.ch/fileadmin/files/regionalgesellschaften/vaud/pcd/PcD_Rapport_activite_2012.pdf

Programme cantonal Diabète. (2013). *Rapport d'activités.* Retrieved October 31, 2016, from http://pcd.diabete-vaud.ch/fileadmin/files/regionalgesellschaften/vaud/pcd/PcD_-_Rapport_activite_2013_-OK.pdf

Programme cantonal Diabète. (2014). *Rapport d'activités.* Retrieved October 31, 2016, from http://pcd.diabete-vaud.ch/fileadmin/files/regionalgesellschaften/vaud/pcd/PcD_-_Rapport_activite_2014.pdf

Schaller, P. (2008). Le réseau de soins Delta (RSD) [The Delta physicians network]. *Care Management, 1,* 3–6. (in French).

Swiss Federal Office of Public Health. (2012). *Réseaux de soins intégrés.* Retrieved October 31, 2016, from http://www.bag.admin.ch/themen/krankenversicherung/00305/06506/06664/index.html?lang=fr

Swiss Federal Office of Public Health. (2016). *Health 2020.* Retrieved October 31, 2016, from http://www.bag.admin.ch/gesundheit2020/index.html?lang=en

Zuercher, E., Bordet, J., Burnand, B., & Peytremann-Bridevaux, I. (2015). CoDiab-VD: protocol of a prospective population-based cohort study on diabetes care in Switzerland. *BMC Health Services Research, 15,* 329.

Netherlands: The Potentials of Integrating Care via Payment Reforms

35

The Case of Dutch Diabetes Care

Jeroen N. Struijs, Hanneke W. Drewes, Richard Heijink, and Caroline A. Baan

35.1 Integrated Care in the Netherlands

This chapter provides insight in the potential of integrating care through payment reform in the Netherlands. We begin by briefly outlining the main characteristics of the Dutch health care system, which has been transformed into a system of managed competition in the past decade. We focus on health care, because our case study is situated in this setting. We then describe the implementation of the bundled payment for diabetes care as one main example of stimulating nationwide implementation of integrated diabetes care in the Netherlands. This case study is based on our previous work on integrated care and related issues, which we have described in detail elsewhere (de Bakker et al. 2012; de Bruin et al. 2013; Struijs 2013, 2015a, b; Struijs and Baan 2011; Struijs et al. 2010, 2012a, b, 2015a, b; de Jong-van Til et al. 2013; Lemmens et al. 2015; Mohnen et al. 2015).

35.1.1 The Dutch Health Care Reform in 2006: The Introduction of Managed Competition

In the past decades, the Dutch health care system has been gradually transformed into a system of managed competition in which market forces and competition play

J.N. Struijs (✉) • H.W. Drewes • R. Heijink
Department of Quality of Care and Health Economics, National Instititute of Public Health and the Environment, Bilthoven, The Netherlands
e-mail: jeroen.struijs@rivm.nl

C.A. Baan
Department of Quality of Care and Health Economics, National Instititute of Public Health and the Environment, Bilthoven, The Netherlands

Scientific Centre for Transformation in Care and Welfare (Tranzo), University of Tilburg, Tilburg, The Netherlands

© Springer International Publishing AG 2017
V. Amelung et al. (eds.), *Handbook Integrated Care*,
DOI 10.1007/978-3-319-56103-5_35

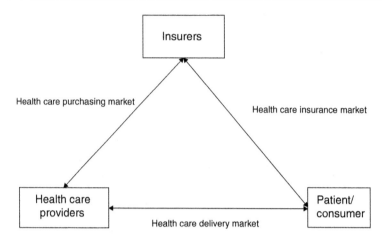

Fig. 35.1 The Dutch health care system and it three interrelated markets. Source: Schäfer et al. (2010)

a prominent role (Van de Ven and Schut 2009). The introduction of managed competition provided a much more prominent role for the three market players in the system, i.e. the patients or consumers, the care providers and the insurance companies. The health care market consists of three interrelated subsidiary markets: the health care provision market, the health care purchasing market and the health insurance market (Fig. 35.1) (Van den Berg et al. 2014).

In the *health insurance market* health insurers provide health insurance policies to all Dutch citizens. Since the introduction of the 2006 Health Insurance Act (Zvw), all health insurers are private companies and allowed to make a profit and pay dividend to shareholders (Schäfer et al. 2010). However, most health insurance companies operate on a non-profit basis. The content of the basic health insurance package to be offered by health insurers is determined by the government. Health insurers can however determine the content (and price) of any additional insurance packages, on which basis they can compete, in addition to the quality of care and the insurance premium. Following the 2006 reform, competition between health insurers led to all insurers incurring losses (Van de Ven and Schut 2009). Under the Zvw, insurers have an obligation to accept all applicants living in the Netherlands or abroad who are compulsorily insured under the Zvw (Van den Berg et al. 2014). To compensate insurers for enrollees with predictably higher care consumption and thereby to prevent risk selection, a risk equalization scheme, which, through the Health Insurance Fund, distributes funds across health insurers on the basis of risk-profiles of enrollees. Residents chose a health insurance policy with the insurer of their choice. They may change their insurer on an annual basis and about 6–8% of enrollees do so.

In the *health provision market* health care providers deliver care services to services users. However, information on quality of care is still hardly available, although some websites, such as Kiesbeter.nl and VolksgezondheidEnZorg.info, provide basic information to inform consumer choice. The suboptimal information on quality makes it difficult for the care consumer to make an informed choice regarding care providers. Besides GPs and other providers' advice, service users are increasingly using the internet to look for information on care providers and quality of care.

In the *health care purchasing market*, health insurers aim to purchase good-quality services at competitive prices. In reality, purchasing services on the basis of quality remains a challenge, given the scarcity of robust information on care quality as mentioned above (Ruwaard et al. 2014), despite efforts by the government to make quality of care more transparent (Van den Berg et al. 2014). Possibilities for negotiating on the price of care were limited at the start of the 2006 health care reform, but have increased gradually over time. For instance, in 2006 about 7% of hospital care was freely negotiated, while in 2014 this figure was about 70%. For the remaining 30%, prices of hospital care rates are, at present, non-negotiable (Van den Berg et al. 2014). In pharmaceutical care, price negotiations between health insurers and pharmacies were implemented in 2012. Health insurers have restricted the reimbursement of pharmaceuticals to preferred medicines (mostly generics) in case a choice can be made between different brands. The price of GP services is negotiable for a small part only and this is presently limited to multidisciplinary integrated care services [diabetes, chronic obstructive pulmonary disease (COPD) and vascular risk management (VRM)] are being negotiated, as we shall see below. Health insurers may also stimulate competition through selective contracting and substitution of care (e.g. services delivered by a nurse rather than a physician), although this option has not been implemented widely thus far.

35.2   Integrated Care in Practice

35.2.1 Problem Definition

The rising burden of chronic disease has been recognised as a challenge in the Netherlands, with for example about 4% of the population diagnosed with diabetes and this proportion is expected to increase in the next coming decades (Van den Berg et al. 2014; Baan et al. 2009). This poses a major challenge to health services, in particular in combination with the rising prevalence of multi-morbidity, involving complex health care needs vis-a-vis a lack of co-ordination between different components and professional groups within health systems. In addition, there was evidence that the quality of care provided to patients with chronic disease was variable, with patients not receiving all the care they needed.

To address these challenges, the Dutch government initiated a range of policies. These included the introduction of integrated care programmes based on multidisciplinary cooperation in primary care, which sought to improve the effectiveness and quality of care and to ensure affordability. The first integrated care programme focused on diabetes care, based on the principles of a bundled payment, developed by the Netherlands Ministry of Health, Welfare and Sport (de Jong-van Til et al.

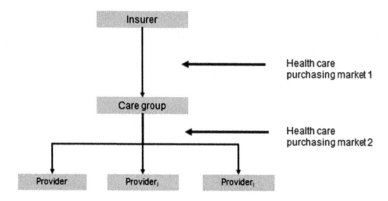

Fig. 35.2 Principle structure of the Dutch bundled payment model. Source: Struijs et al. (2010)

2013). The payment mechanism enables all the necessary services to be contracted as a single package or product. The aim of the new pricing model was to accelerate the implementation of diabetes care programmes, and those for other chronic diseases more widely. In 2007, groups of affiliated health care providers known as care groups began working with bundled payment arrangements for diabetes, initially on an experimental basis. In 2010, bundled payment for the management of diabetes, COPD and VRM was introduced as regular payment mechanism, although contracting under the previous pricing system involving is still permitted. By that year, there were about one hundred care groups operating integrated care programmes for diabetes, covering about 85–90% of all diabetes patients in the Netherlands (Mohnen et al. 2017) (see also Fig. 35.2).

35.2.2 Description of the Bundled Payment Model for Diabetes Care

In the Dutch bundled payment model, insurers pay a bundled payment to a principal contracting entity—the care group—to cover a full range of diabetes-care services for a fixed period of 365 days. The care group, a new legal entity in the Dutch health care system, comprises multiple providers, often exclusively general practitioners (de Jong-van Til et al. 2013). By entering the bundled payment contract, the care group assumes both clinical and financial accountability for all diabetes patients assigned to its care programme. The contract is limited to general diabetes care provided in the primary care setting, that is services to manage the underlying disease and reduce risk for complications, and it does not include services to address complex complications that may arise. General decisions about services covered in the diabetes care bundle were made at a national level and, in 2007, codified in a Health Care Standard for type 2 diabetes (Dutch Diabetes Federation 2007). For the various components of diabetes care, the care group either delivers services itself or subcontracts with other providers (Fig. 35.3). Health insurers and care groups negotiate the price of the bundle, and the care group negotiates with the

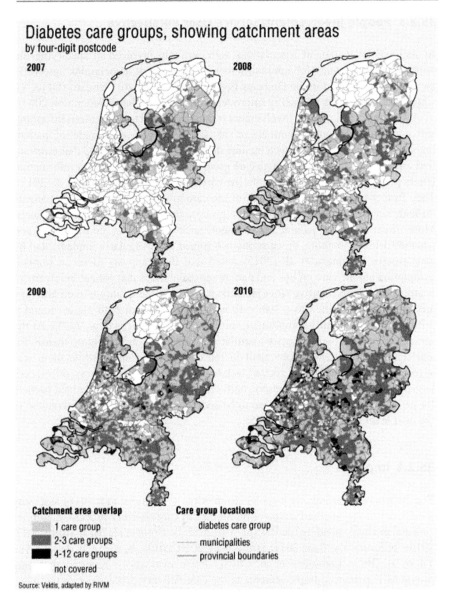

Diabetes care groups, showing catchment areas
by four-digit postcode

2007   2008

2009   2010

Catchment area overlap
- 1 care group
- 2-3 care groups
- 4-12 care groups
- not covered

Care group locations
- diabetes care group
- ------ municipalities
- ------ provincial boundaries

Source: Vektis, adapted by RIVM

Fig. 35.3 Roll out of bundled payment model for diabetes care during 2007–2010. Source: de Jong-van Til et al. (2013)

subcontracted care providers about fees for specific services. All services are covered under the basic insurance package for all Dutch citizens.

35.2.3 People Involvement/Service User Perspective

At national level, patient associations were actively involved in specifying the minimum requirements for optimal diabetes care. Patient associations agreed on the services described in the Diabetes Federation Health Care Standard (DFHCS), which sets the criteria on quality improvement (Dutch Diabetes Federation 2007).

At regional level, patient involvement is mostly limited to care groups informing and consulting patients. Lemmens et al. (2015), in an assessment of patient involvement strategies employed by nine diabetes care groups, found that information was typically accessed through care groups' websites, brochures or information letters provided upon enrolment into the care programme (Lemmens et al. 2015). They further reported that about half of the care groups also consult with patients through surveys, meeting with patient groups, or implementing patient panels. More direct forms of patient involvement, such as advising, co-producing and (shared) decision-making, do currently not appear to be regularly implemented by care groups. Lemmens et al. (2015) noted that there appears to be an implicit assumption among care groups and patient representatives that patient involvement is an instrument to improve (Raaijmakers et al. 2015) the quality of care and they are therefore committed to collaborate with each other but both parties found it difficult to translate this commitment into practice (Lemmens et al. 2015). At the same time, both groups expressed similar preferences regarding future themes for and shaping of patient involvement in the care group context while there was agreement that several issues such as lack of evidence for effectiveness, differences in viewpoints on the role and responsibilities of care groups and perceived barriers for patient involvement would need to be addressed to take patient involvement to the next level (Lemmens et al. 2015).

35.2.4 Impact

The diabetes care groups were subject to multiple evaluations in terms of assessing the impact of the bundled payment on the health care delivery process, quality of care and medical spending (de Bakker et al. 2012; de Bruin et al. 2013; Struijs 2013, 2015a, b; Struijs and Baan 2011; Struijs et al. 2010, 2012a, b, 2015a, b; de Jong-van Til et al. 2013; Lemmens et al. 2015). These evaluations reported that care providers experienced improvements in the care delivery process due to the introduction of bundled payments and related care groups. Providers specifically mentioned that the coordination among care providers improved, as did protocol adherence, attendance at multidisciplinary consultations, and further training of subcontracted providers to facilitate protocol-driven work processes and the use of the electronic health records. For instance, For instance, a survey of providers in 2010 and 2013 found that, in 2013, some 89% reported that they perceived themselves to be working largely or completely in accordance with the Dutch Diabetes Federation Health Care Standard (DFHCS) compared to 79% in 2010 (Raaijmakers et al. 2015). It was also shown that in 2010, 3 years after bundled payments had been introduced, 66% of the care groups had implemented web-based electronic health records (EHRs), requiring subcontracted providers to record their data (de Jong-van Til et al. 2013).

Studies further demonstrated that slight to modest improvements in outcome measures, such as percentage of patients with LDL-levels below target levels and percentage of patients with blood pressure levels below target level, were achieved during the first 3 years after the implementation of the bundled payment model (Struijs et al. 2010). In addition, fewer patients were found to have used specialist care that resulted in a reduction in diabetes-related outpatient specialist and inpatient diabetes hospital spending, but overall hospital care spending and consequently per-patient medical spending increased as compared to care as usual after a 2-year follow-up period (Mohnen et al. 2015). The observed increase in spending growth might have been due to the start-up costs of the bundled payment reform. Also, a 2-year follow-up period may have been too short to gauge the full impact of the bundled payment model as quality improvements within primary care tend to take time. Moreover, development and implementation costs were not included in these analyses and such costs can be substantial. For example, Tsiachristas et al. (2014) demonstrated that development costs varied from €5891 to €274,783 while the implementation costs varied from €7278 to €387,879 across integrated care programmes (Tsiachristas et al. 2014). Key cost drivers were the duration of the development phase and the staff needed to develop and implement an integrated care programme. Overall, empirical evidence of the effects of primary care oriented bundled payments models is scarce, and most support is still based on conceptual grounds.

35.2.5 Lessons Learned

The implementation of the Dutch bundled payment model can be seen to have been a success for three key reasons, which can be summarised as follows (Struijs 2015a, b):

1. *The diabetes care standard was codified.* The DFHCS, agreed on by all national provider and patient associations, specifies the minimum requirements for optimal diabetes care and sets the criteria for improvements. By law, the bundled-payment contract must include all services described in the DFHCS, which identifies *what* services to provide but not *who* delivers those services or *where* and *how* they are delivered (as long as these services are in congruence with national guidelines). This provided care groups with an incentive to adopt innovations and to reallocate tasks so that providers each do the work that best matches their qualifications with lowest costs.

2. *It fostered transparency through the use of electronic health records.* The EHR system made patient data available to primary care providers in real time and helped them to reduce duplicated services. Web-based EHRs also enabled care groups to benchmark the performance of care providers, who could then learn

from one another. Struijs et al. (2012a) reported that the EHRs were used to generate accountability reports for insurers and to inform the public about care groups' achievements. This was seen by most providers to provide greater transparency and as the main achievement of the reform (Struijs et al. 2012a).

3. *It optimised the value of clinical expertise.* Being accountable for both cost and quality as a consequence of the bundled payment creates an incentive to offer effective care and prevent the utilisation of unnecessary care. GPs are incentivised to ensure that their patients receive the right type of care, delivered at the right time, at the right facility, by the right provider, and use their clinical knowledge to do so. For instance, Struijs et al. (2012a) found that following the introduction of bundled payments, diabetes patients with no abnormalities on their annual eye exam were switched to a biannual eye-exam schedule, consistent with Dutch clinical-practice guidelines (Struijs et al. 2012a), which increased the profit margins of care groups. Care groups also made use of various forms of task reallocation and task delegation both within primary care, but also from secondary to primary care as they have an incentive to steer to high-quality low-costs providers. For example, insulin-dependent patients without complications are increasingly being treated in GP practices instead of by specialists in hospital settings, which had been the case prior to introduction of the bundled payment.

Although the bundled payment model realised a more intensified and structured collaboration between care providers and demonstrated modest improvements in outcomes in the early stages after implementation, two main challenges remain (de Bakker et al. 2012). First, the care bundle was limited to primary care and included only to some extent specialist care, while medication was excluded from the bundle. Although this limited scope of the bundle was probably advisable in the early stages of implementation, as GPs were being urged to adopt bundles, it potentially encourages then to refer the more-complex (and more costly) patients to specialists (Struijs 2015a, b). As a result, an incentive for all providers to jointly reduce spending on diabetes care is still lacking, since specialists are not incentivised to do so as their payment model has remained unchanged. Moreover, the bundle does not include an incentive for preventing diabetes since the integrated care programme only commences following a diagnosis of diabetes.

Second, the single-disease approach is not in line with the complex health care needs of many diabetes patients with comorbid diseases and this may lead to new forms of fragmentation. Potentially, substantial parts of diabetes patients' health care needs are not related to their diabetes. However, an assessment of health care providers' views on multimorbid conditions found that the disease-specific approach to diabetes management had not yet resulted in problems for diabetes patients with co-morbid conditions (Struijs et al. 2012a).

35.2.6 Outlook

Considering the aforementioned challenges of the bundled payment model with regard to integration across the care pathway and single-disease approach, two new developments, which are currently being implemented in the Netherlands are worth describing further: (i) the integration of primary, secondary and tertiary care for population subgroups, namely a bundled payment for pregnancy and child birth, and (ii) the move towards population health management through the integration of services across the entire care continuum to address the needs of the whole population.

35.2.6.1 Bundled Payment for Pregnancy and Child Birth

Building on the diabetes care reimbursement model, this new bundled payment model seeks to encourage efficient outcome-focused pregnancy and childbirth care, which is currently hindered by the fragmented funding system. Like diabetes care, insurers will pay a single fee to a contracting entity to cover all services during the antenatal, delivery and postnatal phase for each pregnant woman. The contracting entity will be clinically and financially accountable for the services delivered to enrolled population. By eliminating current funding barriers, the Dutch Minister of Health aims to stimulate the collaboration between providers and settings in order to improve patient value. This bundled payment model will be structurally implemented on a voluntary basis in 2017 (Plexus 2016).

35.2.6.2 Population Health Management

Along with the developments in integrated care for single chronic diseases, it became evident that ideally the scope of integrated care needs to be expanded to bridge the gaps not only within the health system, but also between the health and social systems in order to provide truly population-centred services that improve population health (Struijs et al. 2015a; Steenkamer et al. 2017). In the Netherlands, several regional partnerships have emerged in 2013 in which care providers, insurers, and stakeholders such as municipalities and representatives of citizens participate (Drewes et al. 2015). These initiatives are based on a shared vision, following the Triple Aim (Berwick et al. 2008), with substantial investment in developing relationships between the involved actors in order to build trust for aligning organisations' scope and interest. This complex journey towards population health management is currently being evaluated by the Dutch National Institute of Public Health and the Environment. This evaluation will provide insight in the facilitators and barriers for implementing population health management in order to realize improvements in population health, quality of care and reduce spending growth.

Both the development of population health management and the implementation bundled payment for birth care are strong examples of 'integrating care' along and across the different domains, while at the same time revealing new but comparable challenges. First, both developments will need to create governance arrangements in order to achieve their aims. Whereas the bundled payment requires a contracting entity, this might not be the case within the population health management initiatives. How to best arrange these new governance arrangements, including public-private partnerships, which need to include elements of accountability, oversight and distributed leadership, while at the same time considering the national, regional and local context, is still widely discussed and yet to be resolved (Goodwin et al. 2014). These discussions also bring to the forefront conflicting interests of existing organisations and providers and the overall system-level goal of reducing spending growth.

Second, in both developments questions arise about how to engage the population they serve. In population management initiatives, various strategies to actively involve the local community have already been launched, such as online 'communities', patient representatives as board members of health services, and even new entities led by citizens, which serve as integrator as described by Berwick et al. (2008). These tools and the definitions of underlying concepts vary considerably in scale and scope and more insight is needed to ascertain what works for whom in what context to successfully involve the community (Goodwin et al. 2014; Ferrer, forthcoming).

Thirdly, there is an ongoing debate about the appropriate payment models. Although for birth care a choice has already been made towards a bundled payment approach, involved providers are hesitant to adopt such a disruptive payment model (Struijs et al. 2016). Furthermore, discussions remain regarding the scope of the bundle and the number of modules within the bundle. Moreover, there is still debate within this field whether this is really a stimulus for integrated care or even a threat (Struijs et al. 2016). Currently, empirical evidence underpinning the effects of bundled payments on outcomes is scarce and its support is mostly on conceptual grounds. With the population health management development, the debate on payment models is even more complex (Struijs et al. 2015b). By looking at initiatives experimenting with alternative payment models such as shared savings models (Hayen et al. 2015; Song et al. 2011, 2012; Chernew et al. 2011), lessons can be learned on how to shift financial and clinical accountability from payers towards (groups of) care providers (and potentially in the near future also citizens) in order to incentivize these providers to improve population health, quality of care and reduce costs growth.

References

Baan, C. A., van Baal, P. H., Jacobs-van der Bruggen, M. A., Verkley, H., Poos, M. J., & Hoogenveen, R. T., et al. (2009). [Diabetes mellitus in the Netherlands: Estimate of the current disease burden and prognosis for 2025]. *Nederlands Tijdschrift voor Geneeskunde, 153*(22), 1052–1058.

Berwick, D. M., Nolan, T. W., & Whittington, J. (2008). The triple aim: Care, health, and cost. *Health Affairs (Project Hope), 27*(3), 759–769.

Chernew, M. E., Mechanic, R. E., Landon, B. E., & Safran, D. G. (2011). Private-payer innovation in Massachusetts: The 'alternative quality contract'. *Health Affairs (Millwood), 30*(1), 51–61.

de Bakker, D. H., Struijs, J. N., Baan, C. B., Raams, J., de Wildt, J. E., Vrijhoef, H. J., et al. (2012). Early results from adoption of bundled payment for diabetes care in the Netherlands show improvement in care coordination. *Health affairs (Project Hope)*, *31*(2), 426–433.

de Bruin, S. R., van Oostrom, S. H., Drewes, H. W., de Jong-van Til, J. T., Baan, C. A., & Struijs, J. N. (2013). Quality of diabetes care in Dutch care groups: No differences between diabetes patients with and without co-morbidity. *International Journal of Integrated Care*, *13*, e057.

de Jong-van Til, J. T., Lemmens, L. C., Baan, C. A., Struijs, J. N. (2013). *The organization of care groups in 2011. Current State of affairs and developments during last years* [in Dutch] (Report No.: 260131003/2012). Bilthoven: National Institute for Public Health and the Environment (RIVM).

Drewes, H. W., Heijink, R., Struijs, J. N., & Baan, C. A. (2015). *Working together towards sustainable care*. Bilthoven: National Insitute for Public Health and the Environment (RIVM).

Dutch Diabetes Federation. (2007). *Health Care Standard. Transparency and quality of diabetes health care for patients with diabetes type 2*. Dutch Diabetes Federation: Amersfoort.

Ferrer, L. *Development of the Domain 'People'*. Working paper for the WHO Regional Office for Europe, Copenhagen (forthcoming).

Goodwin, N., Sonola, L., Thiel, V., & Kodner, D. (2014). *Co-ordinated care for people with complex chronic conditions*. Key lessons and markers for success.

Hayen, A. P., van den Berg, M. J., Meijboom, B. R., Struijs, J. N., & Westert, G. P. (2015). Incorporating shared savings programs into primary care: From theory to practice. *BMC Health Services Research*, *15*, 580.

Lemmens, L. C., de Bruin, S. R., Struijs, J. N., Rijken, M., Nijpels, G., & Baan, C. A. (2015). Patient involvement in diabetes care: Experiences in nine diabetes care groups. *International Journal of Integrated Care*, *15*, e044.

Mohnen, S. M., Baan, C. A., & Struijs, J. N. (2015). The impact of bundled payments for diabetes care on curative health care costs growth. A 2-year follow-up study based on Dutch nationwide health claims data. *American Journal of Accountable Care*, *12*, 60–63.

Mohnen, S. M., Molema, C. C., Steenbeek, W., van den Berg, M. J., de Bruin, S. R., Baan, C. A., et al. (2017). Cost Variation in Diabetes Care across Dutch Care Groups? *Health Services Research*, *52*, 93–112.

Plexus, K. (2016). *Advice bundled payment for pregnancy and child birth*. KMPG: Amstelveen.

Raaijmakers, L. G., Kremers, S. P., Schaper, N. C., de Weerdt, I., Martens, M. K., Hesselink, A. E., et al. (2015). The implementation of national action program diabetes in the Netherlands: Lessons learned. *BMC Health Services Research*, *15*, 217.

Ruwaard, S., Douven, R., Struijs, J., & Polder, J. (2014). Hoe kopen zorgverzekeraars in bij ziekenhuizen. Een analyse van de contracten tussen verzekeraars en ziekenhuizen. *TPEdigitaal*, *8*(2), 98–117.

Schäfer, W., Kroneman, M., Boerma, W., van den Berg, M., Westert, G., Devillé, W., & van Ginneken, E. (2010). The Netherlands: Health system review. *Health Systems in Transition*, *12*, 1–229.

Song, Z., Safran, D. G., Landon, B. E., He, Y., Ellis, R. P., Mechanic, R. E., et al. (2011). Health care spending and quality in year 1 of the alternative quality contract. *The New England Journal of Medicine*, *365*(10), 909–918.

Song, Z., Safran, D. G., Landon, B. E., Landrum, M. B., He, Y., Mechanic, R. E., et al. (2012). The 'Alternative Quality Contract,' based on a global budget, lowered medical spending and improved quality. *Health Affairs (Project Hope)*, *31*(8), 1885–1894.

Steenkamer, B. M., Drewes, H. W., Heijink, R., Baan, C. A., & Struijs, J. N. (2017). Defining population health management. A scoping review of the literature. *Population Health Management*, *20*, 74–85.

Struijs, J. N. (2013). Payment reform and integrated care: The need for evaluation. *International Journal of Integrated Care*, *13*, e056.

Struijs, J. N. (2015a). How Dutch Health care Bundled payments are working in the Netherlands. *New England Journal of Medicine Insight Center*.

Struijs, J. N. (2015b). How health care bundled payments are working in the Netherlands. *Harvard Business Review.*

Struijs, J. N., & Baan, C. A. (2011). Integrating care through bundled payments—lessons from The Netherlands. *The New England Journal of Medicine, 364*(11), 990–991.

Struijs, J. N., van Til, J. T., & Baan, C. A. (2010). *Experimenting with a bundled payment system for diabetes care in the Netherlands: The first tangible effects* (Contract No.: 260224002). Bilthoven: National Institut for Public Health and the Environment (RIVM).

Struijs, J. N., de Jong-van Til, J. T., Lemmens, L. C., Drewes, H. W., de Bruin, S. R., & Baan, C. A. (2012a). *Three years of bundled payment for diabetes care in the Netherlands: Impact on health care delivery process and the quality of care* (RIVM rapport 260013002). Bilthoven: Rijksinstituut voor Volksgezondheid en Milieu.

Struijs, J. N., Mohnen, S. M., Molema, C. C. M., De Jong-van Til, J. T., & Baan, C. A. (2012b). *Effects of bundled payment on curative health care costs in the Netherlands. An analysis for diabetes care and vascular risk management based on nationwide claim data, 2007–2010* (Report No.: RIVM rapport 270551008). Bilthoven: Rijksinstituut voor Volksgezondheid en Milieu.

Struijs, J. N., Drewes, H. W., Heijink, R., & Baan, C. A. (2015a). How to evaluate population management? Transforming the Care Continuum Alliance population health guide toward a broadly applicable analytical framework. *Health Policy, 119*(4), 522–529.

Struijs, J. N., Drewes, H. W., & Stein, K. V. (2015b). Beyond integrated care. Challenges on the way towards population health management. *International Jouranal of Integrated Care, 15*(4).

Struijs, J. N., Heijink, R., Kooistra, M., & Baan, C. A. (2016). *Toward bundled payments of birth care* (Report No.: 2016-0031). Bilthoven: National Institute for Public Health and the Environment (RIVM).

Tsiachristas, A., Waters, B. H., Adams, S. A., Bal, R., & Molken, M. P. (2014). Identifying and explaining the variability in development and implementation costs of disease management programs in the Netherlands. *BMC Health Services Research, 14*, 518.

Van de Ven, W. P., & Schut, F. T. (2009). Managed competition in the Netherlands: Still work-in-progress. *Health Economics, 18*(3), 253–255.

Van den Berg, M. J., De Boer, D., Gijsen, R., Heijink, R., Limburg, L. C. M., & SLN, Z. (2014). *Zorgbalans 2014. De prestaties van de Nederlandse gezondheidszorg.* Bilthoven: RIVM.

New Zealand: Canterbury Tales

Integrated Care in New Zealand

Brian Dolan, Carolyn Gullery, Greg Hamilton, and David Meates

36.1 Integrated Care in New Zealand

New Zealand's health and disability system is mainly funded from general taxation. It has a public and private healthcare system, which both offer high standards of care. In the public system, essential healthcare services are provided free or subsidized for some community services (including general practice) for all New Zealanders, people from countries with reciprocal health care provision and people in New Zealand on a work permit valid for 2 years or longer. Emergency care is free as are specialist services and non-urgent surgery although access is prioritised on the basis of clinical need. Alongside the public system, private healthcare offers access to private hospitals for the treatment of urgent and non-urgent conditions. The network of private hospitals and clinics provides a range of services that include recuperative care, elective procedures and a range of general surgical procedures. There are also private radiology clinics and testing laboratories.

The government-funded public health system works on a community-oriented model, with three key sectors. Twenty District Health Boards (DHBs), established in 2001, plan, fund and deliver local services. Primary health care covers a broad range of out-of-hospital services, including first level services such as subsidized general practice and diagnostics, free mobile nursing and community health and dental services which are free for young people. Thirty-two Primary Health Organisations (PHOs) are the local structures for delivering and co-ordinating primary health care services. They are funded by the DHB. PHOs bring together doctors, nurses and other health professionals, in the community to serve the needs

B. Dolan (✉) • C. Gullery • G. Hamilton • D. Meates
Canterbury District Health Board, Canterbury, New Zealand
e-mail: brian@dolanholt.co.uk; Carolyn.gullery@cdhb.health.nz; Greg.hamilton@cdhb.health.nz; David.Meates@cdhb.health.nz

© Springer International Publishing AG 2017
V. Amelung et al. (eds.), *Handbook Integrated Care*,
DOI 10.1007/978-3-319-56103-5_36

of their enrolled patients. There is a co-payment model for general practice, with children under 13 free, and fees for other ages subsidised.

Approximately one quarter of New Zealanders purchase private health insurance in order to receive care in private hospitals and to avoid waiting lists for the treatment of non-urgent medical/surgical conditions. People with private health insurance are still eligible for free public health benefits.

This chapter focuses on Canterbury District Health Board (CDHB), which serves a population of over 540,000 people in a country of some 4.7 million and has a budget of NZD $1.4 billion, or approximately 11% of total state health funding allocated to DHBs. It has a workforce of 9500, supplemented by a further 9000 personnel who are funded in primary health organisations (PHOs), non-governmental organisations (NGOs), for profit providers, aged residential care providers, health related charitable bodies and others.

36.2   Integrated Care in Practice

36.2.1 Problem Definition

The Canterbury Health System is widely considered to be a well integrated health system (Timmins and Ham 2013).

Like many other health systems, Canterbury had to address of growing waiting lists, delays in investigations and treatments and a disengaged and dissatisfied workforce, along with overcrowding in the emergency department, cancelled operations, staff threatening industrial action, a disconnect between general practitioners (GPs) and hospital clinicians, rising locum medical costs and nursing shortages. A substantial shortfall of NZ$ of 20 million in 2005, and the inability to meet performance targets for elective services, a priority area, in any of the preceding four financial years, along with safety concerns around surgery highlighted the significant and complex challenges the system was facing and the need for systemic and systematic change.

At the same time, the primary care system was considered to be highly organised, involving a well-connected network of general practices that were linked by joint education processes, a successful experience of budget-holding for pharmaceuticals and pathology services in the 1990s, and an innovative hospital admission avoidance programme. This had been achieved almost in isolation from the secondary care system. Yet despite the relative successful primary care system, it was estimated that if admissions kept growing at their then current rate, by 2020 Canterbury would have needed a second 450-bed Christchurch Hospital, another 20% more general practitioners (GPs) and 2000 aged care residential beds.

Overall, the Canterbury health system was considered to be highly fragmented, against a backdrop of an ageing population and a scarce and ageing workforce. The transformation of the health system towards an integrated solution was eventually initiated with the appointments of a new Executive Director of Nursing and Chief Medical Officer who created a new focus on patient experience and led to the

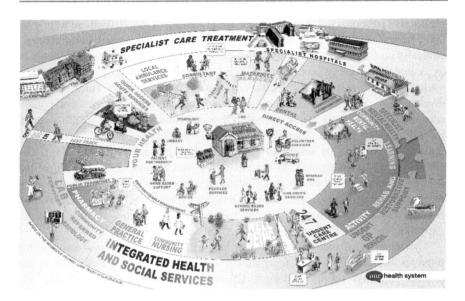

Fig. 36.1 The Canterbury Health System Vision

introduction of the 'Improving the Patient Journey' programme in 2004–2005. This programme sought to re-engineer hospital activities using a 'lean' approach and focusing on identifying and reducing needless waste. The challenge was to change both mind-sets and the system as a whole.

Key strategies to achieve this were a series of *Vision 2020* workshops in 2007 and 2008 (Fig. 36.1). These workshops brought together 80 clinical, managerial and patient representative system leaders and they sought to encourage 'disruptive thinking' and prompt new ways of refocusing the system on home and community delivered care. This led to the emergence of a strategic vision of a connected system, that is centred around people and that aims not to waste their time.

This visionary approach was further strengthened with the appointment of a new General Manager of Planning and Funding in 2007, who introduced a 'one system, one budget' strategy which sought to reconnect the primary and secondary health systems. The interface between general practices and hospital services was recognised as a major area requiring redesign and key to the development of an integrated health system. With the assistance of senior health system managers, community clinicians, funders, and a facilitator, a plan was prepared that proposed changes in pre-referral and post-referral patient management. Following acceptance and implementation of the plan, this process became known as the *Canterbury Initiative* and it is one the examples in Canterbury of using a network of influencers to empower clinically-led change rather than a formal project process or a hierarchical response.

One example of this approach is the process by which GPs and other clinicians (and, more recently, consumers) were brought together to develop what became *HealthPathways*, such as a clinical pathway for the management of chronic obstructive pulmonary disease (McGeoch et al. 2015a, b). By 2016, there were over 800 such pathways that provide locally relevant, evidence informed, iteratively and clinically co-created concise information required for a patient consultation and to overcome the difficulty general practices may experience when organising multiple sources of information. A *HealthPathways* website provides information on investigations, differential diagnosis, acute and conservative management, patient education and links to electronic referral to services across the health system, including specialists, in a standardised format (Kenealy et al. 2015). Important information on possible severe adverse events is highlighted by a 'red flag'. The pathway may include links to resources on background clinical information, aetiology, supporting international guidelines, or the details of the extensive array of educational sessions funded by the DHB for community based clinicians. The *HealthPathways* Community has now expanded to 27 regions in New Zealand, Australia, and the UK to guide the care of some 23 million people.

The majority of pathways include a link to *HealthInfo*, a sister website that provides health information for patients, consistent with that described in the clinical pathways (http://www.healthinfo.org.nz/). Consensus, transparency and equity were key values used during this process with the main focus on what is considered best for patients. The pathways reflect evidence-based best practice while incorporating local expert usual practice and provide a flexible guide outlining 'how we do things around here'.

The Canterbury Clinical Network (CCN), founded in 2009, is a formal collective alliance of healthcare leaders, professionals and providers, from across the Canterbury health system, under the independent Chairmanship of a retired High Court judge (Canterbury Clinical Network 2016). It provides leadership to the transformation of the Canterbury health system in collaboration with system partners and on behalf of the people of Canterbury. The CCN has developed new service delivery models, funding and contracting mechanisms that are based on principles of high trust, low bureaucracy, openness and transparency. It makes decisions for developing new models of care and service delivery across Canterbury. The planning and funding function of the DHB implements the decisions of CCN and ensures that procurement processes are managed to the standard expected in a public system and to minimise the conflicts of interest that are inherent in a clinically led system.

36.2.2 People Involvement/Service User Perspectives

One of the key elements in the success of the Canterbury Health System has been the input of patients, carers and their families. Where new service developments are planned, these are often undertaken in conjunction with the Canterbury District Health Board (CDHB) Consumer Council. This was set up in 2008 to provide consumers with a strong voice in planning, designing and delivering services in the Canterbury Health System (Canterbury District Health Board 2016a, b).

The council is made up of a diverse range of people with ethnic backgrounds and areas of interest that include Māori, Pacific Islanders, people with mental health problems, long term conditions, or physical, intellectual and sensory disabilities, older people, young people, men, women, rural communities, people with visual and hearing impairment and people with alcohol and other drug addictions. The Consumer Council's slogan is "Nothing about us, without us", stipulating that health care should always be planned with consumer involvement, right from the beginning (Canterbury District Health Board 2013).

Listening to the voice of the consumer includes a website, surveys, focus groups, suggestion boxes that invite suggestions, compliments or complaints and family meetings. Minutes of the Consumer Council's monthly meetings are also published on the internet so the wider public can have wider access to the discussions and decision-making.

Consumers also sit on most of the Canterbury Clinical Network's Service Level Alliances, including the overarching group, the Alliance Leadership Team (Canterbury Clinical Network 2016). These Service Level Alliances are made up of groups of people with expertise from across the health system to provide leadership for service development and improvements in the way services are provided. This enables consumers to work in partnership with clinicians and health managers at a senior level, and so influence the transformational change of the health system.

36.2.3 Impact

36.2.3.1 Building a Social Movement

HealthPathways can be seen to be one example of new ways of thinking and enabling people to develop new ways of working. This approach was reinforced upon appointment of a new chief executive in 2009, who ensured visible political support and commitment through media liaison, regular presence at events and activities, a weekly newsletter to the whole system, and holding forums and away days to keep clinicians and other senior staff informed, led by key messages such as 'We need the whole system to be working for the whole system to work'.

Investment in a learning culture had already begun in 2007 with the launch of *Xcelr8*, an 8-day training programme aimed initially at middle-managers and quickly adding senior medical, nursing and allied health leaders from both within and external to the DHB's employed workforce. The programme aims to provide staff with "the tools and techniques for managing processes and resources more effectively" and to equip them with "on-the-job knowledge, skills and tools" to empower them and prepare them for future challenges (Canterbury District Health Board 2016b). Participants were provided with a signed card with the CEO's 'permission to make change to our health system', which can be seen to be a powerful tool for support to implement change.

Xcelr8 was followed by *Collabor8,* a 2-day programme aimed initially at nurses and allied health personnel and then broadened to all staff across the health system and aimed at creating '1000 stories of change'. *Particip8*, a 14-hour programme sought to enable staff to pitch their ideas and give them the tools to make change happen. Each of these '8s' programmes reinforced the same key system messages so that staff at all levels were encouraged and equipped to apply the principles of lean thinking, improvement science and culture change to their workplaces.

The *Vision 2020* workshops mentioned earlier enabled the concept of 'Canterbury Health System' to emerge, as a system based on trust, of 'one system, one budget', being about people, creating a shared purpose (Box 36.1). These were systematically followed up with Showcases to ensure scaling up the spread of new ideas, and highlighting what had already been achieved as in *Showcase 09*. Undertaken in an old warehouse that was fitted out to provide a series of interactive spaces to promote dialogue and discussion, alumni of the *Vision 2020,* by now 80 people, were asked to bring along 10 people to visit *Showcase*. There were to be no official email invites, no social media encouragement, no letters and invitation was by word of mouth only.

Box 36.1 Creating a shared purpose

- Clinicians are trusted
- Care pathways are re-designed
- Funding is arranged to support best practice
- The patient is in the middle of the process
- The system responds well to external shocks
- Adaptive leadership in action

Each group of 10 participants at *Showcase* could experience future scenarios, for instance sitting at the bedside during a specialist consultation via Skype and observe innovative procedures. Each group ended their visit with a debrief asking what they personally would like to change about the health system and how they could make that change happen.

A graphic facilitator translated their views into images, creating a poster summary that participants could take home. Often the posters instantly reappeared in workplaces, prompting more discussion and encouraging more people to see *Showcase*. The season extended into 2010, because by word of mouth the hoped-for 800 participants became over 2000 who eventually had the *Showcase* experience. This experience can be seen to be an example of fostering an engaged social movement that wanted to contribute to change. It can also be seen to be an endorsement of the new Canterbury health system's three strategic goals:

1. **People take greater responsibility for their own health**
   The development of support people/whanau (Maori for family) to stay well and take increased responsibility for their own health and wellbeing

2. **People stay well in their own homes and communities**
   The development of primary care and community services to support people/
   whanau in a community-based setting and provide a point of ongoing continuity,
   which for most people will be general practice
3. **People receive timely and appropriate complex care**
   The freeing-up of hospital based specialist resources to be responsive to episodic
   events and the provision of complex care and support and specialist advice to
   primary care.

By 2011, a transformed health system had successively been put in place, which
was however ultimately put to test by the 2010–2011 earthquakes (Gullery and
Hamilton 2015).

36.2.4 The 2010–2011 Earthquakes

Two major earthquakes, in September 2010 and in particular in February 2011 had
a significant impact causing widespread damage in Christchurch, the second largest
city in New Zealand and the seat of Canterbury region, killing 185 people and
injuring at least 6600 with some 10,000 families permanently displaced due to the
damage to their homes; about 25% of health service staff had damaged homes
(Ardagh et al. 2012). The health system lost 106 acute inpatients beds (17% of its
acute capacity), along with some 635 aged residential care beds. Two hundred
CDHB owned buildings were damaged and 40 were subsequently demolished.
Many non-government organisations were displaced from the central city that
was cordoned off for 12 months.

The February 2011 earthquakes posed significant challenges for the Canterbury
Health System, while at the same time, the system was seen to have demonstrated
remarkable resilience, being organised and connected across Canterbury, and
delivering free care to people in their communities within a short period of time,
a success that was attributed, in large part, to the integrated way of working, which
the Canterbury health system had built up over time (Gullery and Hamilton 2015).

36.2.5 Vision 2020 Becomes Vision 2011

Following the February quakes one general practice was destroyed with staff and
patients killed, while many others were damaged and displaced, 12 pharmacies
were also lost and the Canterbury earthquakes highlighted the risks in holding
electronic information in unconnected systems or relying on paper records. At a
critical time following the earthquakes, access to some patient information was
lost—in some cases permanently.

This prompted the acceleration the introduction of an electronic shared health
record in the form of *HealthOne* (then electronic Shared Care Record Viewer—
eSCRV), launched by mid-2012(healthone.org.nz). It stores and updates at least
hourly key information such as conditions, allergies, medical history, prescribed

medications, test results etc. and enables faster, more informed treatment of patients. In addition to general practice, pharmacy and the hospital services, ambulance services, district nursing and increasingly private sector providers have signed up to *HealthOne* and it is being delivered outside Canterbury and it is expected to cover a population of one million people across the whole South Island in due course.

Also following from the earthquakes was the Community Rehabilitation and Enablement Support Team (CREST) that began as a community-based supported discharge team facilitating earlier discharge from hospital to appropriate home-based rehabilitation services. Introduced just 3 weeks after the February 2011 quakes as a service level alliance it has since been extended to accept referrals directly from general practice, providing older people referred to it with care and support to be rehabilitated in their own homes, so as to avoid hospital admission altogether. As such CREST constitutes a further component of the suite of programmes that influence acute demand, and shift care to community settings.

In parallel, the acute demand management service (ADMS) aims to provide the most appropriate urgent care options for patients, it was expanded from around 14,000 referrals before the 2010/2011 earthquakes to 30,000 after to ease pressure on the hospital. General practice and acute community nursing deliver packages of care that allow people who would otherwise need an emergency department visit and possible hospital admission to be treated in their own homes or community. Services include: practice support; mobile nursing service; home IV therapy; logistical support; extended care management; urgent tests/investigations, doctor visits; and home support.

These examples illustrate that the earthquakes served to accelerate thinking and initiatives that were already in development. However, the earthquakes also challenged financial stability, because the national population based funding formula model did not take into account natural disasters and the rapid fluctuations in population and demand that were consequences of the earthquakes. That noted the disaster became an opportunity to accelerate the introduction of concepts then in development, notably finding ways to treat more people in the community, and making greater use of information shared electronically.

In 2014, the Office of the Auditor General (NZ) rated Canterbury District Health Board's service performance and management controls in the top 4% of all public entities. The New Zealand State Services Commission (2013) further highlighted the innovative nature of the system (Box 36.2). The Canterbury health system has further been recognised by New Zealand's Productivity Commission for its integrated approach to achieving outcomes and in 2015 was awarded with four prizes by the Institute of Public Administration New Zealand including the Prime Minister's supreme award.

> **Box 36.2 Keys to innovation (State Services Commission 2013)**
> Organisations that enable innovation:
>
> - Are customer focused and solicit idea from and engage with diverse internal and external sources
> - Have leadership that is clear about what it's trying to achieve (outcomes/ goals) but flexible about how to reach those goals
> - Have capability, skills and experience in innovation disciplines and methods supported by resources (funding, time, space)
> - Encourage experimentation and bounded and informed risk-taking

36.2.6 Dissemination and Replication

If the 2010–2011 quakes shifted the 2020 vision to a 2011 vision, it also accelerated the need for data to be made available to frontline staff to provide information to plan, predict and improve, such as through the Canterbury DHB's online health dashboards. The dashboards are also displayed in a real-time Operations Centre and in locations around the hospital network. They are reviewed with both operational and patient journey issues addressed as part of broader hospital flow and resource management. The Operations Centre also enables clinicians to work through initiatives to further improve care using predictive data to inform changes and determine the effect of their interventions.

Organisations such as Lightfoot Solutions were commissioned to assist with the development of predictive modelling of data from different healthcare providers in an integrated approach. It enables the measurement of patient outcomes across the whole pathway, linking all of the services in each patient's journey. Using statistical process control, Lightfoot's *Signals from Noise* has provided insights into the behaviours of real-world processes and pathways and contributes to evidence based strategic and operational decision-making.

36.2.7 Lessons Learned and Outlook

Showcase 2012 was borne of the need for new facilities and also further engaging the workforce to redesign its future. From mid-December 2012, visitors to the second iteration of *Showcase*, also set up in a warehouse, which became known as the Design Lab, could walk through the new hospital ward designs, sit on a bed and 'see the view' from the proposed new hospital and leave notes and comments. By the end of the *Showcase 2* season, the moveable walls were festooned with notes and posters on which visitors had written suggestions about everything from the design of bed trays to the cleaning of sliding doors, as well as ideas such as a designated 'end of life' area for each floor.

The second *Showcase* was also designed to bring people up to date with progress and achievements, despite the earthquake, and remind them of future challenges. Like its predecessor, *Showcase* 2 was interactive, but offered different experiences, with a new focus on international demographic and environmental issues likely to impact on health. *Showcase 2* was again a huge success, attended by over 3500 visitors and had to be extended well into 2013. The Design Lab, where Showcase 2 was held, continues to be a space for teaching, events, collaboration with other social services and life-sized mock-ups of facilities such as wards, CT rooms, integrated family health (extended general practice) centres etc. with visitors from all over the world coming to see what's being done in this and the Canterbury Health System space.

In 2013, Canterbury DHB developed an outcomes framework to measure collective impact of the system on population outcomes. It starts with the high level outcome of people being well and healthy in their own homes and communities. From there it identifies key strategies and nine system-level outcomes:

- Improved environment supports health and wellbeing
- Delayed/avoided burden of long-term conditions
- Decreased wait times
- Increased planned care
- Decreased acute care
- Decreased institutionalisation
- Decreased adverse events
- Decreased avoidable mortality
- No wasted resource

Within each of these second tier outcomes lie further levels of detail, which provide a set of coherent outcomes that allow all providers in the system to identify their various operational contributions towards higher-level outcomes. The outcomes framework is a continuation and codification of some of the principles and visions identified in the *Vision2020* process and early health service planning exercise.

The overarching aim of this approach is to support the population to stay well and self-manage in their own homes and communities. There have been measurable impacts of this strategy, with for example the number of beds required by people over 75 years with long stays (14 days or longer) decreasing by 28 beds (14%) with in the space of 12 months between 2013 and 2014 (Gullery and Hamilton 2015). In addition, people over 75 years of age living in care homes having fallen from approximately 16% in 2006 to just above 12% in 2013/2014, equating to over 400 fewer people in such beds despite a growing older population (Box 36.3).

Box 36.3 Benefits of supporting people to stay well in the community in Canterbury Health System

- Achieved the lowest ED attendance rate in Australasia (180 per 1000 in 2015/16).
- Reduction in the proportion of people over 65 who are attending ED, from a high of 32% of the population over 65 attending EDs in 2010/11 to 28% of over 65s attending EDs in 2015/16.
- 29% fewer acute medical admissions in 2015/16 compared to the New Zealand average.
- In 2015/16, if Canterbury health system admitted at the same rate as the rest of the country, there would be 14,000 more people in hospital.
- In 2015/16, over 30,000 people who would previously have been treated in ED or acutely admitted to hospital received their treatment and care in the community.
- Integrated falls prevention strategies are contributing to a reduction in harm from falls in the elderly population. Over the 5 years from the introduction of a community falls prevention program in February 2012 (compared with outcomes expected based on previous trends for over 75s) there were;
  - 2253 fewer people with falls presented to ED.
  - 590 fewer than expected admissions for hip fractures, saving about 30 hospital beds each year.
  - 222 fewer deaths at 180 days post discharge after treatment for a fractured neck of femur (hip).
  - The reduction in hospital beds is approximately one ward reduction each year resulting in reduced expenditure of approximately NZD$34 M over 5 years for an annual investment of around NZD$0.65 M.
- Supporting people in their own homes means 400 fewer people in residential aged care compared to 2006, and a 13 month decrease in the average time spent in aged residential care.
- Increased access to elective surgery by 54% since 2007.
- The number of hospital beds has remained stable, despite a population increase of about 70,000 since 2006.
- Despite significant increases in demand for mental health services after the 2010/11 earthquakes, services, including general practice teams have stepped up and met the demand, with an increased range of flexible, responsive mental health services across community and specialist care.

Love (2015) noted that within the Canterbury Health System, there is a widely-held view that the next level of challenge will be to integrate health and social services such as education and welfare, and to develop the next level of shared information systems, both to support clinical activity and to generate business improvement.

In recent years the focus of further developing integrated services has focused on these key areas

- Mental health services
- Frail older people's pathway
- Enhanced recovery after surgery
- The 100 days program (to reduce waiting time for assessment and treatment)
- Faster cancer treatment
- Enhanced theatre utilisation

Each of these reflects the goals of valuing patient and staff time, enhancing patient experience and wellbeing and building organisational capacity and capability. Evaluating these services, like all others, is based on delivering strategic and operational benefits that are best for patient and best for system. Other measures of impact include reductions in length of stay, enhanced patient safety, timely access to services, closely monitoring readmission rates, undertaking frequent patient surveys, reduced consumable costs etc.

36.3 Conclusion

Good enough never is and the Canterbury Health System is on an ongoing journey for further improvement and while much has been learned in the journey so far, much still needs to be done (Box 36.4). Canterbury seeks to stimulate the curiosity for making better in its people and for its population and continues to value patients' time as the most important currency in healthcare from which all things flow. Canterbury leaders would be the first to say that what cannot be done is to transfer the Canterbury model wholesale into another health system. However, Love (2015) identified some transferrable attributes of the Canterbury Health system and the underlying elements of principle led change and adaptive leadership apply to all complex, adaptive systems (Box 36.4).

> **Box 36.4 Some learnings of the Canterbury Health System journey so far**
>
> - Patient time is the unifying metric of performance
> - Create a vision, and key principles, that shape our behaviour and actions
> - Reignite the passion and commitment
> - Patient and staff stories encourage continuous improvement
> - The language we use connects and aligns groups to create a purposeful identity
> - Integrated networks trump organizational hierarchy for empowering and enabling change
> - Share a problem, to empower and trust people to deliver the solution
> - Shared experiences enhance engagement and learning application

Each system has its own journey and is its own intricate web of layers of processes, plant and people. Bohmer (2016) noted that '[e]xamination of organizations that have achieved and sustained substantial performance improvements requires the relentless hard work of local operational redesign' and that 'major change emerges from aggregation of marginal gains' (p. 709).

There is an oft-cited Maori (the indigenous people of New Zealand) proverb 'He aha te mea nui o te ao. [What is the most important thing in the world?] He tangata, he tangata, he tangata [It is the people, it is the people, it is the people]. And in the end, that really is the most important thing in a health system that is built on trust.

References

Ardagh, M. W., Richardson, S. K., Robinson, V., Than, M., Gee, P., Henderson, S., Khodaverdi, L., McKie, J., Robertson, G., Schroeder, P. P., & Deely, J. M. (2012). The initial health-system response to the earthquake in Christchurch, New Zealand, in February, 2011. *Lancet, 379* (9831), 2109–2115.

Bohmer, R. M. J. (2016). The hard work of health care transformation. *New England Journal of Medicine, 375*(8), 709–710.

Canterbury Clinical Network. (2016). Canterbury clinical network structure. Retrieved December 15, 2016, from http://ccn.health.nz/WhoWeAre/OurStructure.aspx

Canterbury District Health Board. (2013). Consumer Council Terms of Reference, May 2013. "Nothing About Us, Without Us". Retrieved December 15, 2016, from http://www.cdhb. health.nz/About-CDHB/Documents/Terms%20of%20Reference%20May%202013.pdf

Canterbury District Health Board. (2016a). Consumer Council. Retrieved December 15, 2016, from http://www.cdhb.health.nz/About-CDHB/Who-We-Are/Clinical-Board-Consumer-Coun cil/Pages/Consumer-Council.aspx

Canterbury District Health Board. (2016b). Choose a rewarding career. Retrieved December 15, 2016, from http://www.cdhbcareers.co.nz/All-About-Us/How-We-Do-What-We-Do/ Xcelr8/

Gullery, C., & Hamilton, G. (2015). Towards integrated person-centred healthcare – The Canterbury journey. *Future Hospital Journal, 2*, 111–116.

Kenealy, T. W., Sheridan, N. F., & Connolly, M. J. (2015). HealthPathways website: Making the right thing the easy thing to do? *New Zealand Medical Journal, 128*, 6409.

Love, T. (2015). Case study: People centred health care in Canterbury, New Zealand. Final Report. Sapere Research Group. Washington: World Bank.

McGeoch, G., Anderson, I., Gibson, J., Gullery, C., Kerr, D., & Shand, B. (2015a). Consensus pathways: Evidence into practice. *New Zealand Medical Journal, 128*, 6418.

McGeoch, G., McGeoch, P., & Shand, B. (2015b). Is HealthPathways effective? An online survey of hospital clinicians, general practitioners and practice nurses. *New Zealand Medical Journal, 128*, 6413.

New Zealand State Services Commission. (2013). *Designing and growing innovation capability: A case study*. State Services Commission: Wellington.

Timmins, N., & Ham, C. (2013). *King's Fund (2013) The quest for integrated health and social care: A case study in Canterbury, New Zealand*. London: King's Fund.

Israel: Structural and Functional Integration at the Israeli Healthcare System **37**

Ran Balicer, Efrat Shadmi, Orly Manor,
and Maya Leventer-Roberts

37.1 Integrated Care in Israel

The Israel healthcare system was transformed with the enactment of the National Health Insurance Law (NHIL) in 1995. The law states that healthcare in Israel shall be based on three values—justice, equity and solidarity (Gross et al. 1998). To assure these principles are upheld the law enacted several important mechanisms, including a mandatory progressive health tax and universal coverage to all Israeli residents. Universal coverage is provided by one of the four non-profit health funds (also known as health plans, HPs), Clalit, Maccabi, Meuhedet, and Leumit, of which any one of the 8.5 million (current) Israeli residents is free to choose from. HPs serve as insurers and providers of services, providing all outpatient care (primary, specialty, laboratory, imaging and pharmacy services) and some of the inpatient services (about a third of hospital beds, owned and operated by Clalit). All other inpatient services are provided by the Ministry of Health and a mix of non-profit and for-profit organisations. The NHIL determines a broad unified

R. Balicer (✉)
Clalit Research Institute, Clalit Health Services, Tel-Aviv, Israel

Faculty of Health Sciences, Ben-Gurion University of the Negev, Beersheba, Israel
e-mail: rbalicer@gmail.com

E. Shadmi
Clalit Research Institute, Clalit Health Services, Tel-Aviv, Israel

Faculty of Social Welfare and Health Sciences, University of Haifa, Haifa, Israel

O. Manor
The Braun School of Public Health and Community Medicine, Hebrew University, Jerusalem, Israel

M. Leventer-Roberts
Clalit Research Institute, Clalit Health Services, Tel-Aviv, Israel

Icahn School of Medicine at Mount Sinai, New York, USA

© Springer International Publishing AG 2017
V. Amelung et al. (eds.), *Handbook Integrated Care*,
DOI 10.1007/978-3-319-56103-5_37

587

benefits package (also called the "health basket") that each of the HPs is required to provide to its members and which is reviewed and updated annually by a budgeted governmental committee in a thorough and transparent process (Chinitz et al. 2009).

Health spending in Israel is relatively low. In 2013, it was 7.56% of GDP compared to 8.7% for the EU average (2012) and 8.9% for the OECD average. This low level is generally attributable to several factors. First, HPs are financed through a capitated formula that is adjusted for age, sex, and area of residency (periphery vs. central Israel). Israeli residents can freely switch between HPs but yearly movement between HPs is very low, at <1% among those aged 30 years and over. Thus, capitation creates a strong incentive for HPs to provide efficient, effective, preventive and integrated care to keep their member population healthy and reduce costs. Additionally, HPs work as managed care organisations with gatekeeping, and some cost sharing through out-of-pocket payments for visits to specialists and for medications. Finally, in-patient service supply is highly regulated with constraints on costs and bed availability (Van de Ven et al. 2013).

The system is financed mainly through a combination of a progressive payroll based health tax and general taxation. Yet, despite equitable principles asserted by the NHIL, a growing percentage of financing is private, reaching up to 39% in 2012 (Bin-Nun 2013), with a surge in the breadth and scope of services provided by HPs as voluntary health insurance (VHI) benefits and by independent private health insurance companies (Brammli-Greenberg et al. 2014). Thus, while Israeli residents value their freedom to receive care outside the HP scheme, the growing privatisation of healthcare services erodes its equitable nature. Another negative by-product of the surge in private services is fragmentation, as information on the type and content of services privately consumed is unavailable to the HPs, which as insurers and integrative providers, are ultimately accountable for the health of their member population.

In recent years two major reforms that took place in the Israeli healthcare system have significantly contributed to integration. Beginning in 2010, dental services for children are included in the basket of services. This is the first time any type of dental care services (with the exception of limited services for trauma and oncology patients) were added to the health basket. The benefits initially included preventive and preservative dental care for children up to age 8 and this was recently expanded to cover children up to age 14. In 2015, mental health services, which despite numerous efforts since the enactment of the NHIL, were until then provided by the Ministry of Health, were added to the basket of services to be provided by the HPs. This major reform shifted responsibility for inpatient and ambulatory mental health services to the HPs, aiming to provide better access to ambulatory mental health services, reduce psychiatric hospitalisation rates and integrate mental health with all other health care services (Aviram and Azary-Veisel 2015).

Overall, the structure of the Israeli healthcare system can be described as one that is extensively integrated. Nonetheless, fragmentation still exists, in particular as it relates to long-term care and social services, which are provided directly by government social security and welfare services. This structural fragmentation leads to significant challenges in providing integrated care for those with health and social care needs, and while work to reform the infrastructure has been ongoing for some two decades (Asiskovitch 2013), it has yet to materialise.

37.1.1 A National Perspective: How Integration in Practice Can Improve Quality of Outpatient Care

- The National Program for Quality Indicators in Community Healthcare (QICH) was initiated in 2000 as a research project founded by the Israel National Institute for Health Policy Research. The QICH program maintains and updates comprehensive and integrative measures of the quality of primary care provided by the health plans, including selected services in the fields of prevention, diagnosis and treatment. There are 50 indicators in eight domains: health promotion, cancer screening, child and adolescent health, health in older adults, respiratory diseases, cardiovascular health, diabetes, and antibiotic usage.
- Data are continuously collected for the entire population of Israel from the integrated electronic health records of the four health plans using multiple sources such as physicians' and nurses' records, pharmacy claims, laboratory results, hospital procedures and reimbursement claims from private suppliers.
- The indicators are implemented in a cascade-type manner to integrative multiple fields into a single measure. For example, in order to evaluate monitoring of diabetic co-morbidities, an initial filter identifies patients with diabetes, followed by monitoring of renal function and diagnosis of diabetic nephropathy, and only then compliance with appropriate treatment of Angiotensin Converting Enzyme Inhibitors or Angiotensin Receptor Blockers is evaluated.
- The impact of this strategy can be exemplified as follows:
  - The rate of BMI documentation, which increased from less than 6% in 2003 to almost 88% in 2014.
  - The rate of individuals who underwent colorectal cancer screening increased from 11.5% in 2003 to 58.9% in 2014. This level advances Israel to the top position among OECD countries.

37.2 Integrated Care in Practice: Clalit Health Services

Clalit Health Services (Clalit) is the largest health plan in Israel, covering about 4.3 million Israelis, about 52% of the Israeli population. Due to historical reasons, Clalit, relative to the other three HPs, has an overrepresentation of members with lower socioeconomic status, ethnic minorities, elderly, and those with chronic conditions. Clalit insures over 70% of all Israelis aged 85 and over, and about 80% of the non-Jewish minority populations (Social Security report 2015). Clalit owns and operates 30% of the acute hospital beds, over 1500 primary care clinics and specialist clinics, and a complete set of ancillary services (imaging, pharmacy, laboratory). Clalit members mostly receive primary care from salaried physicians at clinics owned and operated by Clalit. Patients are free to choose their general practitioner, or primary care physician (PCP) and can switch as often as they wish. Primary care is also delivered by independent physicians operating their own facilities, mostly in solo but also some in group practices. Clinics' size varies, with some small, rural clinics serving several hundred patients, up to large clinics covering up to about 10,000 members. Specialist services are either provided at speciality care centres located throughout the country or in multidisciplinary clinics that provide both primary and specialty care services (Rosen et al. 2015).

At Clalit, most PCPs are payed a monthly salary, based on the size of their roster, or patient list, plus a capitation fee, which reflects the age composition and morbidity levels of their patient population (Rosen et al. 2015) and is determined according to the case-mix system score of the Adjusted Clinical Groups® system (Shadmi et al. 2011). This payment scheme creates a form of an accountable care system, in which PCPs and primary care clinics are accountable for the health and health care service use of their member population. The scheme does not involve penalties or financial incentives; instead it builds on the performance of the clinics, the health status of the populations and the resources used and costs accrued are monitored by the respective managerial units at the sub-regional and regional levels, and ultimately at the managerial headquarters. That way, the scheme avoids otherwise commonly occurring perverse incentives to seek volume over value, and provides a drive for investing in effective preventive services.

All GPs and specialists use a single electronic health record (EHR) software, and all clinical data, administrative, and claims data are unified into a single data warehouse centre. The data are both ID-tagged and geo-coded. Additionally, to achieve interoperability between its primary, specialty and in-patient care services, a health information exchange (HIE) system, which connects EHR systems across the various clinics and hospitals, has been implemented in Clalit since 2005 (Flaks-Manov et al. 2016). This HIE system (OFEK) links patient health records and allows providers to access critical clinical data at the point of care.

While all HPs in Israel are similar in that they serve as insurers and providers of all services covered by the health basket, Clalit is the only HP structured mostly as an integrated delivery system. It owns and operates most services, including a third of all hospital beds, as mentioned earlier and it is also the only HP in which patients are registered to receive services with a particular PCP, who is accountable for their care and health. Also, in Clalit, the PCP plays a gatekeeper role in which access to all specialty services is contingent upon referral (Tabenkin and Gross 2000), expect for five areas, ear, nose and throat, dermatology, orthopaedics, ophthalmology, and gynaecology. The second largest HP, Maccabi, covers about 25% of the population, and it is structured mostly as a preferred provider organisation, in which PCPs work as independent contractors, mostly in solo practices, and although most patients receive the bulk of their care from one PCP, there is no mandatory registration. In the two other HPs, Leumit and Meuhedet, the majority of PCPs work as independent physicians, and similar to Maccabi, there is no mandatory registration with one PCP, and PCPs do not serve as gatekeepers of specialty services (Rosen et al. 2015). With the exception of one private hospital chain owned by Maccabi, none of the other HPs, own and operate their own hospital system.

It is this structural integration of Clalit, in which ambulatory and a large share of in-patient services are provided by the same organisation, and in which the organisation of management is fully integrated, with the community care division and hospital care division working in close collaboration, in conjunction with the aligned incentives, which creates an important foundation for care integration.

37.2.1 Problem Definition: Unplanned Readmissions

Readmission reduction is a primary focus of healthcare systems worldwide in efforts to improve quality of care and efficiency across care settings (Jencks et al. 2009; Nolte et al. 2012). In Clalit, approximately one out of five older adults who are hospitalised in internal medicine wards return to the hospital for an unplanned readmission within 30 days. Readmission reduction is one of the few strategies that can serve as a prime example for care integration between primary, secondary and tertiary care (Leppin et al. 2014). To maximize clinical relevance and efficiency, interventions should vary according to patients' readmission risk. Patient surveys and computerised risk prediction models are increasingly used for such high-risk patient targeting purposes (Amarasingham et al. 2015).

In 2011, Clalit implemented a comprehensive three-level approach to achieve early identification and readmission prevention in targeted high-risk patients.

37.2.1.1 The Strategy: Vertical Integration
The organisation-wide integrated programme includes three components: (I) development and implementation of a predictive modelling tool for high risk of readmission, which is provided to health care providers (primary care physicians and nurses) at the patients' primary care clinic and upon admission to the hospital; (II) a transitional care intervention in which community care nurses are positioned within the hospital to facilitate complex care transitions; and (III) integrated quality monitoring of key objectives (readmission rates and early post-discharge primary care visit indicators) and patient reported indicators (quality of the transitional process). Each component is detailed below.

37.2.1.2 Predictive Modelling
To guide the strategy and to identify patients who are most likely to benefit from an intensive readmission reduction intervention, a prediction algorithm was developed. This algorithm is based on medical history from EHR and administrative data, the Preadmission Readmission Detection Model (PREADM) and it uses a preprocessing variable selection with decision trees and neural network algorithms in order to identify patients at high-risk for an unplanned subsequent hospitalisation, upon admission to any internal medicine unit at any hospital. The aim was

to achieve a generalisable model that contains data that could potentially be used in any health system with EHRs. Model construction also emphasised the importance of applicability, and weighed the likelihood of data availability at the time of admission. Ultimately, the PREADM included variables such as chronic conditions, prior health services use, body mass index, and geographical location variables to determine each older adults' risk score. This algorithm was introduced into all of Clalit's hospitals and primary care clinics' EHR system to yield a readmission risk score for all patients on admission to an internal medicine department at any hospital in Israel (Shadmi et al. 2015).

37.2.1.3 Transitional Care Interventions

The PREADM risk score is used to target patients for specific interventions in hospitals and primary care clinics. In all general hospitals in Israel, a transitional care nurse (TCN) uses the PREADM score to target high-risk older people aged 65 and above. The TCN role was developed by Clalit's community care division for this programme and implemented country-wide for all Clalit members. The nurse provides in-hospital coordination, discharge planning, and coordination with primary care clinic services for post-discharge follow-up and monitoring. Moreover, primary care nurses from each patients' primary care clinic receive notices that their patients are hospitalised, complete with their PREADM score, enabling them to prioritise reaching out efforts to high-risk patients immediately after discharge. Nurses use a specially tailored EHR embedded screening and action tool to assess patients' needs and plan their post discharge care (e.g. need for a home visit and/or medication reconciliation) and provide or refer them to needed services.

37.2.1.4 Quality Monitoring

Quality monitoring is performed using both objective and patient reported measures. Hospital managers as well as primary care clinics' regional managerial teams receive quarterly reports on the readmission rates and post-discharge follow up (within 3 and 7 days) in their respective areas and compared to other regions. Additionally, patient-reported data from the post-discharge nursing assessments is collected via surveys to evaluate the quality of their post discharge care.

37.2.2 Impact

The vertical integration strategy has produced multiple levels of results. First, the Preadmission Readmission Detection Model (PREADM) has been shown to comparatively accurately identify patients at high-risk for readmission (Shadmi et al. 2015). Second, the TCNs role was implemented in all 27 general hospitals across Israel, including the eight Clalit hospitals, in which approximately 40% of Clalit's member population is hospitalised, and the 19 government owned and operated hospitals. The TCNs helped to tailor the care of individual high-risk patients and to establish mechanisms that improve care transitions in multiple settings, for example improved transitions to rehabilitation services. Finally, quality monitoring identified several areas for improvement: (1) rates of follow up post-discharge, defined as a visit or a phone call with a primary care physicians or nurses within 7 days of discharge, have risen substantially, from an already relatively high rate of 68% in 2012 to a rate of 86% in 2015; (2) most primary care clinics are using patients' assessments of their own post-discharge needs to guide personalised follow-up interventions; and (3) within the patient population hospitalised in Clalit's hospitals, a significant reduction in readmission rates was observed in high-risk older patients, from 34.3% in 2012 to 32.4% in 2015, which translates into approximately 9100 averted hospitalisation days.

37.2.3 Dissemination and Replication

The observed results of the vertical integration strategy implemented by Clalit to effectively address readmission rates point to the potential outcomes of a strategy which establishes links between health care providers and services at different levels, uses the same tools to guide their intervention, and incorporates advanced EHR based predictive algorithms and quality monitoring measures. The favourable results observed for the Clalit health system illustrate the importance of structural integration, which can fully capitalise on the benefits of an integrated delivery system design. The Clalit experience also provides several principles that can be widely disseminated. For example, with the wide-spread adoption of EHRs, there is increasing opportunity for their "meaningful use" by targeting highest-risk patients for interventions and creating feedback mechanism that contribute to a transparent reporting system in which the various managerial units (in Clalit, both at the hospital and community division levels) can act upon.

37.2.4 Lessons Learned and Outlook

As improving continuity of care remains a national priority and given the integrative structure and availability of interoperable electronic HIEs, several trends will likely impact the further implementation of care integration in Israel in the coming years.

With the 2015 mental health reform, an ongoing process of integrating mental health care into the outpatient setting and GP practices is taking place, which is expected to lead to a considerable improvement in the quality of care for mentally ill patients. There is dire need to implement a similar reform to integrate the social and health care aspects of care for older people in particular, which is currently disjointed and so reduces the efficiency, effectiveness and patient centre-edness of care for older people in Israel.

Israel has put a considerable emphasis on embracing digital health on the national level, with a national initiative called 'Digital Israel' now funding innovation in digital health that may increase care effectiveness and patient engagement. With its long tradition as the 'start-up nation', it is likely that the coming years will show new and innovative technologies that can enhance care integration such as through smartphones and immersive technologies (see Chap. 7) These technologies may allow better flow of real-time data between providers, patient guidance within the healthcare system components according to the illness at hand, and predictive/ prescriptive provider and patient decision support based on advanced analytics. The digital infrastructure is there, it is the scaled implementation that will be the upcoming challenge in harnessing these promising technologies to improve care integration and patient-centred care outcomes.

References

Amarasingham, R., Velasco, F., Xie, B., Clark, C., Ma, Y., Zhang, S., et al. (2015). Electronic medical record-based multicondition models to predict the risk of 30 day readmission or death among adult medicine patients: Validation and comparison to existing models. *BMC Medical Informatics and Decision Making, 15*, 39. doi:10.1186/s12911-015-0162-6.

Asiskovitch, S. (2013). The Long-Term Care Insurance Program in Israel: Solidarity with the elderly in a changing society. *Israel Journal of Health Policy Research, 2*(1), 3. doi:10.1186/2045-4015-2-3.

Aviram, U., & Azary-Veisel S. (2015). Mental health reform in Israel: Challenge and opportunity, Taub Center.

Bin, N. G. (2013). Private health insurance policies in Israel: A report on the 2012 Dead Sea Conference. *Israel Journal of Health Policy Research, 2*(1), 25.

Brammli-Greenberg, S., Waitzberg, R., Medina-Artom, T., & Adijes-Toren, A. (2014). Low-budget policy tool to empower Israeli insureds to demand their rights in the healthcare system. *Health Policy, 118*(3), 279–284.

Chinitz, D., Meislin, R., & Alster-Grau, I. (2009). Values, institutions and shifting policy paradigms: Expansion of the Israeli National Health Insurance Basket of Services. *Health Policy, 90*(1), 37–44.

Flaks-Manov, N., Shadmi, E., Hoshen, M., & Balicer, R. D. (2016). Health information exchange systems and length of stay in readmissions to a different hospital. *Journal of Hospital Medicine, 11*(6), 401–406.

Gross, R., Rosen, B., & Chinitz, D. (1998). Evaluating the Israeli health care reform: Strategy, challenges and lessons. *Health Policy, 45*(2), 99–117.

Jencks, S. F., Williams, M. V., & Coleman, E. A. (2009). Rehospitalizations among patients in the Medicare fee-for-service program. *The New England Journal of Medicine, 360*, 1418–1428.

Leppin, A. L., Gionfriddo, M. R., Kessler, M., Brito, J. P., Mair, F. S., Gallacher, K., et al. (2014). Preventing 30-day hospital readmissions: A systematic review and meta-analysis of randomized trials. *JAMA Internal Medicine, 174*(7), 1095–1107. doi:10.1001/jamainternmed.2014.1608.

Nolte, E., Roland, M., Guthrie, S., & Brereton, L. (2012). Preventing emergency readmissions to hospital: A scoping review. Retrieved August 29, 2014, from http://www.rand.org/content/dam/rand/pubs/technical_reports/2012/RAND_TR1198.pdf

Rosen, B., Waitzberg, R., & Merkur, S. (2015). Israel: Health system review. *Health Systems in Transition, 17*(6), 1–212.

Shadmi, E., Balicer, R. D., Kinder, K., Abrams, C., & Weiner, J. P. (2011). Assessing socio-economic health care utilization inequity in Israel: Impact of alternative approaches to morbidity adjustment. *BMC Public Health, 11*, 609.

Shadmi, E., Flaks-Manov, N., Hoshen, M., Goldman, O., Bitterman, H., & Balicer, R. D. (2015). Predicting 30-day readmissions with preadmission electronic health record data. *Medical Care, 53*(3), 283–289.

Social Security Report. (2015). https://www.btl.gov.il/Publications/survey/Documents/seker_271.pdf

Tabenkin, H., & Gross, R. (2000). The role of the primary care physician in the Israeli health care system as a 'gatekeeper'—The viewpoint of health care policy makers. *Health Policy, 52*(2), 73–85.

van de Ven, W. P., Beck, K., Buchner, F., Schokkaert, E., Schut, F. T., Shmueli, A., et al. (2013). Preconditions for efficiency and affordability in competitive healthcare markets: Are they fulfilled in Belgium, Germany, Israel, the Netherlands and Switzerland? *Health Policy, 109*(3), 226–245.